Assistive Technologies, Robotics, and Automated Machines in the Health Domain

Assistive Technologies, Robotics, and Automated Machines in the Health Domain

Editor

Daniele Giansanti

MDPI • Basel • Beijing • Wuhan • Barcelona • Belgrade • Manchester • Tokyo • Cluj • Tianjin

Editor
Daniele Giansanti
Centro Nazionale per le
Tecnologie Innovative in
Sanita Pubblica
Istituto Superiore di Sanità
Roma
Italy

Editorial Office
MDPI
St. Alban-Anlage 66
4052 Basel, Switzerland

This is a reprint of articles from the Special Issue published online in the open access journal *Healthcare* (ISSN 2227-9032) (available at: www.mdpi.com/journal/healthcare/special_issues/Assistive_Technologies_Robotics_Automated_Machines_Health_Domain).

For citation purposes, cite each article independently as indicated on the article page online and as indicated below:

LastName, A.A.; LastName, B.B.; LastName, C.C. Article Title. *Journal Name* **Year**, *Volume Number*, Page Range.

ISBN 978-3-0365-7689-3 (Hbk)
ISBN 978-3-0365-7688-6 (PDF)

Contents

About the Editor

Daniele Giansanti

Dr. Giansanti received an MD in Electronic Engineering at Sapienza University, 1991, Rome; a PHD in Telecommunications and Microelectronics Engineering at Tor Vergata University, 1997, Rome; and an Academic Specialization in Cognitive Psychology and Neural Networks at Sapienza University, Rome, 1997. His Academic Specialization was in Medical Physics, Sapienza University, Rome, 2005. Dr. Giansanti was in charge of the Design of VLSI Asics for DSP in the Civil Field (1991–1997) during his MD and PHD, and he served as a CAE-CAD-CAM system manager and Design Engineer in the project of electronic systems (Boards and VLSI) for the Warfare at Elettronica spa (1992–2000), one of the leaders in the military field. More importantly, he also conducts varied research at ISS (the Italian NIH) (2000–today) in the following fields:

1) Biomedical engineering and medical physics with the development of wearable and portable devices (three national patents).

2) Telemedicine and e-Health: technology assessment and the integration of new systems in the field of telerehabilitation, domiciliary monitoring, digital pathology, and digital radiology.

3) Mhealth: recent interest in the field of the integration of smartphones and tablet technology in health care with particular attention to the opportunities and the relevant problems of risks, abuse, and regulation.

4) Acceptance of and consensus in the use of robots for assistance and rehabilitation.

5) Challenges and acceptance of the use of Artificial Intelligence in Digital Radiology and Digital Pathology.

6) Cybersecurity in the health domain.

Dr. Giansanti is a Professor at Sapienza and Catholic University in Rome and a tutor of theses. He is a Board Editor and reviewer for several journals. He has 152 publications indexed on Scopus and more than 200 contributions, such as monographies, chapters, and congress papers.

Preface to "Assistive Technologies, Robotics, and Automated Machines in the Health Domain"

The field of healthcare is constantly evolving and advancing with new technologies and innovations. Among these, assistive technologies, robotics, and automated machines are rapidly gaining ground as powerful tools to improve the quality of care and enhance patient outcomes. From wearable devices that monitor vital signs to surgical robots that assist in complex procedures or support rehabilitation, these technologies have the potential to revolutionize the way we deliver healthcare. According to the WHO, assistive technologies enable and promote inclusion and participation, especially for persons with disabilities. The primary purpose of assistive technology is to maintain or improve an individual's functioning and independence, thus allowing them to participate in all activities in life, from education to work. The most interesting applications of care robots are divided into four categories: robotic surgery, care and socially assistive robots, rehabilitation systems, and training for health and care workers. Automated machines support healthcare systems in the decision-making, therapeutic, and rehabilitation approaches. Based on automated machines, the perspective of care in the health domain is radically changing with the potential to transform medicine. The development and integration of assistive technologies, care robots, and automated machines are strategic in the health domain. This book explores the latest developments in assistive technologies, robotics, and automated machines in the health domain, providing a comprehensive overview of their applications and potential impact. The book is for the benefit of healthcare professionals, researchers, engineers, and students interested in these rapidly evolving fields. It covers a wide range of topics, including:

·Portable and wearable devices for remote patient monitoring and home healthcare

·Robotics in healthcare.

·Automated machines for diagnosis, imaging, and service automation in the health domain

·Artificial intelligence and machine learning in the health domain

·Ethical and regulatory considerations in the use of these technologies

·Applications of virtual reality in the health domain

·Integration into digital health and telehealth

The articles are written by experts in their respective fields, providing a detailed and authoritative overview of the current state of the art. Each contribution also includes references to the relevant literature, making this book a useful resource and tool for further study and research.

Overall, this reprint aims to provide a timely and comprehensive overview of the rapidly evolving field of assistive technologies, robotics, and automated machines in the health domain. We hope that it will be a valuable resource for healthcare professionals, researchers, engineers, and students working in this exciting and vital field.

Daniele Giansanti
Editor

healthcare

MDPI

Editorial

Assistive Technologies, Robotics, Automatic Machines: Perspectives of Integration in the *Health Domain*

Daniele Giansanti

Centro TISP, Istituto Superiore di Sanità, 00161 Roma, Italy; daniele.giansanti@iss.it

Assistive technologies, robotics, and automatic machines are becoming important elements of the human health domain. The World Health Organization (WHO) is beginning to address the theme of *assistive technologies (ATs)* [1]. According to the WHO, "assistive technology" is an umbrella term covering systems and services related to the delivery of assistive products and services. The tools for AT can maintain or improve human independence and well-being, and these tools have very broad applications in the field of human health. These applications range from pill organization and spectacles up to communication aids, prostheses, wheelchairs, and many other tools. Such tools can also widely use IT and mechatronics and show different levels of automation. Nowadays, more than 1 billion people require at least one AT tool, but with the increase in world population, in 8 years, more than 2 billion people will require such tools. ATs allow people to become healthy, independent, productive, and to participate in all common activities in society (e.g., education, work, civil life). Therefore, the provision of these tools is essential. Unfortunately, today, AT tools are successfully accessed by only 1 in 10 people in need [1]. People who are most in need of ATs are [1,2]:

- People with gradual functional decline;
- Older people;
- People with communication problems;
- People with mental health disabilities;
- People with a wide range of disabilities.

The WHO identified five major *challenges* at the international level [1]:

(1) *The policy*. In most regions of the world, a policy on the ATs is lacking.
(2) *The products*. Unfortunately, the industry is particularly focused on high-income markets. However, these tools should be user-centered and tailored to one's individual needs. According to *the International Classification of Functioning, Disability and Health* [3], two individuals with the same apparent disability are not identical.
(3) *The provision*. In high-income countries, services are not well-integrated but are nearly always independent. For example, multiple appointments at different locations are needed, which is time-consuming, stressful and tiring for both the citizen and the caregiver.
(4) *The personnel*. Trained personnel are crucial for important practices, such as the correct prescription of an AT tool, providing training, and organizing follow-up appointments for the user.
(5) *Assistive technology within universal health coverage*. The 2030 *Agenda of WHO for Sustainability* emphasizes universal health coverage so that everyone in the world can access both services and products without economic restrictions.

Today, the innovative prospects, usefulness and diffusion of *robotics in the health domain* are unconfutable.

The Policy Department for Economic, Scientific and Quality-of-Life Policies of the European Parliament identified the most important applications of care robots [4] to be the following:

Citation: Giansanti, D. Assistive Technologies, Robotics, Automatic Machines: Perspectives of Integration in the *Health Domain*. *Healthcare* **2022**, *10*, 1080. https://doi.org/10.3390/healthcare10061080

Received: 24 May 2022
Accepted: 1 June 2022
Published: 10 June 2022

- The robotic surgery;
- The care and socially assistive robotics;
- The robotic rehabilitation;
- The robotics for training in the health domain.

The debate on both the successes and failures of these tools is widespread both in their industrial use [5,6] and in healthcare [7]. The use of care robots seems to have important advantages for both all those involved in the *health domain* and their users [8].

For example, in surgery, robotics has reduced the probability of infection, blood deficit, and decreased recovery time. The application of care robots in rehabilitation and assistance programs optimizes care and minimizes workload. The general consensus is that care robots are effective, useful, and can work tirelessly. The current use of care robots includes the following [7,8]:

Surgeries—Care robots allow less invasive clinical interventions.

Clinical training—Robotics allow realistic simulations with force feedback due to their haptic technology.

Prescription/dispensing—Special robots can carry out the following with a high precision, accuracy and speed: (a) dispense drug treatment; (b) manage problematic liquids or viscous materials.

Care/services—Dedicated robotic systems can perform daily actions (for example, patient displacement) and daily measurement checks (e.g., pressure, temperature, glycemia).

Disinfection and sanitation—These robots carry out important routine activities in healthcare environments, such as disinfection processes and the air ventilation.

Telepresence—These care robots are properly configured with features related to telemedicine, eHealth and domotics, interacting with patients and/or providing ATs, integrating them into an ambient-assisted living.

Logistic use—Logistics robots perform basic tasks, such as transporting lunches or drug treatments.

Rehabilitation and assistance. The use of care robots to guide the patient in physiotherapy tasks is becoming the subject of increasing research interest. Additionally, the use of robots as companions or for psychological support seems to be very attractive [9]. Moreover, the use of robots as complex mechatronic–IT aids is very promising in the field of the above-described ATs.

Beside the innumerable benefits of these robots, there are also problems. For example, there is a probability of faults due to human error or mechatronic deficits. A single fault could cause physical or psychological damages/harms. Another important problem is the element of cost. Today, the use of care robots is mainly limited to first-world countries. Other problems manifest in the strong impact and implications of ethical concerns in this field [10,11].

These concerns mean that a strong and widespread acceptance of the robots' integration in the health domain is necessary, with the need to obtain consensus initiatives, such as the *Consensus Conferences* [8], which is capable of producing strategic documents, as in the case of rehabilitation in Italy [12].

The introduction of *automatic machines* is radically changing the healthcare landscape with regard to decision-making, therapeutic, and rehabilitation approaches.

Important ethical issues are also being raised [13]. The impact of these machines based on artificial intelligence in the *health domain* is both significant and problematic at the same time, as they have the potential to halter the traditional healthcare–patient relationship, currently centered on the faith and openness of medical opinion and curative decisions. Through algorithms based on artificial intelligence, automatic machines can sometimes make decisions that are not fully transparent [13–16]. Therefore, there is a strong need for transparent approaches in data science, not only to the design of algorithms but also to the insiders, i.e., the clinicians. Automatic machines are increasing their applications in healthcare, for example, in the form of the following: (a) Detecting previously unidentified interferences that reduce the probability of adverse effects in drug interactions [14–16];

(b) integration into digital pathology and digital radiology [17–19]; and (c) working in direct contact with patients in rehabilitation and with social robots, with new practical and ethical implications [20].

We have briefly highlighted the peculiarities of the introduction of *assistive technologies, robotics, and automatic machines into the health domain*. In the healthcare process, these tools can represent single elements but can also be integrated in a cascade; the access to a robot or automatic machine, for example, can be supported in a disabled person by an AT. Assistive technologies, robotics, and automatic machines can also be integrated; think of an AT based on robotics with internal interactive processes derived from the automatic machine learning of artificial intelligence. There is a lot of research for scholars to carry out in the development of these tools in clinical applications. There is also a lot of study and work for ethicists, legislators, economists, and stakeholders.

It will be necessary to allow these solutions to be used for the benefit of an ever-wider audience of citizens; at the same time, it will be necessary to develop a targeted consensus and acceptance initiatives so that their introduction as single, integrated, or coincident elements takes place without trauma or shocks.

With this Special Issue, entitled "Assistive Technologies, Robotics, and Automated Machines in the Health Domain" (https://www.mdpi.com/journal/healthcare/special_issues/Assistive_Technologies_Robotics_Automated_Machines_Health_Domain [21] (accessed on 24 May 2022)), which has just opened, we intend to provide important contributions to this field by creating a forum that showcases the wide-ranging experience of its leading researchers.

Funding: This research received no external funding.

Conflicts of Interest: The author declares no conflict of interest.

References

1. Assistive Technology. Available online: https://www.who.int/news-room/fact-sheets/detail/assistive-technology (accessed on 24 May 2022).
2. What Is AT? Available online: https://www.atia.org/home/at-resources/what-is-at/ (accessed on 24 May 2022).
3. International Classification of Functioning, Disability and Health. Available online: https://www.who.int/standards/classifications/international-classification-of-functioning-disability-and-health (accessed on 24 May 2022).
4. Dolic, Z.; Castro, R.; Moarcas, A. Robots in Healthcare: A Solution or a Problem? Study for the Committee on Environment, Public Health, and Food Safety. Luxembourg: Policy Department for Economic, Scientific and Quality of Life Policies, European Parliament. 2019. Available online: https://www.europarl.europa.eu/RegData/etudes/IDAN/2019/638391/IPOL_IDA(2019)638391_EN.pdf (accessed on 20 November 2021).
5. Advantages and Disadvantages of Robotic Automation. Available online: https://www.granta-automation.co.uk/news/advantages-and-disadvantages-of-robotic-automation/ (accessed on 20 November 2021).
6. Advantages and Disadvantages of Robots. Available online: https://www.futurelearn.com/info/courses/begin-robotics/0/steps/2845 (accessed on 20 November 2021).
7. How Robots Are Introducing A New Dimension to Healthcare Service Delivery. Available online: https://www.delveinsight.com/blog/robotics-in-healthcare (accessed on 20 November 2021).
8. Maccioni, G.; Ruscitto, S.; Gulino, R.A.; Giansanti, D. Opportunities and Problems of the Consensus Conferences in the Care Robotics. *Healthcare* **2021**, *9*, 1624. [CrossRef] [PubMed]
9. Giansanti, D. The Social Robot in Rehabilitation and Assistance: What Is the Future? *Healthcare* **2021**, *9*, 244. [CrossRef] [PubMed]
10. Stahl, B.C.; Coeckelbergh, M. Ethics of healthcare robotics: Towards responsible research and innovation. *Robot. Auton. Syst.* **2016**, *86*, 152–161. [CrossRef]
11. Gordon, J.-S. Building Moral Robots: Ethical Pitfalls and Challenges. *Sci. Eng. Ethics* **2020**, *26*, 141–157. [CrossRef] [PubMed]
12. Consensus Conference CICERONE—Robot-Assisted Rehabilitation: Final Final Document Published. Available online: https://www.simfer.it/consensus-conference-cicerone-documento-finale-conclusivo/ (accessed on 24 May 2022).
13. Morone, G.; Pirrera, A.; Meli, P.; Giansanti, D. Ethics and Automated Systems in the Health Domain: Design and Submission of a Survey on Rehabilitation and Assistance Robotics to Collect Insiders' Opinions and Perception. *Healthcare* **2022**, *10*, 778. [CrossRef] [PubMed]
14. Lötsch, J.; Kringel, D.; Ultsch, A. Explainable Artificial Intelligence (XAI) in Biomedicine: Making AI Decisions Trustworthy for Physicians and Patients. *BioMedInformatics* **2022**, *2*, 1–17.

15. Datta, A.; Matlock, M.K.; Le Dang, N.; Moulin, T.; Woeltje, K.F.; Yanik, E.L.; Swamidass, S.J. 'Black Box' to 'Conversational' Machine Learning: Ondansetron Reduces Risk of Hospital-Acquired Venous Thromboembolism. *IEEE J. Biomed. Health Inform.* **2021**, *25*, 2204–2214. [CrossRef] [PubMed]
16. Datta, A.; Flynn, N.R.; Barnette, D.A.; Woeltje, K.F.; Miller, G.P.; Swamidass, S.J. Machine learning liver-injuring drug interactions with non-steroidal anti-inflammatory drugs (NSAIDs) from a retrospective electronic health record (EHR) cohort. *PLoS Comput. Biol.* **2021**, *17*, e1009053. [CrossRef] [PubMed]
17. Giovagnoli, M.R.; Giansanti, D. Artificial Intelligence in Digital Pathology: What Is the Future? Part 1: From the Digital Slide Onwards. *Healthcare* **2021**, *9*, 858. [CrossRef] [PubMed]
18. Giansanti, D.; Di Basilio, F. The Artificial Intelligence in Digital Radiology: Part 1: The Challenges, Acceptance and Consensus. *Healthcare* **2022**, *10*, 509. [CrossRef] [PubMed]
19. D'Antonoli, T.A. Ethical considerations for artificial intelligence: An overview of the current radiology landscape. *Diagn. Interv. Radiol.* **2020**, *26*, 504–511.
20. Banks, J. The Human Touch: Practical and Ethical Implications of Putting AI and Robotics to Work for Patients. *IEEE Pulse* **2018**, *9*, 15–18. [CrossRef] [PubMed]
21. Special Issue "Assistive Technologies, Robotics, and Automated Machines in the Health Domain". Available online: https://www.mdpi.com/journal/healthcare/special_issues/Assistive_Technologies_Robotics_Automated_Machines_Health_Domain (accessed on 24 May 2022).

healthcare

Review

Artificial Intelligence Systems Assisting in the Assessment of the Course and Retention of Orthodontic Treatment

Martin Strunga *, **Renáta Urban**, **Jana Surovková** and **Andrej Thurzo** *

Department of Orthodontics, Regenerative and Forensic Dentistry, Faculty of Medicine, Comenius University in Bratislava, 81250 Bratislava, Slovakia
* Correspondence: strunga2@uniba.sk (M.S.); thurzo3@uniba.sk (A.T.)

Abstract: This scoping review examines the contemporary applications of advanced artificial intelligence (AI) software in orthodontics, focusing on its potential to improve daily working protocols, but also highlighting its limitations. The aim of the review was to evaluate the accuracy and efficiency of current AI-based systems compared to conventional methods in diagnosing, assessing the progress of patients' treatment and follow-up stability. The researchers used various online databases and identified diagnostic software and dental monitoring software as the most studied software in contemporary orthodontics. The former can accurately identify anatomical landmarks used for cephalometric analysis, while the latter enables orthodontists to thoroughly monitor each patient, determine specific desired outcomes, track progress, and warn of potential changes in pre-existing pathology. However, there is limited evidence to assess the stability of treatment outcomes and relapse detection. The study concludes that AI is an effective tool for managing orthodontic treatment from diagnosis to retention, benefiting both patients and clinicians. Patients find the software easy to use and feel better cared for, while clinicians can make diagnoses more easily and assess compliance and damage to braces or aligners more quickly and frequently.

Keywords: orthodontics; AI; ChatGPT; AI Treatment Assessment; Teledentistry Cephalometrics

Citation: Strunga, M.; Urban, R.; Surovková, J.; Thurzo, A. Artificial Intelligence Systems Assisting in the Assessment of the Course and Retention of Orthodontic Treatment. *Healthcare* **2023**, *11*, 683. https://doi.org/10.3390/healthcare11050683

Academic Editor: Daniele Giansanti

Received: 31 December 2022
Revised: 17 February 2023
Accepted: 23 February 2023
Published: 25 February 2023

1. Introduction

Assistive technologies and automated systems are high-tech elements that are every day reshaping workflows of modern healthcare. Assistive technologies, including virtual reality, are designed to improve or maintain a person's functioning so that they can participate in all aspects of life [1–3]. Automated systems empowered with Artificial Intelligence (AI) can support healthcare decision-making, therapy, and rehabilitation and can also help prevent treatment errors. These technologies can be used individually or can be interconnected to create assisted living solutions or enable rehabilitation at home [4]. Artificial intelligence is essential for advanced computer aided diagnostics' [5] appropriate integration of social robots with the potential to bring benefits to aged care [6] and also future hybrid exoskeleton systems [7]. Various telemonitoring systems will benefit from the AI evaluation of sensor data from mobile phones or wearables, e.g., patient movements in the early diagnosis of Parkinson's disease [8]. AI is not only the future of advanced robotics in healthcare [9,10], but it is also cornerstone of advanced digital radiology [11] in dentistry, including the orthodontic specialty [12–14]. The editorial of the International Journal of Environmental Research and Public Health from September 2022 by Giansanti summarized what is expected from an AI-based system [2] in the public health domain.

Today's rapidly growing desire by dental practices to increase the effectiveness of their treatments has led to the development of numerous tools to achieve this, such as Dental Monitoring software (DM) (Dental Monitoring Co., Paris, France), StrojCHECK by Sangre Azul (3Dent medical Ltd., Bratislava, Slovakia), White teeth, etc. DM is a combination of artificial intelligence and telemedicine that enables easy daily collaboration and communication between the dental practice and the patient via a smartphone software app. This facilitates the coordination and execution of each step and the monitoring of the achieved goals throughout the treatment. It is feasible for both parties to use the maximum potential of this tool. There is an increasing demand for health apps not only in orthodontic dentistry but also in other medical specialties [15,16].

The possibilities of health apps are immense, ranging from promoting an active, healthy lifestyle, assisting with nutrition, preventing diabetes and high blood pressure, and treating depression to changing behavior to stop smoking and drinking alcohol, taking medications regularly, etc. They also enable monitoring and adjustment of calorie intake and output. For this purpose, additional devices such as wristbands and smartwatches are often used alongside smartphones. These sensor systems vary from accelerometers, barometers, geosensors, heart rate sensors, etc. [17,18]. Additionally, current studies have shown that telemedicine also provides a way to improve primary care accessibility, as it can decrease the time to specialty consultation, reduce the number of patients on the waitlist, and it allows the more urgent cases to reach a specialist sooner [19]. The high technological level of sensors in smartphones have led not only to dental monitoring but also to utilizations of optical scanning for 3D face morphology registration [20,21].

This application of telemedicine, specifically teledentistry, has proven to be increasingly popular and acceptable amongst not only adolescent and child patients but also in adults [22]. For some clinical applications of advanced 3D-printed appliances in children with craniofacial syndrome, regular home telemonitoring would be extremely valuable and would minimize the potential risks of appliance damage and treatment failure in complicated cases, such as Pierre Robin Sequence patients with 3D-printed palatal plates or common orthodontic patients with 3D-printed distalizers [21,23,24]. This also brings an economic and efficiency aspect to the usage of various types of telehealth software. Current data from after the COVID-19 pandemic show that treatments monitored with a DM app required 33.1% less appointments than patients without monitoring. In addition, the duration of the first phase of treatment was reduced by 1.7 months on average for the DM group and, finally, although without clinically significant relevance (less than 0.5 mm or less than 2°), there was an increased accuracy of movements expressed on maxillary and mandibular anterior teeth when compared to predicted positions [25,26].

Studies have shown that their use is perceived as feasible for several reasons: the first, and particularly important, reason is the behavioral impact on the patient during usage of these tools. It has been proven that a patient's engagement in the treatment is considerably improved as a direct effect of working with the app. As a result, better compliance is expected; hence, the outlined outcome should be improved accordingly. Compliance is, apart from the quality of treatment planning and difficulty of the teeth movements, increasingly one of the most crucial aspects of achieving treatment goals, especially for aligner treatments, which are on a significant popularity rise. Furthermore, when a patient is being self-scanned on a 4-, 7-, 10-, or 14-day basis, he is also aware that the hygienic status of his teeth will be assessed and visible to the doctor, assistants, and even third party (the software staff as well), which, overall, leads to improvement in his dental hygiene [27–30].

The software uses a knowledge-based algorithm that evaluates the data patients send to the app after taking a series of photos with their smartphone. An automatic preset for feedback and comments is then sent back to the patient, containing a lot of data for the patient about their current dental status [31].

Unlike other telecommunications systems such as Skype, Google Duo, Zoom, and others [14], which cannot provide a standardized evaluation of the clinical situation, the DM system provides process automation through a knowledge-based algorithm that is based on a combination of robotic and deep learning processes, with information systems that act like a semi-intelligent user [25,32].

The aim of this article was to investigate the use of advanced AI software in orthodontics, particularly for the purposes of CBCT diagnosis and assessment, treatment progress assessment, and outcome stability in the follow-up phase. We evaluate the accuracy and efficiency of these AI tools compared to conventional methods and discuss the potential benefits of using such software in orthodontic practice, including the ability to closely monitor each patient, set specific treatment goals and track their achievement, and detect changes in occlusion, jaw translation, and tooth movement.

The secondary objective was to summarize reported limitations of implemented AI-powered systems in orthodontics.

2. Materials and Methods

2.1. The Research Question

The question for the literature research was defined specifically enough to allow the review team to identify relevant studies, but broadly enough to capture the full scope of the topic being reviewed.

How are AI systems currently assisting the assessment of the treatment or retention of orthodontic treatment clinically implemented, and what are their advantages and limitations?

2.2. The Search Strategy

The search strategy aimed to identify all relevant studies on the topic being reviewed. This involved searching databases and grey literature to ensure that this review was as comprehensive as possible. For this review, PubMed, Scopus, the Web of Science—Core Collection, and Google Scholar were queried.

The query was developed in dialogue with AI ChatGPT 3.5 Dec 15 Version (OpenAI Inc., San Francisco, CA, USA). Databases were queried on 20 December 2022 with the following query:

> *(orthodontic treatment OR orthodontics) AND (artificial intelligence OR machine learning OR deep learning) AND (assessment OR evaluation OR prediction) AND (course OR retention OR outcomes)*

The definition of the query was suggested upon drafts of this review title, abstract, and defined research question and was accepted by all four evaluators. This search query would find articles that discuss the use of artificial intelligence systems in evaluating the course and retention of orthodontic treatment and contain the relevant terms "orthodontic treatment", "artificial intelligence", "evaluation", and "course" or "retention".

2.3. The Review Process

All studies returned by search were analyzed for duplicities followed by analysis from four evaluators for title and abstract evaluation. Only studies relevant to the topic were selected, and relevant data were extracted.

3. Results

All articles below dating before 2020 were eliminated from the study, as only the most contemporary and relevant data were to be gathered.

We excluded 17 articles that complied with queried keywords but were not addressing the topic even marginally. Table 1 shows most cited articles relevant to the queried keywords.

Table 1. The most cited articles relevant to the queried keywords in researched topic.

#	Authors	Title	Citations	FWCI	Reference	Published
1	Kunz et al.	Artificial intelligence in orthodontics: Evaluation of a fully automated cephalometric analysis using a customized convolutional neural network	65	12.89	[33]	2020
2	Maspero et al.	Available technologies, applications and benefits of teleorthodontics. A literature review and possible applications during the COVID-19 pandemic	59	3.44	[34]	2020

Table 1. *Cont.*

#	Authors	Title	Citations	FWCI	Reference	Published
3	Yu et al.	Automated Skeletal Classification with Lateral Cephalometry Based on Artificial Intelligence	57	10.21	[35]	2020
4	Lee et al.	Automated cephalometric landmark detection with confidence regions using Bayesian convolutional neural networks	40	7.51	[36]	2020
5	Leite et al.	Radiomics and Machine Learning in Oral Healthcare	38	1.83	[37]	2020
6	Wang et al.	Multiclass CBCT Image Segmentation for Orthodontics with Deep Learning	27	11.36	[38]	2021
7	Bichu et al.	Applications of artificial intelligence and machine learning in orthodontics: a scoping review	20	6.35	[39]	2021
9	Schwendicke et al.	Deep learning for cephalometric landmark detection: systematic review and meta-analysis	18	3.06	[40]	2021
10	Deshpande et al.	Teledentistry: A boon amidst COVID-19 Lockdown—A narrative review	16	1.67	[41]	2021
11	Ahmed et al.	Artificial Intelligence Techniques: Analysis, Application, and Outcome in Dentistry—A Systematic Review	16	1.34	[42]	2021
12	Mohammadad-Rahimi et al.	Machine learning and orthodontics, current trends and the future opportunities: A scoping review	14	4.34	[43]	2021
13	Juerchott et al.	In vivo comparison of MRI- and CBCT-based 3D cephalometric analysis: beginnning of a non-ionizing diagnostic era in craniomaxillofacial imaging?	14	1.44	[44]	2020
14	MacHoy et al.	The ways of using machine learning in dentistry	14	0.84	[45]	2020
15	Ren et al.	Machine learning in dental, oral and craniofacial imaging: A review of recent progress	13	1.39	[46]	2021
18	Dalessandri et al.	Attitude towards telemonitoring in orthodontists and orthodontic patients	11	4.8	[47]	2021
20	Caruso et al.	A knowledge-based algorithm for automatic monitoring of orthodontic patients: The dental monitoring system. Two cases	10	1.81	[27]	2021
21	Impellizzeri	Dental Monitoring Application: I tis a valid innovation in the Orthodontics Pracice?	9	0.86	[48]	2020
22	Monill-González et al.	Artificial intelligence in orthodontics: Where are we now? A scoping review	9	2.58	[49]	2021
23	Thurzo et al.	Where Is the Artificial Intelligence Applied in Dentistry? Systematic Review and Literature Analysis	8	5.15	[12]	2022
24	Bulatova et al.	Assessment of automatic cephalometric landmark identification using artificial intelligence		3.72	[50]	2021
25	Park et al.	Teledentistry platforms for orthodontics	8	3.39	[51]	2021
26	Sangalli et al.	Effects of remote digital monitoring on oral hygiene of orthodontic patients: a prospective study	7	3.05	[52]	2021
27	Achmad et al.	Teledentistry as a solution in dentistry during the covid-19 pandemic period: A systematic review	6	0.78	[53]	2020

3.1. *Cephalometric Landmark Detection and Placement by Artificial Intelligence*

Multiple studies confirmed a wide range of software enabling recognition and detection and automatic placement of cephalometric landmarks, detecting pathologies using CBCT images, pathologies ranging from tumors, cysts, periapical lesions, caries, supernumerary teeth, tissue alterations as present in infectious processes, and abscess formations. In various measurements, they compared the accuracy of these evaluations to the skills of a trained dentist, all showing more than 95% compatibility with the findings of the dentists [33,35–37,40,49,50].

Juerchott et al. are also studying whether MRI can serve as an alternative to CBCT for 3D cephalometric analysis. Mean values were found to be equivalent, which supports this thesis, which could possibly reduce radiation exposure for many patients [44].

Moreover, segmentation of the facial skeleton was carried out by automatized MS-D convolution networks then compared to a segmentation set by orthodontists; the mean difference was insignificant, whereas the amount of time needed for segmentation was about 5 h for 1 CBCT for an orthodontist and 25 s for the CNN. This study showed that an incredible amount of time was possibly saved by this AI [38].

Ren et al. gathered data that also claim AI and deep machine learning is not already utilized for a cephalometric landmark, but it is already being used for determination of cervical vertebrae stages, oral cancer detection, cancer margin assessment, its prognosis, dental caries detection, root morphology, the presence of periapical lesions, and facial attractiveness evaluation [46].

3.2. Dental Monitoring System Applications

A study by Dallesandri et al. studied the approach of patients and dentists toward a DM system throughout their orthodontic treatments. Collected data showed that all dentists judged telemonitoring positively, as 96.25% of them considered telemonitoring indicative of high-tech and high-quality treatment, and 100% considered it a way to reduce the number of in-office visits. In addition, 97.5% of patients judged telemonitoring positively; 81.25% of them considered telemonitoring indicative of high-tech treatment; 81.25% declared themselves to be interested in reducing the number of in-office visits through telemonitoring. Telemonitoring was assessed as plausible both by patients and dentists; it was also understood as a high-tech tool that could improve quality and effectiveness of the treatments. Both groups were also pleased by possibly reducing the number of in-office visits. However, additional funding for this utility from the side of the patient was less welcomed, and compliance would be put to the question if such was the case [47].

Caruso et al. carried out a two-case study where they assessed treatments of patients using DM. Both patients displayed good compliance and successfully reached all established treatment goals. The needed movements were difficult to achieve, yet, owing to being able to be monitored, they completed treatment quickly; they both followed a seven-day exchange protocol, which is slightly faster than the usually observed treatment speed. There were phases in treatment when it was necessary to prolong the time on each aligner, while maintaining adequate tracking. After this period, the speed adaptively returned to the previous schedule. Patients assessed that monitoring was easy to use; it detected debonding auxiliaries and thus improved quality of the treatment [27].

Impellizzeri et al.'s study suggests that using DM with 0.014×0.025 CuNiTi wires in a self-ligating straight-wire appliance successfully reduced the number of appointments for each patient from 3 appointments in 10 weeks to 2 per 10 weeks. Naturally, a reduction in chair time and material costs was observed. Moreover, more precise evaluation of treatment by the doctor was possible [48].

Another study by Sangalli et al. revealed that when patients were equipped with a cheek retractor and scan box by Dental Monitoring and instructed to take monthly intraoral scans, this study group of patients showed a significant improvement in plaque control compared to the control group. A decreased number of emergency appointments in the study group was also registered, although it was not significant. The patients were not orthodontic treatment cases [52].

Maspero et al., in a 2020 article, confirmed that this application saved 5.8 appointments over a 2-year treatment. Its software platform was observed by patients as user-friendly and they noted improvement of communication with the doctor. Moreover, it was observed that stability of the result could also be measured and, if relapse of misalignment of the teeth were to occur, swift measures could be enacted to interfere with relapse development. Measurement was carried out by Moylan et al. in 2019. They compared intercanine and intermolar measurement differences between plaster models based on impressions taken by a dentist versus measurements from data from Dental Monitoring software. The differences ranged from 0.17 mm and −0.02 mm; this was assessed as sufficiently accurate [34,54]. Another publication measured the difference in STL (Stereolithography) files provided from the iTero scanners and STL files generated by DM software. Differences ranged from 0.0148 mm to 0.0275 mm; thus, they safely stated the method is accurate enough for clinical applications [55].

3.3. Other AI and Teldentistry Applications

An article by Achmad utilized teledentistry in order to connect with distant patients for consultations throughout the COVID-19 pandemic, which was exceptionally well-accepted by both groups [53]. Another purpose of teledentistry was documented by Deshpande et al., who found out that if trained general dentists were remotely communicating with orthodontists via teledentistry, more accurate interceptive orthodontic treatments would be made available, which thus led to a reduction in severity of malocclusions in disadvantaged children where referral was not plausible. Moreover, unnecessary referrals were filtered out, which is an advantage both for specialist and patient. They also warn of the risk that diagnosis based on clinical photography made by the patient may not be accurate, and the practitioner may not collect all necessary data, since other diagnostic procedures such as percussion and palpation cannot be performed via photography [41].

Asiri et al. summarized in their review that most commonly utilized AI domains were intended for diagnostics and treatment planning, followed by automated anatomic landmark detection used for cephalometry. Marginally, AI was used for assessment of growth and development and evaluation of treatment outcome [39].

4. Discussion

Contemporary data show that there is a growing trend towards the use of telemedicine in modern dental and orthodontic practices, as it has been proven to increase efficiency and allow dentists to specifically monitor each case and focus on the most important goals for each patient, while saving chairside time and patient resources and preventing deterioration of their dental status, from which they also benefit financially, psychologically, and esthetically. Likewise, the quality of treatment is improved, and the time needed to resolve problems is reduced. Although the benefits for the patient are not yet fully known, since the willingness to use the modern aids is not yet as high as the doctor would like, the demand is increasing [11,25,25,30,32,42,51,56,57].

The availability for the patient and the practice is indeed very high: the only technical requirement for the patient is a smartphone and an internet connection. The rest is provided by the dental practice. Patient compliance is also statistically higher. Undoubtedly, more and more applications will be developed to facilitate the treatments even more and increase the comfort for the user during the treatment [43,45,54,58,59].

In comparison with conventional methods of treatment management, physicians will be able to increase the number of patients they can treat at one time without compromising the quality of the services provided. They can, in fact, observe the patient's dental status more often, with great detail, instruct the patient remotely to aid in his or her treatment, or change instructions for further steps, e.g., change of placement of intra- and inter-maxillary elastics. They do not have to rely on a patient´s observation skills in terms of debonding of brackets, attachments, or other auxilliars, and problems can be detected much sooner than 3–4 weeks of the next appointment. Moreover, the treatment doctor can very quickly detect the first signs of relapse of the malocclusion, even at the slightest movement of a singular tooth. In addition, improved compliance is observed through the use of the new, attractive AI software. Finally, the ability to seek treatment over long distances is highly desirable, both for patients who travel frequently or live abroad and during pandemics such as those that have occurred in recent years [12,14]. Additionally, when comparing traditional diagnostic methods, the use of AI systems can speed up and enhance even the development of complicated orthognathic surgery treatment planning, where fast cephalometric tracing is performed by software. Jaw segmentation is also faster when performed by AI then by even skilled practitioners. Furthermore, dental and skeletal pathologies can be detected easier and not be omitted from an orthodontist's line of sight, as during cephalometric analysis his focus is mostly on the landmarks and bigger picture of a patient´s skeleton rather than singular teeth.

The combination of AI and teledentistry introduces a historical paradigm shift in orthodontic care. Software enhanced by advanced AI provides not only sophisticated evaluations of clinical situation and post-treatment stability but also pre-treatment diagnostics or even automated segmentations of CBCT utilized for cephalometric [36,60–67], airway [68,69], or forensic applications [70,71]. AI-powered software for orthodontic cephalometric analysis recently became a common tool for a reliable and accurate cephalometric tracing method [61,72], which represents a significant evolution from the times of analog cephalometric processing [73].

This review identified several limitations to using AI-powered systems in orthodontics:

1. Accuracy: AI-powered systems can help with diagnosis and treatment planning, but they are not as accurate as a trained orthodontist in identifying and treating complex cases [55,74,75], although some reports have shown that the level of accuracy is nearing the human level.
2. Expertise: AI systems do not have the same level of clinical expertise as a trained orthodontist. They may not be able to fully understand the patient's needs and cannot provide the same level of individualized care [30,48,74].
3. Ethical concerns: There are also ethical concerns about the use of AI in healthcare, including the possibility of biased algorithms and the potential to replace human labor with automation [76–78].
4. Cost: AI systems can be expensive to implement and maintain and may not be accessible to all patients or clinicians.
5. Regulation: the use of AI in healthcare also comes with regulatory challenges. These include the need for oversight to ensure the accuracy and safety of AI-powered systems [11,79,80].

A limitation of this paper is that there is a wide range of different attributes and parameters that could be used to evaluate the benefits to both parties, and further studies should be conducted that explore each parameter in more depth.

This paper also highlights that the use of AI software in orthodontics raises questions about reliability, as these tools can contain errors and bias that can lead to mistakes or mishaps during treatment. The review included most impactful studies on the use of AI in orthodontics and summarized the characteristics of current software alternatives. The accuracy and expertise have been evaluated as sufficient, albeit a sufficient number of studies on this matter have not been published yet. The value of AI-powered monitoring of the orthodontic retention phase is not completely appreciated yet and very few studies are focusing on this aspect. The authors of this paper see unexplored potential in this direction.

Current clinical decision support systems in orthodontics are already supported by AI. Commercial companies that manufacture clear aligners use data from millions of digital intraoral scans sent by clinical providers and apply AI algorithms to predict and plan tooth movement after they perform tooth segmentation. However, such AI algorithms are not validated and require clinicians to exercise caution when using the predictions provided and monitoring treatment outcomes [81,82].

Scientific reviews mapping the clinical application of orthodontic AI show a significant increase since 2020, recognizing the potential to support the assessment of orthodontic treatment and retention in a variety of ways. This has been accelerated by the global pandemic and technological AI breakthroughs. In 2022, AI algorithms were used to analyze and interpret digital images and diagnostic data, such as dental radiographs, photographs, CBCT, or intraoral photos and video scans, to identify problems and predict treatment course, outcome, or stability. AI has also been widely used to monitor patients during treatment and provide real-time feedback and alerts to ensure treatment is going as planned. AI-based systems and their application have even reached university orthodontic curricula [12,14,26,68,83–92].

In addition, AI can be used to help orthodontists track and analyze patient data over time, allowing them to identify trends and patterns that may be useful in predicting treatment outcomes and optimizing treatment plans. This could be especially useful for patients with complex or difficult cases, where traditional methods of assessment may not be sufficient [25,27,27,32].

Non lege artis treatment can take many forms, such as using treatments that have not been proven effective, using treatments in an inappropriate or dangerous manner, or failing to follow accepted protocols for diagnosing or treating a particular condition. Such treatment may also involve exploitation or abuse of patients, such as taking advantage of their vulnerability or trust. AI implementations in orthodontic software are no exception.

In 2023, the European Union announces the idea of creating the world's first comprehensive standards for regulating or prohibiting certain applications of artificial intelligence [79].

The EU's AI law is expected to lead the world in regulating AI. The AI Act is a proposal for a European law on artificial intelligence (AI)—the first law on AI to be passed by a major regulator. The law assigns applications of AI to three categories of risk. First, applications and systems that pose unacceptable risk, including state-run social assessments such as those used in China, are banned. Second, high-risk applications, such as a CV scanning tool that ranks job applicants, are subject to specific legal requirements. Finally, applications that are not explicitly banned or classified as high-risk are largely unregulated [93].

5. Conclusions

The use of AI in the assessment and retention of orthodontic treatment is an emerging area with significant potential for improving patient care and outcomes. It is likely to see many more AI-powered tools and systems being developed and adopted in the field of orthodontics in the coming years.

Literature research concludes that while AI-powered systems already effectively assist in orthodontic treatment, they must be used in conjunction with properly trained orthodontists to achieve the best possible outcomes for patients. Unsupervised applications of AI-assisted systems in orthodontics are not in accordance with the standards of good medical practice or the principles of medical ethics. With current unresolved risks of AI bias and incoming AI governmental regulations, such an unsupervised orthodontic treatment would be considered as non lege artis.

This scoping review proves that the current clinical adoption of AI-powered systems has already reshaped the form of modern orthodontic practice, albeit they are still rife with limitations such as: accuracy, expertise, ethical concerns, cost, and regulatory issues.

Author Contributions: Conceptualization, A.T., M.S., R.U. and J.S.; methodology, A.T.; software, A.T.; validation, A.T., M.S., R.U. and J.S.; formal analysis, A.T.; investigation, resources, A.T.; data curation, A.T. and J.S.; writing—original draft preparation, A.T., M.S., R.U. and J.S.; writing—review and editing, A.T., M.S., R.U. and J.S.; visualization; supervision, A.T.; project administration, A.T.; funding acquisition, A.T. All authors have read and agreed to the published version of the manuscript.

Funding: This work was supported by the Slovak Grant Agency for Science KEGA Thurzo—grant No. 054UK-4/2023.

Institutional Review Board Statement: Not applicable.

Informed Consent Statement: Not applicable.

Data Availability Statement: Not applicable.

Acknowledgments: The authors gratefully acknowledge the technological support of the digital dental lab infrastructure of the 3Dent Medical Ltd. company, (Bernolakovo, Slovakia) as well as the dental clinic, Sangre Azul Ltd., (Chiyoda City, Tokyo).

Conflicts of Interest: The authors declare no conflict of interest.

References

1. Tokgöz, P.; Stampa, S.; Wähnert, D.; Vordemvenne, T.; Dockweiler, C. Virtual Reality in the Rehabilitation of Patients with Injuries and Diseases of Upper Extremities. *Healthcare* **2022**, *10*, 1124. [CrossRef] [PubMed]
2. Giansanti, D. Artificial Intelligence in Public Health: Current Trends and Future Possibilities. *Int. J. Environ. Res. Public Health* **2022**, *19*, 11907. [CrossRef]
3. Hanna, J.J.; Nijhawan, A.E.; Lehmann, C.U.; Medford, R.J. Simulating Facebook Advertisements to Establish Cost per New HIV Diagnosis Using Routine and Targeted Models in a Local Population. *Healthcare* **2022**, *10*, 1195. [CrossRef] [PubMed]
4. Giansanti, D. Assistive Technologies, Robotics, Automatic Machines: Perspectives of Integration in the Health Domain. *Healthcare* **2022**, *10*, 1080. [CrossRef]
5. Samee, N.A.; Ahmad, T.; Mahmoud, N.F.; Atteia, G.; Abdallah, H.A.; Rizwan, A. Clinical Decision Support Framework for Segmentation and Classification of Brain Tumor MRIs Using a U-Net and DCNN Cascaded Learning Algorithm. *Healthcare* **2022**, *10*, 2340. [CrossRef]
6. Leung, A.Y.M.; Zhao, I.Y.; Leung, A.Y.M.; Zhao, I.Y.; Lin, S.; Lau, T.K. Exploring the Presence of Humanoid Social Robots at Home and Capturing Human-Robot Interactions with Older Adults: Experiences from Four Case Studies. *Healthcare* **2022**, *11*, 39. [CrossRef]
7. Kavalieros, D.; Kapothanasis, E.; Kakarountas, A.; Loukopoulos, T. Methodology for Selecting the Appropriate Electric Motor for Robotic Modular Systems for Lower Extremities. *Healthcare* **2022**, *10*, 2054. [CrossRef] [PubMed]
8. Kalafati, M.; Kakarountas, A.; Chroni, E. Testing of Motor Coordination in Degenerative Neurological Diseases. *Healthcare* **2022**, *10*, 1948. [CrossRef]
9. Jin, M.; Choi, H. Caregiver Views on Prospective Use of Robotic Care in Helping Children Adapt to Hospitalization. *Healthcare* **2022**, *10*, 1925. [CrossRef]
10. Pirrera, A.; Meli, P.; de Dominicis, A.; Lepri, A.; Giansanti, D. Assistive Technologies and Quadriplegia: A Map Point on the Development and Spread of the Tongue Barbell Piercing. *Healthcare* **2022**, *11*, 101. [CrossRef]
11. Giansanti, D. The Regulation of Artificial Intelligence in Digital Radiology in the Scientific Literature: A Narrative Review of Reviews. *Healthcare* **2022**, *10*, 1824. [CrossRef] [PubMed]
12. Thurzo, A.; Urbanová, W.; Novák, B.; Czako, L.; Siebert, T.; Stano, P.; Mareková, S.; Fountoulaki, G.; Kosnáčová, H.; Varga, I. Where Is the Artificial Intelligence Applied in Dentistry? Systematic Review and Literature Analysis. *Healthcare* **2022**, *10*, 1269. [CrossRef] [PubMed]
13. Thurzo, A.; Kosnáčová, H.S.; Kurilová, V.; Kosmeľ, S.; Beňuš, R.; Moravanský, N.; Kováč, P.; Kuracinová, K.M.; Palkovič, M.; Varga, I. Use of Advanced Artificial Intelligence in Forensic Medicine, Forensic Anthropology and Clinical Anatomy. *Healthcare* **2021**, *9*, 1545. [CrossRef] [PubMed]
14. Thurzo, A.; Kurilová, V.; Varga, I. Artificial Intelligence in Orthodontic Smart Application for Treatment Coaching and Its Impact on Clinical Performance of Patients Monitored with AI-Telehealth System. *Healthcare* **2021**, *9*, 1695. [CrossRef] [PubMed]
15. Payne, K.F.B.; Wharrad, H.; Watts, K. Smartphone and Medical Related App Use among Medical Students and Junior Doctors in the United Kingdom (UK): A Regional Survey. *BMC Med. Inform. Decis. Mak.* **2012**, *12*, 121. [CrossRef]
16. Helbostad, J.L.; Vereijken, B.; Becker, C.; Todd, C.; Taraldsen, K.; Pijnappels, M.; Aminian, K.; Mellone, S. Mobile Health Applications to Promote Active and Healthy Ageing. *Sensors* **2017**, *17*, 622. [CrossRef] [PubMed]
17. Quinn, C.C.; Shardell, M.D.; Terrin, M.L.; Barr, E.A.; Ballew, S.H.; Gruber-Baldini, A.L. Cluster-Randomized Trial of a Mobile Phone Personalized Behavioral Intervention for Blood Glucose Control. *Diabetes Care* **2011**, *34*, 1934–1942. [CrossRef] [PubMed]
18. Carrasco, M.P.; Salvador, C.H.; Sagredo, P.G.; Márquez-Montes, J.; González de Mingo, M.A.; Fragua, J.A.; Rodríguez, M.C.; García-Olmos, L.M.; García-López, F.; Carrero, A.M.; et al. Impact of Patient-General Practitioner Short-Messages-Based Interaction on the Control of Hypertension in a Follow-up Service for Low-to-Medium Risk Hypertensive Patients: A Randomized Controlled Trial. *IEEE Trans. Inf. Technol. Biomed.* **2008**, *12*, 780–791. [CrossRef] [PubMed]
19. Pfeil, J.N.; Rados, D.V.; Roman, R.; Katz, N.; Nunes, L.N.; Vigo, Á.; Harzheim, E. A Telemedicine Strategy to Reduce Waiting Lists and Time to Specialist Care: A Retrospective Cohort Study. *J. Telemed. Telecare* **2020**, *29*, 10–17. [CrossRef] [PubMed]
20. Thurzo, A.; Strunga, M.; Havlínová, R.; Reháková, K.; Urban, R.; Surovková, J.; Kurilová, V. Smartphone-Based Facial Scanning as a Viable Tool for Facially Driven Orthodontics? *Sensors* **2022**, *22*, 7752. [CrossRef] [PubMed]
21. Thurzo, A.; Urbanová, W.; Neuschlová, I.; Paouris, D.; Čverha, M. Use of Optical Scanning and 3D Printing to Fabricate Customized Appliances for Patients with Craniofacial Disorders. *Semin. Orthod.* **2022**, *28*, 92–99. [CrossRef]
22. Giudice, A.; Barone, S.; Muraca, D.; Averta, F.; Diodati, F.; Antonelli, A.; Fortunato, L. Can Teledentistry Improve the Monitoring of Patients during the COVID-19 Dissemination? A Descriptive Pilot Study. *Int. J. Environ. Res. Public Health* **2020**, *17*, 3399. [CrossRef]
23. Thurzo, A.; Šufliarsky, B.; Urbanová, W.; Čverha, M.; Strunga, M.; Varga, I. Pierre Robin Sequence and 3D Printed Personalized Composite Appliances in Interdisciplinary Approach. *Polymers* **2022**, *14*, 3858. [CrossRef]
24. Thurzo, A.; Urbanová, W.; Novák, B.; Waczulíková, I.; Varga, I. Utilization of a 3D Printed Orthodontic Distalizer for Tooth-Borne Hybrid Treatment in Class II Unilateral Malocclusions. *Materials* **2022**, *15*, 1740. [CrossRef] [PubMed]

25. Hansa, I.; Katyal, V.; Ferguson, D.J.; Vaid, N. Outcomes of Clear Aligner Treatment with and without Dental Monitoring: A Retrospective Cohort Study. *Am. J. Orthod. Dentofac. Orthop.* **2021**, *159*, 453–459. [CrossRef] [PubMed]
26. Thurzo, A.; Urbanová, W.; Waczulíková, I.; Kurilová, V.; Mriňáková, B.; Kosnáčová, H.; Gális, B.; Varga, I.; Matajs, M.; Novák, B. Dental Care and Education Facing Highly Transmissible SARS-CoV-2 Variants: Prospective Biosafety Setting: Prospective, Single-Arm, Single-Center Study. *Int. J. Environ. Res. Public Health* **2022**, *19*, 7693. [CrossRef]
27. Caruso, S.; Caruso, S.; Pellegrino, M.; Skafi, R.; Nota, A.; Tecco, S. A Knowledge-Based Algorithm for Automatic Monitoring of Orthodontic Treatment: The Dental Monitoring System. Two Cases. *Sensors* **2021**, *21*, 1856. [CrossRef] [PubMed]
28. Ben-Omran, M.O.; Livinski, A.A.; Kopycka-Kedzierawski, D.T.; Boroumand, S.; Williams, D.; Weatherspoon, D.J.; Iafolla, T.J.; Fontelo, P.; Dye, B.A. The Use of Teledentistry in Facilitating Oral Health for Older Adults: A Scoping Review. *J. Am. Dent. Assoc.* **2021**, *152*, 998–1011.e17. [CrossRef]
29. Shen, K.L.; Huang, C.L.; Lin, Y.C.; Du, J.K.; Chen, F.L.; Kabasawa, Y.; Chen, C.C.; Huang, H.L. Effects of Artificial Intelligence-Assisted Dental Monitoring Intervention in Patients with Periodontitis: A Randomized Controlled Trial. *J. Clin. Periodontol.* **2022**, *49*, 988–998. [CrossRef] [PubMed]
30. Albalawi, F.; Alamoud, K.A. Trends and Application of Artificial Intelligence Technology in Orthodontic Diagnosis and Treatment Planning—A Review. *Appl. Sci.* **2022**, *12*, 11864. [CrossRef]
31. Singh, P. Orthodontic Apps for Smartphones. *J. Orthod.* **2013**, *40*, 249–255. [CrossRef]
32. Hansa, I.; Semaan, S.J.; Vaid, N.R. Clinical Outcomes and Patient Perspectives of Dental Monitoring® GoLive® with Invisalign®—A Retrospective Cohort Study. *Prog. Orthod.* **2020**, *21*, 16. [CrossRef]
33. Kunz, F.; Stellzig-Eisenhauer, A.; Zeman, F.; Boldt, J. Artificial Intelligence in Orthodontics: Evaluation of a Fully Automated Cephalometric Analysis Using a Customized Convolutional Neural Network. *J. Orofac. Orthop.* **2020**, *81*, 52–68. [CrossRef]
34. Maspero, C.; Abate, A.; Cavagnetto, D.; el Morsi, M.; Fama, A.; Farronato, M. Available Technologies, Applications and Benefits of Teleorthodontics. A Literature Review and Possible Applications during the COVID-19 Pandemic. *J. Clin. Med.* **2020**, *9*, 1891. [CrossRef] [PubMed]
35. Yu, H.J.; Cho, S.R.; Kim, M.J.; Kim, W.H.; Kim, J.W.; Choi, J. Automated Skeletal Classification with Lateral Cephalometry Based on Artificial Intelligence. *J. Dent. Res.* **2020**, *99*, 249–256. [CrossRef]
36. Lee, J.-H.; Yu, H.-J.; Kim, M.; Kim, J.-W.; Choi, J. Automated Cephalometric Landmark Detection with Confidence Regions Using Bayesian Convolutional Neural Networks. *BMC Oral Health* **2020**, *20*, 1–10. [CrossRef] [PubMed]
37. Leite, A.F.; de Faria Vasconcelos, K.; Willems, H.; Jacobs, R. Radiomics and Machine Learning in Oral Healthcare. *Proteom. Clin. Appl.* **2020**, *14*, e1900040. [CrossRef] [PubMed]
38. Wang, H.; Minnema, J.; Batenburg, K.J.; Forouzanfar, T.; Hu, F.J.; Wu, G. Multiclass CBCT Image Segmentation for Orthodontics with Deep Learning. *J. Dent. Res.* **2021**, *100*, 943–949. [CrossRef]
39. Bichu, Y.M.; Hansa, I.; Bichu, A.Y.; Premjani, P.; Flores-Mir, C.; Vaid, N.R. Applications of Artificial Intelligence and Machine Learning in Orthodontics: A Scoping Review. *Prog. Orthod.* **2021**, *22*, 1–11. [CrossRef]
40. Schwendicke, F.; Chaurasia, A.; Arsiwala, L.; Lee, J.H.; Elhennawy, K.; Jost-Brinkmann, P.G.; Demarco, F.; Krois, J. Deep Learning for Cephalometric Landmark Detection: Systematic Review and Meta-Analysis. *Clin. Oral Investig.* **2021**, *25*, 4299–4309. [CrossRef]
41. Deshpande, S.; Patil, D.; Dhokar, A.; Bhanushali, P.; Katge, F. Teledentistry: A Boon Amidst COVID-19 Lockdown—A Narrative Review. *Int. J. Telemed. Appl.* **2021**, *2021*, 1–6. [CrossRef]
42. Ahmed, N.; Abbasi, M.S.; Zuberi, F.; Qamar, W.; bin Halim, M.S.; Maqsood, A.; Alam, M.K. Artificial Intelligence Techniques: Analysis, Application, and Outcome in Dentistry—A Systematic Review. *BioMed Res. Int.* **2021**, *2021*, 1–15. [CrossRef]
43. Mohammad-Rahimi, H.; Nadimi, M.; Rohban, M.H.; Shamsoddin, E.; Lee, V.Y.; Motamedian, S.R. Machine Learning and Orthodontics, Current Trends and the Future Opportunities: A Scoping Review. *Am. J. Orthod. Dentofac. Orthop.* **2021**, *160*, 170–192.e4. [CrossRef] [PubMed]
44. Juerchott, A.; Freudlsperger, C.; Weber, D.; Jende, J.M.E.; Saleem, M.A.; Zingler, S.; Lux, C.J.; Bendszus, M.; Heiland, S.; Hilgenfeld, T. In Vivo Comparison of MRI- and CBCT-Based 3D Cephalometric Analysis: Beginning of a Non-Ionizing Diagnostic Era in Craniomaxillofacial Imaging? *Eur. Radiol.* **2020**, *30*, 1488–1497. [CrossRef] [PubMed]
45. MacHoy, M.E.; Szyszka-Sommerfeld, L.; Vegh, A.; Gedrange, T.; Woźniak, K. The Ways of Using Machine Learning in Dentistry. *Adv. Clin. Exp. Med.* **2020**, *29*, 375–384. [CrossRef]
46. Ren, R.; Luo, H.; Su, C.; Yao, Y.; Liao, W. Machine Learning in Dental, Oral and Craniofacial Imaging: A Review of Recent Progress. *PeerJ* **2021**, *9*, e11451. [CrossRef] [PubMed]
47. Dalessandri, D.; Sangalli, L.; Tonni, I.; Laffranchi, L.; Bonetti, S.; Visconti, L.; Signoroni, A.; Paganelli, C. Attitude towards Telemonitoring in Orthodontists and Orthodontic Patients. *Dent. J.* **2021**, *9*, 47. [CrossRef]
48. Impellizzeri, A.; Horodinsky, M.; Barbato, E.; Polimeni, A.; Salah, P.; Galluccio, G. Dental Monitoring Application: It Is a Valid Innovation in the Orthodontics Practice? *Clin. Ter.* **2020**, *171*, e260–e267. [CrossRef]
49. Monill-González, A.; Rovira-Calatayud, L.; d'Oliveira, N.G.; Ustrell-Torrent, J.M. Artificial Intelligence in Orthodontics: Where Are We Now? A Scoping Review. *Orthod. Craniofac. Res.* **2021**, *24*, 6–15. [CrossRef]
50. Bulatova, G.; Kusnoto, B.; Grace, V.; Tsay, T.P.; Avenetti, D.M.; Sanchez, F.J.C. Assessment of Automatic Cephalometric Landmark Identification Using Artificial Intelligence. *Orthod. Craniofac. Res.* **2021**, *24*, 37–42. [CrossRef]
51. Park, J.H.; Rogowski, L.; Kim, J.H.; al Shami, S.; Howell, S.E.I. Teledentistry Platforms for Orthodontics. *J. Clin. Pediatr. Dent.* **2021**, *45*, 48–53. [CrossRef] [PubMed]

52. Sangalli, L.; Savoldi, F.; Dalessandri, D.; Bonetti, S.; Gu, M.; Signoroni, A.; Paganelli, C. Effects of Remote Digital Monitoring on Oral Hygiene of Orthodontic Patients: A Prospective Study. *BMC Oral Health* **2021**, *21*, 1–8. [CrossRef]
53. Achmad, H.; Tanumihardja, M.; Ramadhany, Y.F. Teledentistry as a Solution in Dentistry during the Covid-19 Pandemic Period: A Systematic Review. *Int. J. Pharm. Res.* **2020**, *12*, 272–278. [CrossRef]
54. Moylan, H.B.; Carrico, C.K.; Lindauer, S.J.; Tüfekçi, E. Accuracy of a Smartphone-Based Orthodontic Treatment-Monitoring Application: A Pilot Study. *Angle Orthod.* **2019**, *89*, 727–733. [CrossRef]
55. Morris, R.S.; Hoye, L.N.; Elnagar, M.H.; Atsawasuwan, P.; Galang-Boquiren, M.T.; Caplin, J.; Viana, G.C.; Obrez, A.; Kusnoto, B. Accuracy of Dental Monitoring 3D Digital Dental Models Using Photograph and Video Mode. *Am. J. Orthod. Dentofac. Orthop.* **2019**, *156*, 420–428. [CrossRef]
56. Sycinska-Dziarnowska, M.; Maglitto, M.; Woźniak, K.; Spagnuolo, G. Oral Health and Teledentistry Interest during the COVID-19 Pandemic. *J. Clin. Med.* **2021**, *10*, 3532. [CrossRef]
57. Roisin, L.-C.; Brézulier, D.; Sorel, O. Remotely-Controlled Orthodontics: Fundamentals and Description of the Dental Monitoring System. *J. Dentofac. Anom. Orthod.* **2016**, *19*, 408. [CrossRef]
58. Siddiqui, N.R.; Hodges, S.; Sharif, M.O. Availability of Orthodontic Smartphone Apps. *J. Orthod.* **2019**, *46*, 235–241. [CrossRef] [PubMed]
59. Vaid, N.R.; Hansa, I.; Bichu, Y. Smartphone Applications Used in Orthodontics: A Scoping Review of Scholarly Literature. *J. World Fed. Orthod.* **2020**, *9*, S67–S73. [CrossRef]
60. Kang, S.H.; Jeon, K.; Kang, S.-H.; Lee, S.-H. 3D Cephalometric Landmark Detection by Multiple Stage Deep Reinforcement Learning. *Sci. Rep.* **2021**, *11*, 1–13. [CrossRef]
61. Khader, D.; Peedikayil, F.; Chandru, T.; Kottayi, S.; Namboothiri, D. Reliability of One Ceph Software in Cephalometric Tracing: A Comparative Study. *SRM J. Res. Dent. Sci.* **2020**, *11*, 35. [CrossRef]
62. Lachinov, D.; Getmanskaya, A.; Turlapov, V. Cephalometric Landmark Regression with Convolutional Neural Networks on 3D Computed Tomography Data. *Pattern Recognit. Image Anal.* **2020**, *30*, 512–522. [CrossRef]
63. Botelho, F.; Davidovitch, M.; Sella-Tunis, T.; Abramovicz, L.; Reiter, S.; Matalon, S.; Shpack, N. Verification of Convolutional Neural Network Cephalometric Landmark Identification. *Appl. Sci.* **2022**, *12*, 12784. [CrossRef]
64. Duman, Ş.B.; Syed, A.Z.; Celik Ozen, D.; Bayrakdar, İ.Ş.; Salehi, H.S.; Abdelkarim, A.; Celik, Ö.; Eser, G.; Altun, O.; Orhan, K. Convolutional Neural Network Performance for Sella Turcica Segmentation and Classification Using CBCT Images. *Diagnostics* **2022**, *12*, 2244. [CrossRef] [PubMed]
65. Le, V.N.T.; Kang, J.; Oh, I.S.; Kim, J.G.; Yang, Y.M.; Lee, D.W. Effectiveness of Human–Artificial Intelligence Collaboration in Cephalometric Landmark Detection. *J. Pers. Med.* **2022**, *12*, 387. [CrossRef] [PubMed]
66. Zhou, J.; Zhou, H.; Pu, L.; Gao, Y.; Tang, Z.; Yang, Y.; You, M.; Yang, Z.; Lai, W.; Long, H. Development of an Artificial Intelligence System for the Automatic Evaluation of Cervical Vertebral Maturation Status. *Diagnostics* **2021**, *11*, 2200. [CrossRef] [PubMed]
67. Kim, C.; Kim, D.; Jeong, H.G.; Yoon, S.J.; Youm, S. Automatic Tooth Detection and Numbering Using a Combination of a CNN and Heuristic Algorithm. *Appl. Sci.* **2020**, *10*, 5624. [CrossRef]
68. Tsolakis, I.A.; Kolokitha, O.-E.; Papadopoulou, E.; Tsolakis, A.I.; Kilipiris, E.G.; Palomo, J.M. Artificial Intelligence as an Aid in CBCT Airway Analysis: A Systematic Review. *Life* **2022**, *12*, 1894. [CrossRef]
69. Fountoulaki, G.; Thurzo, A. Change in the Constricted Airway in Patients after Clear Aligner Treatment: A Retrospective Study. *Diagnostics* **2022**, *12*, 2201. [CrossRef]
70. Thurzo, A.; Jančovičová, V.; Hain, M.; Thurzo, M.; Novák, B.; Kosnáčová, H.; Lehotská, V.; Moravanský, N.; Varga, I. Human Remains Identification Using Micro-CT, Spectroscopic and A.I. Methods in Forensic Experimental Reconstruction of Dental Patterns After Concentrated Acid Significant Impact. *Molecules* **2022**, *27*, 4035. [CrossRef]
71. Matsuda, S.; Yoshida, H.; Ebata, K.; Shimada, I.; Yoshimura, H. Forensic Odontology with Digital Technologies: A Systematic Review. *J. Forensic Leg. Med.* **2020**, *74*, 102004. [CrossRef]
72. Tsolakis, I.A.; Tsolakis, A.I.; Elshebiny, T.; Matthaios, S.; Palomo, J.M. Comparing a Fully Automated Cephalometric Tracing Method to a Manual Tracing Method for Orthodontic Diagnosis. *J. Clin. Med.* **2022**, *11*, 6854. [CrossRef]
73. Thurzo, A.; Javorka, V.; Stanko, P.; Lysy, J.; Suchancova, B.; Lehotska, V.; Valkovic, L.; Makovnik, M. Digital and Manual Cephalometric Analysis. *Bratisl. Med. J.* **2010**, *111*, 97–100.
74. Dot, G.; Rafflenbeul, F.; Arbotto, M.; Gajny, L.; Rouch, P.; Schouman, T. Accuracy and Reliability of Automatic Three-Dimensional Cephalometric Landmarking. *Int. J. Oral. Maxillofac. Surg.* **2020**, *49*, 1367–1378. [CrossRef]
75. Baksi, S.; Freezer, S.; Matsumoto, T.; Dreyer, C. Accuracy of an Automated Method of 3D Soft Tissue Landmark Detection. *Eur. J. Orthod.* **2020**, *43*, 622–630. [CrossRef]
76. Focardi, M.; Pinchi, V.; de Luca, F.; Norelli, G.-A. Age Estimation for Forensic Purposes in Italy: Ethical Issues. *Int. J. Leg. Med.* **2014**, *128*, 515–522. [CrossRef]
77. Obermeyer, Z.; Powers, B.; Vogeli, C.; Mullainathan, S. Dissecting Racial Bias in an Algorithm Used to Manage the Health of Populations. *Science* **2019**, *366*, 447–453. [CrossRef]
78. Livingston, M. Preventing Racial Bias in Federal AI. *J. Sci. Policy Gov.* **2020**, *16*. [CrossRef]
79. EU's Artificial Intelligence Act Will Lead the World on Regulating AI | New Scientist. Available online: https://www.newscientist.com/article/mg25634192-300-eus-artificial-intelligence-act-will-lead-the-world-on-regulating-ai/ (accessed on 31 December 2022).

80. Sfikas, P.M. Teledentistry: Legal and Regulatory Issues Explored. *J. Am. Dent. Assoc.* **1997**, *128*, 1716–1718. [CrossRef]
81. al Turkestani, N.; Bianchi, J.; Deleat-Besson, R.; Le, C.; Tengfei, L.; Prieto, J.C.; Gurgel, M.; Ruellas, A.C.O.; Massaro, C.; Aliaga Del Castillo, A.; et al. Clinical Decision Support Systems in Orthodontics: A Narrative Review of Data Science Approaches. *Orthod. Craniofac. Res.* **2021**, *24*, 26–36. [CrossRef] [PubMed]
82. Faber, J.; Faber, C.; Faber, P.; Faber, J.; Faber, C.; Faber, P. Artificial Intelligence in Orthodontics. *APOS Trends Orthod.* **2019**, *9*, 201–205. [CrossRef]
83. Kasirzadeh, A.; Gabriel, I. In Conversation with Artificial Intelligence: Aligning Language Models with Human Values. *arXiv* **2022**, arXiv:2209.00731. [CrossRef]
84. de Angelis, F.; Pranno, N.; Franchina, A.; di Carlo, S.; Brauner, E.; Ferri, A.; Pellegrino, G.; Grecchi, E.; Goker, F.; Stefanelli, L.V. Artificial Intelligence: A New Diagnostic Software in Dentistry: A Preliminary Performance Diagnostic Study. *Int. J. Environ. Res. Public Health* **2022**, *19*, 1728. [CrossRef]
85. Meghil, M.M.; Rajpurohit, P.; Awad, M.E.; McKee, J.; Shahoumi, L.A.; Ghaly, M. Artificial Intelligence in Dentistry. *Dent. Rev.* **2022**, *2*, 100009. [CrossRef]
86. Ducret, M.; Mörch, C.M.; Karteva, T.; Fisher, J.; Schwendicke, F. Artificial Intelligence for Sustainable Oral Healthcare. *J. Dent.* **2022**, *127*, 104344. [CrossRef]
87. Ramya, Y.; Betha, S.P.; Kauser, A.; Shetty, C. Artificial Intelligence in Orthodontics: A Review. *Int. J. Health Sci.* **2022**, *6*, 9378–9383. [CrossRef]
88. Shan, T.; Tay, F.R.; Gu, L. Application of Artificial Intelligence in Dentistry. *J. Dent. Res.* **2021**, *100*, 232–244. [CrossRef]
89. Ossowska, A.; Kusiak, A.; Świetlik, D. Artificial Intelligence in Dentistry—Narrative Review. *Int. J. Environ. Res. Public Health* **2022**, *19*, 3449. [CrossRef] [PubMed]
90. Thurzo, A.; Stanko, P.; Urbanova, W.; Lysy, J.; Suchancova, B.; Makovnik, M.; Javorka, V. The WEB 2.0 Induced Paradigm Shift in the e-Learning and the Role of Crowdsourcing in Dental Education. *Bratisl. Med. J.* **2010**, *111*, 168–175.
91. Islam, N.M.; Laughter, L.; Sadid-Zadeh, R.; Smith, C.; Dolan, T.A.; Crain, G.; Squarize, C.H. Adopting Artificial Intelligence in Dental Education: A Model for Academic Leadership and Innovation. *J. Dent. Educ.* **2022**, *86*, 1545–1551. [CrossRef]
92. Saghiri, M.A.; Vakhnovetsky, J.; Nadershahi, N. Scoping Review of Artificial Intelligence and Immersive Digital Tools in Dental Education. *J. Dent. Educ.* **2022**, *86*, 736–750. [CrossRef] [PubMed]
93. The Artificial Intelligence Act. Available online: https://artificialintelligenceact.eu/ (accessed on 17 February 2023).

healthcare

MDPI

Article

Functional Improvement and Satisfaction with a Wearable Hip Exoskeleton in Community-Living Adults

Jihye Kim [1,†], Hyelim Chun [1,†], Su-Hyun Lee [1], Hwang-Jae Lee [2,*] and Yun-Hee Kim [1,3,*]

1 Center for Prevention and Rehabilitation, Samsung Medical Center, Department of Physical and Rehabilitation Medicine, Heart Vascular Stroke Institute, Sungkyunkwan University School of Medicine, Seoul 06351, Republic of Korea
2 Robot Business Team, Samsung Electronics, Suwon 16499, Republic of Korea
3 Department of Health Sciences and Technology, Department of Medical Device Management and Research, Department of Digital Health, SAIHST, Sungkyunkwan University, Seoul 06351, Republic of Korea
* Correspondence: hwangjae.lee@samsung.com (H.-J.L.); yunkim@skku.edu or yun1225.kim@samsung.com (Y.-H.K.); Tel.: +82-2-3410-2824 (ext. 2818) (Y.-H.K.)
† These authors contributed equally to this work.

Abstract: Demand for wearable devices and supportive technology is growing as these devices have the potential to enhance physical function and quality of life in users. The purpose of this study was to investigate usability and satisfaction after performing functional and gait exercise with a wearable hip exoskeleton in community-living adults. A total of 225 adults residing in the local community participated in this study. All participants performed 40 min of exercise once with a wearable hip exoskeleton in various environments. The EX1, which functions as a wearable hip exoskeleton, was used. Physical function was assessed before and after exercise with the EX1. After completing exercise with the EX1, the usability and satisfaction questionnaires were evaluated. Gait speed, timed up and go test (TUG), and four square step test (FSST) showed statistically significant improvements after exercise with the EX1 in both groups ($p < 0.05$). In the 6 min walking test (6MWT), a significant increase was observed in the middle-aged group ($p < 0.05$). In the short physical performance battery (SPPB), there was a significant improvement in the old-aged group ($p < 0.05$). On the other hand, positive results in usability and satisfaction were noticed in both groups. These results demonstrate that a single session of exercise with the EX1 was effective in improving physical performance of both middle- and old-aged adults, with positive feedback from most of the participants.

Keywords: exoskeleton device; gait; robot; personal satisfaction; physical fitness

Citation: Kim, J.; Chun, H.; Lee, S.-H.; Lee, H.-J.; Kim, Y.-H. Functional Improvement and Satisfaction with a Wearable Hip Exoskeleton in Community-Living Adults. *Healthcare* **2023**, *11*, 643. https://doi.org/10.3390/healthcare11050643

Academic Editors: Daniele Giansanti and Tin-Chih Toly Chen

Received: 9 November 2022
Revised: 18 February 2023
Accepted: 21 February 2023
Published: 22 February 2023

1. Introduction

Physical activity, which is associated with quality of life, decreases with age due to loss of muscle mass and strength [1], cardiac and respiratory disease [2], and other factors. Decreased physical activity during the aging process leads to metabolic disorders and other chronic diseases, such as cancer, diabetes, and cerebrovascular and cardiovascular diseases [3]. Regular physical activity such as walking, cycling, dancing, and running leads to positive physiological changes. Regular physical activity improves autonomic balance, bone density, capillary density, muscle fiber size, neuromuscular coordination, stroke volume, blood coagulation, and inflammation [4]. Moreover, these physiological changes result in decreased depression, weight gain, fractures, injurious falls, osteoporosis, and mortality, as well as increased physical and cognitive function [4]. A previous study reported that regular physical activity could increase the life expectancy of the world's population [5].

Walking is one of the easiest regular physical activities. Walking is the cheapest and easiest activity for health promotion and consumes larger amounts of energy than other daily sports activities. Gait function refers to the mobility required for daily life performance, which can predict clinical conditions in various aspects [6]. In previous studies, inactive adults experienced 3–8% muscle loss over 10 years with decreased metabolic rate and fat accumulation during rest [7], but walking exercise improved walking economy and functionality [8], muscle size and quality [9], functional balance, and reaction time [10], which are related to gait quality.

Recently, functional exercise has been carried out under various conditions, such as applying a load, using props, or combining various conditions. Resistance gait exercise enhances balance and gait parameters [11] and decreases the fear of falling [12]. A previous study showed that, after resistance gait exercise using an underwater treadmill, gait parameters including step length, velocity, and cadence were significantly increased [13]. In addition, an assistive therapeutic exercise program is effective in improving preferred gait speed [14].

Robot technology in the healthcare field is being actively used in clinical practice as it has been developed in the surgical and rehabilitation medical fields. However, in recent years, the technological advances in daily assistive robots have gone beyond their limited use for patients in the medical field [15]. Wearable exoskeletons are being actively developed to assist and strengthen physical functions for not only disabled, but also non-disabled people. A wearable exoskeleton helps to improve gait by assisting with voluntary movement of the lower extremity joints during gait [16,17]. Furthermore, gait exercise with a wearable hip exoskeleton improves cardiopulmonary function. In a previous study, gait training with an assisted-exoskeleton robot required less oxygen consumption than a home exercise program of self-paced overground walking without a robot at the same speed in the elderly [18].

The EX1, developed by Samsung Electronics (Suwon, Republic of Korea), is a personalized robot with a light weight of 2.1 kg that is worn on the hip joints. In our previous study in the elderly, there were statistically significant improvements in gait speed, excessive muscle activity, respiration, and metabolic energy during gait with the EX1 compared to walking without it [16].

Demand for wearable devices and supportive technology is growing because these devices have potential to enhance physical functions and quality of life of users. Furthermore, among the factors to be considered when using a wearable robot, user stability and fit are important. Previous studies on the EX1 investigated the effect on physical function rather than usability and satisfaction with the wearable robot. Thus, wearable devices need to be evaluated by actual users in terms of wearability [19]. This study was designed to investigate the usability, satisfaction, and physical function from a single session of functional and gait exercise with the EX1 in community-living middle- and old-aged adults.

2. Materials and Methods

2.1. Study Participants

The participants were recruited from local community residents who use silver town or welfare centers. Two-hundred and twenty-five adults who met the following inclusion criteria were enrolled in this study: no history of central nervous system disease and age between 40 and 84 years. Subjects with uncontrolled severe high blood pressure or diabetes, history of uncontrolled cardiovascular disease, severe dizziness that might lead to a fall, and cognitive disorders that hinder the ability to understand or comply with study instructions were excluded. General characteristics of the subjects are summarized in Table 1. The study protocol was approved by the Institutional Review Board of Samsung Medical Center, Seoul, Korea (No. 2021-04-058), and informed consent was provided by all subjects before participating in the study.

Table 1. General characteristics of participants.

Characteristics	Total (*N* = 225)	Middle-Aged (*n* = 75)	Old-Aged (*n* = 150)
Gender (male/female)	80/145	31/44	49/101
Age (year)	67.52 (10.99) [a]	74.31 (4.79)	53.96 (6.30)
Height (cm)	161.53 (8.26)	159.85 (8.85)	164.88 (7.32)
Weight (kg)	61.76 (10.58)	59.93 (9.32)	65.43 (11.98)
BMI (kg/m^2)	23.59 (3.06)	23.42 (2.92)	23.94 (3.33)
MMSE-K	28.16 (1.82)	27.95 (1.93)	28.57 (1.49)
GDS-15	3.71 (3.32)	4.1 (3.43)	2.93 (2.99)
FES-K	99.32 (3.30)	99.07 (3.92)	99.81 (1.24)
EQ-5D	0.90 (0.08)	0.89 (0.92)	0.93 (0.46)

[a] Mean (SD), middle-aged group = 40–64 years, old-aged group = 65–84 years; BMI = body mass index; MMSE-K = Mini-Mental State Examination—Korean; GDS-15 = Geriatric Depression Scale-15; FES-K = Fall Efficacy Scale—Korean; EQ-5D = EuroQol-5 dimension.

2.2. Experimental Protocol

This study protocol was designed as a single group, and all participants performed a single session of exercise with EX1. All participants received 40 min of exercise with the EX1: 20 min of functional exercise including sit-to-stand and balance exercise and 20 min of gait exercise including stair climbing and over-ground and incline walking with the assist and resistance modes of EX1. To confirm the effect of a single session of exercise with EX1, physical functions measured by the 10 m walking test (10MWT), timed up and go test (TUG), four square step test (FSST), 6 min walking test (6MWT), and short physical performance battery (SPPB) were evaluated before and after the exercise program. All outcome measures were performed without the EX1. After completing a single session of exercise with the EX1, the usability and satisfaction questionnaire for EX1 were evaluated (Figure 1).

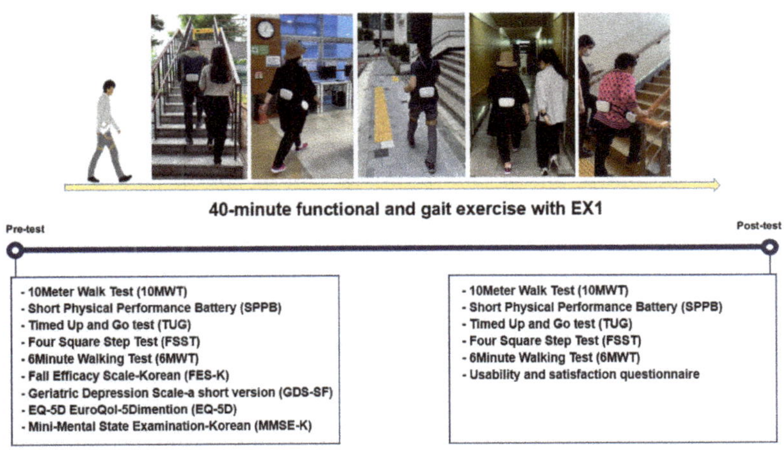

Figure 1. Experimental protocol.

2.3. Wearable Hip Exoskeleton (EX1)

The EX1, which was developed by Samsung Electronics, is a minimized exoskeleton worn on the hip joints. It is very lightweight and user-customizable, weighing approximately 2.1 kg (Figure 2). EX1 can provide assistive or resistive torque forces around both hip joints for both extension and flexion direction during gait as needed, and it promotes physical function in daily life. EX1 consists of a pair of actuators that generate force on the left and right hip joints, a hip brace on the waist, a pair of thigh frames, and a thigh belt [20].

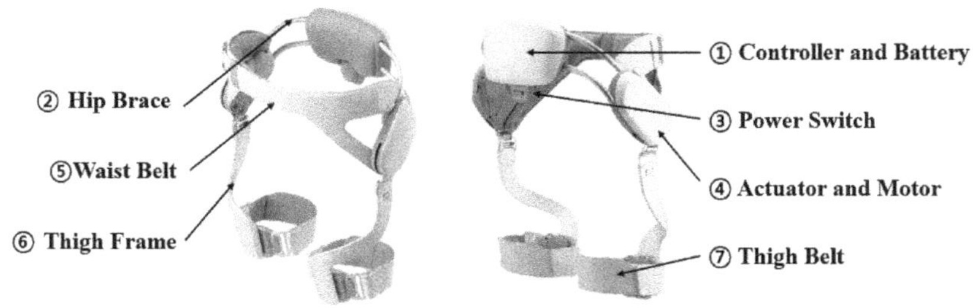

Figure 2. EX1 developed by Samsung Electronics.

2.4. Measurement Tools

2.4.1. Physical Function Evaluation

To measure physical function, 10MWT, TUG, FSST, 6MWT, and SPPB were performed. The 10MWT is the most effective method for predicting falls and evaluating gait ability by measuring gait speed, and it has high test–retest reliability in healthy adults (intra- and inter-tester reliability (ICC) = 0.93–0.91) [21]. For measurement, subjects were asked to walk a total of 15 m at a comfortable speed. The time it took to walk 10 m was measured, excluding the initial 2.5 m acceleration and the final 2.5 m deceleration, and the result in seconds was converted into speed (m/s). Measurements were repeated twice, and the average value was used.

To evaluate the dynamic balance ability among physical functions, TUG and FSST were measured. The TUG test is used as a standard test method in clinical practice as a representative test method for measuring gait ability as well as dynamic balance ability of elderly and brain injury patients, and it has high ICC in the elderly (ICC = 0.92–0.99) [22]. The FSST is a method of evaluating dynamic balance and movement ability. It measures the time it takes to walk forward, backward, and sideways over a low obstacle as fast as subjects can, and it has high test–retest reliability (ICC = 0.87) [23].

To evaluate walking endurance, 6MWT was measured. The 6MWT is a representative method for measuring gait aerobics and endurance in the elderly and patients with cardiopulmonary disease. To measure gait endurance, subjects are asked to walk a set trajectory for 6 min, and the total walking distance is measured. It has excellent test–retest reliability for the elderly (ICC = 0.95) [22].

SPPB is a test that consists of walking speed, sit-to-stand on a chair, and balance tests. It has been used as a predictive tool for dysfunction and can be helpful in functional monitoring in the elderly. The score ranges from a minimum of 0 points to a maximum of 12 points. SPPB has been shown to have validity as a predictor of fall risk and mortality and has excellent test–retest reliability for the elderly (ICC = 0.91) [24].

2.4.2. The Usability and Satisfaction Questionnaire

As there was no appropriate usability and satisfaction questionnaire for evaluating the wearable hip exoskeleton, the questionnaire was developed and applied through previous research [17] and consultation with experts (Table 2). A questionnaire was developed by setting usability and satisfaction evaluation areas. The safety questionnaire is one of the most important parts to determine whether EX1 can be used safely. The operability question is a factor to realize the function of the gait robot. The questionnaire includes operational convenience, effectiveness, and efficiency.

Table 2. The usability and satisfaction questionnaire of the EX1.

Domain	No.	Item	Strongly Disagree	Disagree	Neutral	Agree	Strongly Agree
Safety	1	Did you have any risk of falling when turning or leaning forward while using the EX1?	①	②	③	④	⑤
Safety	2	Did you have a risk of fall or injury while using the EX1?	①	②	③	④	⑤
Safety	3	Do you think you can control the risks posed by EX1 yourself?	①	②	③	④	⑤
Safety	4	Did you fear falling while walking with the EX1?	①	②	③	④	⑤
Satisfaction	1	Was the EX1 easy to use?	①	②	③	④	⑤
Satisfaction	2	Do you think people with healthy people can also use the EX1?	①	②	③	④	⑤
Satisfaction	3	Were you not shamed for using EX1?	①	②	③	④	⑤
Satisfaction	4	Do you think the EX1 will have negative social perceptions?	①	②	③	④	⑤
Satisfaction	5	Was the weight of the EX1 appropriate for walking?	①	②	③	④	⑤
Satisfaction	6	Was the EX1 comfortable to wear?	①	②	③	④	⑤
Satisfaction	7	Were you satisfied with the material of the EX1?	①	②	③	④	⑤
Satisfaction	8	Do you think the assist mode of the EX1 helps with gait?	①	②	③	④	⑤
Satisfaction	9	Do you think the resistance mode of the EX1 helps with gait exercises?	①	②	③	④	⑤
Satisfaction	10	Was there any disturbance caused by noise when using the EX1?	①	②	③	④	⑤
Satisfaction	11	Are you satisfied with the color and design of the EX1?	①	②	③	④	⑤
Satisfaction	12	Are you willing to continue using the EX1?	①	②	③	④	⑤
Satisfaction	13	Between assist and resistance modes of EX1, which was more helpful?	① Resistance mode ② Assist mode				

2.5. Data Preprocessing and Statistical Analysis

All data were analyzed with SPSS version 22.0 program (IBM, Armonk, NY, USA). Results were calculated as mean and standard deviation values. Statistical significance levels for all measurements were set as $p < 0.05$.

Physical function evaluation, usability, and satisfaction tests were analyzed by dividing the age into two subgroups: a middle-aged group 40 to 64 years old and an old-aged group 65 to 84 years old. To evaluate the feasibility of a single session with the EX1, paired t-tests were used to compare outcome measures between pre- and post-exercise.

To evaluate the usability and satisfaction questionnaire, frequency analysis was used. In addition, the usability and satisfaction tests with standardized β coefficients in linear regression analysis were used to investigate the relationship between physical function and questionnaire.

3. Results

3.1. Physical Function

In the 10MWT, TUG, and FSST, significant increases after a single exercise session with the EX1 were observed in both groups ($p < 0.05$) (Figure 3). In the 6MWT, there was a statistically significant improvement only in the middle-aged group ($p < 0.05$). In the SPPB, there was a significant improvement in the old-aged group ($p < 0.05$) but not in the middle-aged group.

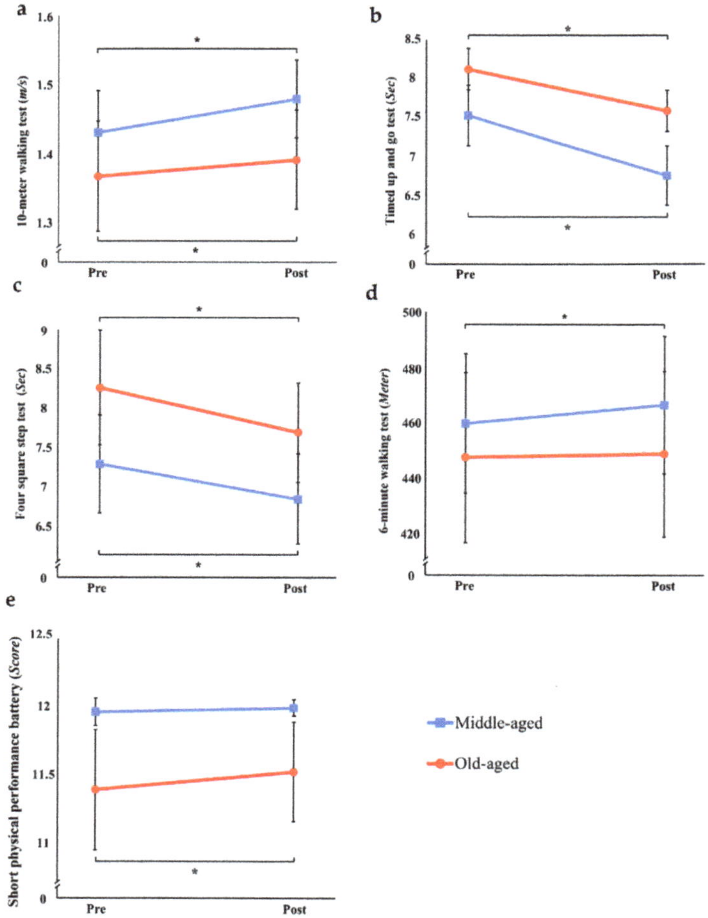

Figure 3. Changes in physical function. (**a**) 10 m walking test; (**b**) timed up and go test; (**c**) four square step test; (**d**) 6 minute walking test; (**e**) short physical performance battery (* $p < 0.05$).

3.2. Usability and Satisfaction of the EX1

In the safety domain (involving items such as risk of falls and control of risk factors), after using the EX1, positive responses were confirmed in both groups. The responses were mostly positive in the satisfaction domain, but there were some items with difference by age group. The middle-aged group showed more positive responses than the old-aged group in the easiness of use, usefulness, and perception of the EX1. In addition, the middle-aged group showed more positive responses than the old-aged group in the questionnaire on whether the assist and resist mode of the EX1 helped with gait exercises. Though the old-aged group tended to prefer the assist mode, the middle-aged group tended to prefer the resistance mode of the EX1 (Figure 4).

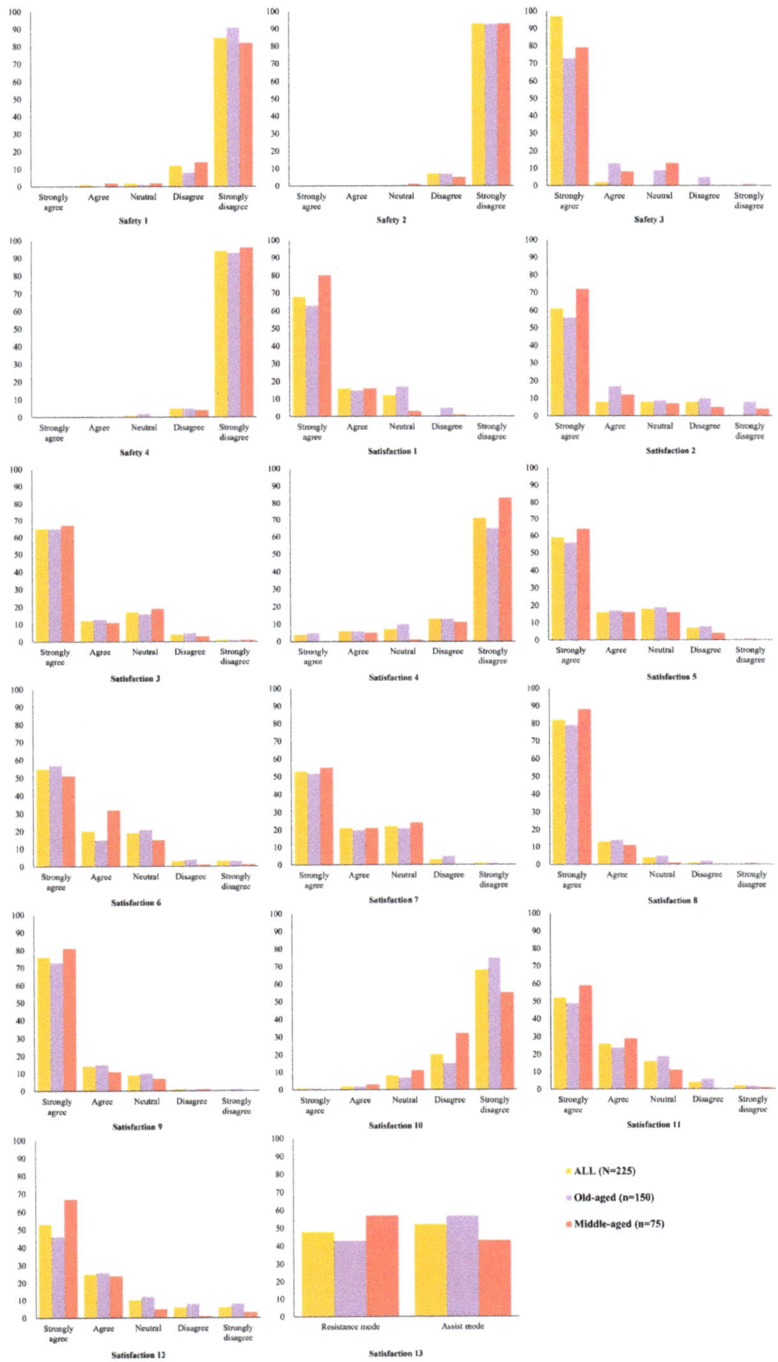

Figure 4. Responses to the questionnaire about usability and satisfaction of the EX1. The items of the usability and satisfaction evaluation include the safety of wearing, the risk of falling, the ease of operation, the feeling of weight, the fit, and the noise of the EX1. Refer to Table 2 for the usability and satisfaction questionnaire.

3.3. Regression Analysis between General Characteristics, Usability, and Satisfaction

As a result of regression analysis of 128 cases with a combination of 16 dependent variables and 8 independent variables, there were 15 significant results (Y = aX + b) (Table 2). The dependent variable (Y) consisted of a total of 16 items related to safety (4 items) and satisfaction (12 items), and the independent variable (X) consisted of a total of 8 items: age, gender, height, weight, body mass index (BMI), health status (2 items; health conditions, level of activity), and experience of fall.

The younger the user, the easier they tend to think the EX1 was to use, they tend to think that the assist mode of the EX1 helps most with gait, and they tend to be willing to continue using the EX1. If the users think they have better health conditions, they tend to think the EX1 was easy to use. If the user is more active, they think that they control the risk posed by the EX1 (Supplementary Table S1).

3.4. Regression Analysis between Usability, Satisfaction, and Physical Function

As a result of regression analysis of 240 cases by combining 10 dependent variables and 24 independent variables, there were 25 significant results (Y = aX + b) (Table 2). The dependent variable (Y) consisted of a total of 10 items regarding functional evaluation baseline (5 items) and difference of functional evaluation between baseline and after single-session exercise with the EX1 (5 items). The independent variable (X) consisted of a total of 24 items related to age, gender, height, weight, body mass index (BMI), health status (2 items; health condition, level of activity), experience of fall, safety (4 items), and satisfaction (12 items).

If the users thought they have better health conditions, they tended to have a faster FSST and TUG. If the users considered themselves active, they tended to have faster gait speed, and walk farther in 6 min. If the users had experience of falling, they tended to have a lower SPPB, slower gait speed, and walk less in 6 min; after gait exercise with the EX1, these users tended to have a higher SPPB than before exercise.

If the users thought there was no risk of falling when they were turning or leaning forward while wearing the robot, after gait exercise with the EX1, they tended to have a lower SPPB. If the users thought the robot was easy to use, they tend to have a higher SPPB, and faster TUG; after gait exercise with the EX1, these users tended to have a faster FSST than before exercise (Supplementary Table S2).

4. Discussion

Our study demonstrates that a single session of exercise with the EX1 improved physical functions. In addition, the positive results of the EX1 were confirmed by conducting a usability and satisfaction survey after exercise with the EX1.

In this study, statistically significant improvements in gait speed, balance ability, and gait endurance were confirmed through a single session of exercise with the EX1. The results of this study suggest that a single session of exercise with the EX1 has several key advantages for physical function and efficiency. Functional exercise that is effective for improving gait function includes gait exercise at various speeds and directions, treadmill gait, and stair climbing. In addition, the resistance and assistance of the EX1 can be adjusted based on individual physical ability. Therefore, it improves physical function gradually by controlling the intensity and duration of the exercise.

To determine gait quality, we used objective, sensitive, and powerful measurement tools that measure gait performance, dynamic balance ability, and gait endurance [25]. In our study, there was a statistically significant improvement in gait speed. Previous studies have shown that lower gait speed is associated with age, education, and particularly modifiable factors such as impairment of activities of daily life, physical inactivity, and cardiovascular disease [26]. Gait speed is a clinical indicator related to survival rate and predicts functional ability in the elderly [27]. In a previous study, it was reported that gait speed increased by 0.1 m/s as the survival rate increased [28]. These results indicate the importance of staying active and healthy for middle- and old-aged people.

Balance ability, an essential factor in gait ability, is the ability to maintain balance against numerical movement and external stimuli, which reduces muscle weakness due to decreased physical activity and is highly associated with risk of fall due to dynamic balance ability during gait [29,30]. Physical changes due to aging lead to a decrease in gait function by reducing balance, and it is highly related to the incidence of injuries in the elderly [31]. In our study, a statistically significant improvement was shown in dynamic balance ability through a single session of exercise with the EX1. Falling is a serious problem that threatens the health of the elderly and can lead to premature death due to physical damage, psychological dysfunction, and onset of various diseases [32]. Preventing falls and improving body function require planned and consistent exercise. Decreased physical activity leads to muscle strength weakness, which causes reduced balance ability. Balance training is an essential element in an exercise program because it is highly correlated with risk of falls according to dynamic balance ability while walking.

Gait endurance is also one of the major factors influencing risk of falls in the elderly. It is known that the weaker the walking endurance, the higher the likelihood of a fall in the elderly. In our study, endurance improved immediately after a single session of exercise with the EX1 in both age groups, but a significant result was found only in the middle-aged group. Endurance is increased through long-term gait training [33], but in our study, the time was insufficient to derive significant results with a single session of exercise with the EX1. However, although it was not significant after a single session of exercise, walking distance for 6 min improved, indicating the potential for positive results with long-term exercise.

The SPPB is a fast and useful measurement tool for predicting falls [34]. In our study, the SPPB improved immediately in the old-aged group after a single session of exercise with the EX1, but no significant result was shown due to the ceiling effect in the middle-aged group.

This study was performed to confirm the usability and satisfaction of the EX1. Considering user physical condition and environment, it was divided into user questionnaire evaluation and user function evaluation, and the safety, operability, and satisfaction of the EX1 were evaluated. If an expert or designer conducts a usability evaluation while listening to users' opinions, it is possible to understand the users' needs, inconveniences, strengths, and expectations in a complex way. Regression analysis showed a difference in the experience feedback for the EX1 by age or physical function. However, there were no implications for usability, perceptions, or satisfaction with general characteristics other than age.

As the results of the questionnaire included usability and satisfaction, both middle- and old-aged groups had positive experience feedback for the EX1. Among them, more positive results were shown in the middle-aged group than the old-aged group in a few items. We think that these results were caused by middle-aged people being more open-minded and faster to learn new technologies than the elderly. In the questionnaire, both the assist and resistance modes of the EX1 helped with gait, with strongly positive answers in the middle-aged group compared to the old-aged group. In addition, in a questionnaire on the preference between the assist and resistance modes of the EX1, the old-aged group preferred the assist mode, but the middle-aged group preferred the resistance mode. These results indicated that the elderly, who have a decline in gait ability, prefer gait assist, but middle-aged people who need gait training prefer the resist mode of the EX1.

In regression analysis between general characteristics and questionnaire, users tended to think that using the EX1 would have no negative social perceptions if they thought they had lower health conditions. Younger users tend to have positive opinions of the EX1. Although there might be perceptions that exercise using robots is applied only to patients or the elderly [35,36], this study confirmed that healthy people had positive perceptions of exercise with robots. Therefore, we think that the EX1 can provide a meaningful exercise program not only for the elderly, but also for young people. In regression analysis between questionnaire and physical function, people who had experienced a fall within the last

6 months had better balance ability and physical function after a single session of exercise with the EX1. It was confirmed that the higher the satisfaction with the function of the robot, the better the physical endurance and dynamic balance. We think that such exercise will bring positive results when applied to people with reduced balance ability, which is a risk factor for falls.

5. Conclusions

This study demonstrated that a single session of exercise with the EX1 in middle- and old-aged persons improved physical performance, including gait and balance, and received positive feedback. A newly developed wearable hip exoskeleton, the EX1, is a potentially useful exercise device for improving gait and physical function not only in the elderly, but also in middle-aged people. In this study, we emphasized short-term usability and satisfaction evaluation of the EX1 for healthy subjects. In future studies, the long-term effects of the EX1, not only in healthy subjects but also in persons with impaired physical function, must be addressed. Additionally, it is necessary to conduct more structured studies and repeat pre–post experiments by repeating specific training protocols in scheduled programs.

Supplementary Materials: The following supporting information can be downloaded at: https://www.mdpi.com/article/10.3390/healthcare11050643/s1, Table S1: Regression analysis between general characteristics, usability, and satisfaction; Table S2: Regression analysis between usability, satisfaction, and physical function.

Author Contributions: Conceptualization, J.K., H.C. and S.-H.L.; methodology, H.-J.L. and Y.-H.K.; software, J.K. and H.C.; validation, S.-H.L., H.-J.L. and Y.-H.K.; formal analysis, J.K., H.C. and S.-H.L.; investigation, J.K., H.C. and S.-H.L.; resources, J.K. and H.C.; data curation, J.K. and H.C.; writing—original draft preparation, J.K. and H.C.; writing—review and editing, S.-H.L., H.-J.L. and Y.-H.K.; visualization, J.K. and H.C.; supervision, H.-J.L. and Y.-H.K.; project administration, Y.-H.K.; funding acquisition, Y.-H.K. All authors have read and agreed to the published version of the manuscript.

Funding: This study was supported by Samsung Electronics (PHO021239).

Institutional Review Board Statement: All participants recruited through Samsung Medical Center provided informed consent before participating in the present study. This study protocol was approved by the ethics committee of the Samsung Medical Center Institutional Review Board (No. 2021-04-058).

Informed Consent Statement: Informed consent was obtained from all subjects involved in the study. Written informed consent has been obtained from the participants to publish this paper.

Data Availability Statement: The data used and/or analyzed during the current study are available from the corresponding author on request.

Conflicts of Interest: The authors declare no conflict of interest.

Abbreviations

10MWT: 10 m walking test, TUG: timed up and go, FSST: four square step test, 6MWT: 6 min walking test, SPPB: short physical performance battery, ICC: intra- and inter-tester reliability

References

1. Milanovic, Z.; Pantelic, S.; Trajkovic, N.; Sporis, G.; Kostic, R.; James, N. Age-related decrease in physical activity and functional fitness among elderly men and women. *Clin. Interv. Aging* **2013**, *8*, 549–556. [CrossRef] [PubMed]
2. Verghese, J.; LeValley, A.; Hall, C.B.; Katz, M.J.; Ambrose, A.F.; Lipton, R.B. Epidemiology of gait disorders in community-residing older adults. *J. Am. Geriatr. Soc.* **2006**, *54*, 255–261. [CrossRef]
3. Suryadinata, R.V.; Wirjatmadi, B.; Adriani, M.; Lorensia, A. Effect of age and weight on physical activity. *J. Public Health Res.* **2020**, *9*, 1840. [CrossRef]
4. Powell, K.E.; Paluch, A.E.; Blair, S.N. Physical activity for health: What kind? How much? How intense? On top of what? *Annu. Rev. Public Health* **2011**, *32*, 349–365. [CrossRef]

5. Lee, I.M.; Shiroma, E.J.; Lobelo, F.; Puska, P.; Blair, S.N.; Katzmarzyk, P.T.; Lancet Physical Activity Series Working Group. Effect of physical inactivity on major non-communicable diseases worldwide: An analysis of burden of disease and life expectancy. *Lancet* **2012**, *380*, 219–229. [CrossRef]
6. Kim, J.; Lee, H.J.; Lee, S.H.; Lee, J.; Chang, W.H.; Ryu, G.H.; Kim, Y.H. Correlation between cardiopulmonary metabolic energy cost and lower-limb muscle activity during inclined treadmill gait in older adults. *BMC Geriatr.* **2021**, *21*, 469. [CrossRef]
7. Westcott, W.L. Resistance training is medicine: Effects of strength training on health. *Curr. Sport. Med. Rep.* **2012**, *11*, 209–216. [CrossRef]
8. Gomenuka, N.A.; Oliveira, H.B.; da Silva, E.S.; Passos-Monteiro, E.; da Rosa, R.G.; Carvalho, A.R.; Costa, R.R.; Rodriguez Paz, M.C.; Pellegrini, B.; Peyre-Tartaruga, L.A. Nordic walking training in elderly, a randomized clinical trial. Part II: Biomechanical and metabolic adaptations. *Sport. Med. Open* **2020**, *6*, 3. [CrossRef] [PubMed]
9. Yoshiko, A.; Tomita, A.; Ando, R.; Ogawa, M.; Kondo, S.; Saito, A.; Tanaka, N.I.; Koike, T.; Oshida, Y.; Akima, H. Effects of 10-week walking and walking with home-based resistance training on muscle quality, muscle size, and physical functional tests in healthy older individuals. *Eur. Rev. Aging Phys. Act.* **2018**, *15*, 13. [CrossRef]
10. Rooks, D.S.; Kiel, D.P.; Parsons, C.; Hayes, W.C. Self-paced resistance training and walking exercise in community-dwelling older adults: Effects on neuromotor performance. *J. Gerontol. A Biol. Sci. Med. Sci.* **1997**, *52*, M161–M168. [CrossRef]
11. Keating, C.J.; Cabrera-Linares, J.C.; Parraga-Montilla, J.A.; Latorre-Roman, P.A.; Del Castillo, R.M.; Garcia-Pinillos, F. Influence of Resistance Training on Gait & Balance Parameters in Older Adults: A Systematic Review. *Int. J. Environ. Res. Public Health* **2021**, *18*, 1759.
12. Wollesen, B.; Mattes, K.; Schulz, S.; Bischoff, L.L.; Seydell, L.; Bell, J.W.; von Duvillard, S.P. Effects of Dual-Task Management and Resistance Training on Gait Performance in Older Individuals: A Randomized Controlled Trial. *Front. Aging Neurosci.* **2017**, *9*, 415. [CrossRef]
13. Kim, M.K.; Lee, S.A. Underwater treadmill training and gait ability in the normal adult. *J. Phys. Sci.* **2017**, *29*, 67–69. [CrossRef]
14. Lim, J.; Lim, J.Y. Responsiveness of gait speed to physical exercise interventions in at-risk older adults: A systematic review and meta-analysis. *Ann. Geriatr. Med. Res.* **2017**, *21*, 17–23. [CrossRef]
15. Lee, H. The change of medical environment & wellness view in the era of the 4th industrial revolution. *J. Korean Soc. Wellness* **2017**, *12*, 215–223.
16. Lee, H.J.; Lee, S.; Chang, W.H.; Seo, K.; Shim, Y.; Choi, B.O.; Ryu, G.H.; Kim, Y.H. A Wearable Hip Assist Robot Can Improve Gait Function and Cardiopulmonary Metabolic Efficiency in Elderly Adults. *IEEE Trans. Neural Syst. Rehabil Eng.* **2017**, *25*, 1549–1557. [CrossRef]
17. Kwon, S.H.; Lee, B.S.; Lee, H.J.; Kim, E.J.; Lee, J.A.; Yang, S.P.; Kim, T.Y.; Pak, H.R.; Kim, H.K.; Kim, H.Y.; et al. Energy Efficiency and Patient Satisfaction of Gait With Knee-Ankle-Foot Orthosis and Robot (ReWalk)-Assisted Gait in Patients With Spinal Cord Injury. *Ann. Rehabil. Med.* **2020**, *44*, 131–141. [CrossRef]
18. Martini, E.; Crea, S.; Parri, A.; Bastiani, L.; Faraguna, U.; McKinney, Z.; Molino-Lova, R.; Pratali, L.; Vitiello, N. Gait training using a robotic hip exoskeleton improves metabolic gait efficiency in the elderly. *Sci. Rep.* **2019**, *9*, 7157. [CrossRef]
19. Chae, U.R.; Kim, K.; Choi, J.; Hyun, D.J.; Yun, J.; Lee, G.H.; Hyun, Y.G.; Lee, J.; Chung, M. Systematic usability evaluation on two harnesses for a wearable chairless exoskeleton. *Int. J. Ind. Ergon.* **2021**, *84*, 103162. [CrossRef]
20. Lee, H.J.; Lee, S.H.; Seo, K.; Lee, M.; Chang, W.H.; Choi, B.O.; Ryu, G.H.; Kim, Y.H. Training for Walking Efficiency with a Wearable Hip-Assist Robot in Patients with Stroke: A Pilot Randomized Controlled Trial. *Stroke* **2019**, *50*, 3545–3552. [CrossRef]
21. Bohannon, R.W. Comfortable and maximum walking speed of adults aged 20–79 years: Reference values and determinants. *Age Ageing* **1997**, *26*, 15–19. [CrossRef]
22. Steffen, T.M.; Hacker, T.A.; Mollinger, L. Age- and gender-related test performance in community-dwelling elderly people: Six-Minute Walk Test, Berg Balance Scale, Timed Up & Go Test, and gait speeds. *Phys. Ther.* **2002**, *82*, 128–137.
23. Gomez, J.F.; Curcio, C.L.; Alvarado, B.; Zunzunegui, M.V.; Guralnik, J. Validity and reliability of the Short Physical Performance Battery (SPPB): A pilot study on mobility in the Colombian Andes. *Colomb. Med.* **2013**, *44*, 165–171. [CrossRef]
24. Olsen, C.F.; Bergland, A. Reliability of the Norwegian version of the short physical performance battery in older people with and without dementia. *BMC Geriatr.* **2017**, *17*, 124. [CrossRef]
25. Bortone, I.; Sardone, R.; Lampignano, L.; Castellana, F.; Zupo, R.; Lozupone, M.; Moretti, B.; Giannelli, G.; Panza, F. How gait influences frailty models and health-related outcomes in clinical-based and population-based studies: A systematic review. *J. Cachexia Sarcopenia Muscle* **2021**, *12*, 274–297. [CrossRef]
26. Busch Tde, A.; Duarte, Y.A.; Pires Nunes, D.; Lebrao, M.L.; Satya Naslavsky, M.; dos Santos Rodrigues, A.; Amaro, E., Jr. Factors associated with lower gait speed among the elderly living in a developing country: A cross-sectional population-based study. *BMC Geriatr.* **2015**, *15*, 35. [CrossRef]
27. Van Abbema, R.; De Greef, M.; Craje, C.; Krijnen, W.; Hobbelen, H.; Van Der Schans, C. What type, or combination of exercise can improve preferred gait speed in older adults? A meta-analysis. *BMC Geriatr.* **2015**, *15*, 72. [CrossRef]
28. Studenski, S.; Perera, S.; Patel, K.; Rosano, C.; Faulkner, K.; Inzitari, M.; Brach, J.; Chandler, J.; Cawthon, P.; Connor, E.B.; et al. Gait speed and survival in older adults. *JAMA* **2011**, *305*, 50–58. [CrossRef]
29. Osoba, M.Y.; Rao, A.K.; Agrawal, S.K.; Lalwani, A.K. Balance and gait in the elderly: A contemporary review. *Laryngoscope Investig. Otolaryngol.* **2019**, *4*, 143–153. [CrossRef]

30. Gill-Body, K.M.; Hedman, L.D.; Plummer, L.; Wolf, L.; Hanke, T.; Quinn, L.; Riley, N.; Kaufman, R.; Verma, A.; Quiben, M.; et al. Movement System Diagnoses for Balance Dysfunction: Recommendations From the Academy of Neurologic Physical Therapy's Movement System Task Force. *Phys. Ther.* **2021**, *101*, pzab153. [CrossRef]
31. Gusi, N.; Carmelo Adsuar, J.; Corzo, H.; Del Pozo-Cruz, B.; Olivares, P.R.; Parraca, J.A. Balance training reduces fear of falling and improves dynamic balance and isometric strength in institutionalised older people: A randomised trial. *J. Physiother.* **2012**, *58*, 97–104. [CrossRef] [PubMed]
32. Jaul, E.; Barron, J. Age-Related Diseases and Clinical and Public Health Implications for the 85 Years Old and Over Population. *Front. Public Health* **2017**, *5*, 335. [CrossRef] [PubMed]
33. Wang, R.Y.; Wang, Y.L.; Cheng, F.Y.; Chao, Y.H.; Chen, C.L.; Yang, Y.R. Effects of combined exercise on gait variability in community-dwelling older adults. *Age* **2015**, *37*, 9780. [CrossRef]
34. Welch, S.A.; Ward, R.E.; Beauchamp, M.K.; Leveille, S.G.; Travison, T.; Bean, J.F. The Short Physical Performance Battery (SPPB): A Quick and Useful Tool for Fall Risk Stratification Among Older Primary Care Patients. *J. Am. Med. Dir. Assoc.* **2021**, *22*, 1646–1651. [CrossRef] [PubMed]
35. Kim, Y.-H. Robotic assisted rehabilitation therapy for enhancing gait and motor function after stroke. *Precis. Future Med.* **2019**, *3*, 103–115. [CrossRef]
36. Schwartz, I.; Meiner, Z. Robotic-assisted gait training in neurological patients: Who may benefit? *Ann. Biomed. Eng.* **2015**, *43*, 1260–1269. [CrossRef] [PubMed]

healthcare

Article

The Potential of the Remote Monitoring Digital Solutions to Sustain the Mental and Emotional Health of the Elderly during and Post COVID-19 Crisis in Romania

Marilena Ianculescu [1,2], Adriana Alexandru [1,3] and Elena-Anca Paraschiv [1,4,*]

1 National Institute for Research and Development in Informatics, 011455 Bucharest, Romania
2 Faculty of Automatic Control and Computer Science, Politehnica University of Bucharest, 060042 Bucharest, Romania
3 Faculty of Electrical Engineering, Electronics and Information Technology, Valahia University of Targoviste, 130004 Targoviste, Romania
4 Faculty of Electronics, Telecommunications and Information Technology, Politehnica University of Bucharest, 060042 Bucharest, Romania
* Correspondence: elena.paraschiv@ici.ro; Tel.: +40-755657973

Abstract: The COVID-19 pandemic amplified the elderly's aging-related dysfunctionalities and vulnerabilities. Research surveys, aimed at evaluating the socio–physical–emotional state of the elderly and obtaining data on their access to medical services and information media services during the pandemic, were carried out on Romanian respondents aged 65+. Identification and mitigation of the risk of emotional and mental long-term decline of the elderly after SARS-CoV-2 infection, based on the implementation of a specific procedure, can be performed through Remote Monitoring Digital Solutions (RMDSs). The aim of this paper is to propose a procedure for the identification and mitigation of the risk of emotional and mental long-term decline of the elderly after SARS-CoV-2 infection that comprises RMDS. The importance of using the knowledge obtained by COVID-19-related surveys corroborating the necessity of including personalized RMDS in the procedure is highlighted. The Non-invasive Monitoring System and Health Assessment of the Elderly in a Smart Environment (RO-SmartAgeing) is an RMDS designed to address the improved preventative and proactive support for diminishing this risk and to provide suitable assistance for the elderly through a safe and efficient smart environment. Its comprehensive functionalities targeted supporting primary healthcare assistance, specific medical conditions—as the mental and emotional disorders post-SARS-CoV-2 infection—and enlarged access to aging-related information, together with customizable features, illustrated the match with the requirements included in the proposed procedure.

Keywords: Remote Monitoring Digital Solutions (RMDSs); elderly patient; mental and emotional decline; COVID-19

Citation: Ianculescu, M.; Alexandru, A.; Paraschiv, E.-A. The Potential of the Remote Monitoring Digital Solutions to Sustain the Mental and Emotional Health of the Elderly during and Post COVID-19 Crisis in Romania. *Healthcare* **2023**, *11*, 608. https://doi.org/10.3390/healthcare11040608

Academic Editor: Daniele Giansanti

Received: 28 December 2022
Revised: 9 February 2023
Accepted: 16 February 2023
Published: 17 February 2023

1. Introduction

SARS-CoV-2, the virus that causes coronavirus disease 2019 (COVID-19), spread in China in early December 2019. On 12 January 2020, the World Health Organization (WHO) confirmed that COVID-19 was the cause of respiratory illness in China [1], having a case–death ratio much lower than that of SARS in 2003 [2], but a notably greater transmission, with an important total dying rate [3]. The virus affected more than 250 million people globally, with more than five million deaths having been reported by the WHO [4]. The virus spreads human-to-human, causing flu, fever, cough, and respiratory problems [5,6]. The prevalence of the virus has been prevented through constant lockdowns, which highly affected the economy and small businesses [7,8]. In order to stop the pandemic, self-quarantine in their residences was enforced on normal people, and quarantine in hospitals until full recovery was enforced on people affected by the virus.

To better understand the pandemic and the impact of COVID-19 on healthcare services in Romania, a short overview is provided: the actions to prevent the spread of the pandemic started in mid-March 2020 (e.g., interdiction of public gatherings, school closure). A state of emergency in Romania was decided, starting on 16 March 2020 [9]. In mid-May 2020, some restrictions were relieved when the state of emergency ended on 14 May 2020 and was changed to a state of alert. Further restrictions were relaxed in the next months. Since an acute increase in the infection rate was observed in the autumn of 2020, several restrictions were reinforced. Schools were re-opened only on 8 February 2021. Between mid-March 2021 and the beginning of March 2022, three waves of cases were noticed in Romania. The wave of cases between 10 August and 20 October 2021 has been the most severe of all infection waves in the COVID-19 pandemic. The pressure on the Romanian healthcare system that achieved its maximum capacity in this wave led to the authorities asking the European Union for help through its Civil Protection Mechanism [10].

Older people were highly affected by COVID-19, and many of them have died [11]. This is due to their low immunity, which is insufficient to fight against the virus. As the risk of mortality in the older population is much higher compared to younger people, protection with social distancing or, if necessary, social isolation is necessary. Loneliness and social isolation may cause many problems, such as mental and emotional problems, disability, cardiovascular diseases, etc., among seniors [12]. The ongoing COVID-19 pandemic has underlined the need for digital technology solutions to diminish the risk of contamination due to close contact [13]. Smart technology (e.g., IoT, mobile phones) has been important for diminishing social isolation, improving the quality of life and self-care, and providing consultation, remote monitoring, and diagnosis for older adults [14].

The numerous restrictions imposed by COVID-19 in many countries led to a damaging effect on the psychological functioning of the elderly [15], loss of social support due to limited contact with other people [16], higher levels of loneliness, which is significantly associated with depression in the elderly [17,18]. Loneliness is considered to be an important risk factor for the exacerbation of a number of health conditions, such as coronary heart disease and stroke [19], and is associated with a 26–50% increased risk of mortality [20].

There are several instruments for assessing the mental and emotional health of the elderly during and post-COVID-19 crisis. They are used to measure her/his cognitive impairments and to screen for dementia or mild cognitive impairments (MCI) for estimating their severity and progression or for following the course of her/his cognitive changes over time. These instruments are used as screening tests, but they need to be used with multiple other screening tests, rather than an isolated one, to confirm a diagnosis of dementia. Some of them are presented below:

- The *Mini-Mental State Examination (MMSE)* or *Folstein test* is the best-known and the most frequently used screening tool for estimating the cognitive impairment of an individual. It consists of a 30-point questionnaire which takes 7–8 min to complete. Using the MMSE over time, one could better predict the conversion to dementia from MCI stages for people with more pronounced symptoms [21].
- The *Montreal Cognitive Assessment (MoCA)* test for dementia is a brief, simple, and reliable tool to evaluate people with memory loss or other symptoms of cognitive decline or a screening tool for conditions such as Parkinson's disease, brain tumors, and head trauma. It consists of a 30-point questionnaire which takes 10–12 min to complete (taking a few minutes more than MMSE). The MoCA may be a better choice for people with mild symptoms than MMSE. The MoCA test checks language, memory, visual and spatial thinking, reasoning and orientation skills, and executive functions, and implements the clock exercise (that the MMSE does not have). Using it, healthcare providers can quickly decide when someone might need an in-depth diagnostic for Alzheimer's disease or dementia [22].
- *Mini-Addenbrooke's Cognitive Examination (MACE)* is a brief cognitive screening instrument for the identification of dementia and MCI [23]. It is comparable to MoCA, being rapid, accurate, easy to use, and well accepted by seniors. MACE and MoCA are

excellent for dementia diagnosis (both >0.9), but NACE has a slight net benefit on MCI diagnosis [24].

- The term *Activities of Daily Living (ADL)* is used to describe the basic skill necessary for caring for an independent living by oneself. (eating, bathing, mobility, dressing, continence, etc.). ADL indicates the functional status of an individual. It is used as a predictor of functional status deterioration and possible necessity of hospitalization, other living arrangements, or assisted home living. Aging can cause a decline in the functional status of seniors and is the principal cause of ADL damage [25], leading to decreased physical functions. A cognitive or mental decline [26] or social isolation can be associated with impaired engagement in ADL.
- The *Free-Cog* test is a hybrid cognitive screening instrument for assessing both cognitive and functional (executive) functions. It combines questions in both domains: for cognitive deficits, it uses questions related to orientation in time and place, memory, calculation, attention, visuospatial function, language, fluency, etc. (in a 25-point questionnaire), and for functional ones, it uses questions related to daily activities including social functioning, travel, self-care, and safety at home (in a 5-point questionnaire) [27].
- The *Mini-Cog* test is a fast and simple screening method for early detecting the first stages of dementia. It consists of two components: a three-item test for memory evaluation and a clock drawing test. As it can be completed in approximately 3 min, it is often used to detect early stages of dementia in which memory or thinking issues might not be that visible. It proved to be appropriate for use in primary care evaluation [28].

The entire impact of the COVID-19 pandemic on the wellness and health status of the elderly has not been completely assessed; what is certain is that this impact has been perceived keener among the older persons, taking into consideration all the restrictions imposed by the authorities (including the lockdowns) in their attempt to reduce and control the degree of contagion. Moreover, isolation was also imposed on the elderly by their family and friends, most of the time to protect them from getting ill.

A study performed on 254 persons who were hospitalized in Italy due to SARS-CoV-2 infection revealed that the elderly patients with persistent psychiatric and somatic symptoms perceived these symptoms more strongly in the following six months post-infection, followed by a decrease afterward [29]. Another study performed at Daping Hospital in Chongqing, China, on COVID-19 patients aged 60+ stated that 21% of those who had had a severe form of the disease suffered from progressive cognitive decline afterward; the more severe the SARS-CoV-2 infection, the higher the risk of deterioration of mental health [30].

It is almost a general fact that nowadays, the elderly are much less tech-savvy than the younger generations, which directly leads to fewer possibilities for them to have access to information (including medical information) or social interaction; another element that has to be taken into consideration is the lower number of digital devices used by the elderly, as they might be too expensive or not age-friendly enough. It is not to be neglected either the situation in which an exacerbated access to scientifically unverified and alarmist information, combined with social isolation, leads to increased anxiety, depression, and other emotional and mental problems. So, the lockdowns and restricted access to the out-of-home world imposed in different periods of time since the beginning of the COVID-19 pandemic had a strong negative effect on the mental and emotional state of older persons.

Some typical mental health disorders that have been estimated to directly affect people post-SARS-CoV-2 infection are as follows: anxiety, panic attacks, depression, dietary and obsessive–compulsive disorder, personality disorders, paranoia, phobias, psychosis, sleep problems, and suicidal thoughts.

The elderly have been among the most vulnerable group of the population from the point of the mortality and serious physical damage of health status directly associated with SARS-CoV-2 infection; it has already been demonstrated that it is no less true that the degree of morbidity, mortality and accelerated mental decline has increased among them due to social isolation, grown stress and the decrease in cognitive provocation and physical activities.

Since the beginning of the COVID-19 pandemic, a series of surveys have been conducted in Romania regarding how it has affected, especially from a mental and emotional point of view, the population at the global level, but especially the elderly. The isolation and fear of contamination with the SARS-CoV-2 virus, the fear of death, loneliness, the limitation/lack of access to medical services, the accentuation of pre-existing mobility and health problems due to loneliness, as well as the limitations imposed on social life, have affected, in particular, people aged 65+. This was also demonstrated by the surveys carried out by (1) the Romanian Institute for Evaluation and Strategy (IRES)—an independent think tank that conducts surveys on the problems and perceptions of Romanians on current issues; (2) Kantar Romania—a data and evidence-based company that operates in the Marketing Research and Public Opinion Polling sector and provides insights and actionable recommendations to its clients—at the request of the Never Alone Association—Friends of the Elderly—an NGO that supports the cause of the loneliness of the elderly and promotes dignity at any age. The methodology used in such surveys, as well as their results obtained at various times during the COVID-19 pandemic, are presented in the paper.

In order to identify and reduce the effects of the COVID-19 pandemic on older adults (such as emotional and mental decline), the authors propose a procedure for managing the associated risk through RMDS.

Due to the short time since the beginning of the COVID-19 pandemic, no solid assessment of the effects on the mental and emotional state of the elderly following SARS-CoV-2 infection has been performed. Even less, no reliable methodologies have been implemented by which these negative effects, which can significantly influence the health of the elderly in the long term, can be managed, controlled, or annihilated.

As there is a continuous growth of RMDS at the national and international level, in Romania, there are several research gaps in this regard. The lack of correlation between the screening tests for neurodegeneration and evaluating patients' medical data is crucial, as healthcare parameters have an essential role in assessing neurodegeneration. Additionally, considering the fear of contamination with the COVID-19 virus, there are not considerable systems that can remotely monitor the elderly in the comfort of their home. The lack of access or the difficulty in reaching medical services related to prior mobility or healthcare issues composes another gap in providing a good quality of life for the elderly. Moreover, there is also the absence of a complex platform that could not only track health parameters, but also sustain mental or behavioral problems.

According to the above-mentioned gaps, the present research paper aims to meet all the needs that can provide a complex and structured system not only to remotely monitor health parameters, but also to track and screen neurodegenerative-associated patients and sustain them emotionally and socially.

The relevance of such solutions during the pandemic is important in managing older people's wellbeing and mitigating the pressures on the healthcare system [22–28,31–33].

The addressed population mainly consists of older people in need of communication, with mental health problems, and suffering from social isolation [34]. The RMDS has been largely used in the last two years [35,36] for dealing with social isolation and loneliness [37–39] and mental health consultation purposes [40,41] during the crisis. With the help of m-health tools, information [42,43] and self-help [44,45] have been provided to the elderly. Internet access [46,47] and the senior's desire and capabilities [32] are the main factors in the success of such solutions to improve their health and combat the COVID-19 outbreak. Some of the facilitators in the adoption of these solutions are the support from the government and family [33,48,49].

In the context of the COVID-19 pandemic, the Non-invasive Monitoring System and Health Assessment of the Elderly in a Smart Environment (RO-SmartAgeing) is implemented as a tailored patient-centric RMDS aiming at assessing and the health management of older patients that are living at home. While its two main components include quite a large range of functionalities able to address primary healthcare issues and support for healthy, independent, and active aging, the potential mental and emotional disorders of the elderly can be identified, evaluated, and tackled both by the elderly, and their supporting people, including the medical staff. The system gathers health, motion, and environmental data from IoT sensors and devices, transmits them, and stores them to the cloud platform for advanced data analysis applications. The IoT-based sensors and devices are programmed to send the data, via an Application Programming Interface (API), to the RO-SmartAgeing database and can be further visualized and analyzed in the web platform. The services provided to the seniors consist of medical assistance and support provided by using a safe, customizable smart environment. The beneficiaries of such services are older persons, their current healthcare specialists, and caretakers/family [50].

As the COVID-19 crisis had such a dramatic impact on individuals and the societal, medical, and social systems in Romania, the development and implementation of digital solutions and technology targeted to support remote health monitoring of the elderly have been accelerated, and gained larger accessibility among citizens and health professionals. Moreover, the research in this field has been boosted, and digital healthcare solutions have been developed or improved to sustain remote care of the elderly, as briefly illustrated in Table 1.

Table 1. Short synthesis of some projects that reflect the state-of-the-art in Romania in the field of research aimed at the remote health monitoring of the elderly.

"Smart assistant to prevent and detect cognitive decline, promote cognitive function and social inclusion among older adults (ReMember-Me)" Project [51]	
Brief presentation	The solution developed in this project aims to monitor, detect, and prevent the cognitive decline of the elderly. It comprises a robot, computer games, and sensors for gathering data on the seniors' status. A monitoring platform is also provided for connecting the elderly with their caretakers and other seniors.
Bottlenecks	It focuses mainly on cognitive issues, without correlating them with other current or potential co-morbidities of the elderly.
Contribution of RO-SmartAgeing system to the progress beyond the state-of-the-art in Romania	The RO-SmartAgeing system provides a framework and facilities for a broad modern approach to the health management of the elderly. The medical history is corroborated and continuously updated with information and data gathered through the RO-SmartAgeing smart environment in real time. The empowerment and engagement of seniors in the management of their health status are strongly taken into consideration and implemented in various functionalities.
"Red-Button—Integrated services of socio-medical care at home monitored through the telecare system" Project [52]	
Brief presentation	The project aimed to develop an innovative system for the teleassistance of single elderly persons in Romania. The main device used in this system is a smart bracelet with an SOS button able to trigger an alert signal to the Emergency Medical Dispatcher. This one receives access to the medical history of the senior patient and triggers a personalized emergency protocol, as well as informs the family.
Bottlenecks	The system is still under-development, and it does not provide enlarged functionalities for evaluating the health status, such as continuous health monitoring.
Contribution of RO-SmartAgeing system to the progress beyond the state-of-the-art in Romania	The solution proposed by the RO-SmartAgeing system provides comprehensive capabilities for personalized health monitoring of the elderly, and it facilitates access to supporting information for an independent, active, and healthy life. It also provides functionalities for the assessment of the current health status of the elderly, as their mental and emotional ones.

Table 1. *Cont.*

"Inclusive online platform for senior adults (iCan)" Project [53]	
Brief presentation	The solution developed in this project aims to support seniors in their daily life, increasing their motivation to use digital solutions to connect with their families. Some "smart" games, home delivery assistance, and ordering taxis for elderly users are also available.
Bottlenecks	The focus of this solution is to help and entertain the elderly; health monitoring is a secondary target.
Contribution of RO-SmartAgeing system to the progress beyond the state-of-the-art in Romania	The medical component of the RO-SmartAgeing system is its core part, and it aims to support the elderly, their caretakers, and health professionals to non-intrusively monitor the seniors' health status and daily activities in an age-friendly environment and to provide functionalities able to offer a broad range of information regarding the evolution of their health. At the same time, the information provided by the support services component assists its users in gaining knowledge about successful and safe aging.
"Clinically-validated INtegrated Support for Assistive Care and Lifestyle Improvement: the Human Link (vINCI)" Project [54]	
Brief presentation	The solution provided by the vINCI project is based on some technologies developed by the project partners: a smartwatch, smart shoes, and indoor tracking algorithms. It aims to assist the caretakers and the elderly (as out-patients) with smart care.
Bottlenecks	The main scope of remote health monitoring is gathering data for assessing several factors that influence seniors' quality of life. The number of monitoring technology is quite small.
Contribution of RO-SmartAgeing system to the progress beyond the state-of-the-art in Romania	The RO-SmartAgeing system comprises more IoT-based devices, thus allowing a larger range of health parameters to be monitored and used for more comprehensive medical assistance support.
"Smart Big Data Platform to Offer Evidence-based Personalised Support for Healthy and Independent Living at Home (SMART BEAR)" [55]	
Brief presentation	The solution provided by this project aims to optimize the management of the elderly's diseases and associated risks. It assesses the quality of life of the elderly and their independence level. It comprises sensors, assistive medical, and mobile devices to gather health parameters able to support independent and healthy living.
Bottlenecks	The provided solution is not personalized for a specific user. The targeted elderly category is restricted to persons aged 67–80 and with a medical history containing at least two health conditions (from a pre-defined five).
Contribution of RO-SmartAgeing system to the progress beyond the state-of-the-art in Romania	While the SMART BEAR project has been developed by 27 European partners, the RO-SmartAgeing system has been developed by a single team from Romania; therefore, its aims were not so broad. Even so, its comprehensive functionalities cover most of the above-mentioned ones. Moreover, the RO-SmartAgeing system provides in one of its components informative support for the elderly, their caretakers, and any person interested in a healthy, independent, and active life and aging. The RO-SmartAgeing smart environment can be personalized according to the elderly's specificities and health status evolution.
"Ella4Life, your virtual personal assistant for home and on the road" [56]	
Brief presentation	The solution developed in this project is based on a mobile solution (that supports the elderly to have an active and healthy life while connecting them with their caretaker and health specialists), an avatar (that assists through speech the elderly in performing daily activities), and specially developed sensor technology (that allows remote health monitoring).
Bottlenecks	Only several chronic diseases are addressed. No alarm triggers are provided. The targeted elderly are supposed to be in quite a good state of mental health.
Contribution of RO-SmartAgeing system to the progress beyond the state-of-the-art in Romania	Even if the RO-SmartAgeing system is not provided with speaking capabilities, and it is intended to be used only indoors, it provides functionalities able to support both the management of primary care and of several age-related diseases, including the mental and emotional health of the elderly. Furthermore, it can be personalized according to the specific needs of the senior, and alarms are triggered in case of an emergency or abnormal event.

The list of abbreviations used in this paper is presented in Table 2.

Table 2. Abbreviations used in this paper.

Abbreviation	Meaning
ADL	Activities of Daily Living
BPM	Blood pressure monitor
ECG	Electrocardiogram
INS	National Institute of Statistics
IRES	Romanian Institute for Evaluation and Strategy
MACE	Mini-Addenbrooke's Cognitive Examination
MCI	Mild cognitive impairments
MMSE	Mini-Mental State Examination
MoCA	Montreal Cognitive Assessment
RMDS	Remote Monitoring Digital Solutions
RO-SmartAgeing	Non-invasive Monitoring System and Health Assessment of the Elderly in a Smart Environment
WHO	World Health Organization
BPM Core	Withings Blood Pressure Monitor

The aim of this paper is to propose a procedure for the identification and mitigation of the risk of emotional and mental long-term decline of the elderly after SARS-CoV-2 infection that comprises RMDS. The necessity of taking into consideration the results of COVID-19-related surveys and the implementation of appropriate RMDS into this procedure is presented and justified. The RO-SmartAgeing system is an illustration of an RMDS for addressing improved preventative and proactive support for diminishing this risk.

The content of the paper is organized as follows: the methodology used to estimate the effects of the COVID-19 crisis on a sample of the Romanian aged population, obtained from some surveys, is presented in Section 2.1. Issues that can sustain the management of the elderly's risk of emotional and mental long-term decline after SARS-CoV-2 infection and the steps of a procedure for managing the elderly's risk of emotional and mental long-term decline after SARS-CoV-2 infection are proposed in Section 2.2. The importance of involving RMDS in the management of seniors' health and the steps for implementing functionalities provided by them are presented in Section 2.3. The effects of the pandemic on representative samples of the Romanian elderly, obtained as results of some surveys, are presented in Section 3.1. The results of this approach are described in Sections 3.2.1 and 3.2.2 by using the capabilities of the RO-SmartAgeing system to address preventative and proactive support for diminishing this decline. Section 4 is a discussion section dealing with the presentation of the main findings of the paper, strengths, drawbacks, as well as lines for future work. Section 5 concludes the paper. The references are included at the end of the paper.

2. Materials and Methods

2.1. Effects of COVID-19 Crisis on a Sample of Romanian Aged Population—Results of Methodology Used in Some Surveys

According to the data published by the National Institute of Statistics (INS) on the International Day of the Elderly, on 1 January 2020 [57], people aged 65 and over in Romania represented 19% of the country's resident population. Among the elderly, men totaled 15.7% of all men resident in Romania, and women 22.1% of all women resident in Romania. The segment of the population aged 80 and over represented 4.8% of the total population. Of the total number of people aged 80 and over, 34.8% were men, and 65.2% were women. The household structure based on the occupational status of the head of the household shows that pensioners represent 40.9%

The share of the population over 65 years of age in Romania, according to the statistical data from the 2022 Census published by the National Institute of Statistics (INS) [58], represents almost 20% of the total population.

Thus, according to the INS, the demographic aging process has deepened in recent years, noting the increase in the share of the elderly population (aged 65 and over).

The perceptions of Romanians regarding the COVID-19 pandemic have been constantly evaluated, starting from March 2020; until now, more than 30 studies have been carried out focusing on the way in which the life of Romanians, but also of the society perceived as a whole, was affected, in different aspects, by the pandemic. We briefly present the methodology of three of these studies and present aspects related to the influences of the COVID-19 pandemic on a sample of population aged 65+. Sample type was simple, random population satisfying the following criteria of eligibility for participation in this study: (i) people currently residing in Romania (aged 65 years and above) of either gender, (ii) comprehension of this study's goal, and (iii) consent to participate in this study.

The research study included a qualitative part (in-depth interviews with people from the representative age segment) and a quantitative part (survey based on Computer Assisted Telephone Interviewing among the elderly) for a national representative sample. A well-structured, closed-ended, and self-reported questionnaire was created, including questions about COVID-19-related characteristics and perceptions. Each survey takes approximately 10–15 min to finish. Prior to the interview, study participants provided verbal consent over the phone. Participants were thoroughly instructed on the process and purpose of this study and agreed that their information would be kept confidential and anonymous. Participants were not compensated for their participation in the research and were free to withdraw at any moment without providing evidence. Those who refused to consent were not authorized to participate in the survey.

A sample of questions used in the three analyzed Romanian surveys is illustrated in Table 3.

Table 3. A sample of questions used in Romanian surveys.

Name of the Survey	Date	Questions Associated with COVID-19
IRES SURVEY "A month of loneliness" [59]	April 2020	(1) How did you get through the first month of the pandemic? (2) Have you felt any of the following states or feelings: fear of infection or death, fear of a future food crisis
IRES SURVEY "Romanians after 2 years of COVID-19" [60]	27 September–12 October 2021	(1) How worried are Romanians about the current COVID-19 pandemic? (2) When do Romanians think the current COVID-19 pandemic will end? (3) How likely is a new pandemic to occur in the near future? (4) Are Romanians more worried about the pandemic or a war in the region? (5) What changes did the pandemic bring to the lives of Romanians? (6) What have Romanians learned due to the pandemic? (7) What limitations have Romanians experienced due to the pandemic? (8) What would Romanians do when all the restrictions in Romania are lifted?
KANTAR ROMANIA, at the request of the Never Alone—Friends of the Elderly Association [61]	15–18 February 2022	(1) How was the state of physical and mental health affected? (2) Have you felt any of the following states or feelings: fear of loneliness, fear of death? (3) Where did they spend their time during the pandemic?

2.2. *Managing the Elderly's Risk of Emotional and Mental Long-Term Decline after SARS-CoV-2 Infection*

Among the most important issues to be identified in order to define a procedure for better management of the emotional and mental long-term decline after SARS-CoV-2 infection is to determine what the most relevant risk factors considering the specificities of the lifestyle and age-related dysfunctionalities of the elderly are. Since the beginning of the COVID-19 crisis, data and information have been collected or become available from local, regional, national, or international surveys or studies based on surveys from self-reports of the patients infected with SARS-CoV-2 [62]. For a better foundation, research and studies that correlate the medical history of elderly patients with new cognitive symptoms and disorders appeared after the SARS-CoV-2 infection started to develop. Special attention is paid to risk factors before and after infection. For instance, in a recent study addressing the long-term sequelae clustering phenotypes for appropriate care management post this type of infection, associated risk factors have been identified and classified [63].

In this context, the most relevant identified *risk factors* are as follows:

- The degree of autonomy and independence of the older person;
- The residential status: living alone or not;
- The previous and current state of cognition, health, and co-morbidities;
- A low degree of self-esteem, social involvement, and commitment;
- A low level of previous education, including ICT and health literacy;
- The lack or little physical activity and social interaction;
- The sex (28% of senior women in U.S. developed mental disorders during COVID-19 pandemic in comparison with 20% of senior men [64]);
- The age (26% of seniors aged 65–77 in U.S. declared mental disorders versus 19% aged 80+ [64]).

The level of impact on the elderly that these risk factors might have depends directly on both their medical history and cognitive and social status, but also on their adaptability and self-sufficiency.

In order to mitigate the psycho-social and mental wellness impact of SARS-CoV-2 infection on older persons, some basic actions must be performed/initiated:

- Early identification of the first signs of decline in mental and emotional health of an elderly person, corroborated awareness and precise identification of risk factors;
- An accurate and timely diagnosis of mental and emotional disorders;
- Proper management of the identified disease, integrated with the management of the health status of the elderly;
- Comprehensive analysis of mental and emotional health;
- Appropriate longitudinal studies for assessing the long-term efficiency of the above-mentioned actions;
- Tailored framework adapted to the specificities of the elderly persons that can provide them support for having access to reliable information associated with healthcare and daily living;
- Taking into consideration their long-life experience, older patients facing mental and emotional disorders can be constantly sustained by medical specialists or family members to cope with their fears, anxieties, mental blocks, or other cognitive issues.

In the context of the COVID-19 pandemic, *RMDS* proved to be a progressive model of care, as they can ensure, in the safest way, continuous monitoring and management of the health status. The elderly patients have been one of the most important potential target users of RMDSs; because of the imposed restrictions and isolation, these solutions for providing healthcare have been perfectly capable of creating a personalized framework in which an older patient is observed, consulted, and monitored non-invasively, constantly, or periodically, depending on the evolution of their state of health. Thus, unnecessary hospitalization or direct human contact in clinics or medical offices could be diminished.

In terms of monitoring and managing the mental and emotional disorders activated or aggravated by the COVID-19 pandemic, in two years, RMDSs have been able to demonstrate how their functionalities could support adaptive behaviors, social relationships, informational necessities, engagement in usual daily activities, increased self-abilities to cope with cognitive issues, and direct real-time link among healthcare providers, patients, and their families.

It is now time to step forward toward proper management of the risk of the decline that those elderly patients with mental and emotional disorders—that were influenced by the SARS-CoV-2 infection—may have in the long term. Moreover, the opportunities and benefits in this domain brought by ICT in healthcare domain should be reflected by integrating the capabilities of RMDSs among different levels, phases, and activities of this management.

Proposed Procedure for Managing the Risk of Mental and Emotional Long-Term Decline during and after SARS-CoV-2 Infection

Although there are many strategies and procedures recommended by health authorities and specialists for decreasing the cognitive decline of the elderly, taking into consideration the short period of time since the beginning of COVID-19 pandemic, there are not many risk management plans addressing this domain in an integrated way, comprising comprehensive aspects that define the state of cognitive health and its evolution. Most of the strategies, procedures, and programs that aim to manage the mental and emotional status of the elderly refer to recommendations directed towards several health areas: controlling the risk factors, lifestyle (sleep, nutrition, and dietary habits), daily activities (physical activity, social participation, and relationship), and cognitive support and stimulation.

Our proposed procedure for managing the risk of mental and emotional long-term decline during and after SARS-CoV-2 infection is intended to cover a larger range of aspects that are associated with these cognitive disorders, starting with its design, comprising the management of the identified mental dysfunctionalities in conjunction with other comorbidities of the elderly, and periodical assessment of the outcomes and feedback of the procedure, and last but not least, formulating potential proposals for improving medical practices, but also the political instruments that govern the field of medical and social care for the elderly.

As is presented in Figure 1, the proposed procedure is designed to be scalable and able to evolve continuously according to the necessities at the individual or group level of elderly patients or, depending on the social/healthcare context, being provided with several steps that allow its improvement and upgrade.

The diagram presented in Figure 1 is detailed as follows:

The steps in designing the proposed procedure consist of clearly defining the *scope, objectives, estimated results, and target users of the risk management.* Briefly, it aims to better support the elderly with mental and emotional problems induced or aggravated by SARS-CoV-2 infection or COVID-19 pandemic.

It is supposed to become an efficient tool:

- To improve healthcare and social services provided by medical and social specialists;
- For better self-management of the health statuses of elderly patients, who are also assisted to be better aware and empowered regarding their own health.

Not less important is the estimated impact on improved policy instruments, research, education, or other types of clinical practice.

For a real-time response and a clear vision of the current situation of the local healthcare ecosystem (with a focus on mental and emotional issues), *implementation of feasibility and market study* should be performed, followed by *development of businesses and implementing plans.* In this phase, the results of national surveys—targeted for evaluating different issues related to the impact of COVID-19 pandemic on the elderly (as those presented in Sections 2 and 3 of this paper)—are important for identifying the most relevant aspect and approaches. Thus, the risk management plan targeted for the mental and emotional long-term decline is designed, structured, adapted to local conditions, and developed in accordance with the real requirements of this category of vulnerable patients, but also those of medical and social service providers.

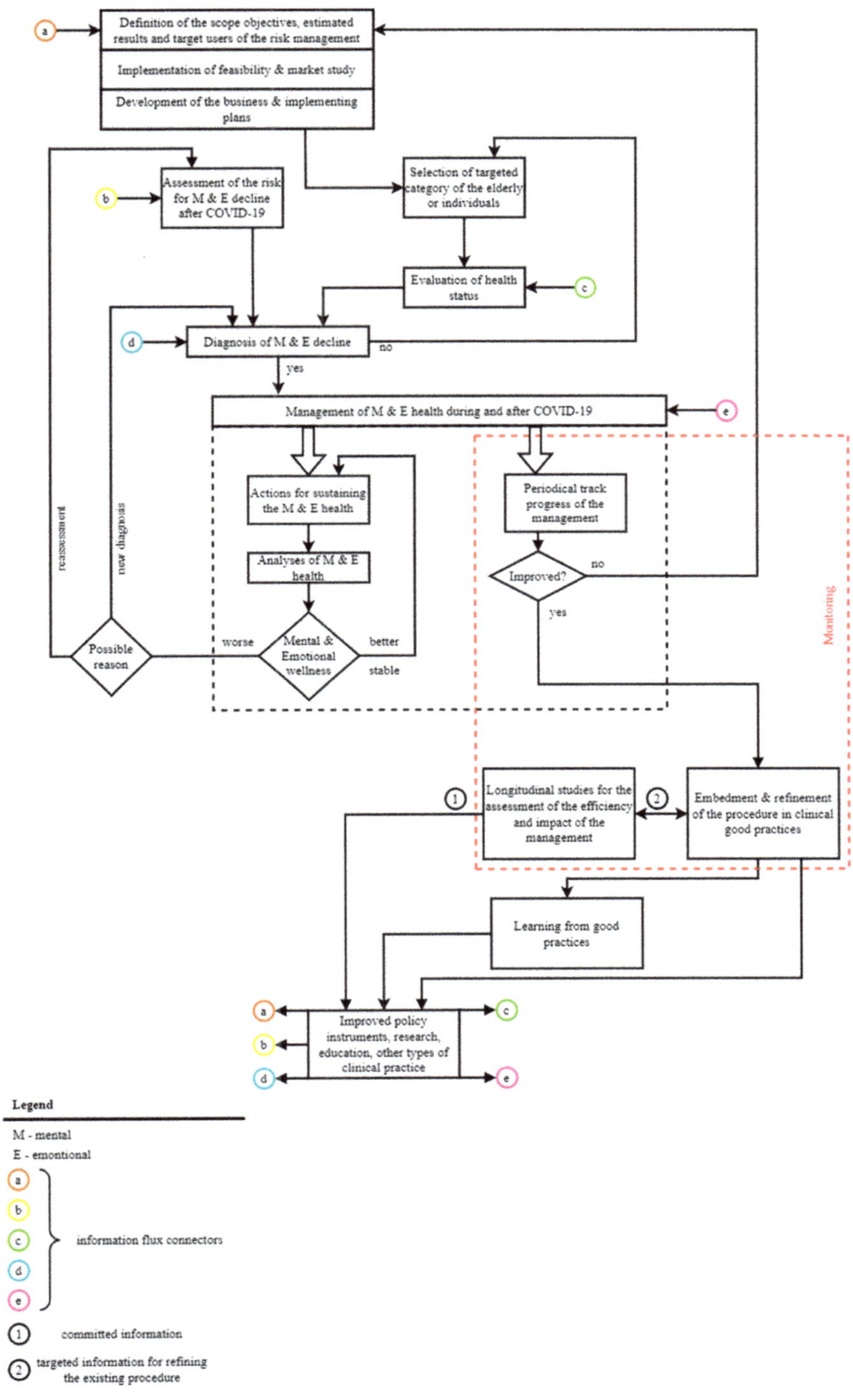

Figure 1. Diagram of the proposed procedure for managing the elderly's risk of mental and emotional long-term decline during and after SARS-CoV-2 infection.

As it was stated previously, *the assessment of the risk for mental and emotional decline after SARS-CoV-2 infection* has crucial importance for managing the associated long-term decline. The results of related surveys, mental status tools for evaluating cognition (such as MMSE, MoCA, ADL, Free-Cog or Anxiety and fear of COVID scale—AMICO), or wearables/smart devices able to assess physiological changes through continuous remote monitoring are sources for generating a reliable identification of these risk factors. These factors should be concatenated with all the other risk factors used for evaluating the mental or emotional status of elderly patients, without necessarily being related to COVID-19.

Some of the above-mentioned risk factors are the same: age, gender, medical history, education, health status (including pre-existing mental and emotional disorders), way of living (with aspects related to loneliness, social relationship, and economic status), access to medical and social assistance, and access to digital technology, level of IT and health literacy, or ageism influences. Once identified, all these risk factors must be prioritized.

The *selection of targeted category of the elderly or individuals* aims to better implement risk management according to the main scope of the healthcare provider that applies this plan. This procedure can be used for improved management of mental and emotional disorders of a particular elderly patient or for a specific category of older patients, depending on the level at which it is applied and by whom it is applied (a physician, a medical unit or at the level of the health insurance system).

Once the targeted elderly patient(s) is/are selected, *an evaluation of their health status* is carried out with the help of traditional medicine, but also with the help of digital technology, including RMDSs.

The results of the evaluation of the health status corroborated the identified and prioritized risk factors are the basis for a reliable *diagnosis of mental and emotional decline*.

In this phase of the procedure, an evaluation of the current situation is performed. If no decline in mental and emotional status of the elderly patients that were previously infected with SARS-CoV-2 is identified, it returns to the step in which a patient or category of patients is selected.

If a decline is identified, the next phase of the procedure is activated, i.e., the management of mental and emotional health during and after COVID-19 pandemic. This one is structured in two parts: (1) appropriate healthcare assistance and services and (2) monitoring of the risk management plan.

(1) Appropriate healthcare assistance and services start with *actions for sustaining mental and emotional health*. Some of these most representative actions are:

- Implementing flexible coping strategies and programs to support the physical and psychological state of the elderly patients, their cognitive status, and physical activity;
- Increasing the participation, awareness, and empowerment of the elderly in the management of their mental, emotional, and health status;
- Supporting long-life learning in appropriate domains such as health or ICT for decreasing the digital divide, ageism influences, age-related dysfunctionalities, etc.;
- Enlarging the access to RMDSs;
- Improving the co-participative design and implementation of customizable remote health monitoring;
- Implementing preventative, proactive, and personalized protocols (including those supported by digital healthcare solutions) aiming to identify early the occurrence of a new risk factor or an abnormal mental/emotional state; act in response to a decline in mental and emotional state or crisis; and predict personalized patterns in the evolution of the elderly's mental and emotional health;
- Ensuring the cognitive, behavioral, and rehabilitation training;
- Facilitating enhanced caretaker support that is personalized according to the elderly's specificities;
- Creating a better framework for targeted mental and emotional screening.

These actions should be followed by *analyses of mental and emotional health*. These analyses imply:

- Checking the conformity of the actions with the current and updated legal framework;
- Correlating the cognitive and emotional distress with other health disorders, daily behavior, and specific issues associated with the COVID-19 pandemic framework;
- Performing correlational research aiming to detect the evolution in mental and emotional health before, during, and after COVID-19 crisis, in order to clearly identify the pandemic-associated disorders;
- Evaluating the role of RMDSs in the management of specific mental and emotional health.

The results of this phase of the procedure are evaluated in order to establish the state of mental and emotional wellness. If it is better or stable, the actions for sustaining mental and emotional health proved to be reliable, and they continue to be applied. If the mental and emotional wellness is worse, the possible reason is looked for:

- A new diagnosis is required or;
- A reassessment of the risk factors should be performed.

In both cases, the procedure is resumed accordingly.

(2) The Monitoring phase implies *periodical track of the progress of the management*. It is performed based on comprehensive questionnaires, surveys, and direct feedback for the implied users/actors. An assessment of the results is performed. If the results are not improved (i.e., the state of mental and emotional health of the elderly patients is not better or the healthcare resources have not become more efficient), it means that the whole risk management plan should be improved, so the procedure is restarted from the beginning in order to be refined or updated.

If the risk management proves to be improved, the next step consists of the *embedment and refinement of the proposed procedure in clinical good practices*.

In parallel, *longitudinal studies for the assessment of the efficiency and impact of risk management* must be performed. Between these two last phases of the procedure, real-time targeted information is shifted, shared, and used, aiming for the refinement of the procedure.

As the procedure is implemented in a medical unit, and in time it demonstrates its efficacy, reliability, and efficiency, it becomes a good clinical practice; the more good practices, the more new *learning from them* can be obtained.

All the committed information, data, and knowledge generated by the embedment and refinement of the proposed procedure in good clinical practices, longitudinal studies for the assessment of the efficiency and impact of risk management, and learning from good practices have great potential to sustain *improved policy instruments, research, education, and other types of clinical practice*. Additionally, starting from these improvements, the proposed procedure itself can be improved starting from different levels, as it is presented in Figure 1 in the areas where the information flux connectors are shown.

This approach sustains the scalability and flexibility of the proposed procedure.

2.3. *Steps for Implementing Functionalities Provided by RMDSs in Accordance with the Proposed Procedure*

Designing and implementing an RMDS targeted to support the management of mental and emotional disorders related to SARS-CoV-2 infection can be naturally integrated into the consecutive phases of the proposed procedure. Some of cases were already mentioned previously. Here are all the phases in the proposed procedure (presented in the diagram from Figure 1 in which the RMDSs can be used/implied:

- *Definition of scope, objectives, estimated results, and target users of the risk management*: the RMDS can be designed in a personalized manner, if possible, in a participative way with the direct involvement of the elderly patients and medical specialists;
- *Assessment of the risk for mental and emotional decline after SARS-CoV-2 infection*: some of the elements on which the assessment is based comprise data and information obtained from remote monitoring performed through RMDSs, as well as the insight obtained from different surveys, statistics, or relevant open data sources with the help

of Artificial Intelligence or Big Data Analytics that can be included as capabilities in RMDSs;

- *Selection of targeted category of the elderly or individuals*: they can be selected via different questionnaires included in RMDSs;
- *Evaluation of health status:* gathering health and lifestyle data based on the primary functionalities of RMDSs is completed with their data processing support functionalities;
- *Diagnosis of mental and emotional decline*: predictive models, personalized differently depending on the elderly individual patient or category, mental or emotional disorders, social environment, etc., are very powerful tools provided by RMDSs and able to support the diagnosis and medical decision making;
- *Management of the mental and emotional health during and after COVID-19 pandemic:* all the functionalities provided by RMDSs (gathering health and lifestyle-associated data, data analytics, predictive models, decision-making and informational support, long-life learning, etc.) are compulsory nowadays for sustaining and analyzing the health status, in our case, the mental and emotional ones;
- *Monitoring of the risk management plan*—namely, the *Periodical track progress of the management* and *the Longitudinal studies for the assessment of the efficiency and impact of the management* can be sustained by specific functionalities provided by RMDSs, such as targeted questionnaires or statistics based on the users' feedback, medical outcomes, and financial and human resources involved in the medical care given to the elderly due to mental and emotional disorders associated with COVID-19.

In conclusion, for a successful implementation of dedicated RMDSs for sustaining long-term personalized management of mental and emotional decline, their targeted users should be involved throughout the entire development cycle, from the definition of technical and (non)functional requirements and specifications, to testing in laboratory and real conditions and, in the longer term, to the upgrades required by the dynamism of the field of smart devices and emerging technologies. No less important is the need for the RMDS architecture to be scalable, flexible, secure, reusable, agile, robust, and age-friendly in order to be easily adapted and integrated into different clinical environments or elderly's homes.

3. Results

3.1. Results from a Sample of Romanian Surveys on COVID-19

(a) Results from IRES SURVEY "A month of loneliness" [59]

The collected data proved that the elderly (aged 65+) are the ones who, during this period, also face greater health problems than before the COVID-19 pandemic, experiencing, in high proportions, feelings of loneliness and fear of death caused by SARS-CoV-2 infection, but also the fear of a food crisis (see Figures 2 and 3).

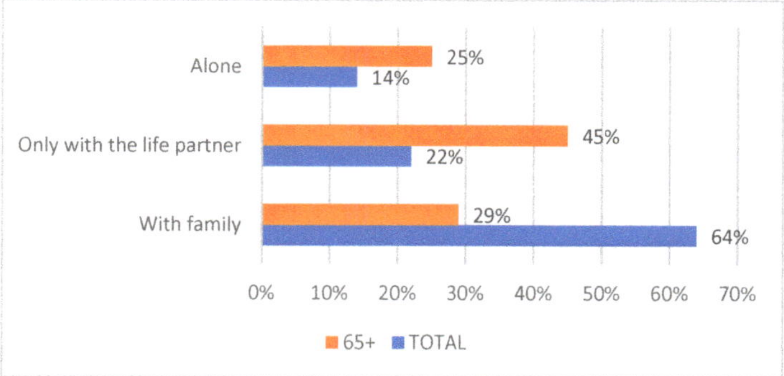

Figure 2. How did you get through most of the first 30 days of the pandemic?

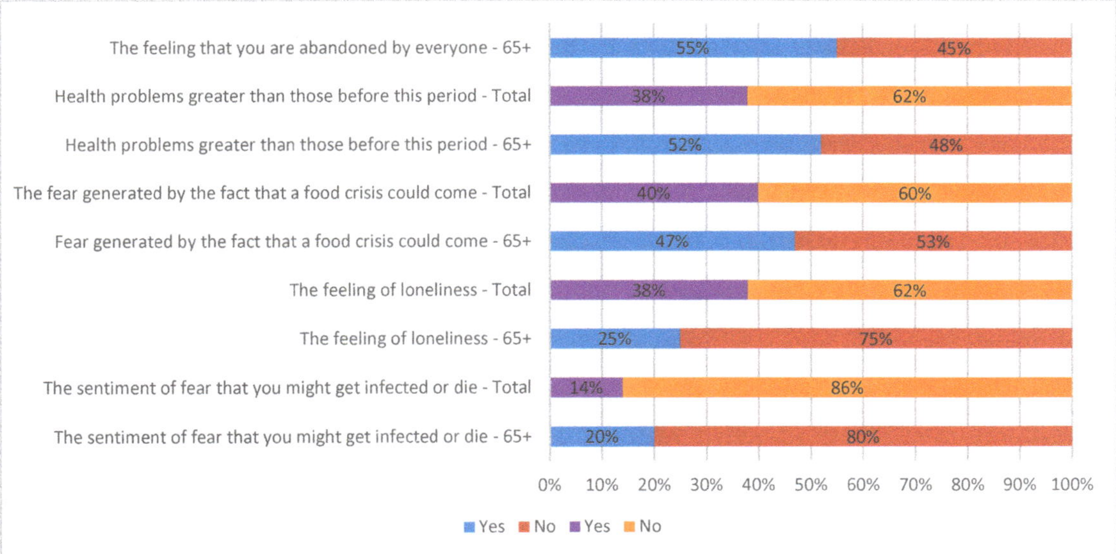

Figure 3. Since declaring the state of emergency, have you felt any of the following states/feelings?

It can be observed from Figure 2 that the fear of infection or death caused by SARS-CoV-2 infection, the feeling of loneliness, the fear of a food crisis, and the existence of bigger health problems have higher percentages in the case of the elderly than in the rest of the entire population. Such problems have a strong impact on their psycho-emotional state.

(b) Results from IRES SURVEY "Romanians after 2 years of COVID-19" [60]

According to the research, one in four people aged 65+ in the urban environment, that is, over 450,000 people, face a high degree of loneliness, and 36% of respondents feel an average degree of loneliness.

Factors such as poor health status or the loss of a life partner contribute to restricting social interactions, such that 28% of the elderly end up socializing with a maximum of four people in a whole month.

Oppressive loneliness affects the elderly, including their health: thus, one in four seniors declare that they have poor physical and mental health. Among people with a high degree of loneliness, 39% have physical problems. Health problems cause one to spend more time indoors: 64% of seniors spend most of their time performing household activities such as cooking or cleaning, occupations used as mechanisms to combat loneliness.

Their routine looks like this: 43% go for a walk exclusively around the house or in the park, 33% watch TV, and only 27% have activities outside the home, including gardening or other hobbies.

Those who experience a high degree of loneliness leave the house even less (18%).

(c) Results from KANTAR ROMANIA, at the request of the Never Alone—Friends of the Elderly Association [61]

In the context of the possibility that the intensity of the current pandemic will decrease in the next period, the survey wanted to evaluate, at the same time, the degree of concern regarding the current pandemic, but also the possibility of a new pandemic, as well as the time horizon in which Romanians expect the current pandemic to end.

The results show that although the COVID-19 pandemic had a significant impact on the health and psycho-emotional state of Romanians, 21% of older Romanians are no longer worried at all about the current pandemic. At the moment, 58% are worried about a war in the region.

More than half (53%) of the elderly participants in the IRES study believe that the current pandemic will end this year. At the same time, however, one in three older people in Romania (36%) believe that the emergence of a new pandemic in the near future is very likely.

The results regarding the degree of concern of the 65+ population relative to the COVID-19 pandemic are presented in Table 4.

Table 4. Degree of concern of the 65+ population relative to the COVID-19 pandemic.

		Age	Gender			Education		Residence	
		65+	M	F	Low	Average	High	Urban	Rural
Thinking about the Covid pandemic, in which of the following situations do you find yourself?	Very + Quite worried	48%	34%	51%	47%	40%	39%	41%	44%
	Neither worried nor unconcerned	1%	1%	0%	1%	1%	0%	1%	1%
	Not at all worried + Rather worried	50%	64%	48%	51%	58%	60%	57%	54%
	I do not know/I do not answer	2%	1%	1%	1%	2%	0%	1%	2%

Regarding the good changes brought about by the COVID-19 pandemic among the elderly, they are mainly related to the time available to be spent with the family and to the way of protecting their health more during the pandemic.

Regarding the bad changes brought about by the COVID-19 pandemic among the elderly, they are mainly related to the restrictions and limitations of movement, the limitations imposed on social life and interaction with others, the limitation of access to medical services, the alteration of the state of health, the states of stress related to the fear of not contacting the virus and the pain related to the death of a close person.

The elderly in Romania believe that they have learned something new thanks to the pandemic, something that they would not have learned in another context. Along with the functional elements related to respecting the hygiene rules and maintaining social distance or those related to health or saving money, many aspects aimed at empathy and the relationship with other people are also included.

Freedom of movement is the first aspect that Romanian seniors have in mind when they are asked what would be the first thing they would do when all the restrictions in Romania are lifted.

3.2. Assistance of the Elderly through Dedicated Functionalities of RO-SmartAgeing System

3.2.1. Brief Presentation of RO-SmartAgeing System

As the isolation and apprehension brought on by the pandemic have strongly influenced the mental health and wellbeing of the elderly, even though it is still an uncertain situation to visit them in person, it is critical to keep a regular connection in order to look after any changes or signs that could lead to a senior's mental or behavioral health concern. In this context, an RMDS for sustaining the mental health of the elderly in their home environment is an enhanced necessity.

RO-SmartAgeing is a system designed to offer personalized in-home services for an elderly person, based on the remote monitoring of various health and ambient parameters and daily activities, across a range of preventative and proactive features targeted to sustain a healthy, independent, and active life; specific requirements for the elderly in order to avoid unexpected concerns related to their mental or behavioral problems.

The smart environment encompassed into the system gathers a set of devices that can be customized and tailored according to elderly patients' health and needs. Their most important technical characteristics are presented as follows:

- Withings MoveECG smartwatch [65]: With a diameter of 38 mm and a weight of 32 g, it can be used to track health parameters (Electrocardiogram—ECG sensor) as well as daily activity information (altimeter and accelerometer sensors). Based on Bluetooth Low Energy (BLE) syncing with a smartphone, it is considered a smartwatch for monitoring day and night activity;

- Withings Sleep Analyzer [66]: Real-time monitoring of sleep-related health data is necessary in order to have an overview of the sleep patterns of the person. It is an easy-to-use device as it is placed under the bed mattress, and it is configured with two sensors: a pneumatic sensor (monitors the body movements across the mattress, cardiac rhythm through ballistocardiography, and respiration rate) and a sound sensor (detects audio signals associated with snoring and any discontinuances in the breathing episodes);
- Withings Thermo [67]: With 16 integrated infrared sensors, this device has a weight of 75 g and a temperature range of 35 °C–43.2 °C (and a clinical accuracy of ±0.2 °C). It is a no-contact device that provides an ultra-hygienic measurement, and the data are automatically synchronized via Wi-Fi into the app;
- Withings Body+ Smart Scale [68]: A full body composition analysis, based on four weight sensors and a body position detector, can be performed using this device. It uses bioelectrical impedance technology to deliver a low-amplitude electrical current through the user's body and measure additional biological tissue resistance;
- Withings Blood Pressure Monitor (BPM Core) [69]: A wireless blood pressure monitor (BPM) is necessary for constantly monitoring systolic and diastolic blood pressure for the elderly. This device has a digital stethoscope and three stainless steel electrodes for monitoring not only blood pressure, but also the ECG and valvular sounds;
- Gait band: It can detect the acceleration of the user's body changes and the speed of the body rotation based on the integrated 6-axis accelerometer and gyroscope sensor that has a 5 V input voltage and an I2C interface which makes it easy to program and configure after the user's specificities.

The HealthMate application collects all the data from the Withings-related devices, and the RO-SmartAgeing system is configured in order to transmit the information into the Cloud database for additional analysis and processing.

The gait band is also programmed to send the relevant data into the Cloud database. The RO-SmartAgeing Cloud database is integrated into the ICIPRO Cloud platform [70], and it is configured to collect a wide range of data (see Figure 4).

←T→	ID	Id_Pacient	Id_Dispozitiv	ClipaInregistrare	ClipaMasurare	Id_Fiziologie	Valore	UM	masurata	unit
Edit Copy Delete	48707	1	NULL	2021-09-02 11:44:26	2021-03-30 10:31:58	1002	1.700	m	1700	-3
Edit Copy Delete	48708	1	NULL	2021-09-02 11:44:26	2021-03-30 10:31:58	1001	56,000	kg	56000	-3
Edit Copy Delete	48709	1	30005	2021-09-02 11:44:26	2021-03-30 11:03:28	1008	59,000	bpm	59	0
Edit Copy Delete	48710	1	30005	2021-09-02 11:44:26	2021-03-30 13:07:43	1008	80,000	bpm	80	0
Edit Copy Delete	48711	1	30005	2021-09-02 11:44:26	2021-03-30 13:21:30	1008	79,000	bpm	79	0
Edit Copy Delete	48712	1	30003	2021-09-02 11:44:26	2021-03-30 13:39:22	1006	65,000	mmHg	65	0
Edit Copy Delete	48713	1	30003	2021-09-02 11:44:26	2021-03-30 13:39:22	1007	92,000	mmHg	92	0
Edit Copy Delete	48714	1	30003	2021-09-02 11:44:26	2021-03-30 13:39:22	1008	74,000	bpm	74	0
Edit Copy Delete	48715	1	30003	2021-09-02 11:44:26	2021-03-30 13:42:06	1006	65,000	mmHg	65	0
Edit Copy Delete	48716	1	30003	2021-09-02 11:44:26	2021-03-30 13:42:06	1007	103,000	mmHg	103	0
Edit Copy Delete	48717	1	30003	2021-09-02 11:44:26	2021-03-30 13:42:06	1008	91,000	bpm	91	0
Edit Copy Delete	48718	1	30003	2021-09-02 11:44:26	2021-03-30 13:54:05	1008	79,000	bpm	79	0
Edit Copy Delete	48719	1	30003	2021-09-02 11:44:26	2021-03-30 13:56:13	1008	74,000	bpm	74	0
Edit Copy Delete	48720	1	30003	2021-09-02 11:44:26	2021-03-30 13:57:26	1006	81,000	mmHg	81	0
Edit Copy Delete	48721	1	30003	2021-09-02 11:44:26	2021-03-30 13:57:26	1007	111,000	mmHg	111	0

Figure 4. ROSmartAgeing Cloud database illustration of a series of consecutive measurements of multiple parameters performed with the devices.

After the data are gathered into the Cloud database, they can be further visualized in the RO-SmartAgeing platform. The RO-SmartAgeing platform has five types of users:

the physician, patient, caregiver, specialist physician, and administrator. Each type of user can access a module corresponding to his role and needs to authenticate in order to visualize/edit the information. The main page of the platform is presented in Figure 5, and it contains both the support services component and the medical component, which are described in the next subchapter.

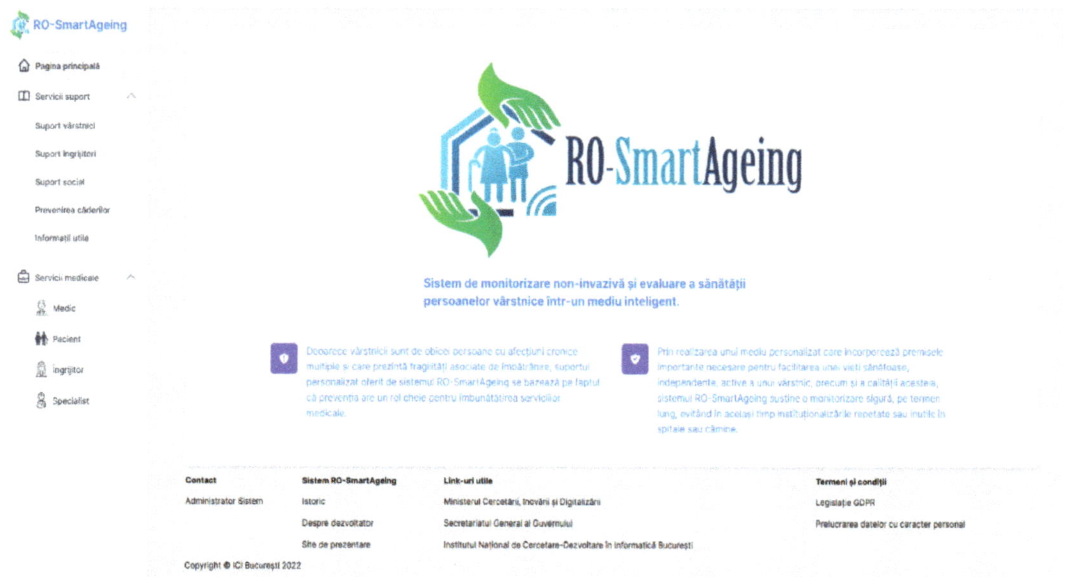

Figure 5. The main page of the RO-SmartAgeing platform (in Romanian).

In the above figure, the left side of the main page describes the menu of the platform: the button towards the Home page, the "Support Services" button (with the following sub-menu options: "Elderly support", "Caretakers support", "Social support", "Fall prevention" and "Useful information") and the "Medical Services" button (with the following sub-menu options: "Physician", "Patient", "Caretaker", "Specialist physician" categories for specific authentication). In the center, there is the logo of RO-SmartAgeing, as well as a description of the system. Other relevant links and information can be found in the footer area of this page.

3.2.2. Specific Capabilities of RO-SmartAgeing System

Various factors can lead to a significant increase in the risk of developing mental health problems. However, a preventative approach through maintaining a good quality of life for one individual can have an enormous impact on his/her behavior and mental state over time. The remote monitoring of a person who is prone to mental decline is a serious aspect that needs to be taken into consideration when it comes to diminishing the risk of emotional and mental long-term decline after a SARS-CoV-2 infection.

The RO-SmartAgeing system is provided with specific capabilities for addressing improved preventative and proactive support for diminishing the risk of emotional and mental long-term decline after SARS-CoV-2 infection.

RO-SmartAgeing has a significant impact through the novel integrated solutions regarding monitoring, wellbeing, and support services enabling an enhanced patient quality of life, especially for the elderly who need to improve and sustain not only their medical health but also their mental health, wellbeing, and behavioral health, as well as their social skills.

The RO-SmartAgeing system encompasses the medical and support service components. The medical component aims to incorporate in a single point, with controlled access, a series of functionalities adapted to each type of user (physician, elderly person, caregiver/family member, specialist physician). It is designed to support personalized monitoring and management of a senior's health in a friendly environment. In addition to this, the support services component is focused on providing specific information and recommendations related to the daily life needs of the elderly: information on aging-related conditions and diseases and recommendations for healthy, independent, social living.

Monitoring mental illness symptoms is very important because they can influence emotions, thoughts, or behaviors among the elderly; there are sensors, wearable devices (RO-SmartAgeing smart environment), questionnaires, and cognitive tests encompassed into the RO-SmartAgeing system that could track and sustain the quality of life of the patients.

- **The Medical Component**

RO-SmartAgeing is a solution that could help in treating and understanding the needs of elderly patients with mental illness or behavioral difficulties. The medical component gathers several Withings devices: the MoveECG smartwatch, Sleep Analyzer device, thermometer, Smart Scale or BPM, as well as integrating a gait band for fall detection and prevention, together with a memo for current activities and a messages service for maintaining strong communication between the elderly, physician, family members and other medical specialists. *The RO-SmartAgeing smart devices* and their capabilities associated with mental or behavioral aspects are described below:

a. *MoveECG smartwatch*: Electrocardiogram (ECG) monitoring and heart rate

The human brain is the most important part of the nervous system. Thus, a reduced heart rate variation is correlated to stress or mental health issues, resulting in loneliness, anxiety, and self-criticism [71,72]. At the same time, an increased heart rate variation implies a solid ability to tolerate stress. However, a high heart rate variation is prone to heart disease. The MoveECG smartwatch is developed to continuously monitor the heart rate, providing real-time data streaming. The smartwatch can be easily placed on the patient's wrist, allowing the continuous transmission of the heart rate and accurately monitoring the ECG when it is needed. This allows healthcare providers to interfere in any emergency related to significant alterations in the patient's heart rate. Meanwhile, measuring the ECG can be of extreme help in order to determine if a patient suffers from depression or bipolar disorder [73].

b. *Withings Sleep Analyzer: Sleep tracker*

The connection between sleep and mental health is considered bi-directional, as low quality of sleep can lead to poor mental health and vice versa [74]. Early waking in the morning, augmented by low energy, distraction, sadness, or loss of appetite, may suggest symptoms related to depression. On the other hand, an incapacity of sleeping or a major decrease in sleep associated with a high level of activity implies several signs of maniacal behavior. Anxiety is also related to sleep problems, represented by awakening, increased sleep onset latency, and low quality of sleep. Sleep deprivation is also related to obsessive–compulsive disorder, as well as detecting sudden awakening through panic episodes during sleep may indicate symptoms of panic disorder. In this context, the Withings Sleep Analyzer can detect any signs related to the movements, sleep cycles, and sleep score (duration, recovery, the number of interruptions, regularity, or time to sleep). The installation of the Sleep Analyzer is firstly based on placing it entirely under the mattress in order to be positioned underneath the chest of the sleeping person. After plugging it into an outlet using the provided adapter, it starts to measure the relevant parameters, making the proper evaluation the next morning. The heart rate is also measured using the Withings Sleep Analyzer as it is an essential parameter to be monitored while sleeping, as it indicates the time covered in the deep sleep phase as well as keeps good management of the heart health.

c. Withings Thermo: body *temperature*

Temperature is another parameter relevant to monitoring the mental health of the elderly. Studies [75] have shown that stress can induce an increase in body temperature. Psychogenic fever can be induced by any kind of stress, a continuous fear of COVID-19 being one cause of social stressors that can eventually trigger a febrile response, significantly impacting the health of the elderly. The Withings thermometer is capable of accurately measuring body temperature and sending the data immediately to the RO-SmartAgeing dashboard. The thermometer is easy to use as it only requires a slide over the patient's forehead. It measures the temperature at the temporal level, considering that the temporal artery is considered the best place to detect any changes in the body temperature. If there are any significant variations being measured (a temperature higher than 37.5 °C), an alarm is triggered in order to alert the healthcare specialists.

d. *Chest band: accelerations and position*

Mobility is linked to the symptoms related to schizophrenia or other neurodegenerative disorders. The risk of falling is also enhanced by mental health issues, but the lack of mobility worsens health problems, reducing social interactions and leading to depression or other mental or behavioral conditions [76]. The RO-SmartAgeing chest band proposes a smart device that could track the position of the elderly. The chest band is placed on the patient's body at the chest level, in order to detect imbalances, movements, positions, and eventual falls, based on accelerations. It can also detect any changes in posture, identifying early the possibility of falling, triggering an instant alarm on the RO-SmartAgeing dashboard. In this sense, the chest band can sustain a social life for the elderly, helping them toward continuous monitoring of eventual falls or movements.

e. *Withings Body+ Smart Scale*: weight and other body composition parameters

Changes in eating habits directly influence weight loss/gain, which can often be correlated with depression [77]. A continuous decrease in weight is interpreted as a diagnostic for depression; depressive people not having a normal appetite due to the lack of pleasure from eating. On the other hand, an increase in weight can be another aspect of depression as the elderly are more likely to not engage in physical activities because of tiredness or age-related aspects even though they consume a large amount of food for their own comfort. In this situation, there is the need to continuously monitor the body composition parameters in order to track any substantial change in weight loss/gain. The Withings Body+ Smart Scale can monitor a wide range of parameters related to the human body composition and transmit the data through the RO-SmartAgeing dashboard to be seen by the health providers in order to take necessary actions: change the patient's environment, current activities memo or treatment plan according to the measured values and diagnostic.

f. *BPM Core:* systolic and diastolic blood pressure

Anxiety associated with the COVID-19 pandemic has proven to have symptoms in blood pressure. Several studies [78,79] have shown an increase in the value of home monitoring systolic blood pressure among the elderly, leading to a much greater risk of cardiovascular issues. Thus, RO-SmartAgeing can help in preventing anxiety aspects in older adults through the easy use of BPM Core. The BPM is placed on the patient's arm and can wirelessly transmit the data to the RO-SmartAgeing system, allowing the healthcare providers to see the home-monitoring of blood pressure variation values over a certain period to detect any significant changes that can occur at the mental level of the patient.

In addition to the smart devices capable of gathering health data for the evaluation and monitoring of mental, behavioral, or emotional features related to the elderly in the context of the COVID-19 pandemic, there are two functionalities of the RO-SmartAgeing system that can improve an elderly patient's quality of life, through *monitoring the current activities* and maintaining a social life by keeping up with the other related users through *messages*.

- *Current activities memo functionality*

In the context in which an elderly patient is prone to problems related to cognitive degeneration and mental imbalances, monitoring the current activities can provide support for maintaining a good social life and self-care, and improve the quality of life.

Generating alerts in case of non-compliance/omission of a recorded activity implies sending reminders for administering pills or respecting the provided treatment. The RO-SmartAgeing functionality of the memo for current activities allows personalized recommendations for the patient's care in terms of sustaining their activities in order to maintain efficient healthcare and good quality of life, as mental and physical health are essential in pursuing a healthful lifestyle to reduce any risks of diseases. Keeping and maintaining an organized schedule for activities can improve the endurance of a person in terms of cardiological functionality, respiratory system, muscular strength, or body composition.

In addition to this, mental health is also sustained through physical activities, having a great impact on boosting the patient's emotional, social, and psychological wellbeing [80].

- *Messages functionality*

Keeping efficient communication between the patient and the physician is mandatory in terms of the post-COVID-19 pandemic, as there is the need to remotely correspond with medical professionals, caregivers, or other medical specialists when any healthcare-related problems may appear. For example, the caregiver, as an authorized user of the RO-SmartAgeing system and being responsible for the elderly person, can send a message, in real time, to the physician if there are any issues regarding the health or the wellbeing of the patient. Once any messages are received by the physician, any further clinical investigations can be based on the measured health data or on the activities the patient is doing.

- **The Support Services Component**

The support services component aims to provide both seniors and caregivers with information and recommendations specific to the daily life needs of the seniors. It attempts to provide the necessary information specific to the older people's conditions and recommendations for a healthy, independent, and social life, and it also allows the possibility of assessing the mental and behavioral capabilities of the elderly using cognitive tests.

A. *Social relationship support and cognitive abilities module*

This module offers the opportunity for the elderly and their caregivers to assess the patient's cognitive abilities and improve their social relationships through interactive tests and relevant information regarding the social aspect of their life. Social networks have a great impact on the quality of life of the elderly, especially in the emotional quality of social relationships. They offer older people the opportunity to renew or develop social contacts and to actively engage in their own community, thus preventing the social isolation of older people and the feeling of loneliness that occurs in the case of retirement, health deterioration, or COVID-19-related quarantine.

The *Social relationship support and cognitive abilities* module covers two sections: (self-)assessment cognitive tests and social support for the elderly.

The purpose of the first section is to allow elderly people to self-assess their cognitive abilities or let their caregivers help them in their evaluation through the provided tests in the RO-SmartAgeing application. Evaluating cognitive abilities or neurological impairments is essential for the elderly, especially in the COVID-19 era, as the mental state or condition can deteriorate.

Among the smart devices encompassed in the smart environment, RO-SmartAgeing has the capability of providing a series of cognitive tests for the patient in order to be evaluated by themselves, or by the caregiver or physician. The cognitive tests integrated into RO-SmartAgeing are either

- developed by medical specialists that use the RO-SmartAgeing system as support in the provision of specialized medical services;

  or

- based on some of the most popular screening tools for cognitive impairments, such as *MMSE* [22], *MoCA* [23], and *Mini-Cog* [29] (see Figure 6).

Figure 6. RO-SmartAgeing (Self-)assessment cognitive tests (in Romanian).

Figure 6 describes the (Self-)assessment cognitive tests (Teste de (auto)evaluare capaciate cognitive) page in the RO-SmartAgeing platform. There are two boxes under the page title for the "Search test (Căutare chestionar)" functionality (the users may search, based on certain keywords, the kind of test that they are looking for) and the "Choose recording (Alege înregistrări)" functionality (the users can select "All the recordings (Toate înregistrările)" option which displays all the tests from the database or choose other options for displaying associated information). Next to these boxes, there is the "Add test (Adăugare test)" button which enables the authorized user to add another test. Below, under the title "Test name (Denumire test)", there is a list of four current available tests: a cognitive assessment test uploaded by one physician (Test de evaluare capacitate cognitive), and the MMSE, MoCA, and Mini-Cog evaluation tests. The "Actions (Acțiuni)" that can be applied to the tests are the following: "Details (Detalii)" (for showing the details of a certain test), "View (Vizualizare)" (for visualizing the test), "Edit (Editare)" (if the physician is authenticated, the "Edit" button is available in order to modify or add information), "Download (Descarcă pdf)" (if the patient wants to download and print the test) and the "Delete (Ștergere)" option (for deleting the test).

The MMSE is easily downloadable from the RO-SmartAgeing platform. It is administered with the assistance of the caregiver in order to assure the robustness of the answers, and via telehealth, it supports the patients for whom distance, expenses, or mobility are considered obstacles to proceeding with face-to-face in-hospital visits. Thus, the elderly patient who is monitored using the RO-SmartAgeing system can be periodically evaluated in terms of the following cognitive functions: time and space orientation, enrollment, awareness and calculation, recall, praxis, and language.

RO-SmartAgeing also provides the possibility of downloading the MoCA test. The test is performed by the elderly patient assisted by the caretaker and, optionally, via videoconference, by the physician. The results of the MoCA test can provide information in addition to the evaluations of the mental state of the patient obtained following the use of other tests accessible through the RO-SmarAgeing system, such as the level of orientation, short-term memory, visuospatial capacity, abstraction, attention, or use of language.

The Mini-Cog test can be easily downloaded from the RO-SmartAgeing platform. As the elderly patient (assisted by the caretaker) has only to repeat three words and draw a clock, this test can be easily performed and interpreted in a step-wise fashion. It provides a neuropsychological evaluation of the patient, which contributes in a reliable way to the early diagnosis of some cognitive disorders.

The second section of the *Social relationship support and cognitive abilities* module aims to synthesize the benefits brought to the elderly by ensuring quality social support (see Figure 7), and thus the advantages brought by the social involvement of the elderly in the community, the facilitation of new social contacts, as well as the benefits of intergenerational activities are provided.

Figure 7. Recommendations regarding the provision of social support for the elderly (in Romanian).

The presented information aims to offer the necessary support for the development of social relationships (with physicians, relatives, friends, and people with similar concerns), such as the elderly's access to support groups.

In the above figure, the page entitled "Recommendations regarding the provision of social support for the elderly (Recomandări privind asigurarea suportului social pentru vârstnic)" enables the user to search for certain information on the webpage, but also to select data based on the "Search information (Căutare informații suport social)" box and "Select recording (Alege înregistrări)" box, respectively. The "Add information (Adăugare informații)" button allows any authorized user to introduce relevant information. The recommendations for social support are displayed under the title "Recommendation name (Denumire recomandare)", containing relevant information about ideas for establishing social interactions among the elderly (for example, information about various seniors' clubs (Clubul Seniorilor "Mihai Eminesccu" – Sectorul 6, București), day centers for old persons (Centrul de zi "Clubul Seniorilor Covasna", Sector 4, București), etc.). Some Actions (Acțiuni) are available for the authorized user. All the recommendations are associated with the "View (Vizualizare)" button that enables the display of the accessed data. Although all the information stored in the RO-SmartAgeing platform can be modified only by the authorized health specialist that introduced it, some recommendations can be edited (the "Edit (Editare)" button) or erased (the "Delete (Ștergere)" button) only by the webpage administrator.

B. *Support services for elderly people*

This category of services will provide informative and interactive support for the conditions and problems faced by the elderly to help them strengthen a healthy and independent life. The subcomponent will allow the elderly to self-assess their quality of life using interactive questionnaires.

The quality of life of the elderly includes both subjective elements (psychological wellbeing, autonomy, the activity carried out pursuing a certain goal, social relationships, spirituality, and identity) and objective elements (physical and care environment, physical and mental health, level of functioning, and socio-economic status).

The *Support services for elderly people* module covers three sections: information on aging-related conditions, healthy and independent living information, and quality of life and wellbeing self-assessment questionnaires.

The purpose of the first section is to provide anyone interested with basic information about the most important conditions, as well as their specificities, associated with aging. It is important that the specifics of a geriatric condition be understood by non-medical, elderly, or other interested people (see Figure 8).

Figure 8. Information on aging-related conditions section (in Romanian).

In the above figure, the "Ageing-related health conditions (Afecțiuni associate îmbătrânirii)" webpage displays the "Search condition (Căutare afecțiune)" and "Select recording (Alege înregistrări)" boxes, as well as the "Add health condition (Adăugare afecțiune)" button for authorized users. Below, under the title "Health condition name (Denumire afecțiune)", a list of such health conditions from the RO-SmartAgeing database is displayed: diabetes (Diabet), hypertension (Hipertensiune arterială), osteoporosis (Osteoporoză), dementia (Demență), and Parkinson's disease (Boala Parkinson). On the right, there are the actions available for these items: the "View (Vizualizare)" button for displaying the stored information, and the "Edit (Editare)" and "Delete (Ștergere)" buttons available for an authenticated user in order to modify that record.

The displayed centralized information on the main conditions associated with aging can be accessed by anyone without the need to be registered. It is the authorized user (physician or healthcare provider) who will enter this structured information in a way that is as accessible as possible to the elderly. In this context, this can increase the level of awareness of the risks associated with aging and offer support for better management of one's own health condition in order to sustain his/her mental health.

The second section, healthy and independent living information, aims to gather all the relevant information for elderly users and their caregivers in order to support the process of active and independent aging through a series of preventive measures and recommendations toward monitoring their health status.

The information is mostly related to chronic conditions and premature aging, considered risk factors for mental and behavioral health degeneration: alcohol and tobacco consumption, unhealthy diets, and the inclusion of physical exercises in daily activities. In addition to this, cognitive health—the ability to think, learn and retain clearly—is an important component of carrying out everyday activities.

Cognitive health is only one aspect of overall brain health. Brain health can be affected by age-related brain changes, injuries such as stroke or traumatic brain injury, mood disorders such as depression, substance use disorder (drug addiction), and diseases such as Alzheimer's disease. While there are some factors that affect brain health that cannot be changed, there are many lifestyle aspects that could make a difference. This section presents information and recommendations to improve the cognitive ability of the elderly (see Figure 9).

Figure 9. Healthy and independent living information section (in Romanian).

Figure 9 displays the "Recommendations for living a healthy and independent life (Recomandări pentru o viață sănătoasă și independentă)" module. The user has access to the boxes for "Search recommendation (Căutare recomandare)" and "Select recording (Alege înregistrare)" functionalities that are useful in the case of a list with a lot of recordings from the database. The button for "Add a recommendation (Adăugare recomandare)" allows the authenticated user to upload the related information into the RO-SmartAgeing database. The displayed list under the title "Recommendation name (Denumire recomandare)", contains three recommendations: "Cognitive health and the elderly (Sănătatea cognitivă și persoanele vârstnice)", "Advices for improving memory (Sfaturi pentru îmbunătățirea memoriei)", and "Minor cognitive deficit (Deficit cognitive minor)". As previously mentioned, the available buttons for these recommendations are as follows: "View (Vizualizare)" to visualize the stored information, "Edit (Editare)" and "Delete (Ștergere)" to modify the information by the authorized users.

The last module, Quality of life and wellbeing self-assessment questionnaires, provides anyone interested with relevant questionnaires to self-evaluate the level of their quality of life and overall wellbeing. This module offers the possibility to increase the awareness of the elderly concerning the risks associated with aging, and as a result, it helps them in making decisions about the management of their own health.

The questionnaires in this module refer to physical and psychological health, social relationships, and the elderly person's home environment.

4. Discussion

The impact of the pandemic on the psycho-emotional state of seniors due to poor physical or mental health and accentuated by several risk factors that generated anxiety, loneliness, depression, fear of health problems, infection, or even death, was mentioned as an outcome of some surveys undertaken in Romania during or after the COVID-19 pandemic. The elderly in Romania say that during this period, they felt anxious and agitated to a greater extent than before the pandemic, they felt sad, depressed, or hopeless more than before the pandemic, and they felt that they could not stop worrying or keep their worries under control.

Such a result constitutes the basis of the participatory design of new RDMSs. The elderly have to be actively involved in the design process to help ensure that the result meets their needs and is usable even during pandemic periods.

Our proposed procedure for managing the elderly's risk of mental and emotional long-term decline after SARS-CoV-2 infection *creates a framework* for the development of personalized, proactive models specific to certain cognitive conditions, aiming to perform the following:

- Prevent the deterioration of the elderly's health or incidents with serious consequences;
- Support and prolong an independent, active, and dignified life for elderly patients;
- Recover in a familiar environment after post-traumatic incidents associated with the COVID-19 pandemic;
- Facilitate ways to migrate the medical system towards personalized and accessible healthcare centered on the elderly and their associated mental and emotional disorders;
- Update the way of interfacing with the elderly and the provision of medical services based on new and innovative digital technologies;
- Improve good clinical practices and their broader implementation, as well as the legal framework associated with the medical consequences of the COVID-19 pandemic over the elderly population.

Among the most representative *barriers* to a successful implementation of the proposed procedure for managing the elderly patient's risk of mental and emotional long-term decline after SARS-CoV-2 infections are the following:

- Digital divide and digital literacy mainly for the elderly, but also for some of the healthcare specialists;
- Ethical issues;
- Physical limitations of the patients;
- Cognitive frailty of the patient;
- Lack of motivation and the existence of feelings of unfair care perceived by the elderly;
- Lack of a fundamental framework for longitudinal studies, considering the relatively short time since the beginning of the COVID-19 pandemic;
- Ensuring compliance with government guidance;
- An unbalanced multidisciplinary approach to the mental and emotional disorders of the elderly.

The efficient management of the risk of mental and emotional long-term decline after SARS-CoV-2 infection is definitively based on the deep implication of the elderly patient and their attending physicians.

As the COVID-19 pandemic may impact not only the elderly's health, but also their mental health and wellbeing, remote health monitoring is necessary to assess and keep them updated with their vital signs and key information regarding social support, their cognitive state, or recommendations for a healthy and independent life.

In order to be proactive, preventative, personalized, and participative, a supporting RMDS must rely on their demands and necessities from the design stage. A participative approach allows the specification of the most appropriate technical and (non-)functional criteria and the identification of a large range of risks (for instance, the risk of triggering false alerts or ignoring age-friendly functionalities).

The RO-SmartAgeing system is an RMDS in which the patient design replaced the patient centricity and in which the elderly patients with potential progressive cognitive impairments are engaged in advanced personalized care models.

RO-SmartAgeing incorporates the development and validation of a system for monitoring and evaluating the health status of the elderly that integrates non-invasive, wearable physiological (Withings MoveECG smartwatch, Withings Sleep Analyzer, Withings Thermo, Withings Body+ Smart Scale, and Withings Blood Pressure Monitor) devices and movement sensors (gait band) to collect medical parameters, to monitor daily activities and lifestyle of the person, all integrated into a smart environment as well as a cloud platform for data storage and aggregation. An added value brought by RO-SmartAgeing is the possibility of (self-)assessing the mental and emotional health of the elderly, considering the vulnerability of their mental state in terms of the COVID-19 pandemic. This assessment is corroborated by physical evaluations, lifestyle, daily activities, and medical history, and thus, a broad range of comprehensive information is established and prepared for further analytics and supporting healthcare functionalities.

Monitoring a wide range of health parameters and offering constant and necessary information regarding the daily life, medical and social needs of the elderly, RO-SmartAgeing is a challenging solution for sustaining mental and behavioral health in times of COVID-19, especially in Romania.

The main functionalities of the RO-SmartAgeing system that can reliably support the management of the elderly's risk of emotional and mental long-term decline after SARS-CoV-2 infection are as follows:

- Centralization of information about health and lifestyle (previous and current);
- Lifestyle monitoring;
- Personalized monitoring of biomedical, environmental, and movement parameters;
- Remote assessment and diagnostics;
- Assistance for elderly patient's autonomy and emotional and mental wellness at home;
- Alerting in case of a physical accident, mental disorder, or in case of detection of an unusual emotional situation;
- Establishing, maintaining, and improving social relationships;
- Support for people who care for the elderly.

Based on the stored data, additional functionalities are implemented that allow the following support services:

- A treatment plan;
- A reminder of the current activity;
- A diagnosis.

The RO-SmartAgeing system has the following main features:

- It is preventive, proactive, and customizable according to the specificities of the elderly, but also according to the evolution of their health condition;
- It supports an integrated and participative management of the health status of the elderly;
- Through its functionalities, it sustains active, independent, and healthy aging, including responsibility, empowerment, and direct involvement of the elderly in managing their health and lifestyle;

- It provides security and confidentiality of medical and personal data;
- It is scalable and flexible.

Limitations: As the RO-SmartAgeing pilot system has just been completed and since it has been tested only in a laboratory environment, only some of the steps from the proposed procedure for managing the elderly's risk of emotional and long-term decline after SARS-CoV-2 infection could be implemented.

Future work: The RO-SmartAgeing system will be implemented in a clinical environment, as it is already discussed with some legal entities and physicians from private and public clinics. In this respect, some preliminary stipulations and action plans have been initiated with the National Institute of Gerontology and Geriatrics "Ana Aslan" and Hospice Care for the Elderly of the Bucharest Municipality "Academician Nicolae Cajal". After a representative number of elderly patients (the target number for the beginning is 100) are enrolled in a legally established trial, we estimate that in three months after the beginning of the monitoring and management of the mental and emotional health of an elderly person with the support of the RO-SmartAgeing system, the first periodical track progress of the management can be initiated. The appropriate periodicity for this tracking will be established according to the physicians' demands and evaluations. The phase for embedment and refinement of the procedure in good clinical practices is estimated to first start after another three months.

5. Conclusions

The COVID-19 pandemic has had a significant impact on the elderly, with potentially dramatic long-term repercussions on their mental and emotional health. The impact of the pandemic on the psycho-emotional state of Romanian seniors is due to the lack of predictability, the avalanche of information, often contradictory, and the imposition of restrictions that some people have never faced during their lives, were elements that generated, in the two years, states of fear, anxiety or stress. Since the spring of 2020, in a relatively short interval, various surveys addressed to the elderly population have revealed multiple negative and aggravating effects on their emotional or mental balance, wellbeing, and quality of life. The results of these surveys can constitute part of a new framework able to support more efficiently elderly patient-centered management, adapted to the dysfunctions and challenges brought by this new pandemic in a society that was already in an accelerated aging.

The proposed procedure for the management of the risk of a mental and emotional long-term decline of the elderly following SARS-CoV-2 infection is based on an integrated and complex system of information, recent research results, and knowledge regarding the mental and emotional health of elderly patients. The proposed procedure is scalable and perfectible through the periodic analysis of the results of the management of mental and emotional health, through sequential reiteration in the case of identifying inappropriate results, and through longitudinal studies for the assessment of the efficiency and impact of the management. The integration of RMDSs in multiple phases of the procedure gives it new capabilities that support the approach to mental and emotional health through personalized, preventive, and proactive healthcare services. An RMDS such as the RO-SmartAgeing system is a concrete example of the benefits that non-intrusive monitoring of the health status, lifestyle, and daily activities of an elderly patient, combined with support services for sustaining some social relationships and an active and independent life, with a real-time dynamic link to the medical staff, can bring to the efficiency of the management of the elderly's mental and emotional health. The RO-SmartAgeing system is to be continuously developed and completed with new functionalities based on new information and requirements resulting from new research, surveys, and medical specifications aimed at remote monitoring of elderly patients.

Author Contributions: Conceptualization, M.I. and A.A.; data curation, E.-A.P.; investigation, M.I., E.-A.P. and A.A.; methodology, M.I. and E.-A.P.; project administration, M.I.; software, E.-A.P.;

supervision, A.A.; writing—original draft, M.I., E.-A.P. and A.A.; writing—review and editing, A.A. All authors have read and agreed to the published version of the manuscript.

Funding: The authors gratefully acknowledge the contribution of the Romanian Ministry of Research, Innovation and Digitization for funding the following project: RO-SmartAgeing—"Non-Invasive Monitoring System and Health Assessment of the Elderly in a Smart Environment" (contract no. 3N/06.02.2019 (PN 19 37 03 01)) for the period 2019–2022.

Institutional Review Board Statement: Not applicable.

Informed Consent Statement: Not applicable.

Data Availability Statement: Not applicable.

Conflicts of Interest: The authors declare no conflict of interest.

References

1. How Coronavirus Started and What Happens Next, Explained. Available online: https://www.wired.co.uk/article/china-coronavirus (accessed on 18 August 2022).
2. Crunching the Numbers for Coronavirus. Available online: https://www.imperial.ac.uk/news/196137/crunching-numbers-coronavirus/ (accessed on 18 August 2022).
3. Coronavirus—Guidance for Anesthesia and Perioperative Care Providers. Available online: https://wfsahq.org/news/latest-news/coronavirus-guidance-for-anaesthesia-and-perioperative-care-providers/ (accessed on 18 August 2022).
4. Report on Coronavirus by World Health Organization (WHO). Available online: https://COVID19.who.int (accessed on 22 August 2022).
5. Xu, Z.; Shi, L.; Wang, Y.; Zhang, J.; Huang, L.; Zhang, C.; Liu, S.; Zhao, P.; Liu, H.; Zhu, L.; et al. Pathological findings of COVID-19 associated with acute respiratory distress syndrome. *Lancet Respir. Med.* **2020**, *8*, 420–422. [CrossRef] [PubMed]
6. Singhal, T. A Review of Coronavirus Disease-2019 (COVID-19). *Indian J. Pediatr.* **2020**, *87*, 281–286. [CrossRef] [PubMed]
7. How Are Small Businesses Adjusting to COVID-19? Early Evidence from a Survey. Available online: https://www.nber.org/papers/w26989 (accessed on 22 August 2022).
8. How is COVID-19 Affecting Businesses in the UK? Available online: https://blogs.lse.ac.uk/businessreview/2020/05/07/how-is-covid-19-affecting-businesses-in-the-uk/ (accessed on 22 August 2022).
9. Romania Enters in State of Emergency from Beginning of Next Week. Available online: https://www.digi24.ro/stiri/actualitate/romania-intra-in-stare-de-urgenta-de-la-inceputul-saptamanii-viitoare-1275543 (accessed on 18 August 2022).
10. Hungary Offers to Care for Romanian COVID-19 Patients. Available online: https://apnews.com/article/coronavirus-pandemic-business-romania-hungary-europe-a12b428393879805b51414b22d57b23b (accessed on 18 August 2022).
11. Kadambari, S.; Klenerman, P.; Pollard, A.J. Why the elderly appear to be more severely affected by COVID-19: The potential role of immunosenescence and CMV. *Rev. Med Virol.* **2020**, *30*, e2144. [CrossRef] [PubMed]
12. Morley, J.E.; Vellas, B. COVID-19 and older adult. *J. Nutr. Health Aging* **2020**, *24*, 364–365. [CrossRef] [PubMed]
13. Smith, A.C.; Thomas, E.; Snoswell, C.L.; Haydon, H.; Mehrotra, A.; Clemensen, J.; Caffery, L.J. Telehealth for global emergencies: Implications for coronavirus disease 2019 (COVID-19). *J. Telemed. Telecare* **2020**, *26*, 309–313. [CrossRef]
14. Martel, D.; Lauzé, M.; Agnoux, A.; de Laclos, L.F.; Daoust, R.; Émond, M.; Sirois, M.-J.; Aubertin-Leheudre, M. Comparing the effects of a home-based exercise program using a gerontechnology to a community-based group exercise program on functional capacities in older adults after a minor injury. *Exp. Gerontol.* **2018**, *108*, 41–47. [CrossRef]
15. Mukhtar, S. Psychological health during the coronavirus disease 2019 pandemic outbreak. *Int. J. Soc. Psychiatry* **2020**, *66*, 512–516. [CrossRef]
16. Armitage, R.; Nellums, L.B. COVID-19 and the consequences of isolating the elderly. *Lancet Public Health* **2020**, *5*, e256. [CrossRef]
17. Bu, F.; Steptoe, A.; Fancourt, D. Who is lonely in lockdown? Cross-cohort analyses of predictors of loneliness before and during the COVID-19 pandemic. *Public Health* **2020**, *186*, 31–34. [CrossRef]
18. Van Tilburg, T.G.; Steinmetz, S.; Stolte, E.; van der Roest, H.; de Vries, D.H. Loneliness and Mental Health During the COVID-19 Pandemic: A Study Among Dutch Older Adults. *J. Gerontol. Ser. B* **2020**, *76*, e249–e255. [CrossRef]
19. Valtorta, N.K.; Kanaan, M.; Gilbody, S.; Ronzi, S.; Hanratty, B. Loneliness and social isolation as risk factors for coronary heart disease and stroke: Systematic review and meta-analysis of longitudinal observational studies. *Heart* **2016**, *102*, 1009–1016. [CrossRef] [PubMed]
20. Holt-Lunstad, J.; Smith, T.B.; Layton, J.B. Social Relationships and Mortality Risk: A Meta-analytic Review. *PLoS Med.* **2010**, *7*, e1000316. [CrossRef] [PubMed]
21. Arevalo-Rodriguez, I.; Smailagic, N.; Roqué-Figuls, M.; Ciapponi, A.; Sanchez-Perez, E.; Giannakou, A.; Pedraza, O.L.; Cosp, X.B.; Cullum, S. Mini-Mental State Examination (MMSE) for the early detection of dementia in people with mild cognitive impairment (MCI). *Cochrane Database Syst. Rev.* **2021**, *2021*, CD010783. [CrossRef]
22. Montreal Cognitive Assessment (MoCA) test for dementia. Available online: https://www.verywellhealth.com/alzheimers-and-montreal-cognitive-assessment-moca-98617 (accessed on 22 August 2022).

23. Williamson, J.C.; Larner, A.J. MACE for the Diagnosis of Dementia and MCI: 3-Year Pragmatic Diagnostic Test Accuracy Study. *Dement. Geriatr. Cogn. Disord.* **2018**, *45*, 300–307. [CrossRef] [PubMed]
24. Larner, A.J. MACE versus MoCA: Equivalence or superiority? Pragmatic diagnostic test accuracy study. *Int. Psychogeriatr.* **2017**, *29*, 931–937. [CrossRef] [PubMed]
25. Geriatric Medicine Research Collaborative. Delirium is prevalent in older hospital inpatients and associated with adverse outcomes: Results of a prospective multi-centre study on World Delirium Awareness Day. *BMC Med.* **2019**, *17*, 229. [CrossRef]
26. Farias, S.T.; Park, L.Q.; Harvey, D.J.; Simon, C.; Reed, B.R.; Carmichael, O.; Mungas, D. Everyday Cognition in Older Adults: Associations with Neuropsychological Performance and Structural Brain Imaging. *J. Int. Neuropsychol. Soc.* **2013**, *19*, 430–441. [CrossRef]
27. Burns, A.; Larner, A.J. Do we need yet another cognitive test? Free-Cog, a novel, hybrid, cognitive screening instrument. *J. Neurol. Neurosurg. Psychiatry* **2021**, *92*, 1359–1360. [CrossRef]
28. Limpawattana, P.; Manjavong, M. The Mini-Cog, Clock Drawing Test, and Three-Item Recall Test: Rapid Cognitive Screening Tools with Comparable Performance in Detecting Mild NCD in Older Patients. *Geriatrics* **2021**, *6*, 91. [CrossRef]
29. Fumagalli, C.; Zocchi, C.; Tassetti, L.; Silverii, M.V.; Amato, C.; Livi, L.; Giovannoni, L.; Verrillo, F.; Bartoloni, A.; Marcucci, R.; et al. Factors associated with persistence of symptoms 1 year after COVID-19: A longitudinal, prospective phone-based interview follow-up cohort study. *Eur. J. Intern. Med.* **2022**, *97*, 36–41. [CrossRef]
30. Liu, Y.-H.; Chen, Y.; Wang, Q.-H.; Wang, L.-R.; Jiang, L.; Yang, Y.; Chen, X.; Li, Y.; Cen, Y.; Xu, C.; et al. One-Year Trajectory of Cognitive Changes in Older Survivors of COVID-19 in Wuhan, China: A Longitudinal Cohort Study. *JAMA Neurol.* **2022**, *79*, 509. [CrossRef] [PubMed]
31. Meinert, E.; Milne-Ives, M.; Surodina, S.; Lam, C. Agile Requirements Engineering and Software Planning for a Digital Health Platform to Engage the Effects of Isolation Caused by Social Distancing: Case Study. *JMIR Public Health Surveill.* **2020**, *6*, e19297. [CrossRef] [PubMed]
32. Padala, K.P.; Wilson, K.B.; Gauss, C.H.; Stovall, J.D.; Padala, P.R. VA Video Connect for Clinical Care in Older Adults in a Rural State During the COVID-19 Pandemic: Cross-Sectional Study. *J. Med. Internet Res.* **2020**, *22*, e21561. [CrossRef] [PubMed]
33. Von Humboldt, S.; Mendoza-Ruvalcaba, N.M.; Arias-Merino, E.D.; Costa, A.; Cabras, E.; Low, G.; Leal, I. Smart technology and the meaning in life of older adults during the Covid-19 public health emergency period: A cross-cultural qualitative study. *Int. Rev. Psychiatry* **2020**, *32*, 713–722. [CrossRef] [PubMed]
34. Abbaspur-Behbahani, S.; Monaghesh, E.; Hajizadeh, A.; Fehresti, S. Application of mobile health to support the elderly during the COVID-19 outbreak: A systematic review. *Health Policy Technol.* **2022**, *11*, 100595. [CrossRef]
35. Jaana, M.; Pare, G. Mobile health technologies use for self-tracking: A survey comparing seniors to the general adult population in Canada. *JMIR Mhealth Uhealth* **2020**, *8*, e24718. [CrossRef]
36. Echeverría, P.; Bergas, M.A.M.; Puig, J.; Isnard, M.; Massot, M.; Vedia, C.; Peiró, R.; Ordorica, Y.; Pablo, S.; Ulldemolins, M.; et al. COVIDApp as an Innovative Strategy for the Management and Follow-Up of COVID-19 Cases in Long-Term Care Facilities in Catalonia: Implementation Study. *JMIR Public Heal. Surveill.* **2020**, *6*, e21163. [CrossRef]
37. van Dyck, L.I.; Wilkins, K.M.; Ouellet, J.; Ouellet, G.M.; Conroy, M.L. Combating Heightened Social Isolation of Nursing Home Elders: The Telephone Outreach in the COVID-19 Outbreak Program. *Am. J. Geriatr. Psychiatry* **2020**, *28*, 989–992. [CrossRef]
38. Prabhu, D.; Kholghi, M.; Sandhu, M.; Lu, W.; Packer, K.; Higgins, L.; Silvera-Tawil, D. Sensor-Based Assessment of Social Isolation and Loneliness in Older Adults: A Survey. *Sensors* **2022**, *22*, 9944. [CrossRef]
39. Joosten-Hagye, D.; Katz, A.; Sivers-Teixeira, T.; Yonshiro-Cho, J. Age-friendly student senior connection: Students' experience in an interprofessional pilot program to combat loneliness and isolation among older adults during the COVID-19 pandemic. *J. Interprof. Care* **2020**, *34*, 668–671. [CrossRef]
40. Kavoor, A.R.; Chakravarthy, K.; John, T. Remote consultations in the era of COVID-19 pandemic: Preliminary experience in a regional Australian public acute mental health care setting. *Asian J. Psychiatry* **2020**, *51*, 102074. [CrossRef] [PubMed]
41. Liu, S.; Yang, L.; Zhang, C.; Xiang, Y.-T.; Liu, Z.; Hu, S.; Zhang, B. Online mental health services in China during the COVID-19 outbreak. *Lancet Psychiatry* **2020**, *7*, e17–e18. [CrossRef] [PubMed]
42. Shura, R.D.; Brearly, T.W.; Tupler, L.A. Telehealth in Response to the COVID-19 Pandemic in Rural Veteran and Military Beneficiaries. *J. Rural Health* **2020**, *37*, 200–204. [CrossRef] [PubMed]
43. Teich, J.; Ali, M.M.; Lynch, S.; Mutter, R. Utilization of Mental Health Services by Veterans Living in Rural Areas. *J. Rural Health* **2017**, *33*, 297–304. [CrossRef]
44. Goodman-Casanova, J.M.; Dura-Perez, E.; Guzman-Parra, J.; Cuesta-Vargas, A.; Mayoral-Cleries, F. Telehealth Home Support During COVID-19 Confinement for Community-Dwelling Older Adults with Mild Cognitive Impairment or Mild Dementia: Survey Study. *J. Med. Internet Res.* **2020**, *22*, e19434. [CrossRef]
45. Brooks, S.K.; Webster, R.K.; Smith, L.E.; Woodland, L.; Wessely, S.; Greenberg, N.; Rubin, G.J. The psychological impact of quarantine and how to reduce it: Rapid review of the evidence. *Lancet* **2020**, *395*, 912–920. [CrossRef]
46. Álvarez-Dardet, S.M.; Lara, B.L.; Pérez-Padilla, J. Older adults and ICT adoption: Analysis of the use and attitudes toward computers in elderly Spanish people. *Comput. Hum. Behav.* **2020**, *110*, 106377. [CrossRef]
47. Wang, J.; Katz, I.; Li, J.; Wu, Q.; Dai, C. Mobile digital divide and older people's access to 'Internet plus social work': Implications from the COVID-19 help-seeking cases. *Asia Pac. J. Soc. Work Dev.* **2021**, *31*, 52–58. [CrossRef]

48. Kavandi, H.; Jaana, M. Factors that affect health information technology adoption by seniors: A systematic review. *Health Soc. Care Community* **2020**, *28*, 1827–1842. [CrossRef]
49. Ghorayeb, A.; Comber, R.; Gooberman-Hill, R. Older adults' perspectives of smart home technology: Are we developing the technology that older people want? *Int. J. Human-Comput. Stud.* **2021**, *147*, 102571. [CrossRef]
50. Ianculescu, M.; Paraschiv, E.-A.; Alexandru, A. Addressing Mild Cognitive Impairment and Boosting Wellness for the Elderly through Personalized Remote Monitoring. *Healthcare* **2022**, *10*, 1214. [CrossRef] [PubMed]
51. ReMember-Me. Available online: https://www.rememberme-aal.eu/about-us/ (accessed on 1 February 2023).
52. Red Button. Available online: https://butonulrosu.ro/#top/ (accessed on 2 February 2023).
53. iCan. Available online: https://www.ican-project.eu/ (accessed on 2 February 2023).
54. vINCI. Available online: http://www.aal-europe.eu/projects/vinci/ (accessed on 2 February 2023).
55. SMART BEAR. Available online: https://www.smart-bear.eu/ (accessed on 3 February 2023).
56. Ella4Life. Available online: http://www.aal-europe.eu/projects/ella4life/ (accessed on 3 February 2023).
57. INS: People Aged 65 and over Represented 19% of the Resident Population of Romania. Available online: https://www.1asig.ro/INS-Persoanele-in-varsta-de-65-de-ani-si-peste-reprezenta-19-din-populatia-rezidenta-a-Romaniei-articol-101-64490.htm (accessed on 2 February 2023).
58. Census Romania's Population Has Aged Strongly. The Share of the Population over 65 Increased by Almost Half a Million People. Available online: https://economedia.ro/recensamant-2022-populatia-romaniei-a-imbatranit-puternic-ponderea-populaiei-de-peste-65-de-ani-a-crescut-cu-aproape-jumatate-de-milion-de-persoane.html#.Y9vYmXZByUk (accessed on 2 February 2023).
59. A Month of Loneliness. Available online: https://www.g4media.ro/sondaj-ires-o-luna-de-singuratate-14-dintre-romani-au-locuit-singuri-in-prima-luna-de-izolare-lipsa-celor-dragi-a-fost-cel-mai-acut-sentiment-resimtit-in-aceasta-perioada-varstn.html (accessed on 29 September 2022).
60. Romanians after 2 Years of COVID-19. Available online: https://ires.ro/articol/436/romanii-dupa-2-ani-de-covid-19 (accessed on 11 September 2022).
61. One in Three Elderly People in the City Lives Alone and Has No One to Socialize with. Available online: https://www.wall-street.ro/articol/Social/279683/sondaj-unul-din-trei-batrani-de-la-oras-traieste-singur-si-nu-are-cu-cine-sa-socializeze.html#gref (accessed on 24 August 2022).
62. Thye, A.Y.-K.; Law, J.W.-F.; Tan, L.T.-H.; Pusparajah, P.; Ser, H.-L.; Thurairajasingam, S.; Letchumanan, V.; Lee, L.-H. Psychological Symptoms in COVID-19 Patients: Insights into Pathophysiology and Risk Factors of Long COVID-19. *Biology* **2022**, *11*, 61. [CrossRef] [PubMed]
63. Zhao, Y.; Le Shi, L.; Jiang, Z.; Na Zeng, N.; Mei, H.; Lu, Y.; Yang, J.; Jin, F.; Ni, S.; Wu, S.; et al. The phenotype and prediction of long-term physical, mental and cognitive COVID-19 sequelae 20 months after recovery, a community-based cohort study in China. *Mol. Psychiatry* **2023**, *28*, 1–9. [CrossRef] [PubMed]
64. Koma, W.; True, S.; Fuglesten Biniek, J.; Cubanski, J.; Orgera, K.; Garfield, R. One in Four Older Adults Report Anxiety or Depression Amid the COVID-19 Pandemic. 2020, KFF (Kaiser Family Foundation). Available online: https://www.kff.org/medicare/issue-brief/one-in-four-older-adults-report-anxiety-or-depression-amid-the-covid-19-pandemic/ (accessed on 25 November 2022).
65. Withings–Smartwatch. Available online: https://www.withings.com/de/en/move-ecg (accessed on 14 December 2022).
66. Withings–Sleep Monitor. Available online: https://www.withings.com/de/en/sleep-analyzer (accessed on 14 December 2022).
67. Withings–Thermo. Available online: https://www.withings.com/ro/en/thermo (accessed on 14 December 2022).
68. Withings–Body+. Available online: https://www.withings.com/eu/en/body-plus (accessed on 14 December 2022).
69. Withings–BPM Core. Available online: https://www.withings.com/it/en/bpm-core (accessed on 14 December 2022).
70. Cloud Computing Services. Available online: https://www.icipro.ro/ (accessed on 20 December 2022).
71. Mental Illness Plays Havoc with Blood Pressure and Heart Rate. Available online: https://www.unisa.edu.au/media-centre/Releases/2022/mental-illness-plays-havoc-with-blood-pressure-and-heart-rate/ (accessed on 14 October 2022).
72. The Connection between Mental Health and Heart Rate Variability. Available online: https://drkumo.com/mental-health-and-heart-rate-variability/ (accessed on 14 October 2022).
73. Hage, B.; Britton, B.; Daniels, D.; Heilman, K.; Porges, S.W.; Halaris, A. Low cardiac vagal tone index by heart rate variability differentiates bipolar from major depression. *World J. Biol. Psychiatry* **2019**, *20*, 359–367. [CrossRef]
74. Wainberg, M.; Jones, S.E.; Beaupre, L.M.; Hill, S.L.; Felsky, D.; Rivas, M.A.; Lim, A.S.P.; Ollila, H.M.; Tripathy, S.J. Association of accelerometer-derived sleep measures with lifetime psychiatric diagnoses: A cross-sectional study of 89,205 participants from the UK Biobank. *PLoS Med.* **2021**, *18*, e1003782. [CrossRef]
75. Imataki, O.; Uemura, M. Psychogenic fever due to worry about COVID-19: A case report. *Clin. Case Rep.* **2021**, *9*, e04560. [CrossRef]
76. Wang, R.; Wang, W.; Aung, M.H.; Ben-Zeev, D.; Brian, R.; Campbell, A.T.; Choudhury, T.; Hauser, M.; Kane, J.; Scherer, E.A.; et al. Predicting Symptom Trajectories of Schizophrenia Using Mobile Sensing. *GetMobile Mob. Comput. Commun.* **2018**, *22*, 32–37. [CrossRef]
77. The Complex Link between Depression and Weight. Available online: https://www.webmd.com/depression/features/depression-and-weight-connection (accessed on 15 October 2022).

78. Zhang, S.; Zhong, Y.; Wang, L.; Yin, X.; Li, Y.; Liu, Y.; Dai, Q.; Tong, A.; Li, D.; Zhang, L.; et al. Anxiety, home blood pressure monitoring, and cardiovascular events among older hypertension patients during the COVID-19 pandemic. *Hypertens. Res.* **2022**, *45*, 856–865. [CrossRef]
79. Nagai, M.; Kato, M.; Keigo, D. Anxiety and hypertension in the COVID-19 era: How is the central autonomic network linked? *Hypertens. Res.* **2022**, *45*, 922–923. [CrossRef]
80. What is Good Health? Available online: https://www.medicalnewstoday.com/articles/150999#types (accessed on 20 October 2022).

healthcare MDPI

Article

Effects of Stroke Rehabilitation Using Gait Robot-Assisted Training and Person-Centered Goal Setting: A Single Blinded Pilot Study

Yeongmi Ha [1] and Mingyeong Park [2,*]

1 College of Nursing, Institute of Health Sciences, Gyeongsang National University, Jinju 52727, Republic of Korea
2 Yeson Rehabilitation Medicine Hospital, Jinju 52717, Republic of Korea
* Correspondence: hongeai@naver.com

Abstract: Many stroke survivors have difficulties due to the mobility and activities required in daily living. A walking impairment negatively affects the independent lifestyle of stroke patients, requiring intensive post-stroke rehabilitation. Therefore, the purpose of this study was to examine the effects of stroke rehabilitation using gait robot-assisted training and person-centered goal setting on mobility, the activities of daily living, stroke self-efficacy, and health-related QoL in stroke patients with hemiplegia. An assessor-blinded quasi-experimental study with a pre-posttest nonequivalent control group was used. Participants who were admitted to the hospital with a gait robot-assisted training system were assigned to the experimental group, and those without gait robots were assigned to the control group. Sixty stroke patients with hemiplegia from two hospitals specialized in post-stroke rehabilitation participated. Stroke rehabilitation using gait robot-assisted training and person-centered goal setting for stroke patients with hemiplegia was conducted for a total of six weeks. There were significant differences between the experimental group and control group in the Functional Ambulation Category (t = 2.89, p = 0.005), balance (t = 3.73, $p < 0.001$), Timed Up and Go (t = −2.27, p = 0.027), Korean Modified Barthel Index (t = 2.58, p = 0.012), 10 m Walking test (t = −2.27, p = 0.040), stroke self-efficacy (t = 2.23, p = 0.030), and health-related quality of life (t = 4.90, $p < 0.001$). A gait robot-assisted rehabilitation using goal setting for stroke patients with hemiplegia improved gait ability, balance ability, stroke self-efficacy, and health-related quality of life in stroke patients.

Keywords: stroke; rehabilitation; gait robot; goal setting

Citation: Ha, Y.; Park, M. Effects of Stroke Rehabilitation Using Gait Robot-Assisted Training and Person-Centered Goal Setting: A Single Blinded Pilot Study. *Healthcare* **2023**, *11*, 588. https://doi.org/10.3390/healthcare11040588

Academic Editor: Daniele Giansanti

Received: 18 January 2023
Revised: 10 February 2023
Accepted: 12 February 2023
Published: 16 February 2023

1. Introduction

Following the rapid aging of the Korean population, the prevalence of stroke in the population over 65 years old has increased from 4.6% in 1998 to 6.6% in 2020 [1]. Despite declining mortality rates from stable stroke incidence, the prevalence of stroke survivors with disabilities has been increasing [2]. According to a population-based study of disability after stroke in the UK, 40% of stroke survivors are disabled between one month and five years after stroke [3]. In Republic of Korea, approximately 9–10% of stroke survivors almost completely recover, and 65–70% of them have shown minor to severe impairments, including speech, swallowing, vision, ambulation, cognition, and coordination [4]. Stroke patients show decreased walking, balance, and daily activity performance caused by lower limb weakness, difficulty controlling movement, and spasticity [5]. Such a problem negatively affects the independent lifestyles of patients and requires continuous rehabilitation [6].

Due to various functional deficits and limitations in stroke survivors, rehabilitation plays an important role in improving functional recovery and minimizing disability by providing a progressive, goal-orientated process aimed at enabling stroke survivors to reach their optimal physical, cognitive, emotional, communicative, social, and functional activity level during the rest of their lives [2,7,8]. A walking impairment is often seen in stroke survivors, and gait recovery after a stroke is an important goal of post-stroke rehabilitation [9]. Therefore, it is recommended that rehabilitation for stroke patients should be aimed at improving not only the gait, balance, and daily activity performance but also the quality of life (QoL) because the decreased performance in daily life activities leads to helplessness, depression, and a lower QoL [10].

Since post-stroke rehabilitation for gait and balance impairments recovery must be provided, research using robotic devices to provide repetitive rehabilitation training is actively adopted [11–13]. Robotic assistance helps stroke patients recover their walking ability and mobility by performing repetitive and mobility-task training at a constant speed and intensity and reducing the physical burden of therapists because they do not need to manually place the paretic limbs or assist in trunk movements [11–15]. In a systemic review of the effects of repetitive gait training in stroke patients, gait training using various electromechanical devices resulted in improved independent walking compared to conventional gait training or treadmill use [11].

Setting goals is essential to stroke rehabilitation and has been recommended in various stroke guidelines [16,17]. A systematic review of the effects of goal setting in the rehabilitation of stroke patients concluded that goal setting contributes to patients' self-efficacy and engagement in rehabilitation, but no rigorous findings could be made on the effects of goal setting in stroke rehabilitation due to the lack of a standard method of goal setting [18]. According to previous studies on the goal setting of stroke patients, the extent of patient involvement in the goal-setting process was unclear, and professionals were involved more in all aspects of goal setting process than patients [18]. Recently, a patient-focused or person-centered goal-setting approach, instead of a health professional-led goal-setting approach, has begun to be interesting due to increasing patient involvement [19]. Considering person-centered goal setting could improve the QoL by strengthening self-efficacy and rehabilitation motivation, it should be included in post-stroke rehabilitation [16,17]. Therefore, this study aimed to examine the effects of stroke rehabilitation using gait robot-assisted training and person-centered goal setting on mobility, activities of daily living, stroke self-efficacy, and health-related QoL in stroke patients with hemiplegia. We hypothesized that the group in the program rehabilitation using gait robot-assisted training and person-centered goal setting would show an improvement in their mobility, activities of daily living, stroke self-efficacy, and health-related QoL.

2. Materials and Methods

2.1. Study Design

An assessor-blinded quasi-experimental study design with a pre-posttest nonequivalent control group was used to examine the effects of stroke rehabilitation using gait robot-assisted training and person-centered goal setting for stroke patients with hemiplegia.

2.2. Participants

The target population was stroke patients getting post-stroke rehabilitation, and the accessible population of this study was hospitalized patients getting post-stroke rehabilitation from two hospitals. Two hospitals that specialized in post-stroke rehabilitation were selected to avoid contamination of the estimated causal effect of the intervention using gait robot-assisted training and person-centered goal setting. The characteristics of patients, bed size of each hospital, and stroke rehabilitation therapies of the two hospitals were similar. Participants who were admitted to the hospital with a gait robot-assisted training system were assigned to the experimental group, and those without gait robots were assigned to the control group. The sampling plan was self-selection and participants had selected the form of open recruitment (Figure 1).

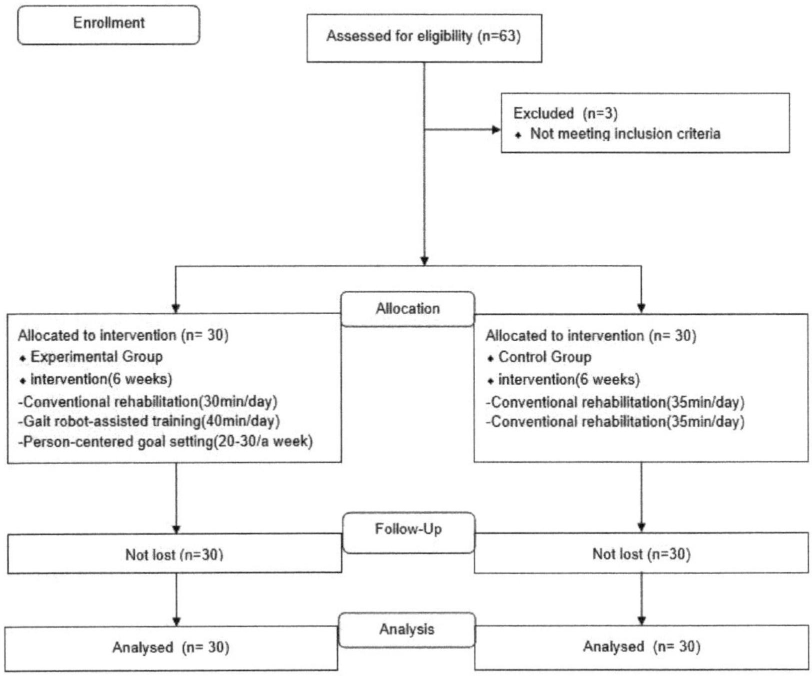

Figure 1. Flow Diagram of the stroke rehabilitation using gait robot-assisted training and person-centered goal setting.

The inclusion criteria of participants were as follows: patients aged above 40 years; patients with the first episode of hemiplegia caused by cerebral infarction or intracerebral hemorrhage; patients who had passed the acute stage of stroke; patients with a score of 1 to 3 in the functional ambulation categories (FAC); and patients with a score of 20 or higher on the Korean Version of Mini-Mental State Examination (K-MMSE) on electronic medical record system. The exclusion criteria were as follows: patients with a score of 0 (non-functional ambulator who could not walk at all) and a score of 4 to 5 (independent ambulator who could walk freely) in the FAC; patients with orthopedic problems that might interfere with walking; patients with underlying neurological disorders such as dementia; and patients with visual or auditory impairment.

Sample size estimation in the t-test, the significant level (α) = 0.05, power (1-β) = 0.080, and the medium effect size (d) = 0.50 were calculated. As a result, 27 patients were required per group. A total of 63 participants were recruited. Three participants were excluded, two participants with cognitive problems (K-MMSE < 20) and one participant who could not walk. Finally, 60 patients participated in this study.

2.3. Measurements

The demographic characteristics of participants were assessed: gender, age, education, job status, marital status, and subjective socioeconomic status. The disease-related characteristics of participants investigated through an electronic medical record system were assessed: subtypes of stroke, stroke-related operation history, underlying disease, medications, numeric rating scale score of pain, and K-MMSE (Korean version of Mini-Mental State Examination). The questionnaire consisted of items with Functional Ambulation Categories, a Timed Up and Go test, the Korean version of the Berg Balance Scale, the Korean version of the Modified Barthel Index, a 10-m Walk Test, Stroke Self-efficacy, and health-related quality of life.

2.3.1. Functional Ambulation Categories (FAC)

The FAC are used to assess ambulation ability. This functional walking test on a six-point scale assessed ambulation status by determining how much human support the patient requires when walking: A score of 0 (non-functional ambulator who could not walk at all); A score of 1 (ambulator with physical assistance level I who requires continuous manual contact to support body weight as well as to maintain balance or to assist coordination); A score of 2 (ambulator with physical assistance level II who requires an intermittent or continuous light touch to assist balance or coordination); A score of 3 (ambulator under supervision who could ambulate on a level surface without manual contact of another person but requires standby guarding of one person either for safety or verbal cueing); A score of 4 (independent ambulator who could ambulate on a level surface but requires supervision to negotiate any of the following: stairs, inclines, or nonlevel surfaces); A score of 5 (independent ambulator who could walk everywhere including stairs) [20]. The inter-rater reliability of the test was high (0.90).

2.3.2. Timed up and Go (TUG) Test

The TUG is a screening tool for basic mobility and balance. The participants were asked to stand from a chair, walk 3 m at a comfortable pace, turn around, walk back to the chair, and return to sit on the chair. The score interpreted that the total time required to perform the test was measured. A total time of fewer than 10 s and 11–20 s indicates independent ambulation and ambulation with little assistance, respectively [21]. Individuals who take longer than 30 s need physical assistance with transfers and generally cannot manage steps [21]. The inter-rater reliability of the test was high (0.95).

2.3.3. Balance

The Korean version of the Berg Balance Scale (K-BBS) assesses sitting, standing, and static and dynamic balance [22]. The scale consisted of 14 functional tasks that focused on the ability to maintain a position and perform postural adjustments to complete functional movements. Each item was scored on a five-point Likert scale from 0 (an inability to complete the task entirely) to 4 points (an ability to complete the task). A global score is calculated out of 56 possible points. Scores of 0 to 20 represent balance impairment, 21 to 40 represent acceptable balance, and 41 to 56 represent good balance. A higher score indicated better balance. The reliability of the K-BBS was high (0.98).

2.3.4. Activities of Daily Living

The Korean version of the Modified Barthel Index (K-MBI) by the Korean Society for Neurorehabilitation was used to assess the activities of daily living [23]. The scale consisted of ten detailed items related to self-care activities: grooming (5 points), bathing (5 points), feeding (10 points), toilet use (10 points), stairs (10 points), dressing (10 points), bowel control (10 points), bladder control (10 points), mobility on level surfaces (15 points), and transfers (15 points). The total score indicated the level of independence according to the disability rating criteria of the Ministry of Health and Welfare [24]: 91–99 points for minimal dependence, 75–90 points for mild dependence, 50–74 points for moderate dependence, 25–49 points for severe dependence, and 0–24 points for complete dependence. A higher score indicated greater independence. The reliability of the K-MBI was high (0.91).

2.3.5. 10-m Walk Test (10 mWT)

The 10-m Walk Test (10 mWT) was conducted to measure the gait speed of stroke patients [25]. The participants traveled a total straight distance of 14 m. The participants started at a point 2 m before the starting point, and the time from the starting point to the endpoint crossed by the front foot was measured. The participants were allowed to conduct the test with a cane or orthosis if needed. A digital stopwatch that measured up to 0.01 s was used for assessment, and two trials were administered at the patient's comfortable walking speed. The average value was used for the final analysis [25]. The inter-rater reliability of the test was high (0.90).

2.3.6. Stroke Self-Efficacy

The stroke self-efficacy scale [26] developed by Fiona Jones (2007) for stroke patients was used in this study. The scale consisted of 13 items on an 11-point scale from 0 points for 'not at all confident' to 10 points for 'very confident. The total score ranged from 0 to 130, and a higher score indicated greater self-efficacy. The reliability of the scale was high (0.95).

2.3.7. Health-Related Quality of Life (QoL)

The Short Form 12 (SF-12) health survey, developed by Ware (1996) [27] and purchased through OPTUM™, was used to evaluate health-related quality of life. The SF-12 covered eight health domains to assess physical and mental health. Physical health-related domains include physical functioning, physical role restriction, pain, and general health. Mental health-related domains include vitality, social function, emotional role restriction, and mental health [27]. The total score of this scale with 12 items ranging from 0 to 100 points and a higher score indicated a higher quality of life. The reliability of the SF-12 was high (0.89).

2.4. Interventions

2.4.1. Development of Interventions

The stroke rehabilitation using gait robot-assisted training and person-centered goal setting was developed. A 6-week rehabilitation using gait robot-assisted training and person-centered goal setting for improving ambulation, balance, activities of daily living, and health-related quality of life was provided to the experimental group. The program consisted of daily gait robot-assisted training and individual education about stroke management. According to the contents of individual education, 'Week 1 (Orientation and Journey of stroke survivors)' consisted of educational content including the stroke recovery process, the importance of exercise in stroke, effective ways of gait training, nutrition, setting long-term and short-term goals, and secondary prevention. 'Weeks 2 and 3 (Lower extremity strength exercise)' consisted of leg exercises such as leg raises, bridges, squats, and superman positions to improve the lower extremity strength. 'Weeks 4 and 5 (Balance exercise)' aimed to improve balance through four exercises: Lean back and forth, Tilt the body left and right, Shifting weight from side to side while standing, Put your feet back and forth and turn your head. Lastly, 'Week 6 (End of the program)' consisted of discussions where participants discussed barriers and facilitators for goal achievement and program performance. The stroke education handbook, including an exercise log, was given to the experimental group to self-monitor their daily exercise and guide stroke recovery. In addition, immediate feedback was provided to improve self-efficacy. For setting person-centered goals to meet patients' individual needs and values, a method of shared decision-making between patients and health professionals was used, such as encouraging patients to actively participate in goal setting, stressing patients' ownership of their goals, and providing information.

2.4.2. Experimental Group

The stroke rehabilitation using gait robot-assisted training and person-centered goal setting was administered to the experimental group from March to May 2021. The Morning Walk® (CUREXO-UMK_MW01, Curexo, Seoul, Republic of Korea), a robot automation system for muscle reconstruction and joint motor function recovery, was used. The experimental group received gait robot-assisted training (once a day for 40 min) combined with conventional rehabilitation (once a day for 30 min) consisting of gait/balance-specific activities such as postural stability training and general gait training. A total of 70 min of combined rehabilitation was provided five days a week. Once the participant boarded the gait robot, information such as the number of steps and walking velocity was automatically recorded in the system. Additionally, patient and caregiver education regarding the stroke rehabilitation process and person-centered goal setting was provided every Saturday in the conference room with a researcher, and short- and long-term goals were reset for each participant after a review of the individual's goal achievement. Once person-centered goals were set, then post-stroke rehabilitation, including gait robot-assisted training, was tailored to each patient. Daily exercise logs and appropriate incentives are also provided to support rehabilitation motivation.

2.4.3. Control Group

The control group received conventional rehabilitation (twice a day, a total of 70 min, five days a week for six weeks) excluding robot-assisted training and goal setting.

2.5. Data Collection

After IRB approval, the pre-survey, a mobility test (FAC, K-BBS, TUG), the activities of the daily living test (K-MBI, 10 mWT), and a post-survey were conducted on participants in two groups. Two rehabilitation therapists and one nurse were hired for data collection. Two of the therapists were professional rehabilitation therapists with a license and working experience of more than five years in clinical practice. They completed the gait ability test and balance test. The survey was performed by a nurse with five years of clinical nursing experience. For data collection, each therapist from the two hospitals completed a mobility test (FAC, K-BBS, TUG) and activities of the daily living test (K-MBI, 10 mWT). The survey data collector visited the wards in two hospitals of two groups and conducted a questionnaire individually. The post-test was conducted by the same therapists and data collector as soon as the intervention was completed. The rehabilitation therapist and nurse are blinded to participants.

2.6. Data Analysis

The collected data were analyzed using the SPSS version 25.0 program. First, the demographic and disease-related characteristics of the patients were analyzed using frequency/percentage and mean/standard deviation. The Shapiro-Wilk test was conducted to test the normality of the study variables. A Chi-square test with Fisher's exact test on categorical variables or an independent *t*-test on continuous variables was conducted to test homogeneity. Second, the effects of a gait robot-assisted rehabilitation on mobility test (FAC, K-BBS, TUG), activities of the daily living test (K-MBI, 10 mWT), stroke self-efficacy, and health-related QoL was analyzed using an independent *t*-test to compare statistical differences between the means of two groups and paired *t*-test to compare statistical differences between two time points before and after completing the program.

3. Results

3.1. Homogeneity Test of Demographic and Disease-Related Characteristics of Participants

There were no significant differences in the demographic and disease-related characteristics between the experimental group and the control group. The mean age of the participants was 63.08 years, and half of the patients graduated from middle school or lower. In addition, 76.7% of patients answered their subjective socioeconomic status as moderate level. Over half of the patients diagnosed their stroke as cerebral hemorrhage; the average K-MMSE and pain scores were 26.45 and NRS 2 points, respectively (Table 1).

3.2. Effects of Stroke Rehabilitation Using Gait Robot-Assisted Training and Person-Centered Goal Setting

There were statistically significant differences between the groups in FAC (t = 2.89, $p = 0.005$), K-BBS (t = 3.73, $p < 0.001$), TUG (t = −2.27, $p = 0.027$), K-MBI (t = 2.58, $p = 0.012$), 10 mWT (t = −2.10, $p = 0.040$), stroke self-efficacy (t = 2.23, $p = 0.030$), and health-related QoL (t = 4.90, $p < 0.001$) (Table 2).

Table 1. Homogeneity test of demographic and disease-related characteristics of the participants.

Characteristics	Categories	Total (n = 60)	Exp (n = 30)	Cont (n = 30)	X^2 or t(p)
Gender	Male Female	36 (60.0) 24 (40.0)	18 (60.0) 12 (40.0)	18 (60.0) 12 (40.0)	0.00 (1.000)
Age(year)		63.08 ± 4.09	63.10 ± 4.34	63.07 ± 3.89	14.34 (0.350)
Education	Elementary Middle High College	13 (21.7) 18 (30.0) 17 (28.3) 12 (20.0)	5 (16.6) 8 (26.6) 11 (36.6) 6 (20.0)	8 (26.6) 10 (33.4) 6 (20.0) 6 (20.0)	2.38 (0.496)
Job status	Yes No	35 (58.3) 25 (41.7)	20 (66.6) 10 (33.4)	15 (25.0) 15 (25.0)	1.17 (0.190)
Marital status	Married Unmarried	56 (93.3) 4 (6.7)	27 (90.0) 3 (10.0)	29 (96.6) 1 (3.5)	1.98 (0.370)
Subjective SES	High Moderate Low	8 (13.4) 46 (76.7) 6 (10.0)	3 (10.0) 25 (83.4) 2 (6.6)	5 (16.8) 21 (70.0) 4 (13.4)	2.67 (0.611)
Subtypeof stroke	Hemorrhage Infarction	27 (45) 33 (55)	13 (43.4) 17 (56.6)	14 (46.6) 16 (53.4)	0.07 (0.795)
K-MMSE		26.45	26.43 ± 1.98	26.47 ± 2.37	5.90 (0.435)
Operation history	Yes No	8 (13.3) 52 (86.7)	4 (13.4) 26 (86.6)	4 (13.4) 26 (86.6)	0.00 (1.000)
Underlying disease	Yes No	31 (51.7) 29 (48.3)	16 (53.2) 14 (46.6)	15 (50.0) 15 (50)	0.37 (0.947)
Medication	Yes No	49 (81.7) 11 (18.3)	24 (80.0) 6 (20.0)	25 (83.2) 5 (16.6)	0.34 (0.987)
NRS score		1.88 ± 0.02	1.86 ± 0.34	1.90 ± 0.31	0.21 (0.640)

Exp = experimental group; Cont = control group; SES = socioeconomic status; K-MMSE = Korean version Mini Mental State Examination; NRS = numeric rating scale of pain.

Table 2. Effects of a gait robot-assisted rehabilitation using goal setting.

Variables		Groups	Pre-Test	Post-Test	Effect by Point †	Intergroup Effect ‡
			M ± SD	M ± SD	t(p)	t(p)
Mobility	FAC	Exp	2.37 ± 0.72	3.13 ± 0.78	−7.399 (0.000) **	2.89 (0.005) **
		Cont	2.20 ± 0.55	2.73 ± 0.64	−5.113 (0.000) **	
	K-BBS	Exp	38.80 ± 5.94	46.03 ± 5.67	−13.197 (0.000) **	3.73 (<0.001) **
		Cont	37.37 ± 6.71	40.70 ± 5.39	−5.976 (0.000) **	
	TUG[4]	Exp	44.75 ± 23.90	33.41 ± 19.89	7.666 (0.000) **	−2.27 (0.027) *
		Cont	44.03 ± 25.61	40.60 ± 26.44	4.857 (0.000) **	
ADL	K-MBI	Exp	61.60 ± 15.75	73.67 ± 16.48	−8.073 (0.000) **	2.58 (0.012) *
		Cont	60.53 ± 11.72	69.00 ± 13.00	−7.429 (0.000) **	
	10 mWT	Exp	40.88 ± 23.11	31.42 ± 16.13	6.615 (0.000) **	−2.27 (0.040) *
		Cont	41.01 ± 34.95	38.83 ± 24.38	3.296 (0.003) **	
Stroke self-efficacy		Exp	59.87 ± 17.33	74.50 ± 20.23	−10.327 (0.000) **	2.23 (0.030) *
		Cont	59.57 ± 17.11	63.87 ± 10.68	−4.552 (0.000) **	
SF-12		Exp	75.02 ± 9.65	96.22 ± 10.68	−15.190 (0.000) **	4.90 (<0.001) **
		Cont	74.55 ± 10.51	83.07 ± 10.15	−6.641 (0.000) **	

* $p < 0.05$; ** $p < 0.01$; † paired t-test; ‡ independent t-test; Exp = experimental group; Cont = control group; FAC = Functional Ambulation Categories; K-BBS = Korean version of Berg Balance Scale; TUG = Timed Up and Go test; ADL = Activity of Daily Living; K-MBI = Korean version of Modified Barthel Index; 10 mWT = 10 meter Walking velocity Test.

4. Discussion

This research provides meaningful findings that stroke rehabilitation using gait robot-assisted training and person-centered goal setting effectively improves mobility, including gait ability and balance, activities of daily living, stroke self-efficacy, and health-related QoL in stroke patients with hemiplegia. Gait impairments negatively affect patients' independent daily life [6], and long-term deterioration in daily activities causes adverse effects on the QoL of stroke patients [10]. Because stroke patients should recover their walking ability and mobility through continuous rehabilitation, person-centered goal setting is essential for successful rehabilitation [16,17]. As a result, the development of post-stroke rehabilitation using gait robot-assisted training and person-centered goal setting could be necessary to rehabilitate stroke patients successfully.

The key findings in this study are that gait ability-related scores, including FAC, 10 mWT, TUG, and K-MBI, of the experimental group are significantly higher than those of the control group. This is consistent with previous studies in which robot-assisted training combined with conventional rehabilitation leads to greater improvement of gait ability-related scores than conventional rehabilitation alone in stroke patients [28–31]. In a systematic review of the effects of repetitive training in stroke patients, robot-assisted training is effective for independent walking by repetitive, high-intensity gait therapy and improves lower extremity muscle strength of the paralyzed leg [11,12]. In this study, the experimental group received a combined intervention consisting of gait robot-assisted training (30 min) and conventional rehabilitation (40 min) for a total of 70 min of rehabilitation a day for five days a week, whereas the control group received conventional rehabilitation twice a day (total 70 min for five days a week). This finding suggests that the task-oriented/repetitive robot-assisted rehabilitation and combined self-exercise for six weeks effectively improve gait ability and mobility.

Another aspect, person-centered goal setting, may have influenced increased gait ability-related scores by improving patient participation and lower adherence to rehabilitation [18–20]. Several studies have demonstrated that person-centered goals have improved patient engagement and daily life activities, ambulation, and mobility in the rehabilitation process [18]. Our results fit with those of previous studies in that the gait ability-related scores of the experimental group were significantly higher than the control group. One plausible reason may be explained by shared goals in the rehabilitation process and customized post-stroke rehabilitation, including robot assistance. For example, the participants and research team actively engaged in the rehabilitation to set individual long-term goals and self-reflected on their performance. Such activities have motivated the participants and positively affected the program performance level, leading to improved gait ability and activities of daily living.

The findings of this study indicate that the balance score has significantly improved with a larger effect size in the experimental group than in the control group. However, a previous study reported conflicting results concerning robot-assisted rehabilitation in stroke patients [28]. Despite mixed findings on the balance function of robot-assisted training, it is obvious that the robot-assisted system totally supports body weight-bearing for patients with hemiplegia, which is beneficial for balance [31]. Body weight support through exoskeletal robots could give an advantage to patients with walking impairments by facilitating balance and gait recovery [31]. In addition, the experimental group received combined self-exercise, including lower extremity strength exercises and balance exercises, and an exercise log for self-monitoring their daily exercise was checked by the research team every Saturday. These findings give meaningful information that combined self-exercise and robot-assisted gait training might contribute to the improvement of balance in the experimental group.

The stroke self-efficacy was significantly more improved in the experimental group than in the control group. It is well-known that stroke self-efficacy is a predictor of functional independence, quality of life, and successful self-management [26]. In particular, a key area of post-stroke rehabilitation is patient-centered goals which are agreed upon between the patient and health professionals [19]. According to the self-efficacy theory, individuals should believe they can perform specific skills in a specific situation to achieve the desired goal [32]. The reason for their significant relationships is that the experimental group had set their own goals and actively participated in the program by continuously reviewing their goal achievement. Additionally, the encouragement, support, and immediate feedback from the researchers would have improved the motivation of the experimental group, leading to the successful achievement of goals and improvement of self-efficacy.

It is noteworthy that the health-related QoL was significantly improved in the experimental group compared to the control group. This agrees with previous studies regarding the improvement in the QoL by robot-assisted ambulation treatment [33]. The health-related QoL of stroke patients is related to the level of daily activities, functional movement, pain, and vitality [10]. Both physical and psychosocial factors must be comprehensively considered to improve health-related QoL [27]. Through face-to-face education in this study, person-centered goal setting was provided, and short- and long-term goals were reset for each participant after reviewing the individual's goal achievement. Additionally, the participants learned combined exercises, including lower limb strength and balance exercises, that were performed independently. As a result, gait ability and activities of daily living in the experimental group are improved, and improved gait-related abilities allow functional movements, thereby increasing the QoL.

This study is meaningful as it is the first trial to identify the effects of stroke rehabilitation using gait robot-assisted training and person-centered goal setting for patients with hemiplegia. There are some limitations despite the significance of our study. First, since a relatively homogeneous and small number of hospitalized stroke patients with hemiplegia from two hospitals have participated in this study, the findings could not be generalized to all hemiplegic stroke patients. Second, there is a threat to internal validity due to a lack of randomization of participants into groups.

5. Conclusions

Our study has demonstrated that the experimental group receiving rehabilitation using gait robot-assisted training and person-centered goal setting has shown significant improvements in mobility tests (FAC, K-BBS, TUG), activities of the daily living test (K-MBI, 10 mWT), stroke self-efficacy, and health-related QoL compared to the control group. For successful rehabilitation of stroke patients, person-centered goals and stroke self-efficacy should be improved by setting realistic short- and long-term goals and a shared vision of the rehabilitation process. This further improves rehabilitation motivation, leading to improved health-related QoL and successful rehabilitation.

Based on the results of this study, there are some implications. First, future studies must evaluate the effects of stroke rehabilitation using gait robot-assisted training and person-centered goal setting from large- and small/medium-sized hospitals such as tertiary and general hospitals. Second, randomization should be adopted for scientifically rigorous trials. Third, when designing the intervention components, it should be tested whether one specific intervention or combined intervention integrating two different strategies is more effective.

Author Contributions: Conceptualization, Y.H. and M.P.; methodology, Y.H.; formal analysis, M.P.; investigation, M.P.; data curation, Y.H. and M.P.; writing—original draft preparation, Y.H. and M.P.; writing—review and editing, Y.H. and M.P.; supervision, Y.H.; project administration, Y.H. and M.P. All authors have read and agreed to the published version of the manuscript.

Funding: This research received no external funding.

Institutional Review Board Statement: The study was conducted in accordance with the Declaration of Helsinki, and approved by the Institutional Review Board of Gyeongsang National University in Republic of Korea (protocol code: GIRB-G20-W-0050/date of approval: 1 September 2020). Clinical trial number: KCTT007391.

Informed Consent Statement: Informed consent was obtained from all subjects involved in the study.

Data Availability Statement: The datasets generated and/or analyzed during the current study are not publicly available due to concerns regarding patient privacy. The data presented in the study can be available from the corresponding author upon reasonable request.

Acknowledgments: We thank all participants for their contribution to this study. Moreover, we would like to thank Director Hyung-Je Cho and the rehabilitation therapists.

Conflicts of Interest: The authors declare no conflict of interest.

References

1. Statistics Korea. Korean Statistical Information Service. Available online: www.kostat.go.kr/korea/index.action (accessed on 14 June 2022).
2. Hankey, G.J. Stroke. *Lancet* **2017**, *389*, 641–654. [CrossRef]
3. Luengo-Fernandez, R.; Paul, N.L.M.; Graym, A.M.; Pendlebury, S.S.T.; Bull, L.M.; Welch, S.J.V. Population based study of disability and institutionalization after transient ischemic attack and stroke: 10-year results of oxford vascular study. *Stroke* **2013**, *44*, 2854–2861. [CrossRef] [PubMed]
4. Korean Academy of Rehabilitation Medicine. Rehabilitation Medicine Health Information. Available online: www.karm.or.kr/info/disease.php (accessed on 7 June 2022).
5. Yavuzer, G.; Geler-Külcü, D.; Sonel-Tur, B.; Kutlay, S.; Ergin, S.; Stam, H.J. Neuromuscular electric stimulation effect on lower-extremity motor recovery and gait kinematics of patients with stroke: A randomized controlled trial. *Arc. Phy. Med. Rehabil.* **2006**, *87*, 536–540. [CrossRef] [PubMed]
6. Balan, B.; Tok, F. Gait disturbances in patients with stroke. *PMR* **2014**, *6*, 635–642. [CrossRef] [PubMed]
7. Herbert, D.; Lindsay, M.P.; Mclntyre, A.; Kirton, A.; Rumney, P.G.; Bagg, S. Canadian stroke best practice recommendations: Stroke rehabilitation practice guidelines, update 2015. *Int. J. Stroke* **2016**, *11*, 459–484. [CrossRef]
8. Winstein, C.J.; Arena, R.; Bates, B.; Cherney, L.R.; Cramer, S.C. Guidelines for adult stroke rehabilitation and recovery. *Stroke* **2016**, *47*, 98–169. [CrossRef]
9. Perry, J.; Garrentt, M.; Gronley, J.K.; Mulroy, S.J. Classification of walking handicap in the stroke. *Stroke* **1995**, *26*, 982–989. [CrossRef]
10. Pound, P.; Gompertz, P.; Ebrahim, S. A patient-centered study of the consequences of stroke. *Clin. Rehabil.* **1998**, *12*, 255–264. [CrossRef]
11. Mehrholz, J.; Thomas, S.; Kugler, J.; Pohl, M.; Elsner, B. Electromechanical-assisted training for walking after stroke. *Cochrane Database Syst. Rev.* **2020**, *5*, CD006185. [CrossRef]
12. Schröder, J.; Truijen, S.; Van riekinge, T.; Saeys, W. Feasibility and effectiveness of repetitive gait training early after stroke: A systematic review and meta-analysis. *J. Rehabil. Med.* **2019**, *51*, 78–88. [CrossRef]
13. Iosa, M.; Morone, G.; Bragoni, M. Driving electromechanically assisted gait trainer for people with stroke. *J. Rehabil. Res. Dev.* **2011**, *48*, 135–146. [CrossRef] [PubMed]
14. Lang, C.E.; MacDonald, J.R.; Gnip, C. Counting repetitions: An observational study of outpatient therapy for people with hemiparesis post-stroke. *J. Neurol. Phys. Ther.* **2007**, *31*, 3–10. [CrossRef] [PubMed]
15. Hesse, S.; Mehrholz, J.; Werner, C. Robot-assisted upper and lower limb rehabilitation after stroke: Walking and arm/hand function. *Dtsch. Arztebl Int.* **2008**, *105*, 330. [CrossRef] [PubMed]
16. Party, I.S.W. *National Clinical Guideline for Stroke*; Royal College of Physicians: London, UK, 2012.
17. Gladstone, D.J.; Lindsay, M.P.; Douketis, J.; Smith, E.E.; Dowlatshahi, D.; Wein, T. Canadian stroke best practice recommendations: Secondary prevention of stroke update 2020. *Can. J. Neurol. Sci.* **2021**, *49*, 315–337. [CrossRef]
18. Sugavanam, T.; Mead, G.; Bulley, C.; Donaghy, M.; Van Wijck, F. The effects and experiences of goal setting in stroke rehabilitation—A systematic review. *Disabil. Rehabil.* **2013**, *35*, 177–190. [CrossRef]
19. Dorfler, E.; Kulnik, S.T. Despite communication and cognitive impairment-person-centered goal setting after stroke: A qualitative study. *Disabil. Rehabil.* **2020**, *42*, 3628–3637. [CrossRef]
20. Holden, M.K.; Gill, K.M.; Magliozzi, M.R.; Nathan Piehl-Baker, L. Clinical gait assessment in the neurologically impaired: Reliability and meaningfulness. *Phys. Ther. Rehabil. J.* **1984**, *64*, 35–40. [CrossRef]
21. Podsiadlo, D.; Richardson, S. The timed "Up & Go": A test of basic functional mobility for frail elderly persons. *J. Am. Geriatr. Soc.* **1991**, *39*, 142–148. [CrossRef]
22. Jung, H.Y.; Park, J.H.; Shim, J.J.; Kim, M.J.; Hwang, M.R.; Kim, S.H. Reliability test of Korean version of Berg balance scale. *J. Korean Acad. Rehab. Med.* **2006**, *30*, 611–618.
23. Korean Society for NeuroRehabilitation. Available online: www.ksnr.or.kr/medical/medical106.html (accessed on 13 June 2022).
24. Ministry of Health and Welfare. Disability Rating Criteria. Available online: www.mohw.go.kr/react/index.jsp (accessed on 14 June 2022).
25. Dean, C.M.; Richards, C.L.; Malouin, F. Walking speed over 10 meters overestimates locomotor capacity after stroke. *Clin. Rehabil.* **2001**, *15*, 415–421. [CrossRef]
26. Jones, F.; Partridge, C.; Reid, F. The Stroke Self-Efficacy Questionnaire: Measuring individual confidence in functional performance after stroke. *J. Clin. Nurs.* **2008**, *17*, 244–252. [CrossRef] [PubMed]

27. Ware, J.E., Jr.; Kosinski, M.; Keller, S.D. A 12-Item Short-Form Health Survey: Construction of scales and preliminary tests of reliability and validity. *Med. Care* **1996**, *34*, 220–233. [CrossRef] [PubMed]
28. Cho, J.E.; Yoo, J.S.; Kim, K.E.; Cho, S.T.; Jang, W.S.; Cho, K.H. Systematic review of appropriate robotic intervention for gait function in subacute stroke patients. *Biomed Res. Int.* **2018**, *2018*, 4085298. [CrossRef] [PubMed]
29. Flansbjer, U.B.; Downham, D.; Lexell, J. Knee muscle strength, gait performance, and perceives participation after stroke. *Arch. Phys. Med. Rebabil.* **2006**, *87*, 974–980. [CrossRef]
30. Susuki, K.; Nakamura, R.; Yamada, Y.; Handa, T. Determinants of maximum walking speed in hemiparetic stroke patients. *Tohoku J. Exp. Med.* **1990**, *162*, 337–344. [CrossRef]
31. Poli, P.; Morone, G.; Rosati, G.; Masiero, S. Robotic technologies, and rehabilitation: New tools for stroke patients' therapy. *Biomed Res. Int.* **2013**, *2013*, 153872. [CrossRef]
32. Bandura, A. Self-efficacy: Toward a unifying theory of behavioral change. *Psychol. Rev.* **1977**, *84*, 191. [CrossRef]
33. Meng, G.; Ma, X.; Chen, P.; Xu, S.; Li, M.; Zhao, Y.; Jin, A.; Liu, X. Effect of early integrated robot-assisted gait training on motor and balance in patients with acute ischemic stroke: A single-blinded randomized controlled trial. *Ther. Adv. Neurol. Disord.* **2022**, *15*, 17562864221123195. [CrossRef]

healthcare

Article

Research of System Design and Automatic Detection Method for Excretion Nursing Equipment

Bingshan Hu [1,2,*], Zhiwei Chen [1], Xinyu Chen [1], Sheng Lu [1], Yingbing Su [1] and Hongliu Yu [1,2]

1 Institute of Rehabilitation Engineering and Technology, University of Shanghai for Science and Technology, Shanghai 200093, China
2 Shanghai Engineering Research Center of Assistive Devices, Shanghai 200093, China
* Correspondence: hubingshan@usst.edu.cn

Abstract: (1) Background: The nursing of the elderly has received more and more attention, especially the nursing of urination and defecation for the elderly. (2) Purpose: Design an excretion nursing equipment that can accurately identify and deal with urine and stool. (3) Methods: In this paper, based on the analysis of the requirements of excretion nursing equipment, a split mechanical design method and a modular control method are used to design the equipment. The Dempster–Shafer (D-S) evidence theory is used in the identification of urine and stool. (4) Results: The excretion nursing equipment designed in this paper works well according to functional test, and the success rate of stool and urine identification method using D-S evidence theory is 20% higher than that of traditional methods, reaching 90%. (5) Conclusions: The urine and stool recognition and detection algorithm based on the D-S evidence theory used in this paper can improve the recognition accuracy of traditional detection methods, and the designed excretion nursing equipment can realize the function of excretion care for patients.

Keywords: urination and defecation care; automation; multi-sensor fusion detection algorithm

Citation: Hu, B.; Chen, Z.; Chen, X.; Lu, S.; Su, Y.; Yu, H. Research of System Design and Automatic Detection Method for Excretion Nursing Equipment. *Healthcare* **2023**, *11*, 388. https://doi.org/10.3390/healthcare11030388

Academic Editor: Giovanni Morone

Received: 2 January 2023
Revised: 19 January 2023
Accepted: 25 January 2023
Published: 29 January 2023

1. Introduction

The rapid development of population aging has attracted the attention of the United Nations and governments around the world. According to the survey, the global population aged 60 and above in 2017 was 962 million. By 2050, the number of people in this age group will be more than twice that of 2017, reaching 2.1 billion. By 2100, it will be more than three times that of 2017, reaching 3.1 billion. China is one of the countries with the fastest aging rate in the world. By the end of 2021, China's elderly population aged 60 and above will reach 267 million, accounting for 18.9% of the total population. By 2035, the elderly population aged 60 and above will exceed 400 million, accounting for more than 30% of the total population, and will enter the stage of severe aging [1]. With the growing trend of population aging, the nursing of the elderly has received more and more attention. Due to the decline of physical function, the elderly is prone to various diseases, including incontinence and other maladies that make them difficult to care for. Therefore, intelligent excretion nursing equipment was developed. Compared with manual urination and defecation care, the intelligent excretion nursing equipment can detect and collect the user's urine and stool in real time, and clean and dry the user's excretion site, which can solve the problems of the dirty and working environment of nursing workers when nursing the defecation and urination of the elderly, awkward situations when the nurse's and patient's genders are different, and invasion of patient privacy. The more established urination and defecation care products on the market include the Smilet automatic excretion treatment robot (Figure 1a) developed in Japan and the China Suzhou Illinois Nursing Robot (Figure 1b). These two types of excretion nursing equipment, which are divided into two parts, i.e., a work head and a host, realize the functions of detecting the user's urine and stool, flushing them, and washing and drying the human skin [2]. However, one problem of the current excretion nursing equipment is that the working head needs to be matched with a special mattress, and the versatility is insufficient. In addition, Omni Medical System has designed a pilot-specific urine collection device AMXDmax (Figure 1c). Macaulay M. et al. designed and developed a portable female excretion nursing device for convenient urine collection in order to solve the problems of difficult cleaning, heavy weight, and unreliability of traditional female excretion nursing equipment [3].

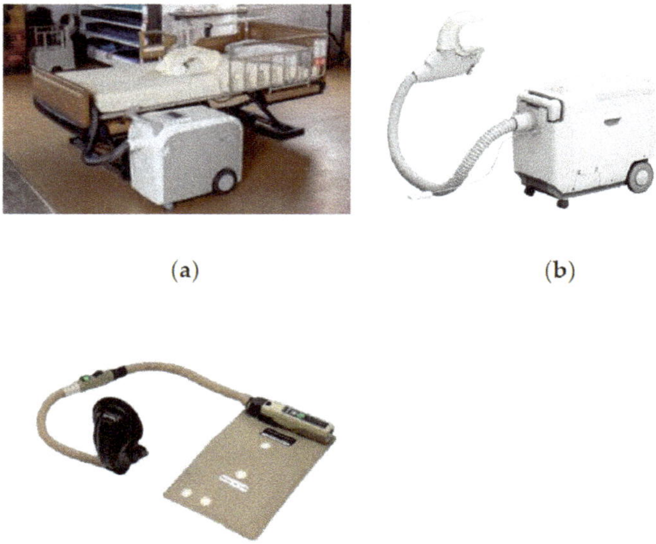

(a) (b) (c)

Figure 1. (**a**) Smilet automatic excretion processing robot; (**b**) Illinois Nursing Robot; (**c**) AMXDmax Urine collecting device [3].

In addition to these products that have been on the market, scholars have also performed a significant amount of related research on urination and defecation care. Since most of the elderly users of urinary incontinence use disposable diapers to solve the problem of incontinence, and the amount of urine that the diapers can absorb is limited, when the diapers absorb enough urine, the problem of overflow and leakage will occur. To this end, B. Fernanders et al. designed an electronic system for urinary incontinence detection. The sensor is sewn into the underwear to detect the overflow of urine on the urine pad and send a signal to the wearer in time [4]. K. Nakajima et al. developed a urinary incontinence warning system for diapers. The entire system is installed outside the diaper, which avoids the cumbersome removal and installation of sensors during replacement. At the same time, it detects the wearer's urinary incontinence and reminds the wearer when incontinence occurs [5]. A. Otero et al. designed an automatic urination recording device in order to help the hospital monitor the user's urine volume and detect the user's treatment effect, which avoids human errors during the operation and reduces the workload of nursing staff [6]. T. Fujimoto et al. developed a new automatic excretion detection system using reflected light sensor and impedance sensor, which can detect the excretion of the user automatically [7].

At present, most of the urinal nursing devices use the sensor to detect the urination and defecation directly. This method determines the type of urination and defecation according to the output data of the sensor directly, and the detection accuracy needs to be improved. The multi-sensor fusion algorithm can perform multi-level fusion processing on multiple different types of sensor data, so as to obtain more accurate detection results [8].

Since the detection object of the excretion nursing equipment is the urine and stool excreted by the user, the data fusion is carried out on the basis of the detection results of each sensor, so the decision layer fusion method is used. The existing decision-level fusion algorithm schemes include the Bayesian theory [9], Dempster–Shafer (D-S) evidence theory, expert system method [10], fuzzy theory [11], and so on. However, due to the real-time changing characteristics of the dynamic environment and the target, the difficulty in obtaining prior knowledge, etc., the application environment of expert system method and fuzzy set theory is relatively complex. Compared with the Bayesian theory, the D-S evidence theory has strong applicability and wide application. Therefore, urination and defecation were detected by the D-S evidence theory fusion method.

Dempster proposed the upper and lower multi-valued mapping criteria to lay the foundation of D-S evidence theory [12], and then G. Shafer extended Dempster's composition rule to more general cases through in-depth research, so that this theory can be applied to a wider range of fields in [13]. After conducting in-depth research on the D-S evidence theory proposed by G. Shafer, Chao Sun et al. proposed a MCDM weight method based on probability distribution negation, which reduces the uncertainty of human subjective factors [14]. Li proposed an improved D-S evidence theory based on orthogonal sum and standard deviation to solve the D-S evidence theory conflict problem, and verified its effectiveness [15]. Ma et al. proposed an improved evidence combination method by studying the combination principle of D-S evidence theory, and verified its fusion performance and reliability [16]. Based on the paradox problem of D-S evidence theory, Wang et al. proposed an improved classifier decision fusion method based on the D-S evidence theory [17]. Kisku D.R. et al. demonstrated the effectiveness of their new face recognition technology by integrating global and local matching methods through the D-S evidence theory [18].

The innovations of this paper are as follows: Aiming at the problem of the large working head and insufficient versatility of the existing excretion nursing equipment, the working head of the excretion nursing equipment designed in this paper adopts a flat design method, which can be used on an ordinary nursing bed. In order to improve the accuracy of urine and stool detection, temperature and humidity sensors and ammonia gas concentration sensors are used, and the D-S evidence theory algorithm is also used to improve the accuracy of urine and stool detection. The rest of this paper is organized as follows: Section 2 introduces the mechanical structure design of the excretion nursing equipment. Section 3 introduces the detection method based on the D-S evidence theory. Section 4 details an experimental study on the function of the excretion nursing equipment and the detection method of the urine and stool. Section 5 contains the conclusions.

2. Materials and Methods

This section will introduce the device we designed in detail. According to the design idea of the device, we will describe the mechanical system and control system in detail. The mechanical system mainly adopts the split design; the whole device is divided into the user directly wearing the working head and as the executive body of the host machine. The control system will introduce the hardware system and the software system: the hardware system mainly shows each module and the connection mode between modules, and the software system mainly introduces the detailed work flow.

2.1. Mechanical System Design

Our previous study revealed that user comfort and safety should be mainly considered when proposing a rehabilitation device [19]. The main target groups of the excretion nursing equipment include disabled and semi-disabled elderly people, users with limited mobility, elderly people who are bedridden for a long time, and people who are worried about infection after surgery. In order to meet the nursing needs of these people, the main functions of the excretion nursing equipment include: intelligent urine and stool detection function, urine and stool flushing function, human body washing function, drying function of human excretory sites, and overall deodorization of the urinal nursing equipment, disinfection function, and human–machine interaction function. The following will design the nursing equipment from the mechanical system and the control system according to the demand analysis. The overall structure of the excretion nursing equipment is shown in Figure 2, and its mechanical structure is mainly divided into two parts: the working head and the host.

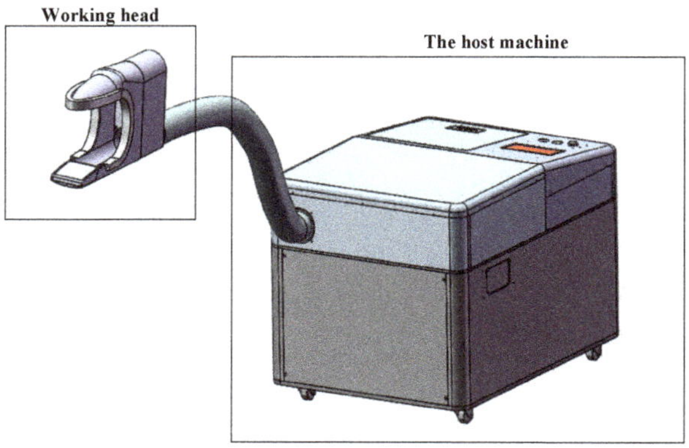

Figure 2. Mechanical structure of nursing equipment.

2.1.1. Working Head of the Excretion Nursing Equipment

As shown in Figure 3, the working head includes a toilet bowl, urine and stool detection sensors, flushing water channels and nozzles, cleaning water channels and nozzles, drying air channels and nozzles, sewage pipes, and externally wrapped soft glue and other components. The working head toilet bowl is composed of the inner upper wall, rear wall, side wall, and bottom of the working head. The bottom is designed in a smooth arc shape, and maintains a 5° inclination angle with the horizontal plane, which is responsible for collecting the urine and stool discharged by the user. The urine and stool detection sensors use temperature, humidity sensors, and ammonia gas concentration sensors, which are respectively installed on the back wall of the toilet bowl and at the mouth of the sewage pipe. An angle sensor is installed behind the back wall of the toilet bowl to detect the side angle of the patient. The flushing water channel, the cleaning water channel and its nozzles are installed on the back wall of the bowl. The flushing nozzles are of two different types: conical and rectangular. The rectangular nozzles are used to flush small particles of stool and urine. The conical nozzles have high water pressure for breaking up hard-to-flush stools. The drying air duct is installed above the back wall of the toilet bucket, and a fan and a heater are also installed behind the air duct. The sewage pipeline is connected with the back wall of the toilet bowl, and is used to discharge the urine and stool collected by the toilet bowl into the dirt bucket. The soft rubber is wrapped on the convex groove on the outside of the toilet bowl to reduce the contact force between the human body and the hard shell of the working head.

2.1.2. Host Machine of the Excretion Nursing Equipment

The host machine is the executive body of the excretion nursing equipment. The host machine is installed with the executive components and main controller of the nursing device, which is mainly responsible for the recovery of dirt, water purification, water purification, heating, negative pressure suction, negative ion deodorization, central control, and other main functions. The internal structure of the host machine is shown in Figure 4, including water purification pumps, ultraviolet sterilizers, vacuum pumps, water purification buckets, sewage buckets, cleaning boxes, solenoid valves, and other components. The water purification pump is installed at the bottom of the host machine, and is connected with the water purification bucket and the ultraviolet sterilizer through the water pipe, and the purified water is pumped out from the purification bucket and sent to the ultraviolet sterilizer for disinfection. The ultraviolet sterilizer is installed on the inner rear wall of the host, and is connected to the water purification pump and the pipeline nozzle through the water pipe. The vacuum pump and the dirt bucket are installed on the side of the clean water pump. The dirt bucket is connected to the vacuum pump, the cleaning box, and the sewage pipeline through the conduit. The dirt bucket stores the collected urine and dirty water. The vacuum pump is responsible for pumping negative pressure in the dirt bucket, and sucking urine and stool from the working head toilet into the dirt bucket through the sewage pipeline. The cleaning box is installed on the bottom side of the host machine, and the inside of the box is equipped with deodorizing activated carbon. The activated carbon is connected to the pipeline of the dirt bucket and is responsible for absorbing odor. The four-way solenoid valve is installed on the clapboard and is responsible for the on-off control of the water circuit. It is divided into four channels, namely the flushing the urine water channel, flushing the stool water channel, cleaning the urine excretion part water channel, and cleaning the stool excretion part water channel. The connection of components is shown in Figure 5. When performing different functions, open the corresponding solenoid valve to work. In order to avoid noise pollution caused by the operation of the internal components of the host, a layer of sound insulation sponge is laid in the shell of the host machine to absorb noise and reduce the impact of noise on the external environment.

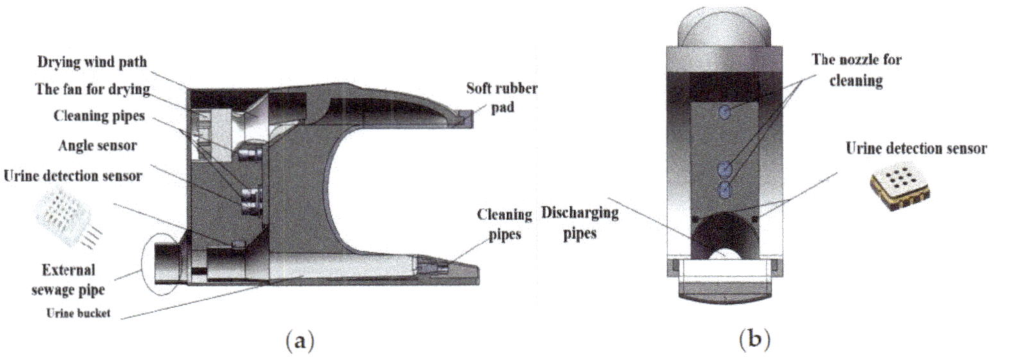

Figure 3. Mechanical structure of the working head. (**a**) Side view; (**b**) Front side view.

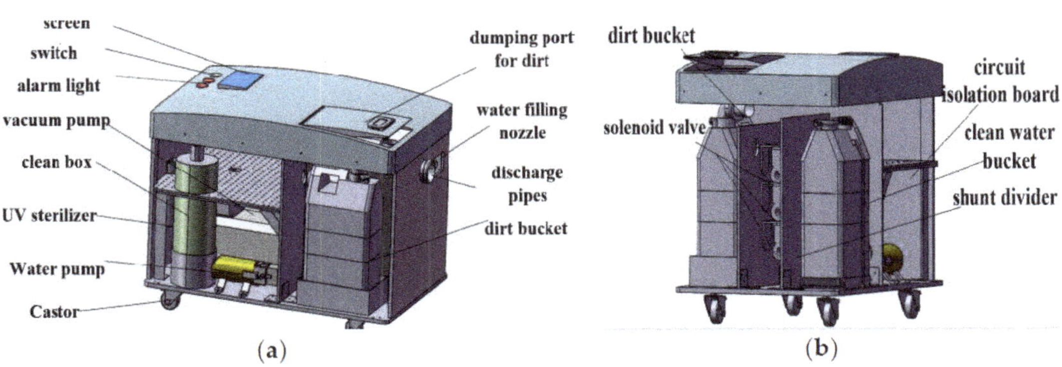

Figure 4. Mechanical structure of main engine. (**a**) Side view; (**b**) Front side view.

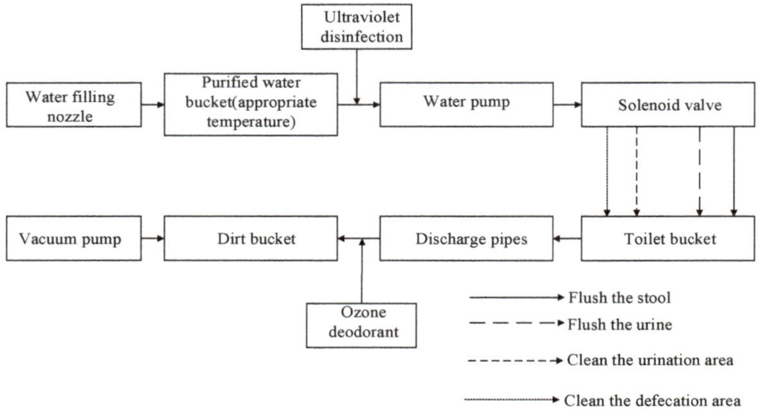

Figure 5. Component connection.

Through the design of the mechanical structure of the excretion nursing equipment in this section, an experimental prototype has been made. Figure 6 is a physical diagram of the prototype.

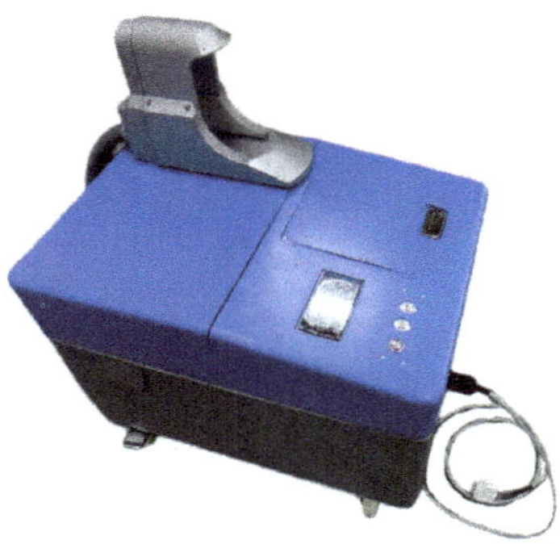

Figure 6. Prototype of excretion nursing equipment.

2.2. Control System Design

The control system design is divided into two parts: hardware design and software design. The hardware design of the control system is analyzed from the aspects of component selection and function realization. The software design is analyzed from the operation process and function realization of the whole equipment.

2.2.1. Control System Hardware Design

The hardware of the excretion nursing equipment control system is mainly divided into the MCU central control module, intelligent detection module, flushing and cleaning control module, drying control module, and other parts.

The MCU central control module uses the Stm32F4 chip as the main control core. Stm32F4 has a powerful peripheral interface, and the chip's operating frequency can reach up to 168 Mhz, which can process the collected data information at a high speed, which satisfies the fast information collection and processing requirements of the experiments in this paper.

The intelligent detection module uses the temperature and humidity sensor and the ammonia gas concentration sensor as the main detection units. After the temperature and humidity sensor and the ammonia gas concentration sensor detect the change data, they are sent to the main control MCU to identify urine and stool by algorithms. The temperature and humidity sensor adopts DHT22. The humidity range that can be detected is 0–99.9%RH, the accuracy is ±2%RH, and the temperature range that can be detected is −40 °C–80 °C. The accuracy is ±0.5% °C. The ammonia gas sensor adopts the MEMS series GM-802B ammonia gas sensor, which can detect the concentration range from 1 ppm to 300 ppm (NH3). These sensor combinations can detect changes in temperature, humidity, and ammonia concentration caused by the user's urination and defecation. The angle sensor is used to detect the patient's sideways angle θ. The MPU6050 angle sensor is selected, and its detection angle range is ±180° for the X and Z axes, and ±90° for the Y axis. When the patient's side angle is not in the range of −30°–30°, the sensor will send a detection signal to the main controller of the host, and the main controller will give an alarm to ensure the normal operation of the excretion nursing device.

The flushing and cleaning control module uses a 24 V diaphragm pump to extract clean water from the clean water bucket for flushing, cleans the waterway, and uses an ultraviolet sterilizer with an efficiency of 0.2 T/H to sterilize the clean water. At the same time, the module sends a level signal through the MCU to control the 24 V normally closed solenoid valve is switched on and off, and then the flushing and cleaning water circuits are controlled on and off, and the vacuum pump with a vacuum degree of 11,000 pa is used to pump the dirt into the dirt bucket. The water temperature in the clean water bucket is controlled by the thermostat and the heating rod to control the temperature in the bucket to the set appropriate temperature. Capacitive non-contact liquid level sensors are installed in the clean water bucket and the dirt bucket to detect the liquid level. When it is detected that the liquid level of the clean water tank is lower than the threshold or the liquid level of the dirt tank is higher than the threshold, it will send an electrical signal to the MCU. After the MCU receives the corresponding sensor signal, it will control the corresponding buzzer to alarm, reminding the nursing staff that they need to add clean water or replace the sewage bucket.

The drying control module uses a 24 V, 300 W PTC ceramic heating element to heat the air, and a 13,500 r/min motor as the drying fan. The MCU sends a level signal to control the on-off of the relay, so as to control the heating element and the motor. The human body is dried in the toilet bowl of the working head. The connection diagram between each module is shown in Figure 7.

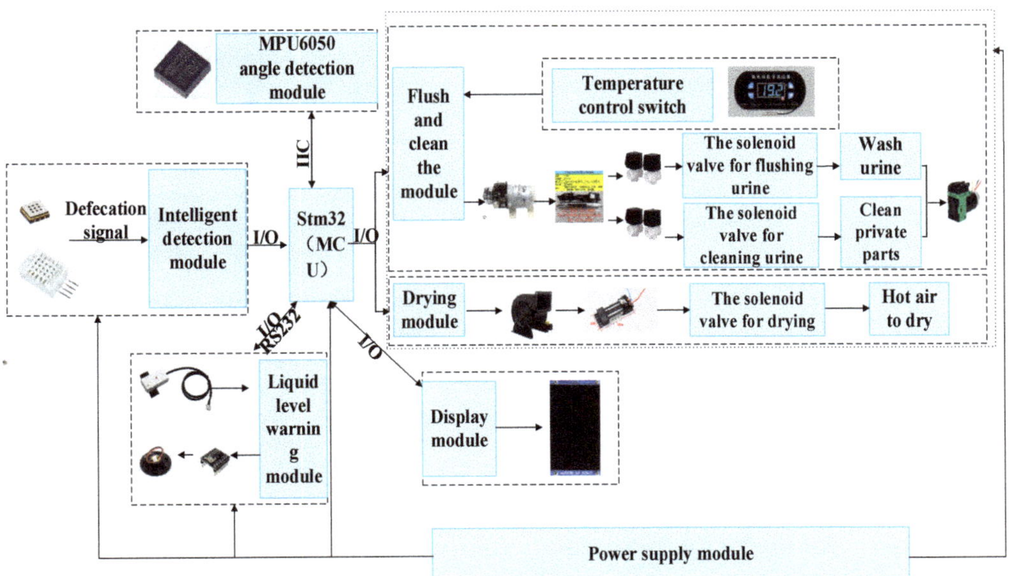

Figure 7. Control system structure diagram of excretion nursing equipment.

2.2.2. Control System Software Design

After the excretion nursing equipment is powered on, the central control module receives the data detected by the temperature, humidity, and ammonia gas concentration sensors, and then judges the type of the patient's urination and defecation. After identifying the excretion type, the MCU will send an instruction to start the flushing process, and the urination and defecation are rushed from the toilet bowl to the dirt bucket. The detailed workflow is shown in Figure 8a. When the identification signal shows that the patient is expelling stool, the MCU will send a flushing command, which will open the solenoid valves for flushing the stool water circuit and the urine water circuit, and control the water pump to flush the inner toilet bowl of the working head (the flushing stool water circuit is used to flush large particles of dirt, and the flushing urine water circuit is used to flush the broken particle dirt). After the pump works for 5 s, the vacuum pump is controlled to start working at the same time, and the dirt and sewage on the working head are sucked into the dirt bucket by negative pressure. After the vacuum pump and the water pump work together for 5 s, the water pump stops working and closes the solenoid valves of the two water circuits. The vacuum pump continues to work for 8 s and then stops. When the identification signal shows that the patient excreted urine, a time delay of 10 s is performed to further detect and determine whether the patient excretes stool. After the patient defecates, the MCU sends a flushing command, opens the solenoid valve for flushing the urine water circuit, and controls the water pump to start flushing the bowl for 5 s. After that, the vacuum pump is controlled to work for 10 s to suck away the remaining sewage in the toilet bowl. Compared with flushing urine, the water pressure to flush the stool will be larger, which is convenient for breaking the stool, making flushing more convenient and further improving the cleanliness of flushing. The working time of the water pump and vacuum pump in the entire detection and flushing process are obtained by multiple experiments.

After finishing the rinsing work, the excretion nursing equipment starts the cleaning and drying process, that is, the process of cleaning the excretory site with heated clean water and drying it with hot air. The operation process is shown in Figure 7b. The washing and drying process is also designed with two different processing modes for stool and urine. When the equipment detects that the patient has discharged the feces, it will wait for the washing to end, then open the solenoid valves for cleaning the stool and cleaning the urine, respectively, start the water pump to flush the patient's urine and stool discharge port, and start the vacuum pump to suck the cleaned sewage into the sewage bucket. After the equipment works for 15 s, the solenoid valve and vacuum pump of the two cleaning water circuits is stopped and closed. After cleaning, the controller controls the fan and the heater to start working. The fan blows through the heater and sends the hot air into the working head. After 8 min, the heater stops working, and the fan stops working after 2 min, after which the drying process ends. When the equipment detects that the patient has discharged urine, the solenoid valve of the cleaning water channel for flushing the urine discharge site of human will be opened after the flushing process. The drying process for stool and urine works the same way.

Although the process of excretion nursing is complicated, for the healthcare professional, it is only necessary to ensure that the user has finished, and then operate the button on the host machine. The working condition information of the device can be displayed to the healthcare professional by the display screen. The healthcare professional only needs to check whether the equipment is working normally. If there are abnormal conditions, such as low water level in the bucket, the abnormal conditions can be removed according to the operation manual.

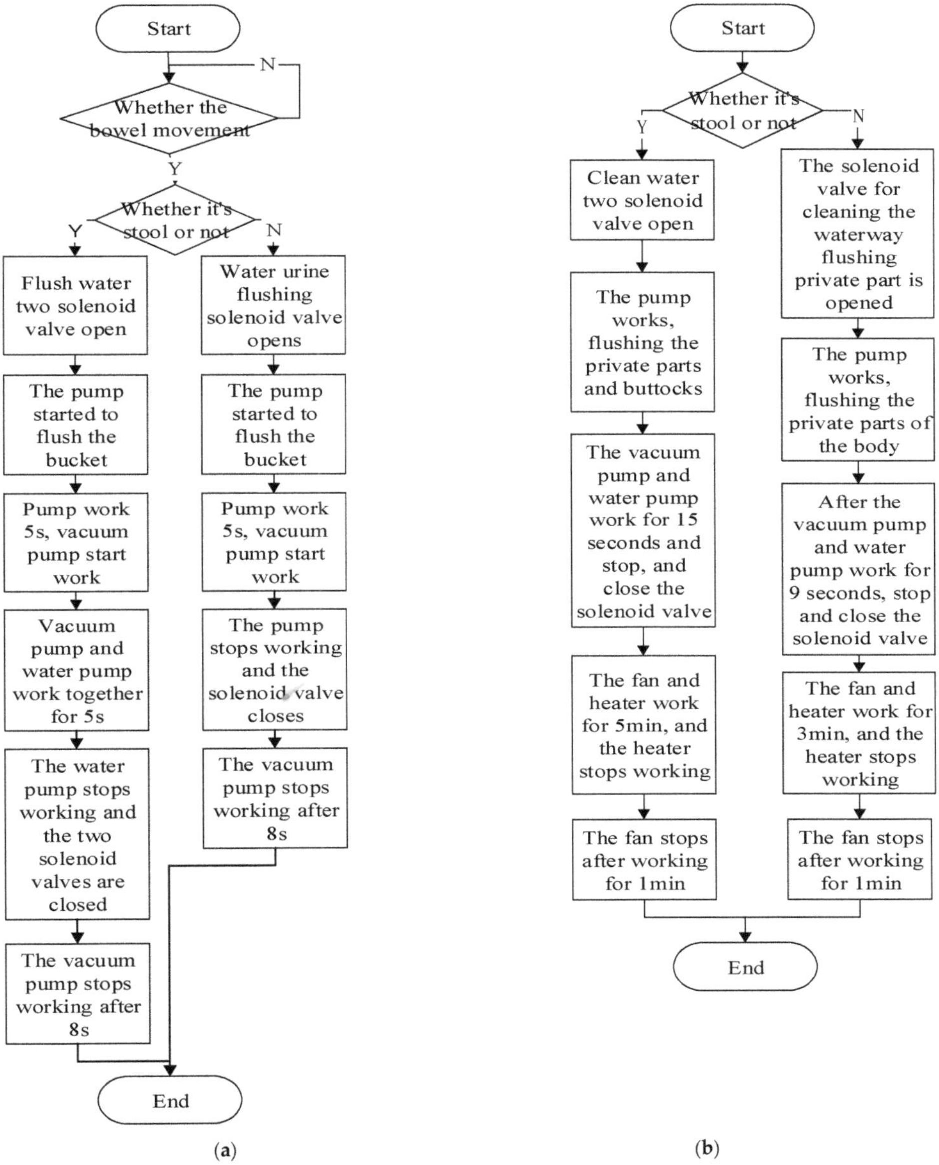

Figure 8. Flowchart of control system of excretion nursing equipment. (**a**) Test flush process; (**b**) Cleaning and drying process.

2.3. Automatic Detection of Urine and Stool Based on Multi-Sensor Fusion

Due to the performance of the sensor itself and the influence of the environment, there will be a certain deviation in the data information obtained by the sensor. When errors occur, the target cannot be identified effectively to obtain results [20]. Therefore, when the sensor is used for direct detection in the nursing device, it is unable to accurately detect whether the user excretes stool or urine. In order to solve this problem, this paper puts the detection results of the temperature and humidity sensor and the ammonia gas sensor into the D-S evidence theoretical model for fusion processing to obtain the final detection result, so as to improve the detection accuracy. As a multi-information source fusion rule, this algorithm can process multiple independent information to obtain the confidence of the proposition, and obtain the accuracy or uncertainty of the final proposition result through comprehensive analysis of the confidence [21,22].

The D-S evidence theory fusion steps are mainly divided into four steps: sensor data collection, data feature extraction, data fusion, and result confirmation [23]. The specific flowchart of the application of D-S evidence theory in this paper is shown in Figure 9.

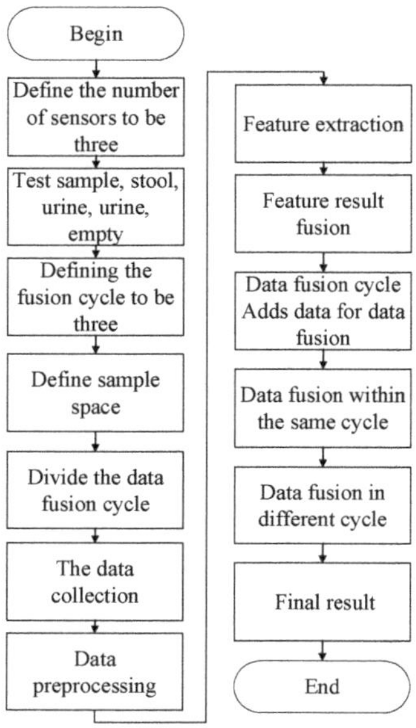

Figure 9. D-S evidence theory model running flowchart.

As mentioned above, this paper uses three kinds of sensors for detection, which defines three types of information source subjects in the D-S evidence theory model. According to the general experience of D-S evidence theory, in order to make the fusion result more favorable for analysis, it is often necessary to perform multiple fusions, which is called multiple fusion cycles. Multiple fusion cycles do not change the results, but only polarize the probability assignment and make the results more salient. In this study, there are three fusion cycles according to the above-mentioned experience, that is, when each sensor collects data for detection, it collects data at nearby moments twice, so that three sets of complete experimental data are finally obtained. Since there are only four final detection results, namely urine (event A), stool (event B), urine and stool (event C), and no detection (event D), the sample space can be determined. Next, multiple sensors collect data, and integrate these data for preprocessing. During the collection, the average value of multiple groups of data is taken, and the obviously unreasonable data are eliminated. The next step is to perform feature extraction on the sorted data, and extract the representative information in the data that can characterize the results. Then, using the data fusion rule of the D-S evidence theory, each cycle is first fused, and finally, the three sets of fusion results are fused, after which the target result is obtained.

According to the above process description, in order to use the D-S evidence theory fusion rule for modeling, it is necessary to preprocess the data obtained by three sensors. First, a large amount of data from three sensors for four possible situations are collected, and four sample spaces are constructed using the data; the data range of the four situations are obtained through analysis as the basis for judging the results (the specific operations are shown in the experiment section). Next, the ratio of the experimental data obtained by each sensor in the actual detection and the judgment basis of the result is taken as the probability of the occurrence of the corresponding event. From this, the basic probability distribution function of urine (event A), stool (event B), urine and stool (event C), and no detection (event D) detected by the temperature sensor is $M_1(A)$, $M_1(B)$, $M_1(C)$, and $M_1(D)$, respectively. The basic probability distribution functions of the humidity and ammonia concentration sensors are $M_2(A)$, $M_2(B)$, $M_2(C)$, and $M_2(D)$, and $M_3(A)$, $M_3(B)$, $M_3(C)$, and $M_3(D)$, respectively.

Then, the D-S evidence theory data fusion formula is used to fuse the characteristic result data. The composite result of two subjects for event A is equal to the ratio of the sum of the product of the probability distribution function values of all events intersecting as A in the data sample space of the two subjects to the normalization coefficient. Taking the result data fusion of temperature sensor and humidity sensor for event A as an example, the synthesis formula is shown in Equation (1):

$$(M_1 \oplus M_2)(A) = \frac{1}{K} \sum_{A \cap C = A} M_1(A) * M_2(C) \tag{1}$$

The orthogonal symbol "$\oplus$" on the left of the equal sign represents the data fusion between different subjects for an event in the sample space, which is the fusion result of the temperature and humidity sensors for urine (event A). The right side of the equal sign is the ratio of the sum of the product of the probability distribution function values of all events intersecting A to the normalized coefficient K. Similarly, the fusion formula (2) for event B is:

$$(M_1 \oplus M_2)(B) = \frac{1}{K} \sum_{B \cap C = B} M_1(B) * M_2(C) \tag{2}$$

In the above two equations, K is the normalization coefficient. Taking the result data fusion of temperature sensor and humidity sensor for event a as an example, the calculation method of K is shown in formula (3):

$$K = 1 - \sum_{A \cap C = \varnothing} M_1(A) * M_2(C) = \sum_{A \cap C \neq \varnothing} M_1(A) * M_2(C) \tag{3}$$

The normalized coefficient K can be understood as the sum of the product of all probability distribution function values whose intersection is not a null set in the sample space of the temperature and humidity sensors. In this study, it is the sum of $M_1(A) * M_2(A)$, $M_1(A) * M_2(C)$, $M_1(B) * M_2(B)$, $M_1(C) * M_2(C)$, $M_1(C) * M_2(B)$, $M_1(C) * M_2(C)$, and $M_1(D) * M_2(D)$.

After the fusion is completed according to formula (1), the fusion result in one cycle can be obtained by fusing the result with the ammonia sensor, that is, a probability matrix of four events. Then, repeat the above steps until the fusion result in three cycles is obtained. Finally, the three results are fused to the final probability matrix, in which the event with the highest probability is the result event.

3. Results

In order to fully verify the feasibility of our equipment, the experiment will be divided into two parts: a detection experiment and a functional experiment. The former is mainly to verify whether the D-S evidence theory can improve the accuracy of stool and urine detection, and the latter is mainly to verify whether the function of our device can be realized.

3.1. Detection Experiments

In order to obtain the judgment basis of the results, firstly, the sensor is used to detect and identify the user's urine and stool directly. In this paper, a 10-day experiment was conducted. According to the four experimental results, a total of 800 datapoints from three sensors were collected and divided into four groups (urine group, stool group, urine and stool group, and no detection group) to establish a sample space. Since the data will be collected multiple times in a short period of time, the data with significant fluctuations are excluded and the average value is taken as one data; all data have been processed similarly. Next, the multi-group averages of the target samples in the data space are used for analysis [24], and the humidity data of all samples in the four sample spaces for 10 days are obtained, as shown in Figure 10a. Figure 10b displays the temperature data. Figure 10c is all the ammonia concentration data in the four sample spaces for 10 days (under normal circumstances, the ammonia concentration is 0, which coincides with the x-axis).

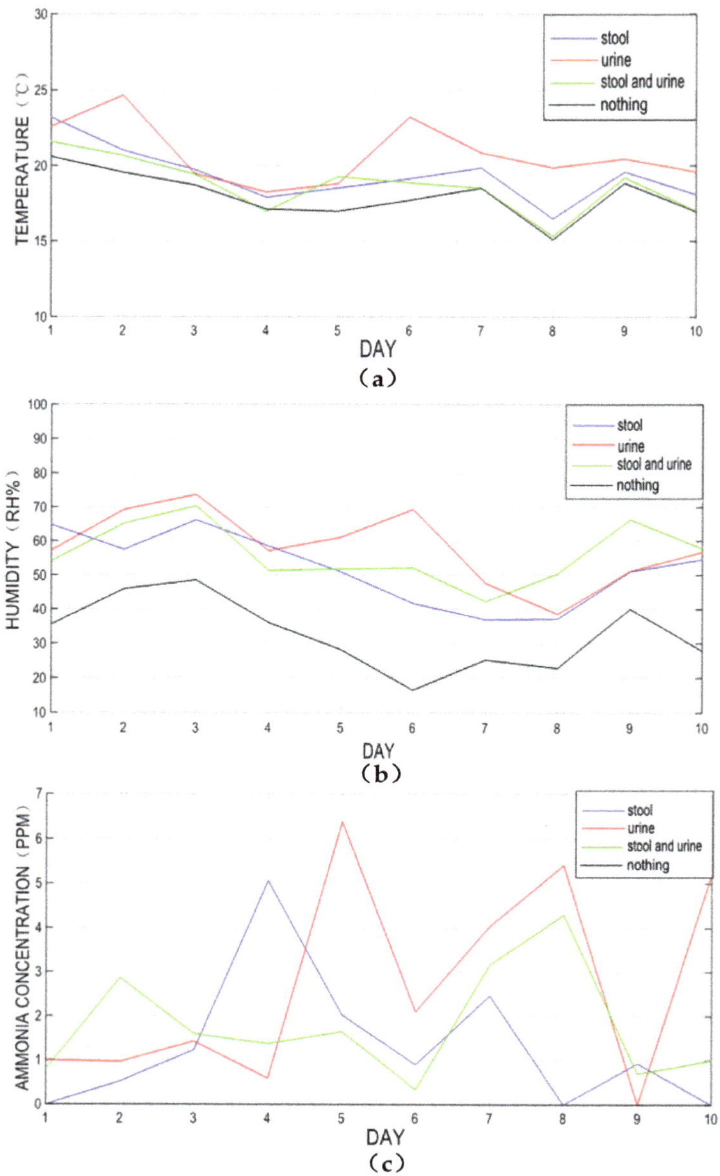

Figure 10. The data value of sample space. (**a**) Temperature data of four sample spaces. (**b**) Humidity data of four sample spaces; (**c**) Ammonia concentration data of four sample spaces.

Through the data collected from the detection target, the value range of the target urine and stool is determined. According to the data obtained from multiple sets of experimental data, it can be seen that the temperature and humidity values detected in the urine are relatively high, and the ammonia concentration in the stool is maintained at around 1 ppm. The humidity of stool and urine is between urine only and stool only, and the ammonia concentration in the blank condition is 0. Based on this, a set of measurement standards is formulated as the detection basis for identifying the occurrence of urination and defecation, as shown in Table 1 (with the indoor temperature and humidity as the reference point, set temperature as x°, humidity as y RH%, and ammonia concentration as z PPM). The temperature range of stool is 0.5°–2° higher than room temperature, the range of urine is more than 1.8° higher than room temperature, and the range of stool and urine is 0°–1°. The test result with a temperature value of 0°–1° higher than room temperature is defined as urine and stool. If the humidity value is 5%–12% higher than the indoor humidity, the test result is defined as stool, the humidity value is higher than 20% above the indoor humidity, the test result is defined as urine, and the humidity value is 12%–20% higher than the indoor humidity, while the test result is defined as urine and stool. When the ammonia concentration value is 1 ppm–2 ppm higher than the ammonia concentration in the air, the test result may be stool or stool and urine. The ammonia concentration value is more than 2 ppm higher than the ammonia concentration in the air, and the test result is defined as urine.

Table 1. Basis for testing urine and stool.

	Stool	Urine	Stool and Urine	No Detection
Temperature (°C)	$0.5 < x < 2$	$1.8 < x$	$0 < x < 1$	0
Humidity (RH%)	$5 < y < 12$	$20 < y$	$12 < y < 20$	0
Ammonia concentration (ppm)	$1 < z < 2$	$z > 2$	$1 < z < 2$	0

Ten groups of detection data are selected randomly from three sensors and put into the sample space, and the urine and stool are identified directly using the sensor data. Experimental results show that the probability of correctly identifying the urine and urine is 70.83%, and there is a situation that the urine and stool are not clearly identified, which will make the nursing equipment have problems in the subsequent washing, cleaning, and drying operations. After the pretreatment of 10 groups of experimental data as described above, the D-S evidence theory is introduced. According to the data fusion process of the D-S evidence theory in Section 2, data fusion decisions are made for temperature, humidity, and ammonia concentration data.

According to the results obtained in Table 2, using the statistical method of Paired χ^2 Test for verification. The χ^2 was calculated and $p < 0.05$ was obtained according to the χ^2 value, which proved that the results were statistically significant. At the level of $\alpha = 0.05$, it was considered that the accuracy of the two methods was different, and the accuracy of the method adopted in this paper reached 90%, which was significantly higher than that of the traditional method.

3.2. Function Test

Experiments were also performed to test the overall function of the excretion nursing equipment. The results show that the nursing equipment can achieve the functions of flushing the dirt in the toilet bowl and washing and drying the human body, and it can satisfy the needs of helping patients to achieve self-care. At the same time, the designed excretion nursing equipment also realizes the function of detecting the patient's sideways angle and reminding the patient to restore their posture. The liquid level of the water bucket and the dirt bucket can be detected, and when the liquid level of the clean water bucket is lower than the threshold or the liquid level of the dirt bucket is higher than the threshold, the alarm reminder function is performed.

Table 2. D-S evidence theory data fusion table.

Num	Humidity (rh%)	Temperature (°C)	Ammonia Concentration (ppm)	Result
1	65.9	20.6	3.0	[Stool and urine]
2	80.4	19.7	1.0	[Stool]
3	63.7	21.1	0.0	[Stool]
4	67.0	17.9	7.0	[urine] (error)
5	55.4	19.2	2.0	[urine]
6	76.0	23.4	2.0	[urine]
7	42.0	19.7	3.0	[Stool]
8	43.3	19.8	8.0	[urine]
9	22.9	15.1	0.0	[no detection]
10	52.8	19.6	5.0	[urine]

3.3. *Safety Instructions*

As a device to be introduced in the health field, safety issues cannot be ignored. According to the provisions of anti-electric shock and other dangerous situations in Part I: General Safety Requirements of "Medical Electrical Equipment", the accessible parts of our equipment are insulating materials. In the host part, according to "Shell Protection Level (IP Code)", the host machine shell of our device has reached IP44 level, which has good protection level for solid liquid. As the working head is directly in contact with human skin, we choose medical soft glue as the material to wrap on the raised groove outside the toilet bowl, according to the biocompatibility requirement of the "Biological Evaluation of Medical Devices", which states that the skin irritation should not be higher than very slight irritation, so as to improve the use experience as much as possible without causing damage to the user's skin.

4. Discussion

Many scholars have done a lot of theoretical research on the problem of excretion nursing, but lack of device to apply these theories. At present, the relatively mature products include the Smilet sleeping automatic excretion treatment robot developed in Japan (Figure 1a) and the product of the Illinois nursing robot in Suzhou, China (Figure 1b). These two types of equipment are also of split design, and are structurally divided into two parts: working head and host machine. It also has the functions of detection, washing, cleaning, and drying. However, they used a single sensor detection method, which directly based on the amount of ammonia as the basis for determining urine and stool, and had a low success rate. In terms of the setting of the working process, the two types of devices are not equipped with the liquid level alarm system of the water purification bucket and the dirt bucket, but rely on manual inspection, which may cause inconvenience in the use of the equipment.

From the experimental results, the design of this paper has achieved a good effect, but this study still has some shortcomings: first, there are few subjects, and there might be significant differences in the data related to urine and stool of different subjects, which makes the test results not general, and it is impossible to identify the urine and stool of most users accurately. Not only that, the subjects' daily different diets will also have an impact on urine and stool, which will further cause confusion. In the later stage of the experiment, it is also necessary to improve the detection equipment and classify and recognize the errors. At the same time, it is necessary to expand the sample size to establish a large database, and neural network technology can be used for integrated analysis to improve the recognition accuracy. In terms of function, the device still has room to be optimized for incontinent users, because wearing the device for a long time will affect the skin of patient's private parts; thus, the nursing staff should be mindful to temporarily remove the device after completing a cleaning or wearing it for a certain time.

As a matter of fact, the D-S evidence theory we used can also be applied to other medical problems, such as medical diagnosis. In the future, we will continue to upgrade the equipment and expand the scope of applications, such as home daily care and so on.

5. Conclusions

This study designed an excretion nursing equipment that uses temperature, humidity, an ammonia concentration sensor, and the D-S evidence theory to detect and identify patients' urine and stool. It has the function of detecting and identifying patients' urine and stool, washing, cleaning, and drying the user's skin, and can help the disabled and semi-disabled elderly, as well as bedridden patients with poor mobility to realize self-care of urine and stool. Based on the detection and function experiments results, the urine and stool recognition and detection algorithm based on the D-S evidence theory used in this paper can obtain a better recognition accuracy than the traditional detection methods, and the excretion nursing equipment can realize the function of excretion care for patients.

Author Contributions: Conceptualization, B.H. and Z.C.; methodology, X.C.; software, X.C. and Z.C.; validation, Z.C., X.C., and B.H.; formal analysis, S.L. and Z.C.; investigation, Y.S.; resources, Z.C.; data curation, B.H., Z.C., and X.C.; writing—original draft preparation, Z.C.; writing—review and editing, Z.C., Y.S., and H.Y.; visualization, B.H. and Z.C.; supervision, H.Y.; project administration, B.H..; funding acquisition, B.H. and H.Y. All authors have read and agreed to the published version of the manuscript.

Funding: This research was funded by the National Key R&D Program of China (2020YFC2005800 & 2020YFC2005804), Natural Science Foundation of Shanghai China(20ZR1437800), and Biomedical Science and Technology Support Project of Shanghai (22S31901400).

Institutional Review Board Statement: Not applicable.

Informed Consent Statement: Informed consent was obtained from all subjects involved in the study.

Data Availability Statement: The data presented in this study are available on request from the corresponding author.

Conflicts of Interest: The authors declare no conflict of interest.

References

1. The United Nations' World Population Prospects 2022 Report: Global Population Reaches 8 Billion and Aging Continues to Ac-celerate. Available online: https://mp.weixin.qq.com/s?__biz=MzI0MzE1MDI0Nw==&mid=2651202854&idx=3&sn=0e86bbbec930dcbc91ca80836f196ae7&chksm=f283f9eec5f470f804260228cf3c9f18f4e84ea7997b4fbd498d3078fa2b9bc0d4eabea50c7b&scene=27 (accessed on 16 January 2023).
2. Sang, S.; Lu, W.; Yuan, F.; Qiang, S.; Li, Z. Inner Bowl of Operating Head of Nursing Machine, and Nursing Machine. U.S. Patent 10,105,271, 23 October 2018.
3. Macaulay, M.; Heuvel, E.; Jowitt, F.; Clarke-O'Neill, S.; Cottenden, A. A noninvasive continence management system: Development and evaluation of a novel toileting device for women. *J. Wound Ostomy Cont. Nurs.* **2007**, *34*, 641. [CrossRef]
4. Bosco, F.; Patrick, G.; Felicity, J.; van den Heuvel, E. Urinary incontinence: A vibration alert system for detecting pad overflow. *Assist. Technol.* **2011**, *23*, 218–224.
5. Nakajima, K.; Hayase, Y.; Tonami, K.; Yamaguchi, G.; Fujimoto, T. Development of a warning system to detect urinary incontinence from outside of a diaper using a reusable sensor. *ABE Adv. Biomed. Eng.* **2014**, *3*, 80–85. [CrossRef]
6. Otero, A.; Palacios, F.; Akinfiev, T.; Fernández, R. A Device for automatically measuring and supervising the critical care patient's urine output. *Sensors* **2010**, *10*, 934–951. [CrossRef] [PubMed]
7. Fujimoto, T.; Hashimoto, T.; Sakaki, H.; Higashi, Y.; Tsuji, T. Automated handling system for excretion. In Proceedings of the 20th Annual International Conference of the IEEE, Hongkong SAR, China, 29 October–1 November 1998.
8. Yang, G.Z.; Andreu-Perez, J.; Hu, X.; Thiemjarus, S. *Body Sensor Networks*, 2nd ed.; Springer: New York, NY, USA; London, UK, 2014; pp. 301–354.
9. Hartigan, J.A. *Bayes Theory*; Springer: New York, NY, USA, 1983; pp. 56–62.
10. Pal, D.; Mandana, K.M.; Pal, S.; Sarkar, D.; Chakraborty, C. Fuzzy expert system approach for coronary artery disease screening using clinical parameters. *Knowl. Based Syst.* **2012**, *36*, 162–174. [CrossRef]

11. Lowen, R. *Fuzzy Set Theory: Basic Concepts, Techniques and Bibliography*; Kluwer Academic Publishers: Hague, The Netherlands, 1996; pp. 1–4.
12. Dempster, A.P. Upper and Lower Probabilities Included by a Multivalued Mapping. *Ann. Math. Stat.* **1967**, *38*, 325–339. [CrossRef]
13. Shafer, G. *A Mathematical Theory of Evidence*; Princeton University Press: Princeton, NJ, USA, 1976; p. 238.
14. Sun, C.; Li, S.; Deng, Y. Determining weights in multi-criteria decision making based on negation of probability distribution under uncertain environment. *Mathematics* **2020**, *8*, 191. [CrossRef]
15. Li, Y.B.; Ning, W.; Chang, Z. Based on D-S evidence theory of information fusion improved method. In Proceedings of the 2010 International Conference on Computer Application and System Modeling, Taiyuan, China, 22–24 October 2010.
16. Ma, Z.G. The application of D-S improving algorithm in data fusion. *Adv. Mater. Res.* **2012**, *1674*, 482–484. [CrossRef]
17. Wang, C.; Guo, F.; Zheng, L.X.; Lai, X.M. Multiple classifiers decision fusion system following improved D-S evidence theory. *J. Chin. Comput. Syst.* **2015**, *36*, 1138–1141.
18. Kisku, D.R.; Tistarelli, M.; Sing, J.K.; Gupta, P. Face recognition by fusion of local and global matching scores using DS theory: An evaluation with uni-classifier and multi-classifier paradigm. In Proceedings of the 2009 IEEE Computer Society Conference on Computer Vision and Pattern Recognition Workshops, Miami, FL, USA, 20–25 June 2009.
19. Zhong, B.; Guo, K.; Yu, H.; Zhang, M. Toward Gait Symmetry Enhancement via a Cable-Driven Exoskeleton Powered by Series Elastic Actuators. *IEEE Robot. Autom. Lett.* **2022**, *7*, 786–793. [CrossRef]
20. Benavoli, A.; Antonucci, A. An aggregation framework based on coherent lower previsions: Application to Zadeh's paradox and sensor networks. *Int. J. Approx. Reason.* **2010**, *51*, 1014–1028. [CrossRef]
21. Koval, V. The competitive sensor fusion algorithm for multi sensor systems. In Proceedings of the International Workshop on Intelligent Data Acquisition and Advanced Computing Systems: Technology and Applications, Crimea, Ukraine, 4 July 2001.
22. Yang, C.; Pu, J.; Dong, Y.; Liu, Z.; Liang, L.; Wang, X. Salient object detection in complex scenes via D-S evidence theory based region classification. *Vis. Comput.* **2017**, *33*, 1415–1428. [CrossRef]
23. Zhao, Q.; Wang, S.; Wang, K.; Huang, B. Multi-objective optimal allocation of distributed generations under uncertainty based on D-S evidence theory and affine arithmetic. *Int. J. Electr. Power Energy Syst.* **2019**, *112*, 70–82. [CrossRef]
24. Liu, M.; Geng, P.; Gao, Y.; An, Y. A regional traffic congestion estimation method based on D-S evidence theory. In Proceedings of the 2021 IEEE International Conference on Networking, Sensing and Control, Xiamen, China, 3–5 December 2021.

healthcare

MDPI

Article

Factors Affecting Continuance Intention in Non-Face-to-Face Telemedicine Services: Trust Typology and Privacy Concern Perspectives

Lin Zhu [1], Xinshu Jiang [1,*] and Junwei Cao [2,*]

[1] Department of Business Administration, Kyung Hee University, Seoul 02447, Republic of Korea
[2] School of Business, Yangzhou University, Yangzhou 225127, China
* Correspondence: jxs7588@khu.ac.kr (X.J.); 008117@yzu.edu.cn (J.C.)

Abstract: As the COVID-19 pandemic progressed, the resulting demand for telemedicine services increased. This research empirically examines the role of trust, privacy concerns, and perceived usefulness in customer confirmation, satisfaction, and continuing intention in telemedicine. A typology of trust was employed to classify trust into three dimensions and explore the mediating role of the three dimensions of trust in the relationship between satisfaction, perceived usefulness, and continued intention. We also examined the moderating role of personal privacy concerns in the relationship between trust and continued intention. For this study, we developed a structural equation model based on expectation confirmation theory and analyzed 465 questionnaires from Chinese online users. The expectancy confirmation theory (ECT) was reaffirmed by empirical evidence. The results showed that the relationship between perceived usefulness and satisfaction with continued intention is moderated by the three dimensions of trust. Privacy concerns can negatively moderate the relationship between structural assurance-based trust and continued intention. This study also identified potential threats to telehealth market growth alongside new insights.

Keywords: telemedicine; expectation confirmation theory; trust typology theory; personal privacy concerns

Citation: Zhu, L.; Jiang, X.; Cao, J. Factors Affecting Continuance Intention in Non-Face-to-Face Telemedicine Services: Trust Typology and Privacy Concern Perspectives. *Healthcare* **2023**, *11*, 374. https://doi.org/10.3390/healthcare11030374

Academic Editors: Daniele Giansanti and Giovanni Morone

Received: 30 November 2022
Revised: 18 January 2023
Accepted: 25 January 2023
Published: 28 January 2023

1. Introduction

COVID-19 represents a major social concern, with increasing numbers of people fearing infection when receiving offline healthcare services, complicating public health governance [1,2]. Telemedicine is increasingly seen as an effective tool to help alleviate this problem [3]. Along with the growing demand for digital healthcare services based on no-contact services, mobile, and easy-to-use individual medical devices and application-based services are on the rise [4,5]. The global telehealth services market was projected to grow significantly from $49.9 billion in 2019 to $459.8 billion in 2030 [6]. In China, telemedicine usage has essentially doubled since 2019, already reaching 47% usage by the end of 2021 [7]. These investments have led to the creation of Pingan Health, Hao Doctor, DingXiang Doctor, ChunYu Doctor, and many other famous applications of telemedicine services [1].

Telemedicine refers to healthcare services that use Internet technology, including connected devices such as computers and mobile phones and platform technologies such as websites and applications [8,9]. By integrating advanced technologies such as IoT, AI, and Big Data with medical technologies, the use of various IT digital devices can facilitate telemedicine services [10]. While researchers have increasingly focused on telemedicine [1,11–14], critical aspects such as privacy, data security, and trust remain unexplored [15–18].

The development of a climate of trust is considered to be an essential task in the field of telemedicine services [11]. Some previous studies have considered trust from two perspectives: confidence in the foreseeability of one's expectations and confidence in the goodwill of others to maintain their commitments [19,20]. From an exchange perspective, trust can be built when one party believes in the exchange partner's reliability and integrity; additionally, trust is complex and should be studied from a multidimensional perspective [21]. Recent literature typically views trust as a one-dimensional concept, failing to specify the unique impact of each type of trust on loyalty behavior [11,22]. It is unclear which types of trust [18,23,24] are most important for customer repurchase intention.

In addition to trust, important factors related to telemedicine processes in the context of IoT adoption include privacy concerns, security concerns, and regulatory issues [25,26]. IoT can be used to collect and process large amounts of telehealth data, but a lack of privacy and confidentiality may prevent users from sharing their data [27]. Concerns about online privacy have grown exponentially due to sweeping changes in the collection, storage, mining, and marketing of consumer data [28–30]. Therefore, the study of privacy concerns in relation to perceptions of data misuse is critical to an understanding of user behavior.

By analyzing these previous studies, we identified the following gaps: (1) There is no multidimensional perspective of trust available to explore why customers continue to use telemedicine; (2) There is no research on privacy issues related to perceived data misuse in telemedicine, which uses IoT as its technical context. To address this problem, in this study, we followed a modified expectation confirmation theory (ECT) [31,32] and employed the typology of trust developed in McKnight [33], which distinguishes between structural assurance-based trust, platform-based trust, and physician-based trust in telemedicine and can determine the relative impact of each category on the relationship of perceived usefulness, satisfaction, and continuance intention [34,35]. We also investigated the moderating effect of privacy issues on the relationship between trust and continuance intention.

The purpose of this study can be summarized as follows: First, to empirically validate the effectiveness of the expectation confirmation theory (ECT) in the process of telemedicine services. Second, to extend trust into three dimensions with the aim of elucidating how these dimensions affect behavioral intention to consistently use telemedicine services. Third, to investigate the moderating role of privacy protection during telemedicine services.

2. Theoretical Background and Hypothesis Development

2.1. Expectation Confirmation Theory

Expectation confirmation theory (ECT) is often used to identify the relationship between customer confirmation, satisfaction, and intention to continue in the marketing field [32]. However, Bhattacherjee extended ECT to the field of information management by arguing that whether users continue to use an information system is a decision similar to the decision-making behavior associated with consumer repurchasing and, therefore, proposed an information system continuity model [31]. ECT can be used to explore the intention to continue using information technology from a utility perspective such as perceived usefulness [31,36,37].

ECT suggests that a positive (negative) confirmation of a product's performance in line with expectations leads to satisfaction (dissatisfaction), and thus, to the (lack of) intention to continue purchasing [31,32]. Previous research applying ECT has shown that user satisfaction is influenced by perceived usefulness and confirmation and that user satisfaction can lead to continuous intention [34,38]. If the expectation of a user to use a telemedicine service is confirmed and a perception of perceived usefulness is created, these factors are likely to satisfy the user and create an intention to continue to use the service. In other words, users will be satisfied and continue to use telemedicine services if they perceive usefulness in the performance of those services, which is in line with the existing literature. Therefore, the following hypotheses are proposed:

H1a. *User confirmation has a positive impact on user-perceived usefulness.*

H1b. *User confirmation has a positive impact on user satisfaction.*

H2a. *User-perceived usefulness has a positive impact on user satisfaction.*

H2b. *User-perceived usefulness has a positive impact on telemedicine continuance intention.*

H3. *User satisfaction has a positive impact on telemedicine continuance intention.*

2.2. Typology of Trust

Trust is involved in every transaction on an Internet platform [39,40], and this factor is relevant to both platform-based trust and service-provider-based trust [41]. The multi-dimensional and multi-functional nature of trust is a very complex issue [42]. The antecedents of trust have been identified as knowledge-based, institutional (structural assurance and situational norms), calculative, cognitive (illusion of control), and personal [43]. Trust based on institutions refers to an individual's overall perception of the transaction environment, including the institutional environment, in which there are structural assurances of trust on the Internet and regulatory environment, and the trust in specific online vendors in which there is platform-based trust [41,44,45]. Researchers have argued that the components of personality-based trust are largely dependent on the personal attitudes, trustworthiness, self-image, and influence of people in society [44,46]. Structural assurance-based trust applies to trust in institutional frameworks, including laws and regulations, rather than trust in the transaction itself [44,45]. Platform-based trust is the perception of a consumer towards a particular application or Internet-based platform in terms of the extent to which that technology is trustworthy, while personality-based trust is defined as trust in individuals, such as Airbnb hosts and DiDi drivers [41,44].

Consumer trust needs to be built both before and after the purchase experience [47,48]. Comparatively, pre-trust has a pivotal role in the initial engagement of the consumer [49,50], while post-trust, which is based on the consumer experience, has a more significant influence in repurchase intention [51,52]. Satisfaction based on a transaction increases trust in the structure and service of the provider's platform [41]. For example, as the driver is the direct service provider during the car-riding process, passenger satisfaction affects the trust of the driver [44]. Thus, the satisfaction and perceived usefulness of telemedicine affect the trust of the structure, platform, and physician. Therefore, if users develop a perception of usefulness by using telemedicine services to their satisfaction, this perception may increase not only their trust in cybersecurity, but also their trust in the platform and the physician as the direct service provider. Therefore, the following hypotheses are proposed:

H4a. *User-perceived usefulness has a positive impact on structural assurance-based user trust.*

H4b. *User-perceived usefulness has a positive impact on platform-based user trust.*

H4c. *User-perceived usefulness has a positive impact on physician-based user trust.*

H5a. *User satisfaction has a positive impact on structural assurance-based user trust.*

H5b. *User satisfaction has a positive impact on platform-based user trust.*

H5c. *User satisfaction has a positive impact on physician-based user trust.*

To investigate the antecedents and impact of trust on (re)purchase intentions, numerous empirical studies have been conducted [41,44,53–55]. Repurchase intentions increase based on trust in structural guarantees and service provider platforms, which has also been shown to increase based on trust in Airbnb hosts and DiDi drivers [41,44]. Thus, in the telemedicine process, increased trust in structural assurance and the service provider platform increases continuance intention, as does increased trust in the physician. In other words, user confidence in structural guarantees can significantly alleviate user concerns about uncertainty in the online environment, as well as increase trust in online platforms and trust in physicians, all of which can positively impact user persistence. Therefore, the following hypotheses are proposed:

H6a. *Structural assurance-based user trust has a positive impact on telemedicine continuance intention.*

H6b. *Platform-based user trust has a positive impact on telemedicine continuance intention.*

H6c. *Physician-based user trust has a positive impact on telemedicine continuance intention.*

2.3. Personal Privacy Concerns

Privacy concerns have been identified as an important antecedent of online behavior, with consumers expressing strong control and protection needs [56]. Using the Internet for transactions often requires the disclosure of large amounts of personal information, whether for business purposes (e.g., credit card data and shipping information) or e-commerce requirements [57]. Routine Internet activities have been shown to correlate with an increased incidence of Internet fraud, and falling victim to Internet fraud is associated with increased online privacy concerns [58].

By modeling privacy concerns as a precursor to trust, a negative correlation between trust and privacy concerns in online transactions has been demonstrated by numerous empirical studies [59–62]. Compared to the risk of actual financial losses due to losses of private data, the perceived risk of losing personal privacy itself is sufficient to negatively affect the intention to perform [63]. In addition, potential moderators of the negative effects of privacy concerns on behavioral intentions in the context of personalized online interactions have previously been examined [64]. When using telemedicine services in the context of Internet technology, users must trust in the structural guarantees and platforms to ensure the security of their private information and also trust that doctors will not disclose patient information. This means that users will be more likely to rely on structural assurance-based trust, platform-based trust, and physician-based trust to ensure privacy and security when using telemedicine in order to eliminate personal privacy concerns. Therefore, the following hypotheses are proposed:

H7a. *The relationship between structural assurance-based user trust and telemedicine continuance intention is negatively moderated by personal privacy concerns.*

H7b. *The relationship between platform-based user trust and telemedicine continuance intention is negatively moderated by personal privacy concerns.*

H7c. *The relationship between physician-based user trust and telemedicine continuance intention is negatively moderated by personal privacy concerns.*

3. Research Model and Questionnaire Survey

3.1. Research Framework

In this study, we proposed a research framework (Figure 1) composed of eight variables. As shown in Figure 1 this study followed a modified expectancy confirmation theory (ECT) and employed a typology of trust, distinguishing between structural assurance-based trust, platform-based trust, and physician-based trust. For the process of using telemedicine, we actively identified whether the actual performance of telemedicine services meets expectations by confirming with users, in order to further identify user satisfaction and perceived usefulness of the platform and to determine the user's intention to continue using such technology. This structural relationship can be influenced by three dimensions of post-trust: structural assurance-based trust, platform-based trust, and physician-based trust. This relationship can also be moderated by the user's personal concerns about privacy issues.

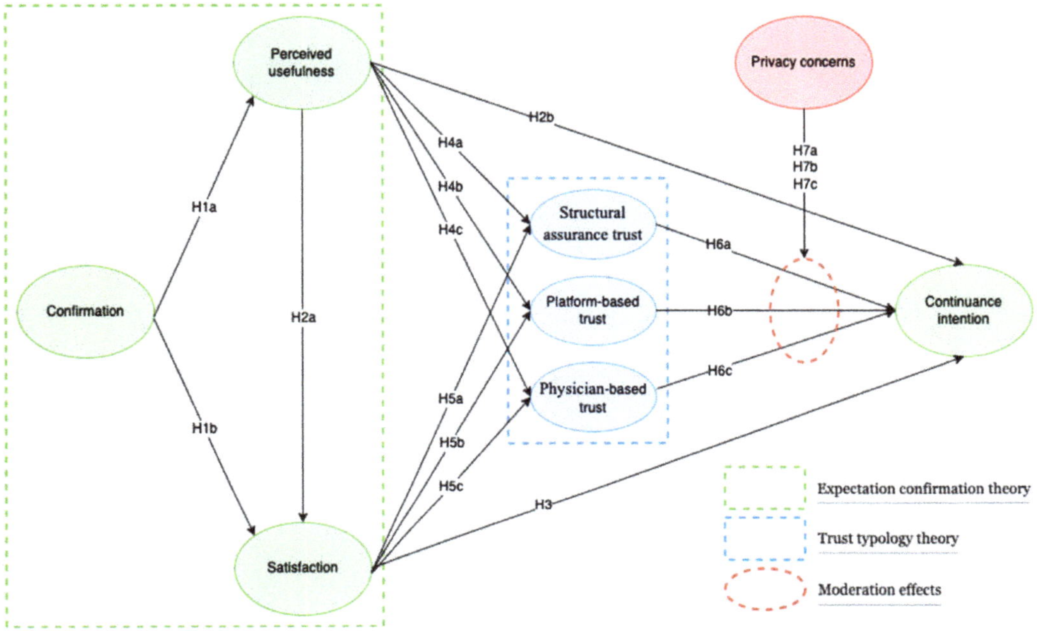

Figure 1. Research model.

3.2. *Questionnaire Survey*

In this study, the scales for all variables were designed based on scales validated by existing research, with some modifications to the items to contextualize telemedicine use by users. The scales used to measure the constructs of confirmation, perceived usefulness, satisfaction, and continuance intention were adapted from research related to expectation confirmation theory [31,65]. The scales used to measure the three types of trust constructs were adapted from research related to trust typology theory [44,45]. The scales used for the measurement of the construct of personal privacy concerns were adapted from past research on privacy concerns [66,67].

In this research, the target population was recent or former users of telemedicine services. As the target population was predominantly users of online platforms, an online survey was employed for this research [68]. The data were collected by the largest online market research company in China, SoJump [69,70], which has a large database of over 6.2 million registered members from different cities across the country and can collect data from a random sample of specific people on request.

The questionnaire consisted of two sections, the first comprising questions about the structure of the study and the second consisting of questions on information about the respondents. The questionnaire was first drafted in English and then translated into Chinese. Once the initial questionnaire design was completed, it was reviewed and revised by experts in the field to check its validity. A small pre-test was also conducted to refine the questionnaire before the final online product was administered by the survey company to a random sample of 506 users who had recently or previously used telemedicine services. It was estimated that the entire questionnaire would take approximately two to five minutes to complete, so we removed 41 invalid responses that took less than two minutes to complete, resulting in 465 valid responses. The general characteristics of the respondents are detailed in Table 1.

Table 1. General characteristics of the respondents.

		N	%
Gender	Male	207	44.52%
	Female	258	55.48%
Age	18–25 years	183	39.35%
	26–35 years	178	38.28%
	36–45 years	103	22.15%
	≥46 years	1	0.22%
Monthly income	<3000 RMB	24	5.16%
	3000–5000 RMB	52	11.18%
	5001–8000 RMB	166	35.70%
	8001–10,000 RMB	138	29.68%
	>10,000 RMB	85	18.28%
Education	Less than high school	34	7.31%
	High school	143	30.75%
	4-year college	268	57.63%
	Graduate student or higher	20	4.30%
Occupation	Students	20	4.30%
	Company employees	272	58.49%
	Civil servants	56	12.04%
	Self-employment	64	13.76%
	Others	53	11.40%
Total		465	100.00%

4. Methods

First, there are two main methods that can be utilized to estimate structural equation models: covariance-based structural equation modeling (CB-SEM) and partial least squares structural equation modeling (PLS-SEM). Additionally, there are a number of options available to determine the choice between PLS-SEM or CB-SEM. CB-SEM is used when the goal is theory testing, theory confirmation, a comparison of alternative theories, or the structural model has circular relationships; alternatively, previous studies have employed a global goodness-of-fit criterion [71,72]. In this study, covariance-based structural equation modeling (CB-SEM) and the corresponding software package Amos 26 were used to test the theoretical models and hypotheses.

Second, to test the mediation effect of the structural model, a bootstrap maximum likelihood method with 2000 bootstrap samples was performed in a bias-corrected confidence interval. In the absence of observed indicators, specific mediating effects of the structure were tested using phantom variables and setting bootstrap confidence intervals corrected for bias at 95% [73].

Moreover, to assess the moderation effect of personal privacy concerns on the relationship of trust and user continuance intention, we adopted Ping Jr.'s (1995) approach [74,75]. We computed means for all of the construct indicators in the study model, mean-centered them, and then computed the variance of each factor loading, error variance, and latent variable variance.

5. Results

5.1. Bias Test Results

Before starting the analysis of the structure, two possible bias phenomena (non-response bias and common method bias) were identified to avoid further affecting the validity in the survey results. This step was performed because the present research was based on a self-administered questionnaire, with both the dependent and independent variables derived from the same sample of respondents. First, to appraise non-response bias, we compared the measurements of early and late responders. The t-test results revealed non-significant differences between the groups, which indicates that a non-response bias was lacking in this research [76]. Second, common method bias is an easily apparent problem in questionnaires. Generally, when survey responses from a single medium (i.e., online) are collected, the survey responses may appear skewed or show a tendency to underestimate or exaggerate results in some way. To appraise common method bias, we applied Harman's single-factor approach. The test results showed that the first factor represented 37.639% of the total variance. This result is below the recommended threshold of 40%, which indicates that there was no common method bias in this research [77,78].

5.2. Measurement Model Results

This study used structural equation modeling to analyze the data, starting with conducting confirmatory factor analysis (CFA) on the structural model to verify the overall fitness of the model and analyze the reliability and validity of the construct. Accordingly, the CFA results are presented in Table 2. The results of the CFA showed a satisfactory model fit, with $\chi^2 = 425.402$, df = 296, $p < 0.001$, $\chi^2/\text{df} = 1.437 < 3$, SRMR = 0.029 < 0.05, RMSEA = 0.031 < 0.05, CFI = 0.982 > 0.96, TLI = 0.979 > 0.96, and IFI = 0.982 > 0.95 [79,80].

Table 2. Measurement model results.

Constructs	Items	Loadings	Cronbach's α	CR	AVE
Confirmation	1. My experience with using telemedicine was better than I expected.	0.821 #	0.887	0.887	0.663
	2. The level of service provided by telemedicine was better than I expected.	0.803 ***			
	3. My expectations for telemedicine services were correct.	0.831 ***			
	4. Overall, most of my expectations for using telemedicine were confirmed.	0.801 ***			
Perceived usefulness	1. I think the telemedicine mobile application is very useful.	0.835 #	0.895	0.897	0.686
	2. I think using telemedicine could help me improve my health.	0.859 ***			
	3. I think the service offered by telemedicine is very useful.	0.823 ***			
	4. On the whole, I think it's useful to use telemedicine.	0.793 ***			
Satisfaction	1. Your thoughts about telemedicine services: Very displeased/Very pleased.	0.777 #	0.886	0.889	0.667
	2. Your thoughts about telemedicine services: Very dissatisfied/Very satisfied.	0.833 ***			
	3. Your thoughts about telemedicine services: Very frustrated/Very contented.	0.845 ***			
	4. You think telemedicine services are: Absolutely terrible/Absolutely delightful.	0.810 ***			
Structural assurance-based trust	1. The Internet has sufficient security measures to allow me to use it for personal matters.	0.872 #	0.839	0.844	0.644
	2. I am sure the legal and technical structures protect me from problems on the Internet.	0.833 ***			
	3. I believe that encryption and other technical advances on the Internet will allow me to do business there more safely.	0.821 ***			
Platform-based trust	1. Telemedicine applications meet my needs as a consumer.	0.843 #	0.844	0.849	0.652
	2. Telehealth applications could provide me with good health services.	0.768 ***			
	3. The services provided by telemedicine applications are reliable.	0.796 ***			
Physician-based trust	1. The telemedicine doctors are very professional.	0.774 #	0.765	0.771	0.530
	2. The telemedicine doctors are honest.	0.794 ***			
	3. The telemedicine doctors have been very helpful to me.	0.852 ***			
Continuance intention	1. I would continue to use telemedicine.	0.729 #	0.873	0.880	0.709
	2. I would be using telemedicine as often as I do now.	0.657 ***			
	3. I would increase the frequency with which I use telemedicine in the future.	0.792 ***			
Personal privacy concerns	1. I feel concerned that the information I have submitted online may be misused.	0.739 #	0.821	0.836	0.629
	2. I feel worried that someone would be able to find information about me on the Internet.	0.832 ***			
	3. I feel concerned that information submitted online will be used in unintended ways.	0.806 ***			

Model fit indexes: $\chi^2 = 425.402$, df = 296, $p < 0.001$, $\chi^2/\text{df} = 1.437$, SRMR = 0.029, RMSEA = 0.031, CFI = 0.982, TLI = 0.979, and IFI = 0.982. Note: *** $p < 0.001$; # factor loading was fixed at 1, so that the p-value is not presented.

As shown in Table 2, we used Cronbach's alpha and composite reliability (CR) to identify reliability and thereby determine the internal consistency of the measurement model. Cronbach's alpha values ranged from 0.765 to 0.895, while the CR values ranged from 0.771 to 0.897, exceeding the recommended value of 0.7 [79,81]. When testing for convergent validity (CV), the common rule is to check that the standard loadings for each item are 0.7 or higher. Additionally, the average variance extracted (AVE) must be higher than the recommended value of 0.5 [79]. Here, all factor loadings exceeded 0.7, and all AVE values exceeded 0.5.

In addition, research constructs should have acceptable discriminant validity (DV), which implies that each construct should represent the square root of AVE values greater than the correlation coefficient value of the constructs [81]. As shown in Table 3, the square root of the AVE values for each construct exceeded the corresponding correlation coefficient values between the constructs.

Table 3. Correlation and square root of the AVE table.

	1	2	3	4	5	6	7	8
1. Confirmation	0.814							
2. Perceived usefulness	0.616	0.828						
3. Satisfaction	0.627	0.656	0.817					
4. Structural assurance-based trust	0.423	0.593	0.567	0.803				
5. Platform-based trust	0.363	0.505	0.540	0.357	0.807			
6. Physician-based trust	0.412	0.553	0.548	0.476	0.361	0.728		
7. Continuance intention	0.538	0.665	0.649	0.617	0.578	0.625	0.842	
8. Personal privacy concerns	0.048	−0.153	−0.064	−0.177	−0.136	−0.171	−0.208	0.793

Note: The square root of AVE for each research construct is presented on the diagonal. Correlations between constructs are under the square root of AVE.

5.3. Structural Model Results

The structural model showed a satisfactory model fit with χ^2 = 338.784, df = 238, $p < 0.001$, χ^2/df = 1.423 < 3, SRMR = 0.031 < 0.05, RMSEA = 0.030 < 0.05, CFI = 0.985 > 0.96, TLI = 0.983 > 0.96, and IFI = 0.985 > 0.95, where the overall model fit indexes all met the recommended values [79,80]. The squared multiple correlations (R2) of the endogenous variables are greater than 0.3. As shown in Figure 2 and Table 4, in the complete structural model, all of the direct paths were significant.

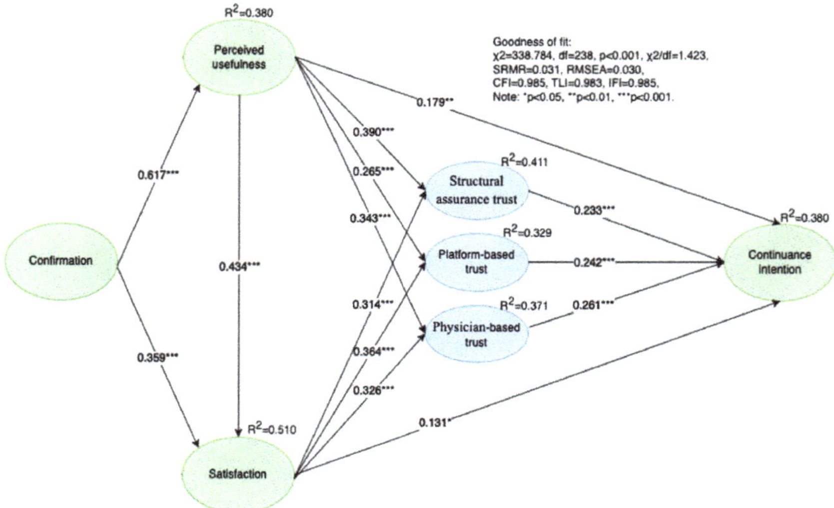

Figure 2. Results of the research model.

Table 4. Results of hypothesis testing and mediation effects.

Hypothesis		β	t-Value	Results
H1a	Confirmation → Perceived usefulness	0.617 ***	12.166	Supported
H1b	Confirmation → Satisfaction	0.359 ***	6.386	Supported
H2a	Perceived usefulness → Satisfaction	0.434 ***	7.613	Supported
H2b	Perceived usefulness → Continuance intention	0.179 **	2.976	Supported
H3	Satisfaction → Continuance intention	0.131 *	2.168	Supported
H4a	Perceived usefulness → Structural assurance-based trust	0.390 ***	6.067	Supported
H4b	Perceived usefulness → Platform-based trust	0.265 ***	4.007	Supported
H4c	Perceived usefulness → Physician-based trust	0.343 ***	4.904	Supported
H5a	Satisfaction → Structural assurance-based trust	0.314 ***	4.895	Supported
H5b	Satisfaction → Platform-based trust	0.364 ***	5.350	Supported
H5c	Satisfaction → Physician-based trust	0.326 ***	4.637	Supported
H6a	Structural assurance-based trust → Continuance intention	0.233 ***	4.486	Supported
H6b	Platform-based trust → Continuance intention	0.242 ***	5.042	Supported
H6c	Physician-based trust → Continuance intention	0.261 ***	4.848	Supported
Mediation Effect of Trust				Indirect
	Perceived usefulness → Structural assurance-based trust → Continuance intention			0.048 ***
	Perceived usefulness → Platform-based trust → Continuance intention			0.034 ***
	Perceived usefulness → Physician-based trust → Continuance intention			0.047 ***
	Satisfaction → Structural assurance-based trust → Continuance intention			0.039 ***
	Satisfaction → Platform-based trust → Continuance intention			0.047 ***
	Satisfaction → Physician-based trust → Continuance intention			0.035 ***

Model fit indexes: $\chi^2 = 338.784$, df = 238, $p < 0.001$, $\chi^2/df = 1.423$, SRMR = 0.031, RMSEA = 0.030, CFI = 0.985, TLI = 0.983, and IFI = 0.985. Note: * $p < 0.05$, ** $p < 0.01$, and *** $p < 0.001$.

Table 4 summarizes the direct and indirect effects. For the direct effects, the relationships between confirmation, perceived usefulness, and satisfaction were statistically significant, and the relationships between perceived usefulness, satisfaction, and continuance intention were also significant. Thus, H1a, H1b, H2a, H2b, and H3 are supported. The effects of perceived usefulness and satisfaction on the three trust components were statistically significant as well, thus supporting H4a–c and H5a–c. Statistical significance was also observed for the effects of structural assurance-based trust, platform-based trust, and physician-based trust on continuance intention, which supported H6a–c.

In terms of the indirect effects, the results showed the mediating effect of the three trust components on the relationship between perceived usefulness and continuance intention, as well as satisfaction and continuance intention, which were all statistically significant. Therefore, structural assurance-based trust, platform-based trust, and physician-based trust play a mediating role between perceived usefulness and continuance intention, and also between satisfaction and continuance intention.

Finally, in terms of moderation effects, among the relationships between the three trust components and continuance intention, only the interaction effects of structural assurance-based trust and privacy concerns were significant, as shown in Table 5. Thus, H7a was supported, while H7b and H7c were rejected.

Table 5. Results of the moderation effects.

	Relationships	β	t-Value
H7a	Structural assurance-based trust × privacy concerns → Continuance intention	−0.084 *	2.161
H7b	Platform-based trust × privacy concerns → Continuance intention	−0.048	1.133
H7c	Physician-based trust × privacy concerns → Continuance intention	−0.049	0.876

Model fit indexes: $\chi^2 = 489.355$, df = 127, $p < 0.001$, $\chi^2/df = 3.853$, SRMR = 0.095, RMSEA = 0.078, CFI = 0.900, TLI = 0.880, and IFI = 0.901. Note: * $p < 0.05$.

6. Discussion and Implications

6.1. Key Findings

This study followed a modified expectancy confirmation theory (ECT) [31,32] to understand why users continue to use telemedicine services based on three dimensions of trust. The moderating influence of privacy concerns on the interrelationship between user trust and the intention to continue using was also explored. Based on the foundation of these elements, we derived the following key findings. First, we found empirical support for the applicability of the modified ECT to telemedicine services in China. Our results show that satisfaction and perceived usefulness of telemedicine services, when confirmed to meet user expectations, lead to an intention to continue using telemedicine services, which is fully consistent with our hypothesis.

Second, we also examined trust as one of the internal mechanisms of ECT [40]. When users are satisfied and find telemedicine services useful, a sense of trust in the institutional environment of the Internet (i.e., structural assurance) and in the Internet platform and service provider (i.e., the physician) is generated, which increases the user's willingness to continue using telemedicine services. According to the typology of trust [33,45], three dimensions of trust (i.e., structural assurance-based trust, platform-based trust, and physician-based trust) were tested in this study.

Third, when examining the moderating effect of privacy concerns on the interrelation between user trust and intention to continue using, we found that privacy concerns have a negative moderating effect between user trust based on the structural guarantees of the Internet and intention to continue using but not on platform- and physician-based trust. This result can be explained by the fact that if users encounter a privacy violation and first consider the weak regulatory environment of the Chinese Internet market [82], there is a significant negative moderating effect between trust based on the structural guarantees of the Internet environment and intention to continue using when users perceive the privacy violation to be serious.

6.2. Theoretical Contributions

The theoretical contributions of this study include, first, new empirical evidence for the applicability of expectancy confirmation theory (ECT) to telemedicine services in the information domain [83], and an advancement of ECT theory by exploring the internal mechanisms linking the relationships between satisfaction, perceived usefulness, and continuance intention, which were able to accurately test the relationship between trust and ECT theory. Taking a multidimensional perspective on trust [33,45], the division of trust into three separate dimensions based on structural assurance-based trust, platform-based trust, and service-provider-based trust showed that all three trust dimensions have different degrees of mediating effects between users' perceived usefulness and satisfaction and continued willingness, providing new evidence for understanding the different types of trust in the telehealth literature.

Second, we provided new insights into the role of trust in the context of telemedicine. As pre-trust purchase intentions have been extensively studied [84,85], we complemented these studies by shifting our focus to post-trust reuse intentions in telemedicine. Our study is also one of the few empirical tests to validate the interactive effects of post-trust types on user intentions to persist in telemedicine from all three dimensions. Thus, this study provides new evidence for understanding different types of post-trust in the sharing economy literature.

Finally, our findings are important because the literature on privacy issues in telemedicine in relation to Internet technologies is sparse [86,87], and our study provides new empirical evidence showing that users who experience privacy violations first consider the weak regulatory environment of the Chinese Internet market, rather than the Internet platform or service provider, thereby providing a useful starting point for future research.

6.3. Practical Contributions

Our findings suggest that user-perceived usefulness and satisfaction are critical to increasing user structural assurance-based trust, platform-based trust, and service-provider-based trust and further influence continued intention to use. User satisfaction has the greatest impact on platform-based trust, while user physician-based trust is the most important factor in continued intention to use telemedicine. Therefore, telehealth companies need to focus on increasing investments in building their platforms and fostering good physician-based trust while maintaining their infrastructure, e.g., by actively and publicly displaying physician research results and recent case outcomes. Platforms could also take a positive stance in responding to some negative user messages about physicians or the platform by explaining and responding to them, understanding the specific reasons for their negative messages, and making targeted improvements. By increasing the perceived usefulness of the platform and the satisfaction of the customer, trust in the platform and the doctor can be increased, which would, in turn, increase willingness to continue using the telemedicine service.

Second, we found that the persistent privacy problems on Internet platforms are still mainly due to the weak regulation of the Internet market. Therefore, Internet regulators need to develop measures to increase the confidence of users in the security of their privacy and the awareness of users by advocating for their protection. Telemedicine platform companies should design comprehensive privacy authorization systems that provide good privacy and security for users so that medical staff have sufficient access to patient information without revealing relatively confidential private information about the patient. Access to patient data, but not patient details (location, name, relevant age, gender, etc.) should be granted to doctors for the purpose of diagnosing a medical condition. In the long run, companies will benefit from adopting a user-centric approach to privacy that gives consumers sufficient control and choice, as these measures can increase user trust and loyalty.

Finally, the higher the perceived usefulness of users, the higher their satisfaction; in order to create a good medical experience, companies need to actively train and supervise doctors, including training in the use of relevant equipment [88–90], to improve medical services, and thus, the user experience through improved operations. The establishment of a supervisory department to regulate conflicts between doctors or the platform and users will help to resolve conflicts at the source and maximize the quality of the healthcare environment. Users also need to be actively informed about telemedicine services, and the information promoted by the company will increase awareness of telemedicine services and, ultimately, the willingness to use such services.

7. Conclusions

7.1. Limitations and Future Directions

The framework of the current study was limited in that it did not consider the influence of other antecedents or consequences on the type of trust and continuance intentions in the current context. Future research should include other elements of the trust typology. In particular, due to the nature of the data collected through the questionnaire, we were unable to examine both the antecedents and consequences of the trust typology in this study. Future research could use different data to examine both the antecedents and consequences of trust in both dimensions of trust. While the social network concept can measure the degree of trust between experts [91,92], the trust relationship between the telemedicine platform and the user influences the evaluation, and future research is required.

Previous research has shown that despite online privacy concerns and worries, online consumers sometimes deliberately disclose personal privacy information for some benefit, accept conditions such as being tracked, and do not take adequate privacy precautions [93]. Future research will include this privacy paradox in which users' behavior runs counter to their privacy concerns.

Moreover, we only measured the intention of the user to continue using the service and did not examine the actual behavior of the user. Although there is no substantial discrepancy between intentions and actual behavior, intentions and actual behavior are not exactly equivalent. Future research could analyze the actual behavior of users by collecting data on their actual activities.

By looking at our research sample, it can be seen that the majority of the sample was young, and, for various reasons, we only conducted an online questionnaire using the largest research company in China. Therefore, our findings do not represent a comprehensive picture of all age groups using telemedicine. In the future, we could use different methods such as combining online and offline data to enrich the diversity of the sample.

7.2. Conclusions

This study employs an integrated research model based on expectancy confirmation theory (ECT), trust type theory, and privacy concerns to comprehend why users of telemedicine services continue to use them from a multifaceted perspective of trust. The expectation confirmation theory (ECT) is again empirically confirmed. According to the findings, telemedicine's perceived usefulness and user satisfaction are positively correlated. The findings imply that users will continue to use the service if they have confidence in the structural assurance, the platform, or the physician, and that this trust is driven by perceived usefulness, satisfaction, and confirmation. In addition, we discovered that the three dimensions of trust act as a moderator in the relationship between perceived usefulness and continued intention satisfaction. Finally, we explored that trust based on structural assurance plays a more positive role in continued intention when users perceive privacy concerns. These findings offer fresh perspectives and insights into potential dangers to the telemedicine market's expansion.

Author Contributions: Conceptualization, L.Z. and X.J.; methodology, L.Z.; software, X.J.; validation, L.Z. and X.J.; formal analysis, L.Z. and X.J.; investigation, L.Z. and X.J.; data curation, X.J.; writing—original draft preparation, L.Z. and X.J.; writing—review and editing, L.Z. and X.J.; visualization, X.J.; supervision, X.J.; project administration, J.C. and X.J. All authors have read and agreed to the published version of the manuscript.

Funding: This research received no external funding.

Institutional Review Board Statement: Not applicable.

Informed Consent Statement: Informed consent was obtained from all subjects involved in the study.

Data Availability Statement: The data presented in this study are available upon request from the corresponding author. The data are not publicly available for ethical reasons.

Conflicts of Interest: The authors declare no conflict of interest.

References

1. Cao, J.; Zhang, G.; Liu, D. The Impact of Using MHealth Apps on Improving Public Health Satisfaction during the COVID-19 Pandemic: A Digital Content Value Chain Perspective. *Healthcare* **2022**, *10*, 479. [CrossRef] [PubMed]
2. Kondylakis, H.; Katehakis, D.G.; Kouroubali, A.; Logothetidis, F.; Triantafyllidis, A.; Kalamaras, I.; Votis, K.; Tzovaras, D. COVID-19 Mobile Apps: A Systematic Review of the Literature. *J. Med. Internet Res.* **2020**, *22*, e23170. [CrossRef] [PubMed]
3. Lee, J.; Kim, B. Social Impacts of the Continuous Usage of Digital Healthcare Service: A Case of South Korea. *Innov. Mark.* **2021**, *17*, 79. [CrossRef]
4. Knörr, V.; Dini, L.; Gunkel, S.; Hoffmann, J.; Mause, L.; Ohnhäuser, T.; Stöcker, A.; Scholten, N. Use of Telemedicine in the Outpatient Sector during the COVID-19 Pandemic: A Cross-Sectional Survey of German Physicians. *BMC Prim. Care* **2022**, *23*, 92. [CrossRef]
5. Papa, A.; Mital, M.; Pisano, P.; Del Giudice, M. E-Health and Wellbeing Monitoring Using Smart Healthcare Devices: An Empirical Investigation. *Technol. Forecast. Soc. Chang.* **2020**, *153*, 119226. [CrossRef]
6. Global Telemedicine Services Opportunities and Strategies Market Report. 2020. Available online: https://www.thebusinessresearchcompany.com/report/telemedicine-services-market (accessed on 22 November 2022).
7. Asia-Pacific Front Line of Healthcare Report. 2022. Available online: https://www.bain.com/insights/asia-pacific-front-line-of-healthcare-report-2022/ (accessed on 22 November 2022).
8. Lepore, L.; Metallo, C.; Schiavone, F.; Landriani, L. Cultural Orientations and Information Systems Success in Public and Private Hospitals: Preliminary Evidences from Italy. *BMC Health Serv. Res.* **2018**, *18*, 554. [CrossRef]
9. Pagliari, C.; Sloan, D.; Gregor, P.; Sullivan, F.; Detmer, D.; Kahan, J.P.; Oortwijn, W.; MacGillivray, S. What Is EHealth (4): A Scoping Exercise to Map the Field. *J. Med. Internet Res.* **2005**, *7*, e391. [CrossRef]
10. Saheb, T.; Izadi, L. Paradigm of IoT Big Data Analytics in the Healthcare Industry: A Review of Scientific Literature and Mapping of Research Trends. *Telemat. Inform.* **2019**, *41*, 70–85. [CrossRef]
11. Arfi, W.B.; Nasr, I.B.; Kondrateva, G.; Hikkerova, L. The Role of Trust in Intention to Use the IoT in EHealth: Application of the Modified UTAUT in a Consumer Context. *Technol. Forecast. Soc. Chang.* **2021**, *167*, 120688. [CrossRef]

12. Cimperman, M.; Brenčič, M.M.; Trkman, P. Analyzing Older Users' Home Telehealth Services Acceptance Behavior—Applying an Extended UTAUT Model. *Int. J. Med. Inf.* **2016**, *90*, 22–31. [CrossRef]
13. Deshkar, S.; Thanseeh, R.A.; Menon, V.G. A Review on IoT Based M-Health Systems for Diabetes. *Int. J. Comput. Sci. Telecommun.* **2017**, *8*, 13–18.
14. Farahani, B.; Firouzi, F.; Chang, V.; Badaroglu, M.; Constant, N.; Mankodiya, K. Towards Fog-Driven IoT EHealth: Promises and Challenges of IoT in Medicine and Healthcare. *Future Gener. Comput. Syst.* **2018**, *78*, 659–676. [CrossRef]
15. Arfi, W.B.; Nasr, I.B.; Khvatova, T.; Zaied, Y.B. Understanding Acceptance of EHealthcare by IoT Natives and IoT Immigrants: An Integrated Model of UTAUT, Perceived Risk, and Financial Cost. *Technol. Forecast. Soc. Chang.* **2021**, *163*, 120437. [CrossRef]
16. Goad, D.; Collins, A.T.; Gal, U. Privacy and the Internet of Things- An Experiment in Discrete Choice. *Inf. Manag.* **2021**, *58*, 103292. [CrossRef]
17. Nicolazzo, S.; Nocera, A.; Ursino, D.; Virgili, L. A Privacy-Preserving Approach to Prevent Feature Disclosure in an IoT Scenario. *Future Gener. Comput. Syst.* **2020**, *105*, 502–519. [CrossRef]
18. Zhao, Y.; Ni, Q.; Zhou, R. What Factors Influence the Mobile Health Service Adoption? A Meta-Analysis and the Moderating Role of Age. *Int. J. Inf. Manag.* **2018**, *43*, 342–350. [CrossRef]
19. Shareef, M.A.; Kumar, V. Prevent/Control Identity Theft: Impact on Trust and Consumers' Purchase Intention in B2C EC. *Inf. Resour. Manag. J. IRMJ* **2012**, *25*, 30–60. [CrossRef]
20. Wicks, A.C.; Berman, S.L.; Jones, T.M. The Structure of Optimal Trust: Moral and Strategic Implications. *Acad. Manag. Rev.* **1999**, *24*, 99–116. [CrossRef]
21. Mayer, R.C.; Davis, J.H.; Schoorman, F.D. An Integrative Model of Organizational Trust. *Acad. Manag. Rev.* **1995**, *20*, 709–734. [CrossRef]
22. Orrange, S.; Patel, A.; Mack, W.J.; Cassetta, J. Patient Satisfaction and Trust in Telemedicine during the COVID-19 Pandemic: Retrospective Observational Study. *JMIR Hum. Factors* **2021**, *8*, e28589. [CrossRef]
23. Nisha, N.; Iqbal, M.; Rifat, A. The Changing Paradigm of Health and Mobile Phones: An Innovation in the Health Care System. *J. Glob. Inf. Manag. JGIM* **2019**, *27*, 19–46. [CrossRef]
24. van Velsen, L.; Tabak, M.; Hermens, H. Measuring Patient Trust in Telemedicine Services: Development of a Survey Instrument and Its Validation for an Anticoagulation Web-Service. *Int. J. Med. Inf.* **2017**, *97*, 52–58. [CrossRef] [PubMed]
25. AlHogail, A.; AlShahrani, M. Building Consumer Trust to Improve Internet of Things (IoT) Technology Adoption. *Int. Conf. Appl. Hum. Factors Ergon.* **2018**, *775*, 325–334. [CrossRef]
26. Martínez-Caro, E.; Cegarra-Navarro, J.G.; García-Pérez, A.; Fait, M. Healthcare Service Evolution towards the Internet of Things: An End-User Perspective. *Technol. Forecast. Soc. Chang.* **2018**, *136*, 268–276. [CrossRef]
27. Younan, M.; Houssein, E.H.; Elhoseny, M.; Ali, A.A. Challenges and Recommended Technologies for the Industrial Internet of Things: A Comprehensive Review. *Measurement* **2020**, *151*, 107198. [CrossRef]
28. Bandara, R.; Fernando, M.; Akter, S. Explicating the Privacy Paradox: A Qualitative Inquiry of Online Shopping Consumers. *J. Retail. Consum. Serv.* **2020**, *52*, 101947. [CrossRef]
29. Martin, K.D.; Murphy, P.E. The Role of Data Privacy in Marketing. *J. Acad. Mark. Sci.* **2017**, *45*, 135–155. [CrossRef]
30. Petrescu, M.; Krishen, A.S. Analyzing the Analytics: Data Privacy Concerns. *J. Mark. Anal.* **2018**, *6*, 41–43. [CrossRef]
31. Bhattacherjee, A. Understanding Information Systems Continuance: An Expectation-Confirmation Model. *MIS Q.* **2001**, *25*, 351–370. [CrossRef]
32. Oliver, R.L. A Cognitive Model of the Antecedents and Consequences of Satisfaction Decisions. *JMR J. Mark. Res.* **1980**, *17*, 460–469. [CrossRef]
33. McKnight, D.H.; Chervany, N.L. What Trust Means in E-Commerce Customer Relationships: An Interdisciplinary Conceptual Typology. *Int. J. Electron. Commer.* **2001**, *6*, 35–59. [CrossRef]
34. Cheng, P.; OuYang, Z.; Liu, Y. Understanding Bike Sharing Use over Time by Employing Extended Technology Continuance Theory. *Transp. Res. Part Policy Pract.* **2019**, *124*, 433–443. [CrossRef]
35. Mou, J.; Shin, D.-H.; Cohen, J. Understanding Trust and Perceived Usefulness in the Consumer Acceptance of an E-Service: A Longitudinal Investigation. *Behav. Inf. Technol.* **2017**, *36*, 125–139. [CrossRef]
36. Dağhan, G.; Akkoyunlu, B. Modeling the Continuance Usage Intention of Online Learning Environments. *Comput. Hum. Behav.* **2016**, *60*, 198–211. [CrossRef]
37. Wang, Y.-T.; Lin, K.-Y. Understanding Continuance Usage of Mobile Learning Applications: The Moderating Role of Habit. *Front. Psychol.* **2021**, *12*, 736051. [CrossRef] [PubMed]
38. Gupta, A.; Dhiman, N.; Yousaf, A.; Arora, N. Social Comparison and Continuance Intention of Smart Fitness Wearables: An Extended Expectation Confirmation Theory Perspective. *Behav. Inf. Technol.* **2021**, *40*, 1341–1354. [CrossRef]
39. Fang, Y.; Qureshi, I.; Sun, H.; McCole, P.; Ramsey, E.; Lim, K.H. Trust, Satisfaction, and Online Repurchase Intention: The Moderating Role of Perceived Effectiveness of e-Commerce Institutional Mechanisms. *MIS Q. Manag. Inf. Syst.* **2014**, *38*, 407–427. [CrossRef]
40. Singh, J.; Sirdeshmukh, D. Agency and Trust Mechanisms in Consumer Satisfaction and Loyalty Judgments. *J. Acad. Mark. Sci.* **2000**, *28*, 150–167. [CrossRef]
41. Liang, L.J.; Choi, H.C.; Joppe, M. Exploring the Relationship between Satisfaction, Trust and Switching Intention, Repurchase Intention in the Context of Airbnb. *Int. J. Hosp. Manag.* **2018**, *69*, 41–48. [CrossRef]

42. Shareef, M.A.; Kumar, V.; Dwivedi, Y.K.; Kumar, U.; Akram, M.S.; Raman, R. A New Health Care System Enabled by Machine Intelligence: Elderly People's Trust or Losing Self Control. *Technol. Forecast. Soc. Chang.* **2021**, *162*, 120334. [CrossRef]
43. Gefen, D.; Karahanna, E.; Straub, D.W. Trust and TAM in Online Shopping: An Integrated Model. *MIS Q.* **2003**, *27*, 51–90. [CrossRef]
44. Jiang, Y.; Lau, A.K. Roles of Consumer Trust and Risks on Continuance Intention in the Sharing Economy: An Empirical Investigation. *Electron. Commer. Res. Appl.* **2021**, *47*, 101050. [CrossRef]
45. McKnight, D.H.; Choudhury, V.; Kacmar, C. Developing and Validating Trust Measures for E-Commerce: An Integrative Typology. *Inf. Syst. Res.* **2002**, *13*, 334–359. [CrossRef]
46. Shareef, M.A.; Dwivedi, Y.K.; Archer, N.; Rahman, M.M. Patient Attitudes toward Physicians: Benchmarking Consumer Perceptions from 15 Countries. *Benchmarking Int. J.* **2018**, *26*, 19–47. [CrossRef]
47. Lin, J.; Wang, B.; Wang, N.; Lu, Y. Understanding the Evolution of Consumer Trust in Mobile Commerce: A Longitudinal Study. *Inf. Technol. Manag.* **2014**, *15*, 37–49. [CrossRef]
48. Venkatesh, V.; Thong, J.Y.; Chan, F.K.; Hu, P.J.-H.; Brown, S.A. Extending the Two-Stage Information Systems Continuance Model: Incorporating UTAUT Predictors and the Role of Context. *Inf. Syst. J.* **2011**, *21*, 527–555. [CrossRef]
49. Kim, D.J.; Ferrin, D.L.; Rao, H.R. Trust and Satisfaction, Two Stepping Stones for Successful e-Commerce Relationships: A Longitudinal Exploration. *Inf. Syst. Res.* **2009**, *20*, 237–257. [CrossRef]
50. Kim, H.-W.; Xu, Y.; Gupta, S. Which Is More Important in Internet Shopping, Perceived Price or Trust? *Electron. Commer. Res. Appl.* **2012**, *11*, 241–252. [CrossRef]
51. Ha, H.-Y.; Janda, S.; Muthaly, S.K. A New Understanding of Satisfaction Model in E-Re-Purchase Situation. *Eur. J. Mark.* **2010**, *44*, 997–1016. [CrossRef]
52. Kim, J.; Hong, S.; Min, J.; Lee, H. Antecedents of Application Service Continuance: A Synthesis of Satisfaction and Trust. *Expert Syst. Appl.* **2011**, *38*, 9530–9542. [CrossRef]
53. Lee, Z.W.; Chan, T.K.; Balaji, M.S.; Chong, A.Y.-L. Why People Participate in the Sharing Economy: An Empirical Investigation of Uber. *Internet Res.* **2018**, *28*, 829–850. [CrossRef]
54. Mou, J.; Cohen, J.F. Trust and Online Consumer Health Service Success: A Longitudinal Study. *Inf. Dev.* **2017**, *33*, 169–189. [CrossRef]
55. Susanto, A.; Chang, Y.; Ha, Y. Determinants of Continuance Intention to Use the Smartphone Banking Services: An Extension to the Expectation-Confirmation Model. *Ind. Manag. Data Syst.* **2016**, *116*, 508–525. [CrossRef]
56. Hoffman, D.L.; Novak, T.P.; Peralta, M. Building Consumer Trust Online. *Commun. ACM* **1999**, *42*, 80–85. [CrossRef]
57. Smith, R.; Shao, J. Privacy and E-Commerce: A Consumer-Centric Perspective. *Electron. Commer. Res.* **2007**, *7*, 89–116. [CrossRef]
58. Chen, H.; Beaudoin, C.E.; Hong, T. Securing Online Privacy: An Empirical Test on Internet Scam Victimization, Online Privacy Concerns, and Privacy Protection Behaviors. *Comput. Hum. Behav.* **2017**, *70*, 291–302. [CrossRef]
59. Castañeda, J.A.; Montoro, F.J. The Effect of Internet General Privacy Concern on Customer Behavior. *Electron. Commer. Res.* **2007**, *7*, 117–141. [CrossRef]
60. Liu, C.; Marchewka, J.T.; Lu, J.; Yu, C.-S. Beyond Concern—A Privacy-Trust-Behavioral Intention Model of Electronic Commerce. *Inf. Manag.* **2005**, *42*, 289–304. [CrossRef]
61. Van Dyke, T.P.; Midha, V.; Nemati, H. The Effect of Consumer Privacy Empowerment on Trust and Privacy Concerns in E-Commerce. *Electron. Mark.* **2007**, *17*, 68–81. [CrossRef]
62. Van Slyke, C.; Shim, J.T.; Johnson, R.; Jiang, J.J. Concern for Information Privacy and Online Consumer Purchasing. *J. Assoc. Inf. Syst.* **2006**, *7*, 1.
63. Dinev, T.; Hart, P. Privacy Concerns and Levels of Information Exchange: An Empirical Investigation of Intended e-Services Use. *E-Service.* **2006**, *4*, 25–60. [CrossRef]
64. Taylor, D.G.; Davis, D.F.; Jillapalli, R. Privacy Concern and Online Personalization: The Moderating Effects of Information Control and Compensation. *Electron. Commer. Res.* **2009**, *9*, 203–223. [CrossRef]
65. Zhao, Y.; Bacao, F. What Factors Determining Customer Continuingly Using Food Delivery Apps during 2019 Novel Coronavirus Pandemic Period? *Int. J. Hosp. Manag.* **2020**, *91*, 102683. [CrossRef]
66. Eastlick, M.A.; Lotz, S.L.; Warrington, P. Understanding Online B-to-C Relationships: An Integrated Model of Privacy Concerns, Trust, and Commitment. *J. Bus. Res.* **2006**, *59*, 877–886. [CrossRef]
67. Milne, G.R.; Boza, M.-E. Trust and Concern in Consumers' Perceptions of Marketing Information Management Practices. *J. Interact. Mark.* **1999**, *13*, 5–24. [CrossRef]
68. Zhang, X.; Wen, D.; Liang, J.; Lei, J. How the Public Uses Social Media Wechat to Obtain Health Information in China: A Survey Study. *BMC Med. Inform. Decis. Mak.* **2017**, *17*, 71–79. [CrossRef]
69. Lien, C.H.; Cao, Y. Examining WeChat Users' Motivations, Trust, Attitudes, and Positive Word-of-Mouth: Evidence from China. *Comput. Hum. Behav.* **2014**, *41*, 104–111. [CrossRef]
70. Wen, D.; Zhang, X.; Lei, J. Consumers' Perceived Attitudes to Wearable Devices in Health Monitoring in China: A Survey Study. *Comput. Methods Programs Biomed.* **2017**, *140*, 131–137. [CrossRef] [PubMed]
71. Rigdon, E.E.; Sarstedt, M.; Ringle, C.M. On Comparing Results from CB-SEM and PLS-SEM: Five Perspectives and Five Recommendations. *Mark. ZFP–J. Res. Manag.* **2017**, *39*, 4–16. [CrossRef]

72. Sarstedt, M.; Hair, J.F.; Ringle, C.M.; Thiele, K.O.; Gudergan, S.P. Estimation Issues with PLS and CBSEM: Where the Bias Lies! *J. Bus. Res.* **2016**, *69*, 3998–4010. [CrossRef]
73. MacKinnon, D.P. *Introduction to Statistical Mediation Analysis*; Routledge: London, UK, 2012.
74. Ping, R.A., Jr. A Parsimonious Estimating Technique for Interaction and Quadratic Latent Variables. *J. Mark. Res.* **1995**, *32*, 336–347. [CrossRef]
75. Ping, R.A., Jr. Latent Variable Interaction and Quadratic Effect Estimation: A Two-Step Technique Using Structural Equation Analysis. *Psychol. Bull.* **1996**, *119*, 166–175. [CrossRef]
76. Armstrong, J.S.; Overton, T.S. Estimating Nonresponse Bias in Mail Surveys. *J. Mark. Res.* **1977**, *14*, 396–402. [CrossRef]
77. Harman, H.H. *Modern Factor Analysis*; University of Chicago Press: Chicago, IL, USA, 1976.
78. Podsakoff, P.M.; MacKenzie, S.B.; Lee, J.-Y.; Podsakoff, N.P. Common Method Biases in Behavioral Research: A Critical Review of the Literature and Recommended Remedies. *J. Appl. Psychol.* **2003**, *88*, 879. [CrossRef]
79. Hair, J.F.J.; Black, W.C.; Babin, B.J.; Anderson, R.E. *Multivariate Data Analysis*, 7th ed.; Springer Science & Business Media: Berlin/Heidelberg, Germany, 2010.
80. Hu, L.; Bentler, P.M. Cutoff Criteria for Fit Indexes in Covariance Structure Analysis: Conventional Criteria versus New Alternatives. *Struct. Equ. Model. Multidiscip. J.* **1999**, *6*, 1–55. [CrossRef]
81. Fornell, C.; Larcker, D.F. Evaluating Structural Equation Models with Unobservable Variables and Measurement Error. *J. Mark. Res.* **1981**, *18*, 39–50. [CrossRef]
82. Chen, Y.; Wang, L. Commentary: Marketing and the Sharing Economy: Digital Economy and Emerging Market Challenges. *J. Mark.* **2019**, *83*, 28–31. [CrossRef]
83. Ayanso, A.; Herath, T.C.; O'Brien, N. Understanding continuance intentions of physicians with electronic medical records (EMR): An expectancy-confirmation perspective. *Decis. Support Syst.* **2015**, *77*, 112. [CrossRef]
84. Dhagarra, D.; Goswami, M.; Kumar, G. Impact of Trust and Privacy Concerns on Technology Acceptance in Healthcare: An Indian Perspective. *Int. J. Med. Inform.* **2020**, *141*, 104164. [CrossRef]
85. Castaldo, S.; Premazzi, K.; Zerbini, F. The Meaning(s) of Trust. A Content Analysis on the Diverse Conceptualizations of Trust in Scholarly Research on Business Relationships. *J. Bus. Ethics* **2010**, *96*, 657–668. [CrossRef]
86. Andrews, L.; Gajanayake, R.; Sahama, T. The Australian general public's perceptions of having a personally controlled electronic health record (PCEHR). *Int. J. Med. Inf.* **2014**, *83*, 889–900. [CrossRef]
87. King, T.; Brankovic, L.; Gillard, P. Perspectives of Australian adults about protecting the privacy of their health information in statistical databases. *Int. J. Med. Inf.* **2012**, *81*, 279–289. [CrossRef] [PubMed]
88. Bouabida, K.; Lebouche, B.; Pomey, M.P. Telehealth and COVID-19 Pandemic: An Overview of the Telehealth Use, Advantages, Challenges, and Opportunities during COVID-19 Pandemic. *Healthcare* **2022**, *10*, 2293. [CrossRef]
89. Massaro, A.; Ricci, G.; Selicato, S.; Raminelli, S.; Galiano, A. Decisional Support System with Artificial Intelligence oriented on Health Prediction using a Wearable Device and Big Data. In Proceedings of the 2020 IEEE International Workshop on Metrology for Industry 4.0 & IoT, Roma, Italy, 3–5 June 2020; pp. 718–723. [CrossRef]
90. Uddin, M.; Syed-Abdul, S. Data Analytics and Applications of the Wearable Sensors in Healthcare: An Overview. *Sensors* **2020**, *20*, 1379. [CrossRef]
91. Cheng, S.; Pain, C.C.; Guo, Y.-K.; Arcucci, R. Optimal vaccination strategies for COVID-19 based on dynamical social networks with real-time updating. *medRxiv* **2021**, *2*, 1–24. [CrossRef]
92. Zhang, M.; Zhang, C.; Shi, Q.; Zeng, S.; Balezentis, T. Operationalizing the telemedicine platforms through the social network knowledge: An MCDM model based on the CIPFOHW operator. *Technol. Forecast. Soc. Change* **2022**, *174*, 121303. [CrossRef]
93. Kokolakis, S. Privacy Attitudes and Privacy Behaviour: A Review of Current Research on the Privacy Paradox Phenomenon. *Comput. Secur.* **2017**, *64*, 122–134. [CrossRef]

healthcare

MDPI

Review

The Use of Sports Rehabilitation Robotics to Assist in the Recovery of Physical Abilities in Elderly Patients with Degenerative Diseases: A Literature Review

Fangyuan Ju [1], Yujie Wang [1], Bin Xie [1], Yunxuan Mi [1], Mengyun Zhao [1] and Junwei Cao [2,*]

1 Department of Physical Education, Yangzhou University, Yangzhou 225012, China
2 Department of Business, Yangzhou University, Yangzhou 225012, China
* Correspondence: 008117@yzu.edu.cn

Abstract: The increase in the number of elderly patients with degenerative diseases has brought additional medical and financial pressures, which are adding to the burden on society. The development of sports rehabilitation robotics (SRR) is becoming increasingly sophisticated at the technical level of its application; however, few studies have analyzed how it works and how effective it is in aiding rehabilitation, and fewer individualized exercise rehabilitation programs have been developed for elderly patients. The purpose of this study was to analyze the working methods and the effects of different types of SRR and then to suggest the feasibility of applying SRR to enhance the physical abilities of elderly patients with degenerative diseases. The researcher's team searched 633 English-language journal articles, which had been published over the past five years, and they selected 38 of them for a narrative literature review. Our summary found the following: (1) The current types of SRR are generally classified as end-effector robots, smart walkers, intelligent robotic rollators, and exoskeleton robots—exoskeleton robots were found to be the most widely used. (2) The current working methods include assistant tools as the main intermediaries—i.e., robots assist patients to participate; patients as the main intermediaries—i.e., patients dominate the assistant tools to participate; and sensors as the intermediaries—i.e., myoelectric-driven robots promote patient participation. (3) Better recovery was perceived for elderly patients when using SRR than is generally achieved through the traditional single-movement recovery methods, especially in strength, balance, endurance, and coordination. However, there was no significant improvement in their speed or agility after using SRR.

Keywords: rehabilitation robot; assistive technology sports rehabilitation; continuation therapy; degenerative diseases; elder

Citation: Ju, F.; Wang, Y.; Xie, B.; Mi, Y.; Zhao, M.; Cao, J. The Use of Sports Rehabilitation Robotics to Assist in the Recovery of Physical Abilities in Elderly Patients with Degenerative Diseases: A Literature Review. *Healthcare* **2023**, *11*, 326. https://doi.org/10.3390/healthcare11030326

Academic Editor: Daniele Giansanti

Received: 13 December 2022
Revised: 18 January 2023
Accepted: 19 January 2023
Published: 21 January 2023

1. Introduction

Currently, the global population is aging. In many countries, life expectancy has increased to 70 years or more. For the first time in history, in 2020, the number of people aged 60 or older exceeded the number of children under five years old, globally. Furthermore, over the coming decades, the greatest increase in aging will occur in developing countries [1]. As one of the largest developing countries, China's adoption of the family planning policy as a basic state policy in 1982 has affected the country's demographic structure and has aggravated the aging problem. The current fertility of the young people in the country has also changed; therefore, low birth rates and low mortality rates have gradually become the main reasons for the aging of Chinese society. According to the projections of the United Nations Development Program (UNDP), the population of those over 65 years old in China will reach 334 million by 2050, and the China Aging Study 2022 has predicted that it will peak at 425 million in 2057. In the future, China will be the country with the largest elderly population in the world and will be facing the serious challenge of its population aging.

The excessive aging of the population will lead to various social problems, such as a lack of economic growth, overburdened public finances, and a sharp increase in the cost of medical care, with medical care becoming the main social burden. As elderly people age further, their physiological functions deteriorate and their physical abilities decline, to some degree [2]. Physical ability is the most basic motor skill necessary for an individual's daily life and labor to be maintained, and it can be classified as strength, endurance, balance, coordination, agility, and speed, according to its nature. In addition, the elderly population is more susceptible to various degenerative diseases, such as Parkinson's disease (PD), stroke, multiple sclerosis (MS), etc. The probability that elderly people will suffer from degenerative diseases will also gradually increase as they continue to age [3–5]. Degenerative diseases not only damage the physical and mental health of the elderly and reduce their quality of life, but they also increase the medical expenses of their families and society. Due to the declining physical ability of the elderly, the process of motor rehabilitation usually requires a significant amount of time and a conducive environment to achieve the desired levels of rehabilitation; however, there is a shortage of rehabilitation nursing staff who are able to provide round-the-clock care, thus, the cost of such rehabilitation is high. This expense and scarcity of care has led to further significant challenges for China's health and social systems in meeting the rehabilitation needs of its elderly population [6,7]. Consequently, the demand for sports rehabilitation robots in the medical rehabilitation field is increasing. "Sport" rehabilitation robots is a rehabilitation robot that can provide motor rehabilitation assistance (including providing assistance or guidance) to patients. Sport rehabilitation robots can help patients with degenerative diseases recover their physical abilities, improve their immune system and metabolic activity [8], return to normal life, and reduce the financial strain on their families due to rehabilitation. Furthermore, the use of sports rehabilitation robots can reduce the burden on rehabilitation instructors, enable data detection during training, and assist in rehabilitation in a controlled and repeatable manner in order to complete quantitative assessments [9]. Previous studies have found that most of the research in this field has focused only on the design and development of devices for medical rehabilitation robots. Furthermore, many of these studies have focused on studying medical rehabilitation robots' role in the physical recovery of PD and stroke patients. However, fewer articles have investigated the use of sports rehabilitation robots in assisting in the recovery of the physical abilities of elderly patients with degenerative diseases.

Most of the previous review papers have been organized and analyzed for the types of rehabilitation robots or their working principles. The novelty of this review is to analyze and compare how different rehabilitation robots work and how effective they are in restoring the physical abilities of elderly patients with degenerative diseases, focusing on the ways in which locomotion-based rehabilitation robots help patients to restore their physical abilities and their effectiveness.

This paper compiles and analyzes the studies related to the high level of motor rehabilitation robots that are being used to promote physical activity in the elderly; compares the advantages and shortcomings of different types of motor rehabilitation robots, in terms of their working methods and their effects; and then proposes feasible suggestions for the application of motor rehabilitation robots in enhancing the physical abilities of elderly patients with degenerative diseases.

2. Materials and Methods

The scope and review of the literature search followed the EQUATOR guidelines, which improve the quality and transparency of research. We ensured that articles related to rehabilitation robots were searched for rather than articles related to rehabilitation and robots, separately. Five databases were searched using the PRSIMA for Protocols guidelines: (1) Web of Science; (2) Engineering Village; (3) Science Direct; (4) the online library, Wiley; and (5) Scopus.

The search was conducted using a Boolean logic combination search for keywords, including the following: 'rehabilitation robotics', 'physical activity, 'human–robot interaction', 'rehabilitation training', 'robotic therapy', 'assistive technology', and 'older people'.

First, a total of 633 articles were obtained from the literature search across the five databases, published over the last five years (2018–2022). In total, 23 duplicate articles were deleted; 134 articles with non-relevant articles were excluded; and 6 articles that could not be downloaded through various sources were deleted. A total of 470 articles were obtained after this screening.

Second, 70 of these articles were read in full. They were chosen out of the 469 articles by screening the titles and abstracts. The last five researchers further screened the remaining 70 articles by reading the full text of the articles separately, and the articles that included conference reports, literature reviews, the introduction of a technology principal, and those that did not contain an experimental design, were excluded. The screening flow chart is shown in Figure 1.

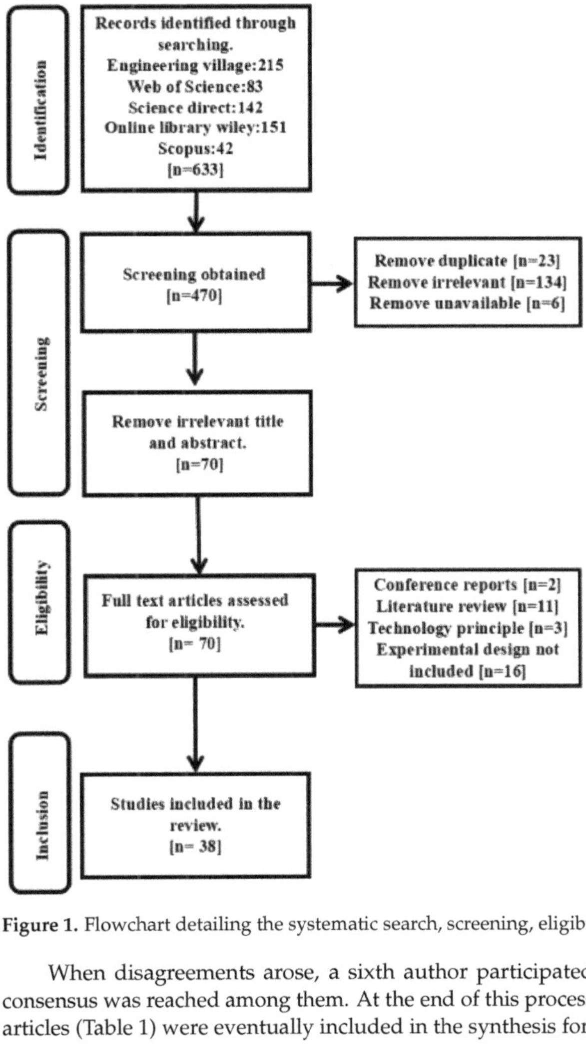

Figure 1. Flowchart detailing the systematic search, screening, eligibility, and inclusion procedure.

When disagreements arose, a sixth author participated in the discussion, until a consensus was reached among them. At the end of this process, 38 qualitatively published articles (Table 1) were eventually included in the synthesis for a narrative review.

Table 1. Characteristics of included studies (n = 38) and information about localization of papers findings in this review.

Author	Year	Country	Study Design
Zhenzhong Zhu, et al. [10]	2022	China	Robot design
Neta Shahar, et al. [11]	2019	Poland	Comparative Trial
Guang Feng, et al. [12]	2022	China	Robot design
Feng Lin, et al. [13]	2019	China	Introduction
Laura Fiorini, et al. [14]	2021	Italy	Needs study
Yuichiro Soma, et al. [15]	2022	Japan	Open-label prospective trial
Sergio D. Sierra M, et al. [16]	2019	Colombia	Robot introduction
Marianna Capecci, et al. [17]	2019	Italy	Randomized controlled trial
Mario F. Jiménez, et al. [18]	2019	Brazil	Robot introduction
George Moustris, et al. [19]	2021	Greece	Evaluation Study
Antonio Frisoli, et al. [20]	2022	Italy.	Clinical control study
Dilber Karagozoglu Coskunsu, et al. [21]	2022	Turkey	Randomized controlled study
Yen-Wei Chen, et al. [22]	2022	China	Randomized cross-over trial
Guotao Li, et al. [23]	2022	China	Robot design
Akim Kapsalyamov, et al. [24]	2020	Australia	Introduction
S.K. Hasan, et al. [25]	2022	America	Robot design
Shuo-Hsiu Chang, et al. [26]	2020	America	Case study
Zlatko Lovrenovic, et al. [27]	2018	Canada	Robot design
Chris McGibbon, et al. [28]	2021	Canada	Open-label randomised cross-over design
Rakel Berriozabalgoitia, et al. [29]	2020	Spain,	Randomized Clinical Trial
Irina Galperin, et al. [30]	2020	Israel;	Cross-sectional study
Simon Christensen, et al. [31]	2021	Denmark	Robot design
Rosaria De Luca, et al. [32]	2020	Italy	Pilot study
Qingming Qu, et al. [33]	2021	China	Functional and clinical experiments
Wonho Choi [34]	2022	Korea	Randomized controlled trial
Lizheng Pan, et al. [35]	2019	China	Preliminary study
Peng Suo, et al. [36]	2022	China	Control algorithm design of mirror rehabilitation training
Jonathan C. Mcleod, et al. [37]	2019	Canada	Robot introduction
Bianca Chinembiri, et al. [38]	2020	China	Randomized clinical trial
Marco Franceschini, et al. [39]	2020	Italy	Follow-up study
Sk. Khairul Hasan, et al. [40]	2020	America	Introduction
Fabian Just, er al. [41]	2020	Switzerland	Robot design
Shih-Ching Chen, et al. [42]	2022	China	Comparative Trial
Silvia Giovannini, et al. [43]	2022	Italy	Randomized controlled trial
Na Ri Yun, et al. [44]	2018	Korea	Randomized controlled trial
Alfredo Manuli, et al. [45]	2020	Italy	Randomized controlled trial
Heejae Kim, et al. [46]	2021	Korea	Randomized controlled trial
Roger Gassert, et al. [47]	2018	Switzerland	Robot design

3. The Value of Robot-Assisted Technology in the Motor Rehabilitation of the Elderly

In the context of global aging, the risk of diseases in the elderly increases as their age advances; therefore, there is a growing demand for robot-assisted motor rehabilitation technology in society. Robot-assisted rehabilitation has, thus, become a prominent research topic, with broad application prospects [10]. Current assistive technologies that utilize robotics include mobility devices (wheelchairs, prosthetics, and external skeletons); specialized assistive devices (visual, auditory, and voice communication); and assistance in accessing information technology and peripherals for people with disabilities.

Most of the communication between devices and users is currently achieved through human–computer interaction systems; however, current human–computer interaction methods usually only have one of these functions, and only the elderly communicated instructions to the robot, meaning that there is no way to obtain feedback from the environment and to adapt to the behavior of the elderly user, accordingly [48]. The design and development of sports rehabilitation robots is not a simple combination of equipment and technology, but it also involves neuroscience; sports biomechanics; sports human body science; ergonomics; robotics, automation, and control; and other professional field knowledge, making it a typical multidisciplinary intersection of complex systems.

Since the operating object of the sports rehabilitation robot is a human, its performance must meet the requirements of adaptability to individual differences and environmental changes, fluency of human-machine interaction, safety in the face of abnormal situations, and adaptability to human physiology and psychology, thus putting higher requirements on the accuracy, reliability, and intelligence level of the control system.

Therefore, the current system of sports rehabilitation robots integrates research fields—such as artificial intelligence, human–computer interactions, and machine learning technology—to achieve intelligent, humanized, and accurate rehabilitation assistance [49]. Elderly patients who are suffering from degenerative diseases—such as Parkinson's disease, stroke, and multiple sclerosis—account for a large number of the users of motor rehabilitation robots. These patients mainly present with upper and lower limb dysfunction, trunk weakness, decreased proprioception, decreased balance and postural control, gait abnormalities, and abnormal movement patterns [11]. Patients with multiple sclerosis also commonly experience impaired mobility and mobility limitations, which are caused by a combination of several factors—such as increased susceptibility to muscle fatigue, pain, abnormal tone, and falls [50].

Compared with the traditional manual, assisted rehabilitation training, robot-assisted motor rehabilitation and neurological rehabilitation training has unique advantages. Firstly, sports rehabilitation robots can provide high-intensity and repeatable rehabilitation training. Once popularized, they will be able to greatly relieve the pressure on the level of staff input in rehabilitation institutions and will be able to reduce the workload of clinical rehabilitation physicians. However, a more prominent advantage is that robots can provide flexible and precise rehabilitation training, which can enhance the effectiveness of patients' rehabilitation. The main example of this is that the rehabilitation robot can combine modern multimedia and interactive technology in patients' training to stimulate their interest and enthusiasm in participating in the rehabilitation training, and to mobilize their awareness and ability to actively participate in the training, which, thus, promotes the recovery and compensation of patients' neurological functions [12].

At the same time, the sports rehabilitation robot can also combine sensor technology with multiple modalities to accurately detect changes in a patient's physical condition in real-time and then use these data to adjust rehabilitation training strategies [51]. Research on motor rehabilitation robots is important for relieving the pressure on medical resources and rehabilitation manpower investments, and for improving the effectiveness of elderly patients' rehabilitation training.

4. Working Methods and the Effects of the Assistance of Different Types of Sports Rehabilitation Robots

Degenerative diseases can have an impact on the physical abilities of strength, agility, balance, endurance, coordination, and speed for elderly patients. In particular, they can lead to limb dysfunction and to the inability to perform basic physical activities. Different types of sports rehabilitation robots have emerged in the market to assist with the dysfunction of different parts of the human body. These robots meet the different rehabilitation needs of patients through their range of different working methods to help restore limb functions and to return the patient to normal life.

4.1. Classification and Characteristics of Sports Rehabilitation Robots

According to the results of our literature analysis and according to previous classification methods (Figure 2), we found that the sports rehabilitation robots are currently classified into the following groups: upper extremity rehabilitation system, end-effector robot, smart walker, intelligent robotic rollator, and robotic exoskeletons. These classifications help them to respond to the rehabilitation needs of patients with different diseases.

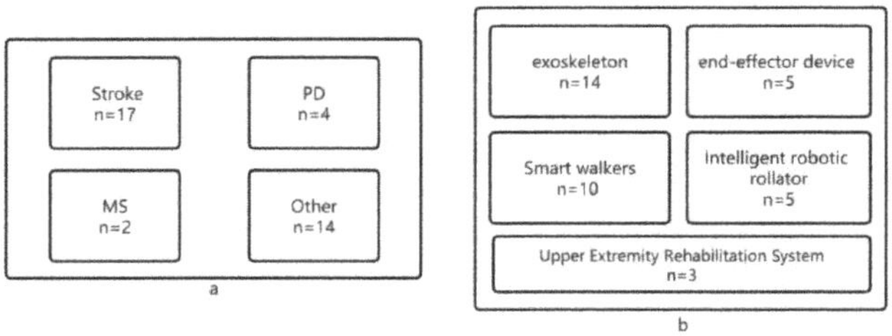

Figure 2. (**a**) Number of literature accounted for by different diseases; (**b**) number of literature accounted for by different types of rehabilitation robots.

4.1.1. Upper Extremity Rehabilitation System: Helps Patients Recover Upper Extremity Function

Among the robots used for upper limb function recovery is the QM-FOrMS, a portable and cost-effective upper limb rehabilitation system. The system is able to give some exercise instruction to help patients perform active upper extremity activities; however, it only provides a small amount of assisted strength, which is a limitation for patients with low levels of physical ability [13].

This system, first proposed by Lin (2016), advocates the acquisition of EMG signals from the patient's upper limb muscle groups to identify their motor intent and drive them to active training in order to complete the training task, through a combination of electrical stimulation and robot-assisted technology [52]. It is evident that the upper extremity rehabilitation system has a role in enhancing patients' initiative. Moreover, the integrated sports intervention approach, which combines different assistive technologies, has a different training focus and, thus, has different training advantages. Due to the complex structure of the upper limb, the restoration of the structural function of the upper limb requires comprehensive consideration of the functional characteristics of each part of the shoulder, elbow joint, wrist, and hand. Therefore, Lin's (2019) study modified and pointed out that the upper limb recovery system is characterized by its open and novel approach to recovery, and that the system's unique training feedback system would further increase patients' motivation and participation [13,53], by allowing them to actively engage in diverse training, based on light cues. Ultimately, Lin argued that this would lead to a holistic recovery of the patient's upper limb function.

4.1.2. End-Effector Robot Promotes the Range of Motion and Flexibility of the Patient's Hand Joints

The end-effector robot uses assistive devices to assist in the movement of more than 20 free flexible joints in the hand, which helps patients to record the recovery process of their small muscles and nerves, and helps them, to a certain extent, to achieve dexterity and coordination in their hand functions. For example, REO-GO includes a telescopic arm and a screen, and offers different movement therapy modalities, according to the patient's motor ability and motivation. This robot has two types of handles, spherical and platform, and places EMG electrodes on the patient's upper limbs to record their muscle activity [11]. In a literature collection analysis, the scholar Moggio (2022) noted that end-effector rehabilitation robots can assist patients with stretching and flexion movements within a range of motions close to that of normal human fingers and can generate enough assisted force at the fingertips to provide a boost to the patient's rehabilitation [52]. In addition, Fuzzy Sliding Mode Control technology was developed for functional finger rehabilitation. It provides the possibility of rehabilitating each phalanx individually which is very important in the finger rehabilitation process [14,54,55]. VR technology is also gradually being incorporated into the design of rehabilitation robots [56]. Other studies have also pointed out that the recovery of the arm needs to take into account, not only the direction of movement, but also the recovery of the nervous system. In this complexity of movement and motor control, rehabilitation can provide a guide for motor recovery that influences the neurobiology of neuronal plasticity, by providing controlled, repetitive, and variable patterns [57]. Thus, the end-effector robot can promote a range of motions and flexibility in a patient's hand joints; however, its application in restoring the neurological system of the hand is more limited and less impressive.

4.1.3. Smart Walkers Enhance Leg Muscle Strength and Balance

Unlike the two types of robots discussed above (the upper limb rehabilitation system and the end-effector robot), the smart walker is a lightweight robotic assistive device. It is intended as a lower limb function recovery robot. It can provide support and assistance to patients and can improve their autonomy and the effectiveness of their rehabilitation work. In addition, it also has a certain degree of safety and does not restrict the range of motion in the patient's joints or their amplitude, which allows the patients maximum freedom [15]. For elderly patients, leg strength and body balance are the basis for participating in rehabilitation activities. Sierra (2019) pointed out that the smart walker is able to select rehabilitation exercises of different intensities, which are based on the patient's own recovery. This enables them to gain a better understanding of their recovery and to adapt more effectively to real walking conditions [16]. The smart walker can help patients to complete physical activities through assistive devices, can provide personalized exercise programs, and can give different levels of support and assistance to patients with different dysfunctions, which can play an active and effective role in lower limb muscle strength and balance functions [15–17]. Enhancing leg strength and body balance not only improves the ability of the elderly patients to live, but also improves their bodies' neurological connections and speeds up their physical recovery. The smart walker can also help patients to perform rehabilitation exercises for different physical difficulties, can develop new rehabilitation programs, and can provide real-time assessments through built-in sensors, which improves patients' basic mobility [18], thus, helping them to restore their normal ability levels and to improve their quality of life.

4.1.4. Intelligent Robotic Rollator Integrally Enhances Physical and Cognitive Abilities

The intelligent robotic rollator, e.g., i-Walk, is an integrated set of sensing, navigation, and user–robot interaction modules, which are designed in such a way as to enable the real-time operation to support the envisioned user-assisted functions [19]. They are suitable for providing cognitive and walking assistance to people with mild to moderate motor impairments (e.g., the elderly), and they can combine user-adaptive motion control, navigation in dynamic environments, and cognitive assistance. In addition, they can provide stable human posture support, walking assistance, navigation in indoor and outdoor environments, health monitoring, and more [58,59].

The researchers believe that the greatest advantage of this type of robot is its high intelligence—it not only has a verbal human–computer interaction system, but also recognizes the patient's commands and feeds the language back into the system to recognize and respond to the patient's intentions. It breaks through the limitations of the support provided by assistive devices and takes the patient as the main intermediary by incorporating the patient's intentions into a functional rehabilitation training program in order to achieve a holistic improvement in the patient's physical and cognitive abilities.

4.1.5. Robotic Exoskeletons Provide Site-Specific Muscle Training

The research on this topic generally agrees that robotic exoskeletons are one of the most-used motor rehabilitation robots in the rehabilitation field today [60]. Through their bionic design, they connect the human-like mechanical structure's design with the patient, forming an integrated, wearable mobile device, which is driven by an external power source to alleviate movement disorders. Therefore, they achieve the dual purpose of sports rehabilitation and physical function recovery, by effectively providing a second skeleton for the patients [61].

The research in and the development of the technology for exoskeleton rehabilitation robots are currently more mature than they are in other areas. Consequently, there are not only local joint rehabilitation assistance robots, but also full-body, wearable exoskeleton robots. This connects to the individual patient in a wearable way and has multiple points, and, because its joint axis matches human joints, it can control the movement of all the patient's joints and can therefore train muscles in specific areas during the rehabilitation training. Furthermore, it can also provide corresponding training for patients with limb dysfunction to help restore the working ability of their limbs [62]. At present, robotic exoskeletons can be divided into the following four types, according to where they are worn: upper limb robotic exoskeletons [20–24], lower limb robotic exoskeletons [25–30], whole body robotic exoskeletons [15], and ground robotic exoskeletons [31,32].

Compared with the first four types of robot-assisted technology discussed in this paper, the current challenges in robotic exoskeleton research and development are as follows: (1) its rigid structure and multi-link design affects the freedom of movement in a patient's joints—a patient can only execute the angle and speed that has been fixed for their training method; (2) spending a long time repeating single action exercises could easily trigger other parts of a sports injury and, thus, the function of other parts of the body could be weakened; and (3) it is a non-intelligent functional system, which is unable to follow up a patient's rehabilitation progress in a timely manner or adjust the movement strategy.

4.2. How the Sports Rehabilitation Robot Works

The working methods of motor rehabilitation robots can be divided into three categories: assistant tools as the main intermediaries, the patient as the main intermediary, and the sensors as the intermediaries.

The robots in which the assistant tools are the main intermediaries focus on stimulating the patient's motivation for rehabilitation and on guiding the patient to carry out their rehabilitation training. The robots in which the patient is the main intermediary are mainly controlled by the patient's will and they help the patient to complete their rehabilitation training movements. In the robots in which the sensors are the main intermediaries, myoelectric sensors automatically identify the patient's rehabilitation needs and make the rehabilitation process more intelligent. Patients can choose the right exercise rehabilitation robot, according to their needs and to the different stages of their rehabilitation to improve its efficiency.

4.2.1. Assistant Tools as the Main Intermediary: Robotic-Assisted Patient Participation in Motor Rehabilitation

Assistant tools, as the main type of rehabilitation robot, consist of software and hardware tools and generally include not only the robot, but also a rehabilitation system, which work in conjunction with each other. Because there are different types of assistive rehabilitation, the robots' components have different characteristics, and their working methods vary accordingly. Usually, each component is directed towards the device's function to guide the patient through their motor rehabilitation.

As described above (Section 4.1.1), the upper extremity rehabilitation system, QM-FOrMS, consists of a smart pad, a smart canister, and a mobile device, and it directs a patient's arm movements through LED cues on the smart pad to guide them towards completing their rehabilitation movements [53]. In the FELXO-Arm1 rehabilitation system, this upper limb-assisted rehabilitation robot (ULRR), has multiple degrees of freedom, which enables it to provide a full range of assistance to the patient. It has an encoder and sensors attached to it to enable it to record the patient's rehabilitation status. Furthermore, additional power units act on the patient's elbow and shoulder joints. Information on the forces interacting between the patient and the robot is obtained through sensors mounted at the joint locations.

Using this information, the rehabilitation robot actively constructs an inverse dynamic model to precisely calculate and control the starting friction, motion friction, and motion compensation force of the patient's affected limb, laying the foundation for the subsequent development of the treatment plan [33]. Moreover, together with the TOT rehabilitation theory, different virtual reality game training tasks are set to guide patients towards completing the established rehabilitation training program, which can effectively improve stroke symptoms in elderly patients [34]. In contrast, the above two types of assistive device-based robots work in such a way that the patient must undergo rehabilitation training according to the rehabilitation program that is set by the robot and that is inherent in it.

This type of approach can restore the medical staff's motor rehabilitation purpose to a greater extent and does not negatively affect the final rehabilitation of the patient if the they choose to make a change in the rehabilitation's movement trajectory, or if they decide to abandon the program due to the patient's pre-control or insufficient motivation. The FELXO-Arm1 rehabilitation system and the ULRR upper limb assisted robot can personalize the activity parameters according to patients' different needs and abilities, for example, by including the patients' background complexity, the running speed, the training time, the background music. These factors can effectively cultivate patients' motivation for active rehabilitation and can therefore enhance the rehabilitation results.

4.2.2. Patient as the Main Intermediary: Patients Operate Assistive Devices for Motor Rehabilitation Activities

The patient-oriented motor rehabilitation robot is mainly patient-controlled, and the rehabilitation robot is manipulated to perform rehabilitation activities according to the patient's wishes, and with the help of the robot's functions. For example, the REO-GO upper limb rehabilitation robot first uses a platform to stabilize the patient's upper limb, and then relies on the patient to actively apply grip force to the handle, after which the robot assists the patient in achieving the free movement of their upper limb [11]. Similarly, patients can use the HAL-SJ, a wearable exoskeleton robot, to actively assist in their training, by using the muscles' action potentials, which are detected from the patients' muscle fibers. This approach can help elderly patients to improve their knee's mobility and its synergistic contraction. Furthermore, this rehabilitation training method can reduce antagonist musculature and synergistic muscle injuries [18].

The whole-body exoskeleton robot, FB-AXO, connects the upper and lower systems through the lumbar and spine modules. Patients with muscle weakness can remain standing with the external assistance provided by the whole-body exoskeleton robot and they can therefore actively operate the robot to complete the physical activities set in the rehabilitation training program. Ultimately, this enables them to achieve the purpose of their rehabilitation [35].

The motion rehabilitation robot mainly targets elderly patients and can help them with their personalized physical activity exercises, under the active operation of the patient. These robots can supplement the patient's subjective rehabilitation and the corresponding parts of their rehabilitation treatment. They can also allow the patient to perceive the recovery of their corresponding body parts through the feedback that they provide. The patients' choice of an appropriate physical activity program (a choice offered by these robots) is also important for their subsequent rehabilitation. Therefore, this patient-led rehabilitation robot only provides external assistance, which maximizes the patient's initiative in the rehabilitation process, unlike the robot-led rehabilitation approach, which requires patients to passively receive their rehabilitation treatment [32].

4.2.3. Sensors as the Intermediaries: Myoelectric-Driven Robot Promotes Patient Participation in Sports Rehabilitation

Robots in which the sensors are the intermediaries have a significant impact on the way that the motor rehabilitation robot acts [36]. In addition, they contribute, to a certain extent, to the motor rehabilitation of elderly patients. Usually, upper limb exoskeleton robots (Rehab-Robotics) use myoelectric actuation as the mediating mode of action, and bioelectric sensors, such as EMG sensors, can detect the patient's voluntary muscle activation in real-time and trigger the robot-assisted movements [63]. The lower extremity rehabilitation robot (Keeogo) places sensors on the thighs, knees, and calves of the elderly patients and uses a wearable design, which connects the calves to the thighs and suspends them from a lumbar carrier system, enabling the elderly patient's hips to rotate freely and enabling the sensors to transmit data to a terminal for analysis during the rehabilitation exercises. This allows the robot to set up a rehabilitation medical program for them [37]. Ing-Jr Ding and Yu-Jui Chang had confirmed after research, the Kinect-sensor-based sport instructor robot was beneficial to rehabilitation and exercise training of the elderly. A GAD scheme for enhancing Kinect-sensor-based gesture recognition was proposed. In addition, three different types of state machine for formulating certain rehabilitation exercises in the sport instructor expert system were also presented [64].

With the sensors as the intermediaries, the data obtained by using EMG to observe the actual recovery of the patients will be more quantitative and objective than the data obtained through the observation of medical personnel and through personal perception. The use of a myoelectric drive to control the rehabilitation robot enables the patient to execute the rehabilitation movements precisely and enables the maximum possible fit with the patient's rehabilitation wishes. Moreover, it also perfectly demonstrates the effectiveness of the medical rehabilitation program. Of course, how best to use myoelectric-driven rehabilitation robots to assist elderly patients with precise limb rehabilitation activities will become a major research focus in the future.

4.3. *The Effect of the Sports Rehabilitation Robot*

Traditional exercise rehabilitation programs are designed to focus on the characteristics of the patient's disease and do not pay enough attention to the physical and mental characteristics and to the individual differences of the elderly patients [65]. For frail elderly patients, there are many barriers to exercise, including their physical inability to support their own physical activity; negative attitudes towards exercise; and their lack of sufficient exercise confidence [66]. In investigating the effectiveness of the existing motor rehabilitation robots, sports rehabilitation robots were found to be more effective in the treatment of degenerative diseases in the elderly, compared to the traditional rehabilitation methods, especially in secondary medical problems, such as osteoporosis, cardiovascular disease, respiratory problems, and intestinal dysfunction. Seniors who recover with the assistance of a sports rehabilitation robot also exhibit good behavioral characteristics and psychological states [63].

Moreover, the study showed that the exercise rehabilitation robot assisted elderly patients with degenerative diseases. It was found that they exhibited a better recovery of their strength and endurance and a significant improvement in their balance and coordination. However, no significant improvement in their agility or speed was observed. The main areas of the body targeted by the different types of rehabilitation robots and their effects are shown in Figure 3.

4.3.1. Better Recovery of Strength and Endurance

Strength is the basis of all physical activities, and the elderly generally show a gradual weakening of muscle strength as they age. Resistance training is the main way to help the elderly restore muscle strength [67]. However, most elderly patients are unable to perform resistance training to improve their strength. The use of the same robotic assistance that is used for sports rehabilitation both improves the elderly's upper-limb strength and reduces the sports injuries [68] sustained by them [38,39]. This is because these robots can assist the elderly in their progressive resistance training, while monitoring the changes in their physical status during exercise in real-time [20,40]. As shown by their better strength recovery using these methods, compared to traditional recovery training, elderly patients who cannot exercise on their own can improve their muscle strength with the help of these robots [41,69]. The sports rehabilitation robot was found to perform even better in enhancing the endurance of elderly patients. Traditional rehabilitation training is not comparable to robots in terms of the calculation and the control of the load, and the rehabilitation effects of these traditional methods are, thus, not satisfactory [17]. Robotic-assisted gait training was shown to significantly improve the endurance of the elderly patients, compared to traditional treadmill training. Furthermore, the unassisted walking endurance and stair-climbing ability of the elderly patients were also seen to improve [28].

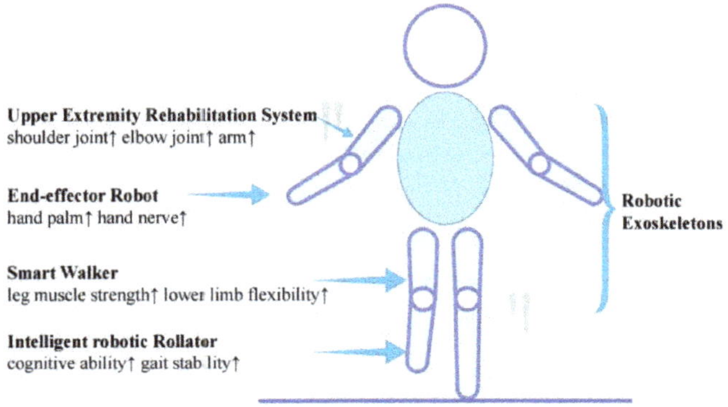

Figure 3. Rehabilitation effects of different types of robots.

4.3.2. Balance and Coordination Improve the Effect Significantly

Balance and gait disturbances are common manifestations of dysfunction in older adults as they age. Professionals need to accompany elderly patients during the exercises necessary for their balance and coordination training, in order to reduce or avoid falls and sports injuries. This requires a significant amount of human and material resources [70]. In contrast, the use of a sports rehabilitation robot can effectively solve the above problems—the higher the involvement of the sports rehabilitation robot, the more effective it will be in improving the ability of the elderly patients to balance, and, thus, the recovery will be much more effective than when using the non-robotic traditional training methods [66]. In addition, studies have also found that rehabilitation training with sports rehabilitation robots can improve the efficiency of elderly patients' balance and coordination recovery, can reduce their rehabilitation time, and can have a better effect on their balance function [42–44].

4.3.3. No Significant Improvement in Agility and Speed

Agility is a unique physical ability that has not received much attention from rehabilitators, and, thus, there are very few agility training methods for improving the agility of older patients [71]. To some extent, sports rehabilitation robots can be used as training aids to help older adults improve their agility. When combined with technologies such as virtual reality, sports rehabilitation robots can substantially improve the cognitive ability and physical state of elderly patients; however, they cannot significantly improve elderly patients' performance in agility-related tests [45]. The sports rehabilitation robot also had limited success in improving the speed of the elderly patients. For example, after using robot-assisted gait training, there was no significant difference observed in the improvement of the elderly patients' gait speed, compared to the traditional treadmill training, and, in some conditions, treadmill training was even seen to yield better results [46]. As a result, there was no significant improvement in the agility and speed of the elderly patients, when they were aided by a sports rehabilitation robot.

5. Optimization Suggestions and Future Perspectives

Currently, sports rehabilitation robots use clinical measurement scales to assess whether patients' functional improvement is significant after receiving the intervention. However, due to the different nature of the ordinal scales used for taking the measurements and their lack of sensitivity in detecting subtle changes in the patient's exercise performance during the assessments, future studies will need to use specific instruments—such as electromyography and kinematic analysis—to accurately assess the effects of the interventions on the exercise performance and on the motor unit recruitment [72]. Because of the characteristics of the current types of sports rehabilitation robots, their working methods, their effects, and the gaps in the current research, we make the following suggestions.

5.1. *Refining Assistive Technology*

Studies have confirmed that patients with physical dysfunction can recover considerably with the aid of a sports rehabilitation robot [47]. This study found and collated the significant effects that this assistive technology had in improving the physical abilities of elderly patients, such as their strength, endurance, balance, and coordination. However, the current motor rehabilitation assistive technology for neurological and cognitive recovery in elderly patients is inadequate. In the future development of robot-assisted rehabilitation technology, we must focus on the neurological function and cognitive recovery of the patients, based on the recovery of their body function, so that patients can truly recover.

5.2. *Classification and Characteristics of Sports Rehabilitation Robots*

Existing sports rehabilitation robots can provide high-intensity, repeatable rehabilitation training for patients, which can greatly relieve the pressure on staff input in rehabilitation facilities, and can reduce the workload of clinical rehabilitation practitioners. However, compared to professional rehabilitation physicians, sports rehabilitation robots are not able to accurately determine a patient's recovery or their motivation to recover, based on the patient's response and physical state, nor are they able to adjust the rehabilitation arrangements in a targeted manner. It is suggested that future sports rehabilitation robots should combine modern multimedia interactive technology to stimulate patients' interest and enthusiasm in participating in rehabilitation training; to mobilize their awareness and ability to actively participate in training; and to combine multiple modal sensor technologies to achieve intelligent recognition of patients' physical status and intentions, while having the ability to adjust the rehabilitation plans in a targeted manner.

5.3. *Enhancing the User Experience*

The service object of a sports rehabilitation robot is a human being, and its user experience determines its value. Because the design of the sports rehabilitation robots mainly uses a mechanical multi-link structure, manufacturing is based mainly on alloys, carbon fiber, and other rigid materials. This results in a poor wearing experience for the user, as the prolonged use of a fixed mechanical structure to carry out activities affects the flexibility of the other joints, making it easier for them to sustain sports injuries. It is hoped that the future development of sports rehabilitation robots will include flexible materials to improve the user's comfort when wearing the devices, based on considerations of safety and support.

6. Conclusions

Robot-assisted technology is of great significance for the rehabilitation of the elderly. Sports rehabilitation robots can assist in the enhancement of the physical ability of elderly patients with degenerative diseases, thus, their development and application will have a significant practical value.

The current types of SRR are generally classified as end-effector robots, smart walkers, intelligent robot rollators, and exoskeleton robots—exoskeleton robots are the most widely used. The working methods of these SRR include the following: (1) assistant tools as the main intermediaries—e.g., the robots assist the patients in participating with their rehabilitation; (2) patients as the main intermediaries—e.g., patients dominate the assistant tools to proactively participate in their rehabilitation; and (3) sensors as the main intermediaries—e.g., myoelectric-driven robots promote patient participation. The robot-assisted rehabilitation method is better than the traditional single-motion recovery method, and the elderly patients' strength and endurance can be better restored through this. In addition, their balance and coordination can also be significantly improved. However, there was no significant improvement in the elderly patients' agility or speed when they were assisted by these robots.

With the continuous innovation of human-computer interactions, the Internet of Things, artificial intelligence, new materials, robot simulation, and other technologies, the sports rehabilitation robot needs to be further improved through the development of assistive technology, intelligent recognition, user perception, and other technologies, to bring new developments into the field of medical rehabilitation [73]. Crucially, this will bring new hope that more elderly patients with degenerative diseases will be able to resume a normal life.

Author Contributions: Conceptualization, F.J. and J.C.; methodology, F.J. and B.X.; validation, Y.W., B.X., and Y.M.; data curation, F.J., Y.W., B.X., M.Z., and Y.M.; writing—original draft preparation, F.J.; writing—review and editing, J.C. and F.J.; visualization, Y.W., M.Z., and B.X.; supervision, J.C.; project administration, F.J. All authors have read and agreed to the published version of the manuscript.

Funding: This research was funded by Yangzhou University, grant number Xjj2021-179; C-c/2021/01/63.

Institutional Review Board Statement: Not applicable.

Informed Consent Statement: Not applicable.

Data Availability Statement: Not applicable.

Conflicts of Interest: The authors declare no conflict of interest.

References

1. Elliott, S.J. Changing geographies of aging on a global scale: The knowledge to action gap. *Can. Geogr.* **2022**, *66*, 60–64. [CrossRef]
2. Falck, R.S.; Davis, J.C.; Best, J.R.; Crockett, R.A.; Liu-Ambrose, T. Impact of exercise training on physical and cognitive function among older adults: A systematic review and meta-analysis. *Neurobiol. Aging* **2019**, *79*, 119–130. [CrossRef]
3. Saftari, L.N.; Kwon, O.S. Ageing vision and falls: A review. *J. Physiol. Anthropol.* **2018**, *37*, 1–14. [CrossRef] [PubMed]
4. Ahn, S.; Oh, J. Effects of a health-belief-model-based osteoporosis-and fall-prevention program on women at early oldage. *Appl. Nurs. Res.* **2021**, *59*, 151430. [CrossRef]
5. Sharif, S.I.; Al-Harbi, A.B.; Al-Shihabi, A.M.; Al-Daour, D.S.; Sharif, R.S. Falls in the elderly: Assessment of prevalence and risk factors. *Pharm. Pract. (Granada)* **2018**, *16*, 1206. [CrossRef] [PubMed]
6. Giovannini, S.; Brau, F.; Galluzzo, V.; Santagada, D.A.; Loreti, C.; Biscotti, L.; Bernabei, R. Falls among older adults: Screening, identification, rehabilitation, and management. *Appl. Sci.* **2022**, *12*, 7934. [CrossRef]
7. Tijsen, L.M.; Derksen, E.W.; Achterberg, W.P.; Buijck, B.I. Challenging rehabilitation environment for older patients. *Clin. Interv. Aging* **2019**, *14*, 1451. [CrossRef]
8. Tang, H.; Dai, Z. Health care intervention measures for the elderly under the smart sports rehabilitation mode under the background of big data. *Wirel. Commun. Mob. Comput.* **2022**, *2022*, 1–10. [CrossRef]
9. Shi, D.; Zhang, W.; Zhang, W.; Ding, X. A review on lower limb rehabilitation exoskeleton robots. *Chin. J. Mech. Eng.* **2019**, *32*, 1–11. [CrossRef]
10. Zhu, Z.; Zheng, G.; Zhang, C. Development and clinical application of robot-assisted technology in traumatic orthopedics. *Chin. J. Reparative Reconstr. Surg.* **2022**, *36*, 915–922. [CrossRef]
11. Shahar, N.; Schwartz, I.; Portnoy, S. Differences in muscle activity and fatigue of the upper limb between Task-Specific training and robot assisted training among individuals post stroke. *J. Biomech.* **2019**, *89*, 28–33. [CrossRef] [PubMed]
12. Feng, G.; Zhang, J.; Zuo, G.; Li, M.; Jiang, D.; Yang, L. Dual-modal hybrid control for an upper-limb rehabilitation robot. *Machines* **2022**, *10*, 324. [CrossRef]
13. Lin, F.; Ajay, J.; Langan, J.; Cavuoto, L.; Nwogu, I.; Subryan, H.; Xu, W. QM-FOrMS: A portable and cost-effective upper extremity rehabilitation system. *Smart Health* **2019**, *14*, 100080. [CrossRef]
14. Fiorini, L.; De Mul, M.; Fabbricotti, I.; Limosani, R.; Vitanza, A.; D'Onofrio, G.; Tsui, M.; Sancarlo, D.; Giuliani, F.; Greco, A.; et al. Assistive robots to improve the independent living of older persons: Results from a needs study. *Disabil. Rehabil. Assist. Technol.* **2021**, *16*, 92–102. [CrossRef] [PubMed]
15. Soma, Y.; Mutsuzaki, H.; Yoshioka, T.; Kubota, S.; Shimizu, Y.; Kanamori, A.; Yamazaki, M. Single-joint hybrid assistive limb in knee rehabilitation after ACL reconstruction: An open-label feasibility and safety trial. *Prog. Rehabil. Med.* **2022**, *7*, 20220036. [CrossRef] [PubMed]

16. Sierra, M.S.D.; Garzón, M.; Múnera, M.; Cifuentes, C.A. Human–robot–environment interaction interface for smart walker assisted gait: AGoRA walker. *Sensors* **2019**, *19*, 2897. [CrossRef]
17. Capecci, M.; Pournajaf, S.; Galafate, D.; Sale, P.; Le Pera, D.; Goffredo, M.; De Pandis, M.F.; Andrenelli, E.; Pennacchioni, M.; Ceravolo, M.G.; et al. Clinical effects of robot-assisted gait training and treadmill training for Parkinson's disease. A randomized controlled trial. *Ann. Phys. Rehabil. Med.* **2019**, *62*, 303–312. [CrossRef]
18. Jiménez, M.F.; Monllor, M.; Frizera, A.; Bastos, T.; Roberti, F.; Carelli, R. Admittance controller with spatial modulation for assisted locomotion using a smart walker. *J. Intell. Robot. Syst.* **2019**, *94*, 621–637. [CrossRef]
19. Moustris, G.; Kardaris, N.; Tsiami, A.; Chalvatzaki, G.; Koutras, P.; Dometios, A.; Mavridis, P. The i-walk lightweight assistive rollator: First evaluation study. *Front. Robot. AI* **2021**, *8*, 677542. [CrossRef]
20. Frisoli, A.; Barsotti, M.; Sotgiu, E.; Lamola, G.; Procopio, C.; Chisari, C. A randomized clinical control study on the efficacy of three-dimensional upper limb robotic exoskeleton training in chronic stroke. *J. NeuroEngineering Rehabil.* **2022**, *19*, 1–14. [CrossRef]
21. Coskunsu, D.K.; Akcay, S.; Ogul, O.E.; Akyol, D.K.; Ozturk, N.; Zileli, F.; Tuzun, B.B.; Krespi, Y. Effects of robotic rehabilitation on recovery of hand functions in acute stroke: A preliminary randomized controlled study. *Acta Neurol. Scand.* **2022**, *146*, 499–511. [CrossRef] [PubMed]
22. Chen, Y.W.; Chiang, W.C.; Chang, C.L.; Lo, S.M.; Wu, C.Y. Comparative effects of EMG-driven robot-assisted therapy versus task-oriented training on motor and daily function in patients with stroke: A randomized cross-over trial. *J. NeuroEngineering Rehabil.* **2022**, *19*, 1–9. [CrossRef] [PubMed]
23. Li, G.; Cheng, L.; Sun, N. Design, manipulability analysis and optimization of an index finger exoskeleton for stroke rehabilitation. *Mech. Mach. Theory* **2022**, *167*, 104526. [CrossRef]
24. Kapsalyamov, A.; Hussain, S.; Jamwal, P.K. State-of-the-art assistive powered upper limb exoskeletons for elderly. *IEEE Access* **2020**, *8*, 178991–179001. [CrossRef]
25. Hasan, S.K.; Dhingra, A.K. Biomechanical design and control of an eight DOF human lower extremity rehabilitation exoskeleton robot. *Results Control. Optim.* **2022**, *7*, 100107. [CrossRef]
26. Chang, S.H.; Zhu, F.; Patel, N.; Afzal, T.; Kern, M.; Francisco, G.E. Combining robotic exoskeleton and body weight unweighing technology to promote walking activity in tetraplegia following SCI: A case study. *J. Spinal Cord Med.* **2020**, *43*, 126–129. [CrossRef]
27. Lovrenovic, Z.; Doumit, M. Development and testing of a passive walking assist exoskeleton. *Biocybern. Biomed. Eng.* **2019**, *39*, 992–1004. [CrossRef]
28. McGibbon, C.; Sexton, A.; Gryfe, P.; Dutta, T.; Jayaraman, A.; Deems-Dluhy, S.; Novak, A.; Fabara, E.; Adans-Dester, C.; Bonato, P. Effect of using of a lower-extremity exoskeleton on disability of people with multiple sclerosis. *Disabil. Rehabil. Assist. Technol.* **2021**, 1–8. [CrossRef]
29. Berriozabalgoitia, R.; Sanz, B.; Fraile-Bermúdez, A.B.; Otxoa, E.; Yeregui, I.; Bidaurrazaga-Letona, I.; Duñabeitia, I.; Antigüedad, A.; Domercq, M.; Irazusta, J. An overground robotic gait training program for people with multiple sclerosis: A protocol for a randomized clinical trial. *Front. Med.* **2020**, *7*, 238. [CrossRef]
30. Galperin, I.; Herman, T.; Assad, M.; Ganz, N.; Mirelman, A.; Giladi, N.; Hausdorff, J.M. Sensor-based and patient-based assessment of daily-living physical activity in people with parkinson's disease: Do motor subtypes play a role? *Sensors* **2020**, *20*, 7015. [CrossRef]
31. Christensen, S.; Rafique, S.; Bai, S. Design of a powered full-body exoskeleton for physical assistance of elderly people. *Int. J. Adv. Robot. Syst.* **2021**, *18*, 17298814211053534. [CrossRef]
32. De Luca, R.; Maresca, G.; Balletta, T.; Cannavò, A.; Leonardi, S.; Latella, D.; Calabrò, R.S. Does overground robotic gait training improve non-motor outcomes in patients with chronic stroke? Findings from a pilot study. *J. Clin. Neurosci.* **2020**, *81*, 240–245. [CrossRef] [PubMed]
33. Qu, Q.; Lin, Y.; He, Z.; Fu, J.; Zou, F.; Jiang, Z.; Jia, J. The effect of applying robot-assisted task-oriented training using human-robot collaborative interaction force control technology on upper limb function in stroke patients: Preliminary findings. *BioMed Res. Int.* **2021**, *2021*, 1–8. [CrossRef] [PubMed]
34. Choi, W. Effects of robot-assisted gait training with body weight support on gait and balance in stroke patients. *Int. J. Environ. Res. Public Health* **2022**, *19*, 5814. [CrossRef]
35. Pan, L.; Song, A.; Wang, S.; Duan, S. Experimental study on upper-limb rehabilitation training of stroke patients based on adaptive task level: A preliminary study. *BioMed Res. Int.* **2019**, *2019*, 2742595. [CrossRef]
36. Suo, P.; Zhu, X.; Wang, S.; Li, M.; Yu, T.; Song, C.; Ning, H.; Xin, Y. A training method for a sensor-based exercise rehabilitation robot. *J. Sens.* **2022**, *2022*, 4336664. [CrossRef]
37. Mcleod, J.C.; Ward, S.J.; Hicks, A.L. Evaluation of the Keeogo™ dermoskeleton. *Disabil. Rehabil. Assist. Technol.* **2019**, *14*, 503–512. [CrossRef]
38. Chinembiri, B.; Ming, Z.; Kai, S.; Xiu, F.Z.; Wei, C. The fourier M2 robotic machine combined with occupational therapy on post-stroke upper limb function and independence-related quality of life: A randomized clinical trial. *Top. Stroke Rehabil.* **2021**, *28*, 1–18. [CrossRef]
39. Franceschini, M.; Mazzoleni, S.; Goffredo, M.; Pournajaf, S.; Galafate, D.; Criscuolo, S.; Posteraro, F. Upper limb robot-assisted rehabilitation versus physical therapy on subacute stroke patients: A follow-up study. *J. Bodyw. Mov. Ther.* **2020**, *24*, 194–198. [CrossRef]
40. Hasan, S.K.; Dhingra, A.K. State of the art technologies for exoskeleton human lower extremity rehabilitation robots. *J. Mechatron Robot* **2020**, *4*, 211–235. [CrossRef]

41. Just, F.; Özen, Ö.; Tortora, S.; Klamroth-Marganska, V.; Riener, R.; Rauter, G. Human arm weight compensation in rehabilitation robotics: Efficacy of three distinct methods. *J. Neuroeng. Rehabil.* **2020**, *17*, 1–17. [CrossRef]
42. Chen, S.C.; Kang, J.H.; Peng, C.W.; Hsu, C.C.; Lin, Y.N.; Lai, C.H. Adjustable parameters and the effectiveness of adjunct robot-assisted gait training in individuals with chronic stroke. *Int. J. Environ. Res. Public Health* **2022**, *19*, 8186. [CrossRef] [PubMed]
43. Giovannini, S.; Iacovelli, C.; Brau, F.; Loreti, C.; Fusco, A.; Caliandro, P.; Castelli, L. Robotic-assisted rehabilitation for balance and gait in stroke patients (ROAR-S): Study protocol for a preliminary randomized controlled trial. *Trials* **2022**, *23*, 1–10. [CrossRef] [PubMed]
44. Yun, N.; Joo, M.C.; Kim, S.C.; Kim, M.S. Robot-assisted gait training effectively improved lateropulsion in subacute stroke patients: A single-blinded randomized controlled trial. *Eur. J. Phys. Rehabil. Med.* **2018**, *54*, 827–836. [CrossRef] [PubMed]
45. Manuli, A.; Maggio, M.G.; Latella, D.; Cannavò, A.; Balletta, T.; De Luca, R.; Naro, A.; Calabrò, R.S. Can robotic gait rehabilitation plus virtual reality affect cognitive and behavioural outcomes in patients with chronic stroke? A randomized controlled trial involving three different protocols. *J. Stroke Cerebrovasc. Dis.* **2020**, *29*, 104994. [CrossRef] [PubMed]
46. Kim, H.; Kim, E.; Yun, S.J.; Kang, M.; Shin, H.I.; Oh, B.; Seo, H.G. Robot-assisted gait training with auditory and visual cues in Parkinson's disease: A randomized controlled trial. *Ann. Phys. Rehabil. Med.* **2022**, *65*, 101620. [CrossRef] [PubMed]
47. Gassert, R.; Dietz, V. Rehabilitation robots for the treatment of sensorimotor deficits: A neurophysiological perspective. *J. NeuroEng. Rehabil.* **2018**, *15*, 46. [CrossRef]
48. Martinez-Martin, E.; Escalona, F.; Cazorla, M. Socially assistive robots for older adults and people with autism: An overview. *Electronics* **2020**, *9*, 367. [CrossRef]
49. Losey, D.P.; McDonald, C.G.; Battaglia, E.; O'Malley, M.K. A review of intent detection, arbitration, and communication aspects of shared control for physical human–robot interaction. *Appl. Mech. Rev.* **2018**, *70*, 010804. [CrossRef]
50. Bove, R.; Musallam, A.; Healy, B.C.; Houtchens, M.; Glanz, B.I.; Khoury, S.; Chitnis, T. No sex-specific difference in disease trajectory in multiple sclerosis patients before and after age 50. *BMC Neurol.* **2013**, *13*, 1–7. [CrossRef]
51. Gu, Y.; Xu, Y.; Shen, Y.; Huang, H.; Liu, T.; Jin, L.; Wang, J. A review of hand function rehabilitation systems based on hand motion recognition devices and artificial intelligence. *Brain Sci.* **2022**, *12*, 1079. [CrossRef] [PubMed]
52. Moggio, L.; de Sire, A.; Marotta, N.; Demeco, A.; Ammendolia, A. Exoskeleton versus end-effector robot-assisted therapy for finger-hand motor recovery in stroke survivors: Systematic review and meta-analysis. *Top. Stroke Rehabil.* **2022**, *29*, 539–550. [CrossRef] [PubMed]
53. Lin, F.; Ajay, J.; Langan, J.; Cavuoto, L.; Nwogu, I.; Subryan, H.; Xu, W. A portable and cost-effective upper extremity rehabilitation system for individuals with upper limb motor deficits. In Proceedings of the 2016 IEEE Wireless Health (WH), Bethesda, MD, USA, 25–27 October 2016. [CrossRef]
54. Abbasimoshaei, A.; Mohammadimoghaddam, M.; Kern, T.A. Adaptive fuzzy sliding mode controller design for a new hand rehabilitation robot. In Proceedings of the 12th International Conference on Human Haptic Sensing and Touch Enabled Computer Applications, Leiden, The Netherlands, 6–9 September 2020; Springer: Cham, Switzerland, 2020; pp. 506–517. [CrossRef]
55. Moshaii, A.A.; Moghaddam, M.M.; Niestanak, V.D. Fuzzy sliding mode control of a wearable rehabilitation robot for wrist and finger. *Ind. Robot.* **2019**, *46*, 839–850. [CrossRef]
56. Aly, A.A.I.; Abbasimoshaei, A.; Kern, T.A. Developing a VR Training Environment for Fingers Rehabilitation. In Proceedings of the13th International Conference on Human Haptic Sensing and Touch Enabled Computer Applications (EuroHaptics 2022), Hamburg, Germany, 22–25 May 2022; TUHH Universitätsbibliothek: Hamburg, Germany, 2022. [CrossRef]
57. Molteni, F.; Gasperini, G.; Cannaviello, G.; Guanziroli, E. Exoskeleton and end-effector robots for upper and lower limbs rehabilitation: Narrative review. *PMR* **2018**, *10*, S174–S188. [CrossRef]
58. Chalvatzaki, G.; Koutras, P.; Tsiami, A.; Tzafestas, C.S.; Maragos, P. I-Walk intelligent assessment system: Activity, mobility, intention, communication. In Proceedings of the European Conference on Computer Vision, Glasgow, UK, 23–28 August 2020; Springer: Cham, Switzerland, 2020; pp. 500–517. [CrossRef]
59. Moustris, G.; Kardaris, N.; Tsiami, A.; Chalvatzaki, G.; Koutras, P.; Dometios, A.; Mavridis, P. The I-walk assistive robot. In Proceedings of the 13th International Workshop on Human-Friendly Robotics, Innsbruck, Austria, 22–23 October 2020; Springer: Cham, Switzerland, 2020; pp. 31–45. [CrossRef]
60. Weber, L.M.; Stein, J. The use of robots in stroke rehabilitation: A narrative review. *NeuroRehabilitation* **2018**, *43*, 99–110. [CrossRef] [PubMed]
61. Rupal, B.S.; Rafique, S.; Singla, A.; Singla, E.; Isaksson, M.; Virk, G.S. Lower-limb exoskeletons: Research trends and regulatory guidelines in medical and non-medical applications. *Int. J. Adv. Robot. Syst.* **2017**, *14*, 1729881417743554. [CrossRef]
62. Gorgey, A.S. Robotic exoskeletons: The current pros and cons. *World J. Orthop.* **2018**, *9*, 112. [CrossRef] [PubMed]
63. Martinek, R.; Ladrova, M.; Sidikova, M.; Jaros, R.; Behbehani, K.; Kahankova, R.; Kawala-Sterniuk, A. Advanced bioelectrical signal processing methods: Past, present, and future approach—Part III: Other biosignals. *Sensors* **2021**, *21*, 6064. [CrossRef] [PubMed]
64. Ding, I.J.; Chang, Y.J. On the use of Kinect sensors to design a sport instructor robot for rehabilitation and exercise training of the elderly. *Sens. Mater.* **2016**, *28*, 463–476.

65. Kropielnicka, K.; Dziubek, W.; Bulińska, K.; Stefańska, M.; Wojcieszczyk-Latos, J.; Jasiński, R.; Pilch, U.; Dąbrowska, G.; Skórkowska-Telichowska, K.; Kałka, D.; et al. Influence of the physical training on muscle function and walking distance in symptomatic peripheral arterial disease in elderly. *BioMed Res. Int.* **2018**, *2018*, 1937527. [CrossRef] [PubMed]
66. Rogers, C.E.; Cordeiro, M.; Perryman, E. Maintenance of physical function in frail older adults. *Nurs. Clin.* **2014**, *49*, 147–156. [CrossRef] [PubMed]
67. Fragala, M.S.; Cadore, E.L.; Dorgo, S.; Izquierdo, M.; Kraemer, W.J.; Peterson, M.D.; Ryan, E.D. Resistance training for older adults: Position statement from the national strength and conditioning association. *J. Strength Cond. Res.* **2019**, *33*, 2019–2052. [CrossRef] [PubMed]
68. Bessler, J.; Prange-Lasonder, G.B.; Schaake, L.; Saenz, J.F.; Bidard, C.; Fassi, I.; Valori, M.; Lassen, A.B.; Buurke, J.H. Safety assessment of rehabilitation robots: A review identifying safety skills and current knowledge gaps. *Front. Robot. AI* **2021**, *8*, 602878. [CrossRef] [PubMed]
69. Der Loos, V.; Machiel, H.F.; Reinkensmeyer, D.J.; Guglielmelli, E. Rehabilitation and health care robotics. In *Springer Handbook of Robotics*; Springer: Cham, Switzerland, 2016; pp. 1685–1728. [CrossRef]
70. Osoba, M.Y.; Rao, A.K.; Agrawal, S.K.; Lalwani, A.K. Balance and gait in the elderly: A contemporary review. *Laryngoscope Investig. Otolaryngol.* **2019**, *4*, 143–153. [CrossRef] [PubMed]
71. Ogilvie, M.; Wallen, M.P.; Talpey, S.W. Agile ageing–A modifiable vital sign to mitigate the risk of falls in older adults? *Med. Hypotheses* **2021**, *148*, 110517. [CrossRef] [PubMed]
72. Porciuncula, F.; Roto, A.V.; Kumar, D.; Davis, I.; Roy, S.; Walsh, C.J.; Awad, L.N. Wearable movement sensors for rehabilitation: A focused review of technological and clinical advances. *PMR* **2018**, *10*, S220–S232. [CrossRef] [PubMed]
73. Kondratenko, Y.P. Robotics, automation and information systems: Future perspectives and correlation with culture, sport and life science. In *Decision Making and Knowledge Decision Support Systems*; Springer: Cham, Switzerland, 2015; pp. 43–55. [CrossRef]

healthcare

Review

Assistive Technologies and Quadriplegia: A Map Point on the Development and Spread of the Tongue Barbell Piercing

Antonia Pirrera [1,*], Paola Meli [1], Alessandra De Dominicis [2], Alessandra Lepri [2] and Daniele Giansanti [1,*]

[1] Centro TISP, Istituto Superiore di Sanità, 00161 Roma, Italy
[2] FARVA, Istituto Superiore di Sanità, 00161 Roma, Italy
* Correspondence: antonia.pirrera@iss.it (A.P.); daniele.giansanti@iss.it (D.G.)

Abstract: The barbell piercing can be used as an assistive device that allows people with severe disabilities, such as tetraplegia, to control their environments using the movement of the tongue. The human tongue can move rapidly and accurately, such that the tip can touch every tooth. Lingual control systems allow people with disabilities to take advantage of their residual skills for easier communication and to improve the control of mobility and the surrounding environment. The aim of this study was to conduct a narrative review of the development and dissemination of the assistive technologies based on tongue control by means of the barbell piercing. The design of the study was based on: (I) an overview of Pubmed complemented with other databases and Web searches (also institutional); (II) an organization according to a standardized checklist for narrative reviews; (III) an arrangement with four different perspectives: the trends in the scientific literature, technological evolution and categorization, dominant approaches, issues of incorporation into the *health domain*—such as acceptance, safety, and regulations. The results have highlighted: (1) that the volume of scientific productions, which started in this sector before the smartphone expansion, has not increased; (2) that it is possible to make a map point of the technological evolution and categorization; (3) that these assistive technologies have a high degree of acceptance and performance, especially when integrated with aid tools with mechatronics; (4) and the complexity of the regulatory framework in this area. The study, from a general point of view, highlighted the high potential of these systems and we suggest investing the energy into agreement tools for assistive technologies (AT)s, such as health technology assessment studies, comparative assessment analysis, or consensus conferences that could allow a better diffusion and use of ATs, including these systems.

Keywords: spinal cord injuries; assistive technology; tongue barbell piercing; tongue drive system; inductive tongue control system

Citation: Pirrera, A.; Meli, P.; De Dominicis, A.; Lepri, A.; Giansanti, D. Assistive Technologies and Quadriplegia: A Map Point on the Development and Spread of the Tongue Barbell Piercing. *Healthcare* **2023**, *11*, 101. https://doi.org/10.3390/healthcare11010101

Academic Editor: Norbert Hosten

Received: 8 November 2022
Revised: 14 December 2022
Accepted: 21 December 2022
Published: 28 December 2022

1. Introduction

This study moves into the sector of severe motor disabilities. Among these disabilities, quadriplegia has an important impact on the autonomy and quality of life of a person. Assistive technologies have enormous potential for supporting the communicative functions of people with tetraplegia and are therefore the theme of important studies relating to engineering developments and clinical applications. Among the assistive technologies used in quadriplegia, it is also possible to find some technologies based on the barbell piercing.

1.1. Spinal Cord Injuries and Tetraplegia: Definition

A spinal cord injury is the result of damage to any portion of the spinal cord or the nerves at the base of the spine. The spinal cord is a bundle of nerve fibers and tissue, which lies within the spine forming the brain's connection to the body.

Damage to any part of the spinal cord can affect sensory, motor, and reflex capabilities if the brain is unable to send information past the location of the injury.

A severe spinal cord injury (SCI) or traumatic brain injury (TBI) can have a variety of impacts [1]. Patients of SCIs and TBIs can suffer a certain type of constant paralysis. An SCI can be complete (totally affecting the spinal cord) or incomplete (partially affecting the spinal cord). Furthermore, it should be considered that the higher the damage is positioned on the spine, the more serious the paralysis will be. We must consider that the spine is divided into four districts: cervical (C1–C7, C8*), thoracic (T1–T12), lumbar (L1–L5), and sacral (S1–S5) (*there is an additional cervical-level injury known as a C8 injury, which relates to damage to the spinal cord root that exits the spinal column between vertebrae C7 and T1). Tetraplegia refers to damage in the cervical district.

The simplest Tetraplegia definition [1] is "a form of paralysis that affects both arms and both legs "This term is often replaced with the term "Quadriplegia". Table 1 reports the neuromotor limitations as a function of the location of the damage [1]. The level of individual disability depends on several factors, such as the position of the injury, its completeness, and the timeliness of the treatment of the injury. Therefore, the technologies must be properly planned and assigned to support the disability considering this.

Table 1. Map between the level of the lesion and the state of neuromuscular functions in quadriplegia.

District/Level	Neuro Respiratory Function	Neuromuscular Function
C1–C4	Need for mechanical breathing	Total paralysis of the arms
C5	Difficulty in coughing, there may be a need for help in cleaning up the secretions	Paralysis of the wrists, hands, and triceps muscles
C6	As above	Paralysis of the wrist flexors, triceps, and hands
C7–C8*	As above	Some muscle weakness in the hand, difficulty in grasping and releasing

1.2. The Assistive Technologies and the Tetraplegia

The WHO has addressed the issue of Assistive Technologies (ATs) and reports on its website [2] as they are a fundamental instrument of equity, independence, and dignity. In other words (literal quote),

> *"Assistive technology enables people to live healthy, productive, independent, and dignified lives, and to participate in education, the labour market and civic life. Assistive technology reduces the need for formal health and support services, long-term care and the work of caregivers. Without assistive technology, people are often excluded, isolated, and locked into poverty, thereby increasing the impact of disease and disability on a person, their family, and society."*

According to the Assistive Technology Industry Association (ATIA), an AT is any item, piece of equipment, software program, or product system that is used to increase, maintain, or improve the functional capabilities of persons with disabilities [3]. An AT supports people who have difficulty speaking, typing, writing, remembering, pointing, seeing, hearing, learning, walking, and many other things.

These aids are complex devices that often use special materials and complex mechanics. They are controlled by high-level electronics and information technology (e.g., motorized exoskeletons). In the case of aids for supporting the communication capabilities of people with communication disabilities, so-called devices for "alternative and augmentative communication" (e.g., eye pointers) are used [4]. The ATs for quadriplegia have been greatly affected, as for other forms of disability, by the exceptional technological developments of recent decades, and, more specifically, by the miniaturization of electronics, and the diffusion and integration into the *health domain* of mobile technology, micromechanics, and materials. These ATs allow people with tetraplegia both to interact with the environment and to communicate. They allow for the control of your smartphone, tablet, computer, wheelchair, robotic devices, and more, usually from one singular controller/device. This gives the person control over the Ambient Assisted Living systems for domotics, communication, and displacement.

When quadriplegia is addressed, it is necessary to carefully consider both the different forms of neuromotor disability and other aspects such as age, literacy, and the presence of any cognitive disorders, while also considering other factors such as the patient's ability to accept a certain assistive technology. In this context, it is important to adapt the ATs to the person [5].

All of this is also in compliance with the latest document, the "International Classification of Functioning, Disability and Health" [6], which no longer looks at disabilities but at the *health components* of the person.

1.3. The Barbell Piercing as an Assistive Technology

In recent years, among the various AT solutions that have been developed to support tetraplegia patients with environmental control, communication, and displacement, it is possible to find those based on barbell piercing. Body piercing is defined as the penetration of an ornament into openings made in the skin or mucosa. Intraoral and perioral sites are often selected for piercing with the tongue, lips, and cheeks being the most pierced sites.

The spread of "body art" practices has given rise to increasing concerns.

We previously performed studies and analyses on tattoos and piercings designed to improve the lives of those who suffer from particular diseases [7]. Medical tattoos applied to restore the bodily integrity of cancer patients are an example.

There is also a great interest in the application of piercing in assistive devices, based on tongue control systems that can help to improve the autonomy of people with severe motor disabilities.

The barbell piercing can also be used as an assistive device that allows people with severe disabilities to control the environment using the movement of the tongue. The human tongue can move rapidly and accurately and the tip can touch every tooth. Lingual control systems allow people with disabilities to take advantage of their residual skills for easier communication and to improve the control of mobility and the surrounding environment.

Regarding the sensor in these ATs, an activation unit made of a soft ferromagnetic material magnet can be used to carry out actions based on distance or support with appropriate devices.

Therefore, such an activation unit placed, for example with adhesive, on the tongue can interact with other receiving devices internally or externally from the mouth.

The use of a piercing as an alternative solution guarantees better stability, as the actuator is firmly anchored on the tongue through it. The positioning of the actuator by means of an adhesive solution presents less stability at the price of easier removal.

A technological study proposed at the Micro and Nanotechnology Sensors, Systems, and Applications IX congress in 2017 [8], highlighted the technologies used, and the classification of the devises used in this field.

1.4. Purpose, Organization and Key Questions to Answer

The main objectives of this study are to:

- Investigate the evolution of these devices; the volume of scientific production; describe the use of tongue piercing as a driving tool for AT systems in quadriplegic patients enrolled in the study protocols.
- Analyze the use of these devices and their integration into the *health domain*.

The work is organized into five sections plus the introduction (*section one*).

Section two is the methods.

Section three reports the results. It is divided into *four parts*:

- The *first part* analyses the scientific production in this area, highlighting the progress and the evolutions.

  This part answers the key question: *"How has scientific production evolved in this area?*

- The *second part* reports the technological evolution and categorization of the tongue-based devices.

This part answers the key question: *"What are the technological evolutions of these devices and how can they be categorized?"*

- The third part, reports the consolidated approaches using the barbell piercing.

It answers the key question *"What are the dominant approaches regarding the use of the barbell piercing inside the mouth?"*

- The *fourth part* analyses the integration into the *health domain* with a particular focus on the acceptance, safety, comparison, and regulation issues. It answers the heterogeneous question *"What can be said about the acceptance, comparison, safety, and regulation of these devices?"*

Section four reports a discussion on the evidence gathered also based on the deployment, and the development prospects.

Section five is dedicated to the conclusions.

2. Methods

This study made use of a standardized checklist for narrative reviews (Available online: [9]).

Given that this study investigated the integration in the *health domain,* the search was conducted on Pubmed. The search was also complemented, when necessary based on the topic addressed (for example legislation), by deepening the search using other databases dedicated to technological studies, and websites, including institutional ones. Tables 2 and 4 show the search terms used in the relevant sections.

The design of the study, in line with the objectives, addressed four specific points of view with targeted searches to give the reader a complementary image from multiple angles and perspectives on specific aspects. The first search was dedicated to analyzing the trend of scientific production. The second search addressed the technological evolutions and the categorization of the devices. The third search was dedicated to the dominant approaches in the development of the sensor–actuator chains inside the mouth. The fourth search addressed aspects related to integration into the *health domain,* such as acceptance, comparison, security, and regulatory aspects.

3. Results

3.1. The Development of the Tongue Piercing as a Driver for Assistive Technologies in the Scientific Literature

In line with the purpose of the study, we:

- Turned to the PubMed database to analyze the evolution of scientific production in this area in relation to integration into the *health domain.*
- Defined a search key suitable for the purpose.
- Checked for any reviews.

The composite key is available and can be found in Table 2 [10].

The *first piece of general evidence* to be noted is that the list did not show the presence of reviews. This is certainly a comforting finding for our study in relation to the need to make a map point.

The *second piece of general evidence* is that the search returned 72 contributes, starting from the year 2006 up to the date of this review (the year 2022), a span of about 16 years. This means that the spread of these systems began before the boom of smartphones, as we know them today [11], and followed its evolution. With a few exceptions, regarding studies dealing with the biocompatibility of materials and lingual models (and the related issues), all the studies are focused on this area.

Table 2. Search terms in Section 3.1.

Search Key
"tongue drive system"[Title/Abstract] OR "tongue control system"[Title/Abstract] OR "tongue computer"[Title/Abstract] OR "tongue computer interface"[Title/Abstract] OR (("tongue"[MeSH Terms] OR "tongue"[All Fields] OR "tongues"[All Fields] OR "tongue s"[All Fields]) AND "elaborator"[All Fields] AND ("interface"[All Fields] OR "interface s"[All Fields] OR "interfaced"[All Fields] OR "interfaces"[All Fields] OR "interfacing"[All Fields]))

The *third general* consideration concerns the progress of scientific production.

The peak of scientific production was in 2012 with 10 papers. In the first 5–6 years, up until the year 2012, the year in which the maximum number of studies, 10, was proposed, there was a growth in production. After this period, the trend changed. Figure 1 shows how: (a) up to the year 2013, approximately the first half-period of the scientific production period, we had 41 papers (57% of scientific production). (b) From the year 2014 up to today, approximately the second half-period of the scientific production period, we have had 31 papers (43% of scientific production). Twenty-five (34.7 %) of the total scientific works are contributions to International Congresses.

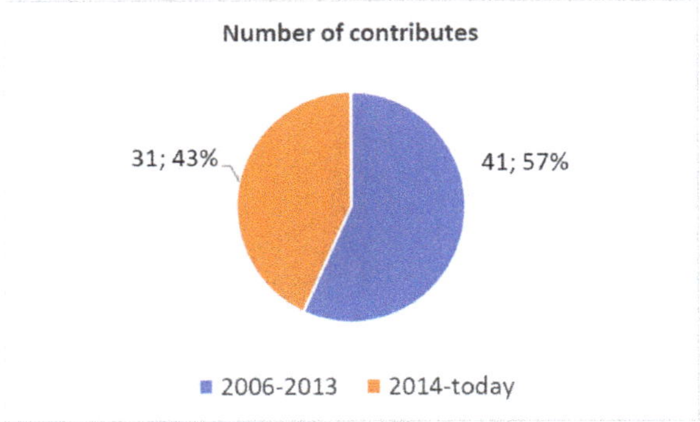

Figure 1. Scientific production for tongue electronic systems.

By addressing the scientific aspects, it is possible to see that the history and evolution of this technology are due to two international groups, which, starting from the year 2006, through initial contributions in [12,13], contributed to the theme with a different approach. In fact, with a few isolated exceptions [14,15], the scientific contributions were made by these scholars.

The technological approaches have evolved and adapted from time to time into different applications for the *health domain* and have shown important potential for integration with Alternative and Augmentative Communication, for integration with the environment (Ambient Assisted Living), and other home automation applications [16–21].

These two intraoral technological approaches produced through the two groups, in their different versions, integrations, and evolutions, demonstrated potential in the field of assistive technologies.

3.2. Applied Technologies and Categorization

In order to analyze the applied technologies and approaches in this area, the search was integrated with other technology-focused databases. Some scholars reported in [8] an interesting categorization useful as a reference. We briefly report the technological evolutions and approaches according to this categorization also resumed in Table 3.

Table 3. Categorization of the tongue-based systems.

	Young Participants	Brief Description	References
1	Tongue drive system	Actuator and receiver use magnetic fields. Sensors are external	[8,22–26]
2	Intraoral tongue drive system	Actuator and receiver use magnetic fields. Sensors placed inside the mouth.	[8,27–32]
3	Standalone tongue drive system	Completely wearable	[8,33–35]
4	Multimodal Tongue Drive System	The system integrates a head-mounted device and a speech recognition device	[8,36]
5	Inductive tongue control system	Actuator and receiver (external) use magnetic fields. Inductive sensors are used (placed on a PCB for the palate)	[8,37–41]
6	Further tongue-based systems	They are emerging technologies based on light emitting diodes and light detectors, the IBM tongue track point technologies, piezoelectric sensors, and a tongue-based Joystick (Jouse3)	[8,42–45]

3.2.1. Tongue Drive System

The first device, the Tongue Drive System (TDS) [8], used a magnetic field generated by a magnetic actuator-tracer on the patient's tongue to detect instructions based on a set of tongue-based gestures [22]. The authors designed a headset with a pair of lateral poles arranged with sensors to detect and measure the variation of the magnetic field, correlated to the tongue-based gestures. The detectors were four tri-axial magnetic sensors. The communication to the receiver was wireless. The authors used a Texas Instrument device. The frequency was set at 2.4 GHZ [23–25]. The interface used the software Labview for both the A/D conversion and display [26].

3.2.2. Intraoral Tongue Drive System

An evolution of the TDS [8,27–29] considered the placement of the receiver in the mouth. This new architectural design improved the detection of the magnetic field correlated to the tongue-based gestures, as the detectors were closer to the actuator-tracer placed on the tongue [30]. The receiver was anchored on the teeth. This allowed for better steadiness and discretion (with the system being hidden inside the mouth) [31]. Two evolutions were proposed. The first version used a custom system-on-chip device placed in the center of the device's printed circuit board (PCB). Four 3-axial magnetic sensors were affixed on the four corners of the PCB. The system used a dual band (27 MHZ, 433 MHZ). The system communicated the data similarly to the previous system. The second version [32] proposed an arch-shape device, placed on the lower jaw, with the electronics located in the buccal shelf area. The frequency used was the same. The reception on the receiver side was improved using a super-regenerative approach.

3.2.3. Standalone Tongue Drive System

The design of a device that could fit completely inside the mouth, i.e., a standalone device, was the next step [8]. The first device used a common open-source miniaturized platform, named Beagle Bone Black (BBB) [8]. The calibration based on an ARM A8 processor included a classifier designed by means of a support vector machine. This system allowed for successful interfacing with an electronically driven wheelchair [33]. Another device included a field programmable gate array (FPGA). The FPGA collected digitized raw information from the detectors using a serial peripheral interface [34,35]. A properly designed classifier algorithm based on the Earth's magnetic field attenuation and logistic regression was implemented in the FPGA. Bluetooth low energy (BLE) was also used to interface with the pc or the smartphone.

3.2.4. Multimodal Tongue Drive System

The integration of the TDS with further assistive technologies has been proposed [8]. The authors named it the Multimodal Tongue Drive System [36]. It integrated a head tracker and a speech recognition system [36]. The head tracker used an Inertial Measurement Unit comprising both one 3D gyroscope and one 3D accelerometer. The Dragon Naturally Speaking tool was used as an interpreter/speech-to-text translator.

3.2.5. The Inductive Tongue Control System

A further device used inductive sensors [8,37–41]. It was proposed at Alborg University in Denmark. It comprised: (a) a ferromagnetic actuator-tracer placed on the tongue; and (b) a group of 18 inductive switches placed on a PCB designed to be affixed on the palate. When the actuator touches the switches, the result is a voltage change and therefore a command. We will return to this later in the paper (see Section 3.3).

3.2.6. Further Tongue-Based Systems

Further approaches [8] in progress are using light-emitting diodes and light detectors [42], the IBM tongue-track-point technologies [43], piezoelectric sensors [44], and a tongue-based Joystick (Jouse3) [45].

3.3. *The Tongue Piercing in Assistive Technologies in Quadriplegia Today: The Two Most Important Approaches*

Different technological approaches have been followed in the use of assistive systems based on the movement of the tongue. It was possible to carry out the categorization shown in Table 4. Surely, future efforts will be directed towards the bringing of all the ICT inside the mouth, and pushing towards miniaturization, towards greater comfort of the Stand-Alone Tongue drive system (*Position 3*, Table 3), and towards the expansion of Multimodal Tongue Drive Systems (*Position 4*, Table 3).

Looking from another perspective, however complementary, in line with the objectives of the study, which intends to address the processes of inserting the barbell piercing into these systems, we can focus on the Tongue Drive System and its intraoral evolution (*Position 1-2*, Table 3) and on the Inductive Tongue-Based System (*Position 5*, Table 3). In fact, two different approaches [12,13] have been proposed by scholars in the past, evolving in the recent two decades that use the movement and the multiple capabilities of the tongue, providing a specific tongue cockpit, which led to the insertion of the barbell piercing. One approach is the Tongue Drive System device, also available in the intraoral version (iTDS). Another approach is the Inductive Tongue Control System (Itongue). A description of the functioning and of the evolution of the two systems is provided below.

3.3.1. The Tongue Drive System (TDS) in detail

The TDS designed and developed initially at the North Carolina State University is a wireless and portable human–computer interface. The device consists of a small magnetic disk, attached by means of a dental adhesive onto the tongue, capable of generating a magnetic field [13]. The movements of the tongue induce variations in the magnetic field, which are detected using a kit of sensors positioned on an earphone. The signals are then sent wirelessly from a control unit, placed in the headset, to a receiver that processes them and translates each movement into a specific function defined by the user, such as moving the cursor on the screen of a computer, dialing a phone number, driving a wheelchair, or turning the light on and off. The TDS was capable of detecting six positions in the mouth, which are activated when reached by the tongue and translated into six commands. The TDS featured several important upgrades. Figure 2 shows a sketch of the first release. We report here two *important upgrades* (see in Figure 3 the sketch of the two upgrades).

Table 4. The Search Keys in Section 3.4.

	Search Key
1	*("tongue drive system"[Title/Abstract] OR "tongue control system"[Title/Abstract] OR "tongue computer"[Title/Abstract] OR "tongue computer interface"[Title/Abstract] OR (("tongue"[MeSH Terms] OR "tongue"[All Fields] OR "tongues"[All Fields] OR "tongue s"[All Fields]) AND "elaborator"[All Fields] AND ("interface"[All Fields] OR "interface s"[All Fields] OR "interfaced"[All Fields] OR "interfaces"[All Fields] OR "interfac-ing"[All Fields]))) AND ("accept"[All Fields] OR "acceptabilities"[All Fields] OR "ac-ceptability"[All Fields] OR "acceptable"[All Fields] OR "acceptably"[All Fields] OR "acceptance"[All Fields] OR "acceptances"[All Fields] OR "acceptation"[All Fields] OR "accepted"[All Fields] OR "accepter"[All Fields] OR "accepters"[All Fields] OR "accepting"[All Fields] OR "accepts"[All Fields])*
2	*("tongue drive system"[Title/Abstract] OR "tongue control system"[Title/Abstract] OR "tongue computer"[Title/Abstract] OR "tongue computer interface"[Title/Abstract] OR (("tongue"[MeSH Terms] OR "tongue"[All Fields] OR "tongues"[All Fields] OR "tongue s"[All Fields]) AND "elaborator"[All Fields] AND ("interface"[All Fields] OR "interface s"[All Fields] OR "interfaced"[All Fields] OR "interfaces"[All Fields] OR "interfacing"[All Fields]))) AND ("comparison"[All Fields] OR "comparisons"[All Fields])*
3	*("tongue drive system"[Title/Abstract] OR "tongue control system"[Title/Abstract] OR "tongue computer"[Title/Abstract] OR "tongue computer interface"[Title/Abstract] OR (("tongue"[MeSH Terms] OR "tongue"[All Fields] OR "tongues"[All Fields] OR "tongue s"[All Fields]) AND "elaborator"[All Fields] AND ("interface"[All Fields] OR "interface s"[All Fields] OR "interfaced"[All Fields] OR "interfaces"[All Fields] OR "interfacing"[All Fields]))) AND ("legislation and jurisprudence"[MeSH Subheading] OR ("legislation"[All Fields] AND "jurisprudence"[All Fields]) OR "legislation and juris-prudence"[All Fields] OR "regulations"[All Fields] OR "social control, formal"[MeSH Terms] OR ("social"[All Fields] AND "control"[All Fields] AND "formal"[All Fields]) OR "formal social control"[All Fields] OR "regulate"[All Fields] OR "regulates"[All Fields] OR "regulating"[All Fields] OR "regulation s"[All Fields] OR "regulative"[All Fields] OR "regulator"[All Fields] OR "regulator s"[All Fields] OR "regulators"[All Fields] OR "regulated"[All Fields] OR "regulation"[All Fields])*
4	*("tongue drive system"[Title/Abstract] OR "tongue control system"[Title/Abstract] OR "tongue computer"[Title/Abstract] OR "tongue computer interface"[Title/Abstract] OR (("tongue"[MeSH Terms] OR "tongue"[All Fields] OR "tongues"[All Fields] OR "tongue s"[All Fields]) AND "elaborator"[All Fields] AND ("interface"[All Fields] OR "interfaces"[All Fields] OR "interfaced"[All Fields] OR "interfaces"[All Fields] OR "interfacing"[All Fields]))) AND ("safety"[MeSH Terms] OR "safety"[All Fields] OR "safeties"[All Fields]))*

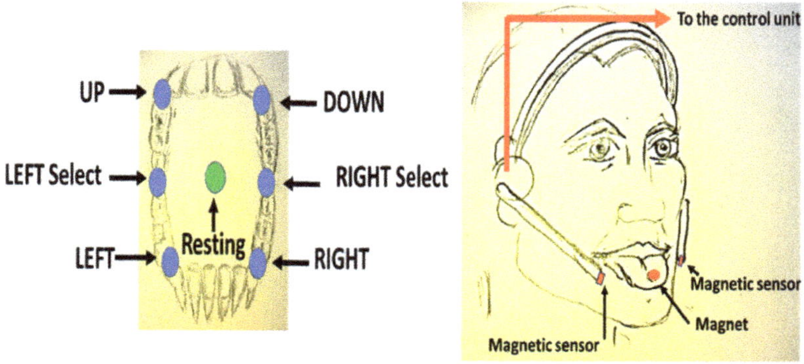

Figure 2. Sketch (realized by D.G.) of the first version of the TDS.

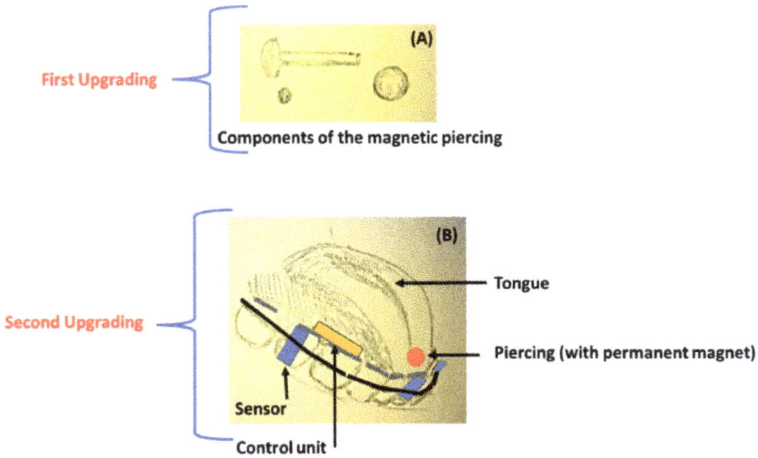

Figure 3. Sketch (realized by D.G.) of the upgrade to the TDS: (**A**) the introduction of the magnetic piercing; (**B**) the introduction of the oral control unit.

The *first important upgrade* in the year 2014 consisted of inserting a magnet inside a barbell piercing to maintain the greatest level of efficiency over time. The magnet that generates the magnetic field was placed inside the dorsal sphere of a titanium barbell piercing, internally drawn, to which, after insertion into the tongue, a retainer is screwed in the ventral position, like a common lingual piercing. A medically performed tongue-piercing method was developed and tested for use with the TDS by people with high-level SCIs [46,47]. The piercing attached to the magnetic disc with adhesive has different implications due to the stable implant inserted into a body part (the tongue). The adhesive disk is not a stable device; however, it is useful for running some proof-of-concept experiments. The patients involved in the study evaluated the TDS as effective in interfacing with computers, driving wheelchairs, dialing telephone numbers, and other tasks, as described later in the paper. This device turned out to be even easier to use than the sip-n-puff device, as described later in the paper (see Section 3.4).

The second important upgrade eliminated the headset. In this device, named Internal TDS (iTDS), the control unit was inserted into an apparatus similar to an orthodontic appliance (Figure. 3). The use of the iTDS by patients showed better compliance in comparison with the TDS, due to the absence of the earpiece [34].

3.3.2. The Inductive Tongue Control System (Itongue) in Details

The Itongue was developed at the Center for Sensory–Motor Interaction at Aalborg University in Denmark [39,48–50].

This device, like the previous one, allows persons with severe motor impairments and loss of limb functionality to directly type a text or command a pointing device in order to control, for example, an electric wheelchair or a personal computer. The system consists of an orthodontic appliance (OA) placed on the palate (see the sketch in Figure 4) which contains two blocks of inductive sensors (in total 18) organized in a front panel (8 sensors) that can be used as a pointing device (mouse, joystick) and a rearmost panel (10 sensors) that can function as a keyboard.

Inductive sensors are activated using an activation unit on the OA, which changes the inductance. The activation unit consists of a small cylinder of ferromagnetic material. The activation unit is placed inside the upper sphere of a barbell piercing which is inserted into the tongue and activates a given sensor every time the tongue selects it. The raw activation signals are sent wirelessly to an integrated electronic component (embedded controller) which processes and transforms the data, and sends them to a composite USB peripheral.

The USB peripheral then interacts with the PC through a standard USB interface [48]. The high number of sensors and their particular arrangement allows the system to be used both for writing, by the use of each sensor as a key (keyboard mode), and to obtain the functionality of the joystick (mouse mode) combining sensor signals. In addition, the ability of the system to interact with the PC through the USB interface, and therefore without customized software, means that the device can be used with any PC, even one that is not your own. The use of this device gave encouraging results in terms of speed and accuracy from the point of view of the acceptance [39] as described later in the paper (see Section 3.4).

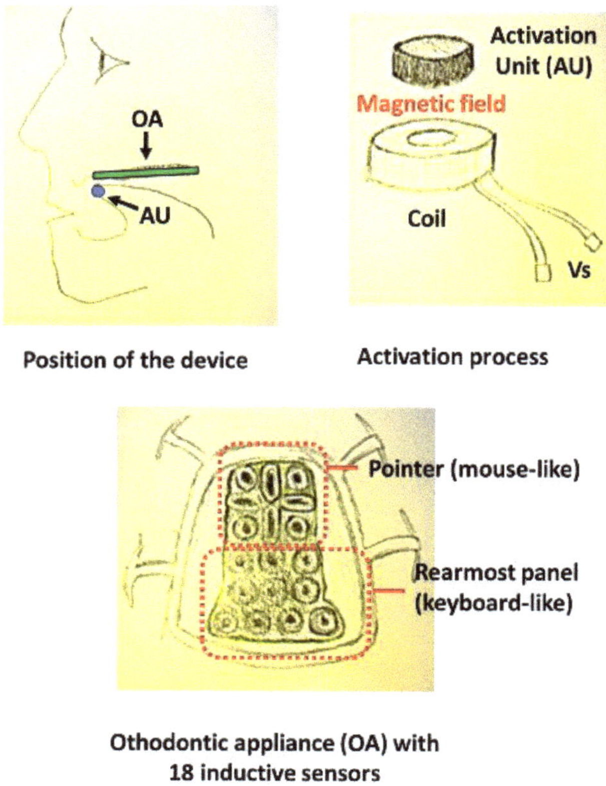

Figure 4. Sketch (realized by D.G.) of the Itongue and its components.

3.4. *Incorporation in the Health Domain: Acceptance, Safety, Comparison, Regulation Issues*

One of the key aspects of the use of these devices is integration into the *health domain*. This integration is based on an accurate assessment of aspects related to interoperability, comparison with the other devices, safety, and the regulations. Targeted searches were carried out on Pubmed, as it is the reference database for the subject of integration into the *health domain*. Other databases and websites (including institutional ones) were also analyzed in order to complement and integrate the available information. Table 4 shows the key search terms used.

3.4.1. Acceptance

The search of studies on acceptance was performed by means of the key in *Position 1* of Table 4. The study reported in [51] analyzed the acceptance of the intraoral inductive tongue system interface in typing text. Both able-bodied and tetraplegic persons were recruited. The experimentation lasted five days. The average error-free typing rate ranged between 11.6 correct characters/min for all participants and 15.5 correct characters/min for those participants familiar with the piercing. The functionality of inductive systems was demonstrated in two quadriplegic subjects and two able-bodied participants in a study reported in [41]. It was particularly appreciated that the device was invisible. A maximum speed of 1.4 s has been reached for the repeated typing of a correct character with the use of the mouse function. The results highlighted both the effectiveness and the aesthetic acceptability of the device. The effectiveness of these devices was also evaluated in an application that involved both the interaction of the TDS with the computer and interaction with the driving systems of an electric wheelchair [52]. Moreover, in this case, both able-bodied participants and participants with spinal cord injuries were recruited [52]. Comparisons were also made with the sip-and-puff (SnP) system, with which patients with spinal cord injuries were already familiar. These comparisons showed that the lingual device obtained three times better speed performance than the SnP. The acceptance of these systems was also investigated in the control of Apps available in the stores for smartphones. A Bluetooth module was used that emulated the interactions of the fingers on the touchscreen [53]. The study was carried out on able-bodied people. The errors were negligible at the typing speed measured.

3.4.2. Comparison

The search of studies on comparison was performed by means of the key in *Position 2* of Table 4. The search returned studies focused on comparison with other systems and on the learning process of the use of these ATs [21,54,55], also highlighting in some cases that these systems could be useful in healthy people to fast control elaborators and mechatronics (e.g., robots). In the study reported in [21], the authors suggested that the inductive tongue control system allowed the user control over the environment. The Cartesian control of an assistive robotic arm was mapped with the device. Two healthy participants were recruited. Trials compared the tongue interface with the manual control based on a keyboard. The results showed that the tongue-based system performed better than the keyboard with an increase in the task duration of up to 30%. The study available in [54] assessed in 18 health participants the ability of the tongue tip to accurately select intraoral targets enclosed in a palatal device. The outcome showed: (a) that the performances were faster and more accurate for targets located farther away from the base of the tongue; (b) an improvement in the speed and accuracy of the learning and familiarity; (c) the evolution of the medical knowledge on the processes of learning related to tongue interaction. Nine able-bodied participants, who already had tongue piercings, were enrolled in another study lasting 5 weeks. The study was focused both on the learning processes on this device and on the limiting factors [55]. Medical knowledge on the human factors affecting the use of these ATs was obtained thanks to the comparison with the index-finger-keypad tools.

3.4.3. Regulation and Safety

The search on regulations with the key in *position 3* of Table 4 did not produce results. This indicates: (a) the need for scholars to focus internationally on these aspects; (b) fragmentation and non-uniformity at an international level, with regard to the applicable regulations. This fragmentation is already present with regard to medical devices, for those with high technological innovation [56]. This causes scarce initiatives and scholarly interest in these issues [56].

The paths for the process of the commercial introduction of these devices, as with the other ones, depend on the country or area (for example, Europe) where they are used, and on the intended use and the relevant application. In fact, there are different legislative frameworks introduced as the country or area changes. These different regulatory frameworks determine different approval and insertion procedures. Thus, the approach, just to give an example, is different if we are in the USA, where the FDA follows a certain road map, than if we are in England, where Nice follows a different approval process, or if we are in Europe where, at the community level, the regulations are determined and must then be implemented in the countries belonging to the community.

These ATs can be used in different applications and with different intended uses. They can be used in clinical or non-clinical applications. They can be used in home automation both to drive electric wheelchairs and to interact generally with the automated home environment. They can be used as a high-tech medical aid to help with expressive language and for communication, or as a part of a mobility or rehabilitation aid. They can be used in a standalone mode or in connection with a network (e.g., local area network, world area network), with different potential implications for cybersecurity.

Regarding safety, AT systems have some requirements to consider relating to the insertion of sensors, actuators (e.g., the barbell piercing), and electronics into the oral cavity.

With these devices being based on electronics, electronic medical safety and electromagnetic compatibility must also be considered. In light of all these considerations, it is evident that a detailed analysis would be impossible and far from the scope of this study given the multifaceted characteristics of the possible applications and their intended uses. With the idea of considering a more general and less specific possible framework, we report the European regulatory framework as an example that is applicable here.

If we focus on the European reality, we find that all the systems in free commerce must follow both the General Product Safety Directive [57] on general product safety and the Directive 85/374/EEC on liability for defective products [58], which together regulate the safety of products on the market and the responsibility for their defects. Furthermore, these AT systems, based on their destination of use, can be classified as a specific medical device (MD). Medical Devices are regulated by (Regulation (EU) 2017/745) [59], which from the year 2020 replaces the previous directive. As electro-medical devices, based on the application, they must comply with the CEI EN 60601-1 standard in force in Europe [60]. As far as electromagnetic compatibility is concerned, the reference standard is Directive 2014/30 /UE EMC [61]. There are three documents that regulate cybersecurity in the EU [62–64]:

- The EU Cybersecurity Act (Regulation (EU) 2019/881) which launched an EU certification path dedicated to cybersecurity [62].
- The directive on the security of the network and the information systems (commonly referred to as the NIS Directive) that provides procedures for improving cybersecurity [63].
- The General Data Protection Regulation (GDPR) which necessitates the design of suitable actions to counter cyber risks [64].

The first document made available a procedure for a purely voluntary certification process. The last two documents delegate and pass on security matters to the providers in the *health domain*.

As for biocompatibility, there is ISO 10993 [65], although it is not mandatory, (this is also applicable in dentistry). It establishes the parameters for the biological evaluation of all medical devices in contact with the human body.

A search on Pubmed, dedicated to safety (*Position* 4, Table 4), highlighted three important studies [46,66,67] in this field. The study reported in [66] investigated the biological consequences of the titanium-magnet tongue implants of the TDS. The authors reported an oromotor and tongue-tissue response in the miniature pig, having a tongue similar to the human tongue. The results suggested the safety of the material used in the implants. Another study addressed this issue [67]. The authors analyzed the behavior of a smooth steel spherical implant in the anterior tongue of the rat. The study showed that the device did not create migration problems or tissue biocompatibility problems. Furthermore, it also showed that tongue functionality was not affected. The study also supports the use of these devices in humans.

In the study reported in [46], the authors designed and tested a tongue-piercing protocol and the application of the magnet barbell piercing to the tongue. They concluded that by using both careful procedures and medical protocols, the risk could be controlled and strongly minimized.

The regulatory framework, with reference to Europe, is of a general nature. It was reported considering the most general and broadest possible cases. It is not certain that, according to the intended use and applications, all regulations must always be applied to these ATs, such as for example what is reported for cybersecurity and electromagnetic compatibility.

Based on the above, an assessment of the marketing status of these devices requires a country-by-country analysis. For the sake of completeness, we report that an inductive operating device is marketed in Europe and is accessible at the site https://tks-technology.dk/en/produkter/#itongue/ (accessed on 7 November 2022) [68].

4. Discussion

4.1. Highlights from the Study

The study in the first part recalled that: - quadriplegia has an important impact on the autonomy and quality of life of the citizen.-The assistive technologies have both an enormous potential for supporting the communicative functions of people with tetraplegia and are the theme of important studies relating to engineering developments and clinical application. -Among the assistive technologies used in quadriplegia, there are technologies based on the tongue barbell piercing. In the second part of the study it was analyzed the evolution of the tongue piercing as an assistive technology, reporting *four points of view*. The true added values of the study are the *four points of view*.

The *first point of view* made a map point on the evolution of the scientific literature on Pubmed. It reported the scientific production trends. It showed that the scientific production in this sector (see Figure 1) started before the smartphone boom [9] and has not increased, unlike other technologies that the tongue-based systems are capable of controlling, such as the robots used in assistance and rehabilitation. In fact, a search on Pubmed by means of the key *"robotics"[Title/Abstract] AND ("assistance"[Title/Abstract] OR "rehabilitation"[Title/Abstract])"* shows how in the latter sector, the growth up to the year 2021 (the year 2022 is not yet closed) of the scientific production shows a positive pseudo-exponential trend [69]. On the contrary, in the sector of rehabilitation and assistance robots, which these ATs are able to pilot, there has been a disruptive growth of interest. It is therefore important to ask ourselves about the reasons for this disinterest and the factors that influenced it.

The *second point* of view reported the technological advances and the categorization (see Table 3) according to the position of the scientific literature [8]. These systems have evolved, from time to time, with the evolution of the technologies and processes of miniaturization and have relied on the use of specific microprocessors, FPGAs, protocols based on Bluetooth LTE, interface systems, advanced software (see for example Labview), and typical algorithms of artificial intelligence.

The *third point of view*, with reference to the barbell piercing, described the two dominant architectural approaches in mouth sensorization (of which, however, there are different evolutions and additions), without the aim of finding the best of the bunch, (it was not the objective of the study). One of these approaches was based on magnetic sensors arranged on orthodontic equipment [32], while another approach was based on palatal equipment with inductive sensors [37]. Even if it was not the objective of the overview to find the best of the bunch, the study suggests that HTA or comparative assessment technology (CAT) studies, focused on the two different systems, could bring a benefit to the development and diffusion of these ATs for the assistance of frail people. Of course, the feasibility of a CAT depends on the availability of both scholars in general and of the two groups responsible for the history of these systems.

The fourth and last *point of view* discussed the integration of these ATs into the *health domain* focusing on the *acceptance, comparison, safety, and* the *regulatory issues*. From one side, the interesting acceptance characteristics of these devices were highlighted, such as:

- The invisibility, which can improve privacy aspects and compliance [41].
- The high typing-speed performances [21,41,51–53].
- The better performances than the *SnP* systems in subjects with SCIs [52].
- The ability to improve the use with the increasing time of practice and learning [58,59].
- The effectiveness of control in home automation applications, such as in the control of the electronic wheelchair or of a robotic arm [21,52–54].

On the other side, the fragmentation of the legislation at an international level was highlighted. Some key considerations were reported, in some cases with reference to clinical studies [46,66,67] and in other cases with reference to the European regulatory situation [57–64]. It was highlighted that:

- The Pubmed search did not report specific studies on the legislation, useful as an indication for these devices.
- These devices may have different applications and destinations of use. Furthermore, regulatory reference requirements change based on this and according to the country/area of reference.
- Safety covers various aspects (which must be respected in the processes of inclusion in free commerce based on adherence to regulatory requirements) such as, by way of non-exhaustive example and even if not all of these are always applicable: electrical safety and electromagnetic compatibility [60,61]; cybersecurity [62–64]; and the biocompatibility of materials [65]. Regarding this last point, in some studies, also based on animal models, scholars have shown how with such systems it is possible to obtain the risk control based on accurate procedures and appropriate medical protocols [46,66,67].

4.2. The Tongue-Based Systems versus the Other Assistive Technologies: Pros and Cons

Many technical and psychophysical factors influence the degree of acceptance of a given assistive technology. Among the important factors are the ease of use and the simplicity of learning how the AT works. The device should also be small, discreet, aesthetically acceptable, and of a low cost.

There are currently several AT solutions, with *pros and cons* [5,16].

The *Brain–Computer Interface* (BCI), for example, is a technology based on the ability to read neuronal activity, to process signals, and to send commands to the outside world.

Two approaches are used in the BCI. The first one is Electrocorticography, (ECoG) which is based on intracortical electrodes allowing access to even more intense brain signals. However, these electrodes often cause reactions in the neural tissue in the insertion area. For this reason, the use of these systems is limited to a few cases in which their use is justified, such as in epilepsy. The second approach uses electroencephalography (EEG). In this case, the signals are distant from neurons, resulting in signal attenuation limitations and unreliable performance.

The *Eye Tracker* (ET) captures the movement of the eye and in particular the position of the pupil using a digital camera. This system is influenced by the lighting conditions, sometimes generates eye fatigue, and requires a high level of concentration. There are also alignment problems. In fact, it is necessary, when using it, to maintain the front position with respect to the monitor. False detections may also happen because it is sometimes difficult to distinguish if a point is really of interest for the user or if it is casually pointed.

Head pointers (HP) are only suitable for subjects with good residual ability in neck and head movement. They often cause fatigue in the neck and shoulder muscles.

The *Voice recognition systems (VRS)*, dedicated to subjects with an intact ability to speak, are efficient for writing but are slow and not very intuitive when you want to carry out home automation control.

The *SnP system* is one of the most popular ATs. It is based on the pressure value applied to a tube and whether negative or positive pressure is applied (inhalation and exhalation, respectively). This device, although easy, only allows a few direct commands. It also assumes that the user has good control of the diaphragm and airflow, a condition that, for example, limits its use in people who need mechanical ventilation.

These tongue-based systems have shown important potential [8,70–72] for wheelchair navigation, computer access, robotic rehabilitation, exoskeleton-based rehabilitation, home automation applications, and in the control of the home environment.

These systems, unlike the tools already in widespread use, seem very flexible and discreet, since they are also able to be hidden [41]. The tongue is connected to the brain by the hypoglossal nerve, which generally escapes serious damage even in spinal cord injuries. The tongue is also the last organ to be affected in most neuromuscular degenerative disorders. It has many degrees of freedom and can move very quickly and accurately within the oral cavity. With the tip of the tongue, you can touch every single tooth, so it is an organ suitable for manipulating this type of auxiliary device. The tongue muscle tires slowly. Therefore, a device based on the tongue motion can be used continuously for long periods, guaranteeing the user a certain degree of privacy, since it remains hidden in the mouth.

These systems: (I) are less invasive than *BCI-ECoG* using intracortical electrodes; (II) can be used on subjects without voice (who cannot use VRSs); (III) can be used on subjects who do not have head movement (who cannot use head pointers); (IV) are totally wearable and invisible; (V) do not need complex alignments as in the case of the *ETs*; and (V) can be used on subjects with displacement problems in the diaphragm (who cannot use the SnP).

However, as highlighted, the paths of adherence to the regulations are complex. The device, with the control electronics, sensors, and an actuator, goes into a cavity of the human body, the oral cavity. This makes the initiatives to be undertaken around regulation certainly more complex than those envisaged for other devices such as HP, VRS, SnP, and ET. Furthermore, the high and complex technology together with the low diffusion increases the costs and engenders a vicious circle that hinders the diffusion of these ATs.

4.3. Recommendations from the Study

The WHO is suggesting changing the vision [2] for the better diffusion of ATs, giving great attention to both the needs and acceptance of citizens.

According to the ICDH-2 [2], great attention must be given to the components of health and to the residual capacities of the citizen. The designers of the tongue-based-systems have shown great kindness to persons with tetraplegia through both the improvement and the adaptation of the technology to the various application environments [8,16–21], also comprising in some cases the integration of augmented reality and of artificial intelligence [73]. The most commercially available devices are not automatically suitable for everyone as there are different residual capacities, health components, and psychological acceptance aspects to consider in a person.

There is a lack of studies that address the use and applications of these technologies in multiple domains. They must include comparisons, costs, acceptance, dissemination problems, regulatory aspects, ethical aspects, and other issues important for integration into the *health domain*. Studies on health technology assessment, comparative technology assessment, and consensus conferences are therefore now recommended. This would also allow for a better tailoring of the AT devices to the citizen and a wider diffusion of niche devices, such as the ones investigated in this study.

There is therefore the need to invest energy into agreement tools that both support the actors in the *health domain* through recommendations and give a stimulus for stakeholders and researchers. In robotic rehabilitation (a theme that we have seen connected to this topic), for example, the need to face consensus conferences that include experts from various sectors (usually hundreds) was highlighted, and the experiment in progress in Italy that was reported in [74], later concluded in [75]. The issues that should be addressed in a desirable consensus conference for these ATs should include: classification and intended use; clinical and not-clinical use; models of use and research direction: organizational models; training; regulations and ethics.

We hope that this review can be a stimulus for this topic.

4.4. Limitations

This study based on a narrative review focused on the integration of these devices into the *health domain* and used Pubmed as the main database, as it is the reference for the interoperability of the devices in the *health domain*. In some search integrations, other databases focused on technologies and websites (including institutional ones) have been used. As far as the regulatory aspects are concerned, we wanted to give a local example, as the search showed that the international situation is fragmented. We referred to the European situation. Further studies are encouraged to expand the regulatory theme to include other local realities.

5. Conclusions

This overview was intended to make a map point on the development of ATs based on lingual control with barbell piercing and their integration into the *health domain*.

The overview provides four points of view. The *first point* of view highlights how: (a) the scientific production, which began in this area in the year 2006, has not grown over time; (b) two international research groups have given the greatest impetus in this area. The *second point of view* reported the categorization of these devices together with the relevant elements of technological evolutions. It has been highlighted here that both the emerging innovations of microelectronics and the improvements of the miniaturization processes have been used to achieve the performing results. The *third point of view*, with reference to the use of barbell piercing, reports the two dominant approaches in the device design of the sensorization–activation chain in the mouth. These approaches have been proposed by two international research groups. The *fourth point of view* addresses the aspects of integration into the *health domain*: acceptance, comparison, safety, and the regulatory approach. Important studies and results were highlighted, with concern to performance (three times better than SnP), the learning processes, the high study participant approval of the invisibility of the device, and the biocompatibility and safety studies of the device components. The fragmentation of the legislation on medical devices, for this device, as with all highly innovative technologies, does not help with diffusion. This study highlighted the high potential of these devices. They can also be used by those patients with very low residual capacities, who, for example, cannot use the VRS, HP, or SnP. Stakeholders are advised to invest energy in agreement tools for ATs, such as consensus conferences that allow for, through specific recommendations, the centered and targeted diffusion and use of ATs, including these devices.

Author Contributions: Conceptualization, A.P. and D.G.; methodology, D.G. and A.P.; software (excel), D.G.; validation, P.M., A.L. and A.D.D.; formal analysis, D.G., A.P., P.M., A.L. and A.D.D.; investigation, A.D.D., D.G., A.P., P.M. and A.L.; resources, D.G., A.P., P.M., A.L. and A.D.D.; data curation, D.G.; writing—original draft preparation, D.G. and A.P.; writing—review and editing, D.G., A.P., P.M., A.L. and A.D.D.; schemes: D.G.; visualization, P.M., A.L. and A.D.D.; supervision, D.G. and A.P.; project administration, D.G. and A.P.; funding acquisition, D.G., A.P., P.M., A.L. and A.D.D. All authors have read and agreed to the published version of the manuscript.

Funding: This study was also supported and funded by the Italian Ministry of Health-Ricerca Corrente.

Institutional Review Board Statement: Not applicable.

Informed Consent Statement: Not applicable.

Conflicts of Interest: The authors declare no conflict of interest.

References

1. Cervical Spinal Cord Injuries. Available online: https://www.spinalcord.com/cervical-spinal-cord-injury (accessed on 7 November 2022).
2. World Health Organization, Assistive Technologies. Available online: https://www.who.int/news-room/fact-sheets/detail/assistive-technology (accessed on 7 November 2022).

3. Assistive Technology Industry Association. Available online: https://www.atia.org/home/at-resources/what-is-at/ (accessed on 7 November 2022).
4. ASHA Association. Available online: https://www.asha.org/public/speech/disorders/aac/ (accessed on 8 November 2022).
5. Fager, S.K.; Fried-Oken, M.; Jakobs, T.; Beukelman, D.R. New and emerging access technologies for adults with complex communication needs and severe motor impairments: State of the science. *Augment. Altern. Commun.* **2019**, *35*, 13–25. [CrossRef] [PubMed]
6. ICDH-2, International Classification of Functioning, Disability and Health. Available online: https://unstats.un.org/unsd/disability/pdfs/ac.81-b4.pdf (accessed on 8 November 2022).
7. Renzoni, A.; Pirrera, A.; Lepri, A.; De Dominicis, A.; Cammarata, P.; Meli, P.; Grigioni, M. Tatuaggi E Piercing: Non Solo Potenziali Rischi, ma Anche Benefici Per I Pazienti. Not Ist Super Sanità. 2018, Volume 31, pp. 3–7. Available online: https://www.iss.it/documents/20126/45616/online_aprile_maggio.pdf/7124816f-e1b0-9a7b-96a1-9ab9f8154316?t=1581100961706 (accessed on 7 November 2022).
8. Ghovanloo, M.; Sahadat, M.N.; Zhang, Z.; Kong, F.; Sebkhi, N. Tapping into tongue motion to substitute or augment upper limbs. In *Micro-and Nanotechnology Sensors, Systems, and Applications IX*; SPIE: Bellingham, WA, USA, 2017; p. 1019413.
9. ANDJ Narrative Checklist. Available online: https://it.scribd.com/document/434616519/ANDJ-Narrative-Review-Checklist (accessed on 8 November 2022).
10. Pubmed Search. Available online: https://pubmed.ncbi.nlm.nih.gov/?term=%28%28%28%28tongue+drive+system%5BTitle%2FAbstract%5D%29+OR+%28tongue+control+system%5BTitle%2FAbstract%5D%29%29+OR+%28tongue+computer%BTitle%2FAbstract%5D%29%29+OR+%28tongue+computer+interface%5BTitle%2FAbstract%5D%29+OR+%28tongue+elaborator+interface%29%29&sort=pubdate&size=100 (accessed on 7 November 2022).
11. Giansanti, D.; Grigioni, M. (Eds.) *La Salute in un Palmo di Mano: Nuovi Rischi da Abuso di Tecnologia*; Istituto Superiore di Sanità: Roma, Italy, 2018; Rapporti ISTISAN 18/21.
12. Struijk, L.N.S.A. An Inductive Tongue Computer Interface for Control of Computers and Assistive Devices. *IEEE Trans. Biomed. Eng.* **2006**, *53*, 2594–2597. [CrossRef] [PubMed]
13. Huo, X.; Wang, J.; Ghovanloo, M. A Wireless Tongue-Computer Interface Using Stereo Differential Magnetic Field Measurement. *Annu. Int. Conf. IEEE Eng. Med. Biol. Soc.* **2007**, *2007*, 5723–5726. [CrossRef]
14. Peng, Q.; Budinger, T.F. ZigBee-based Wireless Intra-oral Control System for Quadriplegic Patients. *Annu. Int. Conf. IEEE Eng. Med. Biol. Soc.* **2007**, *2007*, 1647–1650. [CrossRef] [PubMed]
15. Chou, C.-H.; Hwang, Y.-S.; Chen, C.-C.; Chou, S.-W.; Chen, Y.-L. Noninvasive tongue-motion controlled computer mouse for the disabled. *Technol. Health Care* **2016**, *24*, 401–408. [CrossRef]
16. Zhang, Z.; Prilutsky, B.I.; Butler, A.J.; Shinohara, M.; Ghovanloo, M. Design and Preliminary Evaluation of a Tongue-Operated Exoskeleton System for Upper Limb Rehabilitation. *Int. J. Environ. Res. Public Health* **2021**, *18*, 8708. [CrossRef]
17. Kong, F.; Sahadat, N.; Ghovanloo, M.; Durgin, G.D. A Stand-Alone Intraoral Tongue-Controlled Computer Interface for People With Tetraplegia. *IEEE Trans. Biomed. Circuits Syst.* **2019**, *13*, 848–857. [CrossRef]
18. Kim, J.; Park, H.; Bruce, J.; Rowles, D.; Holbrook, J.; Nardone, B.; West, D.P.; Laumann, A.; Roth, E.J.; Ghovanloo, M. Assessment of the Tongue-Drive System Using a Computer, a Smartphone, and a Powered-Wheelchair by People With Tetraplegia. *IEEE Trans. Neural Syst. Rehabilitation Eng.* **2015**, *24*, 68–78. [CrossRef] [PubMed]
19. Mohammadi, M.; Knoche, H.; Struijk, L.N.S.A. Continuous Tongue Robot Mapping for Paralyzed Individuals Improves the Functional Performance of Tongue-Based Robotic Assistance. *IEEE Trans. Biomed. Eng.* **2021**, *68*, 2552–2562. [CrossRef]
20. Struijk, L.N.S.A.; Bentsen, B.; Gaihede, M.; Lontis, R. Speaking Ability while Using an Inductive Tongue-Computer Interface for Individuals with Tetraplegia: Talking and Driving a Powered Wheelchair-A Case Study. *Annu. Int. Conf. IEEE Eng. Med. Biol. Soc.* **2018**, *2018*, 2483–2486. [CrossRef]
21. Struijk, L.N.S.A.; Lontis, R. Comparison of tongue interface with keyboard for control of an assistive robotic arm. In Proceedings of the 2017 International Conference on Rehabilitation Robotics (ICORR), London, UK, 17–20 July 2017; Volume 2017, pp. 925–928. [CrossRef]
22. Huo, X.; Wang, J.; Ghovanloo, M. Introduction and preliminary evaluation of the tongue drive system: Wireless tongue-operated assistive technology for people with little or no upper-limb function. *J. Rehabil. Res. Dev.* **2008**, *45*, 921. [CrossRef] [PubMed]
23. Huo, X.; Wang, J.; Ghovanloo, M. A Magneto-Inductive Sensor Based Wireless Tongue-Computer Interface. *IEEE Trans. Neural Syst. Rehabil. Eng.* **2008**, *16*, 497–504. [CrossRef] [PubMed]
24. Kim, J.; Huo, X.; Ghovanloo, M. Wireless control of smartphones with tongue motion using tongue drive assistive technology. In Proceedings of the 2010 Annual International Conference of the IEEE Engineering in Medicine and Biology, Buenos Aires, Argentina, 31 August–4 September 2010; IEEE: Piscataway, NJ, USA, 2010; pp. 5250–5253.
25. Huo, X.; Wang, J.; Ghovanloo, M. A Wireless Tongue-Computer Interface Using Stereo Differential Magnetic Field Measurement. In Proceedings of the 2007 29th Annual International Conference of the IEEE Engineering in Medicine and Biology Society, Lyon, France, 22–26 August 2007; Volume 2007, pp. 5723–5726.
26. Huo, X.; Wang, J.; Ghovanloo, M. A Magnetic Wireless Tongue-Computer Interface. In Proceedings of the 2007 3rd International IEEE/EMBS Conference on Neural Engineering, Kohala Coast, Hawaii, 2–5 May 2007; pp. 322–326. [CrossRef]
27. Tang, H.; Beebe, D.J. An oral tactile interface for blind navigation. *IEEE Trans. Neural Syst. Rehabil. Eng.* **2006**, *14*, 116–123. [CrossRef]

28. Randerath, W.J.; Galetke, W.; Domanski, U.; Weitkunat, R.; Ruhle, K.-H. Tongue-muscle training by intraoral electrical neurostimulation in patients with obstructive sleep apnea. *Sleep* **2004**, *27*, 254–259. [CrossRef] [PubMed]
29. Campisi, G.; Giannola, L.I.; Florena, A.M.; De Caro, V.; Schumacher, A.; Göttsche, T.; Paderni, C.; Wolff, A. Bioavailability in vivo of naltrexone following transbuccal administration by an electronically-controlled intraoral device: A trial on pigs. *J. Control. Release* **2010**, *145*, 214–220. [CrossRef]
30. Park, H.; Ghovanloo, M. A Wireless Intraoral Tongue–Computer Interface. *Wirel. Med. Syst. Algorithms: Des. Appl.* **2016**, *56*, 63.
31. Park, H.; Kiani, M.; Lee, H.-M.; Kim, J.; Block, J.; Gosselin, B.; Ghovanloo, M. A Wireless Magnetoresistive Sensing System for an Intraoral Tongue-Computer Interface. *IEEE Trans. Biomed. Circuits Syst.* **2012**, *6*, 571–585. [CrossRef]
32. Park, H.; Ghovanloo, M. An Arch-Shaped Intraoral Tongue Drive System with Built-in Tongue-Computer Interfacing SoC. *Sensors* **2014**, *14*, 21565–21587. [CrossRef]
33. Yousefi, B.; Huo, X.; Kim, J.; Veledar, E.; Ghovanloo, M. Quantitative and Comparative Assessment of Learning in a Tongue-Operated Computer Input Device—Part II: Navigation Tasks. *IEEE Trans. Inf. Technol. Biomed.* **2012**, *16*, 633–643. [CrossRef]
34. Viseh, S.; Ghovanloo, M.; Mohsenin, T. Toward an Ultralow-Power Onboard Processor for Tongue Drive System. *IEEE Trans. Circuits Syst. II Express Briefs* **2015**, *62*, 174–178. [CrossRef]
35. Jafari, A.; Buswell, N.; Page, A.; Mohsenin, T.; Sahadat, M.N.; Ghovanloo, M. Live demonstration: Towards an ultra low power on-board processor for Tongue Drive System. In Proceedings of the 2015 IEEE Biomedical Circuits and Systems Conference (BioCAS), Atlanta, GA, USA, 22–24 October 2015.
36. Sahadat, M.; Alreja, A.; Srikrishnan, P.; Ghovanloo, M. A multimodal human computer interface combining head movement, speech and tongue motion for people with severe disabilities. In Proceedings of the 2015 IEEE Biomedical Circuits and Systems Conference (BioCAS), Atlanta, GA, USA, 22–24 October 2015.
37. Struijk, L.N. A tongue based control for disabled people. In *International Conference on Computers for Handicapped Persons;* Springer: Berlin/Heidelberg, Germany, 2006; pp. 913–918.
38. Struijk, L.N.S.A.; Lontis, E.R.; Bentsen, B.; Christensen, H.V.; Caltenco, H.A.; Lund, M.E. Fully integrated wireless inductive tongue computer interface for disabled people. In *2009 Annual International Conference of the IEEE Engineering in Medicine and Biology Society;* IEEE: Piscataway, NJ, USA, 2009; Volume 2009, pp. 547–550. [CrossRef]
39. Lontis, E.R.; Lund, M.E.; Christensen, H.V.; Bentsen, B.; Gaihede, M.; Caltenco, H.A.; Struijk, L.N.S.A. Clinical evaluation of wireless inductive tongue computer interface for control of computers and assistive devices. In Proceedings of the 2010 Annual International Conference of the IEEE Engineering in Medicine and Biology, Buenos Aires, Argentina, 31 August–4 September 2010; Volume 2010, pp. 3365–3368.
40. Lund, M.E.; Christiensen, H.V.; Caltenco, H.A.; Lontis, E.R.; Bentsen, B.; Struijk, L.N.A. Inductive tongue control of powered wheelchairs. In Proceedings of the 2010 Annual International Conference of the IEEE Engineering in Medicine and Biology, Buenos Aires, Argentina, 31 August–4 September 2010; pp. 3361–3364.
41. Struijk, L.N.S.A.; Lontis, E.R.; Gaihede, M.; Caltenco, H.A.; Lund, M.E.; Schioeler, H.; Bentsen, B. Development and functional demonstration of a wireless intraoral inductive tongue computer interface for severely disabled persons. *Disabil. Rehabil. Assist. Technol.* **2016**, *12*, 631–640. [CrossRef] [PubMed]
42. Saponas, T.; Scott, D.; Kelly, B.A.; Tan, D.S. Optically sensing tongue gestures for computer input. In Proceedings of the 22nd Annual ACM Symposium on User Interface Software and Technology, Victoria, BC, Canada, 4–7 October 2009; Association for Computing Machinery: New York, NY, USA, 2009; pp. 177–180.
43. Salem, C.; Zhai, S. An isometric tongue pointing device. In Proceedings of the ACM SIGCHI Conference on Human Factors in Computing Systems, New York, NY, USA, 24 April 1994; Association for Computing Machinery: New York, NY, USA, 1997.
44. Nutt, W.; Arlanch, C.; Nigg, S.; Staufert, G. Tongue-mouse for quadriplegics. *J. Micromech. Microeng.* **1998**, *8*, 155. [CrossRef]
45. Jouse3. Compusult Limited. Available online: http://www.jouse.com/ (accessed on 8 November 2022).
46. Laumann, A.; Holbrook, J.; Minocha, J.; Rowles, D.; Nardone, B.; West, D.; Kim, J.; Bruce, J.; Roth, E.; Ghovanloo, M. Safety and Efficacy of Medically Performed Tongue Piercing in People with Tetraplegia for Use with Tongue Operated Assistive Technology. *Top Spinal. Cord Inj. Rehabil.* **2015**, *21*, 61–76. [CrossRef] [PubMed]
47. Minocha, J.S.; Holbrook, J.S.; West, D.P.; Ghovanloo, M.; Laumann, A.E. Development of a Tongue-Piercing Method for Use With Assistive Technology. *JAMA Dermatol.* **2014**, *150*, 453–454. [CrossRef] [PubMed]
48. Lontis, E.R.; Struijk, L.N. Design of inductive sensors for tongue control system for computers and assistive devices. *Disabil. Rehabil. Assist. Technol.* **2010**, *5*, 266–271. [CrossRef]
49. Bentsen, B.; Gaihede, M.; Lontis, R.; Struijk, L.N.A. Medical tongue piercing – development and evaluation of a surgical protocol and the perception of procedural discomfort of the participants. *J. Neuroeng. Rehabil.* **2014**, *11*, 44. [CrossRef] [PubMed]
50. Lund, M.E.; Caltenco, H.A.; Lontis, E.R.; Christiensen, H.V.; Bentsen, B.; Struijk, L.N.S.A. A framework for mouse and keyboard emulation in a tongue control system. In Proceedings of the 2009 Annual International Conference of the IEEE Engineering in Medicine and Biology Society, Minneapolis, MN, USA, 3–6 September 2009; Volume 2009, pp. 815–818.
51. Struijk, L.N.S.A.; Bentsen, B.; Gaihede, M.; Lontis, E.R. Error-Free Text Typing Performance of an Inductive Intra-Oral Tongue Computer Interface for Severely Disabled Individuals. *IEEE Trans. Neural Syst. Rehabil. Eng.* **2017**, *25*, 2094–2104. [CrossRef]

52. Kim, J.; Park, H.; Bruce, J.; Sutton, E.; Rowles, D.; Pucci, D.; Holbrook, J.; Minocha, J.; Nardone, B.; West, D.; et al. The Tongue Enables Computer and Wheelchair Control for People with Spinal Cord Injury. *Sci. Transl. Med.* **2013**, *5*, 213ra166. [CrossRef]
53. Kim, J.; Park, H.; Ghovanloo, M. Tongue-operated assistive technology with access to common smartphone applications via Bluetooth link. In Proceedings of the 2012 Annual International Conference of the IEEE Engineering in Medicine and Biology Society, San Diego, CA, USA, 28 August–1 September 2012; Volume 2012, pp. 4054–4057. [CrossRef]
54. Caltenco, H.A.; Lontis, E.R.; Boudreau, S.A.; Bentsen, B.; Struijk, J.; Struijk, L.N.S.A. Tip of the Tongue Selectivity and Motor Learning in the Palatal Area. *IEEE Trans. Biomed. Eng.* **2011**, *59*, 174–182. [CrossRef]
55. Yousefi, B.; Huo, X.; Veledar, E.; Ghovanloo, M. Quantitative and Comparative Assessment of Learning in a Tongue-Operated Computer Input Device. *IEEE Trans. Inf. Technol. Biomed.* **2011**, *15*, 747–757. [CrossRef]
56. Giansanti, D. The Regulation of Artificial Intelligence in Digital Radiology in the Scientific Literature: A Narrative Review of Reviews. *Healthcare* **2022**, *10*, 1824. [CrossRef] [PubMed]
57. Directive 2001/95/EC of the European Parliament and of the Council of 3 December 2001 on General Product Safety. 2001. Available online: https://eur-lex.europa.eu/legal-content/EN/TXT/?uri=celex%3A52003PC0048 (accessed on 8 November 2022).
58. Directive 85/374/EEC-Liability for Defective Products. Available online: https://osha.europa.eu/it/legislation/directives/council-directive-85-374-eec (accessed on 7 November 2022).
59. Regulation (EU) 2017/745 of the European Parliament and of the Council of 5 April 2017 on Medical Devices, Amending Directive 2001/83/EC, Regulation (EC) No 178/2002 and Regulation (EC) No 1223/2009 and Repealing Council Directives 90/385/EEC and 93/42/EEC. 2017. Available online: https://eur-lex.europa.eu/legal-content/EN/TXT/HTML/?uri=CELEX:32017R0745&from=IT (accessed on 7 November 2022).
60. IEC 60601-1 Edition 3.1 2012-08. INTERNATIONAL STANDARD. Available online: http://www.pacificcrn.com/Upload/file/201705/06/20170506193715_57243.pdf (accessed on 7 November 2022).
61. DIRECTIVE 2014/30/EU of the European Parliament and of the Council of 26 February 2014 on the Harmonisation of the Laws of the Member States Relating to Electromagnetic Compatibility. Available online: https://eur-lex.europa.eu/legal-content/EN/TXT/PDF/?uri=CELEX:32014L0030&rid=4#:~{}:text=This%20Directive%20regulates%20the%20electromagnetic,adequate%20level%20of%20electromagnetic%20compatibility (accessed on 7 November 2022).
62. Shaping Europe's Digital Future. Available online: https://digital-strategy.ec.europa.eu/en/policies/cybersecurity-act (accessed on 7 November 2022).
63. NIS Directive (The Directive on Security of Network and Information Systems). Available online: https://www.itgovernance.eu/fi-fi/nis-directive-fi (accessed on 25 November 2021).
64. Complete Guide to GDPR Compliance. Available online: https://gdpr.eu/ (accessed on 7 November 2022).
65. ISO 10993-23:2021 Biological Evaluation of Medical Devices. Available online: https://www.iso.org/standard/74151.html (accessed on 7 November 2022).
66. Sokoloff, A.J.; Yang, Z.; Sargolzaei, S.; Strait, K.; Krasnopeyev, A.; Easley, K.A.; Mimche, S.; Ghovanloo, M. Magnetic implants in the tongue for assistive technologies: Tests of migration; oromotor function; and tissue response in miniature pigs. *Arch. Oral Biol.* **2017**, *81*, 81–89. [CrossRef] [PubMed]
67. Mimche, S.; Ahn, D.; Kiani, M.; Elahi, H.; Murray, K.; Easley, K.; Sokoloff, A.; Ghovanloo, M. Tongue implant for assistive technologies: Test of migration, tissue reactivity and impact on tongue function. *Arch. Oral Biol.* **2016**, *71*, 1–9. [CrossRef] [PubMed]
68. Itongue, Communication and Wheelchair Controller in One Product. Available online: https://tks-technology.dk/en/produkter/#itongue (accessed on 7 November 2022).
69. Pubmed Search. Available online: https://pubmed.ncbi.nlm.nih.gov/?term=%28robotics%5BTitle%FAbstract%5D%29+AND+%28%28+assistance%5BTitle%2FAbstract%5D%29+OR+%28rehabilitation%5BTitle%FAbstract%5D%29%29&sort=date&size=200 (accessed on 7 November 2022).
70. Palsdottir, A.A.; Mohammadi, M.; Bentsen, B.; Struijk, L.N.S.A. A Dedicated Tool Frame Based Tongue Interface Layout Improves 2D Visual Guided Control of an Assistive Robotic Manipulator: A Design Parameter for Tele-Applications. *IEEE Sensors J.* **2022**, *22*, 9868–9880. [CrossRef]
71. Thøgersen, M.B.; Mohammadi, M.; Gull, M.A.; Bengtson, S.H.; Kobbelgaard, F.V.; Bentsen, B.; Ali Khan, B.A.; Severinsen, K.E.; Bai, S.; Bak, T. User Based Development and Test of the EXOTIC Exoskeleton: Empowering Individuals with Tetraplegia Using a Compact, Versatile, 5-DoF Upper Limb Exoskeleton Controlled through Intelligent Semi-Automated Shared Tongue Control. *Sensors* **2022**, *22*, 6919. [CrossRef]
72. Lontis, E.R.; Bentsen, B.; Gaihede, M.; Biering-Sørensen, F.; Struijk, L.N.A. Wheelchair Control with Inductive Intra-Oral Tongue Interface for Individuals with Tetraplegia. *IEEE Sens. J.* **2021**, *21*, 22878–22890. [CrossRef]
73. Chu, F.J.; Xu, R.; Zhang, Z.; Vela, P.A.; Ghovanloo, M. Vela, and Maysam Ghovanloo The Helping Hand: An Assistive Manipulation Framework Using Augmented Reality and Tongue-Drive Interfaces. In Proceedings of the 2018 40th Annual International Conference of the IEEE Engineering in Medicine and Biology Society (EMBC), Honolulu, HI, USA, 18–21 July 2018; Available online: https://arxiv.org/pdf/1802.00463 (accessed on 8 November 2022).

74. Maccioni, G.; Ruscitto, S.; Gulino, R.A.; Giansanti, D. Opportunities and Problems of the Consensus Conferences in the *Care Robotics*. *Healthcare* **2021**, *9*, 1624. [CrossRef]
75. Consensus Conference Cicerone, Document Finale. Available online: https://www.simfer.it/consensus-conference-cicerone-documento-finale-conclusivo/ (accessed on 7 November 2022).

healthcare MDPI

Article

Exploring the Presence of Humanoid Social Robots at Home and Capturing Human-Robot Interactions with Older Adults: Experiences from Four Case Studies

Angela Y. M. Leung [1,2,*], Ivy Y. Zhao [1,2], Shuanglan Lin [1] and Terence K. Lau [1,2]

1 WHO Collaborating Centre for Community Health Services, School of Nursing, The Hong Kong Polytechnic University, Hong Kong 999077, China
2 Research Institute of Smart Aging (RISA), The Hong Kong Polytechnic University, Hong Kong 999077, China
* Correspondence: angela.ym.leung@polyu.edu.hk; Tel.: +852-2766-5587

Abstract: Background: Social robots have the potential to bring benefits to aged care. However, it is uncertain whether placing these robots in older people's home is acceptable and whether human-robot interactions would occur or not. Methods: Four case studies were conducted to understand the experiences of older adults and family caregivers when humanoid social robot *Ka Ka* was placed in homes for two weeks. Results: Four older adults and three family caregivers were involved. Older adults interacted with the social robot *Ka Ka* every day during the study period. 'Talking to *Ka Ka*', 'listening to music', 'using the calendar reminder', and 'listening to the weather report' were the most commonly used features. Qualitative data reported the strengths of *Ka Ka*, such as providing emotional support to older adults living alone, diversifying their daily activities, and enhancing family relationships. The voice from *Ka Ka* (female, soft, and pleasing to the ear) was considered as 'bringing a pleasant feeling' to older adults. Conclusions: In order to support aging-in-place and fill the gaps of the intensified shortage of health and social manpower, it is of prime importance to develop reliable and age-friendly AI-based robotic services that meet the needs and preferences of older adults and caregivers.

Keywords: humanoid social robot; older adults; living alone; loneliness; social isolation; home-based

Citation: Leung, A.Y.M.; Zhao, I.Y.; Lin, S.; Lau, T.K. Exploring the Presence of Humanoid Social Robots at Home and Capturing Human-Robot Interactions with Older Adults: Experiences from Four Case Studies. *Healthcare* **2023**, *11*, 39. https://doi.org/10.3390/healthcare11010039

Academic Editor: Daniele Giansanti

Received: 21 November 2022
Revised: 14 December 2022
Accepted: 20 December 2022
Published: 22 December 2022

1. Introduction

The global population is rapidly aging. In Hong Kong, 2.37 million (31.1%) people will be aged 65 or over in 2036 [1]. In 2016, about 150,000 older adults in Hong Kong lived alone, and almost 300,000 lived with their older spouse [2]. Living alone or with a spouse (who is also an older adult) may exacerbate loneliness in old age [3]. Moreover, 75% of older adults and 45% of soon-to-be-aged (aged 45 to 64) people in Hong Kong were suffering from one or more chronic diseases [4]. It is well reported that older adults are vulnerable to loneliness due to health deterioration and age-related losses, which prevent them from participating in social activities and engaging in interpersonal relationships [5].

In the concept of healthy aging, person-centered holistic care highlights the importance of enabling older people and their significant others (e.g., older spouses or other family caregivers) to establish healthy relationships so as to improve older adults' physical and psychosocial wellbeing [6]. Daily communication within the family and with friends is crucial for older people and this is impactful on their psychological and mental health [6]. Given the complexity of providing care to older adults living alone at home, which typically involves family companionship or social connection, personalized services such as healthy lifestyle promotion, chronic disease management, and adopting and integrating robotic technology in home-based aging care, seems to be reasonable and potentially benefits the older people [7]. Researchers have been exploring ways to utilize different robotic technologies to help and provide care for older adults, particularly socially-assistive robots, which are used to assist older adults with specific physical tasks and meet social and psychological needs [8,9]. Social robots are designed to interact autonomously with people through various application features which adopt the same repertoire of social signals used by humans [10]. Studies suggest that social robots contribute to the reduction of loneliness and social isolation in old age and become a kind of social capital in their homes [11,12]. For example, the Japanese-made baby seal shape *Paro* was tested in cognitively impaired individuals and was found to significantly reduce negative emotions and behavioral symptoms, and improve social engagement and the quality of life of older participants [9,13,14].

There were numerous clinical trials on the application of robots in aged care, in particular for people with dementia and those who are living in residential care facilities [15]. Research on home-based robotic support is very limited. Robotic pets were tested among community-dwelling older adults in New York and suggested that it could be an effective solution for alleviating loneliness in older adults, especially among those who live alone, have fewer social connections, and live less active lifestyles [16]. A recent study showed that older Chinese adults were highly interested in having social robots during dining and entertainment in home-based aged care [17]. However, more evidence is needed to examine the acceptance and feasibility of a social robot at home [18]. Especially whether older adults, their spouses, or other family caregivers at their homes accept, use, and even live with a robot. Their experiences and perspectives on using robots are important to determine the use of technology in supporting ageing-in-place. Therefore, the aim of these case studies was to understand the experiences and perspectives of older adults and their family caregivers on using a humanoid social robot over a two week period at home and to explore the potential benefits and barriers of human-robot interactions at home.

2. Materials and Methods

2.1. Description of the Humanoid Social Robots

The main platform utilized in this study was the robotic-mediated interactive system embedded in a humanoid social robot called *Ka Ka*, which is around 30 cm tall, 20 cm wide, and weighted 2 kg (Figure 1). This robot is designed in a way that it simulates human-robot interactions with a human voice from the robot responding to a human's verbal instructions or initiating conversations by the robot to a human at a specific time. This cultivates an environment for human-robot interactions and human-human interactions via the robot. There are many features in this robot. However, for the sake of testing the acceptance of the robots by older people, we minimize the features of the robot in this study. Four features were selected based on the findings of the literature review as well as the comments from the potential users of the robot (the community-dwelling older adults): (1) interactive modalities, (2) calendar planning and task reminder, (3) promoting healthy lifestyle, and (4) puzzle games. The interactive modalities allow older people to listen to music, stories, weather reports, and the news, and this is initiated by voice commands (that is, older people instruct the robots to turn on the music players by saying '*Ka Ka*, listen to Teresa Teng [a pop singer who sang Chinese songs in 1970s]'. Using the feature 'calendar planning and task reminder', older adults received voice reminders from the robot for the scheduled important events (such as meeting friends on 12 September 2022 at 10 am) and health-related activities (such as taking medicines at 11am, drinking water, and doing exercise). Moreover, schedules can be set up in the robots to guide older adults when and how to work out (doing stretching exercise). The robot also provides puzzle games and quizzes for older adults to stimulate and practice their cognitive functioning.

Figure 1. The participant was engaging with *Ka Ka* at home.

2.2. Recruitment

Purposive sampling was adopted in study recruitment. Advertisements (in Chinese) were distributed in media and community elderly centers. Those who were interested in participating in the study were directed to contact the study team. People with different genders, ages, educational backgrounds, and occupations were included to reflect a diversity of views. The inclusion criteria for older adults were (1) ethnic Chinese aged 60 years and above, (2) need home-based care/assistance from family caregivers, including spouse, (3) live with a family caregiver in the same household or in another household but with regular contacts (at least once per week), and (4) are able to communicate in Cantonese or Putonghua. The exclusion criteria were those with (1) acute mental illness (such as PTSD) or severe physical disabilities (such as cerebral palsy), and (2) those who have limited access to electricity and no Wi-Fi at home. HKD$200 (~U$26) supermarket shopping vouchers were provided to each participant as incentives to compensate the time they spent on interviews after using the robot.

2.3. Ethical Approval

We obtained ethics approval from the Human Subjects Ethics Sub-committee of the [anonymized] University (Reference No. HSEARS20220113001). An information sheet was provided to participants and written consent was gained before commencing data collection. The purpose and methods used in the study were explained to them. Pseudonyms were used in the reporting of findings to protect the confidentiality of participants.

2.4. Robot Set-Up

For the sake of personalized the features of the robot, we collected information about the preference of the user (older adult). For example, the older adult's profile, favorite songs, and important events (including the time to take medicines and the date for next medical appointment). All information was installed into the robots through the *Aged Care* app (see Figure 2). To increase the affiliation with the robot, we introduce the robots to the older adults/family caregivers by naming *'Ka Ka'* which is a common name in Chinese society. Older adults/family caregivers were encouraged to update and manage the calendar reminder by themselves. When setting up *Ka Ka* at home, we carefully assessed the environment, older adults' daily activities and preferences, and we identified a safe and comfortable place together with the older adult/family caregiver to make *Ka Ka* visible and accessible to the users.

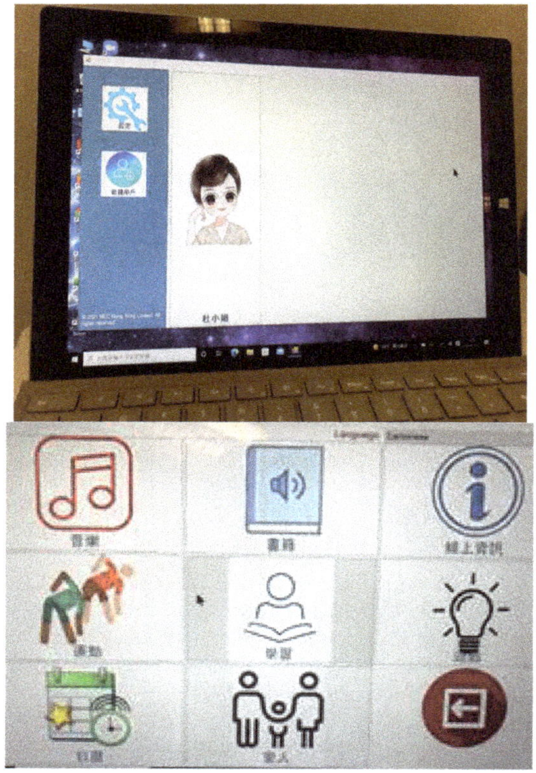

Figure 2. The *Aged Care* app captures the older person's preferences in music, books, news reading, physical activities and the family members' contacts.

2.5. Train Older Adults and Family Caregivers

We provided on-site training and showed older adults and family caregivers how to operate *Ka Ka* through verbal commands and how to update the calendar through the *Aged Care* app. We set up a technical support hotline so that older adults can easily contact the technical support team at any time. If necessary, the technical support team paid home visits to solve the technical issues.

2.6. Data Collection

We encouraged each older adult engage with different features of *Ka Ka* every day for 2 weeks. Login frequency and duration of the human-robot interaction was collected in the backend management system. We utilized the data to examine older adults' engagement with the robot and preference of specific features. Upon completion of the 2-week trial, we conducted individual face-to-face interviews with the older adults at their home and telephone-interviews with the family caregivers. We selected a qualitative descriptive methodology, which enabled participants to describe their experiences of engaging with *Ka Ka* in their own language [19]. Each interview lasted for approximately 20 min and all of them were digitally recorded. Semi-structured interview guidelines for older adults and family caregivers were developed and derived from the literature (Table 1).

Table 1. Interview guide for older adults and family caregivers.

No.	Interview Guide for Older Adults
1	What is your experience when the robot is placed at your home? (can you tell me how you think about this robot, which feature do you think is the most helpful and which one is not very helpful)?
2	What do you think about the acceptability or satisfaction of using the robot at home?
3	Do you think the robot can be used as part of your daily life activities? How does the robot help you in daily life?
4	Do you think the robot is easy to use? What are the difficulties when you are using it?
5	Have you tried to use the robot to contact other people? How do you feel about it? Do you think you would like to keep this robot at home in the future (shall we give this kind of robot to other older people living by themselves)?
No.	**Interview Guide for Family Caregivers**
1	What do you observe when the robot is placed at your mum's/dad's home?
2	Which features do you consider as helpful to your mum/dad/spouse?
3	Did the robot help to promoteyour relationship with your mum/dad/spouse?
4	What other features should be included into this kind of robot?
5	Do you think the robot is suitable for older people living alone at home?

2.7. Data Analysis

Descriptive statistics were utilized to summarize the sociodemographic characteristics of older adults and the human-robot interaction. Descriptive data were presented in frequency (n) and percentage (%). Interviews were transcribed verbatim by a trained research assistant and independently checked by the project team. Thematic coding and content analysis were undertaken independently by two project team members to inductively explore older adults and family caregivers' experiences of engaging with the robot *Ka Ka* at home [20]. An audit of 15% of the coded segments was performed, discussions were made, and agreements were reached.

2.8. Rigor

Rigor was established through credibility, confirmability, and transferability [20]. The interviewers were young adults, trained registered nurses, familiar with *Ka Ka*, and situated themselves as outsiders throughout the interview sessions. To achieve credibility, they bracketed themselves and did not assume how acceptable or user-friendly *Ka Ka* was and held frequent debriefing meetings and encouraged peer scrutiny to reflect on their positioning [21]. Secondly, data sources triangulation (collected data form older adults and their family caregivers) were carried out to gain multiple perspectives in the study [22]. Confirmability was established by recording coding and further supporting quotations from participants for each theme. Transferability was achieved by providing a detailed study design and process to enable readers to understand the findings from the dataset.

3. Results

3.1. Case Information

Four older adults completed this 2-week trial. Case 1 was an 81-year-old woman who lived alone and independently at home. She spent most of her time at home by herself. Her favourite things to do every day at home were to watch TV and listen to a radio station. Her daughter, who lived in another flat in the same neighbourhood, visited her every day. She was concerned about changes in her mother's memory and the lack of external stimulus to her which may have impacts on brain activities. Case 2 was a 76-year-old woman, living by herself at home. Her husband lived in a local nursing home, but she has not seen him in person for a long time due to the COVID-19 visitor restriction policy. She participated in community and church group activities actively. She was well-connected with her daughter, who provided regular visits and assistance with domestic matters. Case 3 was an 86-year-old woman living alone in a retirement village. She had worked and lived in the United States before she retired. She sometimes joined activities arranged by the retirement village. She showed her worries about using a laptop and the internet. Case 4 was a 65-year-old man living with his spouse. This couple support and look after each other. They used to have a dog as a pet but they lost it. They still missed the dog's companion and kept its photos at home. Due to the social distancing of the COVID-19 pandemic, they mostly stayed at home. See Table 2 for the detailed demographic information of the participants.

Table 2. The demographics of the participants.

	Case 1	Case 2	Case 3	Case 4
Age	81	76	86	65
Gender	Female	Female	Female	Male
Living status	Living alone	Living alone	Living alone	Living with spouse
Occupation	Retired	Retired	Retired	Retired
Marital status	Widowed	Married	Widowed	Married
Education level	Primary	Primary	Secondary	Secondary

3.2. Interaction with the Robot in Two Weeks

We collected data on the engagement with *Ka Ka* by the participants (see Figure 3). Records from the robotic system showed that older adults used the features of *Ka Ka* every day, but the frequency of human-robot interaction varied, ranging from 2 to 26 times per older adult per day. A total of 506 human-robot interactions were recorded in these two weeks (with an average of 126 interactions per older adult). There was a significant increase in human-robot interactions in the last two days of the trial.

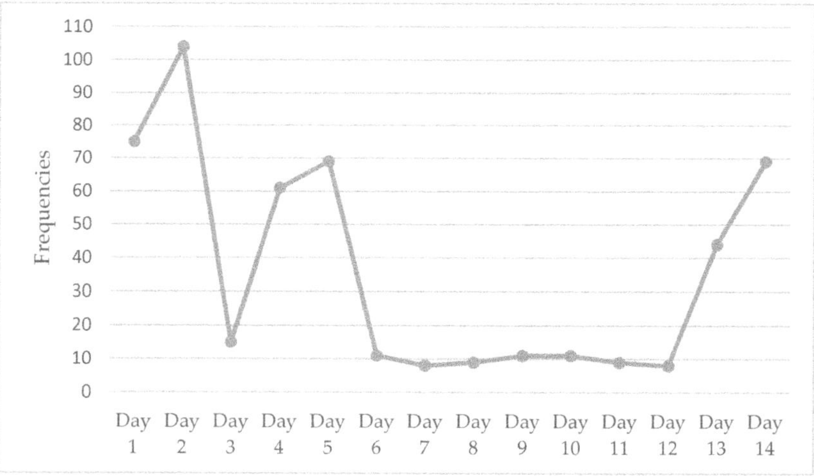

Figure 3. Frequencies of human-robot interactions in two weeks.

Figure 4 shows the timeslots of participants interacted with *Ka Ka* in a typical day. A general timeframe for human-robot interactions was from 6:00 AM to 8:00 PM. All participants preferred to interact with *Ka Ka* from 2:00 PM to 5:00 PM. Other two peak time slots were from 8:00 AM to 1:00 PM and from 7:00 PM to 8:00 PM, respectively. The majority of the participants stopped interacting with *Ka Ka* after 9:00 PM.

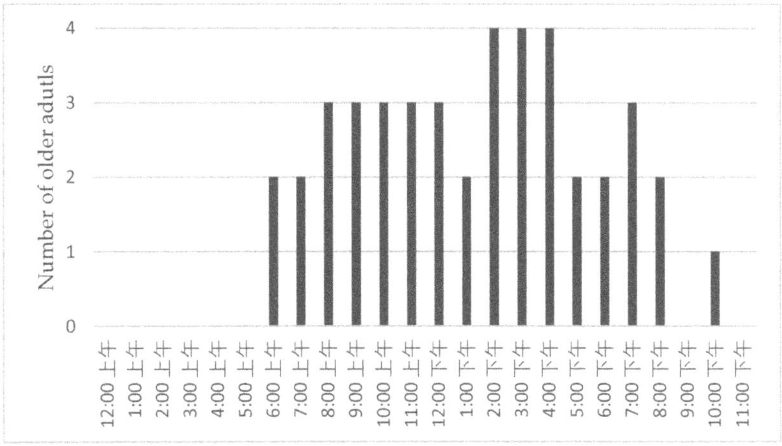

Figure 4. Older adults' interaction with *Ka Ka* during a typical day.

'Talking to *Ka Ka*', 'listening to music', calendar reminders, and weather report were the most commonly used features. All participants listened to music via *Ka Ka,* although the frequency varied across the participants. Two participants (50%) listened to the stories and only one watched the videos in *Ka Ka* on how to do physical exercise. Figure 5 shows the frequencies of use in each feature of the robot by the four participants in two weeks.

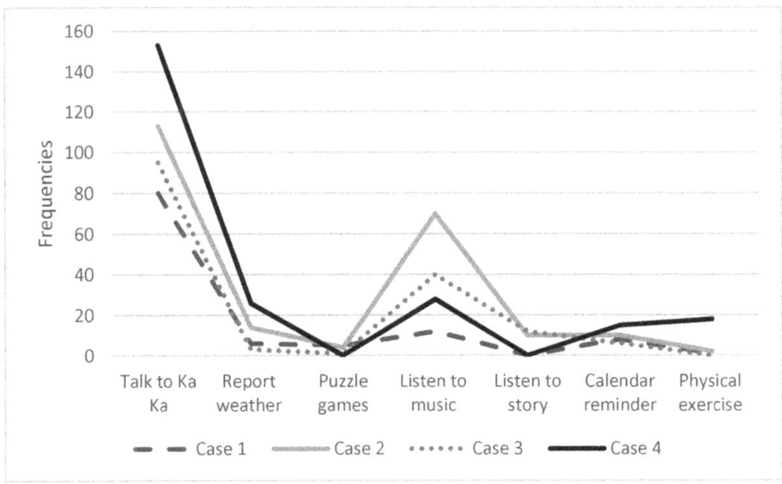

Figure 5. The use of different features by the four older adults over two weeks.

3.3. *Qualitative Findings*

Three key benefits and two aspects for improvement were identified in the qualitative interviews. The strengths of *Ka Ka* include providing emotional support to older adults living alone, diversifying older people's daily activities, and enhancing the dyadic relationship between older adults and family caregivers.

3.3.1. Providing Emotional Support to Older Adults Living Alone

The utilization of *Ka Ka* was reported to reduce feelings of loneliness and boredom among older adults living alone. As a family caregiver stated: *'having a short conversation with Ka Ka, even just asking Ka Ka to report weather could be a kind of external stimulation for my mother and this probably reduces her feelings of loneliness'* (Family caregiver 1). Verbal interactions with *Ka Ka* provided older people with a sense of warmth and encouraged older people to live more actively, especially for the older people who did not have any friends and were unwilling to socialize with others or had no hobbies. An older lady expressed her experience as *'Ka Ka reminded me to eat food every day, which made me feel so warm. I am happy to follow Ka Ka's reminder'* (Case 2). One older man appraised *Ka Ka* as *'a family member'* because it played a companion role in providing daily reminders and talking to him at any time. This benefit was expressed by both older men and his spouse as follows:

> *'Ka Ka presents an extra voice at our home. We regard Ka Ka as another family member'* (Case 4). *'Ka Ka's voice was soft and charming, which made us feel comfortable and calmed us. I think the female voice of robot is adorable. The reminder function is helpful for my husband's decreased memory.'* (Family caregiver 4)

3.3.2. Diversifying the Daily Activities of Older Adults

To the participants, *Ka Ka* was found to diversify and enrich the lives of older adults who live alone and improve their quality of life. *Ka Ka* as a platform provides different categories of audio and videos, covering music, voice-led physical exercises, voice-led interactive puzzle games, and storytelling. Older adults can ask *Ka Ka* to play a song directly through verbal command, which is considered 'simple and convenient'. In addition, *Ka Ka* has functions such as reporting daily news and weather forecasts. One older adults described:

> *'I am highly satisfied with the music function, and I used it every day'* (Case 1); *'I followed the video to do some physical exercises every day. Ka Ka even encouraged me and cheered me up when I was doing it'* (Case 2); and *'I found that the news reported by Ka Ka was the timely ones, which is useful for me to know what has happened in the community.'* (Family caregiver 4).

3.3.3. Enhancing the Dyadic Relationship between Older Adults and Family Caregivers

Some family caregivers indicated that they received direct benefits from the utilization of and interaction with *Ka Ka*. To them, *Ka Ka* is a channel to enhance the dyadic relationship between older adults and family caregivers. In the interviews, some family caregivers asserted that they worked with their care recipients (older adults) to explore how to interact *Ka Ka* (make Ka Ka react with them), discuss the functions in *Ka Ka*, share their experiences of engagement with *Ka Ka* and find out solutions to issues, if any. The mutual relationship was improved by sharing experiences and having more common languages. As one older adult asserted:

> *'Ka Ka has amplified my conversations with my wife'* (Case 4). A family caregiver also *shared* that *'Ka Ka is a new member, and it has become a new and common topic among the family members'* (Family caregiver 4).

3.4. Two Aspects for Improvement in the Design of the Robot

Older adults and family caregivers suggested two main aspects of design that could be improved to enhance the acceptability of robots at home. They raised a connection issue between the robot and tablet, hoping that the robot can be more user-friendly and its response to a human could be enhanced.

3.4.1. Connection between Robots and Tablets

Ka Ka does not have a monitor; therefore, it is connected to a tablet or a laptop so that pictures or videos could be shown to the robot users. Some older adults criticized that such an external device was inconvenient to them. On a few occasions, *Ka Ka* and the laptops/tablets were disconnected, and the older adults were very worried. As the older adults and their family caregivers stated:

> *'The connection with a laptop made it quite hard for me to use it.'* (Case 3)

> *'My mom tried her best to explore the features of robot; however, I felt there were too many technical issues for her to handle.'* (Family caregiver 2)

Technical issues related to the robot seem to be a concern to the participants. Some participants suggested connecting the robot with a phone or web-based application rather than a laptop or tablet, as they felt that they were more familiar with their own mobile phone than a laptop.

3.4.2. Enhancing Robot's Response to Human

Another suggestion was to enhance *Ka Ka*'s ability to respond to humans' verbal commands. Older adults expected *Ka Ka* to be *'smarter'* and be able to respond to their questions instantly. Some older adults indicated that the voice volume of *Ka Ka* was not loud enough, and they have difficulties hearing what *Ka Ka* said. Another older adult wished that *Ka Ka* could be moveable in the future so that they can hear *Ka Ka*'s voice in another room.

Older adults wanted *Ka Ka* to help them in their daily lives as if it was a private secretary (e.g., scheduling daily activities for them and reminding them to take medicine), or serve as an encyclopedia where they could easily find information. As two older adults expressed their expectations:

> *'I hope Ka Ka can entertain my life but also help me with household chores, read stories or long novels for me'* (Case 3).

> *'I hope the robot can remind older adults about health and safety matters, such as take medicine, measure blood pressure . . . , in a timely manner. She could remind me turn off the gas fire and electrical appliances'* (Case 4).

Although older adults expressed their wishes to involve *Ka Ka* in their daily lives, one family caregiver (Case 4) exclaimed that *'the feeling of freshness with a robot could last for one week maximum'*.

4. Discussion

This study provided evidence of the presence of a humanoid social robot *Ka Ka* at home for four older adults. This contributes to the limited knowledge we have in the field of gerontechnology and social robotics in a home-based setting. We found that older adults interacted with *Ka Ka* every day during the whole study period, continuously engaging with *Ka Ka* as if it is one of the family members at home. Both older adults and family caregivers agreed that *Ka Ka* was a good companion for older adults at home, and they expected some other features that can support older adults living alone or only with their spouses. This finding was consistent with the finding of a cross-sectional study in which 67% of the Chinese immigrants (including older adults) who felt lonely accepted the companionship of robots and considered technology as a way to alleviate loneliness [7].

The participants in this study indicated positively with regard to the feasibility and usability of *Ka Ka* in their own homes, which was aligned with a recent scoping review that older adults reported good feasibility and usability of using social robots in care home settings [23]. According to a recent systematic review, acceptance of social robots in healthcare was found to be mixed and can vary considerably in relation to the function and appearance of the robot [24]. The use of artificial intelligent (AI) in social robots is uncommon. Previous studies only reported the use of AI in diagnostic procedures like AI olfactory systems or medical images [25,26]. The current study added our new understanding of the feasibility of using technology to support older adults in real-life settings (their own homes) where no professionals are available. The interaction with the robot solely rests on older adults' self-initiatives or the pre-set timer when the robot talks to the older adults at specific time (such as reminding them to take medications or take their breakfast). Such interactions are valuable to older adults who live alone by themselves or with their spouses, because the robot act as a member of the family. The personalized feature of *Ka Ka*, such as calendar planning and reminders, was helpful in supporting older adults' daily home life. It was beyond the function of companion robots (such as *Paro*) in which Paro's companions were evidenced to reduce older people's emotional loneliness effectively [11]. As medication adherence and good nutritional intake are two big issues in aged care, *Ka Ka* seems to play an important role in these particular aspects of care.

While identifying various benefits of social robots for therapies or companionships [27], previous studies also pointed out that social robots could never replace human presence, especially their family members [28]. A recent experimental study provided evidence that our brain reacted differently in human-human and human-robot eye contact [29], indicating that humans can easily distinguish communication with social robots from humans. Nonetheless, social robots could be an option when human-being care is not available. The contradiction could be overcome by personalizing the older adult's real situations.

In this study, the most frequently used features of *Ka Ka* were verbal interactions and playing music. One possible reason was that older people can instruct the robot through verbal commands, which fits older people's abilities. They found that the feature of verbal interaction and listening to music was easy to access. This was consistent with a previous study that many older people did not prefer text messaging due to their lower writing ability than the younger generation [30]. The interaction of older adults with robots was reported to require effective verbal feedback, which was significantly preferable and increased the engagement with the robot of the older participants [31]. The second reason was that verbal interactions with and remainders from *Ka Ka* played an essential role in providing emotional support to older adults in this study, particularly those living alone at home. The qualitative interview suggested that *Ka Ka* enriched the daily activities of older adults who lived alone and spent most of their time at home watching TV or listening to radio stations. A novel finding of this study was that the robot's voice (female, soft, and pleasing to the ear) could also bring a pleasant feeling to older adults. An older adult and his family caregiver regarded *Ka Ka* as a family member due to the voice of a *'new member'* presented at home. An emotional tie was built up among them, and they even wanted to keep the robot for a longer time. The finding that *Ka Ka* might positively impact upon the person's mood is consistent with previous studies concluding that social robot-mediated intervention was promising to improve interaction/engagement and reduce loneliness and depressive symptoms for older adults [15]. The last possible reason was that personalized content in the robot enhanced its usage. For example, the songs were prepared according to the users' recommendations and preferences. Except for offering some entertainment value, the personalized robot features could create some feelings of being cared for by older adults [23].

We have observed that the frequencies of engagement with *Ka Ka* were comparatively high during the first week and the last two days when we contacted older adults to schedule a time to complete the study and return the robot to the research team. Older adults seem to engage with *Ka Ka* in a regular manner, usually in the morning after breakfast and in the afternoon between lunch and dinner. We found that older people were more likely to follow a stable and fixed rhythm of life. They seemed to use features of verbal communication and listening to music more frequently during this time to fill their spare time. Moreover, some older adults showed activity when we contacted them but became passive afterwards in using *Ka Ka*, and this pattern was consistent to previous studies that technology-related fear might inhibit older people to engage with technologies [32,33]. The fear includes the possibility that technology may be hard or impractical to use, the possible negative effects of sensor radio waves on their personal health, and that extra burden may be brought to their adult children [33]. We have observed a fear of breaking the robot as indicated by an older adult at the time when we intend to recruit her to the study. Two older adults in this study expressed their barriers to using the laptop connecting to the robot. In future studies, more attention should be paid to supporting their acceptance through hands-on training and providing a clear user guide to meet their unique personal needs [34].

Hearing ability may affect the use of robots at home. We found that older adults in this study had different requirements on the voice volume of *Ka Ka* due age-related hearing loss problems. A cross-sectional study in Hong Kong reported that about 28% of older adults living in the community had hearing impairments [35]. It suggests that hearing, as well as other sensory function changes, should be considered by robot designers.

Although *Ka Ka* has artificial intelligence, its responses are based on a verbal command database and this can only be enriched by frequent interactions with humans. *Ka Ka* is the first Cantonese-speaking humanoid robot, and this first trial inspires the subsequent establishment of a verbal command database in the Cantonese-speaking community. A further study is needed to examine the research gap in science and inform subsequent robotic development works.

Limitations

There are some limitations of this study. First, users' experiences might have been disturbed by technical issues and Chinese older adults may have had hesitations about contacting the project team for concern of 'botheriing' others. The challenges in technology may hinder older adults from using the robots. Second, this sample cannot represent the heterogeneous aging population, as we only have four cases in this study. Further investigation should be made with more people with different age ranges, socioeconomic status, and cognitive levels. Moreover, due to the 'Hawthorne' effect [36], participants might modify their behaviours or performance when they are aware that they are being observed. To avoid this effect, establishing rapport and making the subjects feel relaxed in the presence of a participant observer are warranted in future studies. Third, the involvement of family caregivers is limited in this study and cannot represent all caregivers. The current findings should be considered as exemplars. It remains unclear if the results could be applied to other aged populations in Chinese society. Further research is clearly necessary.

5. Conclusions

Older adults and family caregivers in this study were open to the use of social robots in their daily lives. In order to support aging-in-place and fill the gaps of intensified shortage of health and social manpower, it is of prime importance to develop reliable and age-friendly robotic services that are tailored based on the needs and preferences of an older adult.

Author Contributions: Conceptualization, A.Y.M.L. and I.Y.Z.; methodology, A.Y.M.L. and I.Y.Z.; validation, A.Y.M.L., I.Y.Z. and S.L.; formal analysis, A.Y.M.L., I.Y.Z. and S.L.; investigation, A.Y.M.L., I.Y.Z. and T.K.L.; writing—original draft preparation, I.Y.Z. and S.L.; writing—review and editing, A.Y.M.L., I.Y.Z., S.L. and T.K.L.; funding acquisition, A.Y.M.L. All authors have read and agreed to the published version of the manuscript.

Funding: The robots were donated by the NEC Hong Kong Ltd. and the project was funded by Research Matching Grant Scheme (RMGS) offered by the Hong Kong University Grants Committee (ref. no.: P0041148).

Institutional Review Board Statement: The study was approved by the Human Subjects Ethics Sub-committee of the Hong Kong Polytechnic University (Reference No. HSEARS20220113001).

Informed Consent Statement: Informed consent was obtained from all subjects involved in the study.

Data Availability Statement: Data is available per requisition.

Acknowledgments: Special thank goes to Elsa Wong (NEC HK) and Kelvin Chan (NEC HK) for their full support and cooperation in investigations and to Sally Lay (NEC HK) for technical support to the project. The authors also thank the Hong Kong University Grants Committee for financial support and the participants who shared their experiences.

Conflicts of Interest: The authors declare no conflict of interest. The funders had no role in the design of the study; in the collection, analyses, or interpretation of data; in the writing of the manuscript; or in the decision to publish the results.

References

1. Census and Statistics Department. Hong Kong Population Projections for 2017 to 2066. Hong Kong, 2017. Available online: https://www.censtatd.gov.hk/en/EIndexbySubject.html?pcode=FA100061&scode=190 (accessed on 19 September 2022).
2. Census and Statistics Department. Snapshot of the Hong Kong Population. Hong Kong, 2016. Available online: https://www.bycensus2016.gov.hk/en/Snapshot-04.html (accessed on 19 September 2022).
3. O'Súilleabháin, P.S.; Gallagher, S.; Steptoe, A. Loneliness, Living Alone, and All-Cause Mortality: The Role of Emotional and Social Loneliness in the Elderly During 19 Years of Follow-Up. *Psychosom. Med.* **2019**, *81*, 521–526. [CrossRef]
4. Elderly Commission. Report on Healthy Ageing Executive Summary 2021. Hong Kong, 2021. Available online: https://www.elderlycommission.gov.hk/en/library/Ex-sum.htm (accessed on 19 September 2022).
5. Gasteiger, N.; Ahn, H.S.; Fok, C.; Lim, J.Y.; Lee, C.; MacDonald, B.A.; Kim, G.H.; Broadbent, E. Older adults' experiences and perceptions of living with Bomy, an assistive dailycare robot: A qualitative study. *Assist. Technol.* **2022**, *34*, 487–497. [CrossRef] [PubMed]
6. He, A.J.; Tang, V.F.Y. Integration of health services for the elderly in Asia: A scoping review of Hong Kong, Singapore, Malaysia, Indonesia. *Health Policy* **2021**, *125*, 351–362. [CrossRef] [PubMed]
7. Chiu, C.J.; Lo, Y.H.; Ho, M.H.; Montayre, J.; Zhao, I.Y. Association between loneliness and acceptance of using robots and pets as companions among older Chinese immigrants during the COVID-19 pandemic. *Australas. J. Ageing* **2022**, *41*, 414–423. [CrossRef] [PubMed]
8. Henschel, A.; Laban, G.; Cross, E.S. What Makes a Robot Social? A Review of Social Robots from Science Fiction to a Home or Hospital Near You. *Curr. Robot. Rep.* **2021**, *2*, 9–19. [CrossRef]
9. Hung, L.; Liu, C.; Woldum, E.; Au-Yeung, A.; Berndt, A.; Wallsworth, C.; Horne, N.; Gregorio, M.; Mann, J.; Chaudhury, H. The benefits of and barriers to using a social robot PARO in care settings: A scoping review. *BMC Geriatr.* **2019**, *19*, 232. [CrossRef]
10. Vollmer, A.L.; Read, R.; Belpaeme, T. Children conform, adults resist: A robot group induced peer pressure on normative social conformity. *Sci. Robot.* **2018**, *3*, eaat7111. [CrossRef]
11. Chen, S.C.; Moyle, W.; Jones, C.; Petsky, H. A social robot intervention on depression, loneliness, and quality of life for Taiwanese older adults in long-term care. *Int. Psychogeriatr.* **2020**, *32*, 981–991. [CrossRef]
12. Barbosa Neves, B.; Franz, R.; Judges, R.; Beermann, C.; Baecker, R. Can Digital Technology Enhance Social Connectedness Among Older Adults? A Feasibility Study. *J. Appl. Gerontol.* **2019**, *38*, 49–72. [CrossRef]
13. Shibata, T.; Hung, L.; Petersen, S.; Darling, K.; Inoue, K.; Martyn, K.; Hori, Y.; Lane, G.; Park, D.; Mizoguchi, R.; et al. Paro as a biofeedback medical device for mental health in the COVID-19 era. *Sustainability* **2021**, *13*, 11502. [CrossRef]
14. Wang, X.; Shen, J.; Chen, Q. How PARO can help older people in elderly care facilities: A systematic review of RCT. *Int. J. Nurs. Knowl.* **2022**, *33*, 29–39. [CrossRef] [PubMed]
15. Pu, L.H.; Moyle, W.; Jones, C.; Todorovic, M. The Effectiveness of Social Robots for Older Adults: A Systematic Review and Meta-Analysis of Randomized Controlled Studies. *Gerontologist* **2019**, *59*, e37–e51. [CrossRef] [PubMed]
16. Hudson, J.; Ungar, R.; Albright, L.; Tkatch, R.; Schaeffer, J.; Wicker, E.R. Robotic pet use among community-dwelling older adults. *J. Gerontol. Ser. B* **2020**, *75*, 2018–2028. [CrossRef] [PubMed]
17. Chen, N.; Song, J.; Li, B. Providing Aging Adults Social Robots' Companionship in Home-Based Elder Care. *J. Healthc. Eng.* **2019**, *2019*, 2726837. [CrossRef] [PubMed]
18. Leung, L. Validity, reliability, and generalizability in qualitative research. *J. Fam. Med. Prim. Care* **2015**, *4*, 324–327. [CrossRef] [PubMed]
19. Sandelowski, M. What's in a name? Qualitative description revisited. *Res. Nurs. Health* **2010**, *33*, 77–84. [CrossRef]
20. Klimova, B.; Poulova, P. Older people and technology acceptance. In *Human Aspects of IT for the Aged Population. Acceptance, Communication and. Participation (ITAP 2018)*; Lecture Notes in Computer Science; Zhou, J., Salvendy, G., Eds.; Springer: Cham, Switzerland, 2018; Volume 10926.
21. Shenton, A.K. Strategies for Ensuring Trustworthiness in Qualitative Research Projects. *Educ. Inf.* **2004**, *22*, 63–75. [CrossRef]
22. Moon, M.D. Triangulation: A Method to Increase Validity, Reliability, and Legitimation in Clinical Research. *J. Emerg. Nurs.* **2019**, *45*, 103–105. [CrossRef]
23. Mahmoudi Asl, A.; Molinari Ulate, M.; Franco Martin, M.; van der Roest, H. Methodologies Used to Study the Feasibility, Usability, Efficacy, and Effectiveness of Social Robots For Elderly Adults: Scoping Review. *J. Med. Internet Res.* **2022**, *24*, e37434. [CrossRef]
24. Naneva, S.; Sarda Gou, M.; Webb, T.L.; Prescott, T.J. A Systematic Review of Attitudes, Anxiety, Acceptance, and Trust Towards Social Robots. *Int. J. Soc. Robot.* **2020**, *12*, 1179–1201. [CrossRef]
25. Fu, W.; Xu, L.; Yu, Q.; Fang, J.; Zhao, G.; Li, Y.; Pan, C.; Dong, H.; Wang, D.; Ren, H.; et al. Artificial Intelligent Olfactory System for the Diagnosis of Parkinson's Disease. *ACS Omega* **2022**, *7*, 4001–4010. [CrossRef] [PubMed]
26. Pang, S.; Wang, S.; Rodríguez-Patón, A.; Li, P.; Wang, X. An artificial intelligent diagnostic system on mobile Android terminals for cholelithiasis by lightweight convolutional neural network. *PLoS ONE* **2019**, *14*, e0221720. [CrossRef] [PubMed]
27. Belpaeme, T.; Kennedy, J.; Ramachandran, A.; Scassellati, B.; Tanaka, F. Social robots for education: A review. *Sci. Robot.* **2018**, *3*, eaat5954. [CrossRef] [PubMed]

28. Niemelä, M.; Määttä, H.; Ylikauppila, M. Expectations and experiences of adopting robots in elderly care in Finland: Perspectives of caregivers and decision-makers. In Proceedings of the 4th International Conference on Serviceology, ICServ 2016, Tokyo, Japan, 6–8 September 2016; Society for Serviceology: Tokyo, Japan, 2016.
29. Kelley, M.S.; Noah, J.A.; Zhang, X.; Scassellati, B.; Hirsch, J. Comparison of Human Social Brain Activity During Eye-Contact With Another Human and a Humanoid Robot. *Front. Robot. AI* **2021**, *7*, 599581. [CrossRef] [PubMed]
30. Zhou, J.; Salvendy, G. Human aspects of IT for the aged population. In Proceedings of the Acceptance, Communication and Participation: 4th International Conference, ITAP 2018, Las Vegas, NV, USA, 15–20 July 2018.
31. Markfeld, N.; Olatunji, S.; Gutman, D.; Givati, S.; Sarne-Fleischmann, V.; Edan, Y. Feedback modalities for a table setting robot assistant for elder care. *arXiv* **2021**, arXiv:2103.08428. [CrossRef]
32. Chen, K.; Lou, V.W.; Tan, K.C.; Wai, M.; Chan, L. Changes in technology acceptance among older people with dementia: The role of social robot engagement. *Int. J. Med. Inform.* **2020**, *141*, 104241.
33. Peek, S.T.; Wouters, E.J.; van Hoof, J.; Luijkx, K.G.; Boeije, H.R.; Vrijhoef, H.J. Factors influencing acceptance of technology for aging in place: A systematic review. *Int. J. Med. Inform.* **2014**, *83*, 235–248. [CrossRef]
34. Bong, W.K.; Bergland, A.; Chen, W. Technology Acceptance and Quality of Life among Older People Using a TUI Application. *Int. J. Environ. Res. Public Health* **2019**, *16*, 4706. [CrossRef]
35. Leung, A.Y.M.; Su, J.J.; Lee, E.S.H.; Fung, J.T.S.; Molassiotis, A. Intrinsic capacity of older people in the community using WHO's Integrated Care for Older People (ICOPE) framework: A cross-sectional study. *BMC Geriatr.* **2022**, *22*, 304. [CrossRef]
36. McCarney, R.; Warner, J.; Iliffe, S.; van Haselen, R.; Griffin, M.; Fisher, P. The Hawthorne Effect: A randomised, controlled trial. *BMC Med. Res. Methodol.* **2007**, *7*, 30. [CrossRef]

healthcare

MDPI

Article

Clinical Decision Support Framework for Segmentation and Classification of Brain Tumor MRIs Using a U-Net and DCNN Cascaded Learning Algorithm

Nagwan Abdel Samee [1], Tahir Ahmad [2], Noha F. Mahmoud [3,*], Ghada Atteia [1,*], Hanaa A. Abdallah [1] and Atif Rizwan [4,*]

1 Department of Information Technology, College of Computer and Information Sciences, Princess Nourah bint Abdulrahman University, P.O. Box 84428, Riyadh 11671, Saudi Arabia
2 Department of Computer Science, COMSATS University Islamabad, Attock Campus, Attock 43600, Pakistan
3 Rehabilitation Sciences Department, Health and Rehabilitation Sciences College, Princess Nourah bint Abdulrahman University, P.O. Box 84428, Riyadh 11671, Saudi Arabia
4 Department of Computer Engineering, Jeju National University, Jejusi 63243, Republic of Korea
* Correspondence: nfmahmoud@pnu.edu.sa (N.F.M.); geatteiaallah@pnu.edu.sa (G.A.); atifrizwan@jejunu.ac.kr (A.R.)

Abstract: Brain tumors (BTs) are an uncommon but fatal kind of cancer. Therefore, the development of computer-aided diagnosis (CAD) systems for classifying brain tumors in magnetic resonance imaging (MRI) has been the subject of many research papers so far. However, research in this sector is still in its early stage. The ultimate goal of this research is to develop a lightweight effective implementation of the U-Net deep network for use in performing exact real-time segmentation. Moreover, a simplified deep convolutional neural network (DCNN) architecture for the BT classification is presented for automatic feature extraction and classification of the segmented regions of interest (ROIs). Five convolutional layers, rectified linear unit, normalization, and max-pooling layers make up the DCNN's proposed simplified architecture. The introduced method was verified on multimodal brain tumor segmentation (BRATS 2015) datasets. Our experimental results on BRATS 2015 acquired Dice similarity coefficient (DSC) scores, sensitivity, and classification accuracy of 88.8%, 89.4%, and 88.6% for high-grade gliomas. When it comes to segmenting BRATS 2015 BT images, the performance of our proposed CAD framework is on par with existing state-of-the-art methods. However, the accuracy achieved in this study for the classification of BT images has improved upon the accuracy reported in prior studies. Image classification accuracy for BRATS 2015 BT has been improved from 88% to 88.6%.

Keywords: clinical decision; U-Net; CNN; CAD system; brain tumor; classification; segmentation

Citation: Samee, N.A.; Ahmad, T.; Mahmoud, N.F.; Atteia, G.; Abdallah, H.A.; Rizwan, A. Clinical Decision Support Framework for Segmentation and Classification of Brain Tumor MRIs Using a U-Net and DCNN Cascaded Learning Algorithm. *Healthcare* **2022**, *10*, 2340. https://doi.org/10.3390/healthcare10122340

Academic Editors: Daniele Giansanti and Hermann Nabi

Received: 7 October 2022
Accepted: 15 November 2022
Published: 22 November 2022

1. Introduction

Multiple stakeholders are involved in providing intelligent healthcare, including medical professionals, patients, hospitals, and academic research institutions. It is an organic totality that incorporates numerous dimensions, such as the prevention and monitoring of diseases, the diagnosis and treatment of illnesses, the management of hospitals, the making of decisions regarding health care, and the conducting of medical research [1]. Smart healthcare employs technology such as wearable sensors, artificial intelligence, and the internet to dynamically access healthcare-related information. This information is then used to intelligently control and respond to medical ecosystem demands. Smart healthcare can encourage interaction among all healthcare stakeholders, ensuring that participants receive the services they require, assisting parties in making informed decisions, and facilitating the logical allocation of resources [2]. Smart healthcare's utilization of these technologies has the potential to drastically lower healthcare costs and risks while simultaneously making tailored medical treatment the norm [3]. Clinical decision support systems, disease prevention and risk monitoring, and patient self-management [4] are some examples of the services that may be provided by smart healthcare systems. Artificial intelligence (AI) has the ability to improve the quality and safety of clinical decision-making systems. Currently, AI is successfully integrated into decision support systems for diagnosis in data-intensive disciplines, such as pathology and radiology. These systems, which include computer-aided diagnosis systems for classifying lesions in a variety of diseases [5,6], are examples of the types of clinical applications that have recently benefited from the application of artificial intelligence.

Tumors of the central nervous system (CNS) are a form of cancer that are uncommon but deadly. These tumors frequently rob patients of their basic quality of life. Patients who have CNS tumors have a poor prognosis, notwithstanding the progress that has been made in our understanding of the disease processes that are associated with CNS tumors. In order to aid in the detection and treatment of CNS malignancies, improved techniques for characterization, diagnostics, and monitoring are required. Utilizing more recent imaging methods is an essential component of neuro-oncology's toolbox of available options for treatment. Magnetic resonance imaging and computed tomography (CT) are the two imaging techniques that are currently considered to be the best models for the radiographic evaluation of neuro-oncological diseases [7]. Imaging and computer-aided diagnosis systems in medicine assist in avoiding the need for diagnostic biopsies.

The early diagnosis of brain tumors not only saves lives but also reduces the likelihood of disability. With early detection, there will be less manipulation and surgical removal of tissue from the brain, the most delicate organ in the body [8]. The manual diagnosis of the condition requires a radiologist to record a 3D image for initial understanding. Then, a specialist is consulted for image analysis and treatment planning. As reported by Johnson et al. [9], examining the accuracy of manual brain tumor diagnosis indicates that expert reviewers differ. According to reports, between 90% and 95% of professionals agree on the diagnosis of a brain tumor manually. For multiclass classification, such as medulloblastoma, and glioma, the experts' agreement drops to 77% and 58%, respectively [9]. As a result, developing AI-based assistive tools for accurate detection of brain tumors is required.

MRI is recommended for the CAD system of brain tumors, because there is no risk of ionizing radiation and it can identify blood flow in veins correctly [10]. Several strategies for CAD systems for brain tumors have been developed in recent years, including conventional machine learning (ML) [11] and deep learning (DL) [12–14]. The identification, segmentation, and classification of brain tumors have been the focus of numerous research efforts to date, but studies in this field are only getting started. The comprehensive review conducted by Ali et al. [15] of the relevant literature revealed that deep learning technology ultimately produces fantastically realistic performances in the processing of brain tumor images. Classical machine learning, such as the support vector machine (SVM) is a dominant method for the classification of brain MRI. Deep learning algorithms, on the other hand, are the most successful, with deep convolutional neural networks leading the pack.

The primary modules of the CAD system for detecting brain cancers are image preprocessing and enhancement, brain skull stripping, brain tumor segmentation, feature extraction and selection, and classification of benign and malignant tumors [16–18]. The most crucial stage in the entire CAD system is brain image segmentation, which affects the yielded accuracy [19]. Image segmentation is the process of extracting regions of interest (ROIs) from 3D image data (MRI). The primary purpose of segmenting these data is to identify parts of the anatomy that are needed for a specific study [16]. Manual segmentation for a huge number of MRIs is time-consuming, but new advancements in AI techniques are making it quicker to execute regular tasks [20,21]. This study introduces deep learning-based automatic segmentation of brain MRI images for developing a computer-aided diagnosis of brain tumors—gliomas. Specifically, we propose a modified version of the U-Net convolutional neural network architecture that should improve the performance of automatic brain MRI segmentation. The architecture of U-Net convolutional neural networks has been used in this study since it has demonstrated superior performance in comparison to the present state of the art in the segmentation of MRI images [22]. The phase of image segmentation is preceded by automatic feature extraction and classification, both of which are accomplished through the utilization of a five-layer convolutional neural network.

This article proposes a lightweight, effective U-Net deep network implementation, with the ultimate goal being precise real-time segmentation. To do this, U-Net's input layer had to be modified to accommodate images of a smaller resolution. In contrast to the initial version of U-Net, where input images were always 572 by 572 pixels in size, we have used images as small as 32 × 32 pixels. The U-Net model accepts images of 32 × 32 pixels. The encoding part of the U-Net model decreases the pixels of the image and extracts tiny features from low-resolution images. The U-Net model, which consists of an encoder and a decoder, is utilized for the segmentation stage, while the CNN model is employed for the classification. We believe that our method is more efficient and less time-consuming than competing methods. Our approach was tested and proven accurate on a benchmarking dataset—BRATS 2015.

In order to highlight the significance of the work that we are introducing, the following is a list of the contributions provided by the present study:

- Introducing an enhanced lightweight and effective U-Net deep network architecture, with the ultimate goal being precise real-time segmentation of brain MRIs.
- A simplified CNN-based architecture for BT classification is presented for automatic feature extraction and classification of the extracted regions of interest.

The manuscript is organized as follows. Section 2 is devoted to the literature review. In Section 3, the suggested methodology, proposed framework, and description of the data used are provided. The findings are analyzed in Section 4. Sections 5 and 6 present the study's conclusion and suggestions for future research, respectively.

2. Literature Review

Healthcare organizations are starting to implement AI and related technologies, since they are becoming increasingly common in industry [23–27] and society broadly [28]. Many areas of patient care and administrative procedures within provider, payer, and pharmaceutical organizations stand to benefit from these innovations [29]. Medical diagnosis [30–32] is an area where numerous studies have shown AI to be on par with or even superior to human practitioners. ML/DL algorithms [33–35] are currently more accurate than radiologists in detecting cancerous tumors, and they are also helping researchers figure out how to build study populations for expensive clinical trials. Machine learning is a branch of AI that is dedicated to constructing methods that "learn from data to improve performance on some set of tasks." Machine learning is one of the most widespread types of AI: 63% of companies surveyed in 2018 [36] whose organizations were already pursuing AI used machine learning in their operations [26,29]. The most prevalent use of conventional machine learning in the healthcare field is precision medicine, which predicts the treatment protocols that are likely to be effective on a patient based on numerous patient traits and the treatment context [37]. The vast number of machine learning and precision medicine solutions need a training set with predefined outcome variables—supervised learning. The foundation of machine learning and deep learning in medical imaging is the artificial neural network (ANN). Layers of nodes in an ANN can range from the hundreds to the millions. Deep learning makes use of multilayered artificial neural networks (for example, >8), and is generally considered a more advanced version of ML that can analyze more data and sophisticated inputs [38]. Each node is fed by data from the other nodes, and the contributions of each node are taken into account when calculating the final score. When used properly, the ANN should increase the proportion of right responses.

Because of the increased computing power of today's graphics processing units (GPUs), such models may contain thousands or even tens of thousands of features that have been concealed from view. The detection of possibly malignant tumors in medical imagery is one of the most common applications of deep learning in the healthcare industry [6,39–45]. Radiomics, the detection of clinically significant patterns in imaging data that are invisible to the naked eye, is becoming an increasingly popular use of deep learning [46]. Oncology-specific image analysis typically employs both radiomics and deep learning. Together, they offer improved diagnostic precision and accuracy in CAD systems.

Many researchers have lately advocated the use of artificial intelligence to automatically discover and diagnose brain abnormalities in MRI scans. Table 1 summarizes the present state of the field and the weaknesses of each strategy based on recent research that has used ML/DL algorithms to detect brain cancers. The table helps to highlight the most important features of the new system. The table helps to highlight the most important features of the new system.

Amulya and Prathibha [47] proposed an ML-based method for distinguishing between tumors and non-tumors in brain MRI images by making use of a KNN machine learning algorithm and extracting features using scale invariant feature transform (SIFT) and speeded up robust features (SURF). They conducted their experiments on a total of 101 MRI scans obtained from the MR-TIP database. Accuracy was 94% when utilizing SURF alone and 96% when using SURF and SIFT together. They conducted experiments using several classifiers, including the fuzzy C-mean and SVM, but found that their own proposed technique yielded the best results overall. The detection of brain tumors using another classical ML-based method was introduced by Virupakshappa and Amarapur [48]. Gabor wavelets [49] and a statistical feature extraction method were used to extract the texture features. When separating objects, they turned to the fuzzy C-mean method. One hundred MRIs were utilized to evaluate the system, with sixty images used for testing and forty used for training. Artificial neural networks (ANNs) were used for tumor classification. The performance of the system was measured using precision, recall, and accuracy, with an overall accuracy of 85% being achieved in this study.

Raj et al. [50] have created a system for the classification of MRI obtained from District Hospital Palakkad, Department of Neurosurgery, India. They have applied four phases on the images: image preprocessing, segmentation, feature extraction and classification of brain tumors. For segmentation, they used K-means clustering. For feature extraction, the GLCM and Gabor filters were used, and KNN was used to classify brain tumors. The accuracy was determined by comparing the obtained results to ground truth values, and this study achieved 95% accuracy. Ahmet et al. used novel techniques for brain tumor detection [51]. The primary goal of this study was to clearly identify the tissue that had been damaged by cancer. For preprocessing, they used morphological operations. The threshold-based approach was used for segmentation, and the median filter was used for filtering. In this study, 100 MR images from the TCIA database were used. They achieved a 96% average accuracy. Devkota et al. [52] proposed a CAD method for early-stage detection of brain tumors. They segmented 19 brain MR images affected by four different types of tumors (glioma, metastatic adenocarcinoma, meningioma and sarcoma). The median filter was used for preprocessing, and Mathematical morphological operations were used for MR image segmentation. They classified brain tumors using SVM and achieved an accuracy of 92% on a small dataset.

The work done in [53] presented a framework for brain tumor classification in MRIs. For feature selection, they combined 2D DWT and 2D Gabor Filter techniques. Backpropagation neural network classifier was used to classify such tumors as meningioma, glioma, and pituitary. They used 3064 slices of T1-weighted MRI scans. They achieved an overall accuracy of 91.9% for meningioma, glioma, and pituitary. In [54], a novel method for brain tumor classification and segmentation using genetic algorithms was introduced. For preprocessing, adaptive constraint enhancement was used, and for enhancement, skull scripting was used. A total of 22 images from the DICOM dataset and 44 images from the web brain dataset were used in the analysis. They used various techniques in this paper, including watershed segmentation, FCM, direction cosine transform (DCT) segmentation, and bakery wavelet transform (BWT), and the technique with the highest segment score was chosen. They were 92.03% accurate.

Rajesh et al. proposed a new method for feature extraction based on rough set theory in [55]. For preprocessing, differential-based adaptive filtering (DAF) was used, and the region growing algorithm was used for segmentation. For classification, the PSONN technique was used. The MRI dataset comprised 90 MR images, 60 of which were tumorous and 30 of which were not. The data were obtained from the Government Medical College Hospital in Trivandrum, India. Sensitivity, specificity, and accuracy were used as evaluation metrics to assess the system's performance. They achieved a 96% accuracy rate. In [56], Shree et al. proposed a method for detecting brain tumors. PNN was used to classify tumors from MR images. In this study, two datasets were used: one for training and one for testing. The training dataset was obtained from the DIACOM website. They removed noise and smoothened the images during preprocessing. DWT was used for image decomposition, and GLCM was used to extract textural features. On the test dataset, 95% accuracy was achieved.

Recent research has shown that the CAD system for brain tumors can be much improved with the help of deep learning algorithms [57–65]. Brain images were classified into four types of tumors using a DCNN [66]. Fuzzy C-means was used to segment the images, and DWT was used to extract the features. PCA was used to reduce the features. The sevenfold cross-validation technique was used for classification and training of the seven-hidden-layer DNN model. The dataset used in this study comprised 66 brain MRIs with four types of brain tumors: normal, sarcoma, metastatic bronchogenic carcinoma, and glioblastoma. It was obtained from the website of Harvard Medical School. Recall, precision, F-measure, classification rate, and area under the curve were used to evaluate the proposed method's performance. They achieved an average classification rate of 97.96% for all four tumor classes. A CNN-based deep learning algorithm was used to classify tumor type from a collection of MRIs [67]. In this study, three different datasets were used: REMBRANDT from Cancer Imaging, Brain Images of Normal Subjects (BRAINS) Image Bank repository of the University of Edinburgh, and MIRIAD. The images are classified into five categories: astrocytoma, glioblastoma, oligodendroglioma, healthy tissue, and unknown tumor. The overall average F1 score was 99.46%. Jude et al. introduced a modified architecture of the DCNN model [68] for the classification of abnormal brain MRI scans. They used an assignment method for estimation of weights in the fully connected layer instead of gradient descent to update the weights, and modification in the conventional DCNN was performed in this layer. They used 220 brain MR scans that were obtained from M/s. Devaki Scan Centre in order to carry out the experiment, and as a result, they were able to achieve an accuracy rate of 96.4%.

We have compared the proposed U-Net–CNN approach to other studies that have used the same dataset, BRATS 2015, to better illustrate the unique features of our proposed end-to-end segmentation and classification system for brain tumor MRIs. With this, we were able to gauge the significance of the U-Net–CNN method. BRATS 2015 is a challenging dataset encompassing many types of brain MR images. The BRATS challenge was held in connection with an international conference on medical image computing (MICCAI) to assess the present state of the art in automatic BT segmentation and to compare alternative methodologies. The BRATS dataset was generated for this aim as a one-of-a-kind collection of MR scans of LGG and HGG glioma patients with successive manual tumor categorizations by different human experts. Quantitative assessments demonstrated significant disagreement among human raters in segmenting distinct cancer subregions (Dice ratings ranging from 74% to 85%), highlighting the difficulties of this task. As a result, much effort has been expended on this benchmarking dataset. Some of them are mentioned in Table 1 and reviewed in this section to demonstrate the current state of the art for the accuracies attained with it to the present time. In 2015, Vinay Rao [69] suggested a DCNN model for brain tumor classification and segmentation. For this investigation, they employed the BRATS 2015 dataset. They used pixel-by-pixel categorization. Each pixel joins to generate a multimodal image based on its surroundings. They employed a stochastic gradient to classify each pixel that was surrounded by patches. ReLu was employed in association with the final hidden layer to enhance gradients and obtained 67% accuracy.

In 2016, Pereira et al. [70] used the DCNN for tumor segmentation and detection using BRATS 2015 data. They acquired a greater sensitivity rate of 86% by using neural network hyperparameters such as dropout, leaky rectifier linear units, and tiny convolutional kernels. They trained two architectures, one for each, to ensure the HGG and LGG. After combining LGG and HGG, they reached 0.87 DSC for the entire tumor (LGG, and HGG together). Utilizing data from the BRATS 2015 challenge, Casamitjana et al. [71] developed a 3D convolutional neural network (CNN) for segmenting BT. This work established a robust connection between three separate models. Two fully convolutional 3D CNN architectures were presented, both of which took their inspiration from popular 2D models employed for generic image segmentation. A third model was trained, and it was a two-pathway deep medic network variation. By subtracting the volume's mean and dividing by the volume's standard deviation, they normalized the data inside each input volume. Training data with up-sampling layers can enhance effective batch size with low memory and computational costs. They achieved 84% for the Dice score for segmenting the whole tumor subregion of single-resolution images.

In 2017, Dong et al. [72] introduced the U-Net framework for the segmentation of the BRATS brain MR images dataset. This study made use of the BRATS 2015 dataset, which included HGG and LLG. They employed fivefold cross-validation and obtained a DSC of 0.86 for the combined results of HGG and LGG to properly identify the entire tumor. Mengqiao et al. suggested a 3D CNN for glioma segmentation [73]. They developed a 22-layer network and employed leaky rectifier linear units as activation functions in each activation layer until the last one, which used softmax as an activation function. The model was trained using 20 MR pictures and tested using 100 MR images collected from the BRATS challenge repository. DSC, PPV, and sensitivity were utilized to evaluate the model, and they reached 0.84, 0.88, and 0.82 for the entire tumor region, respectively.

In 2018, Wang et al. [74] employed CNN to detect brain tumors with an accuracy of 80%. This investigation was carried out using a dataset of 480 MR images obtained from the BRATS challenge. A total of 320 MR scans were used for training and 160 for testing. They preprocessed the input before submitting them to the CNN. They eliminated noise and tissue that were not part of the brain during preprocessing and then improved the contrast to assure the quality of medical images. They employed active contour to separate the tumor area from the surrounding areas, and the segmented images were then fed into CNN for classification. In this study, fourfold cross-validation was performed and the attained sensitivity, specificity, and accuracy were 85.7%, 86.5%, and 86.0%, respectively. In [75], Cui et al. introduced an automatic segmentation method from MRI data containing brain gliomas. The work that was proposed was founded on a cascaded deep learning convolutional neural network. This network was comprised of two subnetworks: a tumor localization network (TLN) and an intratumor classification network (ITCN). Determining the location of the tumor on an MRI slice was the primary objective of the first subnetwork. After that, the ITCN was utilized to assign labels to multiple subregions within the previously defined tumor region. On the datasets from BRATS 2015, the proposed method was evaluated. On the combined HGG and LGG MRIs, the DSC and sensitivity values obtained from the experiments came in at 0.89 and 0.80, respectively. A CNN-based classification model for brain tumors was introduced through the work of Lang et al. [76]. This method combines the CNN model that was optimized with the SVM model in order to make full use of the strengths of both methods. The newly proposed method was tested on the BRATS 2015 database, and the results showed that it had an accuracy of 0.88%. Li et al. [77] developed a U-Net-based model for the segmentation of MRIs taken of brain tumors. The newly presented model is capable of automatically generating segmentation maps slice by slice. The proposed model has been shown to be accurate by both the BRATS 2015 and BRATS 2016 studies. The experimental results have achieved a DSC of 0.89 for the BRATS 2015 training dataset and 0.87 for the BRATS 2017 training dataset.

Table 1. A summary of the current state of the art and the limitations of each technique.

Author	Techniques	Dataset/Database	Strengths	Weaknesses
Amulya and Prathibha [47]	SURF, SIFT, KNN	101 Brain MRIs, MR-TIP and overcode.yak.net	• In order to perform well, deep networks need very huge datasets. Classical ML methods typically perform better than deep networks on smaller datasets. • Classical ML algorithms are straightforward to comprehend and interpret because to their reliance on direct feature engineering. • In addition, with a deeper comprehension of the data and algorithms, tweaking hyper-parameters and making other changes to the model designs is much less of a challenge. However, deep networks have a lot of "black box" characteristics, meaning that their "insides" are not fully understood even now by academics. Because of this absence of theory, dealing with hyper-parameters and designing networks is also difficult.	• The significant features are extracted from the input image using some feature extraction algorithm, and the classical machine learning model is trained to recognize the tumor from normal tissues. • This is just one of the three steps that make up the framework for classifying brain tissues into normal/abnormal ones. • Algorithms for extracting features, edge-related characteristics, and other required information might be time-consuming to run. This is especially true when the lines between healthy tissue and tumors are unclear or fuzzy, as is the case with many cancers.
Virupakshappa and Amarapur [48]	FCM, Gabor Wavelet, ANN	60 MR Images Source was not mentioned		
Raj et al. [50]	K-mean, GLCM Gabor Filter, KNN	T1-weighted MRIs, District Hospital Palakkad, Department of Neurosurgery, India		
Ahmet [51]	Morphological Operations, Threshold-based Segmentation, Median Filter	100 MR Images, TCIA		
Shree et al. [56]	PNN, DWT, GLCM	DICOM		
Devkota et al. [52]	Median filter, Mathematical Morphological Operations, SVM	19 MR Images, Source was not mentioned		
Ismael et al. [53]	DWT, Gabor Filter, BPNN	3064 T1-weighted MRI scans, Figshare		
Bahadure et al. [54]	Watershed Segmentation, FCM, Direction Cosine Transform Segmentation, Bakery Wavelet Transform, Genetic Algorithm	22 MRIs from DICOM, 44 MRIs from Web Brain		
Rajesh et al. [55]	Differential based Adaptive Filtering (DAF), Region Growing Algorithm, PSONN	90 MRI scans, Government Medical College Hospital, Trivandrum, India		

Table 1. *Cont.*

Author	Techniques	Dataset/Database	Strengths	Weaknesses
Mohsen et al. [66]	DCNN, DWT, PCA, FCM	66 MRIs, Harvard Medical School Website	• There is no requirement for feature engineering with DL-based methods. • In contrast to traditional ML algorithms, deep learning methods can be readily customized to serve a variety of purposes and domains.	The following deficiencies are common to most DL-based methods: 1. Firstly, the classification systems based on convolutional neural networks (CNNs) have a complex structure that necessitates a lot of computing power. 2. The present state of the art for segmentation and classification on the aforementioned BRATS 2015 dataset demonstrates poor to medium segmentation and classification's performance.
Balasooriya et al. [67]	CNN	REMBRANDT BRAINS MIRIAD		
Hemanth et al. [68]	Modified DCNN	220 Brain MRIs, M/s. Devaki Scan Centre		
Vinay Rao et al. [69]	CNN	BRATS 2015		
Sergio Pereira et al. [70]	DCNN	BRATS 2015		
Casamitjana et al. [71]	3D CNN	BRATS 2015		
Dong et al. [72]	U-Net	BRATS 2015		
Mengqiao et al. [73]	3D CNN	BRATS 2015		
Heng wang [74]	CNN	BRATS 2015		
Cui et al. [75]	Cascade DCNN	BRATS 2015		
Lang et al. [76]	CNN, SVM	BRATS 2015		
Li et al. [77]	Modified U-Net model	BRATS 2015		
Peng et al. [78]	3D U-Net model	BRATS 2015		
Proposed method	U-Net and CNN Cascaded framework	BRATS 2015	• In this work, we present a lightweight and easy-to-use end-to-end segmentation and classification system for BT MRIs. • Precision in real-time segmentation was the driving force behind the introduction of a lightweight, effective implementation of the U-Net deep network. • Further, we provide a simplified CNN-based architecture for BT classification in an effort to enhance performance.	

In 2019, Peng et al. developed a deep learning model for segmenting brain tumor MR images. The model is built on a 3D U-Net architecture that employs many U-Net blocks to record long-distance spatial features at various resolutions. They attained Dice scores of 0.85, 0.72, and 0.61 for the whole tumor, tumor core, and enhancing tumor, respectively, on the BRATS 2015 testing set.

3. Materials and Methods

3.1. Clinical Brain Image Dataset

The data used in this work were obtained from a public dataset—the Multimodal Brain Tumor Segmentation Benchmark (BRATS 2015) [79]. The clinical image data are comprised of 65 multicontrast MR scans obtained from glioma patients [80]. Magnetic resonance imaging (MRI) is one of the most commonly utilized medical imaging analysis techniques for diagnosing problems of the nervous system [81] and the brain due to its outstanding soft tissue resolution and lack of potentially dangerous radiation effects [82]. Since each glioma is unique in terms of its size, form, and structure, several MRI sequences, such as T1-weighted, T1c, and T2-weighted, as well as FLAIR, are utilized in order to examine the tumors. These sequences are analyzed to determine the various subregions of the tumor and offer information relating to those findings. Therefore, appropriately segmenting gliomas and the structures found inside the tumor through the application of various MRI sequences is important for research and can provide extra assistance to medical professionals when formulating a diagnosis strategy.

A total of 65 multicontrast MR scans from glioma patients make up the clinical image data utilized in this study, 14 of which were taken from patients with low-grade gliomas (astrocytomas or oligoastrocytomas) and 51 from patients with high-grade gliomas (anaplastic astrocytomas and glioblastoma multiforme tumors). The scans were taken both before and after treatment, with resections visible in two of the volumes. They were gathered over the course of several years from four institutions (Bern University, Debrecen University, Heidelberg University, and Massachusetts General Hospital) using MR scanners from four different vendors, with two different field strengths of 1.5T and 3T, and two different implementations of the imaging sequences—2D and 3D.

The training dataset includes the ground truth as an input. The image dataset is found in the file format known as Meta Image (.mha). All of the images have already had the skull removed, and the resolution in all of the MRI sequences is very clear. Within this particular dataset, each patient undergoes a total of four MRI sequences. The acronyms FLAIR, T1-weighted, T1c, and T2-weighted describe these images. Necrosis, edema, enhancing, and nonenhancing are the four categories that are used to classify the tumor tissue in this set of data. Image processing techniques can be used to identify the different class regions, since each region in the class has unique radiological features that can be distinguished from one another. Different sequences can provide crucial information about the different intratumoral locations due to the complicated nature of gliomas. The quantitative evaluations were carried out on the basis of three different tumor regions: the whole tumor, the core tumor, and the enhancing tumor. Complete tumor consists of all tumor regions, including necrosis, edema, enhancing, and nonenhancing, while core tumor consists of all three regions save edema, and enhancing tumor consists of only enhancing region. The BRATS 2015 dataset includes a total of 220 MRIs of high-grade gliomas as well as 54 MRIs of low-grade gliomas. FLAIR, T1, T1-contrast, and T2 are the four different MRI sequences that can be performed on each individual participant. For the purpose of determining how well our model works, we employ a 10-fold cross validation. Specifically, the data are divided at random into three sets: training, validation, and testing, with 70%, 15%, and 15% the percentages of division between the training, validation, and testing sets, respectively. In Table 2, we list the total number of images that were used across all three phases of the experiment: training, validation, and testing.

Table 2. The distribution of BT data throughout the several classes that are used in training, validation, and testing.

	High Grade Gliomas MRIs	Low Grade Gliomas MRIs
Training (70%)	616	120
Validation (15%)	132	28
Testing (15%)	132	28

3.2. Experimental Setup

Python 3.7.3 (64-bit) is used as the implementation language for this study. Conv3D, MaxPooling3D, UpSampling3D, concatenation, flatten, and dense are some of the Keras layers utilized by the U-Net and CNN model. We used a 16 GB Intel Core i5 machine with a 2.00 GHz x64-based processor.

3.3. Proposed Framework

In this study, an integrated framework based on U-Net CNN and DCNNs is introduced for CAD of brain MRI images. Such a CAD system involves five main stages including image preprocessing and enhancement, brain skull stripping, brain tumor segmentation, feature extraction and selection, and classification of benign and malignant tumors. The proposed U-Net and CNN cascaded framework for the segmentation and classification of brain tumor MRIs is depicted in Figure 1. During the image preprocessing step, many operations on the data are performed. Some examples of these operations include image scaling, removing noise from an image, and enhancing contrast. Improving the data so that it can be processed further is the goal of this step. The original image resolution for the BRATS data used in this investigation was $240 \times 240 \times 155$. The data contained four different MR sequences: T1, T1c, T2, and FLAIR. After being scaled down to a format measuring $32 \times 32 \times 32$, these images are then provided as input to the segmentation model. The MRI sequences that make up this data are presented as a 3D color image and in the format of Meta Image. The U-Net model is used to automatically segment the preprocessed brain MRIs and hence extract the regions of interest (ROIs). After the ROIs have been automatically extracted, they are used to train and test a deep CNN that can distinguish between tumor and healthy tissue samples.

3.3.1. U-Net Model for Brain MRI Segmentation

The goal of brain tumor segmentation is to automatically and precisely locate a brain tumor in MR images. In contrast to ML [83] and non-AI [84] methods, the DL segmentation methods MRNet [85], and U-Net [86] are fully automated. Further, DL techniques are superior to ML and non-AI approaches when it comes to segment medical images [87,88].

U-Net is a convolutional neural network (CNN) that is fully connected and is utilized for effective semantic segmentation of images [86]. The architecture of U-Net is founded on an autoencoder architecture, which means that the network will duplicate its inputs to its outputs. An autoencoder is a deep NN that compresses the input matrix into a latent-space representation. This is just a demonstration of the images in compact form that indicates which pixels are the closest together. In order to produce an output, the compressed data must first be reconstructed. An encoder and a decoder make up each of the two pathways that make up an autoencoder network. The data is first compressed into a latent-space representation by the encoder, and then the decoder is employed to recreate the inputs from the latent-space representation. U-Net makes use of a convolutional autoencoder architecture, which means that the convolutional layers are utilized both during the encoding process as well as during the decoding process. The input image to U-Net is captured by its encoder route, which contains a stack of convolutional and pooling layers. Accurate localization is achieved by transposed convolutions in the decoder path. U-Net consists solely of stacks of convolutional layers and max-pooling layers—it lacks a fully linked feedforward layer. U-Net can be simply adjusted to function with any image dimension [89], despite being created for 572 × 572 images. Adding many stacked convolutional layers allows the network to acquire more accurate information from the input images with less compression [90].

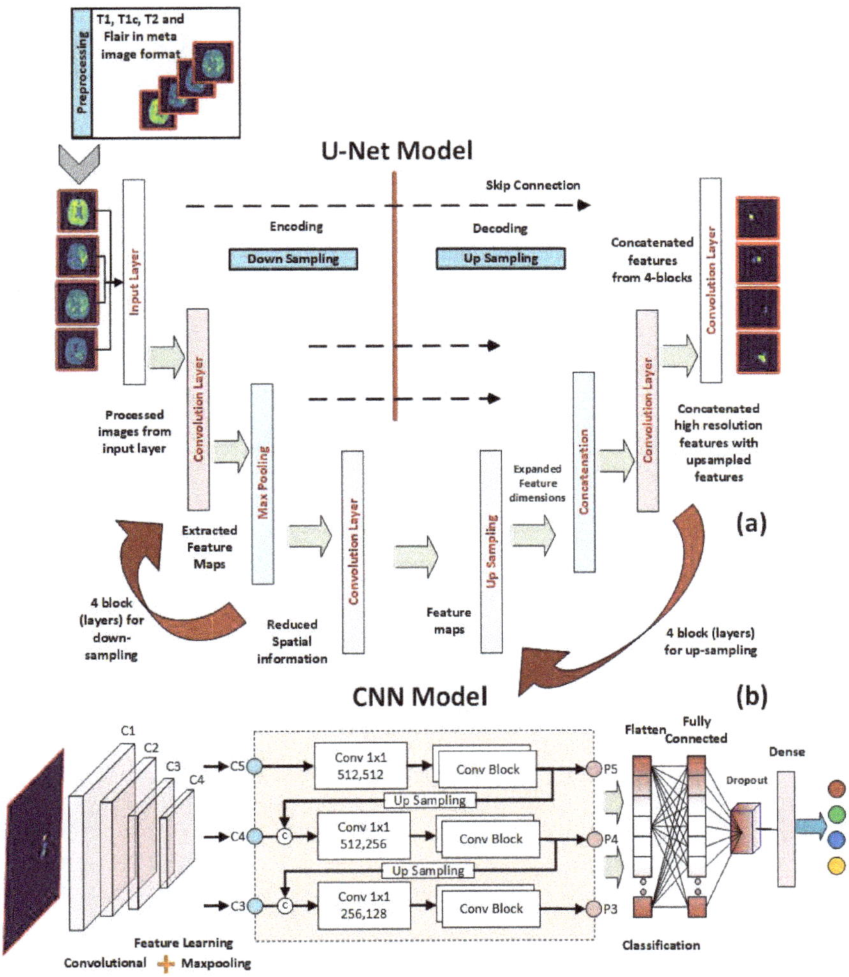

Figure 1. The proposed U-Net and CNN cascaded framework for the segmentation and classification of brain tumor MRIs. (**a**) The U-Net layers for the segmentation of input images. (**b**) The CNN layers for the classification of the segmented ROIs.

In this work, an efficient lightweight implementation of U-Net deep networks is proposed with the goal of providing accurate real-time segmentation. This has been accomplished by altering the input layer of U-Net to accept lower sizes of input images. The results have been quite promising. Instead of working with the default size of input images in the original version of U-Net, which was 572 by 572 pixels, we have utilized images of smaller sizes, including 32 by 32 pixels. In addition, we have incorporated a more extensive and deeper stack of convolutional layers into the proposed architecture (four convolutional blocks, where each block has two convolutional layers). This has assisted us in obtaining more precise information from the input images while also reducing the amount of compression.

The architecture of the proposed U-Net model is shown in Figure 1a. Along the encoding path, which is sometimes referred to as the down-sampling path, there is a total of four convolutional blocks. Each block has two convolutional layers, each of which has a filter size of 3 × 3, and they are separated from one another by a stride size of 1. Although the ReLU is typically used as an activation function in convolutional layers, the ELU has been used in this study as an activation function because it is more suitable for use in applications involving image segmentation. This is in contrast to the general practice, which is to use the ReLU. Because of this, the ELU activation function plays a significant role in the segmentation model that we provide. A convolutional layer that contains an activation function has the potential to increase the number of feature mappings from 4 to 64. Every single convolutional block uses a max-pooling layer that has a stride of 2 × 2 in order to cut down on the overall size of the feature maps that are needed for the process. After decoding, a feature map with 32 × 32 pixels is shrunk to one with only 2 × 2 pixels. In addition, the extraction technique makes use of four convolutional blocks to handle the data. At the start of each block, a Conv3D layer is added, and its stride size is set to 2 × 2, and its filter size is set to 3 × 3. The feature maps included in this section range in size from 2 × 2 grids to 32 × 32 grids (the original size of the input image). The feature maps that were generated by the decoding path and the upsampling path are concatenated in a concatenation that occurs later in each block after the convolutional layer has been processed. Padding of a similar nature is utilized in order to keep the spatial dimensions of the input and output layers consistent with one another. Finally, a Conv3d 1 × 1 layer is utilized to partition the original feature map into the tumor region and the rest of the brain. At the final convolutional stage, Sigmoid is employed as the activation function. We tested the network's functionality at 2, 3, and 4 depths.

3.3.2. DCNN Classification Model

After the ROIs have been automatically extracted using the U-Net model described in the preceding subsection, the ROIs are utilized to train and test a deep CNN that is able to differentiate between samples of healthy and malignant tissue. The deep convolutional neural network has quickly become the most popular tool for usage in the field of image processing due to its better pattern-recognition capabilities [91–95]. CNNs have a variety of different layers. Convolutional layers, pooling layers, and completely connected layers are the most common [96]. The primary layer of a CNN architecture is the convolutional layer. Image features such as edges and colors can be extracted with its help. The dimension of the collected features is reduced through the use of the pooling layer, which reduces the complexity and the processing time. The fully connected layer is the final stage of the CNN model, which aims towards linearity within the networks.

A schematic of the proposed CNN model architecture for BT tissue classification is shown in Figure 1b. The input layer of the proposed model takes in the input images, ROIs, which have the size of 32 × 32. The input layer is followed by a set of convolutional layers. The proposed model contains five convolutional layers to extract the significant features from the ROIs. As segmented images are input to our model, we chose max pooling because we only cared about the most informative features in the tumor tissue. Using a max-pooling layer after each convolutional layer is used to improve the accuracy of the final result. The convolutional layer we utilized has 3 kernels and 2 strides. ReLU is used in all convolution layers. Edges can be protected from data loss by using padding. The padding applied to inputs and outputs is identical. After each convolution layer, a batch normalization is applied to further optimize the findings and hasten the network's convergence. "Fully linked layers" of 64 neurons are used. Softmax classifier is used at the output layer.

4. Results and Discussion

Because of the large dimensionality of deep neural networks, solving the challenge of choosing the parameters that should be used to train them in order to achieve the maximum possible performance is a challenging optimization problem. As a direct consequence of this, techniques based on stochastic optimization are utilized frequently. In this work, the adaptive moment estimation (ADAM) optimizer is used using the learning parameters that are laid out in Table 3. These parameters were determined by keeping an eye on the test results for validation, and they were used for all networks for easy comparison of their outputs and computational costs.

Table 3. Hyperparameters for training the proposed model.

Hyperparameter	Value
Initial Learning rate	10^{-3}
No. of Epochs	200
Image Batch size	16
L2-Regularization	0.0004

In order to assess the effectiveness of the suggested CAD framework, the Dice similarity coefficient (Dice) [97], accuracy, and sensitivity have been utilized. DSC is a performance indicator that can be used to evaluate how significant the autonomous segmentation actually is. The Dice coefficient, depicted by Equation (1), is a measurement that determines how similar two sets of data are to one another. The primary application for it is in the analysis of the segmentation models. We put it to use to determine how closely the segmented image and the ground truth image were related to one another.

$$Dice = \frac{2TP}{2TP + FP + FN} \quad (1)$$

TP is for "true positive," *FP* stands for "false positive," which indicates that the number was actually negative, but our model predicts it as positive, and *FN* stands for "false negative."

Sensitivity is utilized for the purpose of predicting the real positive cases that were predicted as positive. It is also referred to as recall, and it is expressed as Equation (2).

$$Sensitivity = \frac{TP}{TP + FN} \quad (2)$$

The accuracy refers to how well the predicted value and the actual value match up with one another. It is utilized in the method of performance analysis of the system. It is expressed as Equation (3), specifically.

$$Accuracy = \frac{TP + TN}{TP + TN + FP + FN} \quad (3)$$

Experiments were performed on three-dimensional MR images of a brain tumor. Images in three dimensions are those whose colors are produced by combining the red, green, and blue color channels. The information for each of the three channels—red, green, and blue—is stored in the image's individual pixels. By providing the height, breadth, and depth dimensions, we are able to conceptualize a three-dimensional image. As stated in the dataset section, there are four types of tumor necrosis, edema, enhancing, and non-enhancing tumors, and the MRI sequences used to detect these tumors are FLAIR, T1, T1c, and T2. To detect these cancers, the image annotation is provided for all of these sequences. There is just one annotated image that includes all of these kinds as intratumor areas.

To demonstrate the quality of input images, we represent several renderings of the input images in various sizes (Figures 2–4). Figure 2 displays the visualization of HGG BRATS data for the MR sequences of T1, T1c, T2, and FLAIR at a resolution of 32 × 32 × 32. Images were transformed in the preprocessing phase. Tumor details were more easily discerned by viewing the identical pictures in a 64 × 64 × 64 matrix (Figure 3). A clearer view of brain tumor images with dimension of 128 × 128 × 128 is presented in Figure 4.

The illustration depicts the afflicted area of brain that may be evaluated better than the prior dimensions.

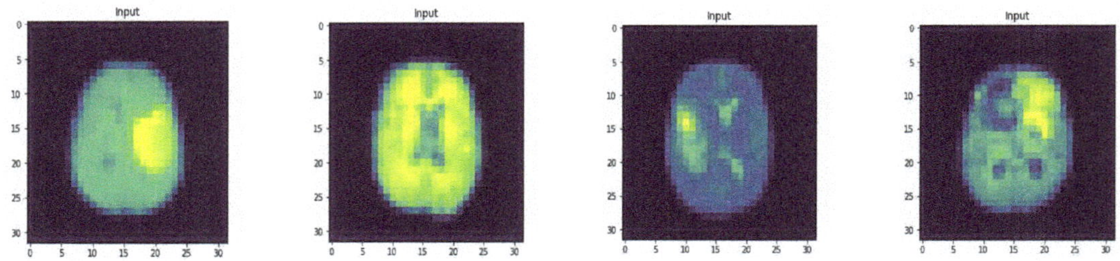

(a) T1 **(b)** T1c **(c)** T2 **(d)** Flair

Figure 2. Rendering of T1, T1c, T2, and FLAIR at a resolution of $32 \times 32 \times 32$.

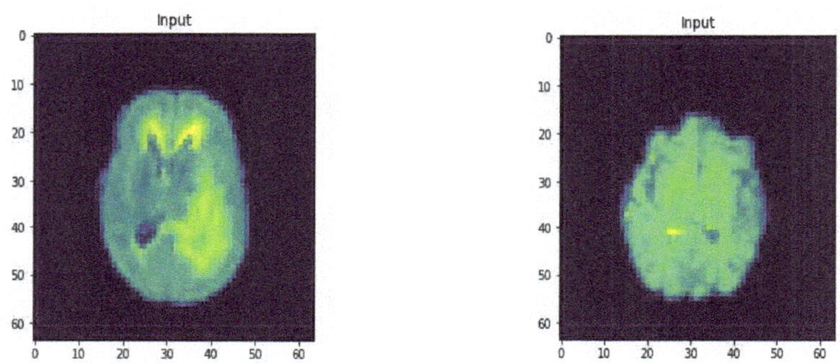

(a) T1 **(b)** T1c

Figure 3. Rendering of T1, T1c, T2, and FLAIR at a resolution of $64 \times 64 \times 64$.

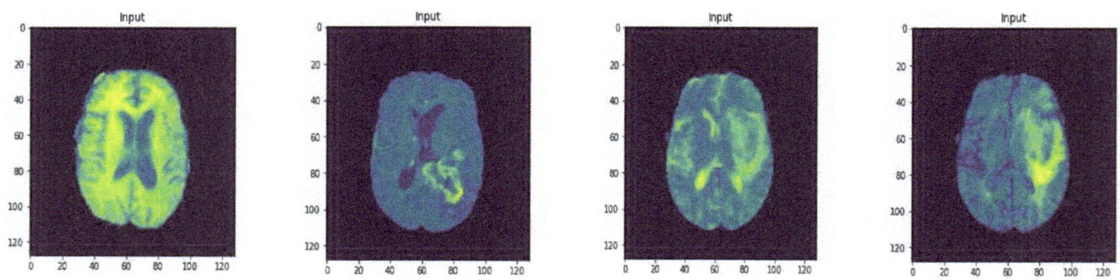

(a) T1 **(b)** T1c **(c)** T2 **(d)** Flair

Figure 4. T1, T1c, T2, and FLAIR rendered at a resolution of $128 \times 128 \times 128$.

We fed the preprocessed images into the U-Net model, which segmented out the brain tumor regions. At first look, the model appears to be divided into two phases: encoding and decoding. The goal of the encoding is to reduce spatial information while improving feature mapping by utilizing various blocks of the convolution and max-pooling layers. Following the encoding phase, the decoding step uses upsampling, convolution, and concatenation layers in blocks to split the input image into two parts—the tumor and the background. As a result, the suggested model will provide us with a segmented view of the brain tumor region. We conducted the experiment on both high-grade gliomas (HGG) and low-grade gliomas (LGG). Figures 5 and 6 illustrate the segmentation of HGG and LGG brain tumors from four MRI sequences (FLAIR, T1, T1C, and T2), respectively, using the U-Net model. Each MRI sequence (FLAIR, T1, T1C, and T2) is displayed in three different views: the input view, the ground truth view, and the segmented view.

By calculating the Dice score and the sensitivity performance metrics, we were able to assess the feasibility of the U Net architecture for the task of segmenting brain tumors for HGG and LGG cases. The results that were retrieved were accomplished through the utilization of a 10-fold cross-validation test. Table 4 provides an illustration of the cross validation test by outlining the retrieved Dice score, sensitivity, and accuracy metrics for the complete type of the BT during the course of a 10-fold test.

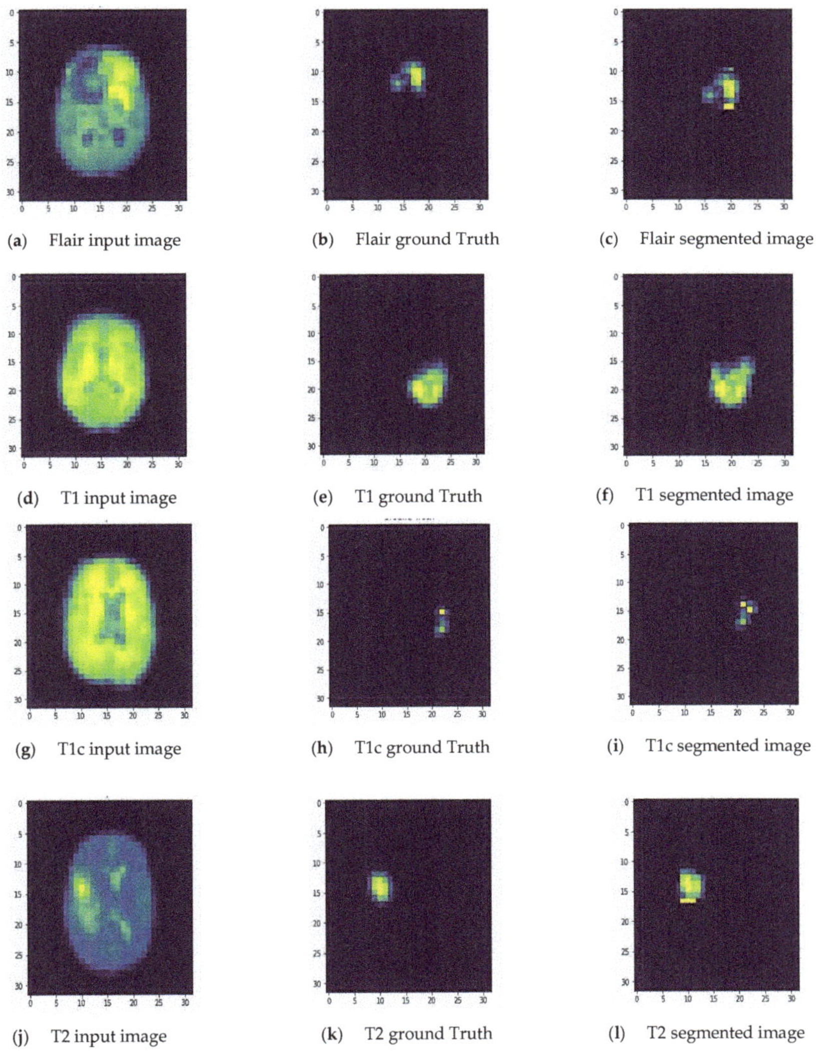

(**a**) Flair input image (**b**) Flair ground Truth (**c**) Flair segmented image
(**d**) T1 input image (**e**) T1 ground Truth (**f**) T1 segmented image
(**g**) T1c input image (**h**) T1c ground Truth (**i**) T1c segmented image
(**j**) T2 input image (**k**) T2 ground Truth (**l**) T2 segmented image

Figure 5. Segmentation of high-grade gliomas (HGG) from four MRI sequences (FLAIR, T1, T1C, and T2), respectively, using the U-Net model. Left column: input image; middle column: ground truth images; right column: segmented images.

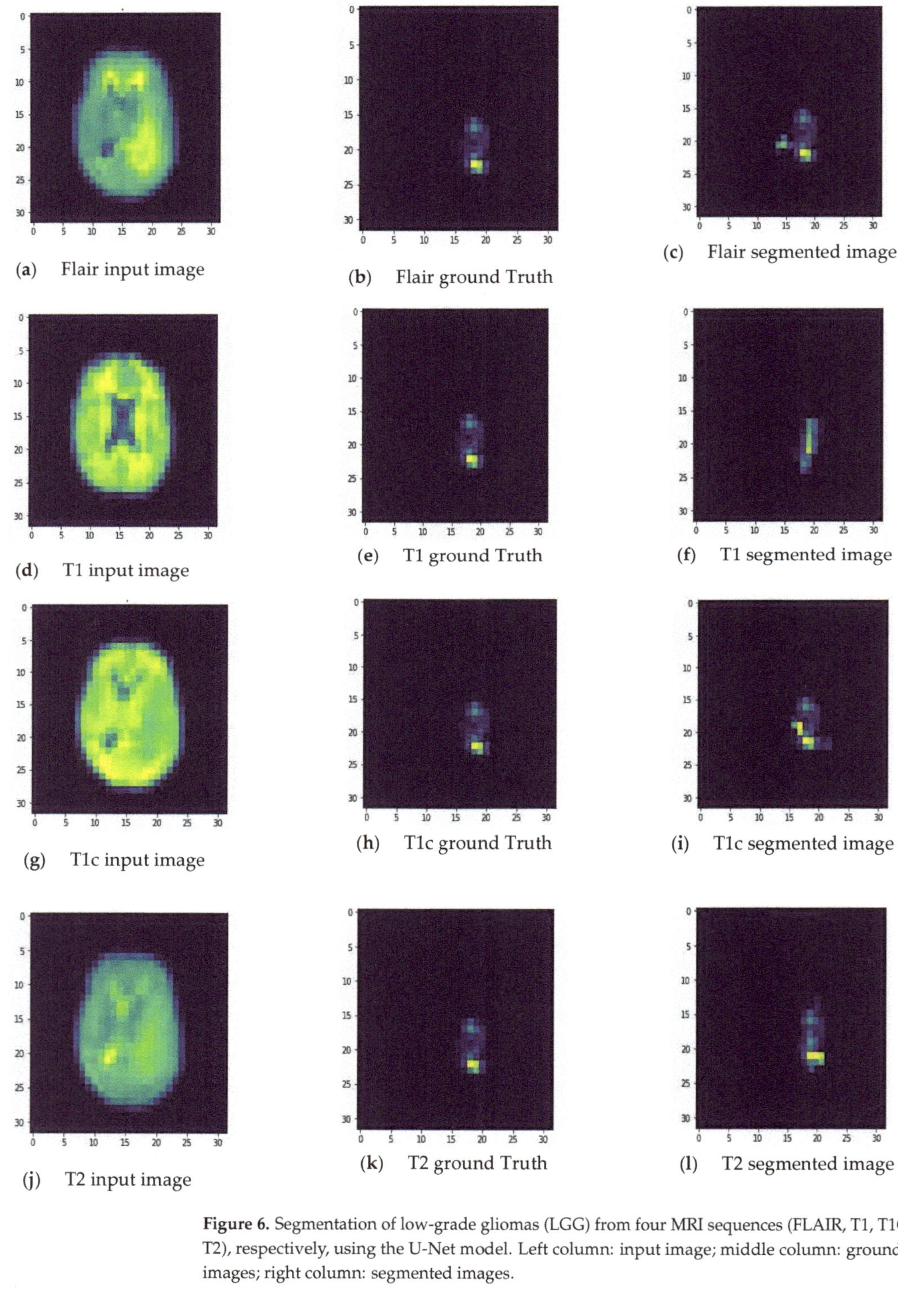

(**a**) Flair input image (**b**) Flair ground Truth (**c**) Flair segmented image

(**d**) T1 input image (**e**) T1 ground Truth (**f**) T1 segmented image

(**g**) T1c input image (**h**) T1c ground Truth (**i**) T1c segmented image

(**j**) T2 input image (**k**) T2 ground Truth (**l**) T2 segmented image

Figure 6. Segmentation of low-grade gliomas (LGG) from four MRI sequences (FLAIR, T1, T1C, and T2), respectively, using the U-Net model. Left column: input image; middle column: ground truth images; right column: segmented images.

Table 4. Evaluation of the proposed U-Net–CNN over 10-fold tests.

Fold	HGG			LGG		
	Dice Score (%)	Sensitivity (%)	Classification Accuracy (%)	Dice Score (%)	Sensitivity (%)	Classification Accuracy (%)
Fold 1	87.16%	88.61%	85.54%	80.5%	77.02%	80.04%
Fold 2	89.1%	88.92%	88.76%	85.3%	79.5%	79.96%
Fold 3	87.98%	89.8%	89.03%	83.6%	80.64%	80.2%
Fold 4	88.74%	89.53%	89.2%	82.1%	81.2%	81.4%
Fold 5	88.95%	88.76%	88.12%	85.84%	79.14	83.5%
Fold 6	88.97%	88.81%	89.98%	86.23%	80.65%	84.6%
Fold 7	88.47%	89.5%	88.73%	86.41%	80.12%	86.73%
Fold 8	88.62%	90.14%	88.91%	85.33%	80.79%	84.1%
Fold 9	89.68%	89.94%	87.66%	85.98%	80.2%	85.9%
Fold 10	89.83%	89.97%	90.22%	85.96%	80.74%	85.3%
Avg. (%)	88.8	89.4	88.6	84.7	80	83.1

The attained results for all types of BT are summarized in Table 5 for the segmentation and classification of several brain tumor regions, including complete, core, and enhancing, for both low-grade gliomas and high-grade gliomas. As can be seen in Table 5, the greatest possible values for the DSC, the sensitivity, and the classification accuracy for HGG patients in the complete brain tumor region are 88.8%, 89.4%, and 88.6%, respectively. These figures represent the best conceivable values in each of these categories. The learning model is adequate when seen through the lens of these values. The values 84.7%, 80%, and 83.1% are produced for the same measures when they are applied to the cases of low-grade gliomas that are found in the same location. The learning model's accuracy in detecting malignancies in other brain tumor regions, such as the core and enhancing brain tumors, is lower than the values achieved for the complete brain tumor region. This is because the core and enhancing brain tumors are part of the complete brain tumor region. The obtained values for the DSC score, sensitivity, and classification accuracy for the core brain tumor are 83.2%, 80%, and 85.1% for high-grade gliomas, and 70.5%, 69%, and 71.5% for low-grade gliomas, respectively. In addition, the obtained values for the DSC score, sensitivity, and classification accuracy for the enhancing brain tumor are as follows: 71.8%, 73%, and 74.31% in the high-graded gliomas, and 60.2%, 64.3%, and 65.4% in the low-graded glioma.

Table 5. The attained Dice score, sensitivity, and accuracy metrics of the U-Net architecture for the task of segmenting and classifying the brain tumors for HGG and LGG cases in the BRATS 2015 MRI scans.

Brain Tumor Regions	HGG			LGG		
	Dice Score (%)	Sensitivity (%)	Classification Accuracy (%)	Dice Score (%)	Sensitivity (%)	Classification Accuracy (%)
Complete	88.8%	89.4%	88.6%	84.7%	80%	83.1%
Core	83.2%	80%	85.1%	70.5%	69%	71.5%
Enhancing	71.8%	73%	74.3%	60.2%	64.3%	65.4%

We evaluated the relevance of the U-Net–CNN approach by comparing its accuracy to that of the most advanced segmentation and classification systems for brain tumor MRI scans by utilizing the BRATS 2015 database. This allowed us to determine how significant the U-Net–CNN approach is. The comparison between the suggested method and the existing standard of practice is presented in Table 6. The obtained values for the DSC and sensitivity performance metrics are significant compared to the current state of the art for deep learning-based segmentation of brain tumors in the public BRATS 2015 benchmarking dataset. This comparison takes place using the dataset that was made public in 2015.

Table 6. Comparing the attained segmentation, and classification accurateness to the state-of-the-art brain tumor MRI scans using the BRATS 2015 database.

Author	Techniques	Task	BT Type	Accuracy	Dice Score	Sensitivity	Specificity
Vinay Rao et al. [69]	CNN	Classification	HGG	67%	-	-	-
Sergio Pereira et al. [70]	DCNN	Segmentation	HGG	-	87%	86%	-
Casamitjana et al. [71]	3D CNN	Segmentation	HGG	-	84%	-	-
Dong et al. [72]	U-Net	Segmentation	HGG	-	86%	-	-
Mengqiao et al. [73]	3D CNN	Segmentation	HGG	-	84%	82%	
Heng Wang [74]	CNN	Classification	HGG	86.0%	-	85.7%	86.5%
Cui et al. [75]	Cascade DCNN	Segmentation	HGG	-	89%	80%	-
Lang et al. [76]	CNN, SVM	Classification	HGG	88%	-	-	-
Li et al. [77]	Modified U-Net model	Segmentation	HGG	-	89%	-	-
Peng et al. [78]	3D U-Net model	Segmentation	HGG	-	85% (Whole BT) 72% (Core BT) 61% (Enhancing BT)	-	-
Proposed method	U-Net and CNN Cascaded frame-work	End-to-end system for the segmentation and classification of BT	HGG	88.6% (Whole BT) 85.1% (Core BT) 74.3% (Enhancing BT)	88.8% (Whole BT) 83.2% (Core BT) 71.8% (Enhancing BT)	89.4% (Whole BT) 80% (Core BT) 73% (Enhancing BT)	-
			LGG	83.1% (Whole BT) 75.5% (Core BT) 65.4% (Enhancing BT)	84.7% (Whole BT) 70.5% (Core BT) 60.2% (Enhancing BT)	80% (Whole BT) 69% (Core BT) 64.3% (Enhancing BT)	-

When we assess the efficacy of our presented framework in light of the studies that were covered earlier in this part, we discover the following. The newly developed framework has achieved a level of performance that is superior to that accomplished by Vinay Rao et al. [69], Mengqiao et al. [73], and Casamitjana et al. [71]. When contrasted with the work done by Sergio Pereira et al. [70], Dong et al. [72], Heng Wang [74], Cui et al. [75], Lang et al. [76], Li et al. [77], and Peng et al. [78], the presented framework has acquired somewhat higher values for the Dice score, sensitivity, and accuracy.

5. Conclusions

This research introduces a unified framework for CAD of brain MRI images, with support from U-Net and deep convolutional neural networks. Image preprocessing and enhancement, brain skull stripping, brain tumor segmentation, feature extraction and selection, and benign/malignant tumor classification are the five basic stages of this type of computer-aided diagnosis system. We have created a model that is based on deep learning techniques so that automatic tumor segmentation and detection are performed using MRI scans of the brain. The model has two phases. In the first phase, ROIs are segmented. In the second phase, the tumor is classified into one of four categories: necrosis, edema, enhancing, or nonenhancing. The U-Net model is applied to the BRATS dataset to segment the image into the regions of interest.

The introduced lightweight U-Net model is composed of four convolutional layers. Two convolutional layers, each with a filter size of 3 × 3, are separated by a stride size of 1 within each block. The proposed CNN model's input layer takes 32 × 32 ROIs. Convolutional layers follow the input layer. Five convolutional layers are used to extract information from ROIs. We picked max pooling because we only care about the most informative tumor tissue traits. After each convolutional layer, a max-pooling layer improves accuracy. We used three kernels and two strides in convolutional layers. Convolution layers use ReLU. Padding protects data at edges. Inputs and outputs have identical padding. After each convolution layer, batch normalization optimizes the findings and speeds network convergence. Connected layers of 64 neurons are used, as well as output layer Softmax classifier. In conclusion, the obtained results showed that the proposed model achieves better performance than existing models in terms of DSC and sensitivity on segmentation results and classification accuracy as well.

6. Limitations and Future Work

There is always opportunity for progress in the realm of research, and the medical sciences in particular have a pressing need for a highly precise model. The model can be applied to other datasets to extract and categorize the tumor types, expanding the suggested work of tumor identification in the medical area and assisting clinicians. There are a variety of ways in which this model could be improved. First, the U-Net model we used for tumor segmentation in BRATS 15 is transferable to the newer versions of the dataset that can be downloaded from the Multimodal BRATS website. BRATS 20, the latest and greatest edition, now features 3D graphics. The model can be adjusted to fit new datasets. Improved segmentation results on the BRATS 20 dataset are attainable by modifying the model's featured layers. Second, different activation functions and CNN model layers can be tried out to find what produces the most reliable predictions. One can also offer the hybrid model by making use of the already existing one. Tumor detection in 3D images may potentially benefit from the U-Net model trained with GNN. Additional preprocessing techniques can be used for the hybrid model as a last resort for improved segmentation and classification results utilizing the current model.

Author Contributions: Conceptualization, N.A.S., G.A., H.A.A., A.R. and T.A.; methodology, N.A.S., G.A., H.A.A., A.R. and T.A.; software, A.R. and T.A.; validation, N.A.S., G.A., H.A.A., A.R. and T.A.; formal analysis, N.A.S., N.F.M., G.A., H.A.A., A.R. and T.A.; investigation, N.A.S., N.F.M., G.A., H.A.A., A.R. and T.A.; resources, N.A.S. and N.F.M.; data curation, A.R. and T.A.; writing—original draft preparation, N.A.S., N.F.M., G.A., H.A.A., A.R. and T.A.; writing—review and editing, N.A.S., N.F.M., G.A., H.A.A., A.R. and T.A.; visualization, N.A.S., A.R. and T.A.; supervision, N.A.S. and N.F.M.; project administration, N.A.S. and N.F.M. All authors have read and agreed to the published version of the manuscript.

Funding: Princess Nourah bint Abdulrahman University Researchers Supporting Project number PNURSP2022R206, Princess Nourah bint Abdulrahman University, Riyadh, Saudi Arabia.

Institutional Review Board Statement: Not applicable.

Informed Consent Statement: Not applicable.

Data Availability Statement: Not applicable.

Acknowledgments: Princess Nourah bint Abdulrahman University Researchers Supporting Project Number PNURSP2022R206, Princess Nourah bint Abdulrahman University, Riyadh, Saudi Arabia.

Conflicts of Interest: The authors declare no conflict of interest.

References

1. Tian, S.; Yang, W.; Le Grange, J.M.; Wang, P.; Huang, W.; Ye, Z. Smart Healthcare: Making Medical Care More Intelligent. *Glob. Health J.* **2019**, *3*, 62–65. [CrossRef]
2. Gong, F.F.; Sun, X.Z.; Lin, J.; Gu, X.D. Primary Exploration in Establishment of China's Intelligent Medical Treatment. *Mod. Hosp. Manag.* **2013**, *11*, 28–29.
3. Farahani, B.; Firouzi, F.; Chang, V.; Badaroglu, M.; Constant, N.; Mankodiya, K. Towards Fog-Driven IoT EHealth: Promises and Challenges of IoT in Medicine and Healthcare. *Future Gener. Comput. Syst.* **2018**, *78*, 659–676. [CrossRef]
4. Nawaz, A.; Abbas, Y.; Ahmad, T.; Mahmoud, N.F.; Rizwan, A.; Samee, N.A. A Healthcare Paradigm for Deriving Knowledge Using Online Consumers' Feedback. *Healthcare* **2022**, *10*, 1592. [CrossRef] [PubMed]
5. Samee, N.A.; Alhussan, A.A.; Ghoneim, V.F.; Atteia, G.; Alkanhel, R.; Al-antari, M.A.; Kadah, Y.M. A Hybrid Deep Transfer Learning of CNN-Based LR-PCA for Breast Lesion Diagnosis via Medical Breast Mammograms. *Sensors* **2022**, *22*, 4938. [CrossRef] [PubMed]
6. Alhussan, A.A.; Abdel Samee, N.M.; Ghoneim, V.F.; Kadah, Y.M. Evaluating Deep and Statistical Machine Learning Models in the Classification of Breast Cancer from Digital Mammograms. *Int. J. Adv. Comput. Sci. Appl.* **2021**, *12*, 304–313. [CrossRef]
7. O'neill, B.E.; Hochhalter, C.B.; Carr, C.; Strong, M.J.; Ware, M.L. Advances in Neuro-Oncology Imaging Techniques. *Ochsner J.* **2018**, *18*, 236–241. [CrossRef] [PubMed]
8. Kelly, P.J. Gliomas: Survival, Origin and Early Detection. *Surg. Neurol. Int.* **2011**, *1*, 96. [CrossRef] [PubMed]
9. Johnson, K.J.; Schwartzbaum, J.; Kruchko, C.; Scheurer, M.E.; Lau, C.C.; Woehrer, A.; Hainfellner, J.A.; Wiemels, J. Brain Tumor Epidemiology in the Era of Precision Medicine: The 2017 Brain Tumor Epidemiology Consortium Meeting Report. *Clin. Neuropathol.* **2017**, *36*, 255–262. [CrossRef] [PubMed]
10. Fernandes, S.L.; Tanik, U.J.; Rajinikanth, V.; Karthik, K.A. A Reliable Framework for Accurate Brain Image Examination and Treatment Planning Based on Early Diagnosis Support for Clinicians. *Neural. Comput. Appl.* **2020**, *32*, 15897–15908. [CrossRef]

11. Alfonse, M.; Salem, A.-B.M. An Automatic Classification of Brain Tumors through MRI Using Support Vector Machine. *Egypt. Comput. Sci. J.* **2016**, *40*, 11–21.
12. Saba, T.; Mohamed, A.S.; El-Affendi, M.; Amin, J.; Sharif, M. Brain Tumor Detection Using Fusion of Hand Crafted and Deep Learning Features. *Cogn. Syst. Res.* **2020**, *59*, 221–230. [CrossRef]
13. Swati, Z.N.K.; Zhao, Q.; Kabir, M.; Ali, F.; Ali, Z.; Ahmed, S.; Lu, J. Brain Tumor Classification for MR Images Using Transfer Learning and Fine-Tuning. *Comput. Med. Imaging Graph.* **2019**, *75*, 34–46. [CrossRef] [PubMed]
14. Muhammad, K.; Khan, S.; Del Ser, J.; de Albuquerque, V.H.C. Deep Learning for Multigrade Brain Tumor Classification in Smart Healthcare Systems: A Prospective Survey. *IEEE Trans. Neural Netw. Learn. Syst.* **2021**, *32*, 507–522. [CrossRef]
15. Ali, S.; Li, J.; Pei, Y.; Khurram, R.; Rehman, K.U.; Rasool, A.B. State-of-the-Art Challenges and Perspectives in Multi-Organ Cancer Diagnosis via Deep Learning-Based Methods. *Cancers* **2021**, *13*, 5546. [CrossRef]
16. Dandil, E.; Çakiroğlu, M.; Ekşi, Z. Computer-Aided Diagnosis of Malign and Benign Brain Tumors on MR Images. In *Advances in Intelligent Systems and Computing, Proceedings of the International Conference on ICT Innovations, Macedonia, 9–12 September 2014*; Springer: Berlin/Heidelberg, Germany, 2015; Volume 311, pp. 157–166.
17. Ullah, N.; Khan, J.A.; Khan, M.S.; Khan, W.; Hassan, I.; Obayya, M.; Negm, N.; Salama, A.S. An Effective Approach to Detect and Identify Brain Tumors Using Transfer Learning. *Appl. Sci.* **2022**, *12*, 5645. [CrossRef]
18. Ullah, N.; Khan, M.S.; Khan, J.A.; Choi, A.; Anwar, M.S. A Robust End-to-End Deep Learning-Based Approach for Effective and Reliable BTD Using MR Images. *Sensors* **2022**, *22*, 7575. [CrossRef] [PubMed]
19. Despotović, I.; Goossens, B.; Philips, W. MRI Segmentation of the Human Brain: Challenges, Methods, and Applications. *Comput. Math. Methods Med.* **2015**, *2015*, 450341. [CrossRef]
20. Wang, L.; Chitiboi, T.; Meine, H.; Günther, M.; Hahn, H.K. Principles and Methods for Automatic and Semi-Automatic Tissue Segmentation in MRI Data. *Magn. Reson. Mater. Phys. Biol. Med.* **2016**, *29*, 95–110. [CrossRef]
21. Mirzaei, G.; Adeli, H. Segmentation and Clustering in Brain MRI Imaging. *Rev. Neurosci.* **2019**, *30*, 31–44. [CrossRef]
22. Jiang, Y.; Ye, M.; Wang, P.; Huang, D.; Lu, X. MRF-IUNet: A Multiresolution Fusion Brain Tumor Segmentation Network Based on Improved Inception U-Net. *Comput. Math. Methods Med.* **2022**, *2022*, 6305748. [CrossRef] [PubMed]
23. Atteia, G.E.; Mengash, H.A.; Samee, N.A. Evaluation of Using Parametric and Non-Parametric Machine Learning Algorithms for Covid-19 Forecasting. *Int. J. Adv. Comput. Sci. Appl.* **2021**, *12*, 647–657. [CrossRef]
24. Samee, N.A.; Osman, N.H.; Seoud, R.A.A.A.A. Comparing MapReduce and Spark in Computing the PCC Matrix in Gene Co-Expression Networks. *Int. J. Adv. Comput. Sci. Appl.* **2021**, *12*. [CrossRef]
25. Khan, U.; Khan, S.; Rizwan, A.; Atteia, G.; Jamjoom, M.M.; Samee, N.A. Aggression Detection in Social Media from Textual Data Using Deep Learning Models. *Appl. Sci.* **2022**, *12*, 5083. [CrossRef]
26. Alhussan, A.A.; Gaafar, M.S.; Alharbi, M.; Marzouk, S.Y.; Alharbi, S.; ElRashidy, H.; Mabrouk, M.S.; AlEisa, H.N.; Samee, N.A. Prediction of the Judd–Ofelt Parameters of Dy3+-Doped Lead Borosilicate Using Artificial Neural Network. *Electronics* **2022**, *11*, 1045. [CrossRef]
27. Alhussan, A.A.; AlEisa, H.N.; Atteia, G.; Solouma, N.H.; Seoud, R.A.A.A.A.; Ayoub, O.S.; Ghoneim, V.F.; Samee, N.A. ForkJoinPcc Algorithm for Computing the Pcc Matrix in Gene Co-Expression Networks. *Electronics* **2022**, *11*, 1174. [CrossRef]
28. Davenport, T.; Kalakota, R. The Potential for Artificial Intelligence in Healthcare. *Future Healthc. J.* **2019**, *6*, 94–98. [CrossRef]
29. Samee, N.A.; Atteia, G.; Alkanhel, R.; Alhussan, A.A.; AlEisa, H.N. Hybrid Feature Reduction Using PCC-Stacked Autoencoders for Gold/Oil Prices Forecasting under COVID-19 Pandemic. *Electronics* **2022**, *11*, 991. [CrossRef]
30. Samee, N.M.A. Classical and Deep Learning Paradigms for Detection and Validation of Key Genes of Risky Outcomes of HCV. *Algorithms* **2020**, *13*, 73. [CrossRef]
31. Atteia, G.; Samee, N.A.; Hassan, H.Z. DFTSA-Net: Deep Feature Transfer-Based Stacked Autoencoder Network for DME Diagnosis. *Entropy* **2021**, *23*, 1251. [CrossRef]
32. Samee, N.M.A.; Solouma, N.H.; Kadah, Y.M. Detection of Biomarkers for Hepatocellular Carcinoma Using a Hybrid Univariate Gene Selection Methods. *Theor. Biol. Med. Model.* **2012**, *9*, 34. [CrossRef] [PubMed]
33. Atteia, G.; Alhussan, A.A.; Samee, N.A. BO-ALLCNN: Bayesian-Based Optimized CNN for Acute Lymphoblastic Leukemia Detection in Microscopic Blood Smear Images. *Sensors* **2022**, *22*, 5520. [CrossRef] [PubMed]
34. Samee, N.A.; El-Kenawy, E.-S.M.; Atteia, G.; Jamjoom, M.M.; Ibrahim, A.; Abdelhamid, A.A.; El-Attar, N.E.; Gaber, T.; Slowik, A.; Shams, M.Y. Metaheuristic Optimization Through Deep Learning Classification Of COVID-19 in Chest X-Ray Images. *Comput. Mater. Contin.* **2022**, *73*, 4193–4210. [CrossRef]
35. Atteia, G.; Samee, N.A.; El-Kenawy, E.-S.M.; Ibrahim, A. CNN-Hyperparameter Optimization for Diabetic Maculopathy Diagnosis in Optical Coherence Tomography and Fundus Retinography. *Mathematics* **2022**, *10*, 3274. [CrossRef]
36. Loucks, J.; Davenport, T.; Schatsky, D. State of AI in the Enterprise. Deloitte Insights Report 2018. Available online: https://www2.deloitte.com/us/en/pages/consulting/articles/state-of-ai-2022.html (accessed on 6 October 2022).
37. Lee, S.-I.; Celik, S.; Logsdon, B.A.; Lundberg, S.M.; Martins, T.J.; Oehler, V.G.; Estey, E.H.; Miller, C.P.; Chien, S.; Dai, J.; et al. A Machine Learning Approach to Integrate Big Data for Precision Medicine in Acute Myeloid Leukemia. *Nat. Commun.* **2018**, *9*, 42. [CrossRef]
38. Currie, G.; Hawk, K.E.; Rohren, E.; Vial, A.; Klein, R. Machine Learning and Deep Learning in Medical Imaging: Intelligent Imaging. *J. Med. Imaging Radiat. Sci.* **2019**, *50*, 477–487. [CrossRef]

39. Mohamed, W.A.; Kadah, Y.M. Computer Aided Diagnosis of Digital Mammograms. In Proceedings of the ICCES'07-2007 International Conference on Computer Engineering and Systems, Cairo, Egypt, 27–29 November 2007; pp. 299–303.
40. Abduh, Z.; Wahed, M.A.; Kadah, Y.M. Robust Computer-Aided Detection of Pulmonary Nodules from Chest Computed Tomography. *J. Med. Imaging Health Inform.* **2016**, *6*, 693–699. [CrossRef]
41. Mohamed, W.A.; Alolfe, M.A.; Kadah, Y.M. Microcalcifications Enhancement in Digital Mammograms Using Fractal Modeling. In Proceedings of the 2008 Cairo International Biomedical Engineering Conference, Cairo, Egypt, 18–20 December 2008.
42. Kadah, Y.M.; Farag, A.A.; Zurada, J.M.; Badawi, A.M.; Youssef, A.-B.M. Classification Algorithms for Quantitative Tissue Characterization of Diffuse Liver Disease from Ultrasound Images. *IEEE Trans. Med. Imaging* **1996**, *15*, 466–478. [CrossRef]
43. Alolfe, M.A.; Mohamed, W.A.; Youssef, A.B.M.; Mohamed, A.S.; Kadah, Y.M. Computer Aided Diagnosis in Digital Mammography Using Combined Support Vector Machine and Linear Discriminant Analyasis Classification. In Proceedings of the Proceedings-International Conference on Image Processing (ICIP), Cairo, Egypt, 7–10 November 2009; pp. 2609–2612.
44. Al-antari, M.A.; Al-masni, M.A.; Park, S.-U.; Park, J.H.; Metwally, M.K.; Kadah, Y.M.; Han, S.M.; Kim, T.-S. An Automatic Computer-Aided Diagnosis System for Breast Cancer in Digital Mammograms via Deep Belief Network. *J. Med. Biol. Eng.* **2018**, *38*, 443–456. [CrossRef]
45. Al-Masni, M.A.; Al-Antari, M.A.; Park, J.-M.; Gi, G.; Kim, T.-Y.; Rivera, P.; Valarezo, E.; Choi, M.-T.; Han, S.-M.; Kim, T.-S. Simultaneous Detection and Classification of Breast Masses in Digital Mammograms via a Deep Learning YOLO-Based CAD System. *Comput. Methods Programs Biomed.* **2018**, *157*, 85–94. [CrossRef]
46. Vial, A.; Stirling, D.; Field, M.; Ros, M.; Ritz, C.; Carolan, M.; Holloway, L.; Miller, A.A. The Role of Deep Learning and Radiomic Feature Extraction in Cancer-Specific Predictive Modelling: A Review. *Transl. Cancer Res.* **2018**, *7*, 803–816. [CrossRef]
47. Amulya, C.; Prathibha, G. MRI Brain Tumour Classification Using SURF and SIFT Features. *Int. J. Mod. Trends Sci. Technol.* **2016**, *2*, 123–127.
48. Virupakshappa; Amarapur, B. An Automated Approach for Brain Tumor Identification Using ANN Classifier. In Proceedings of the 2017 International Conference on Current Trends in Computer, Electrical, Electronics and Communication (CTCEEC), Mysore, India, 8–9 September 2017; pp. 1011–1016.
49. Wicaksono, Y.; Wahono, R.S.; Suhartono, V. Color and Texture Feature Extraction Using Gabor Filter-Local Binary Patterns for Image Segmentation with Fuzzy C-Means. *J. Intell. Syst.* **2015**, *1*, 15–21.
50. Samjith Raj, C.P.; Shreeja, R. Automatic Brain Tumor Tissue Detection in T-1 Weighted MRI. In Proceedings of the 2017 International Conference on Innovations in Information, Embedded and Communication Systems (ICIIECS), Coimbatore, India, 17–18 March 2017; pp. 1–4.
51. Ilhan, U.; Ilhan, A. Brain Tumor Segmentation Based on a New Threshold Approach. In Proceedings of the 9th International Conference on Theory and Application of Soft Computing, Computing with Words and Perception, ICSCCW 2017, Budapest, Hungary, 24–25 August 2017; Volume 120, pp. 580–587.
52. Devkota, B.; Alsadoon, A.; Prasad, P.W.C.; Singh, A.K.; Elchouemi, A. Image Segmentation for Early Stage Brain Tumor Detection Using Mathematical Morphological Reconstruction. *Procedia Comput. Sci.* **2018**, *125*, 115–123. [CrossRef]
53. Ismael, M.R.; Abdel-Qader, I. Brain Tumor Classification via Statistical Features and Back-Propagation Neural Network. In Proceedings of the 2018 IEEE International Conference on Electro/Information Technology (EIT), Rochester, MI, USA, 3–5 May 2018; pp. 252–257.
54. Bahadure, N.B.; Ray, A.K.; Thethi, H.P. Comparative Approach of MRI-Based Brain Tumor Segmentation and Classification Using Genetic Algorithm. *J. Digit. Imaging* **2018**, *31*, 477–489. [CrossRef]
55. Rajesh, T.; Malar, R.S.M.; Geetha, M.R. Brain Tumor Detection Using Optimisation Classification Based on Rough Set Theory. *Clust. Comput.* **2019**, *22*, 13853–13859. [CrossRef]
56. Shree, N.V.; Kumar, T.N.R. Identification and Classification of Brain Tumor MRI Images with Feature Extraction Using DWT and Probabilistic Neural Network. *Brain Inform.* **2018**, *5*, 23–30. [CrossRef]
57. Al-Masni, M.A.; Kim, D.-H. CMM-Net: Contextual Multi-Scale Multi-Level Network for Efficient Biomedical Image Segmentation. *Sci. Rep.* **2021**, *11*, 10191. [CrossRef]
58. Rajeev, S.K.; Rajasekaran, M.P.; Vishnuvarthanan, G.; Arunprasath, T. A Biologically-Inspired Hybrid Deep Learning Approach for Brain Tumor Classification from Magnetic Resonance Imaging Using Improved Gabor Wavelet Transform and Elmann-BiLSTM Network. *Biomed. Signal Process. Control.* **2022**, 78. [CrossRef]
59. Tandel, G.S.; Tiwari, A.; Kakde, O.G. Performance Enhancement of MRI-Based Brain Tumor Classification Using Suitable Segmentation Method and Deep Learning-Based Ensemble Algorithm. *Biomed. Signal Process. Control.* **2022**, *78*, 104018. [CrossRef]
60. Anaraki, A.K.; Ayati, M.; Kazemi, F. Magnetic Resonance Imaging-Based Brain Tumor Grades Classification and Grading via Convolutional Neural Networks and Genetic Algorithms. *Biocybern. Biomed. Eng.* **2019**, *39*, 63–74. [CrossRef]
61. Kazemi, A.; Shiri, M.E.; Sheikhahmadi, A.; Khodamoradi, M. Classifying Tumor Brain Images Using Parallel Deep Learning Algorithms. *Comput. Biol. Med.* **2022**, *148*, 105775. [CrossRef] [PubMed]
62. Mehrotra, R.; Ansari, M.A.; Agrawal, R.; Anand, R.S. A Transfer Learning Approach for AI-Based Classification of Brain Tumors. *Machine Learning with Applications* **2020**, *2*, 100003. [CrossRef]
63. Sultan, H.H.; Salem, N.M.; Al-Atabany, W. Multi-Classification of Brain Tumor Images Using Deep Neural Network. *IEEE Access* **2019**, *7*, 69215–69225. [CrossRef]

64. Abiwinanda, N.; Hanif, M.; Hesaputra, S.T.; Handayani, A.; Mengko, T.R. Brain Tumor Classification Using Convolutional Neural Network. In Proceedings of the World Congress on Medical Physics and Biomedical Engineering, Prague, Czech Republic, 3–8 June 2018; pp. 183–189. [CrossRef]
65. Díaz-Pernas, F.J.; Martínez-Zarzuela, M.; Antón-Rodríguez, M.; González-Ortega, D. A Deep Learning Approach for Brain Tumor Classification and Segmentation Using a Multiscale Convolutional Neural Network. *Healthcare* **2021**, *9*, 153. [CrossRef]
66. Mohsen, H.; El-Dahshan, E.-S.A.; El-Horbaty, E.-S.M.; Salem, A.-B.M. Classification Using Deep Learning Neural Networks for Brain Tumors. *Future Comput. Inform. J.* **2018**, *3*, 68–71. [CrossRef]
67. Balasooriya, N.M.; Nawarathna, R.D. A Sophisticated Convolutional Neural Network Model for Brain Tumor Classification. In Proceedings of the 2017 IEEE International Conference on Industrial and Information Systems (ICIIS), Peradeniya, Sri Lanka, 15–16 December 2017; pp. 1–5.
68. Hemanth, D.J.; Anitha, J.; Naaji, A.; Geman, O.; Popescu, D.E.; Son, L.H. A Modified Deep Convolutional Neural Network for Abnormal Brain Image Classification. *IEEE Access* **2019**, *7*, 4275–4283. [CrossRef]
69. Rao, V.; Sharifi, M.; Jaiswal, A. Brain Tumor Segmentation with Deep Learning. *MICCAI Multimodal Brain Tumor Segm. Chall. (BraTS)* **2015**, *59*, 1–4.
70. Pereira, S.; Pinto, A.; Alves, V.; Silva, C.A. Brain Tumor Segmentation Using Convolutional Neural Networks in MRI Images. *IEEE Trans. Med. Imaging* **2016**, *35*, 1240–1251. [CrossRef]
71. Casamitjana, A.; Puch, S.; Aduriz, A.; Vilaplana, V. 3D Convolutional Neural Networks for Brain Tumor Segmentation: A Comparison of Multi-Resolution Architectures. *arXiv* **2017**, arXiv:1705.08236v1.
72. Dong, H.; Yang, G.; Liu, F.; Mo, Y.; Guo, Y. Automatic Brain Tumor Detection and Segmentation Using U-Net Based Fully Convolutional Networks. In *Medical Image Understanding and Analysis*; Springer: Cham, Switzerland, 2017; Volume 723, pp. 506–517. [CrossRef]
73. Wang, M.; Yang, J.; Chen, Y.; Wang, H. The Multimodal Brain Tumor Image Segmentation Based on Convolutional Neural Networks. In Proceedings of the 2017 2nd IEEE International Conference on Computational Intelligence and Applications (ICCIA), Beijing, China, 8–11 September 2017; pp. 336–339.
74. Wang, H. A CNN Based Method for Brain Tumor Detection. Master's Thesis, Carleton University, Ottawa, ON, Canada, 2018.
75. Cui, S.; Mao, L.; Jiang, J.; Liu, C.; Xiong, S. Automatic Semantic Segmentation of Brain Gliomas from MRI Images Using a Deep Cascaded Neural Network. *J. Healthc. Eng.* **2018**, *2018*, 4940593. [CrossRef]
76. Lang, R.; Jia, K.; Feng, J. Brain Tumor Identification Based on CNN-SVM Model. In Proceedings of the 2nd International Conference on Biomedical Engineering and Bioinformatics, Tianjin, China, 19–21 September 2018; Association for Computing Machinery: New York, NY, USA, 2018; pp. 31–35.
77. Li, H.; Li, A.; Wang, M. A Novel End-to-End Brain Tumor Segmentation Method Using Improved Fully Convolutional Networks. *Comput. Biol. Med.* **2019**, *108*, 150–160. [CrossRef]
78. Peng, S.; Chen, W.; Sun, J.; Liu, B. Multi-Scale 3D U-Nets: An Approach to Automatic Segmentation of Brain Tumor. *Int. J. Imaging Syst. Technol.* **2020**, *30*, 5–17. [CrossRef]
79. Menze, B.H.; Jakab, A.; Bauer, S.; Kalpathy-Cramer, J.; Farahani, K.; Kirby, J.; Burren, Y.; Porz, N.; Slotboom, J.; Wiest, R.; et al. The Multimodal Brain Tumor Image Segmentation Benchmark (BRATS). *IEEE Trans. Med. Imaging* **2015**, *34*, 1993–2024. [CrossRef] [PubMed]
80. Ohgaki, H.; Kleihues, P. Population-Based Studies on Incidence, Survival Rates, and Genetic Alterations in Astrocytic and Oligodendroglial Gliomas. *J. Neuropathol. Exp. Neurol.* **2005**, *64*, 479–489. [CrossRef]
81. Louis, D.N.; Ohgaki, H.; Wiestler, O.D.; Cavenee, W.K.; Burger, P.C.; Jouvet, A.; Scheithauer, B.W.; Kleihues, P. The 2007 WHO Classification of Tumours of the Central Nervous System. *Acta Neuropathol.* **2007**, *114*, 97–109. [CrossRef]
82. O'Shea, K.; Nash, R. An Introduction to Convolutional Neural Networks. *arXiv* **2015**, arXiv:1511.08458.
83. Kabade, R.S.; Gaikwad, M.S. Segmentation of Brain Tumour and Its Area Calculation in Brain MR Images Using K-Mean Clustering and Fuzzy C-Mean Algorithm. *Med. Comput. Sci.* **2013**, *4*, 524–531.
84. Mustaqeem, A.; Javed, A.; Fatima, T. An Efficient Brain Tumor Detection Algorithm Using Watershed & Thresholding Based Segmentation. *Image Graph. Signal Process.* **2012**, *10*, 34–39. [CrossRef]
85. Bien, N.; Rajpurkar, P.; Ball, R.L.; Irvin, J.; Park, A.; Jones, E.; Bereket, M.; Patel, B.N.; Yeom, K.W.; Shpanskaya, K.; et al. Deep-Learning-Assisted Diagnosis for Knee Magnetic Resonance Imaging: Development and Retrospective Validation of MRNet. *PLoS Med.* **2018**, *15*, e1002699. [CrossRef]
86. Walsh, J.; Othmani, A.; Jain, M.; Dev, S. Using U-Net Network for Efficient Brain Tumor Segmentation in MRI Images. *Healthc. Anal.* **2022**, *2*, 100098. [CrossRef]
87. Kouli, O.; Hassane, A.; Badran, D.; Kouli, T.; Hossain-Ibrahim, K.; Steele, J.D. Automated Brain Tumor Identification Using Magnetic Resonance Imaging: A Systematic Review and Meta-Analysis. *Neuro-Oncol. Adv.* **2022**, *4*, 1–13. [CrossRef] [PubMed]
88. Das, S.; Nayak, G.K.; Saba, L.; Kalra, M.; Suri, J.S.; Saxena, S. An Artificial Intelligence Framework and Its Bias for Brain Tumor Segmentation: A Narrative Review. *Comput. Biol. Med.* **2022**, *143*, 105273. [CrossRef] [PubMed]
89. Ronneberger, O.; Fischer, P.; Brox, T. U-Net: Convolutional Networks for Biomedical Image Segmentation. In *Lecture Notes in Computer Science, Proceedings of the International Conference on Medical Image Computing and Computer-Assisted Intervention, Munich, Germany, 5–9 October 2015*; Springer: New York, NY, USA, 2015; Volume 9351, pp. 234–241.

90. Yin, X.X.; Sun, L.; Fu, Y.; Lu, R.; Zhang, Y. U-Net-Based Medical Image Segmentation. *J. Healthc. Eng.* **2022**, *2022*, 4189781. [CrossRef] [PubMed]
91. Hsu, L.-M.; Wang, S.; Walton, L.; Wang, T.-W.W.; Lee, S.-H.; Shih, Y.-Y.I. 3D U-Net Improves Automatic Brain Extraction for Isotropic Rat Brain Magnetic Resonance Imaging Data. *Front. Neurosci.* **2021**, *15*, 1674. [CrossRef]
92. Kalaiselvi, T.; Padmapriya, S.T. Multimodal MRI Brain Tumor Segmentation-A ResNet-Based U-Net Approach. In *Brain Tumor MRI Image Segmentation Using Deep Learning Techniques*; Chaki, J., Ed.; Academic Press: Cambridge, MA, USA, 2021; pp. 123–135.
93. Goyal, S.; Kotambkar, D.M. Exploring Unet Architecture for Semantic Segmentation of the Brain MRI Scans. In *Lecture Notes in Electrical Engineering, Proceedings of the Machine Intelligence and Signal Processing, Allahabad, India, 7–10 September, 2019*; Springer Science and Business Media Deutschland GmbH: Berlin, Germany, 2022; Volume 858, pp. 569–578.
94. Hmeed, A.R.; Aliesawi, S.A.; Jasim, W.M. Enhancement of the U-Net Architecture for MRI Brain Tumor Segmentation. In *Lecture Notes in Networks and Systems, Proceedings of the International Conference on Next Generation of Internet of Things (ICNGIoT 2021), Odisha, India, 5–6 February 2021*; Springer Science and Business Media Deutschland GmbH: Berlin, Germany, 2021; Volume 201, pp. 353–367.
95. Rehman, M.U.; Cho, S.; Kim, J.H.; Chong, K.T. BU-Net: Brain Tumor Segmentation Using Modified U-Net Architecture. *Electronics* **2020**, *9*, 2203. [CrossRef]
96. Ayadi, W.; Elhamzi, W.; Charfi, I.; Atri, M. Deep CNN for Brain Tumor Classification. *Neural Process. Lett.* **2021**, *53*, 671–700. [CrossRef]
97. Vanderbecq, Q.; Xu, E.; Ströer, S.; Couvy-Duchesne, B.; Melo, M.D.; Dormont, D.; Colliot, O. Comparison and Validation of Seven White Matter Hyperintensities Segmentation Software in Elderly Patients. *NeuroImage Clin.* **2020**, *27*, 102357. [CrossRef]

healthcare

MDPI

Article

Methodology for Selecting the Appropriate Electric Motor for Robotic Modular Systems for Lower Extremities

Dimitrios Kavalieros *, Evangelos Kapothanasis, Athanasios Kakarountas and Thanasis Loukopoulos

Department of Computer Science and Biomedical Informatics, University of Thessaly, 35131 Lamia, Greece
* Correspondence: dkavalieros@uth.gr

Abstract: Torque calculation is essential for selecting the appropriate motor to achieve the required torque at each joint of a hybrid exoskeleton. In recent years, the combined use of functional electrical stimulation (FES) and robotic devices, called hybrid robotic rehabilitation systems, has emerged as a promising approach for the rehabilitating of lower limb motor functions. Specifically, the implementation strategy of functional electrical stimulation walking aid combined with the design of the exoskeleton part is the main focus of our research team. This work copes with issues of the design process of a robotic exoskeleton. The importance of robotic exoskeletons for providing walking aid to people with mobility disorders or the elderly is discussed. Furthermore, the approaches to calculating the joint torques are investigated, and the mathematical models and parameters of interest are identified. This further includes the comparative data for servo motors: robotic exoskeleton characteristics and actuator analysis in the robotic exoskeleton. The aforementioned is used to propose a mathematical model based on previous models (Zatsiorsky BSP and Dempster BSP body segment parameters models, forward kinematics models), which was extended to include added adjustable parameters such as length, area, volume, mass, density, the centre of mass, human body characteristics, and considering both static and dynamic parameter extraction. Then, an analytic method is presented, exploiting the results from the mathematical model to select the appropriate motor for each joint of the lower extremities. The detailed description of the method is followed by examples, experimental measurements, and statistical analysis of qualitative and quantitative characteristics. The results showed deviations from typical calculation methods, offering a better understanding of the motor requirements for each joint of the exoskeleton and avoiding selections of marginal functionality features of the motors. In addition, researchers are offered a tool for replicating the results of this work, allowing them to configure the parameters associated with the servo motor features. The researcher can either use the embedded library developed for this work or enter new data into it, affecting the calculated torques of the model joints. The extracted results assist the researcher in choosing the appropriate motor among commercially available brushed and brushless motors based on the torques applied at each joint in robotic articulated systems.

Keywords: robotic exoskeletons; servo motor; brushless; brushed; actuators; torque; centre mass

Citation: Kavalieros, D.; Kapothanasis, E.; Kakarountas, A.; Loukopoulos, T. Methodology for Selecting the Appropriate Electric Motor for Robotic Modular Systems for Lower Extremities. *Healthcare* **2022**, *10*, 2054. https://doi.org/10.3390/healthcare10102054

Academic Editor: Daniele Giansanti

Received: 18 August 2022
Accepted: 9 October 2022
Published: 17 October 2022

1. Introduction

Lately, exoskeletons are designed to provide strength in gait and heavy transport loads. There are also designs for assisting people with disorders in motion or older adults. Gait rehabilitation is one of the most significant challenges for society in the coming years due to population ageing and the increase of diseases affecting motion. Partial or total paralysis of one side of the body due to injuries in the motor centres of the brain is called Hemiplegia. Hemiplegia is a disorder that causes one-half of the human body to fail to perform its functions. This disorder is caused mainly due to stroke, and in many cases, it is hereditary. Recovery from a stroke is complex, and the treatment is prolonged. Wearable robotics is an area that provides solutions for such problems. A wearable robot extends, complements, or empowers the human limb where it is worn. These kinds of robots are classified according to the function they perform:

- **Empowering robotic exoskeletons:** These kinds of robots are known as extenders since they extend the strength of the human hand beyond its natural ability while maintaining human control of the robot.
- **Orthotic robots:** An orthosis maps the anatomy of a limb to restore lost functions. The robotic counterpart of orthosis is robotic exoskeletons that complement the ability of the limbs. Exoskeletons are also capable of restoring handicapped functions.
- **Prosthetic robots:** These robots are devices that fully substitute lost limbs [1].

Figure 1 shows two examples of wearable robots. The scientific community differentiates exoskeletons from orthosis by defining the former as the devices that enhance the physical capabilities of wholesome users and the latter as the devices that assist persons with limb impairments [2]. Specifically, in Figure 1, the lower extremity of an orthotic exoskeleton for mobility problems is presented as developed by the authors, and the lower extremity of a prosthetic robot, according to work in [1], is presented in Figure 1b. Despite their differences, both devices act in parallel with the limb. In the medical field, in combination with rehabilitation therapies, exoskeletons can help patients with spinal cord injuries, strokes, and lower limb paralysis caused by hemiplegia [1].

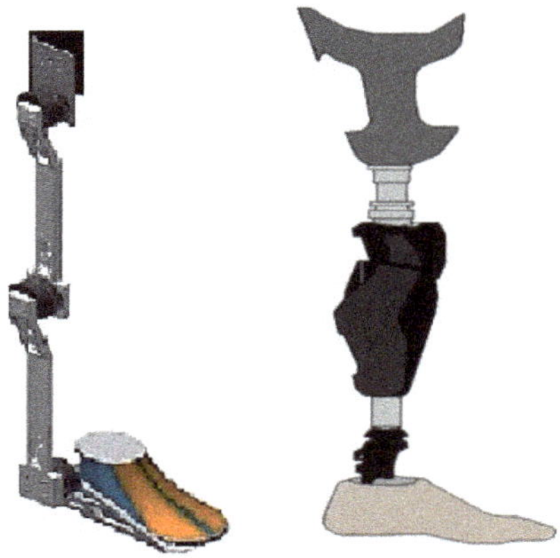

(a) (b)

Figure 1. (**a**) Lower limb orthotic exoskeleton, (**b**) lower limb prosthetic robot [1].

The studies of the calculation of torque equations in each lower extremity exoskeleton joint were based on the kinematic analysis. Specifically, in [3], forward kinematics was applied to find the foot's position when values were given for the corners of the joint. The torque required on each joint is determined using free-body diagrams of different joints. The work found in [4] proposed the lower limb robotic exoskeletons (LLRE) model. The free-body diagram of force on the knees and hips was constructed. Dynamic hip and knee models were obtained, considering the hips and knees as support points. The torque equations of the lower limb joints were calculated according to the parameters of the specific model. Another approach to calculating the joint torques was also based on kinematics. The kinematic analysis is applied through forward and inverse kinematics as proposed in [1]. The Euler–Lagrange method is used to obtain the dynamic equations of the exoskeleton. The literature review was performed by querying the Google Scholar database. To identify papers on robotic lower limb exoskeletons, we mainly focused on electric actuation technologies. The results were filtered based on the officially used torque calculation models to determine the percentages. Nearly 600 scientific articles have been published in the last three years on robotic exoskeletons for the lower extremities based on kinematics (thus, excluding the upper extremities cases).

Nearly 32% are surveyed on the topic, and 35% mainly present simulations of proposed models based on the formally used torque calculation models. The rest include works on reducing cost or power dissipation and applications of ML in the control of the exoskeleton. As the works above show, the researchers of robotic exoskeletons calculate the torques of the lower limb exoskeleton joints based on their model's kinematic analysis.

It was noted by the authors that there is a lack in the international literature on the measurement of lower extremity joint torques embedding the physical part of the implementation, which differentiates significantly by both the building components of the exoskeleton and the user's physical characteristics.

Thus, the following are issues that motivated this work, and the proposed approach to offer a combined solution is presented in the rest of this work.

1. Lack of a well-defined framework for calculating the torques of the joints based on multiple factors.
2. Creation of a set of parameters for simulating the operation and calculating the torques.
3. Inclusion of the user's physical data in the calculation of the parameters for calculating the torques.
4. Use of the motor characteristics to assess their suitability or not for the targeted solution (exoskeleton).

Most authors seem to agree that clinical gait analysis (CGA) data sources are a good start for the initial design of the actuation to be used in their prototypes [5]. However, Beyl, in his work [6], remarks on the large variability observed in gait data and cautions designers of actuated exoskeletons to be careful in interpreting CGA data and formulating design recommendations based on those data. Joint torque data determine the required characteristics for the actuation to be applied at each assisted joint. The intensity of the joint torques fluctuates within the gait cycle [5–8], and therefore, in most cases, designers use maximum values (peaks) as requirements for the sizing of their actuators [5–7]. However, in [9], the authors used optimisation methods and models of human motion to estimate the required torques for their passive, assistive systems. The aforementioned shows the need for a method to optimise the torque calculation based on the characteristics of the human, the exoskeleton, and the motors selected to decrease the time-to-production and achieve smooth motion.

According to the above literature references, the mathematical model in this article differs from other models in terms of its variability. First, the user can configure multiple parameters that affect the robotic exoskeleton, taking into account the characteristics of the human body (weight, height, etc.) and the characteristics of the robotic exoskeleton (exoskeleton weight, actuator weight, etc.). Second, the proposed solution considers the self-correction of the model by allowing its dynamic modification.

Figure 2 shows the robotic exoskeleton drawing showing the joints of the actuators. We are developing a hybrid rehabilitation system (FesRobex) combining Functional Electrical Stimulation (FES) and an exoskeleton to control patients' gait with lower limb mobility problems. This study aims to use the mathematical model to calculate the torque at each joint and analyse the individual characteristics that influence the mathematical model for the appropriate selection of motors in exoskeleton joints.

First, in Section 1.1, an introduction to servo motors is offered, and Section 2 presents the proposed approach. Then, in Section 3, the evaluation of the proposed model and the calculations are offered, as well as its effectiveness in selecting the appropriate motors for embedding on a targeted exoskeleton. Finally, the paper concludes with Section 4 featuring the discussion and Section 5 outlining the conclusions of the mathematical model.

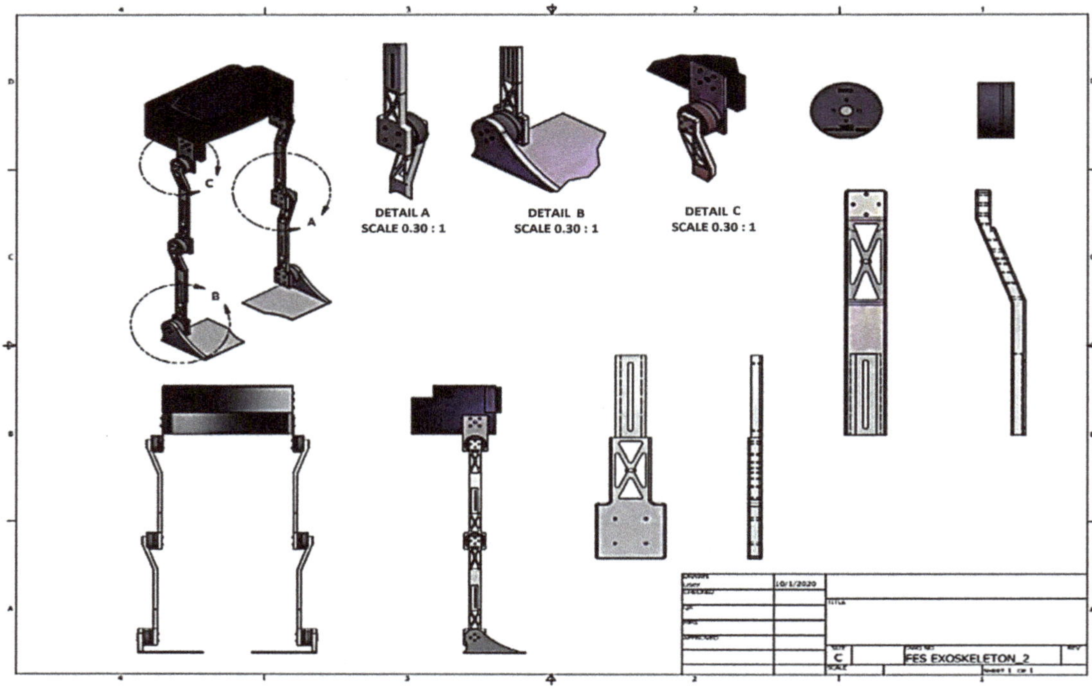

Figure 2. Robotic exoskeleton design plan of the Hybrid Exoskeleton FesRobex (Autocad design).

1.1. Introduction to Servo Motors

In this section, an introduction to servo motors that are used in the design and implementation of exoskeletons is provided. This part of the work is considered significant to highlight the variety of the available servo motors and emphasise the parameters that need to be considered when embedded in an exoskeleton.

1.1.1. Research on Servo Motors

Servo motors have been used in automatic control systems for many years, especially in applications that require speed, position and torque control of the motor shaft. Classic examples include robotic arms, automatic machine tools, remote-controlled models, and automatic navigation systems for ships and aircraft [10].

The essential characteristics of the servo motor

- The motor torque is proportional to the applied control voltage that the amplifier develops due to the error at its input.
- The direction of the torque is determined by the control voltage's polarity (instantaneous value).

Servo motors are structurally very similar to ordinary motors but are not identical. They differ because they contain measurement devices and a feedback system that is used in conjunction with a servo-drive mechanism to control torque, speed, or position [11].

1.1.2. Criteria for the Selection of Servo Motors

The criteria for selecting servo motors are response speed, accuracy, and errors due to external distortions combined with the cost, availability, and reliability of the motor. Another important selection criterion is that the performance should cover both the power of the load (due) and the friction (losses) of the device. In addition, the servo motor must operate at the desired speeds and provide the required acceleration for the rotor and the load [12].

1.1.3. Characteristics of the Servo Motor

(a) Mechanical and geometric

- The size, weight and inertia of the motor.
- The placement of the motor and the way it is connected to the moving mechanism.

(b) Electromechanical

- Required power and concentration of motor power (power to mass ratio).
- Torque requirements and characteristics.
- Speed range and response to changes.
- Sensitivity to changes in servo motor parameters [13].

1.1.4. Features of Electric Servo Motors

- **DC Servo motors**

There are various types of electric servo motors, such as permanent magnet servo motors, rotor-controlled servo motors, stator-controlled servo motors, and stator and rotor servo motors in series.

- **R/C Servo motors**

R/C servo motors are special compact servo motors that include a complete servo motor system consisting of a motor, a gearbox, a feedback device, and a drive and control circuit (Figure 3). The main parts constituting it are the following:

- DC electric motor;
- An electronic circuit controls the end drive shaft and gearbox position.

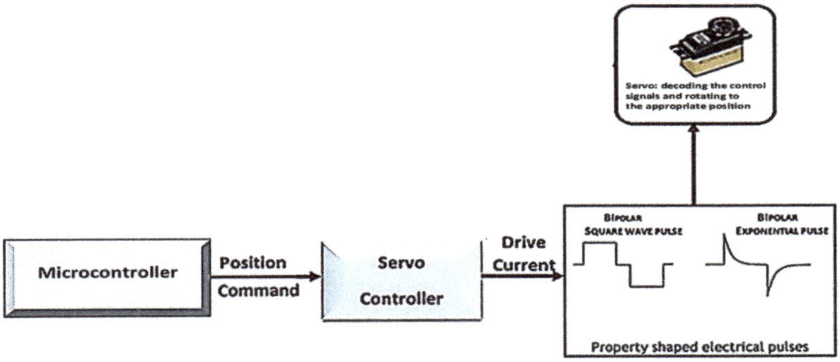

Figure 3. Operation RC Servo.

The final drive shaft does not perform complete rotations but rotates between two extreme positions. The servo operation requires (Figure 3) the provision of the appropriate electrical voltage and a signal that determines the position of rotation of the final shaft. The control of the servo requires a specialised controller, and the open-loop control method is used. The main disadvantage of RC servo motors is the inability to perform complete and continuous rotation (Figure 4).

Nevertheless, these servomechanisms have essential advantages such as:

- Low cost.
- Small dimensions and easy-to-use shape, which surrounds all parts.
- Produce high torque values.
- The use of sensors and feedback circuits is not required to determine the position of the driveshaft.

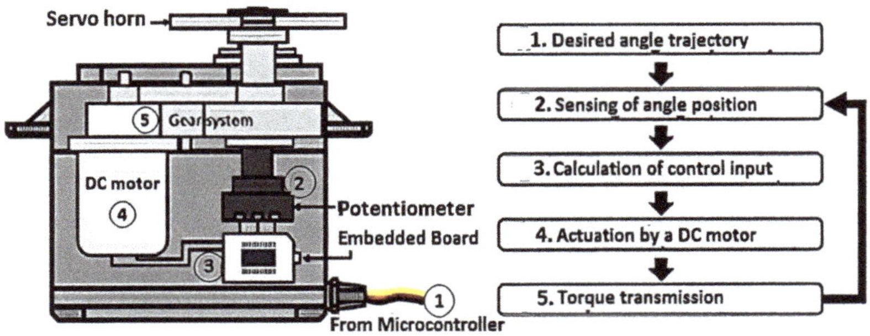

Figure 4. Schematic of an RC servo motor [14].

Servo motors are essential in robotics as they facilitate intelligent and natural movement. They are used in robotic systems of all kinds and can transmit information about the rotation of the motor on its axis so that the robot can "know" the movements of its various parts. The realisation of the desired movement of a robotic mechanism requires the combined movement of its joints. This is achieved by using a servo motor, which drives a mechanical system as a whole. In recent years, with the development of biomedical technology, servo motors have had broad applications in medicine and specifically in robotic medical systems [12].

1.2. Brushless and Brushed DC Motors

DC motors are used in applications where DC power sources are available, such as aircraft, automobiles or robotic systems. However, this type of small motor has some drawbacks. The main disadvantage is the excessive scintillation and wears on the brushes. Small and fast DC motors are too small to use compensation winding and auxiliary poles. The reinforcement reaction and the effects L $\frac{di}{dt}$ tend to create sparks in the transducer brushes. In addition, the high rotation speed of these motors increases the wear of the brushes, thus requiring shorter maintenance. In some applications, the maintenance required by the brushes of these DC motors may not be acceptable. A typical example is the DC motor in an artificial heart, where an incision must be made in the patient's chest for maintenance. In addition, sparks in the brushes are dangerous, as they can cause an explosion and excessive RF noise. This developed a fast, small and reliable direct current motor with low noise and long life. This is a combination of a small motor that is very similar to a permanent stepper motor and has:

1. A cursor position sensor; and
2. An electronic circuit breaker.

These motors are called brushless DC motors (S.R.) because they are powered by a direct current source without switches and brushes. They are also called Modern Permanent Magnet Motors [15].

The S.R. motors without brushes have many advantages such as:

1. Size and low weight.
2. Relatively high performance.
3. Long service life and reliability.
4. Minimal or no maintenance.
5. Very low RF noise level compared to S.R. motors with brushes.
6. High-speed capability (50,000 rpm).
7. High torque.

Their main disadvantage is the high purchase cost.

Finally, in the introduction, we note that most studies use clinical gait analysis (CGA) data and human motion models to estimate the required torques for their passive support systems. As a result, there is no possibility of parameter variability (mass, length of body parts, height and weight of a person, the mass of actuators, etc.). Most studies use ready-made data from libraries and data they extract from their model with specific characteristics, as we mentioned in the introduction to the bibliographies. Therefore, they do not have the option to vary the characteristics of the robotic exoskeleton or the characteristics of the human body over a wide range to calculate the joint torque. The aim of the article is to fill the gap that has been created, i.e., the computation of torque with the possibility of changing parameters of the exoskeleton and human characteristics. The purpose of this work is to model the best choice of the appropriate motor (in the physical implementation phase) for each lower limb joint of the hybrid exoskeleton.

2. Materials and Methods

In this section, the materials of interest are initially presented along with their parameters. Then, the theoretical approach, according to the evidence from the literature, is explored, aiming at the comparative data for servo motors. Collecting the servo motors' data is critical since introducing any servo motor to a robotic component dynamically affects the system's characteristics, especially in the case of the inclusion of heterogeneous servo motors to various joints of the exoskeleton. The collected data are organised in a database to allow the selection of the appropriate motor for the targeted joint. The following two subsections refer to the parameters of the exoskeleton that should be considered for calculating the joints' torques and the characteristics of the actuators that may be used. This concludes the extraction of the parameters and values of interest, developing the proposed mathematical model to calculate the torques of heterogeneous motors installed on an exoskeleton's joints.

After the presentation of the materials and their characteristics, the methodology to select the appropriate motor for each joint follows. Next, the mathematical model is analysed, and the steps to be followed are presented. The proposed methodology has two steps. During initialisation, the parameters of the user are set based on the user's characteristics (e.g., weight, height, etc.) and the coefficients derived from known models. In the first step (A), the masses for the exoskeleton are calculated, and the motors' characteristics are considered as a penalty on masses. In the second step (B), the joint torque is calculated and verified with the desired one. If the achieved torque is sufficient, then the motor is selected. Otherwise, the process is repeated until an appropriate configuration is found.

2.1. Comparative Study of Servo Motors

In many automation control applications, the main competitors of servo motors are stepper motors. Both types of motors have their advantages and disadvantages. Their differences relate mainly to their performance because they are differently designed. For example, a rotor motor's poles are much larger than the poles of a servo motor, so a rotation requires a larger current to flow through its windings. In addition, the stepper motor at high speeds degrades its torque, which is a phenomenon that can be reduced using a higher supply voltage. In contrast, the large number of poles of a stepper motor has a beneficial effect at lower speeds, thus giving it a torque advantage over a servo motor of the same size. Another difference is the way each type of motor is controlled. The open-loop method is used to control the stepper motors. This reduces the cost, as no feedback device is required (e.g., encoder for most positioning applications). However, in stepper motor systems, the excess power is converted into heat, thus generating a significant amount of heat in the motor and drive, which must be considered in various applications, especially those in the medical and healthcare field. Servo control solves this problem by supplying the motor with the current needed to move or hold the load. It can also provide maximum acceleration torque, which is often more significant than the maximum continuous torque of the motor. However, an encoder can also control a stepper motor in a complete closed-loop servo system. In terms of equipment, stepper motors are more superficial than servo motors.

Therefore, they are much easier to maintain and cost less, especially in small motor applications. When they operate within the design parameters, they do not lose their steps and do not require encoders. At the same time, when they are at rest, they remain stable, holding their position without any fluctuations, especially in dynamic loads. Specifically, a Brushless Direct Current (BLDC) generally operates better for speeds below 2000 RPM, lower acceleration values, and high retention torque. Servo motors are best in applications that require speeds above 2000 RPM and high torque at high speeds or where a high dynamic response is required. In conclusion, servo motor control systems respond better to high speeds and high torque applications involving dynamic load changes. BLDC motor control systems are less expensive than their respective servo motors and are ideal mainly for applications that require relatively low acceleration values, high holding torque, and flexibility to operate in an open or closed-loop system. For a complete picture of the differences between a Servo Motor SR (Brushed) and Step Motor (Hybrid) or BLDC motor, the table below shows the characteristics of a DC servo motor with a collector–brush system and a BLDC brushless motor (Table 1) [16].

Table 1. Comparison of SR servo motor with brushes and hybrid stepper motor or BLDC motor.

Features	Servo Motor SR (Brushed)	Step Motor (Hybrid) or BLDC Motor
Cost	The cost of a servo motor or servo system is greater than the cost of a step motor system with the same rated power.	Step motors are generally cheaper than servo motors that have the same rated power value.
Size	They are available in a wide variety of sizes from small to very large motors and can operate huge machines.	In the step motors, there are not as many size options as in servo motors, especially for large sizes.
Noise	Servo motors produce very little noise compared to step motors.	They produce a small hum due to the screening process. However, a high-quality driving system reduces the level of this noise.
Power range	They are available in DC and AC motors and thus have a very wide range of available power.	The range of available power in step motors is smaller than in servo motors.
Performance	In general, servo motors are very efficient motors. In small loads mainly, a yield of 80–90% is reported.	The step motors consume enough power, a lot of which is converted into heat. Usually, their performance is at about 70% and depends on the driving system.
Life	Coolers every 2000 h of operation must be replaced. Codecs may also be needed to replace them	The only place that wears out is the bearing. This gives the step motors a slight lead.
Low speed high torque	They work very well in low-speed applications, mainly due to very low friction.	They provide more torque at low speeds (RPM).
High speed high torque	They maintain rated torque at about 90% of their speed without load.	Step motors lose up to 80% of their maximum torque, at 90% of their maximum speed.
Power ratio by weight/size	Given the effectiveness of the servo motors, they have an excellent power ratio in terms of weight and size.	Step motors are less efficint than servo motors. This usually means a lower motor size power–weight ratio.

We consider that the two motors are of the same quality and have the same rated power. There are many designs of robotic exoskeletons proposed for different purposes in the literature. Table 2 summarises some of the primary active projects in the scientific community with the types of motors they use, which have been reported in journals and conferences [1].

Table 2. Robotic exoskeletons around the world.

Foundation	Name	Purpose	Technical Data	Control Method
Yonsei University South Korea	Help walking an exoskeleton of the lower extremity	Patients with lower limb paralysis	1. 200 W DC motor without brushes 2. Harmonic movements 3. Torques: Hip: 79.3 nm Knee: 42.2 nm	1. Active kinematic control 2. Stability check
Tsukuba University Japan	HAL3	Patients with lower limb paralysis	1. Servo Motor DC 2. Harmonic joint reducers	1. Conscious recognition based on plant pressure and torso angle
Automation Robotics Centre Hispania	ATLAS	Quadriplegic patients	1. Brushless motors (Maxon) 2. Harmonic reducers 3. Maximum torque 57 nm (hip)	1. CoP stability check 2. Conscious recognition
Berkeley Robotics and Human Engineering Laboratory USA	Lower extremity exoskeleton (BLEEX)	Allow personnel the ability to carry major loads such as food, rescue equipment, first-aid supplies	1.DC brushless motors 2.Harmonic reducers	1. CoP stability control 2. Conscious recognition

2.2. Robotic Exoskeleton Features

Exoskeletons are anthropomorphic mechanical devices worn by an operator that closely match the body's anatomy and work in coordination with the user's movements. Among the main requirements of an exoskeleton to be taken into account when designing are the following:

- **The design must be anthropomorphic:** Current designs have an abnormal shape; another limitation of exoskeletons is the lack of direct exchange of information between the human nervous system and the wearable robotic part.
- **The design must be flexible:** The length of the thigh, stem, and waist must be adjustable, and the variation in length and the stem is approximately 6 cm for average people, from 1.60 to 1.80 m. The length of the torso is approximately 0.246 times the height, and the length of the thigh is about 0.245 times the height.
- **Increase joint strength:** Exoskeletons do not transfer the substantial load to the ground but augment joint torque. This consideration might be used to reduce joint pain or increase joint strength in paralysed or weak joints.
- **Selection of Degrees of Freedom (DoF):** The exoskeleton must comply with the free movement of the joints. Table 3 shows the DoF of a lower extremity exoskeleton.
- **The exoskeleton robot actuator:** It must have a high output-to-weight power ratio and features such as low inertia, fast response, high accuracy, etc. [1].

The joints in the lower limb of the human body are the hips, knees, and ankles. Each joint has different abilities to move or DoF, as shown in more detail in Table 3. The types of lower limb exoskeletons based on joint motions are differentiated into several types based on how the actuators drive the exoskeleton. The actuators can drive just the hips, the knees, or the ankles.

In a small number of studies, exoskeletons have multiple actuators to drive a combination of joints. These combinations of actuators are hips and knees, knees and ankles, and all three joints (hips, knees, and ankles) [17].

Table 3. DOF design for lower extremity exoskeleton.

Joints	DOF/ Movement	Freedom Range	Driving Power Required (N/m)
Hip	3/Flexion–extension	−120°/65°	80–100
Hip	3/Addition–abduction	−30°/40°	Spring
Hip	3/Rotation	−30°/30°	Spring
Knee	2/Flexion–extension	−30°/40°	45–70
Ankle	2/Pretonation–rotation	−15°/30°	Spring
Ankle	3/Dorsal bending–bending of the fingersn	−20°/50°	Spring
Ankle	3/Dorsal bending–bending of the fingersn	−30°/20°	Spring

2.3. *Analysis of Actuators in Robotic Exoskeletons*

Most types of actuators used in robotics cannot be used in exoskeletons since this application requires high speeds during operation at higher speeds than most actuators can provide. Electric, pneumatic, hydraulic, and Series Elastic Actuators (SEA) are the leading candidates available for use as actuators in exoskeletons. The design and selection of actuators was based on the average torque and power of each subject during normal walking (not pathological) at average speed. In addition, a study of different potential candidates was evaluated. The most relevant criteria for selecting activation technology for driving human joints were specific strength (activator power ratio to actuator weight) and portability. In this respect, linear hydraulic and pneumatic actuators have a high power density but are usually massive and present internal leakage and friction problems.

They have been used in some recovery devices but still face a standard limitation on the constant spring of the tyre element that is stable. Harmonic coordination of strength and position between patient and exoskeleton is complex between different subjects. The literature shows that the use of electric motors provides a reduction in energy consumption during walking. DC motors meet the criteria of the necessary power with a compact and portable solution for portable devices. Based on this, brushless DC motors connected to a harmonic drive gearbox were selected. Torque calculation is necessary to construct robotic exoskeletons and specialised robotic devices using servo and DC brushless motors [18].

2.4. *Methodology of Selecting the Appropriate Motor*

As mentioned in this section, the proposed methodology comprises two steps. Initially, the characteristics of the user are set, and the parameters regarding the skeleton are set. Then, the coefficients are calculated based on known models, namely the Zatsiorsky BSP and the Dempster BSP (body segment parameters). In Step A, the masses of the exoskeleton's parts are calculated, considering the collateral effect of installing a specific motor at a joint. This is a novel approach, since this effect was included (or not) in the mass of the body parts. The approach allows a more precise exploration of the motor under consideration, its effect on movement, and the motor's verification (hence, selection) with the desired behaviour. In Step B, the torques are calculated using additional parameters set by the user or a group of sensors to calculate more precise data during kinematic analysis. At the end of this step, the torques are reported, and the motor is either characterised as appropriate, or the process is repeated from the start, rejecting the motor as unsuitable. Steps A and B have been implemented in the LabView for verification reasons and to facilitate researchers to implement these steps (see Figure 5, flow chart). The calculations include the extensive mathematical model and the database of DC motor characteristics. In this way, selecting the appropriate DC motor per articulation is automated. The implementation of the mathematical model for calculating lower extremity joint torques may be found on GitHub [19]. The fact guarantees the commonality of this methodology that it utilises the extended mathematical model, takes into account the characteristics of the available DC motors, takes into account their effect on the behaviour of the robotic exoskeleton and automates the selection of the appropriate DC motor at the joints' lower extremity.

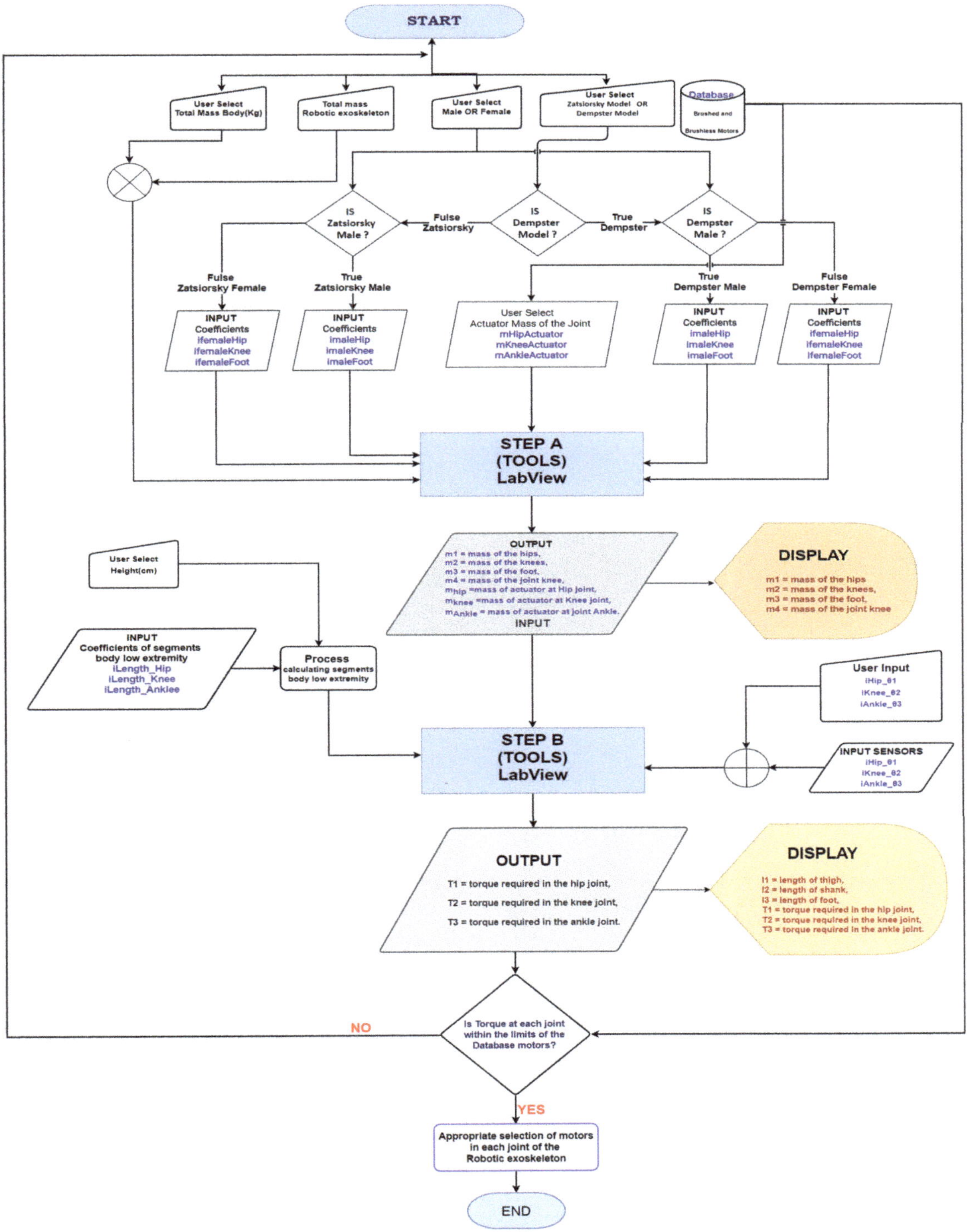

Figure 5. Flow chart Model.

The calculations are based on the proposed extended mathematical model, which has as its fundamental principle that each lower limb robotic exoskeleton is an interconnected part of the human body. According to this assumption, every variable of the human body, such as weight, and height, affects the calculation of the mathematical model. Accordingly, the variables of the robotic exoskeleton, such as its total weight and the weight of actuators in the joints, should also be considered. It is essential to point out that the mathematical model can be used by any lower limb robotic exoskeleton researcher who wants to calculate the joint torques to choose correctly between brush and brushless DC motors at each joint. It has the ability to configure the parameters of the human body and corresponding variables of the robotic exoskeleton. It can also use a database of data on electric motors DC for robotic exoskeletons.

In Section 2.4.1, the extended mathematical model is presented in detail regarding calculating the masses of the variables that affect each part's mass, as shown in Figure 6. Then, in Step B of the methodology, as depicted in Figure 7, the calculation of the length of parts and torques of each part of the lower limb to the total mass (kg), its height (cm) and the change of the angles of each joint, as it is analysed in Section 2.4.2, is performed. The methodology allows the user to interact with a database containing characteristics of brush or brushless, as analysed in Section 2.4.3.

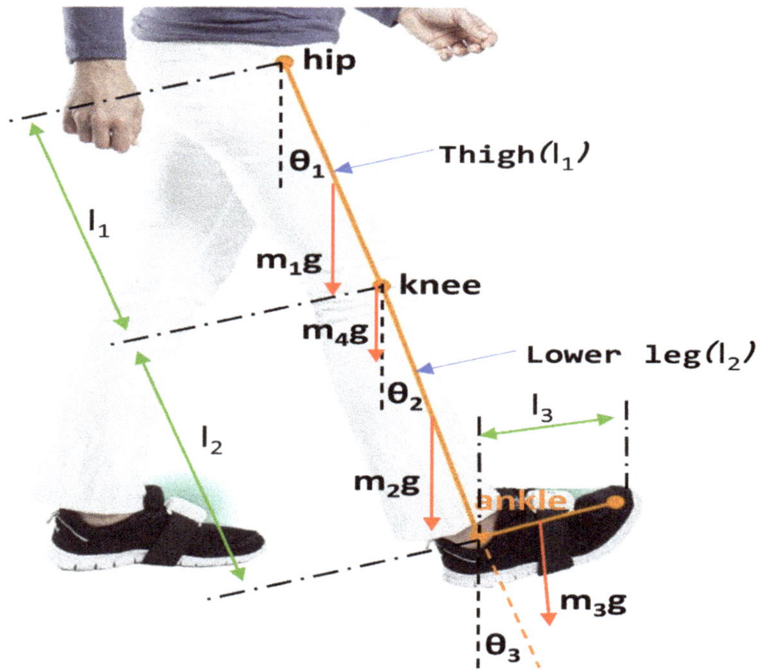

Figure 6. Force balance diagram of the lower leg.

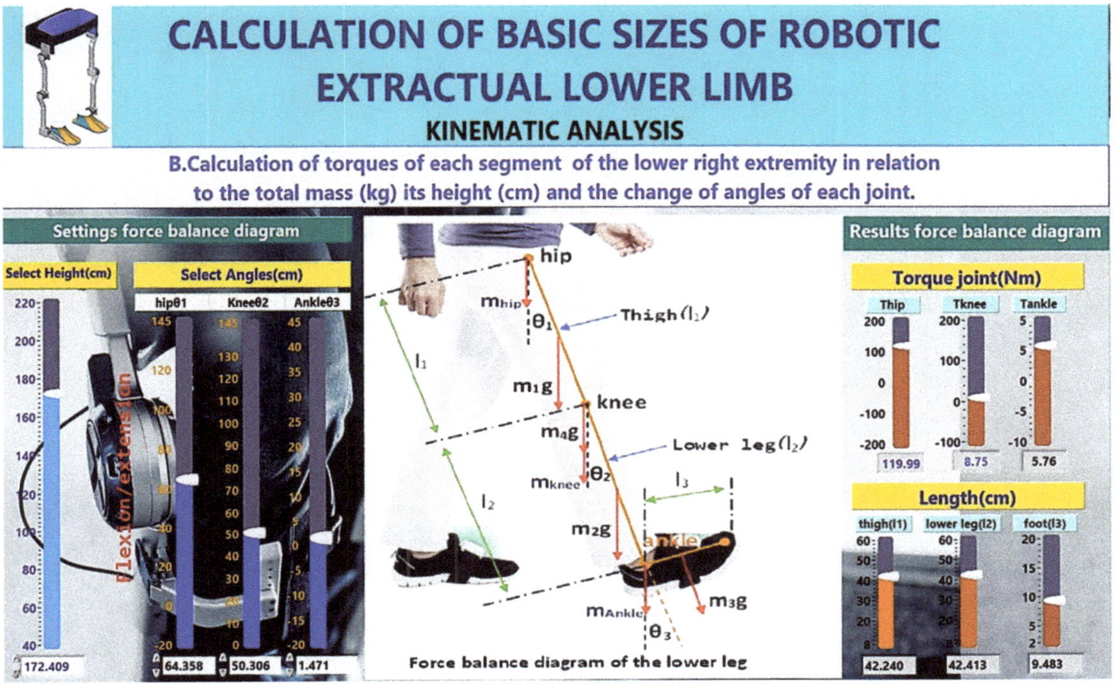

Figure 7. Calculation of the torques of each joint of the lower extremity.

2.4.1. Extended Mathematical Model for Calculation of Segment Masses, Centres of Mass

The mathematical model in Step A calculates the masses and centres of mass (COM) of the lower limb of the human body, such as the hip centre of mass (COM_{hip}), the knee centre of mass (COM_{knee}), the foot centre of mass (COM_{foot}), and mass of the knee joint. The user can choose between two mass calculation models, the Zatsiorsky BSP and the Dempster BSP, and the gender (male or female), as seen in Figure 8, which is the Graphical User Interface (GUI) developed in LabVIEW.

Dempster's method is reflected in Table 4, which gives the coefficients affecting body parts' mass or centre mass. Cadaver data from Dempster (1955) are applied to water displacement data obtained from 135 living subjects (35 men and 100 women) to obtain the weight, centre of gravity, and radius of gyration for the segmented extremities. Some subjects (33 in total, 15 men and 18 women) were examined to obtain the weight of the segments of the trunk using the water displacement method, and 16 of these subjects (7 men and 9 women) were examined to locate the centre of gravity of each trunk segment [20]. In 1990, Zatsiorsky et al. determined the centre of mass for different human body segments. Each human body segment was divided according to the bony landmarks defined by Zatsiorsky. Data for this operation were collected via means of gamma-ray scanning, and the measurements were completed on 100 male and 15 female Caucasian subjects aged between 19 and 25 years old [21]. In 1993, de Leva observed that data provided by Zatsiorsky lead to many errors in the body COM calculation of USA college athletes. The source of those errors was caused by the body segmentation method, specifically by setting the reference points at bony landmarks. To obtain more precise results, de Leva decided to change the reference points from bony landmarks to the axis of rotation of body segments. To simulate the kinematic and dynamic behaviour of the body in movement, the body should be simulated. Segmentation methods allow the body to be modelled as connected segments are reduced to their centre of mass [22]. Zatsiorsky's method is reflected in Table 5, where the coefficients affecting body parts' mass or centre mass are given.

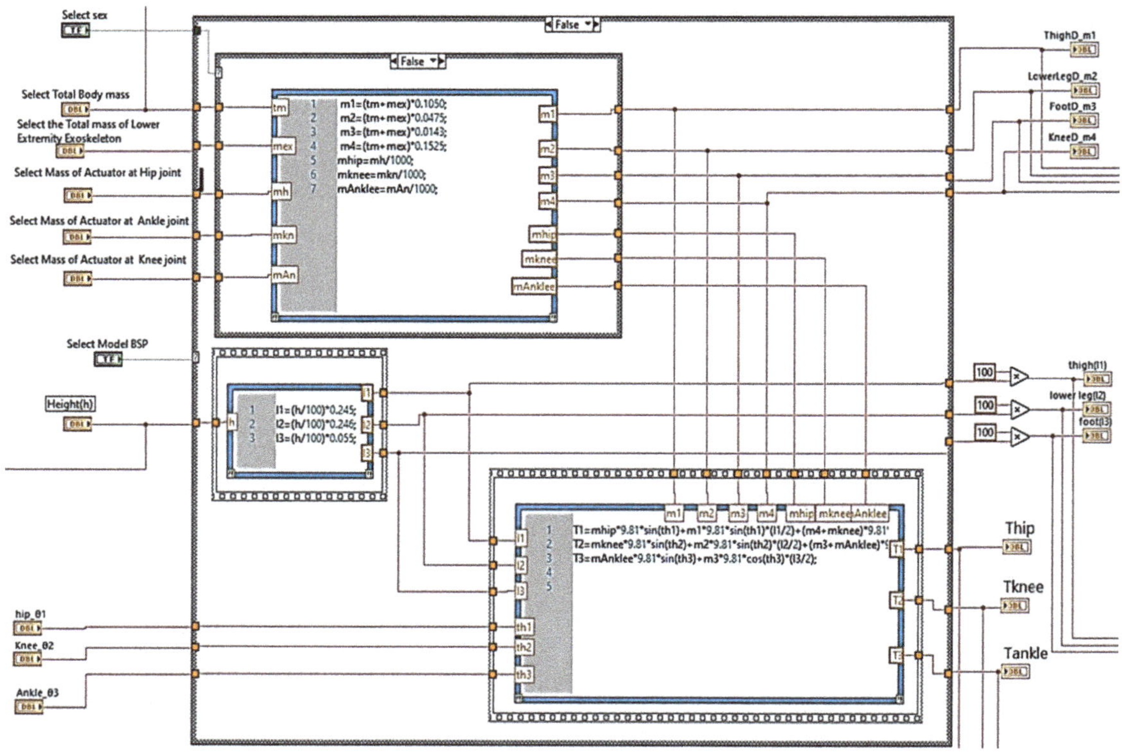

Figure 8. Calculation of Segment Masses, Centres of Mass and Length of Segment in LabView.

Table 4. Body segment coefficients as calculated for Dempster model.

	Dempster [b]					
Segment	**Weight/Total Body Weight**		**Centre of Mass/ Segment Length**		**Length Relative to Height**	
	Female	**Male**	**Female**	**Male**	**Female**	**Male**
Thigh	0.1050	0.1175	0.428	0.433	0.242	0.245
Knee	0.1525	0.1710				
Foot	0.0143	0.0133	0.500	0.500	0.151	0.152

[b] Based on Plagenhoef et al. (1983), based on Drillis and Contini (1966), based on Dempster et al. (1955) [23].

Table 5. Body segment coefficients as calculated for Zatsiorsky model.

	Zatsiorsky [a], as Modified by de Leva					
Segment	**Weight/Total Body Weight**		**Centre of Mass/ Segment Length**		**Length Relative to Height**	
	Female	**Male**	**Female**	**Male**	**Female**	**Male**
Thigh	0.1478	0.1416	0.3612	0.4095	0.3685	0.422
Shank–Lower Leg	0.0481	0.0433	0.4416	0.4459	0.4323	0.434
knee	0.1849	0.1959				
Foot	0.0129	0.0137	0.4014	0.4415	0.2283	0.258

[a] Zatsiorsky et al. (1990), as modified by de Leva.

In addition, the user sets the total body mass in kg (see Figure 9). In Figure 8, the code for calculating the masses in LabVIEW is shown by applying the above coefficients to each calculation of mass and centres of mass of lower body parts (see Figure 7). Masses are calculated according to the following general relationship:

$$m = t_m + m_{ex} \times Coef \tag{1}$$

t_m = Total mass body
m_{ex} = Total mass robotic exoskeleton - mass actuator ($m_{actuator}$)
Coef = Coefficients affecting the mass or centre of mass of body parts.

It is possible to adjust the mass of actuators at each lower limb joint (actuator mass selection at hip joint, actuator mass selection at knee joint, actuator mass selection at ankle joint) for each brushless motor or brushed motor (grams). The user in Figure 9 defines them according to the motor selection present in the database (see Figure 10).

Therefore, according to the above, the mass of the hip, the mass of the knee, the mass of the leg, the mass of the knee joint, the mass of the actuator at the hip joint, the mass of the actuator at the knee joint, and the mass of the actuator at the ankle joint are considered. They will then be used in the calculation of the torques that are analysed in the following section.

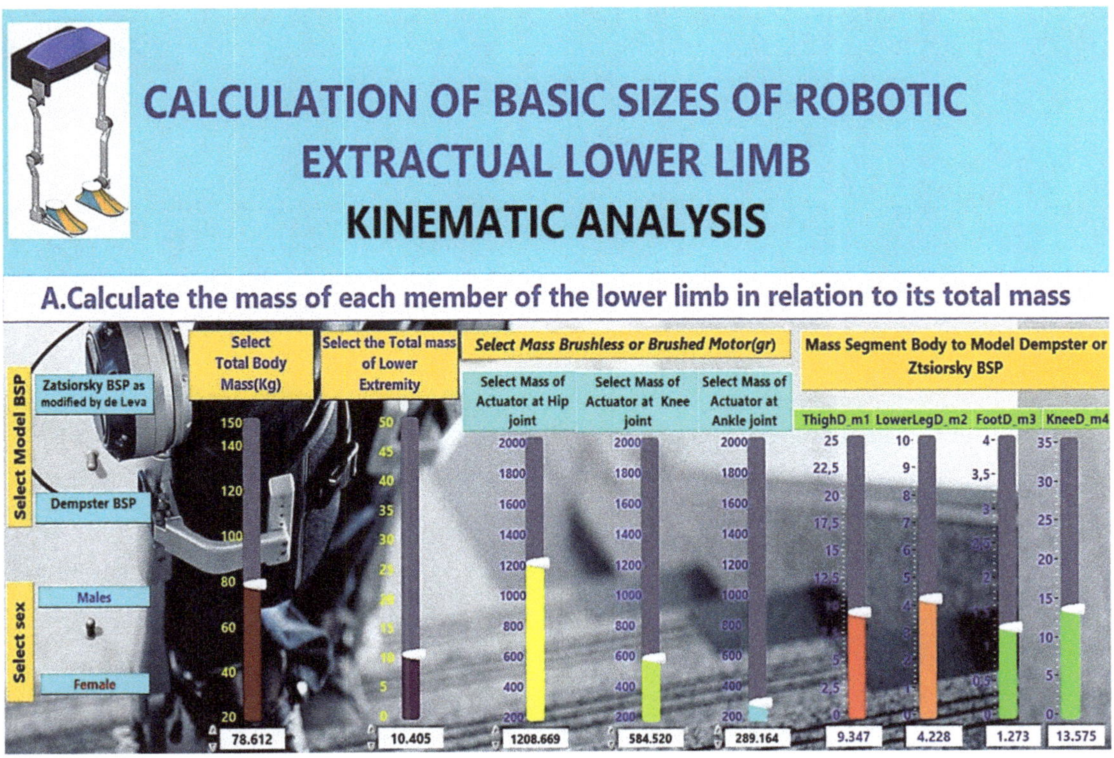

Figure 9. The mass of each part of the lower limb is calculated in relation to its total mass.

DataBase Model

I. *(Import of characteristic motor from the database)*

Data Brushless Motors

A/A	PartNo	Torque(mNm)	Weight(gr)	Power(W)	Speed(rpm)	Voltage(V)	Price(€)
1	500269	1010	985	2110	260	18	217.27
2	597974	1560	988	2080	600	30	234.28
3	597975	1490	988	1960	600	48	234.28
4	597976	1500	988	1980	600	60	234.28
5	607325	1010	985	2100	260	18	223
6	607930	1260	964	2080	400	30	228
7	607931	1210	964	1960	400	48	228
8	607932	1220	964	1980	400	60	228
9	607933	1300	964	2080	400	18	234.73
10	607934	1260	964	2080	400	30	234.73

Data Brushed Motors

A/A	PartNo	Torque(mNm)	Weight(gr)	Power(W)	Speed(rpm)	Voltage(V)	Price(€)
1	353295	501	2100	250	4090	24	789.74
2	353296	751	2100	250	3970	36	789.74
3	353297	800	2100	250	3670	48	789.74
4	353298	813	2100	250	3680	60	789.74
5	353299	832	2100	250	3440	70	789.74
6	353300	839	2100	250	3190	70	789.74
7	353301	836	2100	250	2690	70	789.74
8	388986	684	2100	250	3960	36	789.74
9	388987	742	2100	250	3660	48	789.74
10	388988	754	2100	250	3670	60	789.74

Figure 10. Characteristics of motors from database.

2.4.2. Calculation of the Torque of Robotic Exoskeleton Joints

Figure 6 shows the Power Balance Chart of the lower leg, which shows the forces acting on the hip, knee, and ankle joints, that help determine the torque required on each joint. Using the robotic exoskeleton, the authors have designed and considered similar exoskeleton robots, such as robotic exoskeleton (LLRE) [4], and the following torque equations were calculated.

- **Hip torque calculation model equation:**

$$\begin{aligned} T_1 = {} & m_{hip}\times g\times sin(\theta_1) + m_1\times g\times sin(\theta_1)\times(l_1/2) + (m_4 + m_{knee})\times g\times sin(\theta_1)\times l_1 + m_2\times \\ & g\times(sin(\theta_1)\times l_1 + sin(\theta_2)\times l_2/2) + m_3\times g\times(sin(\theta_1)\times l_1 + sin(\theta_2)\times l_2 + cos(\theta_3)\times(l_3/2)) \\ & + (m_3 + m_{Ankle})\times g\times(sin(\theta_1)\times l_1 + sin(\theta_2)\times l_2) \end{aligned} \quad (2)$$

- **Knee torque calculation model equation:**

$$\begin{aligned} T_2 = {} & m_{knee}\times g\times sin(\theta_2) + m_2\times g\times sin(\theta_2)\times(l_2/2) + (m_3 + m_{Ankle})\times g\times(sin(\theta_1)\times(l_1) + sin(\theta_2) \\ & \times(l_2)) + m_3\times g\times(sin(\theta_2)\times l_2 + cos(\theta_3)\times(l_3/2)) \end{aligned} \quad (3)$$

- **Ankle torque calculation model equation:**

$$T_3 = m_{Ankle}\times g\times sin(\theta_3) + m_3\times g\times cos(\theta_3)\times(l_3/2) \quad (4)$$

- **Parameters of calculations:**
  m_1 = centre of mass of the hips;
  m_2 = centre of mass of the knees,
  m_3 = centre of mass of the foot;
  m_4 = mass of the knee joint;
  m_{hip} = mass of actuator at hip joint;
  m_{knee} = mass of actuator at knee joint;
  m_{Ankle} = mass of actuator at ankle joint;
  g = 9.81m/s^2 gravitational acceleration;
  l_1 = length of thigh;
  l_2 = length of shank;

l_3 = length of foot;
T_1 = torque required in the hip joint;
T_2 = torque required in the knee joint;
T_3 = torque required in the ankle joint.

In Step B of the mathematical model, the torques at each joint of the lower limb are calculated, as shown in Figure 7, which is the GUI. In this step, the lengths of the lower limb body segments are calculated, selecting the person's height. The user adjusts the angles (θ_{hip}, θ_{knee}, θ_{ankle}) of the lower limb joints or with motion sensors. Since calculating all the above quantities, the mathematical model calculates the torques in each joint using the equations of motion mentioned above, which are integrated into the proposed mathematical model (see Figure 8).

2.4.3. Reference Database

The proposed methodology considers the characteristics of brushed and brushless motors from the database storing the motor characteristics. Figure 10 depicts the GUI of LabVIEW, in which the elements of the motors are entered in the panels brushless and brushed. The GUI allows collecting torque data (torque hip, torque knee, and torque ankle) and deleting and plotting the torques from the mathematical model, as shown in Figure 11. According to the data collected in the database, a researcher can choose the appropriate actuator needed in each joint of the robotic exoskeleton he will implement. It can also change every element in the mathematical model, as already mentioned in the flow chart of the model in Figure 5, and feedback of the robotic exoskeleton.

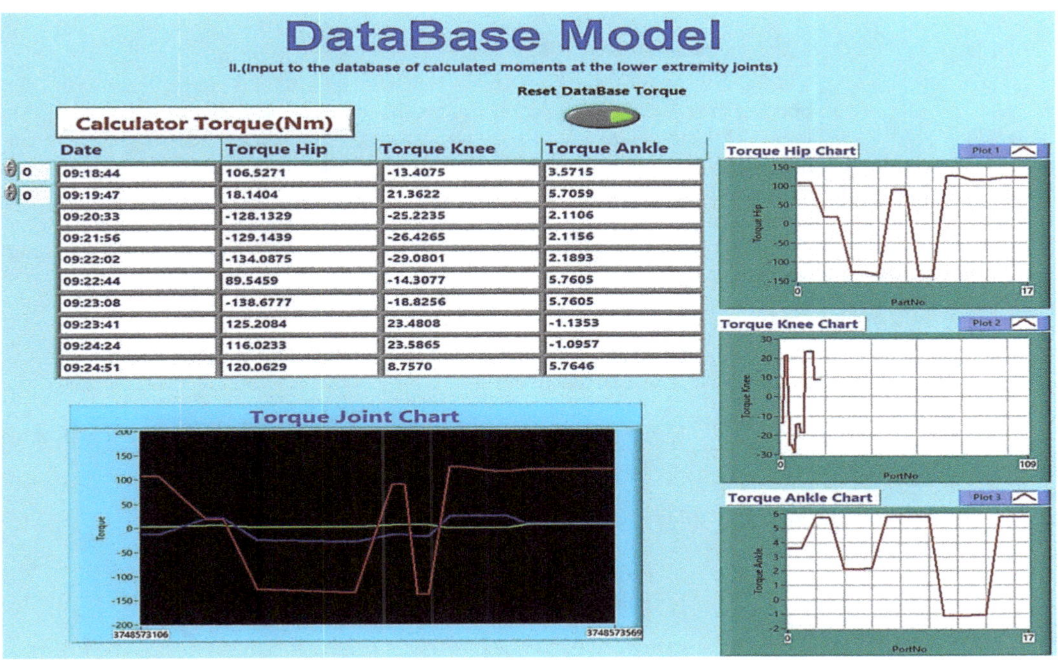

Figure 11. Joint torque calculations and SQL database storage (GUI).

3. Results

Experimental measurements were performed for the proposed methodology, implementing it in LabView. Groups of males and females were considered, considering each individual's height and weight parameters and the Dempster and Zatsiosky models, as shown in Tables 4 and 5. All parameters are adjusted by the mathematical model as described before. According to the data collected, the following descriptive statistics for qualitative and quantitative characteristics were reported, exploiting the SPSS statistical analysis suite.

3.1. Quality Characteristics of Motors

Table 6 presents the quality characteristics of the brushless and brushless motors. The advantage of brushless over brushed is the greater lifetime, the high efficiency, the low inertia of the rotor, and the low electrical noise. Brushless motors have many positive quality features. The question is whether they cover the needs of the parameters (torque, weight) of the joints of the body's lower extremities. The following subsection explores the use of the brushless over brushed motors by analysing the quantitative characteristics.

Table 6. Quality Characteristics of Brushless and Brushed Motors.

Commutation	BLDC Motor Electronic Commutation Based on Hall Sensors	Brushed Motor Brushed Commutation
Maintenance	Less	Periodic
Life	Longer	Shorter
Efficiency	High	Moderate
Rotor inertia	Low	Higher
Electric Noise	Low	Arcs in brushes generate noise
Control	Complex, expensive	Simple, inexpensive

3.2. Quantitative Characteristics of Motors

Table 7 contains a comparison of brushless quantitative characteristics (BLDC) and brushed motors. The characteristics of brushless and brushed motors are from the Maxon library [24] and are registered in the database (SQL Server). Additionally, the user can add motor data from other company libraries to the database. This allows them to be compared with the data collected and processed in the mathematical model. In the descriptive statistics of Table 8, the maximum values of torques that can be used for each motor are found, allowing a numerical comparison. Finally, in the table, the results derived from the mathematical model in LabView are offered regarding the torques at each joint of the body's lower limbs.

Table 7. Comparison Quantitative Characteristics: Brushless (BLDC) and Brushed Motors.

Servo Motor		Min	Max	Mean	Std. Deviation
Brushless	Torque (mNm)	1010.00	1560.0	1282.00	190.42
(BLDC)	Weight (gr)	964.00	988.00	975.40	12.00
	Power (W)	269.00	600.00	432.00	128.60
	Speed (rpm)	1960.00	2110.00	2041.00	62.20
	Voltage (V)	18.00	60.00	36.00	16.70
	Price (€)	217.00	235.00	229.60	5.90
Brushed	Torque (mNm)	501.00	839.00	1282.00	190.42
	Weight (gr)	2100.00	2100.00	2100.00	0.00
	Power (W)	250.00	250.00	250.00	0.00
	Speed (rpm)	2960.00	4090.00	3602.00	414.75
	Voltage (V)	24.00	70.00	52.20	16.42
	Price (€)	790.00	790.00	789.74	0.00

Table 8. Report Torque (Nm).

Sex		Torque Hip	Torque Knee	Torque Ankle
Male	Mean	78.9534	19.2694	2.6254
	Std. Dev/tion	38.2399	9.5207	2.0741
	Minimum	7.2119	2.3286	0.1082
	Maximum	145.7430	33.9808	5.9167
Female	Mean	45.4926	11.5044	2.4046
	Std. Dev/tion	24.2209	5.6196	1.3984
	Minimum	13.8903	4.6761	0.5725
	Maximum	91.8309	19.9213	5.8193
Total	Mean	69.0198	16.9642	2.5598
	Std. Dev/tion	37.7666	9.2258	1.8904
	Minimum	7.2119	2.3286	0.1082
	Maximum	145.7430	33.9808	5.9167

The mathematical model calculates the torques of the joints, the masses and the central masses of the parts of the lower extremities, as well as their lengths. It is essential that for the correct choice of motors in the joints, all the parameters related to the robotic exoskeleton must be taken into account: that is, the weight of the motors (entered in the mathematical model from the database) and the individual weights that are calculated by adjusting the weight of each body. This is the necessity of the descriptive statistics in Table 8 with the SPSS software in groups of men and women. The torques at each lower extremity joint through Table 8 give important information regarding the difference in motors selection at each joint, specifically a maximum torque at 145.75 Nm for males and 91.83 Nm for females, 34 Nm the knee for males and 20 Nm for females, and at the ankle 6 Nm for both groups.

The parameters of the mass and the centres of mass of the lower extremity parts of the body are essential. Therefore, they are also considered in calculating the extended mathematical model as a function of the body's total mass and separate masses of parts. Furthermore, they are also considered in the calculation from the extended mathematical model as a function of the body's total mass and separate masses of parts. Therefore, the descriptive statistics of the masses in Table 9 allow selecting the appropriate motors based on the torque and considering the weight of each joint of the body.

Table 9. Report Mass and Centre Mass (Kg).

Sex		Total Mass	Thigh m1	Knee m4	Lower Leg m2	Foot m3
Male	Mean	79.141	11.697	15.504	3.806	3.806
	Std. Dev.	15.151	2.239	2.967	0.728	0.728
	Min	60.640	8.960	11.880	2.920	2.920
	Max	108.800	16.080	21.310	5.230	5.230
Female	Mean	54.214	7.154	9.561	2.407	2.407
	Std. Dev.	7.019	1.668	1.870	0.251	0.251
	Min	47.590	5.000	7.260	2.060	2.060
	Max	63.650	9.010	11.770	2.760	2.760
Total	Mean	66.021	9.306	12.376	3.070	3.070
	Std. Dev.	17.034	3.008	3.867	0.884	0.884
	Min	47.590	5.000	7.260	2.060	2.060
	Max	108.800	16.080	21.310	5.230	5.230

4. Discussion

Below, we mention methods of selecting electric actuators and calculating joint torques. Calanca et al. in [25], presented a methodology based on a graphical tool that matches the actuator's capabilities with the task's requirements. The proposed approach obtains the operating torques and speeds through experimental tests. A motion capture system allows positions and velocities to be acquired, while joint torques are calculated via inverse dynamics in a multi-body human exoskeleton model. Similarly, Barjuei et al. in [26], proposed an approach for selecting a brushless BLDC motor and a gearbox transmission based on optimisation through an analytical human–robot dynamic interaction model and a mathematical relationship between the weight and technical characteristics of its components. Finally, Belogusev and Egorov in [27] proposed an automatic measurement procedure for determining the starting torque of an electric gear actuator for an exoskeleton. In this work, a methodology is proposed for selecting the appropriate motor during the design phase, hence, at a higher abstraction level, avoiding experimental tests of the exoskeleton. Additionally, this work considered not only the characteristics of the human–robot interaction model but also the effect of candidate motors at each joint.

In the results presented in Table 7, the maximum torques of brush and brush motors in mNm were obtained from the database, as shown in Figure 12. Furthermore, the graph in Figure 13 calculates torques at each joint at the lower end over time, according to the extracted parameters resulting from the mathematical model. Therefore, according to the previous data, a thigh motor is suitable if it offers a maximum torque of at least 150 Nm. Similarly, a knee motor is suitable if it offers a maximum torque of at least 35 Nm, and an ankle motor is suitable if it offers a maximum torque of at least 10 Nm.

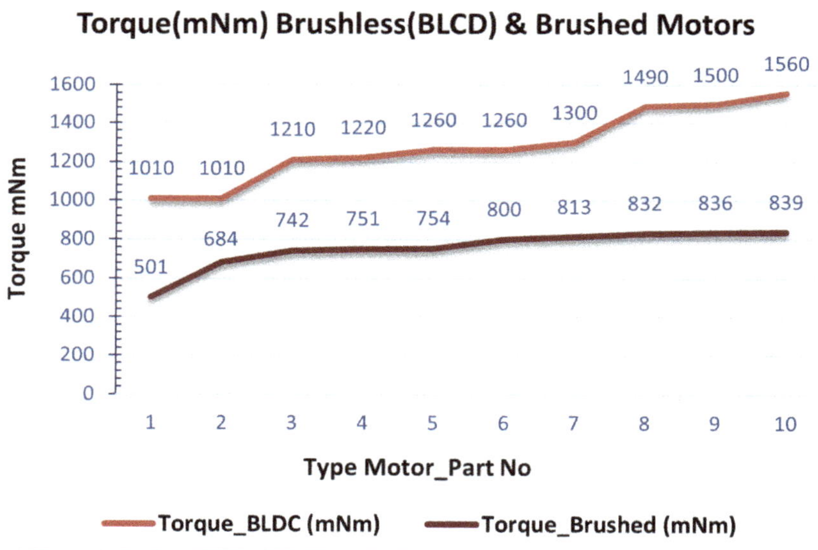

Figure 12. Comparison Torque (mNm) Brushless (BLDC) and Brushed Motor.

Since the maximum torque range, as shown in Figure 13 (torques at each joint per time from the mathematical model), does not achieve the target torque, a gearbox (Harmonic Drive, CSD-20-160-2AGR [28]) is connected to the motor shaft to reduce speed and increase torque. So, at the peak torque from Figure 12, the 1560 mNm (1.56 Nm) brushless motors will be closer to the desired thigh torque values. A ratio of 160:1 gives each combination a continuous net torque of 71 Nm and peak torques of 180 Nm. Therefore, the average hip actuator torque of 71 Nm is considered sufficient for most patients.

The choice of brushless motors is an option because of the coverage of the maximum torque and other factors such as their weight. According to Table 7, there is less weight (1000 g) in brushless motors compared to brushed motors (2000 g). Conversely, choosing heavier motors will increase the overall weight of the robotic chassis. The weight of the robotic exoskeleton is critical to the system's human factor stability, which highlights this work's impact.

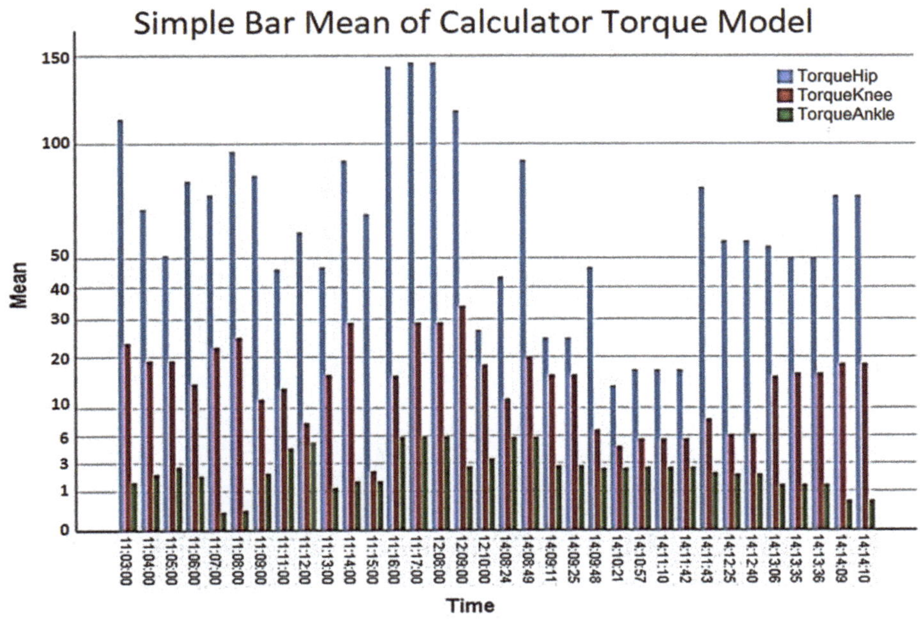

Figure 13. Simple Bar Mean of Torque Model Calculator.

In Figure 14 and Table 8 (Total torque), the calculation of the joints of the lower extremities in the male and women groups is shown. The torques at the knee and ankle joints have negligible differences in their maximum value between males and females, Tknee = 34 Nm and Tankle = 6 Nm. Thus, the motor required for the knee joint should perform a maximum torque Tknee = (34 + std. Deviation = 10N m) = 44 Nm. Likewise, the motor required for the ankle joint should perform a maximum torque Tankle = (6 Nm + std. Deviation = 2 Nm) = 8 Nm. According to Table 7, the torques of the joints in nominal torque (max. Continuous torque) = 1560 mNm or 1560 Nm.

The above calculations of the torques at the joints of the lower limbs of the human body and the calculation of the masses of the lower limbs and the masses of the actuator joint of the robotic exoskeleton, combined with the qualitative characteristics, were compared between brushless and brushed motors, as reported in Section 2.1. The following motor choices result in each joint of the robotic lower limb exoskeleton.

Initially, a choice of a motor (EC 90 flat Ø90 mm, brushless, 600 W [24]) for the thigh and knee was made at 15,600 mNm with the addition of a gearbox (Harmonic Drive [28], CSD-20-160-2AGR) connected to the motor shaft to reduce speed and increase torque. Regarding the ankle, the motor choice was based on a brushless one (EC 60 flat Ø60 mm, brushless, 100 Watt [29]) with the addition of a gearbox (Harmonic Drive [28], CSD-20-160-2AGR), which is connected to the motor shaft to reduce the speed and increase the torque, i.e., Tankle = (nominal torque, max. continuous torque = 227 mNm); (transmission ratio 160: 1) = 36Nm. Regarding the choice of the specific motors, their masses have been taken into account (1000 gr, brushless < 2000 gr, brushed) and nominal speed 1620 rpm (EC90), 3840 rpm (EC60) due to the use of a gear unit.

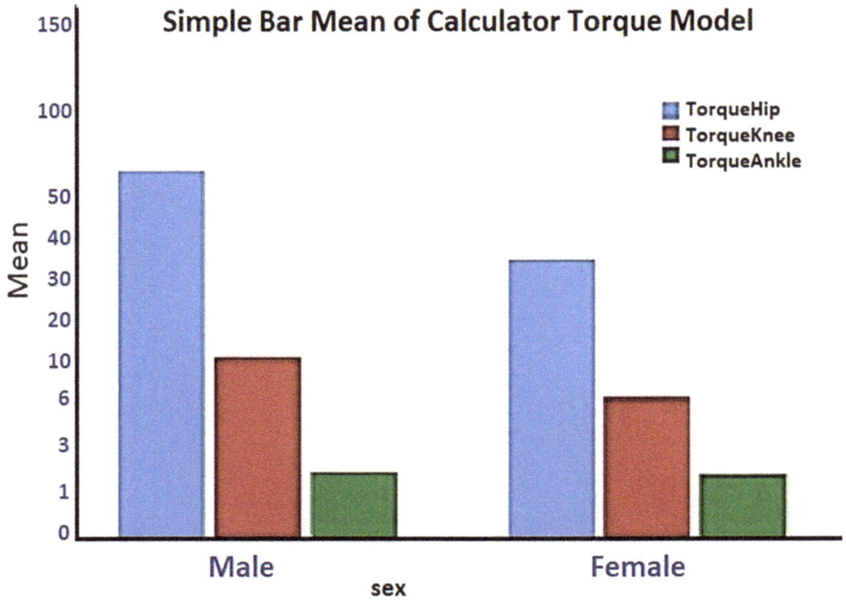

Figure 14. Simple Bar Mean of Calculated Torque—Male, Female.

5. Conclusions

As we presented in the Introduction, the mathematical model proposed in this paper differs from other models in terms of its variability. As from the discussion above, the mathematical model has several positive elements. In the automated mathematical model, researchers for the lower limb robotic exoskeleton experiment with various parameters (centres of mass, common masses, total body weight, mechanical exoskeleton weight, actuator masses at each joint, human body height, and joint angles). Based on the mathematical model, the methodology calculates the torques at the joints of the lower limb and compares them with the motor database elements. So, it selects the appropriate motor at each joint.

Weaknesses in the mathematical model were also identified, such as the need to evaluate more parameters affecting the stability of the robotic exoskeleton. However, due to the uniqueness of the walking pattern, it is difficult for the lower limb exoskeleton robot to adapt to the different walking patterns of users. Therefore, embedding an AI model for walking patterns may be considered for future improvement. This will adjust the mathematical model based on the different walking patterns of the users and provide the appropriate motor selection in each joint for achieving the optimal solution.

Author Contributions: Conceptualization, D.K.; methodology, D.K.; software, D.K.; validation, A.K. and T.L.; formal analysis, D.K. and E.K.; investigation, D.K.; resources, D.K.; data curation, A.K.; writing—original draft preparation, D.K.; writing—review and editing, A.K. and T.L.; visualization, D.K.; supervision, A.K.; project administration, A.K.; funding acquisition, D.K. All authors have read and agreed to the published version of the manuscript.

Funding: This research received no external funding.

Institutional Review Board Statement: Not applicable.

Informed Consent Statement: Not applicable.

Conflicts of Interest: The authors declare no conflict of interest.

References

1. Minchala, L.I.; Astudillo-Salinas, F.; Palacio-Baus, K.; Vazquez-Rodas, A. Mechatronic design of a lower limb exoskeleton. In *Mechatronic Systems in Engineering: Design, Control and Applications*; IntechOpen: London, UK, 2017; pp. 111–134. http://doi.org/10.5772/67460.
2. Tucker, M.R.; Olivier, J.; Pagel, A.; Bleuler, H.; Bouri, M.; Lambercy, O.; Millán, J.d.R.; Riener, R.; Vallery, H.; Gassert, R. Control strategies for active lower extremity prosthetics and orthotics: A review. *J. Neuroeng. Rehabil.* **2015**, *12*, 1–2. [CrossRef] [PubMed]
3. Shaari, N.L.A.; Isa, I.S.M.; Jun, T.C. Torque analysis of the lower limb exoskeleton robot design. *ARPN J. Eng. Appl. Sci.* **2015**, *10*, 9140–9149.
4. Pan, C.T.; Chang, C.C.; Sun, P.Y.; Lee, C.L.; Lin, T.C.; Yen, C.K.; Yang, Y.S. Development of multi-axis motor control systems for lower limb robotic exoskeleton. *J. Med. Biol. Eng.* **2019**, *39*, 752–763. [CrossRef]
5. Chu, A.; Kazerooni, H.; Zoss, A. On the Biomimetic Design of the Berkeley Lower Extremity Exoskeleton (BLEEX). In Proceedings of the 2005 IEEE International Conference on Robotics and Automation, Barcelona, Spain, 18–22 April 2005; pp. 4345–4352. [CrossRef]
6. Beyl, P. Design and Control of a Knee Exoskeleton Powered by Pleated Pneumatic Artificial Muscles for Robot-Assisted Gait Rehabilitation. Ph.D. Thesis, Vrije Universiteit Brussel, Ixelles, Belgium, 2010.
7. Dollar, A.M.; Herr, H. Design of a quasi-passive knee exoskeleton to assist running. In Proceedings of the 2008 IEEE/RSJ International Conference on Intelligent Robots and Systems, Nice, France, 22–26 September 2008; pp. 747–754.
8. Banala, S.K.; Agrawal, S.K.; Fattah, A.; Krishnamoorthy, V.; Hsu, W.L.; Scholz, J.; Rudolph, K. Gravity-balancing leg orthosis and its performance evaluation. *IEEE Trans. Robot.* **2006**, *22*, 1228–1239. [CrossRef]
9. Walsh, C.J.; Endo, K.; Herr, H. A quasi-passive leg exoskeleton for load-carrying augmentation. *Int. J. Humanoid Robot.* **2007**, *4*, 487–506. [CrossRef]
10. Chapman, S. *Electric Machinery Fundamentals*; McGraw-Hill Series in Electrical and Computer Engineering; McGraw-Hill: New York, NY, USA, 2005. ISBN 0–07- 246523–9.
11. Chapman, S.J. *Electric Machinery and Power System Fundamentals*; McGraw-Hill Series in Electrical and Computer Engineering; McGraw-Hill: New York, NY, USA, 2002. ISBN:9780072291353.
12. Tziamalis, A. Servomotors and Servo motive Systems. Thesis, National Technical University of Athens-School of Electrical and Computer Engineering, Zografou, Greece, 2012. http://dx.doi.org/10.26240/heal.ntua.10388.
13. Firoozian, R. *Servo Motors and Industrial Control Theory*; Science + Business Media: New York, NY, USA, 2009. 07/978-3-319-07275-3. [CrossRef]
14. Hwang, Y.; Minami, Y.; Ishikawa, M. Virtual Torque Sensor for Low-Cost RC Servo Motors Based on Dynamic System Identification Utilizing Parametric Constraints. *Sensors* **2018**, *18*, 3856. [CrossRef] [PubMed]
15. Kenjō, T.; Nagamori, S. *Permanent-Magnet and Brushless DC Motors*; Electrical and Electronic Engineering Monographs, Oxford University Press: New York, NY, USA 1985.
16. Yedamale, P. *Brushless DC (BLDC) Motor Fundamentals*; Microchip Technology Inc.: Chandler, AZ, USA, 2003; Volume 20, pp. 3–15.
17. Pamungkas, D.S.; Caesarendra, W.; Soebakti, H.; Analia, R.; Susanto, S. Overview: Types of lower limb exoskeletons. *Electronics* **2019**, *8*, 1283. [CrossRef]
18. Bortole, M.; Venkatakrishnan, A.; Zhu, F.; Moreno, J.C.; Francisco, G.E.; Pons, J.L.; Contreras-Vidal, J.L. The H2 robotic exoskeleton for gait rehabilitation after stroke: early findings from a clinical study. *J. Neuroeng. Rehabil.* **2015**, *12*, 1–14. [CrossRef] [PubMed]
19. GitHub. Developer:Kavalieros, Dimitrios. Model Torque Calculation Fesrobex. Available online: https://github.com/jimkava/model-torque-calculation-fesrobex (accessed on 20 December 2021).
20. Plagenhoef, S.; Evans, F.G.; Abdelnour, T. Anatomical data for analyzing human motion. *Res. Q. Exerc. Sport* **1983**, *54*, 169–178. [CrossRef]
21. De Leva, P. Adjustments to Zatsiorsky-Seluyanov's segment inertia parameters. *J. Biomech.* **1996**, *29*, 1223–1230. [CrossRef]
22. Adolphe, M.; Clerval, J.; Kirchof, Z.; Lacombe-Delpech, R.; Zagrodny, B. Center of mass of human's body segments. *Mech. Mech. Eng.* **2017**, *21*, 485–497.
23. Winter, D.A. *Biomechanics and Motor Control of Human Movement*; John Wiley & Sons: Hoboken, NJ, USA, 2009. ISBN 978-0-470-39818-0.
24. Maxon. Maxon Motors, EC90 Flat Brushless. Available online: https://www.maxongroup.com/maxon/view/product/323772 (accessed on 12 March 2022).
25. Calanca, A.; Toxiri, S.; Costanzi, D.; Sartori, E.; Vicario, R.; Poliero, T.; Di Natali, C.; Caldwell, D.G.; Fiorini, P.; Ortiz, J. Actuation selection for assistive exoskeletons: matching capabilities to task requirements. *IEEE Trans. Neural Syst. Rehabil. Eng.* **2020**, *28*, 2053–2062. [CrossRef]
26. Barjuei, E.S.; Ardakani, M.M.G.; Caldwell, D.G.; Sanguineti, M.; Ortiz, J. Optimal selection of motors and transmissions in back-support exoskeleton applications. *IEEE Trans. Med. Robot. Bionics* **2020**, *2*, 320–330. [CrossRef]
27. Belogusev, V.; Egorov, A. Development of a method and instruments to assess the build quality and the technical condition of an electric gear actuator for an electromechanical orthosis of a lower limb exoskeleton. *J. Appl. Eng. Sci.* **2019**, *17*. [CrossRef]

28. Drive, H. CSG-20-160-2A-GR. Available online: https://www.harmonicdrive.net/products/component-sets/cup-type/csg-2a/csg-20-160-2a-gr (accessed on 12 March 2022).
29. Maxon. Maxon Motors, EC60 Flat Brushless. Available online: https://www.maxongroup.com/maxon/view/product/motor/ecmotor/ecflat/ecflat60/408057 (accessed on 12 March 2022).

healthcare

MDPI

Article

Testing of Motor Coordination in Degenerative Neurological Diseases

Maria Kalafati [1,†], Athanasios Kakarountas [1,†,*] and Elisabeth Chroni [2,†]

[1] Department of Computer Science and Biomedical Informatics, University of Thessaly, Papasiopoulou 2-4, 35131 Lamia, Greece
[2] Department of Medicine, University of Patras, 26504 Patras, Greece
* Correspondence: kakarountas@uth.gr; Tel.: +30-2231-066-723
† These authors contributed equally to this work.

Abstract: Parkinson's disease (PD) is a progressive movement disorder caused by the death of dopamine-producing cells in the midbrain. PD is the most prevalent movement disorder of the central nervous system and affects more than 6.3 million people in the world. The changes in the motor functions of patients are not easy to be clearly and on-time observed by the clinicians and to make the most well-informed decisions for the treatment. The aim of this paper is the monitoring PD by designing, developing, and evaluating a prototype mobile App using a pressure pen, which collects quantitative and objective information about PD patients, thus allowing clinicians to understand better and make assumptions about the severity and the stage of Parkinson's disease. This study presents a dynamic spiral test that can only be performed with tablet and pen pressure. Furthermore, the handwriting samples by PD patients and healthy controls individuals are collected by a computerized system, and the measurements of Spiral Deviation, Total Time, and Pen Pressure are processed. The results showed an accurate evaluation of the stage of Parkinson's disease. Thus, the clinician may use the proposed PD telemonitoring system as a screening test, storing the history of all the patient's measurements.

Keywords: testing; motor coordination; screening tool

Citation: Kalafati, M.; Kakarountas, A.; Chroni, E. Testing of Motor Coordination in Degenerative Neurological Diseases. *Healthcare* **2022**, *10*, 1948. https://doi.org/10.3390/healthcare10101948

Academic Editors: Daniele Giansanti and Norbert Hosten

Received: 23 July 2022
Accepted: 29 September 2022
Published: 5 October 2022

1. Introduction

Parkinson's disease (PD) is a long- term degenerative disorder of the central nervous system that mainly affects the motor system. As the disease worsens, non-motor symptoms become more common. The symptoms usually emerge slowly. Early in the disease, the most obvious symptoms are shaking, rigidity, slowness of movement, and difficulty with walking. Thinking and behavioral problems may also occur. Dementia becomes common in the advanced stages of the disease. Depression and anxiety are also common, occurring in more than a third of people with PD. Other symptoms include sensory, sleep and emotional problems. The main motor symptoms are collectively called "parkinsonism", or a "parkinsonian syndrome". The cause of Parkinson's disease is unknown but is believed to involve both genetic and environmental factors. The motor symptoms of the disease result from the death of cells in the substantia nigra, a region of the midbrain. The results are not enough dopamine in this region of the brain. The cause of this cell death is poorly understood, but it involves the build-up of proteins into Lewy bodies in the neurons. Diagnosis of typical cases are mainly based on symptoms, with tests such as neuroimaging used to rule out other diseases. There is no cure for Parkinson's disease. Treatment aims to improve the symptoms. Initial treatment is typically with the antiparkinson medication levodopa (L-DOPA), followed by dopamine agonists when levodopa becomes less effective [1]. As the disease progresses and neurons continue to be lost, these medications become less effective while at the same time they produce a complication marked by involuntary writhing movements. Evidence for treatments for the non-movement-related symptoms of PD, such as sleep disturbances and emotional problems, is less strong [2]. In 2015, PD affected 6.2 million people and resulted in about 117,400 deaths globally. Parkinson's disease typically occurs in people over the age of 60, of whom about one percent are affected. Males are more often affected than females at a ratio of around 3:2.

Today, many researchers have turned their attention to upgrading the medical approach to understanding the stage and the severity of PD via medical equipment or introducing innovative extra examinations, except from CT tomography, biomarkers, and other blood tests. In fact, the research "A novel computer-based technique for the assessment of tremor in Parkinson's disease" is focused on the suitability and clinical value of a low-cost computer-based system as an aid to the diagnosis of PD, in particular the presence of tremor. All participants (12 patients and 10 controls) performed a shape-tracing task using a graphic tablet attached to a laptop. To assess the presence of tremors in the collected data, a statistical spectral analysis of the moment-to-moment fluctuations in the position signal of the output from the digitizing tablet was performed. This allowed the comparison of power spectrums obtained from the control and patient responses respectively. A peak in log power between the 5 Hz and 6 Hz can clearly be identified in the patient's spectrum and is indicative of Parkinson's related tremor and no similar peak could be seen in the control's spectrum, suggesting this type of sequential task and automated data analysis may be useful in the diagnosis of tremor [3].

Moreover, Muhammed Erdem Isenkul et al. [4] proposed an alternative solution to the traditional method of paper and pencil of Spiral Static Test drawings (SST), which can be replaced by Dynamic Spiral Test (DST) that is realized on a tablet. They collected handwriting samples of patients who have been admitted to the Department of Neurology in Cerrahpaşa Faculty of Medicine, Istanbul University via a graphics tablet and the researchers compared SST and DST drawings of PD patients and healthy control subjects. The analysis demonstrates that the acceleration of SST is statistically closer to that of DST for control subjects when compared to the PD patients. It can be concluded that the SST and DST tests can be applied together in order to measure the cortical and motor performance of the subjects and can find use in diagnosis and telemonitoring applications of PD and some other similar neuropathological conditions.

Poonam Zham at al. [5] has proposed the use of the Composite Index of Speed and Pen-pressure (CISP) of sketching as for analyzing the severity level (SL) of PD. The participants drew an Archimedean spiral and speed, pen-pressure, and CISP were measured and analyzed to obtain their correlation with the severity of the disease. The correlation of speed, pen-pressure, and CISP with the severity of PD was −0.415, −0.584, and −0.641, respectively. The Mann–Whitney U test confirmed that CISP was suitable to distinguish between PD patients and healthy subjects, while the non-parametric k-sample Kruskal–Wallis test confirmed that it was significantly different for PD SL-1 and PD S-3. This shows that CISP during spiral sketching may be used to differentiate between CG and PD and between PD SL-1 and PD SL-3 but not SL-2.

Somayeh Aghanavesi et al. studied the measurement of temporal irregularity score (TIS) for patients at different stages of PD during each medication time points [6]. Both PD patients and healthy controls participated in the survey and the spiral tests on a smartphone were investigated before a single levodopa dose and at specific time intervals after the dose. Three movement disorder specialists rated videos of the patients based on UPDRS and the Dyskinesia scale. The differences in mean TIS between patients and healthy controls were estimated and there were proven when PD patients were in an advanced stage as well the capacity of TIS to detect changes from baseline (before medication) to later time points was assessed. TIS had good test-retest reliability and it was responsive to single-dose levodopa treatment. Since TIS is an upper limb high-frequency-based measure, it cannot be detected during clinical assessment.

Manuel Gil-Martín et al. [7] proposed the use of analyzing a convolutional neural network (CNN) for PD detection from drawing movements, which combines the feature extraction (convolutional layers) and classification (fully connected layers). The CNN has inputs which are the module of the Fast Fourier transform in the range of frequencies between 0 Hz to 25 Hz. Using the public dataset: Parkinson Disease Spiral Drawings Using Digitized Graphics Tablet dataset, they analyzed into X and Y directions the discrimination capability during drawing movements of individuals. The accuracy of this work is 96.5%, a F1-score of 97.7%, and an area under the curve of 99.2%.

Iqra Kamran et al. presented an approach of patients' handwriting samples for early diagnosis of PD [8]. They include different Parkinson's datasets, which are PaHaW dataset, HandPD dataset, NewHandPD dataset, and Parkinson's Drawing Datasetand, and applied deep transfer learning algorithms to overcome the challenge of high variability in the handwritten material. In their analysis, they evaluated six main transfer learning architectures, namely AlexNet, GoogleNet, VGGNet-16/19, and ResNet-50/101. They succeed in excellent PD identification performance with 99.22% accuracy on the illuminated tasks of combined HandPD, NewHandPD, and Parkinson's Drawing datasets, demonstrating the superiority of our approach over current state-of-the-art methods.

Elina Kuosmanen et al. [9] proposed a work related to this work, which describes the implementation of the digitized version of the spiral drawing test for Android devices. In this application, they have introduced both the spiral test and the square-shape drawing and in the survey eight PD patients and six healthy controls participated and the error rate and the drawing speed were measured. The results of the trials were a clearly different accuracy between the PD patient and the healthy individuals between the two drawing tasks.

Besides focusing only on Parkinson's disease, Andrius Lauraitis et al. [10] presented a new approach which addressed other degenerative disorders of the central nervous system, such as Huntington's disease, Alzheimer's Disease, mild cognitive impairment, and dementia. They proposed a smart application, called "Neural Impairment Test Suite" (NITS), for Android smartphones and tablets which concerns the self-administered cognitive testing (SAGE) methodology that used finger tapping and voice features acquired from the sensors of the device. The experiments were realized in patients with neurological disorders (one with Parkinson's disease, three with Huntington's disease, one with early dementia, one with cerebral palsy, one post-stroke) and eight healthy controls. The data are collected in an Android device and measure cognitive, hand tremor, energy expenditure, and speech features of subjects. According to the statistical analysis, they used 13 classifiers for combined finger tapping and SAGE features, and 96.12% accuracy was achieved and using bidirectional long short-term memory (BiLSTM) (94.29% accuracy) for speech analysis features.

Benjamin I Ferleger et al. [11] proposed a pilot study about a tablet and a mobile-based application for remote diagnosis and analysis of movement disorder symptoms. More specifically, in this application, the patients are called to follow, with a pen, a drawing task, especially with the spiral and line-drawing tasks of the Fahn–Tolosa–Marin tremor rating scale serving as the task in this survey. The data are collected in a cloud, which is analyzed quantitatively, and drawing smoothness, pressure applied, and other measures are estimated. The maximum cross-validated classification accuracy on a preliminary sample set was 98.3%.

Except for applications that specialize only in spiral drawings, Hung N. Pham et al. [12] introduces a novel study that incorporates voice and spiral drawing for better detection of PD severity level. In their study, they use various machine learning models and succeed with a great accuracy level for PD recognition. Using pairwise correlation and k-means clustering techniques the highest accuracy of 95.89% is obtained using an ensemble of 3 classification models. The best accuracy of 99.6% is achieved using the k-Nearest Neighbors classifier in the Dynamic Spiral Test (DST) and accuracy of 98.8% and 94.9% are achieved using the Logistic Regression classifier and the Adaptive Boosting classifier on the Static Spiral Test (SST) and Stability Test on Certain Point (STCP). Finally, the trials were implemented into a touch-enabled smartphone-based application.

The objective of this study is to design, develop, and evaluate a prototype digital application for mobile appliances and tablets using a pressure pen, which collects quantitative and objective information about the PD patients' handwriting dexterities, thus allowing clinicians to monitor the deterioration of motion or response to treatment and to make assumptions about the prognosis severity and the stage of Parkinson's disease. A cardinal sign of PD is the lack of coordination of fine movements of the hand for a common procedure such as writing or drawing. Clinicians often offer a piece of paper to the patient and ask them to draw geometric shapes in order to decide the effect of the disease on this function. A digital tool, easy to be used in routine visits (and even at home), characterized for accuracy and reproducibility, would be a valuable asset to neurologists and caregivers.

2. Materials and Methods

2.1. Description of the Mobile App

As described in Section 1, the aim of this study is to design a novel mobile application, which will be a useful tool to the medical society and will be effective in the diagnosis and monitoring of Parkinson's disease. The main novelty of the presented tool is that it may be used for generating real-time data on the writing ability of the patient and creating datasets in historical order. The data are then read by the neurologist and the evolution of the PD is assessed. In contrast to other works adopting the spiral test, the digital application is offering an accurate and timely assessment of the PD patient status. The use of the application by the PD user may occur in any environment, apart from the clinic, with the assistance of the caregiver.

For the evaluation of the application, it was installed on a tablet. Then, the handwriting dataset was constructed using a pressure pen as the input device, for recording the movement and the applied pressure. Specifically, the tablet is connected with the Sonar Pen, which is a pressure pen that estimates the pressure or the applied force by the patient on the screen of the tablet. Unlike the traditional tests, using a pencil and paper, the patient's digitized handwriting gives valuable digital features which are accurate x-y-z coordinates, the precise pressure applied to the screen, the pen grip angle, and the total time that the patient required to complete the drawing task.

The procedure to initiate the test and capture the results is simple and is described in the following. Initially, the clinician launches the app, which is found in the installed apps of the mobile or tablet, and fills in the fields with the required information, such as "surname", "name", "birth year", "sex" and "patient type", as seen in Figure 1. In the field "patient type" the clinician indicates if the Parkinson's test is realized in a healthy person or a PD patient. The application, also, gives in every addition a unique "code number", which is incremental, to indicate the new registered patient/user. Selecting the option "ADD" the addition of a new patient is confirmed. The clinician then has the option to search for any registered patient, by surname or code number, and access the previous tests and assessments associated with the particular patient. There is also the option to delete an addition using the "DEL" option. The last option available to the clinician is to perform a new test, that is recording new data regarding the handwriting movement of the user, by selecting the option "NEW RECORD", which brings to the forefront the spiral test screen.

In the spiral drawing task screen, the clinician initiates the test by selecting the "START" option. Then the patient, using the pressure pen, follows the spiral line trying to draw accurately the spiral shape. The movement is inwards out, as seen in Figure 2.

When the patient completes the spiral test, the clinician selects the "STOP" option to indicate the completion of the test. Then, the drawn shape is depicted over the initial spiral shape, to indicate the deviations in the drawing and also the pressure (red for high pressure and shades of red for low pressure), as shown in Figure 3.

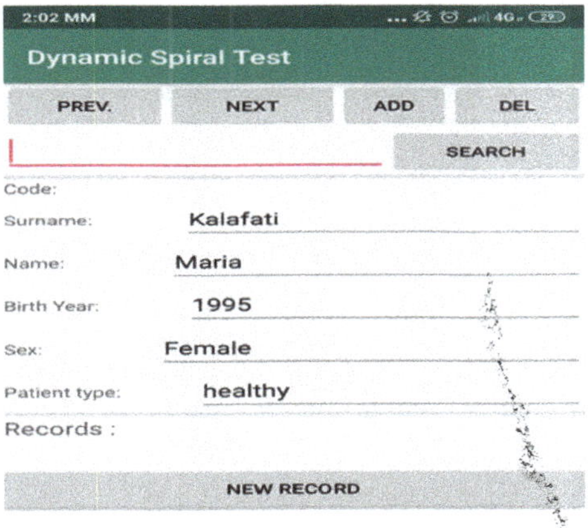

Figure 1. The initial screen of the Dynamic Spiral Test.

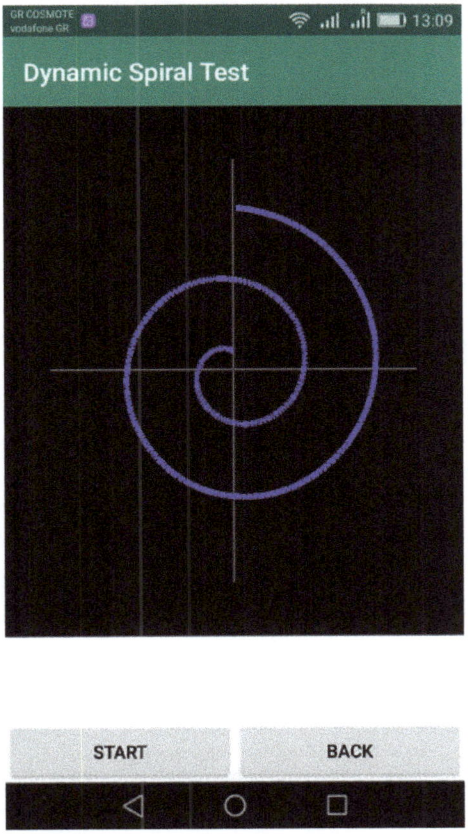

Figure 2. Second screen of Dynamic Spiral Test—the spiral drawing task.

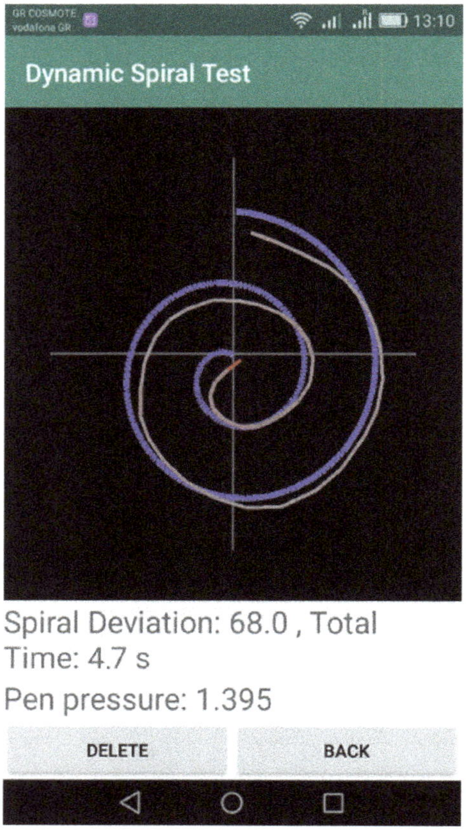

Figure 3. Screenshot of the application showing the spiral drawn by the patient using the SonarPen.

The Dynamic Spiral Test application offers three different assessments of the completed task:

- The measurement "Spiral Deviation" is the ratio of the area between two lines of the spiral test to the screen size multiplied by 10,000. With this value, the clinician can draw the right conclusions about the ability of the patient to lead the line of the spiral. More specifically, the malfunction of the fingers is observed due to tremor and in combination with the above two measurements, the symptoms of bradykinesia, tremor, and malfunction are examined by the clinician.
- The measurement "Time" relates to the total time needed by the patient to complete the spiral test. A long time for a patient to complete the task is directly associated with the stage of the PD disease, as described in previously mentioned works.
- The calculation "Pen Pressure" relates to the exercised pressure by the patient. If the pressure is greater than the expected one (as derived by tests by healthy users), then the line is more intense, red, and thicker, whereas if the exercised pressure is weak then the color of the line approaches the pink color, as in the Figure above. If the patient has tremor at a great scale, the exercised pressure, which is expected by the pen on the tablet will be weaker, so the patient will try to increase the pressure to achieve the stability of the pen.

Thus, the suggested three values of the application offer an indication of the severity of Parkinson's disease.

2.2. Application Program Design

The proposed application was developed targeting Android-based smartphones and tablets. It was developed in Java with Android Studio v3.52 for Linux, using an object-oriented methodology.

The application contains five main parts:

- The first part handles the graphic user interface (GUI). It uses Android SDK functions and consists of two screens, the one that shows the patient's data and the other the spiral sketch graph (API level 29). This approach is the most popular and common way for Android App development, supported by Google Inc., Mountain View, CA, USA.
- The second part is responsible for the calculation of the surface between the curve drawn by the patient and the spiral displayed on the screen (Spiral Deviation). A special algorithm is used for this. For each point of the curve drawn by the patient (curve with red color in screenshot) the application stores the following values: x position, y position, time in milliseconds, pressure on this point, and its spiral angle. The Spiral angle is a value that starts with the value of 90 (the polar angle of the first point) and it is increased by 720 degrees (two full circles up to the final point). In this way, each point of the patient's curve is related to a point of the test spiral. The calculation of the spiral deviation uses the distance of these two points.
- The third part is responsible for acquiring and displaying the relative pressure values of the Sonar pen as sampled from the Tablet's microphone input.
- A fourth part is aimed to generate a dedicated audio signal/tone, which is forward to the stereo audio output (L-R) of the Tablet. This signal is used to implement the battery-less pressure sensing of the Sonar Pen.
- Finally, a fifth part is used to store and fetch data from internal storage.

2.3. The Pressure Pen

The pressure pen selected for the application is the Sonar pen. The Sonar pen is a smart stylus, which is used for digital drawing and has all the standard features (e.g., position, angle, and pressure capturing), at a relatively low cost (compared to other similar devices). The de facto standard of a smart pen is to offer the following functions (if not all): pressure sensing, palm rejection, and shortcut button. The technology of the Sonar pen is based on the earphone solution, which eliminates the costs of expensive electronics, controlling circuits, Bluetooth, and rechargeable batteries and replaced them with a circuit that communicates with the tablet through the standard audio channel. To detect the pressure, the Tablet sends a dedicated audio signal waveform to the stereo audio output (L-R), the signal waveform passes through a simple voltage divider circuit using a force-sensitive resistor which changes according to the pressure applied to it, such in Figure 4. The modulated waveform is then sent back to the Tablet using the microphone input, for reading the voltage drop over the force-sensitive resistor which relates to the applied pressure.

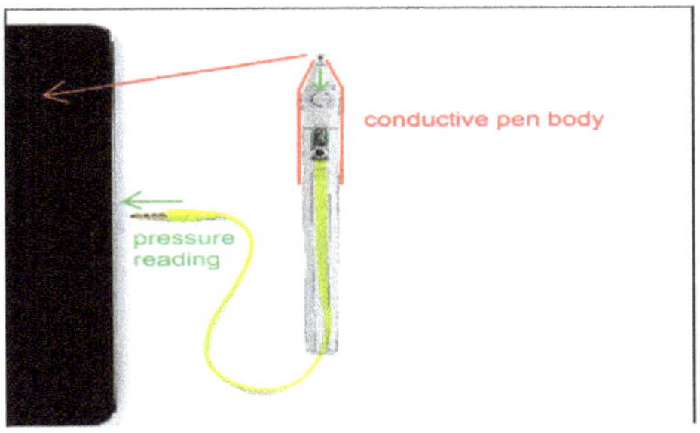

Figure 4. Connection between the Sonarpen and the Tablet.

2.4. Assessment of the Test Procedure for the PD Patients

The tests took place at the University General Hospital of Patras "Panagia h Bohthia" at the Neurological Clinic with the guidance of Dr Zinovia Kefallopoulou, Neurologist, and Dr. Elisabeth Chroni, Neurology Professor of the Department of Medicine. The tests were realized by PD patients and a healthy control group. The patients signed a detailed informed consent form before participating in the tests and they had the opportunity of rejection. The form assured participants of medical confidentiality and concealment of their personal information. The patients who participated in the tests were selected with two criteria. The first is that all the PD patients were in the same severity stage of the disease. It was complicated to discriminate among all the patients of the clinic the patients who presented the same behavior and characteristics, limiting the patients, however, to adequate sample size. In addition, the second criterion was that the patients follow the same medication for a quite long time. It is important to be noticed that all the patients suffered from PD for over a decade. Twelve PD patients and twelve healthy controls participated in the tests. For PD patients, there were 4 women, 2 in the decade of 40–50 and 2 in the decade of 50–60, and 8 men, 4 in the decade of 40–50 and 4 in the decade of 50–60, and for healthy controls, there were 6 women, 3 in the decade of 40–50 and 3 in the decade of 50–60 and 6 men, 3 in the decade of 40–50 and 3 in the decade of 50–60, were recruited in repeated spiral drawings of the application using the tablet with the Sonarpen. The tablet has 9.6 inches touch screen with a screen resolution of 1280 × 800 and recorded both positions (x and y coordinates). No participant in the study had cognitive or visual problems to the extent to which it could influence their test performance. Firstly, the clinician was noticing the personal information of the patient or the individual from the healthy control group. The subjects were informed by the clinician how to draw the spiral test and afterward, they performed the test. They were seated on a chair and performed the tests using the pressure pen with the tablet, which was on a stable spot. All data collected was then stored in a file of the application in the device's storage memory. Figures 5 and 6 are examples of dynamic spiral tests of healthy controls and PD patients respectively.

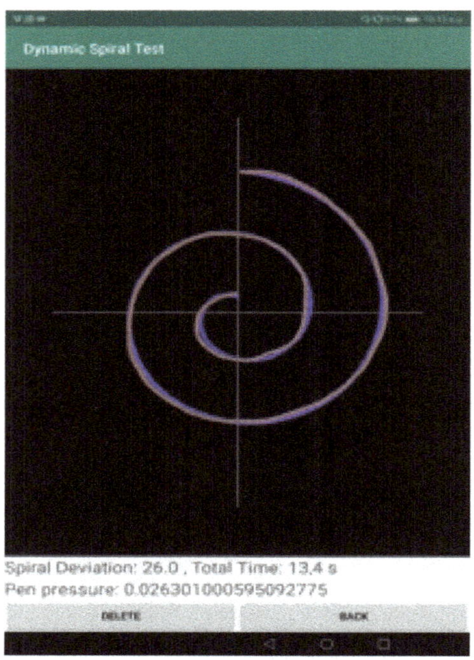

Figure 5. Spiral Tests of Healthy Control.

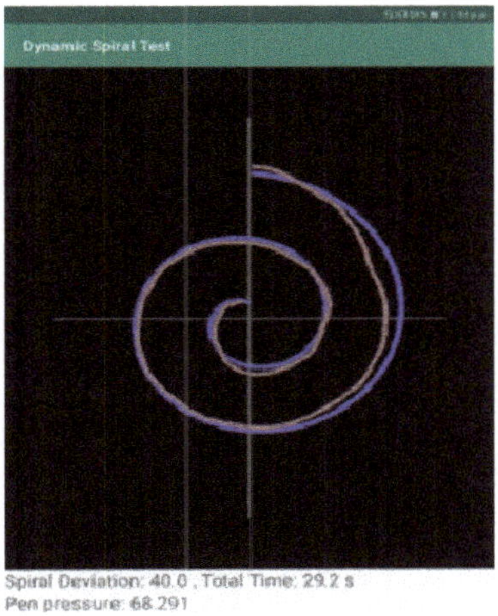

Figure 6. Spiral Tests of PD Patient.

Statistical analysis was performed using the parametric statistical procedure T-test. In the study, T-test hypothesis tests were performed for statistical analysis of the parameters of independent samples in the following different cases. In each different case mean, Standard Deviation, and Standard Error Mean were observed and their values are placed in each table separately. Moreover, Levene's test is also used in the study, which is an inferential statistic used to assess the equality of variances for a variable calculated for two or more groups.

3. Results

- In Table 1, which is organized as follows, the independent variable is HEALTH (indicating whether the tests were performed by PD patients or healthy individuals) and dependent values are Standard Deviation (SD in %), Total Time (TT in sec), and Pen Pressure (PP as a number corresponding to the sum of the pixels multiplied by the difference of the force applied force (Newton—N) to the typical pen pressure (1.4–1.5 N)—the bigger the number the higher the pressure in many points, while typical handwriting pressure tends to zero) separately:

Table 1. Group Statistics—HEALTH variable.

	HEALTH	N	MEAN	Std. Deviation	Std. Error Mean
SD	PATIENTS	12	33.1750	7.2267	2.0862
(% pixels)	HEALTHY	12	29.8333	5.3229	1.5366
TT	PATIENTS	12	20.1250	7.1106	2.0526
(sec)	HEALTHY	12	12.7250	5.1517	1.4872
PP	PATIENTS	12	47,696.1080	26,647.0019	7692.3269
(N * pixels)	HEALTHY	12	0.0191	0.0088	0.0026

- In Table 2, for PD patients the mean value of SD was 33.175 and for healthy was 29.833. As expected, PD patients present a greater deviation in SD value in drawing test, as result of the tremor and difficulty in moving of the hand of the disease. Additionally, the mean value of the TT variable, for PD patients, is 20.13 while for healthy it is 12.73. The total time to complete the spiral test is quite longer in the patient, as opposed to the healthy controls due to bradykinesia and other motor symptoms of Parkinson's disease. In PD patients the mean PP is 47,696.11 and for healthy it is 0.02. Because of the motor symptoms of the disease, PD patients exercise significantly greater pressure in their attempt to complete the dynamic spiral test in comparison with the healthy controls, who have no difficulties.

For SD: Testing for comparison of sample variances: Levene's Test for Equality of Variances (H0: variances do not differ). From the importance of this control Sig. = 0.286 > 0.05 we conclude that there is no significant difference in variances and therefore we conclude that variances do not differ. The significance of the test is Sig. = 0.211 > 0.05 we conclude that the variance SD does not depend from the health. The results are not statically significant. Thus, we infer that both of healthy controls and patients present spiral deviation of the dynamic spiral test of our application. From our sample it follows that the SD does not depend on whether you are healthy or PD patient.

For TT: Testing for comparison of sample variances: Levene's Test for Equality of Variances (H0: variances do not differ). From the importance of this control Sig. = 0.235 > 0.05 we conclude that there is no significant difference in variances and therefore we conclude that variances do not differ. Because the significance of the test is Sig. = 0.008 < 0.05 we reject the null hypothesis and conclude that the total time depend from the health and there is a statistically significant difference in the value of TT between patients and healthy. Indeed, once again we confirm that patients need more time to complete the dynamic spiral test in relation with healthy subjects.

For PP: Testing for comparison of sample variances: Levene's Test for Equality of Variances (H0: variances do not differ). From the importance of this control Sig. = 0.00 < 0.05 we conclude that there is a significant difference in variances and therefore we conclude that variances differ. From the statistical analysis we observe that the the significance of the test is Sig = 0.00 < 0.05, so the pen pressure depends from whether is healthy control or PD patient. Actually, there is a statistical difference between healthy and patients regarding the variable PP.

Table 2. Independent Samples Test—HEALTH.

		Levene's Test for Equality of Variances		T-Test for Equality of Means						
								95% Confidence Interval of the Difference		
		F	**Siq.**	**t**	**df**	**Sig.** [1]	**Mean Difference**	**Std. Error Difference**	**Lower**	**Upper**
SD	Equal variances assumed	1.195	0.286	1.290	22.000	0.211	3.3416	2.5909	−2.0317	8.7150
	Equal variances not assumed			1.290	20.221	0.212	3.3416	2.5909	−2.0592	8.7426
TT	Equal variances assumed	1.490	0.235	2.919	22.000	0.008	7.4000	2.5347	2.1432	12.6567
	Equal variances not assumed			2.919	20.054	0.008	7.4000	2.5347	2.1134	12.6865
PP	Equal variances assumed	28.269	0.000	6.200	22.000	0.000	47,696.0892	7692.3268	31,743.1797	63,648.9987
	Equal variances not assumed			6.200	11.000	0.000	47,696.0892	7692.3268	30,765.3919	64,626.7865

[1] Sig. (2-tailed).

- In Table 3, only PD patients are analyzed and the age is considered as the independent variable, while SD, TT, PP are dependent variables (separately).

Table 3. Group Statistics—PD patients—age variable.

	Age	N	MEAN	Std. Deviation	Std. Error Mean
SD	50–60	6	37.8667	5.18716	2.11765
	40–50	6	28.4833	5.92973	2.42080
TT	50–60	6	20.8167	8.00185	3.26674
	40–50	6	19.4333	6.78636	2.77052
PP	50–60	6	59,088.3666	20,674.8706	8440.4805
	40–50	6	36,303.8500	28,691.5870	11,713.2913

- The results for the age variable are summarized in Table 4: For people aged 50–60 years, the mean SD is 37.87 while for 40–50 years it is 28.48. Here, we can conclude that the age affects the SD of the patients and is probably due to the fact as the age group increases, the tremor and the other motor symptoms, such as instability, are increased too.
  For people aged 50–60 years, the mean of the TT variable is 20.82 while for the 40–50 years old it is 19.43. We notice that the longer a patient has been affected by the disease, despite being under the influence of medication, the more complicated it is to complete the test, and therefore it takes longer to complete the dynamic spiral test.
  For people aged 50–60 years, the average of the PP variable is 59,088.37 while for 40–50 years it is 36,303.85. As it is mentioned above, and at this point we observe that the greater age group needs more pressure to performing the dynamic spiral test. We come to the conclusion that although medication reduces and exacerbates the symptoms of the disease, it appears from our analysis that over time all three variables are affected. **For SD**: Testing for comparison of sample variances: Levene's Test for Equality of Variances (H0: variances do not differ). From the importance of this control Sig. = $0.740 > 0.05$ we conclude that there is no significant difference in variances and therefore we conclude that variances do not differ. The significance of the test is Sig. = $0.015 < 0.05$, thus we conclude that the variance of SD depends from the age of patients there is a statistically significant difference in the value of SD between the patient group of 50–60 years and patient group of age between 40–50. Actually, as the age of the patients increases, we notice that the value of the spiral deviation increases too.
  For TT: Testing for comparison of sample variances: Levene's Test for Equality of Variances (H0: variances do not differ). From the importance of this control Sig. = 0.511 > 0.05 we conclude that there is no significant difference in variances and therefore we conclude that variances do not differ. The significance of the test is Sig. = 0.753 > 0.05 and we make the conclusion that there is no statistically significant difference in the value of TT between 50-60 years and 40-50. The SD variance does not depend from the age of the patient.
  For PP: Testing for comparison of sample variances: Levene's Test for Equality of Variances (H0: variances do not differ). From the importance of this control Sig. = 0.281 > 0.05 we conclude that there is no significant difference in variances and therefore we conclude that variances do not differ. The significance of the test is Sig. = 0.146 > 0.05, so we conclude that the PP variance does not depend from the age group of patients.

Table 4. Independent Samples Test—PD patients—age.

		Levene's Test for Equality of Variances		T-Test for Equality of Means						
									95% Confidence Interval of the Difference	
		F	**Siq.**	**t**	**df**	**Sig.** [1]	**Mean Difference**	**Std. Error Difference**	**Lower**	**Upper**
SD	Equal variances assumed	0.116	0.740	2.917	10.00	0.015	9.3833	3.2163	2.2169	16.5497
	Equal variances not assumed			2.917	9.83	0.016	9.3833	3.2163	2.1997	16.5669
TT	Equal variances assumed	0.464	0.511	0.323	10.00	0.753	1.3833	4.2833	−8.1606	10.9273
	Equal variances not assumed			0.323	9.74	0.754	1.3833	4.2833	−8.1952	1.9619
PP	Equal variances assumed	1.300	0.281	1.578	10.00	0.146	22,784.5166	14,437.5519	−9384.3538	54,953.3871
	Equal variances not assumed			1.578	9.09	0.149	22,784.5166	14,437.5519	−9826.3746	55,395.4080

[1] Sig. (2-tailed).

- In Table 5, only PD patients are analyzed and the sex is considered as the independent variable, while SD, TT, PP are dependent variables.

Table 5. Group Statistics—PD patients—sex variable.

	Sex	N	MEAN	Std. Deviation	Std. Error Mean
SD	FEMALE	4	35.2750	3.51888	1.75944
	MALE	8	32.1250	8.54296	3.02039
TT	FEMALE	4	18.3250	7.72933	3.86466
	MALE	8	21.0250	7.14638	2.52663
PP	FEMALE	4	45,035.0500	27,235.2282	13,617.6141
	MALE	8	49,026.6375	28,139.7772	9948.9136

- The results for the sex variable are summarized in Table 6: For women, the mean of SD is 35.28 while for men it is 32.13. The women present a little greater SD in comparison with men.
  For women, the mean of TT is 18.33 while for men it is 21.03.
  For women, the average PP is 45,035.05 while for men it is 49,026.64.
  From these three valuable variables emerge the conclusion that the symptoms of the disease affect a greater percentage of women compared to men. However, in women, the development of symptomatic PD may be delayed by higher physiological striatal dopamine levels, possibly due to the activity of estrogens. This could explain the epidemiological observations of a lower incidence and higher age at onset in women. Women also presented more often with tremor which, in turn, is associated with milder motor deterioration and striatal degeneration. Taken together, these findings suggest a more benign phenotype in women with PD, according to [13]. So, combining these results with our conclusions, the treatment of Parkinson's disease which is focused on oestrogens works more effectively on symptoms in men than in women although the disease occurs more in the male population.
  For SD: Testing for comparison of sample variances: Levene's Test for Equality of Variances (H0: variances do not differ). From the importance of this control Sig. = 0.138 > 0.05 we conclude that there is no significant difference in variances and therefore we conclude that variances do not differ. The significance of the control is Sig. = 0.503 > 0.05 we conclude that there is no statistically significant difference in the value of SD between women patients and men patients. **For TT**: Testing for comparison of sample variances: Levene's Test for Equality of Variances (H0: variances do not differ). From the importance of this control Sig. = 0.807 > 0.05 we conclude that there is no significant difference in variances and therefore we conclude that variances do not differ. The significance of the control is Sig. = 0.561 > 0.05 we conclude that there is no statistically significant difference in the value of TT between women and men in our sample. The value of TT does not depend from the sex of patients.
  For PP: Testing for comparison of sample variances: Levene's Test for Equality of Variances (H0: variances do not differ). From the importance of this control Sig. = 0.799 > 0.05 we conclude that there is no significant difference in variances and therefore we conclude that variances do not differ. The significance of the control is Sig. = 0.820 > 0.05, so we conclude that there is no statistically significant difference in the value of PP between women and men in our sample.

Table 6. Independent Samples Test—PD patients—sex.

		Levene's Test for Equality of Variances		T-Test for Equality of Means						
									95% Confidence Interval of the Difference	
		F	Siq.	t	df	Sig. [1]	Mean Difference	Std. Error Difference	Lower	Upper
SD	Equal variances assumed	2.598	0.138	0.69	10.00	0.50	3.150	4.533	−6.951	13.251
	Equal variances not assumed			0.90	9.90	0.39	3.150	3.495	−4.649	10.949
TT	Equal variances assumed	0.063	0.807	−0.60	10.00	0.56	2.700	4.486	−12.696	7.296
	Equal variances not assumed			−0.58	5.67	0.58	2.700	4.617	−14.160	8.760
PP	Equal variances assumed	0.068	0.799	−0.23	10.00	0.82	−3991.587	17,067.735	−42,020.872	34,037.697
	Equal variances not assumed			−0.23	6.29	0.82	−3991.587	16,864.765	−44,802.306	36,819.131

[1] Sig. (2-tailed).

- In Table 7, only healthy individuals are analyzed and the age is considered as the independent variable, while SD, TT, PP are dependent variables.

Table 7. Group Statistics—Healthy individuals—age variable.

	Age	N	MEAN	Std. Deviation	Std. Error Mean
SB	50–60	6	30.0000	4.81664	1.96638
	40–50	6	29.6667	6.25033	2.55169
TT	50–60	6	12.7167	3.63891	1.48558
	40–50	6	12.7333	6.71913	2.74307
PP	50–60	6	0.0194	0.00919	0.00375
	40–50	6	0.0187	0.00932	0.00381

- The results for the age variable are summarized in Table 8:
  For people aged 50–60 years, the mean of SD is 30.00 while for 40–50 years it is 29.67.
  For people aged 50–60 years, the mean of the TT variable is 12.72 while for the 40–50 years old it is 12.73.
  For individuals aged 50-60 years, the mean of the PP variable is 0.01943 while for the age group 40–50 it is 0.1869.
  Comparing, the tables of the second case with the present case, where in both the age is the analyzing variable, we observe that exist an important difference in SD, TT and PP measurements, as we expected. Although the patients are under their medication for a long time, there is exist difficulties due to motor symptoms.
  For SD: Testing for comparison of sample variances: Levene's Test for Equality of Variances (H0: variances do not differ). From the importance of this control Sig. = 0.277 > 0.05 we conclude that there is no significant difference in variances and therefore we conclude that variances do not differ. The importance of control is Sig. = 0.920 > 0.05. We make the conclusion that the SD variance does not depend from the age group of 40–50 and 50–60.
  For TT: Testing for comparison of sample variances: Levene's Test for Equality of Variances (H0: variances do not differ). From the importance of this control Sig. = 0.219 > 0.05 we conclude that there is no significant difference in variances and therefore we conclude that variances do not differ. The significance of the test is Sig. = 0.996 > 0.05, so we conclude that there is no statistically significant difference in the value of TT between 50–60 years and 40–50.
  For PP: Testing for comparison of sample variances: Levene's Test for Equality of Variances (H0: variances do not differ). From the importance of this control Sig. = 0.686 > 0.05 we conclude that there is no significant difference in variances and therefore

we conclude that variances do not differ. The significance of the control is Sig. = 0.92 > 0.05 and we conclude that there is no statistically significant difference in PP value between 50–60 years and 40–50. The value of PP is not affected from the age group on healthy controls.

Table 8. Independent Samples Test—Healthy individuals—age.

		Levene's Test for Equality of Variances		T-Test for Equality of Means						
									95% Confidence Interval of the Difference	
		F	**Siq.**	**t**	**df**	**Sig.** [1]	**Mean Difference**	**Std. Error Difference**	**Lower**	**Upper**
SD	Equal variances assumed	1.321	0.277	0.103	10.00	0.920	0.3333	3.2214	−6.8445	7.5111
	Equal variances not assumed			0.103	9.39	0.920	0.3333	3.2214	−6.9082	7.5748
TT	Equal variances assumed	1.716	0.219	−0.005	10.00	0.996	−0.0166	3.1195	−6.9673	6.9340
	Equal variances not assumed			−0.005	7.70	0.996	−0.0166	3.1195	−7.2592	7.2259
PP	Equal variances assumed	0.174	0.686	0.139	10.00	0.892	0.0007	0.0053	−0.0111	0.0126
	Equal variances not assumed			0.139	9.99	0.892	0.0007	0.0053	−0.0111	0.0126

[1] Sig. (2-tailed).

- In Table 9, only Healthy individuals are analyzed and the sex is considered as the independent variable, while SD, TT, PP are dependent variables.

Table 9. Group Statistics—Healthy individuals—sex variable.

	Sex	N	MEAN	Std. Deviation	Std. Error Mean
SD	FEMALE	6	30.5000	4.03733	1.64823
	MALE	6	29.1667	6.70572	2.73760
TT	FEMALE	6	13.2000	4.85551	1.98225
	MALE	6	12.2500	5.85414	2.38994
PP	FEMALE	6	0.0215	0.01024	0.00418
	MALE	6	0.0167	0.00728	0.00297

- The results for the sex variable are summarized in Table 10:
  For women, the mean of SD is 30.50 while for men it is 29.17.
  For women, the mean of the TT variable is 13.20 while for men it is 12.25.
  For women, the mean of PP is 0.0214 while for men it is 0.0167.
  We observe that there is no significant difference between healthy men and women
  For SD: Testing for comparison of sample variances: Levene's Test for Equality of Variances (H0: variances do not differ). From the importance of this control Sig. = 0.143 > 0.05 we conclude that there is no significant difference in variances and therefore we conclude that variances do not differ. The significance of the test is Sig. = 0.685 > 0.05 we conclude that there is no statistically significant difference in the value of SD between women and men. The SD variance does not depend from the sex of healthy controls.
  For TT: Testing for comparison of sample variances: Levene's Test for Equality of Variances (H0: variances do not differ). From the importance of this control Sig. = 0.763 > 0.05 we conclude that there is no significant difference in variances and therefore we conclude that variances do not differ. The significance of the control is Sig. = 0.766 > 0.05 we conclude that there is no statistically significant difference in the value of TT between women and men. Thus, the TT value between women and men remains unaffected.
  For PP: Testing for comparison of sample variances: Levene's Test for Equality of Variances (H0: variances do not differ). From the importance of this control Sig. = 0.323

> 0.05 we conclude that there is no significant difference in variances and therefore we conclude that variances do not differ. According the significance of the control is Sig. = 0.371 > 0.05, so we conclude that there is no statistically significant difference in the value of PP between women and men.

Table 10. Independent Samples Test—Healthy individuals—sex.

		Levene's Test for Equality of Variances		T-Test for Equality of Means 95% Confidence Interval of the Difference						
		F	Siq.	t	df	Sig. [1]	Mean Difference	Std. Error Difference	Lower	Upper
SD	Equal variances assumed	2.526	0.143	0.417	10.00	0.685	1.3333	3.1954	−5.7866	8.4533
	Equal variances not assumed			0.417	8.204	0.687	1.3333	3.1954	−6.0037	8.6703
TT	Equal variances assumed	0.096	0.763	0.306	10.00	0.766	0.9500	3.1050	−6.9673	7.8684
	Equal variances not assumed			0.306	9.669	0.766	0.9500	3.1050	−6.0006	7.9006
PP	Equal variances assumed	1.080	0.323	0.937	10.00	0.371	0.0048	0.0051	−0.0066	0.0162
	Equal variances not assumed			0.937	9.027	0.373	0.0048	0.0051	−0.0067	0.0164

[1] Sig. (2-tailed).

Visualization of the Statistical Analysis

The following is a statistical analysis using bar charts. In Figures 7–9 the Patients' Frequency bar charts for the three parameters are depicted.

In Figure 7 we observe that most patients of the sample present a value between 35–40 of Spiral Deviation measurement.

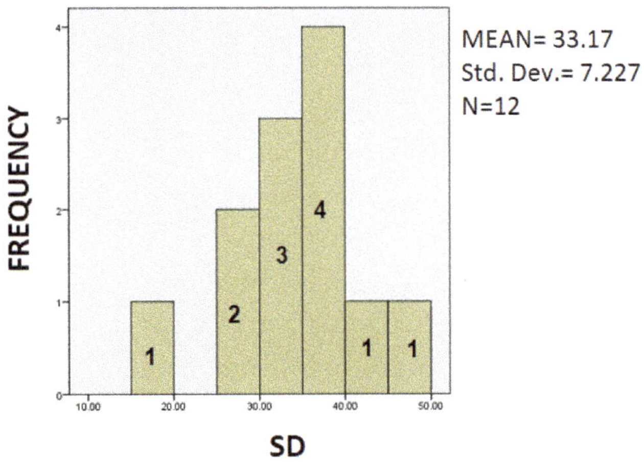

Figure 7. Barchart showing the frequency of the PD patients and the clustering of SD values.

In Figure 8 we observe that most patients of our sample use a total time of 15–20 s for completion of the spiral test, whereas the mean value of the total time is greater, i.e., the most patient of our sample use less time than the total mean time of the group to complete the motive test.

In Figure 9 we observe that most patients achieve values between 60,000–80,000, but the total mean value of Pen Pressure measurement is the lowest, which means that most patients exercise more pressure on the pen to draw the spiral test.

Following are bar charts (as depicted in Figures 10–12) for patients with the mean values of the variables depending on the age group.

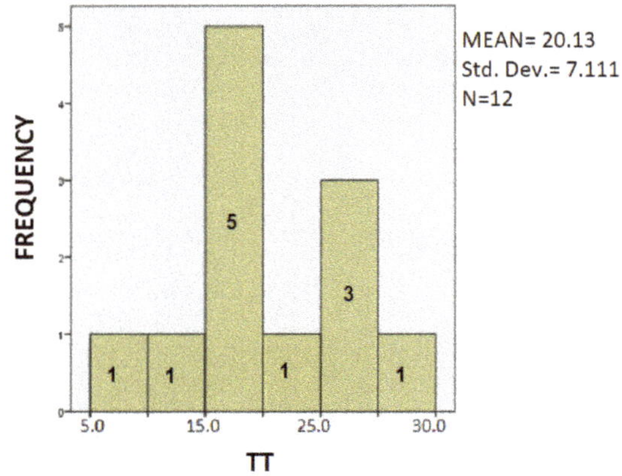

Figure 8. Barchart showing the frequency of the PD patients and the clustering of TT values.

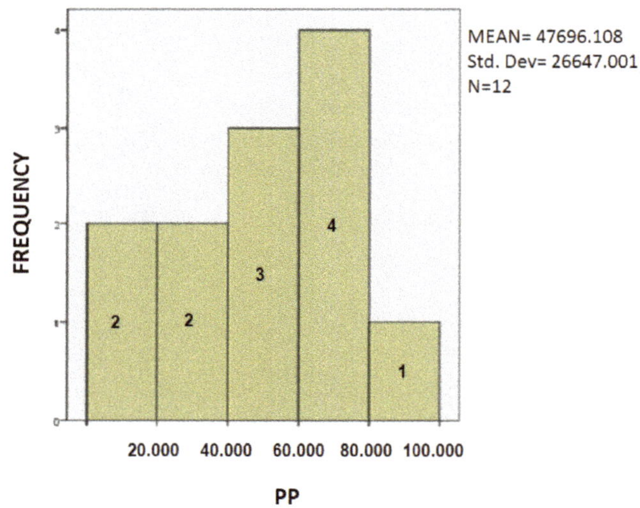

Figure 9. Barchart showing the frequency of the PD patients and the clustering of PP values.

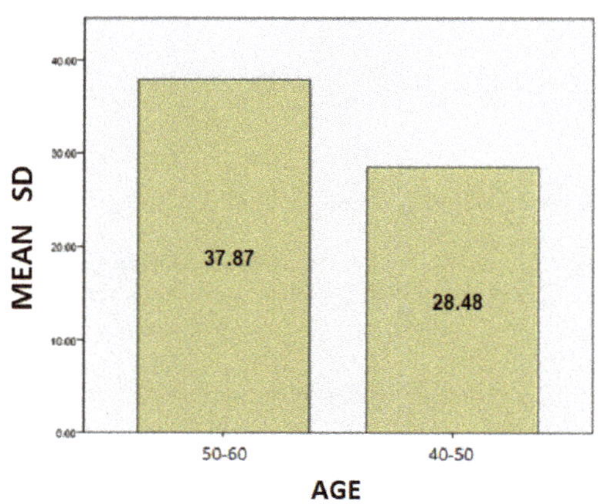

Figure 10. Barchart for patients with the mean value of SD by age.

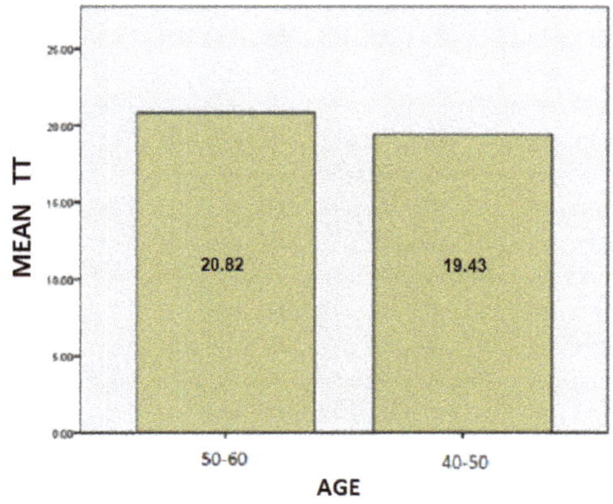

Figure 11. Barchart for patients with the mean value of TT by age.

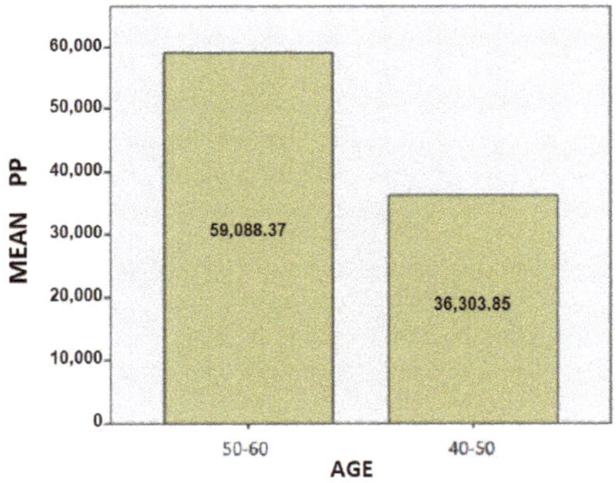

Figure 12. Barchart for patients with the mean value of PP by age.

4. Discussion and Conclusions

This study presents a novel tool for the quantitative estimation of movement disorders. The aim was to develop a flexible test, suitable for clinical practice that will allow monitor of certain muscle activities during the progress of the disease. It could also be useful for the assessment of drug or surgery treatment response. The preliminary application of the developed tool in several PD patients was successful. All patients as well as healthy controls followed the instructions and perform the test. No more than three repetitions were necessary in order to complete the task.

The main conclusion was that there is a statistically significant difference between healthy and PD patients for total time and pen pressure, reflecting the bradykinesia and rigidity of the patients respectively. Specifically, the poverty movement and the slow reaction to perform daily activities, which are characteristics of PD resulted in increased time spent to complete this specific task. Another characteristic of PD, i.e., increased muscle tone, known by the term rigidity was reflected by the enhanced pressure exerted on the pen. On the other hand, inter-group comparison of the spiral deviation did not reach a significant level, possibly because in PD voluntary activity is not predominately affected. The coordination of hand movements and is not deranged in PD, at least early on. Likewise, a tremor is often called a resting tremor, since it is not interfered with the intended motion as in an idiopathic senile tremor. It would be interesting to perform the same test in patients with idiopathic tremor or ataxia where it is expected to find severely abnormal values of spiral deviation.

The spiral deviation was higher in older patients, perhaps suggesting the greater disease severity. No other meaningful statistical results were obtained. In addition, one technical advantage of the application is the digitization and the automation of the results. In the traditional way, clinicians who are occupied with Parkinson's disease, such as physiotherapists etc., could observe only the tremor of the patient with the observation of the distance between the patient's line and the motive's line. Now with the application, clinicians can observe automatically the exercised pressure of the patient on the tablet and the time that the patient needs to complete the test, except from the distance. The main limitation of this study is the small sample size both for patients and healthy volunteers. It is possible that PD patients at a later stage of the disease demonstrate higher deviation from normality. The role of age should be examined in a future study as well. The next step would be the application of this test in a large sample of patients with extrapyramidal syndrome, as well as in patients with spasticity (pyramidal syndrome) or cerebellar ataxia in order to detect disease-specific differences.

The contribution of this work in relation to the other projects is not only the digitization of the quantitative measurements, such as the spiral deviation, the motive completion time, and the pressure that the patient exercise on the tablet with the pen, but this work is observing and analyze statically the differences between the age groups of patients and the differences between the sex of patients, each time different dependent and independent variable.

In brief, a novel custom-made software was developed in order to provide clinicians with a practical tool for the evaluation of movement disorders. Its preliminary application was successful allowing differentiation between PD and healthy subjects. Estimation of its specificity and sensitivity would require future studies in a large cohort of patients.

Author Contributions: Conceptualization, E.C.; methodology, E.C.; software, M.K.; validation, A.K. and E.C.; formal analysis, M.K.; investigation, M.K.; resources, E.C.; data curation, M.K.; writing—original draft preparation, M.K.; writing—review and editing, A.K.; visualization, M.K.; supervision, E.C.; project administration, E.C. All authors have read and agreed to the published version of the manuscript.

Funding: This research received no external funding.

Institutional Review Board Statement: The study was conducted in accordance with the Declaration of Helsinki, and approved by the Ethics Committee of the University of Patras (protocol code 14106).

Informed Consent Statement: Informed consent was obtained from all subjects involved in the study.

Data Availability Statement: Not applicable.

Conflicts of Interest: The authors declare no conflict of interest.

References

1. Vazquez-Velez, G.E.; Zoghbi, H.Y. Parkinson's Disease Genetics and Pathophysiology. *Annu. Rev. Neurosci.* **2021**, *44*, 87–108. [CrossRef] [PubMed]
2. German, D.; Dubach, M.; Askari, S.; Speciale, S.; Bowden, D. 1-Methyl-4-phenyl-1,2,3,6-tetrahydropyridine-induced Parkinsonian syndrome in Macaca fascicularis: Which midbrain dopaminergic neurons are lost? *Neuroscience* **1988**, *24*, 161–174. [CrossRef]
3. Aly, N.M.; Playfer, J.R.; Smith, S.L.; Halliday, D.M. A novel computer-based technique for the assessment of tremor in Parkinson's disease. *Age Ageing* **2007**, *36*, 395–399. Available online: https://academic.oup.com/ageing/article-pdf/36/4/395/7291977/afm061.pdf (accessed on 3 August 2022). [CrossRef] [PubMed]
4. Isenkul, M.; Sakar, B.; Kursun, O. Improved spiral test using digitized graphics tablet for monitoring Parkinson's disease. In Proceedings of the 2nd International Conference on E-Health and TeleMedicine, Istanbul, Turkey, 22–24 May 2014; pp. 171–175. [CrossRef]
5. Zham, P.; Kumar, D.K.; Dabnichki, P.; Poosapadi Arjunan, S.; Raghav, S. Distinguishing Different Stages of Parkinson's Disease Using Composite Index of Speed and Pen-Pressure of Sketching a Spiral. *Front. Neurol.* **2017**, *8*, 435. [CrossRef] [PubMed]
6. Aghanavesi, S.; Memedi, M.; Dougherty, M.; Nyholm, D.; Westin, J. Verification of a Method for Measuring Parkinson's Disease Related Temporal Irregularity in Spiral Drawings. *Sensors* **2017**, *17*, 2341. [CrossRef] [PubMed]

7. Gil-Martin, M.; Montero, J.M.; San-Segundo, R. Parkinson's Disease Detection from Drawing Movements Using Convolutional Neural Networks. *Electronics* **2019**, *8*, 907. [CrossRef]
8. Kamran, I.; Naz, S.; Razzak, I.; Imran, M. Handwriting dynamics assessment using deep neural network for early identification of Parkinson's disease. *Future Gener. Comput. Syst.* **2021**, *117*, 234–244. [CrossRef]
9. Kuosmanen, E.; Kan, V.; Visuri, A.; Boudjelthia, A.; Krizou, L.; Ferreira, D. Measuring Parkinson's Disease Motor Symptoms with Smartphone-Based Drawing Tasks. In *Proceedings of the Adjunct Proceedings of the 2019 ACM International Joint Conference on Pervasive and Ubiquitous Computing and Proceedings of the 2019 ACM International Symposium on Wearable Computers*; Association for Computing Machinery: New York, NY, USA, 2019; pp. 1182–1185. [CrossRef]
10. Lauraitis, A.; Maskeliunas, R.; Damasevicius, R.; Krilavicius, T. A Mobile Application for Smart Computer-Aided Self-Administered Testing of Cognition, Speech, and Motor Impairment. *Sensors* **2020**, *20*, 3236. [CrossRef] [PubMed]
11. Ferleger, B.I.; Sonnet, K.S.; Morriss, T.H.; Ko, A.L.; Chizeck, H.J.; Herron, J.A. A tablet- and mobile-based application for remote diagnosis and analysis of movement disorder symptoms. In Proceedings of the 42nd Annual International Conference of the IEEE Engineering in Medicine & Biology Society (EMBC), Montreal, QC, Canada, 20–24 July 2020; pp. 5588–5591. [CrossRef]
12. Pham, H.N.; Do, T.T.T.; Jie Chan, K.Y.; Sen, G.; Han, A.Y.K.; Lim, P.; Loon Cheng, T.S.; Nguyen, Q.H.; Nguyen, B.P.; Chua, M.C.H. Multimodal Detection of Parkinson Disease based on Vocal and Improved Spiral Test. In Proceedings of the 2019 International Conference on System Science and Engineering (ICSSE), Dong Hoi, Vietnam, 20–21 July 2019; pp. 279–284. [CrossRef]
13. Haaxma, C.A.; Bloem, B.R.; Borm, G.F.; Oyen, W.J.G.; Leenders, K.L.; Eshuis, S.; Booij, J.; Dluzen, D.E.; Horstink, M.W.I.M. Gender differences in Parkinson's disease. *J. Neurol. Neurosurg. Psychiatry* **2007**, *78*, 819–824. [CrossRef]

healthcare

MDPI

Article

Caregiver Views on Prospective Use of Robotic Care in Helping Children Adapt to Hospitalization

Meiling Jin [1] **and Hanna Choi** [2,*]

[1] Research Institute of Nursing Science, Seoul National University, Seoul 08826, Korea
[2] Department of Nursing Science, Nambu University, Gwangju 62271, Korea
* Correspondence: hanna.choi.kr@gmail.com

Abstract: Children in hospitals endure a variety of stressful situations. Children feel friendly toward and have fun with robots. Care robots are considered to be an alternate technique to relieve stress after hospitalization. A mixed-methods study was conducted on caregivers to understand the ideal care robot. One hundred and fifty caregivers of pediatric patients participated in a quantitative online survey, and eleven participated in focus group interviews for qualitative analysis. Quantitative data underwent descriptive statistics. Content analysis was conducted for qualitative data. Regarding the overall awareness and necessity of a care robot, the caregivers thought it would help patients adapt to the hospital environment more quickly. The caregivers' preferred character-shaped robots of child height. For sound, they preferred an animated character's voice. For movement, they preferred the robot to roll on wheels. Regarding functions, medicine was the item for which they most wanted to use game elements. For the educational element, the caregivers wanted to teach children the reasons for and methods of medicine administration. Four themes were derived from the qualitative results. The findings are expected to contribute to the future development of care robots that can assist pediatric patients.

Keywords: child patient; care robot; caregiver; hospitalization

Citation: Jin, M.; Choi, H. Caregiver Views on Prospective Use of Robotic Care in Helping Children Adapt to Hospitalization. *Healthcare* **2022**, *10*, 1925. https://doi.org/10.3390/healthcare10101925

Academic Editor: Daniele Giansanti

Received: 31 August 2022
Accepted: 27 September 2022
Published: 30 September 2022

1. Introduction

Children in hospitals endure a variety of stressful situations, including physical discomfort and fear, which make it difficult for them to adjust to their new surroundings [1]. Pain from treatment, in which attention conversion therapy is an example of a pain reduction approach, is one of the most common pressures faced by pediatric patients [2].

Using robotics technology, care robots follow individual health goals and promote health [3]. Because children feel friendly towards and have fun with robots, care robots are considered to be an alternate technique to relieve stress after hospitalization [4]. The following are the different types of care robots that have been developed and utilized in hospitals for children.

The Probo robot was created to provide knowledge and spiritual support to children, as well as to console children undergoing treatment [5]. The MediRobbi robot is an interactive robot designed to assist and guide medical procedures [6]. The Nao robot is a humanoid robot that relieves children's physical discomfort during flu vaccines [7]. Pleo is a dinosaur robot that helps children have a cheerful attitude while fighting disease, which enhances therapy effectiveness and the well-being of hospitalized children [8,9]. A bear-shaped, huggable robot was made to help children with stress, worry, and pain [10]. The Arash robot was created to help children cope with the discomfort of cancer treatment by entertaining and supporting them [11]. The Pepper robot helps children learn in the home environment, serve as a companion to older adults, and coach elderly people with psychiatric disorders through rehabilitation and recreational activities [12]. The above robot studies mainly targeted children with autism spectrum disorder, and most of them focused on the emotional aspects of children, except for the Pepper robot. According to the literature review, previous studies have focused on evaluating children's distraction potential during medical procedures using robots, as well as the emotional support and well-being of children during hospitalization [13]. Therefore, this study tried to develop a new robot that helps with children's general hospitalization in detail. We determined at which age they most need robots, where to place them, what functions the robots should have, and what role the robot should play.

For understanding the potential use before development, researchers have identified care robots' proactive role in children's hospitals from the nurse's point of view through interviews [14]. There are many limitations to the ability of health care providers to understand the full needs of children with limited communication skills.

The system-development life-cycle methodology is used in the development of new technologies. It consists of four steps: needs analysis, design, implementation, and evaluation [15]. Needs analysis is the first step in this process. We intended to analyze the need for robots that help children adapt to hospital life through the use of caregivers who take care of the children closest to them.

This study intended to provide basic data for the development of care robots that help children adapt to hospitalization by examining the need for robots. However, toddlers are limited in their ability to express themselves freely and have limitations due to their lack of understanding of terms. According to the research conducted so far, children are used to playing with robots that have already been developed and analyzed through very simple yes or no questions [16]. Moreover, in Korea, when a child is hospitalized, it is the cultural norm that their caregiver stays in the room with them and looks after them, so parents are effective in verbal and nonverbal communication with the child [17]. Therefore, it is meaningful to investigate and analyze the needs of the caregivers who understand them best because they care for the children closest to them.

Scholars have pointed out that it is necessary to use different methods of data collection or analysis according to the content, object, and purpose to be grasped through demand analysis. In existing papers, most of the statistical processing uses questionnaires, so it is necessary to use a mixture of two or more methods to find a complementary relationship, rather than using one method [18]. For effective data collection, it is necessary to use two or more methods (e.g., questionnaire and interview) [19].

The mixed research method, which combines both methods, is a disadvantage of quantitative research, in that it is difficult to understand the research subjects' situational context, and it is difficult for direct opinions and statements to reflect the research data. The disadvantage of qualitative research is researcher bias. As a research method that overcomes the excessive reflection of this problem or the difficulty in generalizing research results, it has the advantage of complementing the shortcomings of the two research methods [20].

While building a care robot, it is critical to understand what kind of robot children require from the perspective of the caregivers who are closest to them. From the perspective of caregivers, the goal of this study was to suggest the appearance, function, and role of a care robot that could be deployed in children's hospitals.

2. Materials and Methods

2.1. Study Design

This mixed-methods study included caregiver questionnaires and focus group interviews with children aged 3 to 18 who had been hospitalized in the previous 3 months. The research questions were as follows:

- Quantitative Question 1: Do you think care robots are needed in children's hospitals?
- Quantitative Question 2: What do you think the appearance of the care robot should be for hospitalized children?
- Quantitative Question 3: What do you think is the most necessary function of a care robot for hospitalized children?

- Quantitative Question 4: Where would be the best place to locate the care robot?
- Qualitative Question 5: What do you think a care robot's role should be for hospitalized children?

2.2. Participants

The participants in this study were caregivers of children aged 3 to 18 who had been hospitalized for at least 3 days within the previous 3 months. Caregivers of children with chronic diseases, cancer, or in need of intensive care were excluded from the study. All participants filled in consent forms for participation in the study.

2.3. Data Collection

The online survey for caregivers of hospitalized children was commissioned by Korea Research, a specialized research institute, and the survey period was from 16 March to 21 March 2020. The researcher sent the research participant selection criteria, research participant recruitment letter, research participant explanation and consent form, and questionnaire to the academic research officer of Korea Research, and then the person in charge produced it according to the survey frame of Korea Research. The researcher then confirmed it. In addition, Korea Research established an online survey web link for to be sent to the survey subjects for testing, and the researcher launched the survey after checking the contents of the web link. The subjects of the survey read the research participant recruitment statement and the research participant explanation presented through the online survey web link from Korea Research. If they did not click a button indicating they agreed to participate, then the survey automatically closed and the session ended. We did not use demonstration programs or videos to investigate the need to develop a robot that helps children adapt to hospitalization. If the caregiver saw or experienced a video or demonstration of a robot that was already developed, they may have preconceived thoughts about it. We recognized that these are suitable for usability evaluation research. For the qualitative focus group, interviewees were recruited through Korea Research, and an online survey was conducted from 16–21 March 2020. On 31 January 2020, the researcher divided 11 participants into two groups and interviewed them for about 60–90 min each in the seminar room of Seoul National University's College of Nursing; all contents were recorded.

Participants were also asked seven open-ended questions about the experience of their children's hospitalization and the need for and role of a care robot (Table 1).

Table 1. Guiding Questions for the Focus Groups.

Type	Question Topics
Introduction	• Share the sociodemographic characteristics (gender, age, child's age, child's diagnosis, period of hospitalization)
Opening	• During hospitalization, share your daily routine with your child • What was the most memorable challenge you faced while in the hospital?
Exploratory	• Do you think care robots are helpful to your child during hospitalization? • Could you recommend a care robot's functions that would help with the difficulties of hospitalization? • Please describe in detail the role of the robot you expect in the ward.
Closing	• Share a summary of the discussed content. • (After summarization) Was it well summarized? • Do you have any comments you would like to add?

2.4. Data Analysis

The results of the online survey were analyzed using SPSS 23.0 for Windows. The percentages, means, and standard deviations were calculated according to the survey items for each field of the questionnaire. Interview data recorded in the focus group interviews were transcribed and analyzed in the language used to establish the reliability of the data. Qualitative content analysis was used to analyze the collected interview data.

Qualitative content analysis is a research method that analyzes the patterns and topics of content through a coding process and a systematic classification method based on the overall understanding of vast textual data, such as interview data [21]. Without using a software program, two researchers analyzed the content in the following way. The specific analytical steps were as follows: First, the researcher repeatedly read the transcription and tried to understand it. Second, the representative main concepts and contexts were coded in the overall content. Third, if commonalities were found between the extracted codes, they were grouped separately and classified into topics.

2.5. Verifying the Validity of the Research Results

After revising a questionnaire developed by the researcher for nurses to suit the purpose of this study, four experts modified it to ensure content validity [22]. The experts consisted of one person enrolled in a PhD program in child nursing, one with a PhD in child nursing, and two professors of nursing informatics. Each expert calculated the content validity score for each item, assigning 4 points if it was valid, 3 if it was somewhat valid, 2 if it was somewhat invalid, and 1 if it was not valid at all. We then calculated the content validity index for each item and guided the experts to present their opinions freely. Three items with a content validity index of 0.8 or less, and those with ambiguous meanings, were excluded. As a result, quantitative data were used to define seven questions on general characteristics, seven on overall awareness and necessity of care robot, four on the appearance of care robots, two on the function of care robots (one on game elements and one on educational elements), and one on the place for a care robot.

As for qualitative data, findings of the care robot role were verified according to credibility, auditability, fittingness, and confirmability suggested by Sandelowski [23]. For the credibility of the data, subjects were recruited using the random sampling method from a Korean company that conducts research. To ensure auditability, we recorded all processes of the actual steps from the planning to the reassurance of all study findings from the participants. Six professionals who were experts in their fields (three nursing researchers, two health researchers, and one qualitative researcher) refined the final contents for testing fittingness and confirmability. As for the validity of the qualitative results, we asked each focus group the same set of questions.

3. Results

3.1. Quantitative Result

3.1.1. General Characteristics

A total of 150 participants took the online survey for quantitative data collection. The online survey of caregivers drew a total of 63 men and 87 women. Regarding age, 47.3% were in their thirties, and most of the caregivers had school-aged children. The average age of the participants was 40 ± 5.9 years. The average length of stay in the hospital was 6 days, ranging from 3 to 26 days, and many children were primarily hospitalized for pneumonia (Table 2).

3.1.2. The Overall Awareness and Necessity of Care Robots

The participants responded based on a five-point scale (1—definitely no, 2—no, 3—yes, 4—definitely yes, 5—neither). The scores for each category were all over 3 when it came to general perceptions and the requirement of a care robot. "A care robot is needed in pediatric wards" scored 3.41 ± 0.94; "A care robot will reduce the fear of hospitalization" scored 3.33 ± 0.82; "A care robot will assist child patients to adapt to the hospital environment more quickly" scored 3.33 ± 0.73; "A care robot will enhance child patients' cooperation with treatment" scored 3.37 ± 0.71; "A care robot will reduce the fear of treatment" scored 3.32 ± 0.73; and "A care robot will ease the burdens of parents looking after their children" scored 3.25 ± 0.77.

Table 2. General Characteristics of the Caregivers in the Quantitative Analysis (n = 150).

Characteristics		*n* (%)
Gender	Male	63 (42)
	Female	87 (58)
Age	20 s	2 (1.3)
	30 s	71 (47.3)
	40 s	66 (44)
	≥50 s	11 (7.3)
	Mean ± SD = 40 ± 5.9	
Education	High school	14 (9.3)
	College	16 (10.7)
	University	101 (67.3)
	≥Graduate school	19 (12.7)
Job	Homemaker	39 (26.0)
	Office clerk	64 (42.7)
	Tradesperson	3 (2.0)
	Professional	26 (17.3)
	Public official	6 (4.0)
	Private business	10 (6.7)
	Other	2 (1.3)
Hospitalization Experience	Currently hospitalized for 3 days or more	16 (10.7)
	Have been hospitalized within the last 3 months	134 (89.3)
Child' age	Preschool	50 (33.3)
	School	63 (42)
	Adolescence	37 (24.7)
Child's diagnosis	Pneumonia	35 (23.3)
	Enteritis	25 (16.7)
	Fracture	22 (14.7)
	Influenza	21 (14.0)
	Other	47 (31.3)

Kindergarteners (37.9%) were the age group most in need of a care robot according to the caregivers. Daycare was 26.4%, lower elementary school was 22%, upper elementary school was 5.1%, middle school was 5.4%, and high school was 3.2%. The caregivers thought children in kindergarten were the right age to benefit from a care robot, claiming that children would like to have one. They also stated that children in hospitals become frustrated and bored, but that if they had a care robot, they could be friends with it. Hospital beds, according to the caregivers, are the places where care robots are most needed.

3.1.3. The Appearance of Care Robots

Character-shaped robots were the most popular among the caregivers (including animation characters). When asked why they preferred character-based robots (including animated characters), the caregivers said it was because they seemed comforting and nice to the children.

When asked what size the care robot should be, 42.3% said it should be the same height as the young patients; 46.5% indicated an animated character's voice would be preferred for the care robot's sound. In terms of the way the care robot should move, 56.9% thought it should be on wheels (Table 3).

3.1.4. The Function and Place of a Care Robot

When asked if gaming elements relating to nursing services should be utilized to encourage taking medicine, 32.3% of the caregivers said yes. The caregivers' arguments for choosing this item were that they would enjoy it if children were encouraged as if they were being rewarded for taking medicine, and that children would be more willing to take medicine if they were made to feel better through games (Table 4).

Table 3. Care Robot Appearance: Choosing Children's Preferred Robot Characteristics from Caregivers' Perspectives (Multiple Choice).

Type	Ranking	Item	*n* (%)
Design	1	Character-shaped robot (including animated characters)	138 (45.5)
	2	Animal-shaped robot	108 (35.6)
	3	Humanoid robot	35 (11.6)
	4	Other (monitor-shaped robot, etc.)	22 (7.3)
Size	1	The height of the pediatric patients	90 (42.3)
	2	Taller than the height of the pediatric patients	52 (24.4)
	3	Smaller than the height of pediatric patients	36 (16.9)
	4	Pediatric patient is sitting on a bed	28 (13.1)
	5	The height of an adult	7 (3.3)
Sound	1	Animated character voice	128 (46.5)
	2	Familiar to pediatric patients	83 (30.2)
	3	A sound that expresses various types of music	37 (13.5)
	4	Sound like a real animal	27 (9.8)
Movement	1	Rolls on wheels	111 (56.9)
	2	Walking	67 (34.4)
	3	Fixed form	17 (8.7)

Table 4. Care Robot Function (Multiple Choice).

Element	Ranking	Item	*n* (%)
Game (Items to be implemented using game elements in nursing procedures)	1	Medication	103 (32.3)
	2	Injections	90 (28.2)
	3	Measure blood pressure, body temperature, and pulse	44 (13.8)
	4	Food rejection	42 (13.2)
	5	Diet survey	19 (6.0)
	6	Inspection	11 (3.4)
	7	Changing clothing in hospital	10 (3.1)
Educational (Topics to be taught to the children through care robot)	1	Reason for and method of medicine administration	68 (20.7)
	2	Overall description of the disease	48 (14.6)
	3	Reason for and method of inspection	42 (12.8)
	4	Infection management education	40 (12.2)
	5	Inpatient education	21 (6.4)
	6	Other (discharge education, type of inspection, result of inspection, etc.)	110 (33.4)

When asked what information they would like their pediatric patients to learn via a care robot, 20.7% of the caregivers said the reason for and method of medicine administration. When asked why they chose this item, the caregivers replied that children would listen better if the care robot explained the purpose for medicine administration (Table 4).

The caregivers of hospitalized children accounted the hospital bed to be the place where a care robot was needed 30% of the time. This was followed by the treatment room (25.5%), hospital corridor (20.1%), nurse station (9.9%), EMR (electronic medical record) cart (9.6%), and school in hospital (4.8%).

3.2. Qualitative Result

3.2.1. General Characteristics

We interviewed eleven participants in the focus group for the qualitative research. The caregivers who took part in the focus group interviews were all full-time, stay-at-home mothers, with an average age of 41 ± 4.2. The children were divided into six girls and five boys, with an average age of 9 years and a 6-day hospitalization. The most common reason for hospitalization was pneumonia (Table 5).

Table 5. General Characteristics of the Caregivers in the Qualitative Analysis (n = 11).

Number	Gender	Age	Period of Hospitalization	Child' Gender	Child' Age	Child's Diagnosis
1	F	31	5	F	3	Bronchopneumonia
2	F	40	6	M	3	Bronchopneumonia
3	F	43	4	M	9	Supernumerary Teeth
4	F	44	9	F	12	Mycoplasma Pneumonia
5	F	46	4	M	14	Acute appendicitis
6	F	39	5	F	7	Pneumonia
7	F	45	4	M	14	Fracture
8	F	44	9	F	6	Obstructive pulmonary Disease
9	F	39	10	F	10	Pneumonia
10	F	42	8	M	15	Accessory Navicular Syndrome
11	F	39	6	F	6	Pneumonia

3.2.2. The Role of a Care Robot

The following are the outcomes of the focus group interviews, which provide the perspectives of both hospitalized children and their caregivers (Table 6).

Table 6. The role of care robot in children's hospital.

Domain	Sub-Domain	Quote
Children's perspective	Relieving fear by providing familiar elements	*I believe that a care robot would be ideal for removing the fear of being admitted to the hospital for the first time*
	Expecting that care robot can be a friend	*I hope the care robot is like a friend. My child is anxious, (..) even child is left alone for a short time. A robot can communicate when a child asks something*
	Educating tool	*I'd like a care robot to explain the disease to the child in a timely manner*
Caregivers' perspective	Relieving stress to provide a little break	*If [the care robot] plays with their child for even an hour, I believe it will be lot less stressful and more pleasant for caregivers*

3.2.3. Children's Perspective

- Relieving fear by providing familiar elements

According to the caregivers, hospitalization is a scary event for children. The caregivers claimed that the kind expression of a care robot could help decrease fear in children on the day of their admission. Children would prefer it if the familiarly characterized care robot complimented, cheered, or encouraged them when they had to do tasks they disliked, such as taking medicine or traveling to the treatment room.

> *"I believe that a care robot would be ideal for removing the fear of being admitted to the hospital for the first time .... He was unwell and sensitive, but he was abruptly placed in an unknown atmosphere, so the odd devices and injections were terrifying to him. I believe the care robot will be beneficial to youngsters"* (Participant 5, Focus Group 1).

> *"You had a rough day today, right?' the care robot asked. 'Isn't it excruciating? Let us, on the other hand, take good care of ourselves today.' ... I felt [the care robot] would be able to help people cope with their fear"* (Participant 1, Focus Group 1).

- Expecting a care robot to be a friend

The caregivers expressed their desire for a care robot to be a friend who speaks to and plays with the child patients. Patients admitted to the hospital said that boredom was one of the biggest difficulties they faced because they spent most of their time watching YouTube without any activity. In particular, the unfamiliar environment maximizes the fear of the first day of hospitalization. At this time, friends other than family could alleviate this fear. Therefore, they hoped care robots could be friends who talk to or connect with patients.

> *"I hope the care robot is like a friend. My child is anxious, so when I go to restroom, she worries and tells me to come right away, even child is left alone for a short time. At times like this, a robot can communicate when a child asks something. If the care robot with no reaction, I think it's not much different from tablet PC."* (Participant 2, Focus Group 2).

> *"Some children have cell phones, but many do not. I think it would be good to use the [robot's] Wi-Fi function to make video calls possible and connect to talk with or see the faces of their friends or mother."* (Participant 4, Focus Group 2).

- Educating tool

Children are fascinated by care robots, so if the robots teach them lessons to which they ordinarily do not listen (e.g., hand cleaning or respiratory therapy), they are likely to accept them. The caregivers also suggested that a care robot could explain to children why they should do tasks they dislike, such as taking medicine or receiving injections. Furthermore, in this scenario, children may forget information shortly after learning it; therefore, it would be beneficial to reinforce it is using a care robot. The caregivers expressed their desire for the care robot to assist children in navigating an unfamiliar environment when they were admitted to the hospital.

> *"I'd like a care robot to explain disease to the child in a timely manner at a level the child could understand. "Could a child be taught to wash his or her hands if the lesson were presented as a children's animation? The surgery will proceed in this manner. Therefore, don't worry when you're done, do something with me."* (Participant 5, Focus Group 1).

3.2.4. Caregivers' Perspective

- Relieving stress to provide a little break

One caregiver said she could not sleep because she had to care for her child 24 h a day and that it was very difficult to feed their child and administer medicine to them when the child was hospitalized. Furthermore, the caregiver stated that she struggled physically and mentally when her child was unwell, cranky, or upset. In this scenario, the caregiver stated that she would be able to rest briefly if the care robot talked to or played with the child.

> *"The mother can take a break while the child converses with the robot. As a result, I believe it will benefit me emotionally because I will be able to take a break."* (Participant 5, Focus Group 1).

> *"If [the care robot] plays with their child for even an hour, I believe it will be lot less stressful and more pleasant for caregivers."* (Participant 2, Focus Group 2).

3.3. *Suggestion for the Adaption of a Care Robot for Children's Hospitalization*

From the perspective of the caregivers, the installation location, the care robot's appearance, the type of care robot that hospitalized children are most likely to prefer, and the care robot's implementation function are proposed as follows (Table 7).

Table 7. Suggestion for the adaption of a care robot for children's hospitalization.

Category	Sub-Category		Detail
Main target population	3–10 years old (daycare, kindergarten, lower elementary school)		
Care robot location	Hospital bedside		
Care robot's appearance	Design	Character-shaped robot (including animated characters)	A round monitor in the face part allows children to set their favorite cartoon character on their own.
	Size	The pediatric patient's height	A height adjuster is installed on the robot's leg so that the height can be adjusted based on the child's height.
	Sound	Animated character voice	Children can choose from kindergarten and lower elementary characters and franchises, such as Pororo and Marvel.
	Movement	Rolls on wheels	Wheel-based legs are utilized, as on the Pepper robot.
Care robot's function	Game element	Medication Injections Measure blood pressure, body temperature, and pulse Food rejection	The care robot functions as a serious game. A child administers medicine to a character. Every time the character administers medicine, the child's health level will increase. The child will receive coins, badges, etc., each time they take medication or undergo a medical procedure.
	Educational element	Reason for and method of medicine administration Overall description of the disease Reason for and method of inspection Infection-management education	The care robot functions as a serious game. The child receives training from the chosen character through a face-shaped monitor. If the child listens carefully to the educational content and solves a problem, they will receive a coin or badge.

4. Discussion

4.1. Overall Awareness and Necessity of a Care Robot

Regarding the overall perception of and necessity for care robots, in the category of "Using care robots, the burden on parents caring for hospitalized children will be reduced", the caregivers of hospitalized children scored high. This result was also consistent with the theme of "Relieving stress to provide a little break"; therefore, it is judged that care robots are expected to relieve the stress of care.

The caregivers of hospitalized children said that preschool age is the age at which care robots are most needed. Preschool is a time when peers are important, and children can play with friends using rules [24]. Moreover, during this stage, they begin to feel interested in playing with their friends. Based on these characteristics, it is said that if a care robot becomes a friend and plays with a pediatric patient, it will help the child's adaptation to hospitalization life by aiding cognitive and emotional development by accepting roles and resolving realistic frustration.

4.2. The Care Robot Appearance

From the standpoint of the caregivers, a cartoon character-based robot was the favored type of care robot. A character-based robot was also the favored form of care robot in a study of pediatric nurses [22]. This result was the same as another study of children aged 4–7 years [25]. The preferred size was discovered to be around the same height as the child in this investigation.

Other research has revealed that children prefer smaller robots to larger robots [26]. When it came to the movement of the care robot, the caregivers favored it rolling on wheels. According to previous surveys, nurses and doctors preferred that the robot move on wheels (71.1%) [27]. The robot's movement, according to Jin and Kim [22], preferred walking shape. The researchers believe that rolling with wheels is more stable and does not hurt patients. As a result, we believe it is important to develop a care robot around these requirements. According to Arnold et al. [26], when designing products for children, their opinions need to be gathered if they are to be considered. Therefore, young patients should be included in the design of care robots.

4.3. The Care Robot Function

The caregivers preferred medication in the game elements to provide a reason for and method of medicine administration in an educational manner via a care robot. Medication was the second-most prevalent item that might be implemented when utilizing game features according to pediatric nurses [22]. Baek et al. [28] found that, among children aged 6 to 12, 32.6% of children owned a smartphone and used game functions the most.

For children, games are a very familiar tool. Therefore, it is believed that if children experience taking medicine as a serious game, they will be more willing to actively participate in treatment. The other recommendations in the survey included discharge education, type of inspection, result of inspection, outpatient treatment, medication precautions, bedsore education, hospital tours (location), fall prevention education, explanation of surgery, education before and after surgery (deep breathing, fasting, and position), wound dressing, nursing method according to disease, and growth and development (characteristics of each age group).

Robots that employ game elements have an emotionally supportive effect on children. Pourteimour and Kazemi [29] showed that, when preschool children were hospitalized, a robotic game kit could be used to lower the children's separation anxiety and fears of physical injury.

4.4. The Role and Place of a Care Robot

The caregivers anticipated that their children would be friends with a care robot. They wanted a robot that could converse with children, as well as encourage and play with them. The most significant responsibilities of a care robot are to bring comfort to inpatients, reducing anxiety, discomfort, and suffering, while enhancing the motivation to be treated and raising attentiveness [30]. Liang et al. [14] reported that nurses thought care robots were efficient and effective in providing hospital guidance for hospitalized children and their guardians, and that care robots programmed for education provided education for patients in the absence of nurses. Nurses thought robots could play a role in complementing the reinforcement of a patient's knowledge and their self-management ability.

4.5. Limitations

This study investigated the necessity for a care robot that can assist children in adjusting to hospitalization. However, children were not included in this study due to being unable to identify differences in need due to these variables. Future research should consider various factors related to the characteristics of various age groups, disease severity, and disease type.

5. Conclusions

In this study, we used a mixed research method with the caregivers of hospitalized children so that we could understand the needs for the development of care robots regarding children's adaptation to hospitalized life. As a result of this study, we discovered that the preferred care robot for children's adaptation to hospitalization was a character robot with the voice of an animated character, a height similar to that of a hospitalized child, and wheels for movement. For developing a care robot, we required software that selects a child's favorite animated cartoon character, hardware that utilizes a face-shaped monitor representing the selected character and possesses the capability of height adjustment. In addition, we found that there was a high demand for education on the reasons for and methods of medicine administration by adding an element of fun through serious games. The caregivers hoped that a care robot could relieve fear by providing familiar elements, serving as a friend and an educational tool for hospitalized children, and relieving stress in order to provide a little break to caregivers.

Based on the findings of this study, it is envisaged that care robots that assist hospitalized pediatric patients will be produced in the future.

Author Contributions: Conceptualization, methodology, formal analysis, investigation, M.J.; writing—original draft preparation, writing—review and editing, Visualization M.J. and H.C. All authors have read and agreed to the published version of the manuscript.

Funding: This work was supported by the National Research Foundation of Korea (NRF), South Korea (No. 2019R1F1A1058969, 2019R1F1A1049523, 2020R1F1A1077151).

Institutional Review Board Statement: This research was approved by the internal review board of S National University (Institutional Review Board No.1912/001-010).

Informed Consent Statement: Participates received detailed announcement about study aim, process, taking time, reward, and confidentiality. All participants gave their informed consent.

Data Availability Statement: Data are available on request due to restrictions. The data presented in this study are available on request from the corresponding author.

Conflicts of Interest: The authors declare no conflict of interest.

References

1. Díaz-Boladeras, M.; Angulo, C.; Domènech, M.; Albo-Canals, J.; Serrallonga, N.; Raya, C.; Barco, A. Assessing pediatrics patients' psychological states from biomedical signals in a cloud of social robots. In Proceedings of the XIV Mediterranean Conference on Medical and Biological Engineering and Computing 2016, Paphos, Cyprus, 31 March–2 April 2016; Springer: Berlin/Heidelberg, Germany, 2016; pp. 1185–1190. [CrossRef]
2. Cho, H.; Lee, J.; Kim, S.-J. An integrative literature review on pain alleviation interventions for hospitalized children. *Child Health Nurs. Res.* **2020**, *26*, 254–266. [CrossRef] [PubMed]
3. Hong, E.; Shin, S. Nurses' perceptions of care robots in long-term care facilities. *J. Korean Gerontol. Nurs.* **2019**, *21*, 22–32. [CrossRef]
4. Moerman, C.J.; van der Heide, L.; Heerink, M. Social robots to support children's well-being under medical treatment: A systematic state-of-the-art review. *J. Child Health Care* **2019**, *23*, 596–612. [CrossRef] [PubMed]
5. Goris, K.; Saldien, J.; Vanderborght, B.; Lefeber, D. The huggable robot Probo: Design of the robotic head. In Proceedings of the Second AISB Symposium on the Role of Virtual Creatures in a Computerised Society, from AISB 2008 Proceedings, Aberdeen, UK, 1–4 April 2008; Volume 1, pp. 23–29.
6. Lu, S.-C.; Blackwell, N.; Do, E.Y.-L. mediRobbi: An interactive companion for pediatric patients during hospital visit. In Proceedings of the International Conference on Human-Computer Interaction, Orlando, FL, USA, 9–14 July 2011; Springer: Berlin/Heidelberg, Germany, 2011; pp. 547–556. [CrossRef]
7. Beran, T.N.; Ramirez-Serrano, A.; Vanderkooi, O.G.; Kuhn, S. Reducing children's pain and distress towards flu vaccinations: A novel and effective application of humanoid robotics. *Vaccine* **2013**, *31*, 2772–2777. [CrossRef]
8. Larriba, F.; Raya, C.; Angulo, C.; Albo-Canals, J.; Díaz, M.; Boldú, R. Externalising moods and psychological states in a cloud based system to enhance a pet-robot and child's interaction. *Biomed. Eng. Online* **2016**, *15*, 187–196. [CrossRef]
9. Moerman, C.J.; Jansens, R.M. Using social robot PLEO to enhance the well-being of hospitalised children. *J. Child Health Care* **2021**, *25*, 412–426. [CrossRef]
10. Jeong, S.; Logan, D.E.; Goodwin, M.S.; Graca, S.; O'Connell, B.; Goodenough, H.; Anderson, L.; Stenquist, N.; Fitzpatrick, K.; Zisook, M. A social robot to mitigate stress, anxiety, and pain in hospital pediatric care. In *Proceedings of the Tenth Annual ACM/IEEE International Conference on Human-Robot Interaction Extended Abstracts*; Association for Computing Machinery: New York, NY, USA, 2015; pp. 103–104. [CrossRef]
11. Meghdari, A.; Shariati, A.; Alemi, M.; Vossoughi, G.R.; Eydi, A.; Ahmadi, E.; Mozafari, B.; Amoozandeh Nobaveh, A.; Tahami, R. Arash: A social robot buddy to support children with cancer in a hospital environment. *Proc. Inst. Mech. Eng. Part H J. Eng. Med.* **2018**, *232*, 605–618. [CrossRef]
12. Kyrarini, M.; Lygerakis, F.; Rajavenkatanarayanan, A.; Sevastopoulos, C.; Nambiappan, H.R.; Chaitanya, K.K.; Babu, A.R.; Mathew, J.; Makedon, F. A survey of robots in healthcare. *Technologies* **2021**, *9*, 8. [CrossRef]
13. Cifuentes, C.A.; Pinto, M.J.; Céspedes, N.; Múnera, M. Social robots in therapy and care. *Curr. Robot. Rep.* **2020**, *1*, 59–74. [CrossRef]
14. Liang, H.-F.; Wu, K.-M.; Weng, C.-H.; Hsieh, H.-W. Nurses' views on the potential use of robots in the pediatric unit. *J. Pediatr. Nurs.* **2019**, *47*, e58–e64. [CrossRef]
15. Cohen, S.; Dori, D.; de Haan, U. A software system development life cycle model for improved stakeholders' communication and collaboration. *Int. J. Comput. Commun. Control* **2010**, *5*, 20–41. [CrossRef]
16. Logan, D.E.; Breazeal, C.; Goodwin, M.S.; Jeong, S.; O'Connell, B.; Smith-Freedman, D.; Heathers, J.; Weinstock, P. Social robots for hospitalized children. *Pediatrics* **2019**, *144*, e20181511. [CrossRef]
17. Bae, M.-J.; Shin, N.-M. Effects of skill teaching of oral administration for caregivers of hospitalized toddler on dose loss and administration behavior. *Korean J. Adult Nurs.* **2017**, *29*, 333–342. [CrossRef]
18. Shin, E.; Hyun, Y. A study about the research trends of needs analysis: Centered on the articles published in Korean journals from 2006 to 2016. *Korean J. Hum. Resour. Manag.* **2017**, *19*, 65–97. [CrossRef]
19. Cho, D. The state of need analysis research for building programs for adults: 1990-2005. *Andragogy Today Int. J. Adult Learn. Contin.* **2006**, *9*, 85–106.
20. Hayes, B.; Bonner, A.; Douglas, C. An introduction to mixed methods research for nephrology nurses. *Ren. Soc. Australas. J.* **2013**, *9*, 8–14.

21. Hsieh, H.-F.; Shannon, S.E. Three approaches to qualitative content analysis. *Qual. Health Res.* **2005**, *15*, 1277–1288. [CrossRef]
22. Jin, M.; Kim, J. A survey of nurses' need for care robots in children's hospitals: Combining robot-care, game-care, and edu-care. *Comput. Inform. Nurs.* **2020**, *38*, 349–357. [CrossRef]
23. Sandelowski, M. The problem of rigor in qualitative research. *Adv. Nurs. Sci.* **1986**, *8*, 27–37. [CrossRef]
24. Kim, H.; Ahn, H.; Cho, G.; Lee, J.; Kim, J.; Jung, Y.; Lee, Y.; Park, S.; Kim, S.; Choi, H.; et al. *Health Promotion Throughout the Life Span;* HYUNMOON Publishing Co.: Seoul, Korea, 2016.
25. Yang, S.; Kim, M.; Byun, J.; Seo, J. A research on the appearance design for a robot based on children' preference. *Proc. Korea Soc. Des. Stud. Conf.* **2007**, 24–25.
26. Arnold, L.; Lee, K.J.; Yip, J.C. Co-designing with children: An approach to social robot design. In Proceedings of the 11th AMC/IEEE International Conference on Human-Robot Interaction, Christchurch, New Zealand, 7–10 March 2016.
27. Lee, H.; Kim, J.; Kim, S.; Kong, H.-J.; Ryu, H. Investigating the need for point-of-care robots to support teleconsultation. *Telemed. J. E Health* **2019**, *25*, 1165–1173. [CrossRef] [PubMed]
28. Baek, H.W.; Shin, Y.M.; Shin, K.M. Emotional and behavioral problems related to smartphone overuse in elementary school children. *J. Korean Neuropsychiatr. Assoc.* **2014**, *53*, 320–326. [CrossRef]
29. Pourteimour, S.; Kazemi, S. The effectiveness of the robotic game kit on anxiety among hospitalized preschool children: A non-randomized controlled trial. *Nurs. Pract. Today* **2021**, *8*, 273–283. [CrossRef]
30. Dawe, J.; Sutherland, C.; Barco, A.; Broadbent, E. Can social robots help children in healthcare contexts? A scoping review. *BMJ Paediatr. Open* **2019**, *3*, e000371. [CrossRef] [PubMed]

healthcare

MDPI

Review

The Regulation of Artificial Intelligence in Digital Radiology in the Scientific Literature: A Narrative Review of Reviews

Daniele Giansanti

Centro TISP, Istituto Superiore di Sanità, 00161 Roma, Italy; daniele.giansanti@iss.it

Abstract: Today, there is growing interest in artificial intelligence (AI) in the field of digital radiology (DR). This is also due to the push that has been applied in this sector due to the pandemic. Many studies are devoted to the challenges of integration in the health domain. One of the most important challenges is that of regulations. This study conducted a narrative review of reviews on the international approach to the regulation of AI in DR. The design of the study was based on: (I) An overview on Scopus and Pubmed (II) A qualification and eligibility process based on a standardized checklist and a scoring system. The results have highlighted an international approach to the regulation of these systems classified as "software as medical devices (SaMD)" arranged into: ethical issues, international regulatory framework, and bottlenecks of the legal issues. Several recommendations emerge from the analysis. They are all based on fundamental pillars: (a) The need to overcome a differentiated approach between countries. (b) The need for greater transparency and publicity of information both for SaMDs as a whole and for the algorithms and test patterns. (c) The need for an interdisciplinary approach that avoids bias (including demographic) in algorithms and test data. (d) The need to reduce some limits/gaps of the scientific literature production that do not cover the international approach.

Keywords: regulation; artificial intelligence; digital radiology; medical devices

Citation: Giansanti, D. The Regulation of Artificial Intelligence in Digital Radiology in the Scientific Literature: A Narrative Review of Reviews. *Healthcare* **2022**, *10*, 1824. https://doi.org/10.3390/healthcare10101824

Academic Editors: Norbert Hosten and Joaquim Carreras

Received: 1 August 2022
Accepted: 20 September 2022
Published: 21 September 2022

1. Introduction

1.1. Background

AI is increasingly bursting into many sectors of the *health domain*. One of the areas where the introduction of AI is increasingly being discussed is that of DR. Many healthcare activities seem to be able to benefit from AI. The benefits range from workload assistance, quality control, and clinical decision automation [1]. However, there are important steps that must be followed before the complete introduction of AI in a standardized way in clinical routine.

This review looks at the evolution of regulations with interest. The regulations are among the topics considered of great interest in the Special Issue "Assistive technologies, robotics and automated machines in the healthcare sector" [2] as they are connected to the standardization processes in the introduction of AI in the healthcare sector.

Recent experiences of use during the pandemic seem to have given an important push towards the affirmation and integration of AI in the health domain [3,4].

It is foreseeable that more and more studies dedicated to the transfer of evidence-based medicine to healthcare will be undertaken. Agreement tools used in the health domain will be useful and have been successfully used in many sectors. It is foreseeable that tools such as health technology assessment or comparative effectiveness research tools [5] will be increasingly used. Other methods, such as consensus conferences, may also have a successful application as in other sectors, such as that of care robots [6,7]. All this will allow us to obtain guidelines [8] on the use of AI in DR. *At the basis of all this, there will be the regulatory aspects that will be essential and preparatory in the processes of integration of consent through the tools listed above.*

1.2. Related Work

The Pubmed search had the following key [9]:

Search: ((artificial intelligence[Title/Abstract]) AND (radiology[Title/Abstract])) AND (regulation) Sort by: Most Recent "artificial intelligence"[Title/Abstract] AND "radiology"[Title/Abstract] AND ("legislation and jurisprudence"[MeSH Subheading] OR ("legislation"[All Fields] AND "jurisprudence"[All Fields]) OR "legislation and jurisprudence"[All Fields] OR "regulations"[All Fields] OR "social control, formal"[MeSH Terms] OR ("social"[All Fields] AND "control"[All Fields] AND "formal"[All Fields]) OR "formal social control"[All Fields] OR "regulate"[All Fields] OR "regulates"[All Fields] OR "regulating"[All Fields] OR "regulation s"[All Fields] OR "regulative"[All Fields] OR "regulator"[All Fields] OR "regulator s"[All Fields] OR "regulators"[All Fields] OR "regulated"[All Fields] OR "regulation"[All Fields]). It is noted that scientific research activity in this area is relatively recent with scientific works starting from 2018, demonstrating that it is a hot topic in relation to regulations and has only recently been addressed.

A total of 41 scientific papers emerge from the search, of which 16 are revisions demonstrating a still-limited scientific production. In the last 2 years (2021–2022), there are 16 contributions including 8 reviews. The contributions based on full scientific articles [10–17] dealt with various issues related to the regulations ranging from barriers for the radiologist [10], to the knowledge of this figure through surveys [13], to local experiences [12–16], to the implication of ethics [14], and the importance of federative activities [11]. Nair et al. [10] highlighted that there are barriers that radiologists should be aware of prior to implementing Artificial Intelligence in daily practice. Barriers include regulatory compliance, ethical issues, data privacy, cybersecurity, AI training bias, and safe integration of AI into routine practice. Castellanos et al. [11] faced the importance of the data federation in this field. Data federation offers a way to get data moving from multiple sources, providing advantages in healthcare systems where medical data is often hard to reach because of regulations or the lack of reliable solutions that can integrate on top of protocols such as FHIR, HL7, and DICOM, among others. They proposed an architectural solution that may provide the core capabilities to implement a data federation approach in a healthcare system to enable AI. Yy et al. [12] reported the regulatory approach proposed in their country, Korea. Eiroa et al. [13] focused on Spain and reported on an experience-based survey of radiologists, where regulation was among the topics. They concluded that, although there is a lack of knowledge about AI among Spanish radiologists, there is a will to explore such topics and a general belief that radiologists should be trained in these matters. Based on the results, a consensus is needed to change the current training curriculum to better prepare future radiologists. The contribution by Batle et al. [14] is a report of the ACR Data Sharing Work group, where the regulation issues are dedicated to Data Ethics of Privacy, Consent, and Anonymization. Allen et al. [15] focused on the algorithms, discussed why regulatory clearance alone may not be enough to ensure AI will be safe and effective in all radiological practices, and reviewed strategies and available resources for evaluation before clinical use and monitoring performance of AI models to ensure efficacy and patient safety. Kenny et al. [16] reported on the ethics and standards in the use of artificial intelligence in medicine based on the Royal Australian and New Zealand College of Radiologists. Harvey et al. [17] discussed the uncertain legal environment. In particular, they examined the nature, exposure, and theories of liability relevant to musculoskeletal radiologist practice with a particular focus on the negligence, vicarious liability, and product liability frameworks.

1.3. Problems, Research Question, and Purpose of the Study

Now, scientific production in this area is rather scarce. As highlighted, scientific works have only recently been recorded in this area [9]. The topic of regulation is very important to allow the introduction of this technology in stable routine applications in the health domain. This regulation must address a wide range of issues that include many aspects, such as, to name a few, the development of algorithms, the certification of medical devices, ethical aspects, and workflows.

In this perspective, scientific studies based on reviews have the task of cataloguing and categorizing the various experiences in the international arena, to provide practical tools both to scholars and also to stakeholders. They can be useful, for example, as a starting point for addressing the production of guidelines, or as a support for consensus conferences. The main objective of this study is, therefore, to analyze how the regulatory aspects have been analyzed by these reviews, and aimed at answering the question "*How it is faced the regulation of artificial intelligence in Digital Radiology in scientific productions based on the reviews*" and make a map point on the issues where scholars have focused most. The main contribution of the study is to understand, through the analysis of these reviews, what the research trends are in this technological sector. The issues addressed by the reviews give an important idea, on the one hand, of the macro-research most faced by the scholars and, on the other hand, indirectly, on what the absent themes are in which it is necessary to insist the gaps be overcome.

2. Methods

The narrative review followed a standard narrative e checklist [18,19] and a qualification approach. The qualification methodology used an assessment based on a scoring scheme (with a score assigned to defined parameters) applied by two external experts not involved in the article, to include each reference. The followed checklist allowed to structure the design according to a standardized structure.

The experts were also required to add a comment to support their assessment.

Table 1 shows the parameters used in the scoring system. The score ranges from "1" (minimum-poor) up to "5" (maximum-excellent). It was also checked and assessed for the exclusion/inclusion the conflicts of interest (declared, not declared, possible, etc.).

The work was included when all parameters had an assessment $\geq$3.

Table 1. Parameters used for the qualification (standardized table).

PARAMETER ASSESSED
Is the rationale for the review in the introduction clear?
Is the design of the review appropriate?
Are the methods described clearly?
Are the results presented clearly?
Are the conclusions based and justified by results

The Pubmed and Scopus Databases were analyzed and only publications in peer reviewed journals were considered.

The following search key was applied [20]:

Search: ((artificial intelligence [Title/Abstract]) AND (radiology [Title/Abstract])) AND (regulations) Filters: Review Sort by: Most Recent

("artificial intelligence"[Title/Abstract] AND "radiology"[Title/Abstract] AND ("legislation and jurisprudence"[MeSH Subheading] OR ("legislation"[All Fields] AND "jurisprudence"[All Fields]) OR "legislation and jurisprudence"[All Fields] OR "regulations"[All Fields] OR "social control, formal"[MeSH Terms] OR ("social"[All Fields] AND "control"[All Fields] AND "formal"[All Fields]) OR "formal social control"[All Fields] OR "regulate"[All Fields] OR "regulates"[All Fields] OR "regulating"[All Fields] OR "regulation s"[All Fields] OR "regulative"[All Fields] OR "regulator"[All Fields] OR "regulator s"[All Fields] OR "regulators"[All Fields] OR "regulated"[All Fields] OR "regulation"[All Fields])) AND (review[Filter]).

3. Results

The search on Pubmed returned 16 papers [21–36] (Scopus returned 4 further works, which, being works at congresses in accordance with the qualification procedure, were excluded), all studies from 2018 to today.

The process of inclusion that was followed showed that:

- The number of reviews produced is very low, which denotes a low interest on the part of researchers in addressing the sector of AI regulations regarding digital radiology.
- No studies showed problems concerning the conflicts of interest.
- Two papers could be excluded [23,32], as they were not completely centered on the theme.

The study in [23] was excluded because radiology was treated marginally (as a neuroimaging tool) in the context of mental health care processes. It was considered from the analysis that the contribution relating to the regulatory aspects in this area was minimal.

The study in [32] was excluded as it was a sentiment analysis based on Twitter. The regulatory aspects were dealt with, but as a necessity that emerged from the tweets. Additionally, in this case it was considered that the contribution was minimal.

Figure 1 shows the outcome of the assessment procedure.

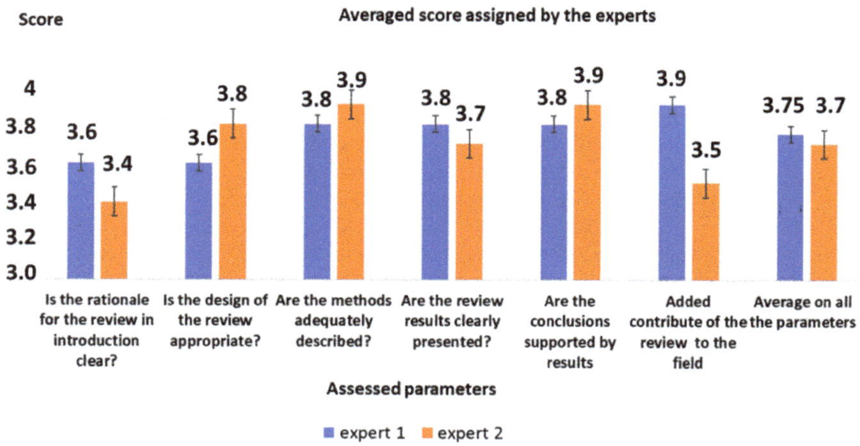

Figure 1. Output from the qualification process.

The analysis showed that the scientific literature has produced important and far-reaching reviews. Twelve reviews [21,25–31,33–36] out of fourteen were focused on radiology in general, two reviews were more specific, one review was focused on nuclear medicine [24], and one on imaging in gastrointestinal pathology [22]. As far as the regulatory aspects were concerned, some interesting issues emerge. Two papers addressed the issue from a more general point of view [21,28] by relating the regulations to the challenges. One focused exclusively on the ethical issues [26], other studies focused on the European [25,33] and American [25,29,33] situations, in some cases also making comparisons [25,33]. One study was related to the Canadian situation [30]. Two other studies offered new and important points of view on the regulatory aspects in this area; one focused on AI in DR, stressing the concept of *software as medical device* (SaMD) [27]; the other one dealt with the importance of providing certified datasets in training AI systems [31]. The three most recent reviews focused on some heterogeneous problems of AI regulation [34–36]. The review proposed in [34] faced the problems of regulating the workloads and the relevant implications. In addition, the hurdles of the legal issues to AI autonomy have been faced in [35], where the ambiguity of the legal management and the impact on all the actors were stressed. The imaging-based algorithms validated by the FDA were analyzed in [36] with the focus also on the emerging problems.

Artificial intelligence/machine learning (AI/ML) algorithms have been analyzed in [36].

What emerged from the search suggests an organized analysis based on the following topics: (a) Ethical issues in the scientific literature. (b) The regulatory framework in the scientific literature. (c) Bottlenecks of the legal issues.

3.1. The Ethical Issues in the Scientific Literature

Mudgal et al. [26] proposed a study entirely focused on the ethical issues. This review covered the different ethical issues of a harmless and justifiable deployment of AI in every part of the training, incorporation in the health domain, and regulation. According to the study, the managed data must: be appropriately evaluated, refined, purified, and managed in a centralized and non-dispersive way; be processed through methods that provide for anonymization, consent, and information to patients; represent all demographics. Transparency and security, according to the authors, must have central roles and all systems must follow authorization processes by the competent authorities. Ethical issues have been extensively addressed together with other issues in three other studies [21,24,30].

The review by Harvey et al. [21] considered both the power to redefine the practice of radiology and the nascent phase with the related largely untested aspects in the clinical space. The uncertainty of the legal-regulatory environment (also related to the ethical issues) according to the authors affected the introduction of AI. The study reported: (a) the challenges, tracing the various pathways toward approval by the FDA. (b) The future of government oversight. (c) The privacy issues. (d) The ethical dilemmas. (e) The practical considerations related to implementation in radiologist practice. The authors highlighted how, for nuclear medicine, careful considerations were needed for reliability, safety, non-maleficence, beneficence, justice and fairness, data privacy, data security, data confidentiality, minimization of bias, clearness, autonomy, and clarification ability. Jaremko et al. [30] produced a study for the Canadian Association of Radiologists focused both on regulatory and on ethical issues. The study reported a framework of the legal and ethical issues, with reference to the Canadian health domain.

The review by Currie et al. [24] focused specifically on nuclear medicine. The study reported the strong opportunities of an "ethical AI" in terms of productivity and workflow, strengthening of the research, and clinical use.

3.2. The Regulatory Framework in the Scientific Literature

Two studies among the overviewed ones faced the regulatory framework both for the European Union and for the US [25,33]. The study by Pesapane et al. [23] analyzed the regulation focusing on the legal framework of the Medical Devices (MDs) in the US and Europe. The study reported that European bodies were producing new regulations on cybersecurity, data protection, regulation of integrations, MDs, and in vitro MDs regulation. The FDA was controlling the scene in the US. The study emphasized that regulations for privacy protection, ethical use, and safety were required, and that AI applications must be considered MDs dedicated to diagnosis/detection. The approach in US and in Europe was different. Europe dedicated, for example, particular space to the cybersecurity, continuity of the services, and to the notification process. The regulations in the US were particularly focused on the processing and consent of the use of data and on the consent of the user/consumer. The review by Muehlematter [25] raised concerns on the approval processes for the AI-based MDs in Europe and the US. They identified 240 MDs approved in Europe and 222 in the US. They found that these numbers had increased considerably since 2015. Very few of these MDs were approved as high-risk MDs. The study concluded that the high number of approved MDs suggested ensuring severe regulation and a well-defined pathway for these MDs was lacking both in Europe and in the US. The authors recommended more transparency on the process of approval and management of these MDs and a complete, freely reachable database dedicated to these MDs.

Harvey et al. [29] focused on the US and remarked on the position in [25,33]. Furthermore, the authors analyzed the process of AI approval by the FDA. They reported that the FDA had proposed an innovative approach capable of minimizing the regulatory burden incumbent on the designers. The proposal of the FDA looked to the current good manufacturing practices and proposed to adopt a total product lifecycle method. Jaremko et al. [30] provided a study focused on Canada on both regulatory and ethical issues. Recommendations for patient data, algorithms, and practice were reported [30] with reference of the healthcare of this country.

The regulation of AI in radiology is increasingly being linked to the concept of MDs as shown by the studies reported in [25,33]. The review by Arora et al. [27] remarked that AI is recognized as a "Software as a Medical Device (SaMD)" and is looked at with this vision by the regulators. Authors turned around this concept, reporting that there is a strong interconnection between these AI systems with the Internet of Things, genetic data, and patient records. These important synergies must therefore be enclosed and considered when facing these MDs. The input data for testing a SaMD are also strategic. When it comes to SaMD, the problems are even more relevant. The study by Allen et al. [31] was in this direction. They reported that commercial algorithms were affected by gender, ethnic, and social bias. This shows important and dramatic implications in the design of algorithms in healthcare. They also reported that it is important to prevent biases in healthcare by means of a strong connection among the actors to assure robust and bias-free algorithms and datasets. They described a proposal solution at the ACR Data Science Institute. Here, a synergy among different institutions allowed the development of robust datasets and algorithms incorporating standards to mitigate biases.

3.3. *The Bottlenecks of the Legal Issues*

The last three reviews published on these issues have focused specifically on bottlenecks in regulatory aspects [34–36] and represent mutually complementary and overall exhaustive contributions. Alexander et al. [34] focused on the impact of workload on the decision correctness. Many studies also focused on biology have shown that the decision speediness is inversely connected to the correctness. The study analyzed this issue in radiology also considering the impact of the AI. The authors concluded that regulating the workloads without a proper scientific approach could be more dangerous than the not regulating them. Mezrich [35] focused on the legal liability on the errors interconnected to AI use. The review identified several critical issues. One of these issues is the enforcement of the AI-based product liability law adopted in the US. The study identified ambiguities in the legal treatment of AI. The authors believe that this could profoundly affect the integration of AI into the health domain and the trust of all actors involved.

Ebrahimian et al. [36] focused on FDA-regulated AI algorithms. They reviewed 127 regulated software with the aim to classify the available and reported information. They recorded (when available) the number of studies included with other parameters, for example, the specificity, the receiver operating characteristic area under the curve, and the sensitivity. They reported an increasing number of MDs regulated by the FDA from the year 2008 up to 2021. Their review, very importantly, concluded that insufficient public data on the validation/testing datasets in different algorithms are not able to justify applications in healthcare as the generalization and/or the incidence of biases cannot be deduced.

4. Discussion

A deep analysis conducted on social media highlighted a growing attention on the integration of AI in DR within the health domain [32]. Surely, the COVID-19 pandemic that people are experiencing has also represented an important push in this direction [37–39] and given an important lesson for the future [40]. An improvement in equity of care is also expected from the integration of AI in DR into the health domain [41]. It is quite clear that integration into the health domain involves major challenges and processes of acceptance of consensus.

In a previous study [42], the following was addressed: (a) the challenges in the growth and incorporation of AI in healthcare. (b) The acceptance and consensus on the integration of AI in healthcare.

Among the many important challenges, the study highlighted the consolidation of an AI system as a MD and of the related regulatory framework, including ethics and emerging risks. Our overview conducted in Pubmed and Scopus focused precisely on this point.

The number of reviews produced is very low, which denotes a low interest on the part of researchers in addressing the sector of AI regulations regarding digital radiology. This denotes a need for more efforts in this area by scholars.

The selected reviews focused on some specific aspects. They, therefore, gave a scientific contribution on certain aspects and problems. Some studies have focused on DR in general [21,25–31,33–36], while other contributions have investigated specific sectors [22,24]. Some studies faced this from the point of view of the challenges [21,28]. Other studies have focused on the European, American, and Canadian conditions [25,29,30,33]. An approach such as SaMD shines through in these studies. In fact, the need to address this issue considering that AI in DR is a SaMD appears evident in specific studies such as in [27]. The need to certify the datasets used in the SaMD is also considered indispensable [31]. Other studies have addressed specific aspects, such as ethics [16] and regulatory bottlenecks [34–36].

4.1. Added Value of the Review

The proposed overview aimed to give an added value by acting as a connector between all the specific issues addressed in this field to date, to give the scholar a vision of the facets that emerge in the research. Precisely all these facets that emerge together with the real fragmentation of regulatory approaches suggest to scholars from all over the world to meet and start consensus conferences to propose important recommendations that trigger both stakeholders and legislators. An indirect added value is represented by the discovery of the gaps/limitations emerging in the scientific literature production analyzed in the form of reviews.

4.2. Limitations of the Reviews

The subject of regulations is a subject that affects all nations and continents. The analysis of the reviews shows that scholars have focused essentially on European, US, and Canadian regulations. What one would expect from these reviews is that they address the problem with a greater angle and a more international and less local vision, i.e., not only the US, Europe, or Canada, which among other things are showing a mixed position. They should answer also to other important key questions, for example: How is the regulation in Asia and Africa? For example, from the National Medical Products Administration (NMPA), the Chinese agency for regulating drugs and medical devices (formerly the China Food and Drug Administration or CFDA)? From the Web, the position of the NMPA on these issues was found. The NMPA released three guidelines to regulate and support the rapid development in digital health also facing AI [43]:

Guideline for Artificial Intelligence in Medical Devices Registration.

Guideline for Medical Device Software Registration.

Guideline for Medical Device Cybersecurity.

These guidelines represent an international harmonization effort. They are partly inspired by the position of the FDA and partly by the position of the IMDRF and are particularly focused on risk factors and product total life cycle management. In addition, additional reports and specific guidance documents are made available on AI and also with reference to DR [44]. It is evident that the international scientific literature should also give space through reviews to these initiatives that move towards processes of a uniformity of approach.

The regulatory impact relating to ethics is also addressed more from a local point of view. In the reviews, experiences and documents of a non-international nature are not shared, which could make a contribution, however, as regards a uniformity of approach.

In Europe, for example, it is possible to find several documents oriented towards this theme produced by the European community, such as a document dedicated to guidelines for a trustworthy AI and a document that addresses the impact [45] on public services [46].

In summary, there seems to be a fragmentation, or rather, a separation, between the production processes of scientific literature and what is present on public services in the governmental WEBs dedicated to this topic.

4.3. Comparison with the Recent Research Trends

If we compare what emerges from the overview of reviews with the dedicated studies based on full scientific articles of 2021–2022 [10–17], it emerges that there is a coincidence of issues, such as the problem of barriers and critical issues of the issues [10] in relation to the introduction of AI in the health domain, the need for a federative approach [11], the importance of ethical aspects [16], and the interest in local situations as in [13,16].

However, what would have been expected from the overview of reviews is a role of cultural and scientific mediation between the various experiences. The analysis did not show this role.

There are studies, for example, on regulations in Korea [13], or studies on regulations in Australia and New Zeland [16], that have not been taken into consideration, preferring a discussion and analysis on the realities in Canada, Europe, and the USA.

The same goes for ethics, where other interesting studies have been found on the Australian continent that have not been resumed [16].

The need to overcome an analysis of regulatory realities with a patchy approach emerges strongly from this comparison with the studies based on full scientific articles [10–17] but also from the survey reported above of some government websites, where the regulatory approach is described [43,44] also with reference to ethics [45,46].

4.4. Limitations

Our study, based on a narrative review, has several limitations. The review considered papers written in English. The reviews in different languages were not considered. PubMed and Scopus databases, and only peer reviewed papers available here, were considered in the review. A possible enlargement of the overview could consider databases including conference papers, preprint sources, and governmental WEBs. The theme faced in this study is very wide and included several sub-themes (e.g., regulations in MDs, regulations in the production of the datasets). Future enlargements could comprise reviews directed in the identified sub-themes.

5. Conclusions

The development of a solid regulatory framework is indispensable today in the field of AI in DR. This study conducted a narrative overview on reviews to make a map point in this field and explore trends and gaps in the scientific literature production.

It is possible to detect some achievements in brief.

5.1. Achievements in Brief

The *first achievement* is that the overview reported a patchy approach limited to some countries showing a not uniform approach.

The *second achievement* is the need of a more transparent approval process, from an international and contemporary point of view, and the need for open database sources for Medical Devices, algorithms, and datasets.

The *third achievement* is the need of a process of harmonization at the international level of the approach.

The *fourth achievement* is for the ethics, where the need of avoiding demographic bias in the datasets and algorithms was highlighted.

The *fifth achievement* consists in the detected bottlenecks, such as, for example, the difficulty in identifying the workloads for the radiologists and the insufficient transparency in the validation of the datasets, not justifying the use in some applications.

5.2. Conclusions in Detail

In conclusion, the overview highlighted a low production (only 16 reviews) in this field and the need for more efforts of the scientists. The review has identified three important areas of intervention: *ethics issues, international regulatory framework, and bottlenecks in the regulatory development*. Regarding ethics, the areas of intervention have been identified, which, in addition to the traditional ones of the use of technologies in healthcare, include new ones due to the specificity of AI connected to the production of the algorithms, datasets, and avoiding the bias in them. Studies on regulations, before all, highlighted that those emerging regulatory approaches were not uniform and differed in the case of the US, Europe, Canada, or other countries. Different approaches were used to address emerging issues, such as cybersecurity in MDs. The studies have revealed several critical issues, and, in particular, the need to assure a well-defined and rigorous pathway for the approval and the maintenance of the AI-based MDs. Among the recommendations for these issues, more transparency on the approval and post-approval process and the design of a full, openly reachable database dedicated to these MDs was proposed. Bottlenecks were also identified with particular reference to the workload, showing that regulating it without a scientific principle may be more dangerous than no regulation at all. Reference was also made to the insufficient public data on the validation/testing of the datasets in different algorithms not justifying applications in healthcare as the generalization and/or the incidence of biases cannot be deduced. Most importantly, *limitations and gaps* emerge in these reviews. It emerged that they limit themselves to considering regulatory experiences that do not cover the international approach. For example, some significant experiences are not considered, such as those of the NMPA, which may have a role of legislative mediation between multiple positions. Also with regard to ethical aspects, it would be advisable to better share important documentary production experiences, such as those available in Europe.

Funding: This research received no external funding.

Institutional Review Board Statement: Not applicable.

Informed Consent Statement: Not applicable.

Data Availability Statement: Not applicable.

Conflicts of Interest: The authors declare no conflict of interest.

Acronyms

AI	Artificial Intelligence
DR	Digital radiology
MD	Medical Device
SaMD	Software as Medical Device
FDA	Food and Drug administration
ML	Machine Learning
ACR	American College of Radiology
NMPD	National Medical Products Administration
IMDRF	International Medical Device Regulators Forum
FHIR	Fast Healthcare Interoperability Resource
DICOM	Digital Imaging and COmmunications in Medicine
HL7	Health Level seven

References

1. Giansanti, D. The Artificial Intelligence in Digital Pathology and Digital Radiology: Where Are We? *Healthcare* **2021**, *9*, 30. [CrossRef] [PubMed]
2. Assistive Technologies, Robotics, and Automated Machines in the Health Domain. Available online: https://www.mdpi.com/journal/healthcare/special_issues/Assistive_Technologies_Robotics_Automated_Machines_Health_Domain (accessed on 5 September 2022).
3. Alsharif, M.H.; Alsharif, Y.H.; Yahya, K.; Alomari, O.A.; Albreem, M.A.; Jahid, A. Deep learning applications to combat the dissemination of COVID-19 disease: A review. *Eur. Rev. Med. Pharmacol. Sci.* **2020**, *24*, 11455–11460. [PubMed]
4. Ozsahin, I.; Sekeroglu, B.; Musa, M.S.; Mustapha, M.T.; Uzun Ozsahin, D. Review on Diagnosis of COVID-19 from Chest CT Images Using Artificial Intelligence. *Comput. Math. Methods Med.* **2020**, *2020*, 9756518. [CrossRef] [PubMed]
5. Luce, B.R.; Drummond, M.; Jönsson, B.; Neumann, P.J.; Schwartz, J.S.; Siebert, U.; Sullivan, S.D. EBM, HTA, and CER: Clearing the confusion. *Milbank Q.* **2010**, *88*, 256–276. [CrossRef]
6. McGlynn, E.A.; Kosecoff, J.; Brook, R.H. Format and conduct of consensus development conferences: Multination comparison. *Int. J. Technol. Assess Health Care* **1990**, *6*, 450–469. [CrossRef] [PubMed]

7. Boldrini, P.; Bonaiuti, D.; Mazzoleni, S.; Posteraro, F. Rehabilitation assisted by robotic and electromechanical devices for people with neurological disabilities: Contributions for the preparation of a national conference in Italy. *Eur. J. Phys. Rehabil. Med.* **2021**, *57*, 458–459. [CrossRef]
8. Evidence Based Guidelines. Available online: https://www.ebm-guidelines.com/dtk/ebmg/home (accessed on 5 September 2022).
9. Pubmed Search. Available online: https://pubmed.ncbi.nlm.nih.gov/?term=%28%28artificial+intelligence%5BTitle%2FAbstract%5D%29+AND+%28radiology%5BTitle%2FAbstract%5D%29%29+AND+%28regulation%29&filter=pubt.review&sort=date&size=100 (accessed on 5 September 2022).
10. Nair, A.V.; Ramanathan, S.; Sathiadoss, P.; Jajodia, A.; Blair Macdonald, D. Barriers to artificial intelligence implementation in radiology practice: What the radiologist needs to know. *Radiologia* **2022**, *64*, 324–332. [CrossRef] [PubMed]
11. Castellanos, J.; Raposo, G.; Antunez, L. Data Federation in Healthcare for Artificial Intelligence Solutions. *Stud. Health Technol. Inform.* **2022**, *295*, 167–170. [CrossRef] [PubMed]
12. Yu, J.Y.; Hong, S.; Lee, Y.C.; Lee, K.H.; Lee, I.; Seo, Y.; Kang, M.; Kim, K.; Cha, W.C.; Shin, S.Y. Stakeholders' Requirements for Artificial Intelligence for Healthcare in Korea. *Healthc. Inform. Res.* **2022**, *28*, 143–151. [CrossRef]
13. Eiroa, D.; Antolín, A.; Fernández Del Castillo Ascanio, M.; Pantoja Ortiz, V.; Escobar, M.; Roson, N. The current state of knowledge on imaging informatics: A survey among Spanish radiologists. *Insights Imaging* **2022**, *13*, 34. [CrossRef]
14. Batlle, J.C.; Dreyer, K.; Allen, B.; Cook, T.; Roth, C.J.; Kitts, A.B.; Geis, R.; Wu, C.C.; Lungren, M.P.; Patti, J.; et al. Data Sharing of Imaging in an Evolving Health Care World: Report of the ACR Data Sharing Workgroup, Part 1: Data Ethics of Privacy, Consent, and Anonymization. *J. Am. Coll. Radiol.* **2021**, *18*, 1646–1654. [CrossRef]
15. Allen, B.; Dreyer, K.; Stibolt RJr Agarwal, S.; Coombs, L.; Treml, C.; Elkholy, M.; Brink, L.; Wald, C. Evaluation and Real-World Performance Monitoring of Artificial Intelligence Models in Clinical Practice: Try It, Buy It, Check It. *J. Am. Coll. Radiol.* **2021**, *18*, 1489–1496. [CrossRef]
16. Kenny, L.M.; Nevin, M.; Fitzpatrick, K. Ethics and standards in the use of artificial intelligence in medicine on behalf of the Royal Australian and New Zealand College of Radiologists. *J. Med. Imaging Radiat. Oncol.* **2021**, *65*, 486–494. [CrossRef]
17. Harvey, H.B.; Gowda, V. Clinical applications of AI in MSK imaging: A liability perspective. *Skeletal Radiol.* **2022**, *51*, 235–238. [CrossRef]
18. ANDJ Checklist. Available online: https://it.scribd.com/document/434616519/ANDJ-Narrative-Review-Checklist (accessed on 5 September 2022).
19. ANDJ Checklist. Available online: https://www.elsevier.com/__data/promis_misc/ANDJ%20Narrative%20Review%20Checklist.pdf (accessed on 5 September 2022).
20. Pubmed Search. Available online: https://pubmed.ncbi.nlm.nih.gov/?term=%28%28artificial+intelligence%5BTitle%2FAbstract%5D%29+AND+%28radiology%5BTitle%2FAbstract%5D%29%29+AND+%28regulation%29&filter=pubt.review&sort=date&size=200 (accessed on 5 September 2022).
21. Harvey, H.B.; Gowda, V. Regulatory Issues and Challenges to Artificial Intelligence Adoption. *Radiol. Clin. N. Am.* **2021**, *59*, 1075–1083. [CrossRef] [PubMed]
22. Yoshida, H.; Kiyuna, T. Requirements for implementation of artificial intelligence in the practice of gastrointestinal pathology. *World J. Gastroenterol.* **2021**, *27*, 2818–2833. [CrossRef]
23. Lee, E.E.; Torous, J.; De Choudhury, M.; Depp, C.A.; Graham, S.A.; Kim, H.C.; Paulus, M.P.; Krystal, J.H.; Jeste, D.V. Artificial Intelligence for Mental Health Care: Clinical Applications, Barriers, Facilitators, and Artificial Wisdom. *Biol. Psychiatry Cogn. Neurosci. Neuroimaging* **2021**, *6*, 856–864. [CrossRef]
24. Currie, G.; Hawk, K.E. Ethical and Legal Challenges of Artificial Intelligence in Nuclear Medicine. *Semin. Nucl. Med.* **2021**, *51*, 120–125. [CrossRef] [PubMed]
25. Muehlematter, U.J.; Daniore, P.; Vokinger, K.N. Approval of artificial intelligence and machine learning-based medical devices in the USA and Europe (2015-20): A comparative analysis. *Lancet Digit. Health* **2021**, *3*, e195–e203. [CrossRef] [PubMed]
26. Mudgal, K.S.; Das, N. The ethical adoption of artificial intelligence in radiology. *BJR Open* **2020**, *2*, 20190020. [CrossRef]
27. Arora, A. Conceptualising Artificial Intelligence as a Digital Healthcare Innovation: An Introductory Review. *Med. Devices* **2020**, *13*, 223–230. [CrossRef] [PubMed]
28. van Assen, M.; Lee, S.J.; De Cecco, C.N. Artificial intelligence from A to Z: From neural network to legal framework. *Eur. J. Radiol.* **2020**, *129*, 109083. [CrossRef] [PubMed]
29. Harvey, H.B.; Gowda, V. How the FDA Regulates AI. *Acad Radiol.* **2020**, *27*, 58–61. [CrossRef] [PubMed]
30. Jaremko, J.L.; Azar, M.; Bromwich, R.; Lum, A.; Alicia Cheong, L.H.; Gibert, M.; Laviolette, F.; Gray, B.; Reinhold, C.; Cicero, M.; et al. Canadian Association of Radiologists White Paper on Ethical and Legal Issues Related to Artificial Intelligence in Radiology. *Can. Assoc. Radiol. J.* **2019**, *70*, 107–118. [CrossRef] [PubMed]
31. Allen, B.; Dreyer, K. The Role of the ACR Data Science Institute in Advancing Health Equity in Radiology. *J. Am. Coll. Radiol.* **2019**, *16*, 644–648. [CrossRef] [PubMed]
32. Goldberg, J.E.; Rosenkrantz, A.B. Artificial Intelligence and Radiology: A Social Media Perspective. *Curr. Probl. Diagn. Radiol.* **2019**, *48*, 308–311. [CrossRef] [PubMed]
33. Pesapane, F.; Volonté, C.; Codari, M.; Sardanelli, F. Artificial intelligence as a medical device in radiology: Ethical and regulatory issues in Europe and the United States. *Insights Imaging* **2018**, *9*, 745–753. [CrossRef]

34. Mezrich, J.L. Is Artificial Intelligence (AI) a Pipe Dream? Why Legal Issues Present Significant Hurdles to AI Autonomy. *AJR Am. J. Roentgenol.* **2022**, *219*, 152–156. [CrossRef] [PubMed]
35. Alexander, R.; Waite, S.; Bruno, M.A.; Krupinski, E.A.; Berlin, L.; Macknik, S.; Martinez-Conde, S. Mandating Limits on Workload, Duty, and Speed in Radiology. *Radiology* **2022**, *304*, 274–282. [CrossRef] [PubMed]
36. Ebrahimian, S.; Kalra, M.K.; Agarwal, S.; Bizzo, B.C.; Elkholy, M.; Wald, C.; Allen, B.; Dreyer, K.J. FDA-regulated AI Algorithms: Trends, Strengths, and Gaps of Validation Studies. *Acad Radiol.* **2022**, *29*, 559–566. [CrossRef] [PubMed]
37. Sideris, G.A.; Nikolakea, M.; Karanikola, A.-E.; Konstantinopoulou, S.; Giannis, D.; Modahl, L. Imaging in the COVID-19 era: Lessons learned during a pandemic. *World J. Radiol.* **2021**, *13*, 192–222. [CrossRef]
38. Pezzutti, D.L.; Wadhwa, V.; Makary, M.S. COVID-19 imaging: Diagnostic approaches, challenges, and evolving advances. *World J. Radiol.* **2021**, *13*, 171–191. [CrossRef]
39. El Naqa, I.M.; Li, H.; Fuhrman, J.D.; Hu, Q.; Gorre, N.; Chen, W.; Giger, M.L. Lessons learned in transitioning to AI in the medical imaging of COVID-19. *J. Med. Imaging* **2021**, *8* (Suppl. S1), 010902. [CrossRef]
40. Giansanti, D.; Rossi, I.; Monoscalco, L. Lessons from the COVID-19 Pandemic on the Use of Artificial Intelligence in Digital Radiology: The Submission of a Survey to Investigate the Opinion of Insiders. *Healthcare* **2021**, *9*, 331. [CrossRef]
41. Currie, G.; Rohren, E. Social Asymmetry, Artificial Intelligence and the Medical Imaging Landscape. *Semin. Nucl. Med.* 2021, *in press*. [CrossRef]
42. Giansanti, D.; Di Basilio, F. The Artificial Intelligence in Digital Radiology: Part 1: The Challenges, Acceptance and Consensus. *Healthcare* **2022**, *10*, 509. [CrossRef]
43. Three Guidelines Published Today, Propelling China to Be World Leader in Digital Health, Artificial Intelligence. Available online: https://chinameddevice.com/digital-health-nmpa-ai/ (accessed on 5 September 2022).
44. Biotech Magazine Cites China Med Device LLC for AI-aided Software Guideline, Chinese Government Provides AI-aided Software Guideline for Health Care Market. Available online: https://chinameddevice.com/ai-aided-software/ (accessed on 5 September 2022).
45. AI Watch-Artificial Intelligence in Public Services in the JRC Publications Repository. Available online: https://publications.jrc.ec.europa.eu/repository/handle/JRC120399 (accessed on 5 September 2022).
46. Ethics Guidelines for Trustworthy AI. Available online: https://ec.europa.eu/futurium/en/ai-alliance-consultation.1.html (accessed on 5 September 2022).

healthcare

MDPI

Article

Simulating Facebook Advertisements to Establish Cost per New HIV Diagnosis Using Routine and Targeted Models in a Local Population

John J. Hanna [1,2,*], Ank E. Nijhawan [1,3], Christoph U. Lehmann [2,3,4,5] and Richard J. Medford [1,2]

1 Division of Infectious Diseases and Geographic Medicine, University of Texas Southwestern, Dallas, TX 75390, USA; ank.nijhawan@utsouthwestern.edu (A.E.N.); richard.medford@utsouthwestern.edu (R.J.M.)
2 Clinical Informatics Center, University of Texas Southwestern, Dallas, TX 75390, USA; christoph.lehmann@utsouthwestern.edu
3 Department of Population and Data Sciences, University of Texas Southwestern, Dallas, TX 75390, USA
4 Department of Bioinformatics, University of Texas Southwestern, Dallas, TX 75390, USA
5 Department of Pediatrics, University of Texas Southwestern, Dallas, TX 75390, USA
* Correspondence: john.hanna@utsouthwestern.edu

Abstract: Background: Undiagnosed human immunodeficiency virus (HIV) infection remains a public health challenge. We explore Facebook (FB) advertisement (Ads) cost per new HIV diagnosis using non-targeted Ads, a routine testing model against targeted Ads, and a focused testing model in Texas. Methods: On 14 October 2021, we created (without launching) Texas-based, USD 10 targeted (using criteria matching HIV populations at risk) and non-targeted FB Ads for 10 days. In the process of creating the Ads, we collected estimated audience size, daily reach, and daily clicks. We estimated Ad cost for each new HIV diagnosis for targeted and non-targeted Ads using new HIV diagnosis rates from focused and routine testing campaigns. Results: The Ad costs per new HIV diagnosis from the targeted model were 4.74, 2.86, 5.28, and 2.88 times lower for men, Black, Hispanic, and all age groups, respectively, when compared to the non-targeted model. The wider the gap was between new HIV diagnosis rates in a population for focused and routine testing, the more cost-effective targeted Ads became. Conclusions: Among HIV populations at risk, targeted FB Ads are more cost-effective for detecting new HIV infections than non-targeted Ads. This cost-effectiveness increases in locations where focused testing increases new HIV diagnosis rates, compared to routine testing.

Keywords: Facebook advertisements; personalized advertisements; social media; precision medicine; public health informatics; public health communications; consumer health informatics; population health; human immunodeficiency virus; diagnosis; acquired immunodeficiency syndrome

Citation: Hanna, J.J.; Nijhawan, A.E.; Lehmann, C.U.; Medford, R.J. Simulating Facebook Advertisements to Establish Cost per New HIV Diagnosis Using Routine and Targeted Models in a Local Population. *Healthcare* **2022**, *10*, 1195. https://doi.org/10.3390/healthcare10071195

Academic Editor: Daniele Giansanti

Received: 31 March 2022
Accepted: 23 June 2022
Published: 26 June 2022

1. Introduction

Human immunodeficiency virus (HIV) morbidity and mortality affect the United States of America (USA) regions disproportionately [1]. Southern states have the highest rates of new HIV diagnoses (estimated to constitute 51% of new HIV cases annually, nationally) and, subsequently, have a larger, more geographically dispersed population of people living with HIV (PLWH) [1]. The high rates of HIV incidence and prevalence in the South are accompanied by high rates of social determinants of health (SDOH) risk indicators, including lack of insurance, vacant housing, household incomes below the federal poverty level, and rural populations [2]. These observations warrant new initiatives to reduce HIV infections in the South [3].

Texas has one of the highest rates of new HIV diagnoses among the Southern states, with 18.2 new cases per 100,000 people. Texas also has a proportionally lower estimated rate of pre-exposure prophylaxis (PrEP) coverage compared to other states. Including the undiagnosed HIV population, Texas has the highest estimated incidence rate of HIV nationally, with 4500 new cases and a prevalence rate of 113,300 HIV cases per 29 million as of 2019 (1 out of every 256 Texans) [2]. With a rate of 18.4%, the state of Texas also has the highest burden of uninsured persons nationally and one of the highest rates of households living below the federal poverty level (10.5%) [2].

The burden of HIV and associated SDOH are not only disproportionately distributed regionally, but are also more likely to affect certain race/ethnicity groups and different age groups. In the South, Black/African Americans and people 25–34 years old have the highest rates of new HIV diagnoses, regardless of urban or non-urban environments [4]. In Texas in 2018, the highest number of new HIV diagnoses were among Hispanic males (42% of all HIV diagnoses + males) and Black females (51% of all HIV diagnoses + females). While the age group of 25–34 years had the highest rates of new diagnoses, women tended to be diagnosed at a later age than males. Among Texas metropolitan areas, Dallas eligible metropolitan area (EMA) (25%) and Houston EMA (31%) accounted for 56% of Texas PLWH in 2018 [5].

New, innovative public health approaches are needed to reach populations at risk for HIV to increase testing and reduce the incidence of undiagnosed and untreated HIV. In the last decade, social media advertisements (Ads) have enabled health organizations to identify populations with characteristics that match risk factors for diseases [6–8] and to reach populations at risk for research recruitment [9–15]. Among social media platforms, Meta Inc., (Menlo Park, CA, USA) continues to lead the market, with 2.91 billion active users monthly in the fourth quarter of 2021 [16]. The platform's high penetration and the wide array of permitted detailed targeting criteria allow researchers to use Facebook (FB) Ads to recruit difficult-to-reach populations [17–19].

Data from a randomized control trial of HIV and substance use interventions showed that gender minority adolescents and young adults were easier to recruit on social media platforms compared to in-person for HIV interventions [20]. Recent international studies that used social media to promote sexual health resulted in increased HIV testing and linkage to care in high-risk and difficult-to-reach young men who have sex with men (MSM) [21,22]. Similarly, the Keeping it LITE study and the START study were nationally successful in recruiting gender minority participants effectively and efficiently from social media Ads [23,24]. Compared to other social media platforms, FB Ads for HIV prevention have yielded the lowest cost per eligible contact for young MSM, and Instagram Ads have yielded the highest proportion of eligible contacts who were racial or ethnic minorities [25].

In this study, we aim to evaluate the feasibility of FB Ads to reach MSM at high risk for HIV infection in Texas. We compare the cost and efficacy between targeted FB Ads followed by the focused HIV testing of individuals at the highest risk of HIV acquisition (targeted model) against non-targeted FB Ads followed by routine HIV testing (non-targeted model). To estimate the cost for each new HIV diagnosis in both models, we use the FB platform Ad estimates, the healthcare industry average conversion rate on FB (percentage of visitors to a website that do what the advertiser wants them to do, e.g., get tested) [26], and the rates of new HIV diagnoses from focused and routine testing [5].

2. Materials and Methods

FB provides estimates for Ad reach and Ad clicks based on adjusted Ad budgets even prior to running the Ads. On 14 October 2021, we created (without actually launching) 10-day, Texas-based, USD 10 targeted and non-targeted FB Ads for different age groups in Texas counties with high HIV prevalence. Ads placements included FB, FB Messenger, and Instagram. For the targeted FB Ads group, we used the following FB criteria to match the MSM population at highest risk for HIV: men with FB-defined interests in LGBT culture, LGBT community, homosexuality, same-sex marriage, and same-sex relationships.

We attempted to target the age group category at highest risk in the 2018 Texas HIV epidemiologic profile. However, we had to adjust the age group from 15–24 to 18–24, as FB does not allow the granular targeting of users younger than 18 years. Similarly, FB does not allow race/ethnicity-based targeting, and we used interests in African American culture and Hispanic cultures as a proxy for the African American and Hispanic populations. For transgender women and men, we used their interest in transgender issues and their corresponding gender for our FB targeting criteria.

For each targeted group/subgroup, we collected the FB-provided estimated audience size, estimated daily reach, and estimated daily clicks per Ad. We then estimated the average Ad cost for each new HIV diagnosis for targeted and non-targeted Ads. We leveraged new HIV diagnosis rates from focused testing and routine testing campaigns in Texas based on the following formula:

Estimated Ad cost per new diagnosis = daily Ad cost/(estimated daily clicks × average healthcare conversion rate × average rate of new diagnosis)

Using a USD 10 budget for a 10-day-long Ad translated into a daily Ad cost of USD 1. We used the daily cost to compare the FB-provided estimated daily reach and estimated daily clicks for all age groups. We used the average healthcare industry conversion rate on Facebook to estimate the percentage of Facebook users who would convert as a result of the Ads, which in this case translated to undergoing HIV testing. Based on subgroups, we estimated the rates of new HIV diagnoses based on the 2018 Texas HIV epidemiologic profile. For the targeted model, we used the rates of new HIV diagnoses from focused testing (testing a population that is more at risk for HIV). For the non-targeted model, we used HIV new diagnosis rates from routine testing (testing patients independent of their HIV risk).

3. Results

On 14 October 2021, the estimated audience size for the model targeting MSM in Texas included 1,350,000 individuals compared with an estimated 11,050,000 Texan men in the non-targeted model. The cost for each new HIV diagnosis was 4.7 times lower for the targeted model (targeting MSM in Texas: USD 33.06) compared with the non-targeted model (targeting all Texan men: USD 156.74).

The average Ad cost per new HIV diagnosis was lower in the targeted model for all subgroups (Table 1). The costs for targeted campaigns were half in all age groups (Figure 1) and 2.4 times lower in the main affected Texan metropolitan areas (Figure 2). In Hispanic and Black/African American men, the targeted model's costs for each new HIV diagnosis were 5.3 and 2.9 times lower, respectively (Figure 3).

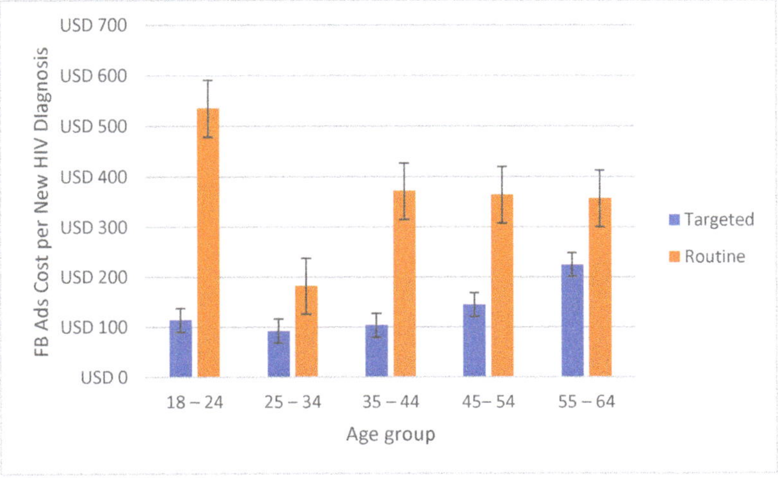

Figure 1. Estimated Ad cost per new HIV diagnosis comparison between targeted and non-targeted models for age groups in Texas, USA.

Table 1. Average Ads cost per new HIV diagnosis among targeted and non-targeted models in Texas, USA.

	Targeted Ads Followed by Focused Testing (Targeted Model)			Non-Targeted Ads Followed by Routine Testing (Non-targeted Model)		
	New Diagnosis Rate	Average Estimated Audience Size on Facebook	Average Cost Per New HIV Diagnosis	New Diagnosis Rate	Average Estimated Audience Size on Facebook	Average Cost Per New HIV Diagnosis
Men	1.0%	1,350,000	USD 33.06	0.2%	11,050,000	USD 156.74
Black	0.8%	289,550	USD 64.94	0.2%	2,100,000	USD 185.53
Hispanic	0.8%	784,300	USD 73.31	0.1%	3,050,000	USD 386.85
18–24	0.8%	326,450	USD 113.64	0.1%	4,800,000	USD 534.76
25–34	0.9%	483,300	USD 91.83	0.2%	6,900,000	USD 181.82
35–44	0.8%	236,250	USD 103.31	0.1%	4,900,000	USD 371.06
45–54	0.6%	125,000	USD 144.30	0.1%	3,400,000	USD 363.64
55–64	0.3%	76,700	USD 224.47	0.1%	2,350,000	USD 356.51
65+	0.2%	60,000	USD 413.22	0.0%	2,050,000	
Austin	0.4%	110,100	USD 206.61	0.1%	1,750,000	USD 443.46
Dallas	1.0%	264,700	USD 86.58	0.3%	4,650,000	USD 114.35
Fort Worth	0.9%	162,000	USD 91.83	0.1%	3,100,000	USD 371.06
Houston	0.7%	288,500	USD 123.69	0.1%	4,750,000	USD 404.04
San Antonio	0.6%	121,400	USD 168.35		2,050,000	
Rest of Texas	0.8%	189,150	USD 126.26	0.1%	9,700,000	USD 356.51

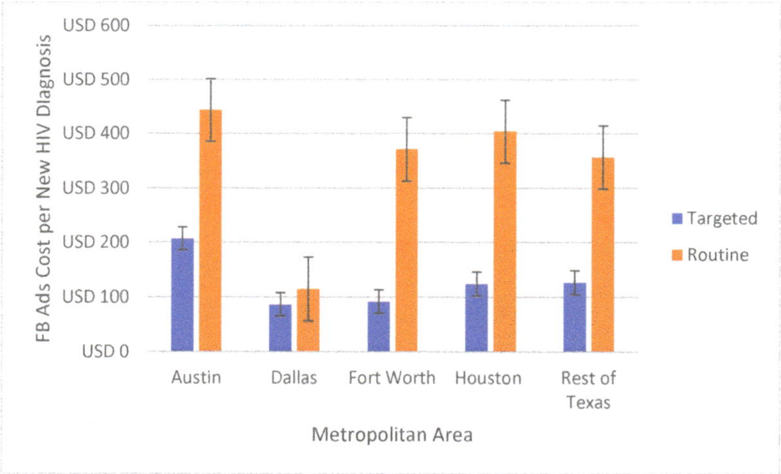

Figure 2. Estimated Ad cost per new HIV diagnosis comparison between targeted and non-targeted models for Texan metropolitan areas in Texas, USA.

Among the Texas metropolitan areas, Dallas had the highest rate of new HIV diagnoses through focused and routine testing. Dallas also had the lowest estimated cost for each new HIV diagnosis for targeted and non-targeted Ads. Austin had the lowest rates for new HIV diagnoses and the highest cost for new HIV diagnoses (targeted or not). The ratio of costs for new diagnoses for the targeted and the non-targeted model was lowest in Dallas, which also had the lowest ratio between new diagnosis rates from focused vs routine testing (1/0.3). The cost ratio was highest in Fort Worth, which also had the highest ratio between new diagnosis rates from focused vs routine testing (0.9/0.1).

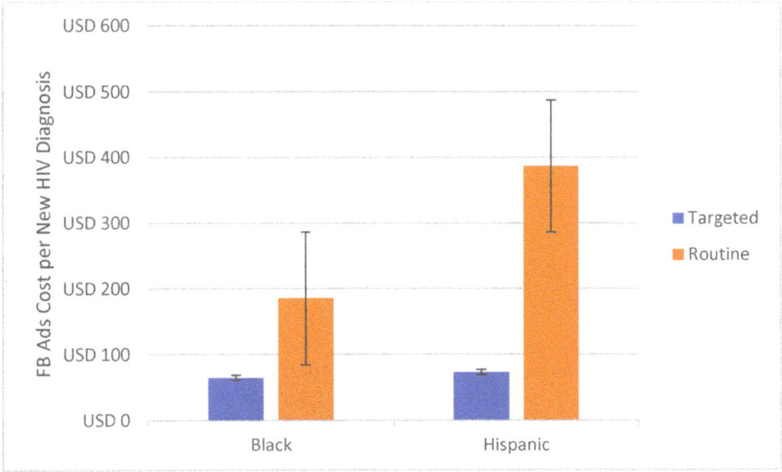

Figure 3. Estimated Ad cost per new HIV diagnosis comparison between targeted and non-targeted models for race/ethnicity in Texas, USA.

4. Discussion

The "Ending the HIV Epidemic: A plan for America" initiative, empowered by the U.S. Department of Health and Human Services (HHS), has launched work with communities, aiming to leverage critical scientific advances in HIV prevention, diagnosis, treatment, and outbreak response and redirect resources to areas where HIV transmission occurs most frequently. The initiative has the goal to reach a 75% reduction in new HIV infections by 2025 and at least a 90% reduction by 2030 [27].

To explore the most cost-effective means of reducing HIV infections, we compared FB Ads' cost per new HIV diagnosis from targeted and non-targeted models in five Texas counties (Bexar, Dallas, Harris, Tarrant, Travis) from the targeted 57 priority jurisdictions in the cross-agency HHS initiative. In all Texas areas, age groups, and race/ethnicity (Table 1), Ad cost per new HIV diagnosis was lower in the targeted model (targeted Ads followed by focused HIV testing) than the non-targeted model (non-targeted Ads followed by routine HIV testing).

The targeted model's lower Ad cost per new HIV diagnosis was in part caused by the higher new HIV diagnosis rates from focused HIV testing. FB Ad cost also varied among each targeted population, as FB uses an Ad auction to determine the best Ad to show to a person at a given point in time [28]. The FB Ad auction is designed to show the Ad with the highest total value to FB users. The Ad total value is based on three major factors: Ad bid, estimated action rates, and Ad quality. The three variables that determine Ad total value, along with seasonality, are the main factors that affect the cost of FB Ads at any point in time. In our study, we collected data on the same day using the same video Ad design and budget to control seasonality and Ad quality among all groups. However, the two other variables that contribute to FB Ads' total value are audience specific: the Ad bid compared to other Ads targeting the same audience, and the estimated action rates based on the FB-estimated probability that showing an Ad to a person leads to the desired outcome of the advertiser.

The results from our study also cast light on the effect of different rates of new HIV diagnoses from routine and focused testing in a certain population on the cost of FB Ads. We observed that the wider the gap in a population between new diagnosis rates from focused HIV testing and new diagnosis rates from routine testing, the more cost-effective targeted FB Ads become in the same population. This finding can guide the allocation of resources based on focused/routine testing rates and can be used to prioritize reach models for each population at risk for HIV.

We focused on populations at risk for HIV in Texas to explore feasibility. However, considering the input variables, this strategy can be applied to any population at risk for a given disease if a population can be represented through a set of targeting criteria/interests on FB Ads and public action rate data are available. In 2021, An et al. [15] proposed a novel precision public health campaign framework to structure and standardize the process of designing and delivering tailored health messages to target population segments on social media, demonstrating their framework through two case studies: breast cancer screening in Qatar, and public health campaigns for promoting flu vaccination in Qatar. In the proposed framework, defining priority audience and evaluation metrics are key factors of the first stages of a social media public health campaign. Our MSM/HIV at-risk audience definitions on FB, FB Messenger, and Instagram, along with our model characteristics, can help public health communities in these first stages of building a public health campaign framework to tackle the HIV epidemic.

Other social media platforms including Twitter, LinkedIn, Snapchat, and TikTok also allow promoters to use basic demographic traits for targeting their audience; however, these rich demographic traits are only available on FB and Snapchat [15]. Platform penetration in a specific population's demographic also plays a key role in selecting the best platform. For example, considering the highest rates of undiagnosed HIV are among the 13–24 age group, platforms such as TikTok or Snapchat that have high penetration in this demographic should also be considered.

While targeted Ads on social media can be effective and cost efficient for HIV prevention, there exists an ethical concern of privacy when targeting vulnerable populations (e.g., Blacks, Hispanics, LGBTQ), whereby an identifiable digital trail is maintained [29,30]. It is thus imperative for researchers and public health officials to act as stewards of this potential untapped resource and to advocate for these vulnerable populations when using these platforms. Additionally, other platforms, including Google and TikTok, have measures in place to protect the privacy and safety of teens. While these measures limit targeting adolescents (where underdiagnosed HIV is highly prevalent), it is important to create collaborative initiatives between public health communities and social media platforms, similar to the COVID-19 response, to aid in ending the HIV epidemic in digital America by 2030.

5. Conclusions

Targeted FB Ads are more cost-effective than non-targeted Ads among HIV populations at risk, across all age groups, and in locations where focused testing yields substantially higher new HIV diagnosis rates compared with routine testing. Our study results can guide public health agencies and local communities in optimizing their resource utilization to address the HIV epidemic, as social media Ad strategies are useful for improving HIV prevention, testing, and treatment. Our future efforts will aim to compare FB Ads' outcomes from launched FB Ad campaigns, including social media Ad metrics, conversion rates, and cost per action among different FB Ad targeting strategies based on FB-defined interests and locations targeting MSM populations at risk for HIV locally in Dallas, TX, in collaboration with a local community initiative.

6. Limitations

Our study has several limitations that must be acknowledged. Firstly, our proposed model is subject to the limitations of the social media platform and will continue to evolve while the platform tools evolve. Our modeling was based heavily on estimates provided by the FB Ads platform without running Ads. The audience size and reach estimates were provided by FB algorithms based on active FB and Instagram users which we were unable to validate. The adjusted targeting criteria were not designed to match a census population. The Ads' estimated daily reach and daily clicks were also subject to the platform algorithms and could vary based on Ad auction factors, as explained in-detail in the discussion section of this study.

Secondly, the conversion rate may also vary based on the Ad quality and its appropriateness to the viewing users. In our model, we used the average healthcare conversion rate on FB by WordStream based on a sample of 256 of their US-based clients in all industries who were advertising on FB between November 2016 and January 2017 [26]. Our study also did not examine the effect of different Ad designs that could variably affect the Ad outcomes, as this would have required user interactions on launched Ads for optimum testing.

Author Contributions: Conceptualization, J.J.H., A.E.N., C.U.L. and R.J.M.; methodology, J.J.H. and R.J.M.; formal analysis, J.J.H.; data curation, J.J.H.; writing—original draft preparation, J.J.H.; writing—review and editing, J.J.H., A.E.N., C.U.L. and R.J.M.; visualization, J.J.H.; supervision, A.E.N., C.U.L. and R.J.M. All authors have read and agreed to the published version of the manuscript.

Funding: This research received no external funding.

Institutional Review Board Statement: Not applicable.

Informed Consent Statement: Not applicable.

Data Availability Statement: Project data available at https://github.com/johnjero/OFBADSHIV.

Conflicts of Interest: RJM has received research grants from the Centers for Disease Control and Prevention and research funding from the Sergey Brin Family Foundation, Verily Life Sciences, and the Texas Health Resources Clinical Scholars Program. For the remaining authors no conflicts of interest are declared.

References

1. Centers for Disease Control and Prevention. Estimated HIV Incidence and Prevalence in the United States, 2010–2016. HIV Surveillance Supplemental Report 2019; 24 (No. 1). Available online: http://www.cdc.gov/hiv/library/reports/hiv-surveillance.html (accessed on 13 March 2022).
2. CDC. NCHHSTP AtlasPlus. Available online: https://www.cdc.gov/nchhstp/atlas/index.htm (accessed on 13 March 2022).
3. HIV in the Southern United States: Issue Brief. Available online: https://www.cdc.gov/hiv/pdf/policies/cdc-hiv-in-the-south-issue-brief.pdf (accessed on 13 March 2022).
4. National Center of HIV/AIDS, Viral Hepatitis, STD, and TB prevention Division of HIV/AIDS Prevention. HIV Surveillance in Urban and nonurban Areas 2018 (Preliminary). Available online: https://www.cdc.gov/hiv/pdf/library/slidesets/cdc-hiv-surveillance-urban-nonurban-2018.pdf (accessed on 13 March 2022).
5. Texas HIV Epidemiologic Profile 2018. Available online: https://dshs.texas.gov/hivstd/reports/epi_profile/files/EpiProfile.pdf (accessed on 13 March 2022).
6. Gittelman, S.; Lange, V.; Gotway Crawford, C.A.; Okoro, C.A.; Lieb, E.; Dhingra, S.S.; Trimarchi, E. A new source of data for Public Health Surveillance: Facebook Likes. *J. Med. Internet Res.* **2015**, *17*, e98. [CrossRef] [PubMed]
7. Chunara, R.; Bouton, L.; Ayers, J.W.; Brownstein, J.S. Assessing the online social environment for surveillance of obesity prevalence. *PLoS ONE* **2013**, *8*, e61373. [CrossRef]
8. Mejova, Y.; Weber, I.; Fernandez-Luque, L. Online health monitoring using Facebook advertisement audience estimates in the United States: Evaluation study. *JMIR Public Health Surveill.* **2018**, *4*, e30. [CrossRef] [PubMed]
9. Ramo, D.E.; Rodriguez, T.M.S.; Chavez, K.; Sommer, M.J.; Prochaska, J.J. Facebook recruitment of young adult smokers for a cessation trial: Methods, metrics, and lessons learned. *Internet Interv.* **2014**, *1*, 58–64. [CrossRef] [PubMed]
10. Burke, R.R.; Weichelt, B.P.; Namkoong, K. Facebook ads manager as a recruitment tool for a health and Safety Survey of Farm Mothers: Pilot Study. *JMIR Form. Res.* **2021**, *5*, e19022. [CrossRef]
11. Ford, K.L.; Albritton, T.; Dunn, T.A.; Crawford, K.; Neuwirth, J.; Bull, S. Youth study recruitment using paid advertising on Instagram, Snapchat, and facebook: Cross-sectional Survey Study. *JMIR Public Health Surveill.* **2019**, *5*, e14080. [CrossRef]
12. Dehlin, J.M.; Stillwagon, R.; Pickett, J.; Keene, L.; Schneider, J.A. #PREP4LOVE: An evaluation of a sex-positive HIV prevention campaign. *JMIR Public Health Surveill.* **2019**, *5*, e12822.
13. Staffileno, B.A.; Zschunke, J.; Weber, M.; Gross, L.E.; Fogg, L.; Tangney, C.C. The feasibility of using Facebook, Craigslist, and other online strategies to recruit young African American women for a web-based Healthy Lifestyle Behavior Change Intervention. *J. Cardiovasc. Nurs.* **2017**, *32*, 365–371. [CrossRef]

14. Gilligan, C.; Kypri, K.; Bourke, J. Social networking versus facebook advertising to recruit survey respondents: A quasi-experimental study. *JMIR Res. Protoc.* **2014**, *3*, e48. [CrossRef]
15. An, J.; Kwak, H.; Qureshi, H.M.; Weber, I. Precision Public Health Campaign: Delivering persuasive messages to relevant segments through targeted advertisements on social media. *JMIR Form. Res.* **2021**, *5*, e22313. [CrossRef]
16. Number of Monthly Active Users Worldwide as of 4th Quarter 2021. Available online: https://www.statista.com/statistics/264810/number-of-monthly-active-facebook-users-worldwide/ (accessed on 9 February 2022).
17. Guillory, J.; Wiant, K.F.; Farrelly, M.; Fiacco, L.; Alam, I.; Hoffman, L.; Crankshaw, E.; Delahanty, J.; Alexander, T.N. Recruiting hard-to-reach populations for survey research: Using Facebook and Instagram advertisements and in-person intercept in LGBT bars and nightclubs to recruit LGBT Young Adults. *J. Med. Internet Res.* **2018**, *20*, e197. [CrossRef] [PubMed]
18. Wozney, L.; Turner, K.; Rose-Davis, B.; McGrath, P.J. Facebook ads to the rescue? recruiting a hard to reach population into an internet-based Behavioral Health Intervention Trial. *Internet Interv.* **2019**, *17*, 100246. [CrossRef] [PubMed]
19. Hibbert, M.P.; Wolton, A.; Weeks, H.; Ross, M.; Brett, C.E.; Porcellato, L.A.; Hope, V.D. Psychosocial and sexual factors associated with recent sexual health clinic attendance and HIV testing among trans people in the UK. *BMJ Sex. Reprod. Health* **2019**, *46*, 116–125. [CrossRef] [PubMed]
20. Parker, J.N.; Hunter, A.S.; Bauermeister, J.A.; Bonar, E.E.; Carrico, A.; Stephenson, R. Comparing social media and in-person recruitment: Lessons learned from recruiting substance-using, sexual and gender minority adolescents and young adults for a randomized control trial. *JMIR Public Health Surveill.* **2021**, *7*, e31657. [CrossRef] [PubMed]
21. Garofalo, R.; Adetunji, A.; Kuhns, L.M.; Omigbodun, O.; Johnson, A.K.; Kuti, K.; Awolude, O.A.; Berzins, B.; Janulis, P.; Okonkwor, O.; et al. Evaluation of the ICARE Nigeria pilot intervention using social media and Peer Navigation to promote HIV testing and linkage to care among high-risk young men. *JAMA Netw. Open* **2022**, *5*, e220148. [CrossRef]
22. Patel, V.V.; Rawat, S.; Dange, A.; Lelutiu-Weinberger, C.; Golub, S.A. An internet-based, peer-delivered messaging intervention for HIV testing and condom use among men who have sex with men in India (chalo!): Pilot randomized comparative trial. *JMIR Public Health Surveill.* **2020**, *6*, e16494. [CrossRef]
23. Stern, M.J.; Fordyce, E.; Hansen, C.; Heim Viox, M.; Michaels, S.; Schlissel, A.; Avripas, S.; Harper, C.; Johns, M.; Dunville, R. Social Media Recruitment for a Web Survey of Sexual and Gender Minority Youth: An Evaluation of Methods Used and Resulting Sample Diversity. *LGBT Health* **2020**, *7*, 448–456. [CrossRef]
24. Gleason, N.; Serrano, P.A.; Muñoz, A.; French, A.; Hosek, S. Limited interaction targeted epidemiology of HIV in sexual and gender minority American adolescents and adults: Feasibility of the keeping it lite study. *JMIR Form. Res.* **2021**, *5*, e30761. [CrossRef]
25. Zlotorzynska, M.; Bauermeister José, A.; Golinkoff, J.M.; Lin, W.; Sanchez, T.H.; Hightow-Weidman, L. Online recruitment of Youth for mHealth Studies. *mHealth* **2021**, *7*, 27. [CrossRef]
26. The WordStream Blog. Facebook Ad Benchmarks for YOUR Industry [Data]. Available online: https://www.wordstream.com/blog/ws/2017/02/28/facebook-advertising-benchmarks (accessed on 31 March 2021).
27. Ending the HIV Epidemic: A Plan for America. Available online: https://www.cdc.gov/endhiv/docs/ending-HIV-epidemic-overview-508.pdf (accessed on 17 March 2022).
28. About Ad Auction. Meta for Business. Available online: https://www.facebook.com/business/help/430291176997542?id=561906377587030&ref=fbb_budgeting (accessed on 17 March 2022).
29. Curtis, B.L. Social Networking and online recruiting for HIV research: Ethical challenges. *J. Empir. Res. Hum. Res. Ethics* **2014**, *9*, 58–70. [CrossRef]
30. Fisher, C.B.; Bragard, E.; Bloom, R. Ethical considerations in HIV ehealth intervention research: Implications for informational risk in recruitment, data maintenance, and consent procedures. *Curr. HIV/AIDS Rep.* **2020**, *17*, 180–189. [CrossRef] [PubMed]

healthcare

MDPI

Review

Virtual Reality in the Rehabilitation of Patients with Injuries and Diseases of Upper Extremities

Pinar Tokgöz [1,2,*], Susanne Stampa [2], Dirk Wähnert [3], Thomas Vordemvenne [3,†] and Christoph Dockweiler [2,†]

1 School of Public Health, Bielefeld University, 33615 Bielefeld, Germany
2 Department of Digital Health Sciences and Biomedicine, School of Life Sciences, University of Siegen, 57068 Siegen, Germany; susanne.stampa@uni-siegen.de (S.S.); christoph.dockweiler@uni-siegen.de (C.D.)
3 Department for Trauma Surgery and Orthopedics, Protestant Hospital of Bethel Foundation, 33617 Bielefeld, Germany; dirk.waehnert@evkb.de (D.W.); thomas.vordemvenne@evkb.de (T.V.)
* Correspondence: pinar.tokgoez@uni-bielefeld.de
† These authors contributed equally to this work.

Abstract: Upper-extremity injuries and diseases rarely have life-threatening consequences, but failure to manage them properly can result in severe dysfunction. This article presents the current state of using virtual reality to support the rehabilitation process of patients with injuries and diseases of the upper extremities and points out their effects on upper-extremity functions. A scoping review was conducted to provide a comprehensive overview of the field of virtual reality for upper-extremity rehabilitation. PubMed, Web of Science, and the Cochrane Library were searched by two independent researchers between April and May 2021 to identify relevant publications and were examined according to inclusion and exclusion criteria. As a result of the literature review, 11 studies of various target groups were identified. Virtual-reality technologies were categorized into multisensory high-end systems and game-based systems. With respect to functional recovery, technologies based on virtual reality were not inferior to traditional rehabilitation. In addition, the users were highly motivated and satisfied. The results emphasize the need for stronger evidence-based virtual-reality technologies for rehabilitation of injuries and diseases of upper extremities.

Keywords: rehabilitation; virtual reality; upper extremity; virtual rehabilitation

Citation: Tokgöz, P.; Stampa, S.; Wähnert, D.; Vordemvenne, T.; Dockweiler, C. Virtual Reality in the Rehabilitation of Patients with Injuries and Diseases of Upper Extremities. *Healthcare* **2022**, *10*, 1124. https://doi.org/10.3390/healthcare10061124

Academic Editor: Daniele Giansanti

Received: 22 April 2022
Accepted: 15 June 2022
Published: 16 June 2022

1. Introduction

Injuries and diseases that concern the apparatus of movement and truss pose a long-term threat to both professional and individual performance, as well as participation in social life. In 2018, diseases of the musculoskeletal system were the most frequent reasons for outpatient rehabilitation among women (74%) and men (67%) in Germany [1]. Most of the complaints affected the upper extremities [2]. Rehabilitation is considered essential for the recovery of patients suffering from injuries and diseases of upper extremities and regaining quality of life.

Rehabilitation is a multifaceted long-term process ranging from inpatient or outpatient rehabilitation up to subsequent rehabilitation services. Accordingly, the conservative treatment includes a multitude of interventions, such as physical therapy, psychological treatment, and activities such as swimming or yoga [3,4]. To maintain the success of rehabilitation, an ongoing execution of acquired changes and a long-term provision of subsequent rehabilitation services are required [5]. With the dissemination of technological innovations, new opportunities arise to redesign rehabilitation services.

A technical innovation highly relevant for rehabilitation is virtual reality (VR). VR is the computer-animated simulation of a three-dimensional environment that can be used in real time [6]. Rehabilitation through VR describes an assistive health technology that is used to recover motor or sensory skills lost due to accident or illness through a virtual but interactive environment [7]. VR consists of a range of technologies that can be used to artificially generate sensory information in the form of a virtual environment that is interactive and perceived as similar to the real world. In addition, audiovisual feedback functions can improve compliance and therapeutic effectiveness [7].

In rehabilitation, VR represents a valid and reliable tool for joint and function [8]. It is a cost-saving alternative and enables personalizing treatment, motivating patients, and increasing their compliance and functional recovery [9]. VR is also generally commercially available and can be used for home-based rehabilitation [10,11]. This may reduce the work burden on professionals, because it requires minimal supervision [12]. An increasing number of VR technologies are supplemented by playful concepts, whereby various elements, dynamics, and mechanics are used. For example, it is possible for virtual environments to be presented on screens or displayed in VR glasses, augmented with simultaneous auditory presentations, closely approximating the complexity of the everyday world [13]. In combination with three-dimensional motion analysis, VR technologies have great potential for the rehabilitation of upper-extremity functions [14]. The design of the systems is often similar; one or more forms of sensor technology record the user's movements, which are presented in a playful and everyday manner [15]. Thorough system design, the patients should be able to implement the idea of movement specification. At the same time, it is possible for professionals to change the structure and severity of training [14].

The effectiveness of VR in neurorehabilitation has been studied extensively in individuals with cerebral palsy [16] and especially stroke [15,17]. In spite of VR´s promising effects for rehabilitation, it lacks routine use in practice. Moreover, its effectiveness for the rehabilitation of upper extremities beyond neurological disorders is insufficiently explored. Patients with neurological diseases might suffer from upper-extremity dysfunction, but there might be differences in treatment goals, which require consideration. Therefore, the aim of this scoping review was to present the current state of VR technologies being used in the rehabilitation of upper-extremity injuries and diseases other than neurological disorders and to examine their impact on functional recovery.

2. Materials and Methods

This scoping review was conducted using the framework of Arksey and O'Malley [18], described in detail by Levac et al. [19]. The databases PubMed, Web of Science, and the Cochrane Library were searched between April and May 2021. The search was updated in January 2022. Using relevant search terms and Medical Subject Headings (MeSH) such as "rehabilitation", "virtual reality", and "upper-extremity diseases", a search syntax was developed.

Two independent reviewers judged the eligibility of retrieved studies by title and abstract, as well as according to inclusion and exclusion criteria. Duplicates were sorted out, and appropriate studies were included in a second screening. Thus, in the next step, the studies were assessed on the basis of full texts and with renewed consideration of inclusion and exclusion criteria. Studies that were not published in English or German, were available as abstracts only, or focused on neurological diseases solely were excluded. Studies that used rehabilitation approaches based on VR as a training tool, reported at least one outcome related to functional recovery, and were published in English or German between the years 2011 and 2021 were included. If disagreement existed, a consensus was reached through discussion.

A standardized data extraction form was used to collect information related to the following aspects:

- Authors,
- Country,
- Study design,
- Sample size,
- Study population,
- Intervention characteristics,

- Relevant outcomes and results.

These data were used for precise planning and preparation of the qualitative synthesis.

3. Results

The initial search procedure retrieved 681 articles. After duplicate removal and screening, 11 studies were considered eligible for inclusion (see Figure 1).

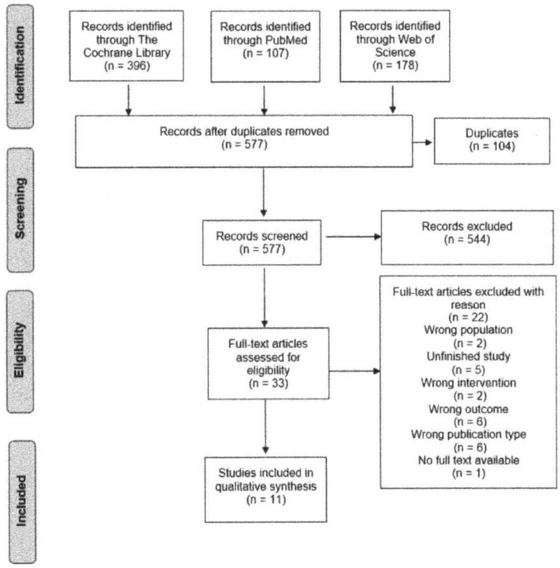

Figure 1. Flow diagram of literature search and selection process.

3.1. Study Characteristics

Of the included studies, five studies were conducted as pilot randomized controlled trials [20–24]. Three studies each were designed as pilot studies [25–27] and randomized controlled trials [28–30]. Sample size ranged from six to 57 participants when intervention and control groups were summed up. There was variability with regard to study population. Four studies considered functional disorders after burns of the upper extremities [21–23,30], while two studies considered functional disorders of the upper extremities after surgical treatment of breast cancer [26,28]. Further indications were chronic pain syndrome of upper extremity [25], shoulder injuries [20], impingement syndrome [29], frozen shoulder [27], and rheumatoid arthritis [24].

Consequently, there was heterogeneity in the parameters measured and assessment methods used in the studies, with a predominant focus on pain perception and dysfunction of the upper extremity. The most common evaluation methodology used was the visual analog scale (VAS) to assess pain and range of motion (ROM) to assess upper-extremity function.

The VR technologies described in the studies can be divided into two categories. The first constituted multisensory high-end systems that enable complete immersion. In the pilot study of Chau et al. (2020), participants used the HTC Vive VR system, which consisted of a wired headset and two handheld motion controllers. Participants were approved for up to 10 sessions of VR therapy, with each session lasting approximately 45 min to 1 h. The sessions consisted of guided visualization exercises and interactions with the virtual environment. Activities included, for example, washing hands, sorting dishware, or arranging utensils [25]. The BrightArm Duo Rehabilitation System in the pilot study of House et al. (2016) is an integrative virtual rehabilitation game system consisting of different exercises for motor, emotive, and cognitive function. For instance, participants were asked to use paddle avatars to bounce a virtual ball toward an array of crates. The duration of the VR therapy sessions progressed from 20 to 50 min of training over a period of 8 weeks, with two sessions every week. All games had progressively higher difficulty levels over the study duration, which were combined with higher gravity loading and longer training sessions to keep the participants challenged [26]. In the study of Lee et al. (2016), an interactive motor training VR system was designed to formulate a goal-directed shoulder rehabilitation, which assisted participants with motor rehabilitation. Sensors were secured to the shoulder joints to measure and record ROM, while participants underwent various exercises consisting of shoulder ROM exercises, shoulder muscle strengthening, and core muscle strengthening. The exercise sessions were 40 min twice a week for 4 weeks. The practice time for each exercise was based on the participants' progress and was determined by the therapists [27]. In the study of Joo et al. (2020), the VR rehabilitation tool RAPAEL Smart Glove was designed for the distal upper extremities. All participants received a 4 week intervention, consisting of 20 sessions for 60 min per day. Participants of the intervention group received 30 min of standard therapy and 30 min of exercises with the VR system. Exercises of the VR system demanded volitional movements such as forearm pronation/supination or wrist flexion/extension. Visual and audio feedback informed participants of success or failure. Participants of the control group received 60 min standard therapy, which comprised ROM exercises or strengthening exercises. The exercises in both groups were comparable and adapted to each participants' performance. The intervention frequency and duration did not differ between both groups. Three therapists who had experience with VR systems and conventional therapy supervised the study [30].

On the other hand, there are commercially available game-based systems, such as Nintendo Wii and Xbox Kinect, which are designed to be lower-threshold and less expensive. The majority of the studies included in this work ($N = 7$) used game-based systems for upper-extremity rehabilitation [20–24,28,29].

Participants in the study of Dahl-Popolizio et al. (2014) performed a protocol of active, active assistivem and passive ROM exercises for six sessions using Microsoft Kinect, where the movements attempted to match the movements of an avatar, which was displayed on a screen. Participants in the control group received similar exercises for six sessions but without Microsoft Kinect and with minimal therapeutically support [20]. In the study of Voon et al. (2016), all participants were requested to attend the study for 1 week and to perform two 30 min exercise sessions daily. Participants in the intervention group were asked, for each session, to perform 15 min of routine physiotherapy exercises followed by a minimum of 15 min of Xbox Kinect game play, consisting of exercises such as darts or bowling. Participants in the control group performed, for each session, a minimum of 30 min of the same routine physiotherapy regime [23]. Similarly, in the study of Feyzioglu et al. (2020), the participants of the intervention group received Xbox Kinect therapy, while the control group received standardized routine physiotherapy. Both groups received the therapy for 45 min per session and two times a week for 6 weeks. Additionally, all participants were given the same home exercise program except for the session days [28].

In the study of Yohannan et al. (2012), all participants received three consecutive sessions of traditional passive ROM and joint-specific exercises for 15 min. This was followed by an additional 15 min of Nintendo Wii exercises consisting of games such as wall finger climbs, overhead ball toss, or bouncing a physioball for those in the intervention group or 15 min of a therapist-chosen exercise for those in the control group. In the control group, although therapy was tailored by interventional therapists, the movements were comparable with the intervention group. Interventional therapists were guided by scripts to provide standardized therapy [21]. The study of Parker et al. (2016) lasted a maximum of 7 days. During this time, in addition to their individualized routine exercises, participants of the intervention group completed up to five individual days of twice-daily exercise with Nintendo Wii, whereby each session lasted 20–30 min. The sessions were self-directed and consisted of an individual playing specific games with a standardized order according to the injury and the limb involved. Participants in the control group received routine individualized exercises that were comparable with the intervention group [22]. In the cross-sectional study of Zernicke et al. (2016), participants of the intervention group started with exercises using Nintendo Wii, while participants in the control group completed conventional physical exercises for 12 weeks. Afterward, participants were crossed over for another period of 12 weeks. Participants in the intervention group could select from at least 46 exercises of different fields such as aerobic, muscle strengthening, or balance. Exercises in the control group were designed by physiotherapists and based on strength training, coordination, joint mobility, and relaxation. According to the training schedule, each participant was stimulated to exercise three times a week for approximately 30 min per session [24]. Participants in the study from Pekyavas and Ergun (2017) were included in the intervention group receiving supervised exercises with Nintendo Wii for 6 weeks, two days per week, and 45 min for day. The sessions consisted of warming and cooling periods and several training games comprising boxing, bowling or tennis games accompanied by an avatar. Participants in the control group received a home exercise program for 6 weeks, two days per week, and 45 min per day. Exercises were similar to the intervention group and consisted of resistive and non-resistive exercises [29].

In two studies, participants using the VR technology received continuous support from trained professionals [21,26]. In another two studies, participants received audiovisual feedback on movement execution [20,30].

3.2. *Effectiveness of VR Technologies*

The results of the pilot studies in pre–post design showed significant improvements with regard to pain and upper-extremity function [26,27]. The study by Chau et al. did not find any statistically significant improvements in the parameters measured [25].

Varying results were obtained in the randomized controlled trials. Rarely, the VR technologies in the included studies were associated with measurable benefits related to pain perception and upper-extremity function. For example, the study results of Parker et al. showed significant improvements in pain ($p = 0.0019$) favoring the intervention group using the VR technology, while no statistically significant differences were detectable in range of motion [22]. In contrast, the intervention group in the study by Joo et al. was associated with statistically significant improvements in the subscales "picking up small objects" ($p < 0.001$) and "pain" ($p = 0.002$) of the Jebsen–Taylor hand function test (JTT) [30]. Pekyavas and Ergun also obtained similar results, where, in terms of single parameters of functionality and pain perception, the intervention group using the VR technology was superior to traditional rehabilitation, while, in other parameters, no statistically significant differences were detectable [29]. Four studies found no statistically significant differences at all with regard to upper-extremity function or pain between participants using the VR technology and participants receiving traditional rehabilitation [20,21,23,24].

Beyond that, results related to user satisfaction and motivation were mostly consistent. Overall, users were satisfied with the interventions used [20,23,30] and motivated to complete training sessions [24–26]. All analyzed studies are summarized in Table 1.

Table 1. Characteristics of included studies.

Study	Country	Study Design	Sample Size	Study Population	Intervention Characteristics	Outcomes	Results
Dahl-Popolizio et al. [20]	USA	Randomized controlled pilot study	IG: 4 CG: 4	Shoulder injuries	IG: Microsoft Kinect motion tracking technology. Participant movement was displayed on a large screen, which was mounted to a motion sensor and could detect in real time. Participants received audiovisual feedback. CG: Standard rehabilitation program.	Shoulder functionality assessed with ROM and FOTO; pain assessed with VAS; satisfaction assessed with a 10-point Likert scale	All measured variables were not significantly different between the two groups. Participants of IG reported high satisfaction with VR system.
Yohannan et al. [21]	USA	Randomized controlled pilot study	IG: 11 CG: 12	Burns	IG: Nintendo Wii fit/sports. Participants first received a standard rehabilitation program for 15 min and then VR exercises mounted to a motion sensor. Participants were supported by trained professionals. CG: Standard rehabilitation program.	Functionality assessed with ROM; pain assessed with VAS	All measured variables were not significantly different between the two groups.
Parker et al. [22]	Australia	Randomized controlled pilot study	IG: 12 CG: 10	Burns	IG: Nintendo Wii fit/sports. Participants first received a standard rehabilitation program and then VR exercises mounted to a motion sensor. CG: Standard rehabilitation program.	Functionality assessed with ROM; pain assessed with VAS	Patients who participated in VR showed significant improvements in pain perception. There were no significant differences in ROM between the two groups.
Voon et al. [23]	Australia	Randomized controlled pilot study	IG: 15 CG: 15	Burns	IG: Xbox 360 Kinect. Participant movement was displayed on a large screen, which was mounted to motion sensor and could detected in real-time, while participants interacted with the virtual environment. Participants first received a standard rehabilitation program for 15 min and then VR exercises for 15 min. CG: Standard rehabilitation program for 30 min.	Functionality assessed with Quick-DASH; satisfaction assessed with VAS; pain assessed with a 10-point Likert scale	Patients who participated in VR showed significant improvements in satisfaction with rehabilitation. There were no significant differences in Quick-DASH and VAS.

Table 1. *Cont.*

Study	Country	Study Design	Sample Size	Study Population	Intervention Characteristics	Outcomes	Results
Zernicke et al. [24]	Germany	Randomized controlled pilot study	IG: 15 CG: 15	Rheumatoid arthritis	IG: Nintendo Wii fit plus. Participants first received different VR exercises for12 weeks and then 12 weeks of standard rehabilitation. CG: Participants first a received standard rehabilitation program for 12 weeks and then VR exercises for the next 12 weeks.	Functionality assessed with HAQ-DI; pain assessed with VAS; quality of life assessed with SF-36; muscle strength assessed with a dynamometer	All measured variables were not significantly different between the two groups.
Chau et al. [25]	USA	Pilot study	$N = 8$	Chronic pain syndrome	HTC Vive. VR system using wired headset, two handheld motion controllers, and two base stations, which provided boundaries and tracking system of the virtual space. Headset and controllers allowed real-time 3D motion tracking. Exercising with virtual activities such as washing hands, sorting dishware, and arranging utensils.	Pain assessed with VAS, SF-MPQ, and WBF	The were no significant changes in measured variables. Participants tolerated the VR system well and were motivated to continue the rehabilitation program until the end.
House et al. [26]	USA	Pilot study	$N = 6$	Chronic pain syndrome after breast cancer surgery	The BrightArm Duo System is an experimental robotic platform that modulates gravity loading on the upper extremities, consisting of a low-friction robotic rehabilitation table, computerized forearm supports, and a screen that displays motion tracking in real time. Participants were supported by trained professionals	Pain assessed with NRS; functionality assessed with Fugl–Meyer assessment, JTT, and ROM; mobility assessed with Chedokee arm and hand activity inventory-9; activities in daily living assessed with UEFI-20	Significant changes in pain perception and functionality assessed with ROM after 4 weeks and significant changes in daily living assessed with UEFI-20 after 8 weeks were observed.

Table 1. *Cont.*

Study	Country	Study Design	Sample Size	Study Population	Intervention Characteristics	Outcomes	Results
Lee et al. [27]	China	Pilot study	$N = 16$	Frozen shoulder	Interactive motor training system involving shoulder joint stretching and muscle strengthening. The 3D game engine software was adopted to formulate a goal-directed shoulder rehabilitation program. Sensors were secured to the shoulder joints to record movement execution while patients were undergoing various exercises.	Shoulder flexibility assessed with CMS; functionality assessed with ROM; muscle strength assessed with a dynamometer	Significant changes in the measured variables were recorded in the study period.
Feyzi-oglu et al. [28]	Turkey	Randomized controlled study	IG: 20 CG: 20	Functional impairment of upper extremities after breast cancer surgery	IG: Xbox 360 Kinect. Participant movement was displayed on a large screen, which was mounted to a motion sensor and could detect in real time, while participants interacted with the virtual environment. CG: Standard rehabilitation program.	Functionality assessed with ROM and DASH; muscle strength and flexibility assessed with a dynamometer	Significant changes in measured variables were seen in both groups, while effect sizes in CG were greater than in IG.
Pekyavas & Ergun [29]	Turkey	Randomized controlled study	IG: 15 CG: 15	Impingement syndrome	IG: Nintendo Wii. Participants received differentVR exercises, which were displayed on a large screen in real time. CG: Standard rehabilitation program.	Pain assessed with VAS; clinical symptoms assessed with Neer and Hawkins tests; functionality assessed with LSST, SRT, and SAT; pain and impairments in daily living assessed with SPADI	Significant differences were observed in Neer test but not Hawkins test, favoring IG. Significant differences were observed in SRT, SAT, and SPADI, favoring IG. No significant differences were seen in pain perception assessed with VAS.

Table 1. *Cont.*

Study	Country	Study Design	Sample Size	Study Population	Intervention Characteristics	Outcomes	Results
Joo et al. [30]	South Korea	Randomized controlled study	IG: 28 CG: 29	Burns	IG: RAPAEL Smart Glove. An exoskeleton type of glove and VR system were used, which could be operated through active movement. The software could be used to visualize the virtual hands in the VR tool according to data gathered by the glove-shaped sensor device. Participants received audiovisual feedback. CG: Standard rehabilitation program.	Functionality assessed by JTT and MHQ; grip strength assessed by grasp and pinch power test	Significant differences in subscales "picking up small objects" and "simulated feeding" of the JTT were recorded, favoring IG. Significant differences in the subscales "daily activity", "pain", "work", and "satisfaction" of the MHQ were recorded, favoring IG. No significant differences were seen in grip strength between both groups.

IG: intervention group, CG: control group, ROM: range of motion, VAS: visual analog scale, FOTO: focus on therapeutic outcome scale, VR: virtual reality, Quick-DASH: disabilities of arm, shoulder, and hand, HAQ-DI: health assessment questionnaire, disability index, SF-36: short-form 36, SF-MPQ: short-form McGill pain questionnaire, WBF: Wong–Baker faces pain rating scale, NRS: numeric rating scale, UEFI-20: Upper-extremity functional index 20, JTT: Jebsen–Taylor hand function test, CMS: constant Murley score, LSST: lateral scapular slide test, SRT: scapular retraction test, SAT: scapular assistance test, SPADI: shoulder pain and disability index, MHQ: Michigan hand questionnaire.

4. Discussion

Numerous reviews [15,17,31] have already shown the successful use of VR technologies for rehabilitation, especially in the field of neurological disorders. For rehabilitation of musculoskeletal diseases, in contrast, only a few publications can be found [32,33]. Therefore, this scoping review aimed to provide an overview of VR technologies used for rehabilitation of upper-extremity injuries and diseases beyond neurological impairments.

Existing evidence of VR technology effectiveness in patients with upper-extremity injuries and diseases is inconclusive yet promising. Findings from this scoping review indicate that VR-based interventions are not inferior to traditional rehabilitation and might have an added advantage for functional recovery and pain reduction. Future studies of high quality are necessary to reach a more solid conclusion.

The number of studies that used game-based VR technologies is remarkable. The integration of low-cost game-based VR technologies can allow healthcare specialists to precisely create, deliver, and control complex and dynamic environments for user interaction. Although such systems were not explicitly developed for rehabilitation, they might be motivating and cost-effective alternatives. As such, game-based VR rehabilitation exercises that are easily adapted to individual user needs will become a valuable adjunct to conventional therapy in inpatient, outpatient, and home-based care settings. However, limited options for customizing and adapting game-based contents to the needs of particular injuries or diseases could also be a disadvantage. Furthermore, visualization of content includes many different elements and stimuli, which might be overwhelming. Additionally, movements to be performed are often too nonspecific and incompatible with therapeutic goals [34].

Future research directions should consider the potential of VR-based systems to increase the efficiency of training in terms of human resources [35]. With VR, therapy sessions can be automated and, therefore, can be completed without the constant supervision of a therapist. Furthermore, a VR system can even be designed for a patient's home, removing the burden of clinical visits. While the vision for home-based rehabilitation is compelling for economic and technical reasons, professional and user-centered issues will also need to be considered concomitantly as the technology evolves [36]. Thus, the appropriate development and use of the VR systems must always be governed by evidence-based guidelines. Indeed, this is also important for user perspectives [37]. Several studies addressed the challenges of VR in a general or specific field from the user's perspective [38,39]. In this context, three categories of technical, practical, and user-based challenges for implementing and using a VR-based system have been discussed [40]. One main limitation includes the requirement for specialist technical skills [41]. It is necessary to educate and train clinical experts, as well as patients, in the proper and professional use of VR systems as useful tools for rehabilitation. The method of training users for the necessary skills should be performed considering their age, level of technical literacy, and previous experience with VR systems [42]. It is obvious to educate specialists to gain an important impact on the more effective use of VR.

Most of the VR technologies used in the studies included motion detection systems, in which the virtual environment is presented on large screens. Thus, the user sees the simulated environment and can interact with it. An advantage of this is that the system might encourage users to perform movements naturally. Consequently, VR-based rehabilitation is an effective way for people with upper-extremity injuries and diseases to cope with their motor impairment and regain the ability of performing activities of daily living (ADL) and self-care, which refer to the activities carried out to live an independent life, e.g., grooming or preparing food [43]. Examples that leverage VR for the rehabilitation of ADL include the use of a virtual kitchen for training meal preparation task or the use of a virtual supermarket for practicing shopping tasks [44] for people suffering from traumatic brain injury [45]. Another example is the training of manual skills with an exoskeleton robot also equipped with an actuator to assist shoulder movement. ADL tasks such as cooking, cleaning, and using a ticket machine were trained using the VR system, where the assist-as-needed strategy was adopted to provide guiding force when necessary [46].

Additionally, for successful rehabilitation, motivation of patients is a driving factor [6]. By embedding repetitive exercises in a playful and everyday manner, through virtual environments, motivation and adherence might be achieved [9]. This provides the opportunity to train in real-world scenarios but in a risk-free, graded fashion. The majority of the studies included in this review consisted of up to 10 training sessions and approximately 30 min of exercise time per session, whereby the difficulty and intensity of exercises were adaptable to individuals' performance. This is important to consider when designing VR exercises since the Yerkes–Dodson law, first explained by Yerkes and Dodson in 1908, describes a relationship between arousal or motivation and performance. It indicates that a low level of task difficulties elicits linear responses. Reaching a higher level of difficulty, the relationship becomes inverse, and increases in arousal or motivation could cause a decrease in performance [47]. An intensive training could reach a point when a higher intensity is necessary to push the functional improvements and patient motivation further, e.g., longer session duration or more sessions per week [48]. Furthermore, the use of VR allows the user's movement to be quantified and saved for analysis and tracking of performance. Specialists can benefit from the recording of performance data to analyze quality of movement and track patient progress within and across sections. Users may benefit from being able to view visualizations of their activity from different perspectives. Additionally, specific and immediate feedback on movement performance might also have a positive effect on motivation and adherence.

It is important to note a few limitations. First, only articles in the English and German language were included. Furthermore, studies that assessed neurological disorders were excluded. Because of this, only 11 studies could be identified, which again highlights that the potential of VR technologies for the rehabilitation of upper-extremity diseases and injuries is still underexplored. The heterogeneity of endpoints and assessment tools, as well as the small sample sizes in the studies, limits the comparability and interpretation of the results. Additionally, it was not possible to obtain conceptual or concrete content-related details of VR technologies.

5. Conclusions

In conclusion, this scoping review showed that especially game-based VR systems are highly prevalent in the context of rehabilitation and seem to be gaining importance to enhance motivation and support therapy. As presented, the literature to date strongly suggests that these technologies are poised to have a major impact on evaluation and intervention for motor and functional rehabilitation because of the unique attributes of VR-based therapy. These attributes make it highly suitable for the achievement of many rehabilitation goals, including the encouragement of active learning, the provision of challenging but safe environments, the flexibility of individualized and graded treatments, the power to motivate patients to perform to their utmost ability, and the capacity to record objective measures of performance.

VR systems are being directed at the rehabilitation of motor deficits to help provide recreational opportunities for people with upper-extremity dysfunction. VR-mediated rehabilitation has yielded significant improvements in upper-extremity recovery, especially regarding range of motion and pain reduction. VR systems show promise for training in activities of daily living, including use of a virtual kitchen, street-crossing, and wayfinding environment. Evidence from this scoping review suggests that VR technologies have the potential to become an effective tool in the rehabilitation of upper-extremity functions. Although the results do not indicate VR systems to be significantly more beneficial than routine physiotherapy, VR systems are comparable with existing traditional rehabilitation procedures and can be used as an alternative or adjunct for the rehabilitation of upper-extremity injuries and diseases. Advantages are mainly seen in the increased motivation to perform therapy tasks and the simulated and risk-free training of functional exercises with a stronger intensity than traditional rehabilitation.

Overall, VR offers a unique medium in which rehabilitation can be offered within a functional, purposeful, and motivation context, which can be readily graded and documented. Especially game-based VR technologies are becoming more accessible and cost-effective; however, they are not yet fully provided in regular care. The successful and extensive implementation of VR technologies in rehabilitation might be possible when the technologies are easily integrated in the everyday life of patients and professionals. For this purpose, it will be necessary to design and evaluate VR technologies in a participatory and user-oriented way. It remains exciting to learn about the effects that future developments will report, including user-specific perspectives.

Author Contributions: Conceptualization and literature search, P.T. and S.S.; data analysis, P.T. and S.S.; writing—original draft preparation, P.T.; writing—review and editing, S.S., D.W. and C.D.; supervision, C.D. and T.V.; funding acquisition, D.W. and T.V.; C.D. and T.V. contributed equally to this paper. All authors have read and agreed to the published version of the manuscript.

Funding: This project was financially supported by a grant from the Medical Research Start-Up Fund of the Medical School OWL. The Medical School OWL played no role in the planning and conceptualization of the manuscript, did not participate in the writing of the manuscript, and played no role in the decision to submit the manuscript. We acknowledge support for the publication costs by the Open-Access Publication Fund of Bielefeld University and the German Research Foundation (DFG).

Institutional Review Board Statement: Not applicable.

Informed Consent Statement: Not applicable.

Data Availability Statement: Not applicable.

Conflicts of Interest: The authors declare no conflict of interest.

References

1. Deutsche Rentenversicherung. Available online: https://www.deutsche-rentenversicherung.de/SharedDocs/Downloads/DE/Statistiken-und-Berichte/Berichte/rehabericht_2019.html (accessed on 20 March 2022).
2. Deutsche Gesetzliche Unfallversicherung. Available online: https://www.dguv.de/ifa/publikationen/reports-download/bgia-reports-2007-bis-2008/bgia-report-2-2007/index.jsp (accessed on 20 March 2022).
3. Greitemann, B.; Stein, V. Praxis der konservativen Orthopädie—Rehabilitation in der Orthopädie. *Orthopädie Und Unf.* **2013**, *8*, 503–522. [CrossRef]
4. Chaitow, L. *Naturopathic Physical Medicine: Theory and Practice for Manual Therapists and Naturopaths*; Elsevier Health Sciences: Edinburgh, UK, 2008; ISBN 978-044-310-902.
5. Bundesarbeitsgemeinschaft für Rehabilitation. Available online: https://www.bar-frankfurt.de/fileadmin/dateiliste/publikationen/arbeitsmaterialien/downloads/Praxisleitfaden_Nachhaltigkeit.pdf (accessed on 20 March 2022).
6. Mehrholz, J.; Elsner, B.; Thomas, S. Virtuelle Realität: Was ist im Einsatz? *Neuroreha* **2017**, *9*, 9–14. [CrossRef]
7. Büro Für Technikfolgenabschätzung Beim Deutschen Bundestag. Available online: https://publikationen.bibliothek.kit.edu/1000134066 (accessed on 13 March 2022).
8. Eini, D.S.; Ratzon, N.Z.; Rizzo, A.A.; Yeh, S.-C.; Lange, B.; Yaffe, B.; Daich, A.; Weiss, P.L.; Kizony, R. Camera-tracking gaming control device for evaluation of active wrist flexion and extension. *J. Hand Ther.* **2017**, *30*, 89–96. [CrossRef] [PubMed]
9. Holden, M.K. Virtual environments for motor rehabilitation. *Cyberpsychol. Behav.* **2005**, *8*, 187–211. [CrossRef] [PubMed]
10. Goble, D.J.; Cone, B.L.; Fling, B.W. Using the Wii Fit as a tool for balance assessment and neurorehabilitation: The first half decade of "Wii-search". *J. Neuroeng. Rehabil.* **2014**, *11*, 12. [CrossRef]
11. Webster, D.; Celik, O. Systematic review of Kinect applications in elderly care and stroke rehabilitation. *J. Neuroeng. Rehabil.* **2014**, *11*, 108. [CrossRef]
12. Stott, I.; Sanders, D. The use of virtual reality to train powered wheelchair users and test new wheelchair systems. *Int. J. Rehabil. Res.* **2000**, *23*, 321–326. [CrossRef]
13. Pfiefke, M.; Ehlers, P. Möglichkeiten der Digitalisierung einer ambulanten neuropsychologischen Rehabilitation und Telemedizin in der Neurologie, Kardiologie und Psychiatrie. In *Digitale Transformation von Dienstleistungen im Gesundheitswesen*; Pfannstiel, M.A., Da-Cruz, P., Mehlich, H., Eds.; Springer: Wiesbaden, Germany, 2019; pp. 311–326. ISBN 978-365-825-460-5.
14. Valle, C.; Schmitt-Sody, M. Was gibt es Neues in der physikalischen Medizin und Rehabilitation? *Knie J.* **2019**, *1*, 151–153. [CrossRef]
15. Laver, K.E.; Lange, B.; George, S.; Deutsch, J.E.; Saposnik, G.; Crotty, M. Virtual reality for stroke rehabilitation. *Cochrane Database Syst. Rev.* **2017**, CD008349. [CrossRef] [PubMed]

16. Ravi, D.K.; Kumar, N.; Singhi, P. Effectiveness of virtual reality rehabilitation for children and adolescents with cerebral palsy: An updated evidence-based systematic review. *Physiotherapy* **2017**, *103*, 245–258. [CrossRef]
17. Neuendorf, T.; Zschäbitz, D.; Nitzsche, N.; Schulz, H. Technikgestützte Bewegungstherapie der oberen Extremitäten nach Schlaganfall—eine aktuelle Übersicht. *Neurotransmitter* **2017**, *28*, 42–47. [CrossRef]
18. Arksey, H.; O'Malley, L. Scoping studies. Towards a methodological framework. *Int. J. Soc. Res. Methodol.* **2005**, *8*, 19–32. [CrossRef]
19. Levac, D.; Colquhoun, H.; O'Brien, K.K. Scoping studies: Advancing the methodology. *Implement. Sci.* **2010**, *5*, 69. [CrossRef]
20. Dahl-Popolizio, S.; Loman, J.; Cordes, C.C. Comparing Outcomes of Kinect Videogame Based Occupational/Physical Therapy Versus Usual Care. *Games Health J.* **2014**, *3*, 157–161. [CrossRef]
21. Yohannan, S.K.; Tufaro, P.A.; Hunter, H.; Orlemann, L.; Palmatier, S.; Sang, C.; Gorga, D.I.; Yurt, R.W. The utilization of Nintendo Wii™ during burn rehabilitation: A pilot study. *J. Burn. Care Res.* **2012**, *33*, 36–45. [CrossRef] [PubMed]
22. Parker, M.; Delahunty, B.; Heberlein, N.; Devenish, N.; Wood, F.M.; Jackson, T.; Carter, T.; Edgar, D.W. Interactive gaming consoles reduced pain during acute minor burn rehabilitation: A randomized, pilot trial. *J. Int. Soc. Burn. Inj.* **2016**, *42*, 91–96. [CrossRef] [PubMed]
23. Voon, K.; Silberstein, I.; Eranki, A.; Phillips, M.; Wood, F.M.; Edgar, D.W. Xbox Kinect™ based rehabilitation as a feasible adjunct for minor upper limb burns rehabilitation: A pilot RCT. *J. Int. Soc. Burn. Inj.* **2016**, *42*, 1797–1804. [CrossRef]
24. Zernicke, J.; Kedor, C.; Müller, A.; Burmester, G.-R.; Reißhauer, A.; Feist, E. A prospective pilot study to evaluate an animated home-based physical exercise program as a treatment option for patients with rheumatoid arthritis. *BMC Musculoskelet. Disord.* **2016**, *17*, 351. [CrossRef]
25. Chau, B.; Phelan, I.; Ta, P.; Chi, B.; Loyola, K.; Yeo, E.; Dunn, J.; Humbert, S.; Hata, J.; Haglund, R.; et al. Immersive Virtual Reality for Pain Relief in Upper Limb Complex Regional Pain Syndrome: A Pilot Study. *Innov. Clin. Neurosci.* **2020**, *17*, 47–52.
26. House, G.; Burdea, G.; Grampurohit, N.; Polistico, K.; Roll, D.; Damiani, F.; Hundal, J.; Demesmin, D. A feasibility study to determine the benefits of upper extremity virtual rehabilitation therapy for coping with chronic pain post-cancer surgery. *Br. J. Pain* **2016**, *10*, 186–197. [CrossRef]
27. Lee, S.-H.; Yeh, S.-C.; Chan, R.-C.; Chen, S.; Yang, G.; Zheng, L.-R. Motor Ingredients Derived from a Wearable Sensor Based Virtual Reality System for Frozen Shoulder Rehabilitation. *BioMed Res. Int.* **2016**, *2016*, 7075464. [CrossRef] [PubMed]
28. Feyzioğlu, Ö.; Dinçer, S.; Akan, A.; Algun, Z.C. Is Xbox 360 Kinect-based virtual reality training as effective as standard physiotherapy in patients undergoing breast cancer surgery? *Off. J. Multinatl. Assoc. Supportive Care Cancer* **2020**, *28*, 4295–4303. [CrossRef] [PubMed]
29. Pekyavas, N.O.; Ergun, N. Comparison of virtual reality exergaming and home exercise programs in patients with subacromial impingement syndrome and scapular dyskinesis: Short term effect. *Acta Orthop. Et Traumatol. Turc.* **2017**, *51*, 238–242. [CrossRef] [PubMed]
30. Joo, S.Y.; Cho, Y.S.; Lee, S.Y.; Seok, H.; Seo, C.H. Effects of Virtual Reality-Based Rehabilitation on Burned Hands: A Prospective, Randomized, Single-Blind Study. *J. Clin. Med.* **2020**, *9*, 731. [CrossRef]
31. Massetti, T.; da Silva, T.D.; Crocetta, T.B.; Guarnieri, R.; de Freitas, B.L.; Lopes, P.B.; Watson, S.; Tonks, J.; de Mello Monteiro, C.B. The Clinical Utility of Virtual Reality in Neurorehabilitation: A Systematic Review. *J. Cent. Nerv. Syst. Dis.* **2018**, *10*, 1–18. [CrossRef]
32. Berton, A.; Longo, U.G.; Candela, V.; Fioravanti, S.; Giannone, L.; Arcangeli, V.; Alciati, V.; Berton, C.; Facchinetti, G.; Marchetti, A.; et al. Virtual Reality, Augmented Reality, Gamification and Telerehabilitation: Psychological Impact on Orthopedic Patients' Rehabilitation. *J. Clin. Med.* **2020**, *9*, 2567. [CrossRef] [PubMed]
33. Gumaa, M.; Rehan Youssef, A. Is Virtual Reality Effective in Orthopedic Rehabilitation? A Systematic Review and Meta-Analysis. *Phys. Ther.* **2019**, *99*, 1304–1325. [CrossRef] [PubMed]
34. Lohse, K.; Shirzad, N.; Verster, A.; Hodges, N.; van der Loos, H.F.M. Video games and rehabilitation: Using design principles to enhance engagement in physical therapy. *J. Neurol. Phys. Ther.* **2013**, *37*, 166–175. [CrossRef]
35. Krasovsky, T.; Lubetzky, A.V.; Archambault, P.S ; Wright, W.G. Will virtual rehabilitation replace clinicians: A contemporary debate about technological versus human obsolescence. *J. Neuro. Eng. Rehabil.* **2020**, *17*, 163. [CrossRef] [PubMed]
36. Rizzo, A.A.; Schultheis, M.T.; Rothbaum, B.O. Ethical issues for the use of virtual reality in the psychological sciences. In *Ethical Issues in Clinical Neuropsychology*; Bush, S., Drexler, M., Eds.; Swets and Zeitlinger Publishers: Lisse, The Netherlands, 2002; pp. 243–280, ISBN 978-902-651-924-6.
37. Lewis, G.N.; Rosie, J.A. Virtual reality games for movement rehabilitation in neurological conditions: How do we meet the needs and expectations of the users? *Disabil. Rehabil.* **2012**, *34*, 1880–1886. [CrossRef]
38. Cao, S. Virtual Reality Applications in Rehabilitation. In *Human-Computer Interaction. Theory, Design, Development and Practice*; Kurosu, M., Ed.; Springer: Cham, Switzerland, 2016; pp. 3–10, ISBN 978-331-939-509-8.
39. Powell, W. Innovations and challenges in the use of virtual reality technologies for rehabilitation. *J. Altern. Med. Res.* **2017**, *10*.
40. Rizzo, A.A.; Strickland, D.; Bouchard, S. The challenge of using virtual reality in telerehabilitation. *Telemed J. E Health* **2004**, *10*, 184–195. [CrossRef] [PubMed]
41. Bohil, C.J.; Alicea, B.; Biocca, F.A. Virtual reality in neuroscience research and therapy. *Nat. Rev. Neurosci.* **2011**, *12*, 752–762. [CrossRef]
42. Halbig, A.; Babu, S.K.; Gatter, S.; Latoschik, M.E.; Brukamp, K.; Mammen, S. Opportunities and Challenges of Virtual Reality in Healthcare—A Domain Experts Inquiry. *Front. Virtual. Real.* **2022**, *3*, 3–837616. [CrossRef]

43. Levin, M.F.; Weiss, P.L.; Keshner, E.A. Emergence of virtual reality as a tool for upper limb rehabilitation: Incorporation of motor control and motor learning principles. *Phys. Ther.* **2015**, *95*, 415–425. [CrossRef] [PubMed]
44. Lee, J.; Ku, J.; Cho, W.; Hahn, W.Y.; Kim, I.Y.; Lee, S.-M.; Kang, Y.; Kim, D.Y.; Wiederhold, B.K.; Wiederhold, M.D.; et al. A virtual reality system for the assessment and rehabilitation of the activities of daily living. *Cyberpsychol. Behav.* **2003**, *6*, 383–388. [CrossRef] [PubMed]
45. Zhang, L.; Abreu, B.C.; Seale, G.S.; Masel, B.; Christiansen, C.H.; Ottenbacher, K.J. A virtual reality environment for evaluation of a daily living skill in brain injury rehabilitation: Reliability and validity. *Arch. Phys. Med. Rehabil.* **2003**, *84*, 1118–1124. [CrossRef]
46. Guidali, M.; Duschau-Wicke, A.; Broggi, S.; Klamroth-Marganska, V.; Nef, T.; Riener, R. A robotic system to train activities of daily living in a virtual environment. *Med. Biol. Eng. Comput.* **2011**, *49*, 1213. [CrossRef] [PubMed]
47. Yerkes, R.M.; Dodson, J.D. The relation of strength of stimulus to rapidity of habit-formation. *J. Comp. Neurol. Psychol.* **1908**, *18*, 459–482. [CrossRef]
48. Lehmann, I.; Baer, G.; Schuster-Amft, C. Experience of an upper limb training program with a non-immersive virtual reality system in patients after stroke: A qualitative study. *Physiotherapy* **2020**, *107*, 317–326. [CrossRef]

healthcare

MDPI

Comment

The Perspective of mHealth in the Self-Assessment of the Parkinson's Disease. Comment on Kalafati et al. Testing of Motor Coordination in Degenerative Neurological Diseases. *Healthcare* 2022, *10*, 1948

Daniele Giansanti

Centre Tisp, The Ialian National Institute of Health, 00161 Rome, Italy; daniele.giansanti@iss.it; Tel.: +39-06-49902701

Citation: Giansanti, D. The Perspective of mHealth in the Self-Assessment of the Parkinson's Disease. Comment on Kalafati et al. Testing of Motor Coordination in Degenerative Neurological Diseases. *Healthcare* 2022, *10*, 1948. *Healthcare* **2023**, *11*, 850. https://doi.org/10.3390/healthcare11060850

Academic Editor: Norbert Hosten

Received: 2 December 2022
Revised: 9 January 2023
Accepted: 6 March 2023
Published: 14 March 2023

Regarding the *research article "Maria Kalafati, Athanasios Kakarountas and Elisabeth Chroni,* Testing of Motor Coordination in Degenerative Neurological Diseases", published in *Healthcare* [1], I found that this is a stimulating work in the field of Biomedical Engineering with interesting clinical perspectives.

As you highlighted in the study [1]:

(1) Parkinson's disease (a progressive movement disorder caused by the death of dopamine-producing cells in the midbrain) is the most prevalent movement disorder of the central nervous system and affects more than 6.3 million people in the world;
(2) Changes in the motor functions of patients are not easy to be clearly observed on time by the clinicians and to make the most well-informed decisions for the treatment;
(3) It is important in light of points (1, 2) to develop bioengineering methods integrated with modern mobile technologies, capable of (a) being easily used by patients with Parkinson's Disease (PD) and (b) providing useful parameters to allow decisions based on quantitative data within the PD.

Your study [1] details the designing, developing, and evaluating of a mobile app using a pressure pen, which collects quantitative and objective information about PD patients, thus allowing clinicians to understand better and make assumptions about the severity and the stage of Parkinson's disease. The app described by you allows the execution of a dynamic spiral test through a pen pressure and obtaining a series of important parameters such as Spiral Deviation, Total Time, and Pen Pressure through a computerized system. The study reports the potential of the system as a telemonitoring method within the PD to remotely perform screening tests and maintain the history of all the patient's measurements.

I believe it is very important to introduce app-based systems and, more generally, *mHealth* solutions that allow the *health domain* to provide quantitative data on a pathology as important as Parkinson's disease. I also believe that these systems are, so to speak, also pioneers based on the introduction of wearable tools for *mHealth-based self-assessment* for PD. Moreover, this is very motivating because *mHealth* seemed to be more concentrated only on specific diseases such as diabetes, heart, and lung diseases [2–4].

When the Special Issue "Assistive Technologies, Robotics, and Automated Machines in the Health Domain" https://www.mdpi.com/journal/healthcare/special_issues/Assistive_Technologies_Robotics_Automated_Machines_Health_Domain (accessed on 5 March 2023) [5] was launched, one of the objectives [6] was to give scholars the opportunity to broaden the boundaries of studies in this area.

mHealth is recently increasingly arousing the interest of scholars in various sectors of the *health domain*. A brief search on Pubmed [7] with the search key (*mobile health [Title/Abstract]) AND (self assessment [Title/Abstract]*) shows reviews of *a growing attraction under different and new perspectives* [8–12].

The study by Alanzi [11] revealed that various applications were developed during the COVID-19 pandemic, also available in Google Play, for different functions such as contact tracing, awareness building, appointment booking, online consultation, etc. However, only a few applications have integrated various functions and features such as self-assessment, consultation, support and access to information.

The study by Claessens et al. [10] reported that numerous digital tools to self-assess visual acuity were introduced and concluded that these have the potential to increase access to eye care, also considering it is expected that the accuracy of the current tools will improve with every iteration in technology development.

Bonnechere et al. [9] highlighted that mHealth is a promising tool for the self-assessment and rehabilitation of people with multiple sclerosis, even if more studies and works are needed to put these solutions in stable routine applications.

Ni et al. [8] faced the use of mHealth for self-assessment in lung cancer. They showed that patients with lung cancer have diversified supportive care needs after discharge. A bottom-up and stepwise approach to developing mobile health-based self-management support tools has been demonstrated to be feasible and valuable.

Santo and Redfern [12] described how recent research has shown that mHealth apps can be beneficial in terms of improving hypertension self-assessment, treatment, and control, being especially useful to help differentiate and manage true and pseudo-resistant hypertension.

I am convinced that it could be useful and stimulating *to enlarge the concept of self-assessment also in PD*. In the past, before the smartphone boom, I was interested in using wearable methods to obtain quantitative parameters in PD.

Together with other coauthors, we developed a specific pedometer for patients with Parkinson's disease, the parameters connected with the path being strategic and also for the diagnostic monitoring of this pathology [13].

Subsequently, other authors and I developed a system for personal computers for monitoring the activity on the video terminal [14], which made it possible to record the trajectories of the movement of the mouse even in the execution of tasks. Nevertheless, with great scientific honesty, I must remember that we never had the idea of using it in PD [8].

I believe that *mHealth* today allows, as you have also highlighted [1], new opportunities in PD monitoring/assessment.

Based on what I wrote above, I would like to open a discussion on this topic with this comment with you or with other authors interested in the discussion.

In particular, I would like to have an opinion on how you or other authors see the development of *mHealth* self-assessment technologies on PD.

I would, therefore, very much appreciate a *reply* in this regard.

Conflicts of Interest: The author declares no conflict of interest.

References

1. Kalafati, M.; Kakarountas, A.; Chroni, E. Testing of Motor Coordination in Degenerative Neurological Diseases. *Healthcare* **2022**, *10*, 1948. [CrossRef] [PubMed]
2. Kramer, E.S.; VanWyk, J.; Holmstrom, H. Telehealth and Diabetes Management. *Prim. Care* **2022**, *49*, 631–639. [CrossRef] [PubMed]
3. Kulbayeva, S.; Tazhibayeva, K.; Seiduanova, L.; Smagulova, I.; Mussina, A.; Tanabayeva, S.; Fakhradiyev, I.; Saliev, T. The Recent Advances of Mobile Healthcare in Cardiology Practice. *Acta Inform. Med.* **2022**, *30*, 236–250. [CrossRef] [PubMed]
4. Sunjaya, A.P.; Sengupta, A.; Martin, A.; Di Tanna, G.L.; Jenkins, C. Efficacy of self-management mobile applications for patients with breathlessness: Systematic review and quality assessment of publicly available applications. *Respir. Med.* **2022**, *201*, 106947. [CrossRef] [PubMed]
5. Special Issue "Assistive Technologies, Robotics, and Automated Machines in the Health Domain". Available online: https://www.mdpi.com/journal/healthcare/special_issues/Assistive_Technologies_Robotics_Automated_Machines_Health_Domain (accessed on 5 March 2023).
6. Giansanti, D. Assistive Technologies, Robotics, Automatic Machines: Perspectives of Integration in the Health Domain. *Healthcare* **2022**, *10*, 1080. [CrossRef] [PubMed]

7. Search on Pubmed. Available online: https://pubmed.ncbi.nlm.nih.gov/?term=%28mobile+health+%5BTitle%2FAbstract%5D%29+AND+%28self+assessment%5BTitle%2FAbstract%5D%29&filter=pubt.review&sort=date&size=200 (accessed on 9 January 2022).
8. Ni, X.; Lou, Y.; Hu, W.; Wang, H.; Xu, H.; Li, S.; Zhou, Y.; Ni, Y. Development of mobile health-based self-management support for patients with lung cancer: A stepwise approach. *Nurs. Open* **2022**, *9*, 1612–1624. [CrossRef] [PubMed]
9. Bonnechère, B.; Rintala, A.; Spooren, A.; Lamers, I.; Feys, P. Is mHealth a Useful Tool for Self-Assessment and Rehabilitation of People with Multiple Sclerosis? A Systematic Review. *Brain Sci.* **2021**, *11*, 1187. [CrossRef] [PubMed]
10. Claessens, J.L.J.; Geuvers, J.R.; Imhof, S.M.; Wisse, R.P.L. Digital Tools for the Self-Assessment of Visual Acuity: A Systematic Review. *Ophthalmol. Ther.* **2021**, *10*, 715–730, Erratum in: *Ophthalmol. Ther.* **2021**, *10*, 731–732. [CrossRef] [PubMed]
11. Alanzi, T. A Review of Mobile Applications Available in the App and Google Play Stores Used During the COVID-19 Outbreak. *J. Multidiscip. Healthc.* **2021**, *14*, 45–57. [CrossRef] [PubMed]
12. Santo, K.; Redfern, J. The Potential of mHealth Applications in Improving Resistant Hypertension Self-Assessment, Treatment and Control. *Curr. Hypertens. Rep.* **2019**, *21*, 81. [CrossRef]
13. Giansanti, D.; Macellari, V.; Maccioni, G. Telemonitoring and telerehabilitation of patients with Parkinson's disease: Health technology assessment of a novel wearable step counter. *Telemed. J. E Health* **2008**, *14*, 76–83. [CrossRef] [PubMed]
14. Morelli, S.; Grigioni, M.; Ferrarin, M.; Boschetto, A.; Brocco, M.; Maccioni, G.; Giansanti, D. A monitoring tool of workers' activity at Video Display Terminals for investigating VDT-related risk of musculoskeletal disorders. *Comput. Methods Programs Biomed.* **2012**, *107*, 294–307. [CrossRef] [PubMed]

MDPI
St. Alban-Anlage 66
4052 Basel
Switzerland
Tel. +41 61 683 77 34
Fax +41 61 302 89 18
www.mdpi.com

Healthcare Editorial Office
E-mail: healthcare@mdpi.com
www.mdpi.com/journal/healthcare

www.ingramcontent.com/pod-product-compliance
Lightning Source LLC
Chambersburg PA
CBHW061823210926
51850CB00006B/791
* 9 7 8 3 0 3 6 5 7 6 8 9 3 *